# SCOTT FORESMAN

## SOCIAL STUDIES

## ALL TOGETHER

### Teacher's Edition

**Editorial Offices:** Glenview, Illinois • Parsippany, New Jersey • New York, New York
**Sales Offices:** Boston, Massachusetts • Duluth, Georgia • Glenview, Illinois •
Coppell, Texas • Sacramento, California • Mesa, Arizona

ISBN: 0-328-23953-4

**Freedom to explore**

Freedom isn't free. Here's the story of
freedom presented in the most powerful
and visually compelling way.

Page SF8

**Freedom to teach**

Who has time to teach social studies?
You do! Check out the Scott Foresman
Quick Teaching Plan and Quick Summary.

Page SF10

★ ★ ★ **SCOTT FORESMAN** ★ ★ ★
SOCIAL STUDIES

**GOLD EDITION**

SF3

# Freedom to read and learn

Reading is the #1 priority. (We understand.) Can you think of a social studies program as content-area reading? Absolutely. *Scott Foresman Social Studies* is designed to extend your reading curriculum. Explicit reading instruction and proven strategies are built into each unit. At Scott Foresman, reading is at the heart of everything we do.

Teach ····▶
Model ····▶
Practice ···▶

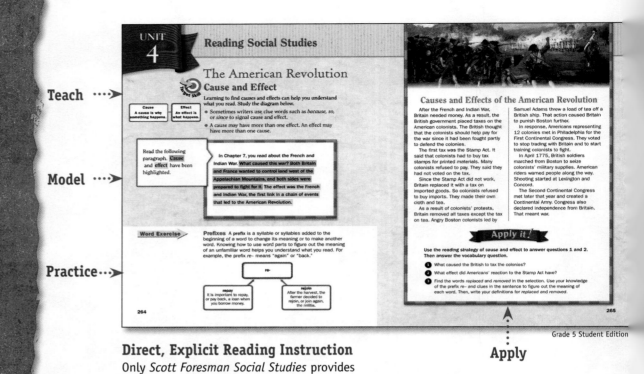

Grade 5 Student Edition

## Direct, Explicit Reading Instruction
Only *Scott Foresman Social Studies* provides explicit, four-step reading instruction in every unit to improve students' comprehension.

Apply

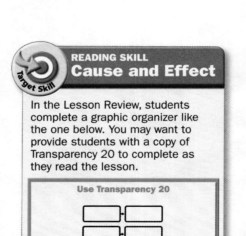

Grade 5 Teacher's Edition

## Practice the Skill
Students practice the reading skill throughout each unit, so they can apply it independently.

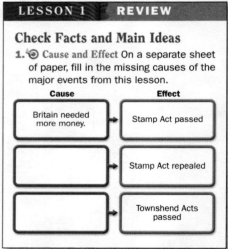

Grade 5 Student Edition

## Review the Skill
The target reading skill is monitored continuously in Lesson, Chapter, and Unit Reviews.

**ree Content Leveled**
**eaders—the Same Topic,**
**ocabulary, and Skill!**

veled readers for each unit of
*ott Foresman Social Studies* help
students access the same grade-
vel skills and content. Compare
is with other social studies
ograms. (There is no comparison!)

The same topic at three
reading levels

The same key content vocabulary

The same reading
comprehension skill

# Leveled Reader Database

## ONLINE
sfsuccessnet.com

### Find the Books You Need with Lightning Speed!

The Scott Foresman online Leveled
Reader Database helps you find
and manage the right books for
every student in your class.

**Select from over 1,000
leveled readers!**

- Search by the criteria you need
- Hear fluently read recordings
- Print out and e-mail assignments
- Teach lessons, use practice pages
- Read online at school or home

## Below-Level

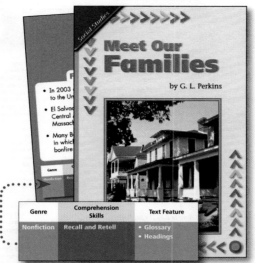

**Meet Our Families**
by G. L. Perkins

| Genre | Comprehension Skills | Text Feature |
|-------|---------------------|--------------|
| Nonfiction | Recall and Retell | • Glossary<br>• Headings |

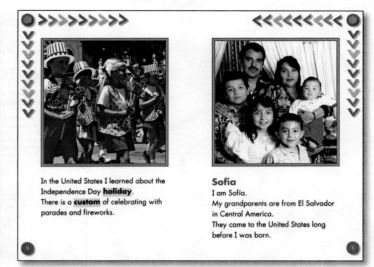

In the United States I learned about the Independence Day **holiday**. There is a **custom** of celebrating with parades and fireworks.

**Sofia**
I am Sofía.
My grandparents are from El Salvador in Central America.
They came to the United States long before I was born.

## On-Level

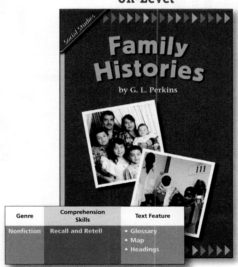

**Family Histories**
by G. L. Perkins

| Genre | Comprehension Skills | Text Feature |
|-------|---------------------|--------------|
| Nonfiction | Recall and Retell | • Glossary<br>• Map<br>• Headings |

**Sofia's Story**
My name is Sofia. I was born in the United States, but my grandparents are from El Salvador. El Salvador is part of Central America, between North America and South America. El Salvador is a small country. It has a tropical climate. El Salvador has several volcanoes. Earthquakes also happen from time to time.

My family is getting used to all of the new things in the United States. The things that were so different when we first came finally seem familiar to us.

## Advanced

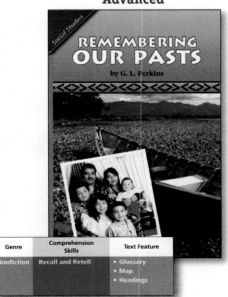

**REMEMBERING OUR PASTS**
by G. L. Perkins

| Genre | Comprehension Skills | Text Feature |
|-------|---------------------|--------------|
| Nonfiction | Recall and Retell | • Glossary<br>• Map<br>• Headings |

**Sofia's Story**
I am Sofia. I was born in the United States, but my ancestors are from El Salvador. El Salvador is part of Central America, the area between North America and South America. El Salvador is a small country and is best known for its coffee crops. It has a tropical climate with rainy and dry seasons. El Salvador is known as the Land of Volcanoes because it has several active volcanoes. Earthquakes also happen from time to time. Both the volcanoes and earthquakes are scary and often damage buildings.

My family is getting used to all of the new things in the United States. Now that we have been here for several years, the things that were so different when we first arrived finally seem familiar to us. My parents often remind me how lucky we are to live in the United States.

# Freedom to act

You don't have to be a president, a soldier, or a famous celebrity to be a citizen hero. You just need to be responsible and caring. *Scott Foresman Social Studies* fosters the notion that every child can be a citizen hero. Good citizenship is about watching out for each other and lending a hand whenever possible.

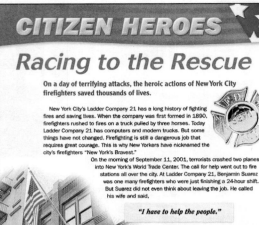

## CITIZEN HEROES

### Racing to the Rescue

On a day of terrifying attacks, the heroic actions of New York City firefighters saved thousands of lives.

New York City's Ladder Company 21 has a long history of fighting fires and saving lives. When the company was first formed in 1890, firefighters rushed to fires on a truck pulled by three horses. Today Ladder Company 21 has computers and modern trucks. But some things have not changed. Firefighting is still a dangerous job that requires great courage. This is why New Yorkers have nicknamed the city's firefighters "New York's Bravest."

On the morning of September 11, 2001, terrorists crashed two planes into New York's World Trade Center. The call for help went out to fire stations all over the city. At Ladder Company 21, Benjamin Suarez was one many firefighters who were just finishing a 24-hour shift. But Suarez did not even think about leaving the job. He called his wife and said,

*"I have to help the people."*

Then he and his fellow firefighters jumped on their trucks and raced to the scene of the attacks.

As firefighters arrived from around the city, they saw that the twin towers of the World Trade Center were on fire. They rushed into the buildings and up the stairs. "We saw them going up the stairs as we were going down," said a woman who escaped from one of the towers. The firefighters helped people who were injured or lost in the smoke. With the firefighters' help, thousands of people escaped to safety.

Not everyone survived, however. About 4,000 people were trapped in the buildings when they collapsed. More than 300 firefighters, including Benjamin Suarez, died while trying saving the lives of others. Like so many heroes on that terrible day, Suarez put the desire to help other people ahead of his own safety. "That's what Benny was about," said Captain Michael Farrell of Ladder Company 21.

In the days following the terrorist attacks, neighbors visited Ladder Company 21 to show their sympathy for the firefighters who had lost their lives. Many people left flowers and made donations to the firefighters' families. Children wrote letters in which they thanked firefighters for saving lives. Some children drew pictures showing firefighters performing brave actions. The firefighters hung these letters and pictures on the wall of the fire station. Similar scenes took place at fire stations all over the city.

Rudolph Giuliani, the mayor of New York City, thanked firefighters for their incredible courage:

*"Without courage, nothing else can really happen. And there is no better example, none, than the courage of the Fire Department of the City of New York."*

New York's firefighters not only saved thousands of lives. Their actions inspired the entire nation. In a time of fear and danger, firefighters helped Americans have the courage to face the difficult times ahead.

#### Courage in Action

Link to Current Events Every day, firefighters, police officers, and other rescue workers perform heroic acts in communities all over the nation. Read a newspaper from your community to find out about the recent actions of your [...] did they take?

**BUILDING CITIZENSHIP**
Caring
Respect
Responsibility
Fairness
Honesty
Courage

667

## Citizen Heroes
Special lessons explore how everyday citizens and well-known Americans show good citizenship.

**BUILDING CITIZENSHIP**

Caring

Respect

Responsibility

Fairness

Honesty

Courage

## Teach the Core Values of Freedom!
Students learn the important responsibilities of citizenship at every grade level.

## Celebrate Freedom
This special resource helps you inspire patriotism through songs, symbols, and sayings of the United States.

# Colonial Williamsburg

the nation's largest living history museum and an exclusive partner of Scott Foresman

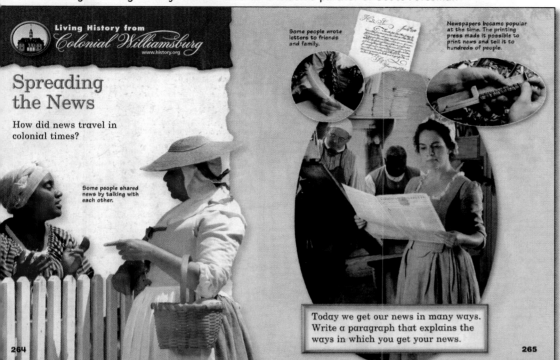

Grade 3 Student Edition

## Living History Lessons

Colonial Williamsburg makes history come alive with artifacts, reenactments, and thought-provoking activities.

*"To be engaged citizens, our children must understand their revolutionary heritage. They must understand that the future of the democracy depends on them."*

**Bill White, Director of Educational Development, Colonial Williamsburg Foundation**

### Primary Sources CD-ROM

Help students think like historians. Produced in cooperation with Colonial Williamsburg, this award-winning multimedia program introduces primary source documents that spark interest in American history and the ideals of citizenship.

"Awards of Excellence"
*Technology And Learning* magazine

"Teachers' Choice Award"
*Learning* magazine

# Freedom to explore

Freedom isn't free. People gave their lives for freedom. (And still do every day.) This is why you teach social studies. Students need to see they are the future defenders of America's freedoms. *Scott Foresman Social Studies* presents the story of our nation, the story of families and cultures, the story of our world.

Grade 5 Student Edition

**You Are There** It is late at night, April 18, 1775. The streets of Boston are quiet.

Most people are at home. You are outside gathering wood for the fire. Suddenly you hear the pounding feet of a young man as he races past you. He looks upset and seems intent on getting somewhere quickly.

You wonder, "Where is he going?" You don't know it at the time, but he carries important information. He is bringing it to Paul Revere. The young man has learned the British soldiers are on the move. Where are they going? What do they plan to do? How will all of this affect the colonists?

▶ Paul Revere warned colo[nists] that the British were adv[ancing]

**AudioText**

## You Are There
Feel the heart-pounding action! The "You Are There" writing style captivates young readers. Dramatic recordings add power and suspense.

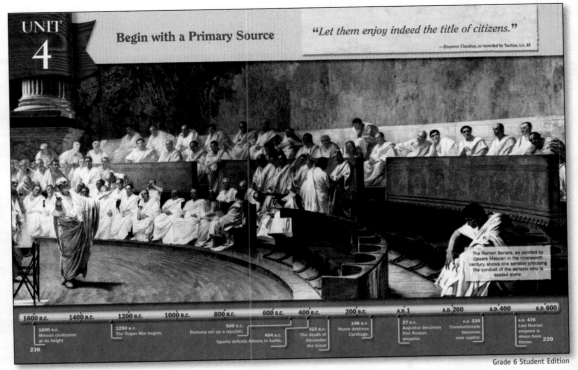

Begin with a Primary Source

*"Let them enjoy indeed the title of citizens."*
—Emperor Claudius, as recorded by Tacitus, A.D. 48

Grade 6 Student Edition

## Stunning, Powerful, Gripping

Erase the notion that a social studies textbook has to be boring. *Scott Foresman Social Studies* is filled with rich, compelling visuals and content.

- Primary sources
- Museum-quality artwork
- Colorful maps and place locators
- Graphs, diagrams, time lines
- Brilliant photographs
- Full-page biographies

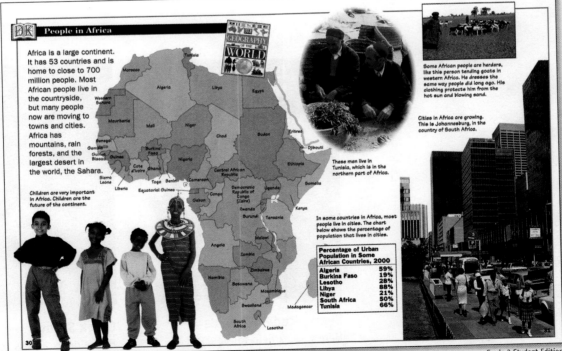

Grade 3 Student Edition

## DK Eyewitness Reference Pages

The Eyewitness Book series has sold 50 million copies. Only Scott Foresman embeds richly illustrated, highly accessible DK Eyewitness reference pages into the text.

# Freedom to teach

Do you feel you have to be a superhero just to teach reading and math? Who has time for social studies? You have time. Scott Foresman's Quick Teaching Plan and Quick Summary make social studies doable when time is short. Of course, Scott Foresman also provides all the tools you need to really dig into a topic. *Enjoy!*

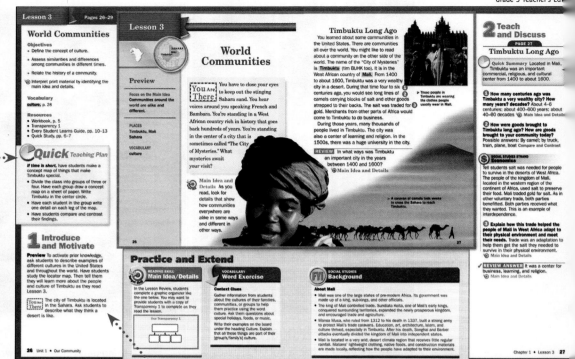

**Quick Teaching Plan**
Use the Quick Teaching Plan to make lessons a breeze.

**Complete Lesson Plan**
Dig into a topic with the three-step lesson plan.

**Quick Summary**
Focus on the key lesson content. It's a snap!

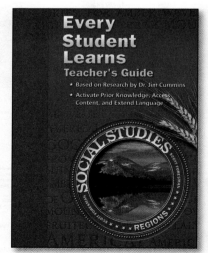

**Every Student Learns**
Here's quick help for your ESL/ELL students.

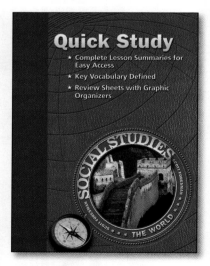

**Quick Study**
Here's quick access to content, vocabulary, and skills.

# Components

## Practice and Assessment

Workbook

Vocabulary Workbook

Test Talk Practice Book

Test Talk Transparencies

Assessment Book

## Map and Globe Skills

• Primary Atlas

• Student Atlas

  Big Book Atlas

• Outline Maps

• Laminated Desk Maps

  Map Sack

• Floor Map

## Supplemental Resources

Ancient Communities

World Communities

Our United States

Latin America and Canada

Native Americans

Learning About Your
State and Community

## Leveled Readers

• Content Leveled Readers
  in English and Spanish

• Online Leveled Readers
  in English and Spanish

## Social Studies Activities

• Celebrate Freedom

• Social Studies Plus!
  A Hands-On Approach

• Read Alouds and
  Primary Sources

• Daily Activity Bank

## Reading Social Studies/ESL

• Quick Study

• Every Student Learns
  Teacher's Guide

• Vocabulary Cards

• Colorful Posters

• Transparencies

• Document-Based Questions

• Multi-Leveled Library

• Literature Library

• Literature Big Books

## Technology

Online Teacher's Edition

Online Student Edition

Digital Learning CD-ROM
Powered by KnowledgeBox®

Colonial Williamsburg Primary
Sources CD-ROM

MindPoint™ Quiz Show CD-ROM

Video Field Trips Package

• Hand in Hand Video Package

• Songs and Music Audio CDs

• AudioText CDs

• Map Resources CD-ROM

• Teacher Resources CD-ROM

• ExamView® Test Bank CD-ROM

• sfsocialstudies.com

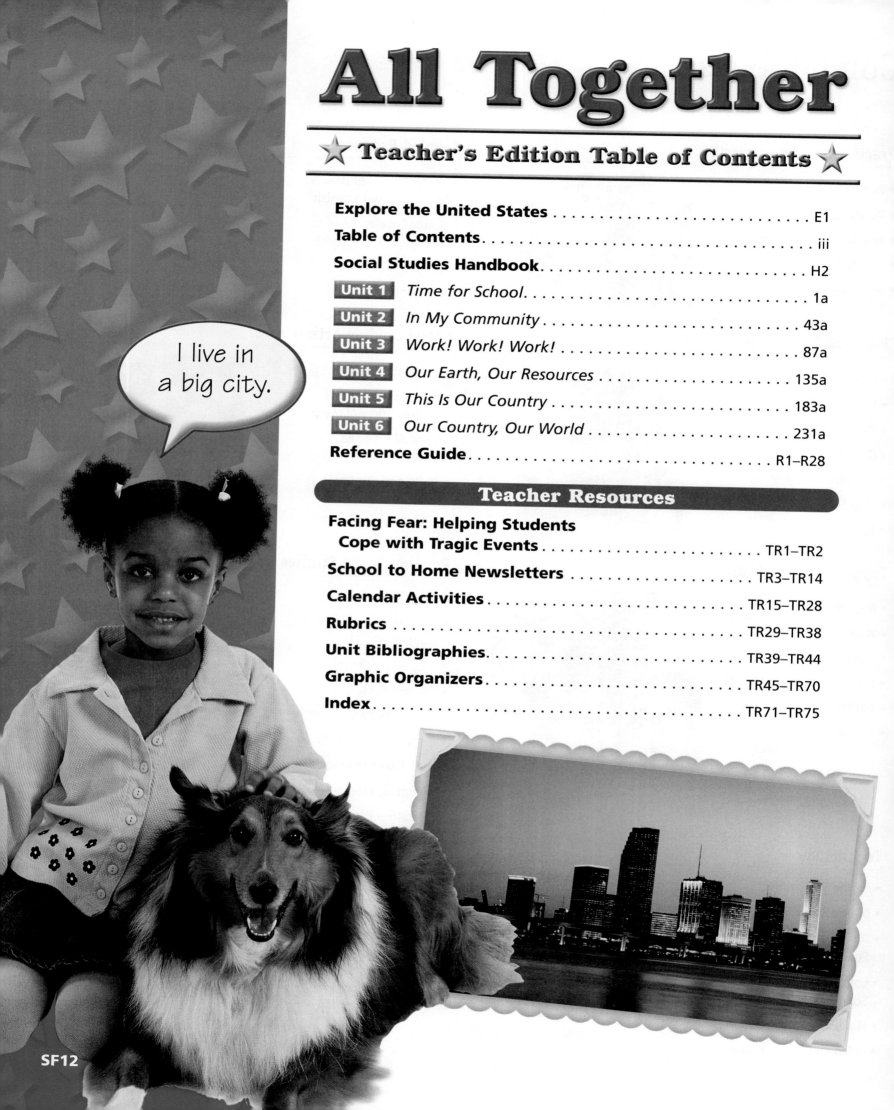

# All Together

## ★ Teacher's Edition Table of Contents ★

## Teacher Resources

I live in a big city.

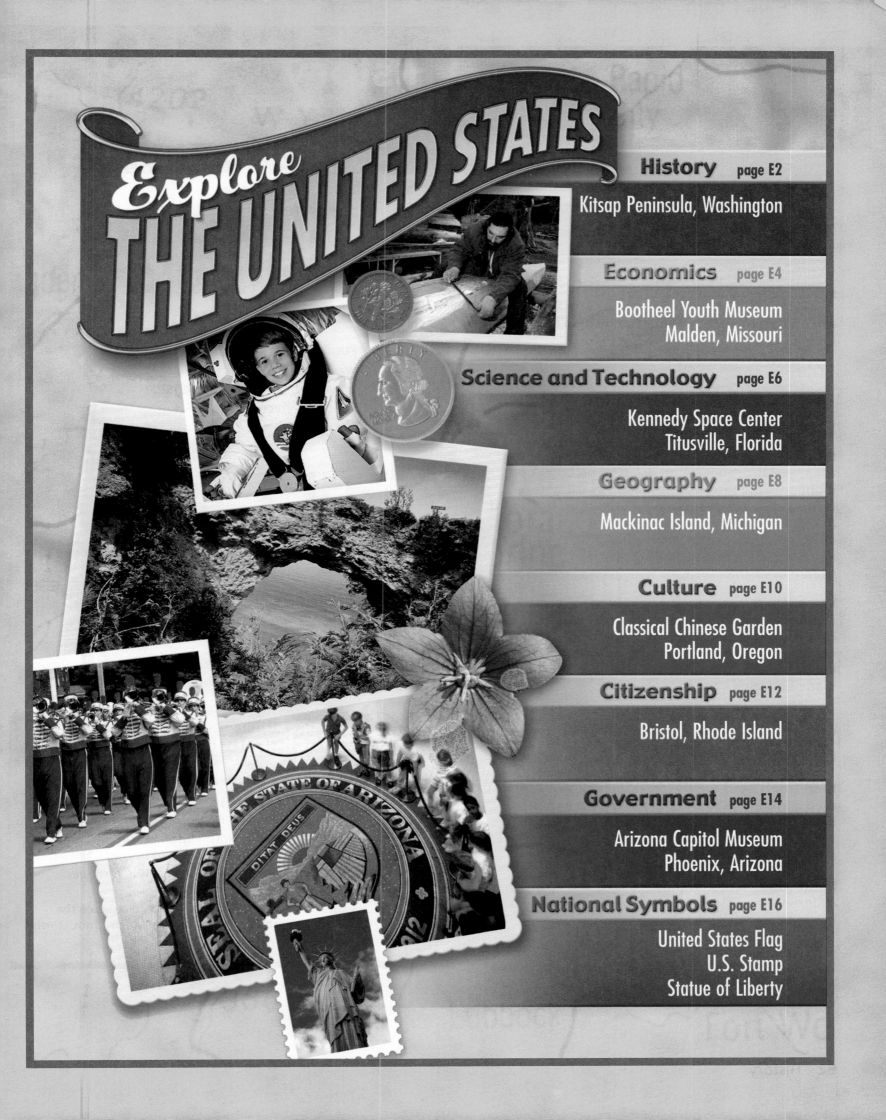

# Explore
# THE UNITED STATES

## Objectives

- Distinguish between past and present.
- Explain how people of the past influence history.

## Vocabulary

**shelter** a home

**ancestor** a member of your family who lived long ago

# 1 Introduce and Motivate

**Preview** Have children preview the pictures on the travel brochure on pp. E2–E3. The brochure highlights the Kitsap Peninsula in Washington. Write the words *shelter* and *ancestor* on the board. Ask children to describe different kinds of shelters, or homes, they have seen. Help children understand that their great-grandparents are examples of their ancestors.

**Warm Up** To activate prior knowledge, ask children if they have ever seen or ridden in a canoe. Explain that some people long ago used canoes to get around. Tell the children that they are going to learn about people in history who made and used canoes.

# 2 Teach and Discuss

**Map Reading** Have the children look at the maps on p. E3. Help them find their state and then locate the state of Washington. Use the map of Washington to point out where the people they are studying lived.

**Read Together** Read the text on pp. E2–E3 with children. Have them point to each image as you read the corresponding text. Then discuss the following questions:

**What did Pacific Northwest Native Americans use to build their homes and canoes?**
Cedar trees

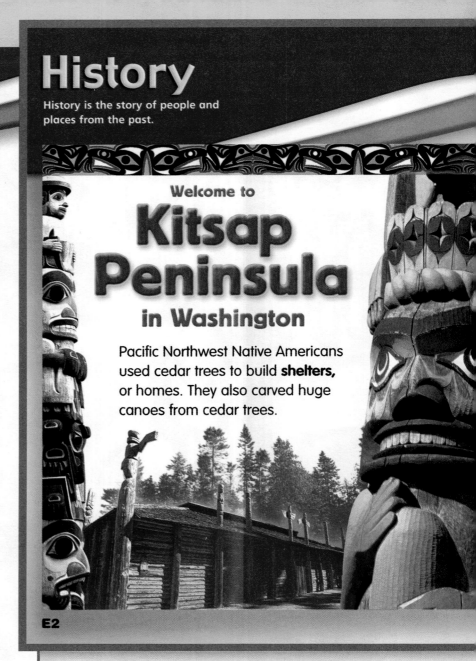

# History

History is the story of people and places from the past.

## Welcome to Kitsap Peninsula in Washington

Pacific Northwest Native Americans used cedar trees to build **shelters,** or homes. They also carved huge canoes from cedar trees.

E2

## Practice and Extend

### SOCIAL STUDIES Background

**Pacific Northwest Native Americans**

- Longhouses of Pacific Northwest Native Americans usually housed several families.
- The city of Seattle in Washington is named after a Pacific Northwest Native American named Chief Seathl.
- Native Americans settled in the Pacific Northwest region more than 10,000 years ago.
- Visitors to the Kitsap Peninsula can experience the Native American culture of the area at the Suquamish Museum.

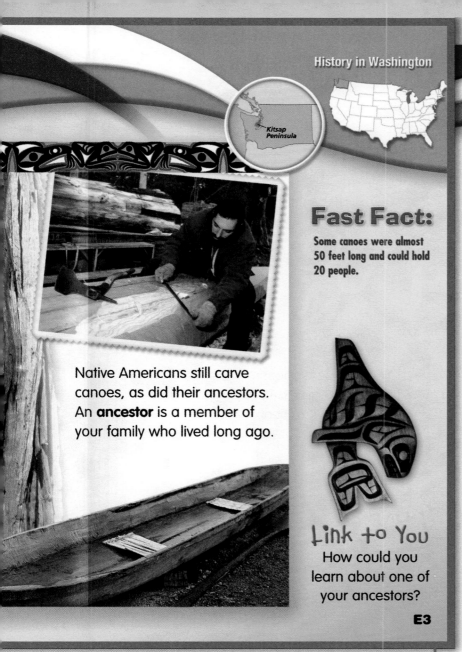

Native Americans still carve canoes, as did their ancestors. An **ancestor** is a member of your family who lived long ago.

## Fast Fact:

Some canoes were almost 50 feet long and could hold 20 people.

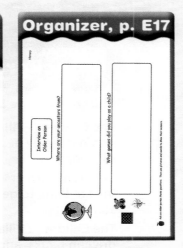

## Link to You

How could you learn about one of your ancestors?

**E3**

---

**How did they learn to make canoes?** Answers should reflect the understanding that the skill was passed on through Native American ancestors.

**What is an ancestor?** A family member who lived long ago

**Why do you think Native Americans used canoes?** Possible answers: They did not have cars long ago; Native Americans lived near water; their ancestors used canoes.

**How is the canoe on p. E3 like and different from boats you see today?** Possible answers: It is made of wood; it was built by hand; it doesn't have a motor or a sail; it doesn't have a steering wheel.

## 3 Close and Assess

Invite children to suggest questions that they would like to ask about the Native Americans who lived on the Kitsap Peninsula long ago. How could they learn the answers to their questions?

### Link to You

Read the question together. Have children use the History graphic organizer to help them interview an older person about ancestors. Answers will vary.

---

**CURRICULUM CONNECTION**
## Writing

**Use Graphic Organizers**

- Use the History graphic organizer to help children answer the Link to You question.
- Direct children to use pictures and words in their answers.
- Have children share their answers with a partner or in a small group.

### Organizer, p. E17

# Economics

### Objectives
- Identify jobs in the community.
- Explain why people have jobs.

### Vocabulary
**job** work people do

**save** to keep

## 1 Introduce and Motivate

**Preview** Have children preview the pictures on the travel brochure on pp. E4–E5. The brochure highlights the Bootheel Youth Museum in Malden, Missouri. Write the words *job* and *save* on the board. Invite children to share different jobs people do. Ask children to talk about things they save and where they keep them. Tell them that in this lesson they will learn about some jobs people do and how money is saved and used to buy things.

**Warm Up** To activate prior knowledge, ask children what kinds of jobs people do at their school. For instance, a teacher helps children learn. Tell children that they will be learning about *economics,* or how money, goods, and services are made and used.

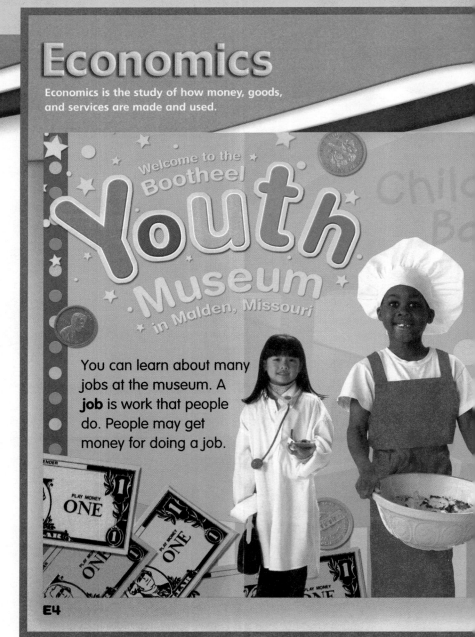

# Economics
Economics is the study of how money, goods, and services are made and used.

Welcome to the Bootheel Youth Museum in Malden, Missouri

You can learn about many jobs at the museum. A **job** is work that people do. People may get money for doing a job.

E4

## Practice and Extend

### FYI SOCIAL STUDIES Background

**Children's Village Bank**

- The Children's Village at the Bootheel Youth Museum also has a play health center, fire house, farm store, and car shop.
- Children learn how to use a bank at the Children's Village Bank to get play money to spend at the grocery store.
- The Children's Village Bank has pneumatic tubes, like drive-in banks, and safe deposit boxes for children to learn how to use.

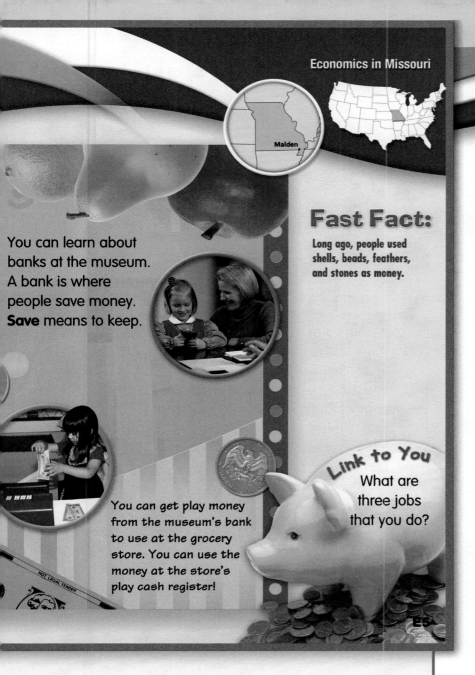

Malden

**Fast Fact:**

Long ago, people used shells, beads, feathers, and stones as money.

You can learn about banks at the museum. A bank is where people save money. **Save** means to keep.

You can get play money from the museum's bank to use at the grocery store. You can use the money at the store's play cash register!

**Link to You**

What are three jobs that you do?

E5

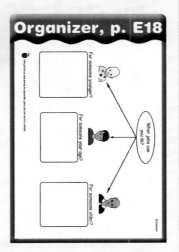

---

## CURRICULUM CONNECTION
### Writing

**Use Graphic Organizers**

- Use the Economics graphic organizer to help children answer the Link to You question.
- Direct children to use pictures or words in their answers.
- Have children share their answers with a partner or in a small group.

### Organizer, p. E18

For someone younger?

For someone your age?

What jobs can you do?

For someone older?

---

## 2 Teach and Discuss

**Map Reading** Use the maps on p. E5 to find Missouri and Malden.

**Read Together** Read the text on pp. E4–E5 with the children. Have them point to each image as you read the corresponding text. Then discuss the following questions:

**What is a job?** Work that people do

**How do you think many people get money to spend?** Possible answer: From doing a job

**Where do many people save money?** In a bank

**What would you use to buy something at the museum grocery store?** Money, play money

**Why might people long ago have used things like shells and beads for money?** Possible answers: Money was not yet invented; these things were valuable to people.

## 3 Close and Assess

Brainstorm with children a list of jobs they want to do when they get older. Have children write about or draw a picture of their job.

---

### Link to You

Read the question together. Have children use the Economics graphic organizer to help them describe three jobs they do. Answers will vary.

## Objectives
- Identify ways that science and technology help us learn about space.
- Describe what astronauts do to help us learn about space.

## Vocabulary
**communicate** to tell about something

**explore** to go to new places and to learn about them

# 1 Introduce and Motivate

**Preview** Have children preview the pictures on the travel brochure on pp. E6–E7. The brochure highlights the Kennedy Space Center in Titusville, Florida. Write the words *communicate* and *explore* on the board. Ask children to describe places they visited for the first time and what they saw there. Point out that they communicate when they describe to others what they saw. Then tell children that in this lesson they will learn about ways scientists explore new places and how they tell others what they have learned. Guide children to understand that science and technology have helped us learn about space.

**Warm Up** To activate prior knowledge, point to the picture of the shuttle launch and the child in a space suit. Ask students if they have seen a space shuttle before and to tell you what it does. Ask the students to suggest why people need to wear suits like the one in the picture when they go outside of the shuttle in space. Explain that space is extremely cold. There is also no air to breathe.

# Science and Technology
Science and Technology change the way we live.

Welcome to the Kennedy

## SPACE CENTER
in Titusville, Florida

Space shuttles lift off from Kennedy Space Center. Rockets help get the shuttles into space. Astronauts learn about space. They communicate what they learn to scientists on Earth. **Communicate** means to tell about something.

*A space shuttle lifts off.*

**E6**

# Practice and Extend

**FYI** SOCIAL STUDIES
**Background**

### Space Exploration
- Astronauts work on experiments in an area of the space shuttle called the Mid-deck. They also sleep and eat there.
- Each astronaut selects all of the food they will eat in space and plans each day's menu. Eating in space can be a challenge due to the weightless conditions. Some foods as we know them cannot be used since they would float around the shuttle. Salt is mixed with water and pepper with oil so they can be used in space.
- Neil Armstrong became the first person to walk on the moon on July 29, 1969.
- During the first moonwalks, astronauts collected 46 pounds of moon rocks for scientists to study. Scientists have learned that the youngest moon rocks are as old as the oldest Earth rocks.

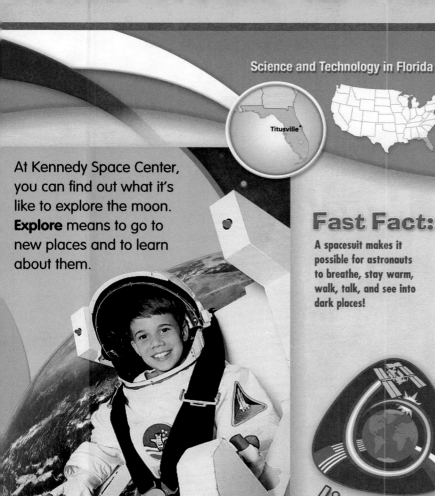

Titusville

At Kennedy Space Center, you can find out what it's like to explore the moon. **Explore** means to go to new places and to learn about them.

## Fast Fact:

A spacesuit makes it possible for astronauts to breathe, stay warm, walk, talk, and see into dark places!

### Link to You

Tell about places you would like to explore.

**E7**

## CURRICULUM CONNECTION
## Writing

### Use Graphic Organizers

- Use the Science and Technology graphic organizer to help children answer the Link to You question.
- Direct children to use pictures and words in their answers.
- Have children share their answers with a partner or in a small group.

## Organizer, p. E19

# 2 Teach and Discuss

**Map Reading** Use the maps on p. E7 to find Florida and then locate Titusville.

**Read Together** Read the text on pp. E6–E7 with the children. Have them point to each image as you read the corresponding text. Then discuss the following questions:

**Where do space shuttles lift off?** Kennedy Space Center

**What do astronauts do?** Possible answers: Learn about space; communicate what they learn to scientists; fly into space

**Why do you think people explore new places?** Possible answers: To learn about them; because they have never been to the place before

**Why does an astronaut wear a spacesuit?** Possible answers: To breathe; stay warm; talk; see into dark places

# 3 Close and Assess

Have children draw a picture showing what it would be like to explore places in space. Ask them to show what they would be wearing and the kinds of machines they would use.

### Link to You

Read the question together. Have children use the Explore Science and Technology graphic organizer to write about or draw a picture of a place they would like to explore. Answers will vary.

# Geography

## Objectives
- Describe ways geography impacts the way people live.
- Identify ways people move from place to place.

## Vocabulary
**map** a drawing of a place

**island** land with water all around it

**transportation** a way of moving people or things from place to place

## 1 Introduce and Motivate

**Preview** Have children preview the pictures on the travel brochure on pp. E8–E9. The brochure highlights Mackinac Island, Michigan. Write the words *map* and *transportation* on the board. Ask children to tell about maps they have seen and the different kinds of transportation they have used. Then tell children that in this lesson they will learn about ways geography influences the lives of people.

**Warm Up** To activate prior knowledge, ask children to describe different kinds of land or landforms that they have seen. Then discuss the types of activities people do there. For instance, what might people do on a mountain, at a beach, or on a lake? Tell children that learning about Earth and the ways people use it is called *geography*.

---

# Geography

Geography is the study of the Earth and the way people use it.

## Welcome to Mackinac Island, Michigan

Arch Rock is a natural rock bridge. Water wore away the middle of the rock!

A **map** is a drawing of a place. This is a map of Mackinac Island. An **island** is land with water all around it.

---

## Practice and Extend

**FYI** SOCIAL STUDIES **Background**

### Life on Mackinac Island
- Mackinac Island is located in the Straits of Mackinac, which connects Lake Michigan and Lake Huron.
- The island is only accessible by ferry or airplane.
- Eighty percent of Mackinac Island is state park.
- There is one school on the island. It has less than 100 students in grades K–12.
- In the winter, students get to school by snowmobile or horse-drawn bus.

## Geography in Michigan

Mackinac Island

## Fast Fact:

Arch Rock is about 150 feet tall—almost as tall as an eleven story building!

There are no cars on Mackinac Island. People walk, use horses, or ride bicycles for transportation. **Transportation** is a way of moving people or goods from place to place.

## Link to You

Tell about transportation where you live. How is it like or different from Mackinac Island?

**E9**

---

#### Use Graphic Organizers

- Use the Geography graphic organizer to help children answer the Link to You question.
- Direct children to use pictures and words in their answers.
- Have children share their answers with a partner or in a small group.

### Organizer, p. E20

---

## 2 Teach and Discuss

**Map Reading** Use the maps on p. E9 to help students see where Mackinac Island is located. Point out that it is located in a body of water that connects two lakes.

**Read Together** Read the text on pp. E8–E9 with children. Have them point to each image as you read the corresponding text. Then discuss the following questions:

**What is a map?** A drawing of a place

Tell children that when a map has a title, it tells what the map is showing.

**What is the title of the map on p. E8?** Mackinac Island Road and Trail Map

**What is an island?** Land with water all around it

**What kinds of transportation do people on Mackinac Island use?** Walking, horses, bicycles

**How did Arch Rock get a hole through it?** Water wore away the middle of the rock.

## 3 Close and Assess

Have children draw a picture of life on Mackinac Island to show ways life is different there from life in their own community.

### Link to You

Read the question together. Have children use the Geography graphic organizer to write or draw pictures of transportation they use and transportation used on Mackinac Island. Possible answers: People where I live drive cars, trucks, and buses; people where I live and on Mackinac Island ride bikes and horses.

# Culture

## Objectives

- Give examples of traditions.
- Identify a holiday celebrated in Chinese culture.

## Vocabulary

**tradition** the way something has been done for a long time

**holiday** a special day

## 1 Introduce and Motivate

**Preview** Read aloud the words *tradition* and *holiday* on the travel brochure about the classical Chinese Garden. Ask children what holidays their community celebrates. Talk about holiday traditions, such as eating turkey on Thanksgiving. Then tell children that in this lesson they will learn about some traditions in Chinese culture. Help children understand that culture is the way a group of people lives.

**Warm Up** To activate prior knowledge, have children preview the pictures on pp. E10–E11. Explain that they are looking at pictures showing what they would see if they visited the Classical Chinese Garden in Portland, Oregon. Ask the children to identify items on the pages. In what ways are they like or not like items they have seen in gardens?

# Culture

Culture is the way a group of people lives.

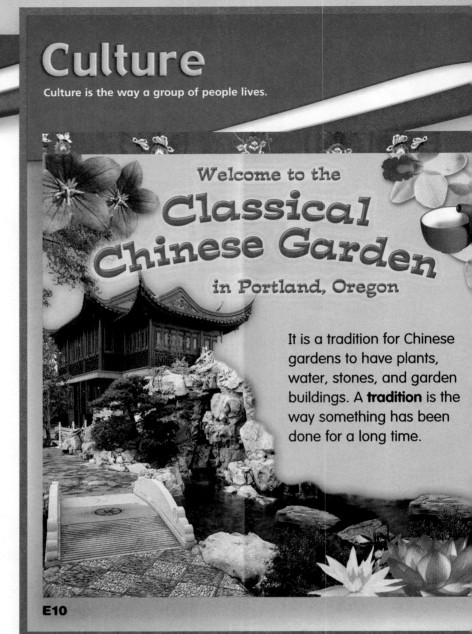

Welcome to the
## Classical Chinese Garden
in Portland, Oregon

It is a tradition for Chinese gardens to have plants, water, stones, and garden buildings. A **tradition** is the way something has been done for a long time.

**E10**

## Practice and Extend

**FYI** SOCIAL STUDIES
**Background**

### Chinese Culture

- Traditional Chinese musical instruments such as the Erhu, a two-stringed violin, are often played in Chinese gardens. Games such as chess are also played.
- The lion symbolizes courage, energy, and wisdom.
- Fireworks are used during the lion dance to chase away bad luck. They were invented in China more than 2,000 years ago.

Visitors can sit and sip tea at the tea house in the garden.

**Fast Fact:**

In China, gardening is a form of art, just like painting and drawing.

People celebrate Chinese New Year at the garden. Chinese New Year is a **holiday,** or special day. The lion dance is a tradition on this holiday.

**Link to You**

Tell about your favorite holiday. What traditions do you have on that day?

**E11**

**Organizer, p. E21**

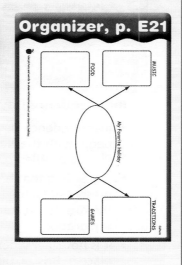

**CURRICULUM CONNECTION**
**Writing**

**Use Graphic Organizers**

- Use the Culture graphic organizer to help children answer the Link to You question.
- Direct children to use pictures and words in their answers.
- Have children share their answers with a partner or in a small group.

# 2 Teach and Discuss

**Map Reading** Use the maps on p. E11 to find Oregon and then locate Portland.

**Read Together** Read the text on pp. E10–E11 with the children. Have them point to each image as you read the corresponding text. Then discuss the following questions:

**What are some Chinese traditions you see in the pictures?** Possible answers: Chinese New Year celebration, the lion dance, drinking tea, Chinese gardens

**What Chinese holiday often has a lion dance?** Chinese New Year

**Why might the lion dance be performed on Chinese New Year?** Possible answer: To bring good luck for the coming year

**What can visitors do at the Tea House?** Drink tea

# 3 Close and Assess

Ask children to give examples of what they have learned about Chinese culture. Write the examples on the board. Discuss as a class how these traditions are similar to or different from traditions in their own culture.

**Link to You**

Read the question together. Have children use the Culture graphic organizer to describe the different traditions of their favorite holidays. Answers will vary.

## Objectives

- Give examples of ways to demonstrate good citizenship.
- Describe ways in which Independence Day is honored.

## Vocabulary

**pride** to feel good about something

**respect** to treat something in a special or nice way

# 1 Introduce and Motivate

**Preview** Read aloud the words *pride* and *respect* from the travel brochure about Bristol, Rhode Island shown on pp. E12–E13. Ask children to tell about a time when they felt proud. Talk with children about how good citizens show respect for people and property. Then tell children that in this lesson they will learn about some ways people practice good citizenship.

**Warm Up** To activate prior knowledge, have children preview the pictures on pp. E12–E13. Ask them to tell what they think is happening in the pictures. Explain that they are going to read about a special Fourth of July celebration. Have children talk about their own Fourth of July experiences. Help them understand how our celebrations show pride in our country.

# Citizenship
Citizenship is being a good member of a nation or community.

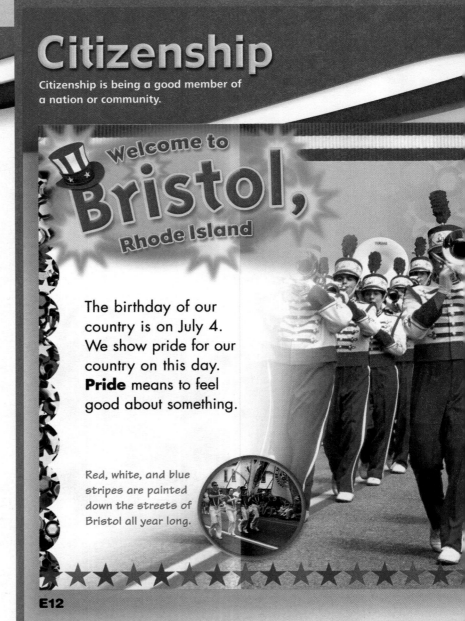

Welcome to **Bristol, Rhode Island**

The birthday of our country is on July 4. We show pride for our country on this day. **Pride** means to feel good about something.

Red, white, and blue stripes are painted down the streets of Bristol all year long.

**E12**

# Practice and Extend

**SOCIAL STUDIES Background**

### Independence Day in Bristol

- Independence Day exercises in Bristol, Rhode Island, begin with the National Anthem followed by the Pledge of Allegiance.
- A U.S. flag that has flown over the nation's Capitol is presented to the Bristol-born person who has traveled the greatest distance to be home for the Fourth of July celebration.
- It is not clear when the first 4th of July parade took place in Bristol, but by 1826 a "Chief Marshal of the Procession" was named, indicating that the parade had become a formal, organized event.

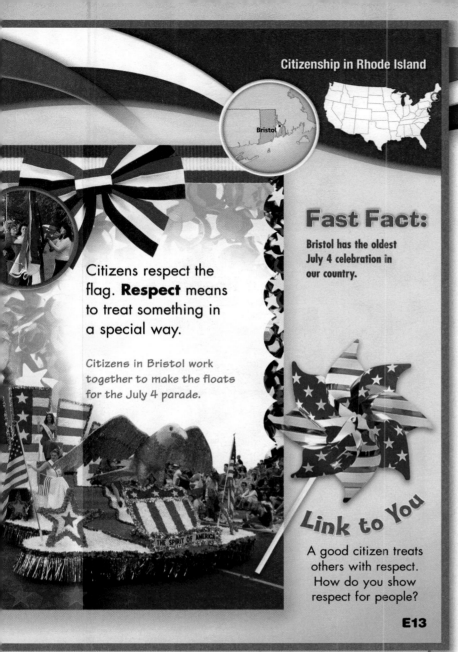

Bristol

Citizens respect the flag. **Respect** means to treat something in a special way.

*Citizens in Bristol work together to make the floats for the July 4 parade.*

## Fast Fact:

Bristol has the oldest July 4 celebration in our country.

## Link to You

A good citizen treats others with respect. How do you show respect for people?

**E13**

## CURRICULUM CONNECTION
## Writing

### Use Graphic Organizers

- Use the Citizenship graphic organizer to help children answer the Link to You question.
- Direct children to use pictures and words in their answers.
- Have children share their answers with a partner or in a small group.

## Organizer, p. E22

YES

RESPECT

NO

## 2 Teach and Discuss

**Map Reading** Have the children use the maps on p. E13 to find Rhode Island and then locate Bristol.

**Read Together** Read the text on pp. E12–E13 with the children. Have them point to each image as you read the corresponding text. Then discuss the following questions:

**Why do we celebrate on the 4th of July?** It is our country's birthday.

**Why do you think red, white, and blue stripes are painted down the streets of Bristol all year long?** Possible answers: The colors of the flag help people in Bristol show how proud they are all year; they want to remind visitors to feel proud.

**Why do you think citizens show respect for the flag?** Possible answers: It is a symbol of our country; they like living in the United States.

## 3 Close and Assess

Ask the class to discuss ways that they could practice good citizenship in their classroom and school.

## Link to You

Read the question together. Have children use the Citizenship graphic organizer to help them show ways they show respect. Possible answers: Saying please and thank you; listening when others are speaking; using kind words.

# Government

## Objectives
- Identify leaders in a state.
- Identify where laws are made.

## Vocabulary

**capitol** a building where people meet to make laws

**citizen** a member of a state and country

# 1 Introduce and Motivate

**Preview** Read aloud the words *capitol* and *citizen* from the travel brochure about the Arizona capitol Museum shown on pp. E14–E15. Explain that there is a capitol building for our country and there are capitol buildings for each state. Tell children that people meet in a capitol to make laws.

**Warm Up** To activate prior knowledge, have children preview the pictures on pp. E14–E15. Ask children if they have ever been to a museum and what they saw there. Tell children that they are going to learn about a museum that was once the capitol building for the state of Arizona.

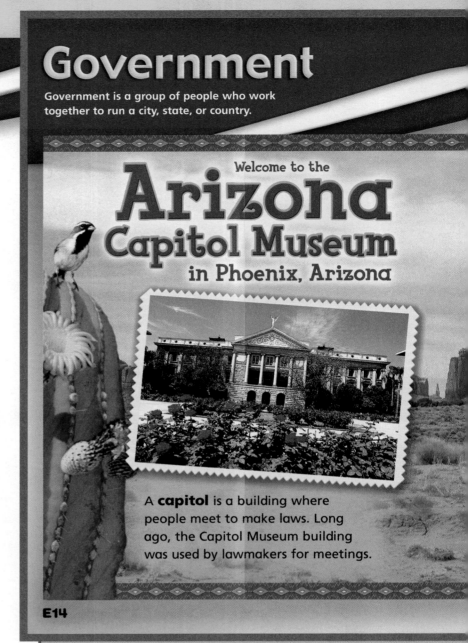

## Government

Government is a group of people who work together to run a city, state, or country.

### Welcome to the Arizona Capitol Museum in Phoenix, Arizona

A **capitol** is a building where people meet to make laws. Long ago, the Capitol Museum building was used by lawmakers for meetings.

E14

# Practice and Extend

### SOCIAL STUDIES Background

**Old Capitol Facts**

- Arizona's state constitution was written in 1910 at Arizona's old State Capitol. The building was the capitol of the Arizona Territory and then the state when Arizona was admitted as a state in 1912. The building became a museum in 1981.

- Arizona's legislature, the governor's office, and the Arizona Supreme Court were all housed in the old capitol.

- Some symbols found on the Arizona state seal include mountains, grazing cattle, a quartz mill, and a miner with a pick and shovel.

## Government in Arizona

Each state has a leader called a governor. Citizens of each state vote for their governor. A **citizen** is a member of a state and country.

Arizona Governor Janet Napolitano

The Arizona State Seal is on the floor of the Capitol Museum.

### Fast Fact:

The Capitol Museum has a lifelike wax figure of the State of Arizona's first governor, George Wiley Paul Hunt.

## Link to You

How does government help people?

E15

---

---

## Teach and Discuss

**Map Reading** Look at the maps on p. E15 and help students find Arizona and then locate Phoenix.

**Read Together** Read the text on pp. E14–E15 with children. Have them point to each image as you read the corresponding text. Then discuss the following questions:

**What happens in a capitol?** People meet to make laws.

**What do we call the leader of a state?** A governor

**How does a person become governor?** Citizens of a state vote for their governor.

## Close and Assess

Ask students to suggest what they might show on a seal for their state. Explain that seals often show more than one item. Have children draw a picture of a seal for their state.

### Link to You

Read the question together. Have children use the Government graphic organizer to draw or write about how government helps people. Possible answers: Makes laws to keep people safe; builds and fixes roads; builds schools.

# National Symbols

## Objectives
- Identify the flag of the United States.
- Explain the meaning of some national symbols.

## 1 Introduce and Motivate

**Preview** Have children preview the pictures on p. E16. Explain that the pictures show symbols of our nation and that a symbol stands for or represents something else. Then tell children that in this lesson they will learn about some important national symbols.

## 2 Teach and Discuss

**Read Together** Read the text on p. E16 with children. Have them point to each image as you read the corresponding text. Then discuss the following questions:

**Which symbol is red, white, and blue?**
The United States flag

**Why do you think the Statue of Liberty is a symbol of America?** Possible answers: It is a symbol of freedom, and many people come to America to find freedom.

**Some U.S. stamps honor important Americans. What other people would you like to see pictured on a U.S. stamp?** Possible answers: government or school leaders, family members, friends

## 3 Close and Assess

Ask children to select their favorite national symbol and tell why it is their favorite. Then have children work in pairs to decide on a symbol they think represents their school. Ask children to share their symbol with the class.

---

## National Symbols

United States Flag

Statue of Liberty

◄ The flag of the United States is red, white, and blue. It is a symbol of our country.

Harriet Tubman

Black Heritage USA 13c

© 1978 USPS

U.S. Stamp

▲ Some U.S. stamps show important Americans. These stamps are a symbol of honor for the different people who have made our country great.

▲ The Statue of Liberty is a very tall statue in New York Harbor. It is a symbol of hope and freedom.

E16

---

## Practice and Extend

**CURRICULUM CONNECTION**
**Writing**

**Organizer, p. E2**

### Use Graphic Organizers
- Use the National Symbols graphic organizer to have children tell what is special about living in the United States.
- Direct children to use pictures and words in their answers.
- Have children share their work with a partner or in a small group.

## Interview an Older Person

Where are your ancestors from?

What games did you play as a child?

Ask an older person these questions. Then use pictures and words to show their answers.

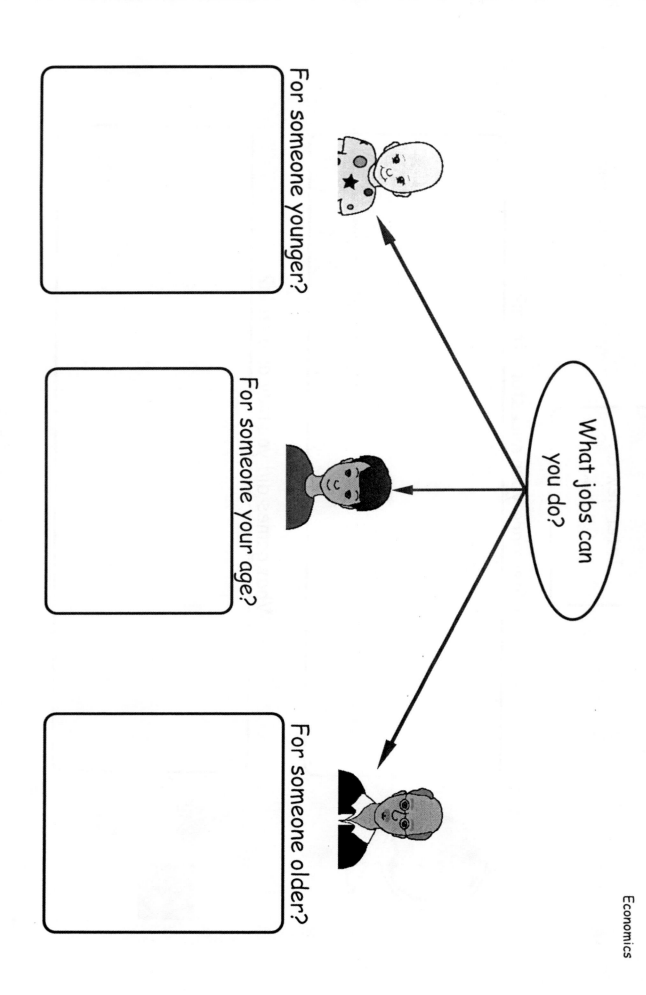

For someone younger?

For someone your age?

For someone older?

What jobs can you do?

Use pictures and words to describe jobs you can do for others.

Economics

How will I get there?

Who will I meet there?

Where do I want to explore?

What will I see there?

Use words and pictures to answer the questions.

**kidspiration** This graphic organizer is also available for use on your school computers. Find this activity and a 30-day Kidspiration trial at www.inspiration.com/sf.

Grade 1 • Explore **E19**

## Transportation for Me

## Transportation for Mackinac Island

*Geography*

In the first box, use pictures or words to show types of transportation you use. In the second box, use pictures or words to show types of transportation on Mackinac Island. Then draw lines connecting any types of transportation that are in both boxes.

TRADITIONS

GAMES

My Favorite Holiday

MUSIC

FOOD

Use picture and words to show information about your favorite holiday.

**kidspiration** This graphic organizer is also available for use on your school computers. Find this activity and a 30-day Kidspiration trial at www.inspiration.com/sf.

Grade 1 • Explore **E21**

In the "YES" box, use pictures and words to show someone acting with respect.
In the "NO" box, use pictures and words to show someone acting without respect.

YES

NO

RESPECT

Citizenship

How does government help us?

Use pictures and words to show how the government helps people.

**kidspiration** This graphic organizer is also available for use on your school computers. Find this activity and a 30-day Kidspiration trial at www.inspiration.com/sf.

Grade 1 • Explore **E23**

What is special to you about living
in the United States?

What is special to you about living in
your state?

Symbols

© Scott Foresman 1

What is special to you about living
in your community?

Use pictures and words to answer the questions.

**kidspiration** This graphic organizer is also available
for use on your school computers. Find this activity and
a 30-day Kidspiration trial at www.inspiration.com/sf.

# SCOTT FORESMAN

SOCIAL STUDIES

ALL TOGETHER

## PROGRAM AUTHORS

**Dr. Candy Dawson Boyd**
**Professor, School of Education**
Director of Reading Programs
St. Mary's College
Moraga, California

**Dr. Geneva Gay**
**Professor of Education**
University of Washington
Seattle, Washington

**Rita Geiger**
**Director of Social Studies and**
**Foreign Languages**
Norman Public Schools
Norman, Oklahoma

**Dr. James B. Kracht**
**Associate Dean for Undergraduate**
**Programs and Teacher Education**
College of Education
Texas A&M University
College Station, Texas

**Dr. Valerie Ooka Pang**
**Professor of Teacher Education**
San Diego State University
San Diego, California

**Dr. C. Frederick Risinger**
**Director, Professional Development**
**and Social Studies Education**
Indiana University
Bloomington, Indiana

**Sara Miranda Sanchez**
**Elementary and Early Childhood**
**Curriculum Coordinator**
Albuquerque Public Schools
Albuquerque, New Mexico

## CONTRIBUTING AUTHORS

**Dr. Carol Berkin**
Professor of History
Baruch College and the Graduate Center
The City University of New York
New York, New York

**Lee A. Chase**
Staff Development Specialist
Chesterfield County Public Schools
Chesterfield County, Virginia

**Dr. Jim Cummins**
Professor of Curriculum
Ontario Institute for Studies in Education
University of Toronto
Toronto, Canada

**Dr. Allen D. Glenn**
Professor and Dean Emeritus
Curriculum and Instruction
College of Education
University of Washington
Seattle, Washington

**Dr. Carole L. Hahn**
Professor, Educational Studies
Emory University
Atlanta, Georgia

**Dr. M. Gail Hickey**
Professor of Education
Indiana University-Purdue University
Fort Wayne, Indiana

**Dr. Bonnie Meszaros**
Associate Director
Center for Economic Education and
Entrepreneurship
University of Delaware
Newark, Delaware

## CONTENT CONSULTANTS

**Catherine Deans-Barrett**
World History Specialist
Northbrook, Illinois

**Dr. Michael Frassetto**
Studies in Religions
Independent Scholar
Chicago, Illinois

**Dr. Gerald Greenfield**
Hispanic-Latino Studies
History Department
University of Wisconsin, Parkside
Kenosha, Wisconsin

**Dr. Frederick Hoxie**
Native American Studies
University of Illinois
Champaign, Illinois

**Dr. Cheryl Johnson-Odim**
Dean of Liberal Arts and Sciences and
Professor of History
African American History Specialist
Columbia College
Chicago, Illinois

**Dr. Michael Khodarkovsky**
Eastern European Studies
University of Chicago
Chicago, Illinois

**Robert Moffet**
U.S. History Specialist
Northbrook, Illinois

**Dr. Ralph Nichols**
East Asian History
University of Chicago
Chicago, Illinois

## CLASSROOM REVIEWERS

**Diana Vicknair Ard**
Woodlake Elementary School
St. Tammany Parish
Mandeville, Louisiana

**Sharon Berenson**
Freehold Learning Center
Freehold, New Jersey

**Betsy Blandford**
Pocahontas Elementary School
Powhatan, Virginia

**Nancy Neff Burgess**
Upshur County Schools
Buckhannon-Upshur Middle School
Upshur County, West Virginia

**Gloria Cantatore**
Public School #5
West New York, New Jersey

**Stephen Corsini**
Content Specialist in Elementary Social Studies
School District 5 of Lexington
and Richland Counties
Ballentine, South Carolina

**Deanna Crews**
Millbrook Middle School
Elmore County
Millbrook, Alabama

**LuAnn Curran**
Westgate Elementary School
St. Petersburg, Florida

**Kevin L. Curry**
Social Studies Curriculum Chair
Hickory Flat Elementary School
Henry County, McDonough, Georgia

**Sheila A. Czech**
Sky Oaks Elementary School
Burnsville, Minnesota

**Louis De Angelo**
Office of Catholic Education
Archdiocese of Philadelphia
Philadelphia, Pennsylvania

**Dr. Trish Dolasinski**
Paradise Valley School District
Arrowhead Elementary School
Glendale, Arizona

**Dr. John R. Doyle**
Director of Social Studies Curriculum
Miami-Dade County Schools
Miami, Florida

**Dr. Roceal Duke**
District of Columbia Public Schools
Washington, D.C.

**Peggy Flanagan**
Roosevelt Elementary School
Community Consolidated School District #64
Park Ridge, Illinois

**Mary Flynn**
Arrowhead Elementary School
Glendale, Arizona

**Odaly Garcia**
Claude Pepper Elementary School
Miami, Florida

**Su Hickenbottom**
Totem Falls Elementary School
Snohomish School District
Snohomish, Washington

**Allan Jones**
North Branch Public Schools
North Branch, Minnesota

**Ruth Rae Koth**
Pinellas County
Bear Creek Elementary School
St. Petersburg, Florida

**Martha Sutton Maple**
Shreve Island School
Shreveport, Louisiana

**Lyn Metzger**
Carpenter Elementary School
Community Consolidated School District #64
Park Ridge, Illinois

**Marsha Munsey**
Riverbend Elementary School
West Monroe, Louisiana

**Christine Nixon**
Warrington Elementary School
Escambia County School District
Pensacola, Florida

**Cynthia K. Reneau**
Muscogee County School District
Columbus, Georgia

**Brandon Dale Rice**
Secondary Education Social Science
Mobile County Public School System
Mobile, Alabama

**Liz Salinas**
Supervisor
Edgewood ISD
San Antonio, Texas

**Beverly Scaling**
Desert Hills Elementary
Las Cruces, New Mexico

**Madeleine Schmitt**
St. Louis Public Schools
St. Louis, Missouri

**Barbara Schwartz**
Central Square Intermediate School
Central Square, New York

**Editorial Offices:**
• Glenview, Illinois
• Parsippany, New Jersey
• New York, New York

**Sales Offices:**
• Boston, Massachusetts
• Duluth, Georgia
• Glenview, Illinois
• Coppell, Texas
• Sacramento, California
• Mesa, Arizona

**www.sfsocialstudies.com**

2 3 4 5 6 7 8 9 10 V057 15 14 13 12 11 10
09 08 07 06

# Contents

## Social Studies Handbook

## UNIT 1

# Time for School

# UNIT 2

# In My Community

# UNIT 3

# Work! Work! Work!

# UNIT 4

# Our Earth, Our Resources

vi

# UNIT 5

# This is Our Country

# Our Country, Our World

**UNIT 6**

# Reference Guide

## Social Studies Handbook

## Biographies

ix

## Maps

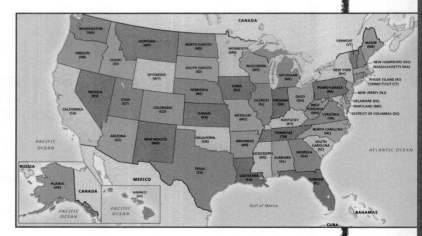

## Skills

# Citizenship Skills

Examining what it means to be a responsible and respectful person will help children to develop an understanding of the ramification of prejudice, racism, and stereotyping.

Read the introductory text to children as they follow along. Then read aloud the definitions of the six citizenship characteristics and talk briefly about the photographs.

Use the following questions to guide children to understand that they can demonstrate each of the characteristics in their own daily lives.

## Respect

**1** **What is a way you can show respect to others?** Possible answer: You can show consideration for what they think and feel. **Apply Information**

## Caring

**2** **What ways can you show you care about a person?** Possible answer: You can help and support a person. **Generalize**

## Responsibility

**3** **How is the boy in the picture showing he is responsible?** He is feeding the dog. **Analyze Pictures**

Citizenship Skills

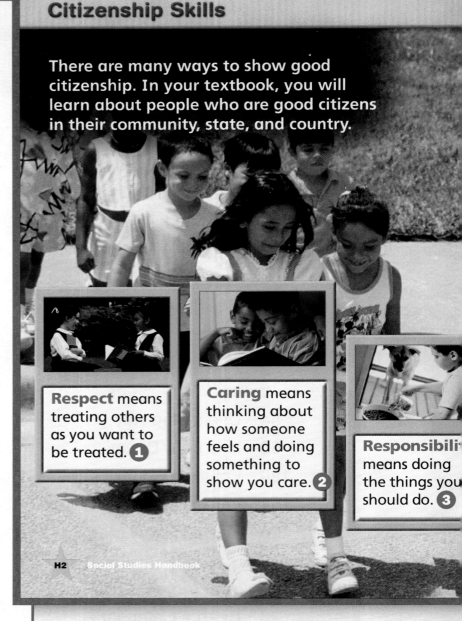

There are many ways to show good citizenship. In your textbook, you will learn about people who are good citizens in their community, state, and country.

**Respect** means treating others as you want to be treated. **1**

**Caring** means thinking about how someone feels and doing something to show you care. **2**

**Responsibili**[ty] means doing the things you should do. **3**

# Practice and Extend

## CURRICULUM CONNECTION
## Drama

**Prejudice Reduction: Playing Together**

- Have small groups of children take turns dramatizing playing a game in the park, and inviting other children they may not know well to join their game.

- Ask a group of three or four children to begin playing a game together. Have another group of the same size to ask to join the game. Encourage children to demonstrate the importance of including everyone in the game.

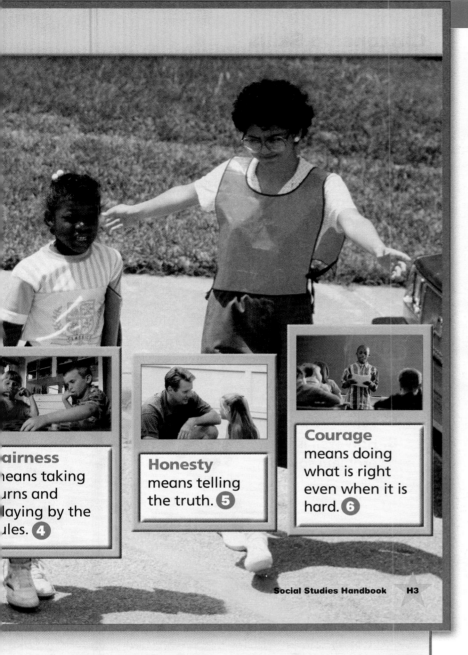

**airness**
**means taking
urns and
laying by the
ules. 4**

**Honesty**
means telling
the truth. 5

**Courage**
means doing
what is right
even when it is
hard. 6

**SOCIAL STUDIES STRAND**
## Citizenship

**Citizen Heroes**

In Grade 1, children will read about the following
Citizen Heroes:

- Ruby Bridges Hall: Courage
- Harriet Tubman: Fairness
- Kid's Kitchen: Caring
- Tree Musketeers: Responsibility
- Eleanor Roosevelt: Honesty
- Joseph Bruchac: Respect

## Fairness

**4 Why is it more important to play a game
by the rules than it is to win?** Possible answer:
A game is something people do together for fun.
**Express Ideas**

## Honesty

**5 What might be the best time for family
members to tell each other the truth about
their feelings?** Possible answer: The best time
might be when they can sit down and quietly talk
to each other. **Express Ideas**

## Courage

**6 Do you think a person who has courage is
never afraid?** Possible answer: Sometimes people
are afraid but still do the right thing. **Express Ideas**

## ★ Citizenship in Action ★

Read aloud the introductory paragraph and then focus children's attention on the two activities. Have children listen and follow along as you read each numbered step in each process.

As you discuss each step individually, encourage children to express a range of ideas they may have. Aside from identifying the problem or decision to be made, make it clear that there is no one correct response to each step.

### Problem Solving

Discuss the problem-solving scenario. Help children solve the problem in a logical way.

1. The problem is that the Art Center is messy.

2. Identify the ways the Art Center is messy, such as crayons aren't in their boxes, and drawing paper is scattered about.

3. Possible solutions: one child or a small group could clean up.

4. One child would not get in people's way. A small group would not be overworked.

5. Children should chose the solution they feel is best.

6. Have children evaluate their solution.

## ★ Citizenship in Action ★

**Good citizens make careful decisions. They learn to solve problems. Help these children act like good citizens. Here are the steps they follow.**

### Problem Solving

The Art Center is messy. What can they do?

1. Name the problem.
2. Find out more about the problem.
3. List ways to solve the problem.
4. Talk about the best way to solve the problem.
5. Solve the problem.
6. How well is the problem solved?

## Practice and Extend

### CURRICULUM CONNECTION
### Literature

**Alexander, Who Used to Be Rich Last Sunday**

• Read this story by Judith Viorst to children (Atheneum; ISBN: 0-689-30602-4). Discuss the fact that Alexander had the problem of how he was going to spend the dollar his grandparents gave him.

• After reading the story, ask children to explain what happened to Alexander's money.

• Ask volunteers to discuss ways they could plan to spend money wisely.

# ★ Citizenship in Action ★

## Decision Making

Open House is tonight. The children want to make a sign to welcome their parents.

1. Tell what decision you need to make.
2. Gather information.
3. List your choices.
4. Tell what might happen with each choice.
5. Make a decision.

**CURRICULUM CONNECTION**
## Writing

### Write a Letter

- Have children write a letter to a parent or family letter inviting that person to attend an Open House at your school.
- If children need assistance, suggest that they include the date and time the Open House will be held, along with the school name, room number, and so on.
- Encourage children to illustrate their letters with drawings.

## Decision Making

Discuss the decision-making scenario. Help children make a careful decision.

1. A decision must be made about what greeting to put on a sign welcoming parents at Open House.
2. Children might brainstorm possible greetings.
3. The choices might include such greetings as "Welcome Parents," "Welcome to Our Class," "Our House is Your House."
4. Have children discuss their responses to different greetings.
5. Have children vote for their favorite greeting.

# The United States

## About "America, the Beautiful"

- Read the title of the song—"America, the Beautiful." Tell children that this song is one of America's most loved patriotic songs.

- Read the songwriter's name—Katharine Lee Bates. Tell children that she was a teacher.

- Tell the following about the history of the song. One day Bates went on a trip to Pikes Peak, a mountain in Colorado. The beautiful view from the top inspired her to write the song. She wrote the original version in 1893, a second version in 1904, and the final version in 1913.

- Read the words to "America, the Beautiful" before singing it with children. Explain any words or phrases children may not understand, such as *spacious*, *amber waves of grain*, and *brotherhood*.

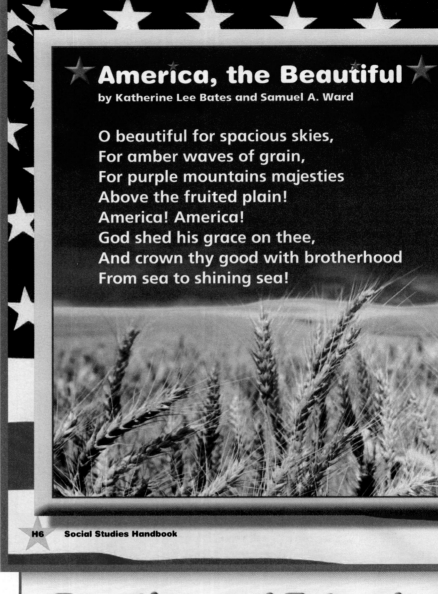

### America, the Beautiful
by Katherine Lee Bates and Samuel A. Ward

O beautiful for spacious skies,
For amber waves of grain,
For purple mountains majesties
Above the fruited plain!
America! America!
God shed his grace on thee,
And crown thy good with brotherhood
From sea to shining sea!

H6   Social Studies Handbook

# Practice and Extend

### AUDIO CD
### Technology

Play the CD, *Songs and Music*, to listen to "America, the Beautiful."

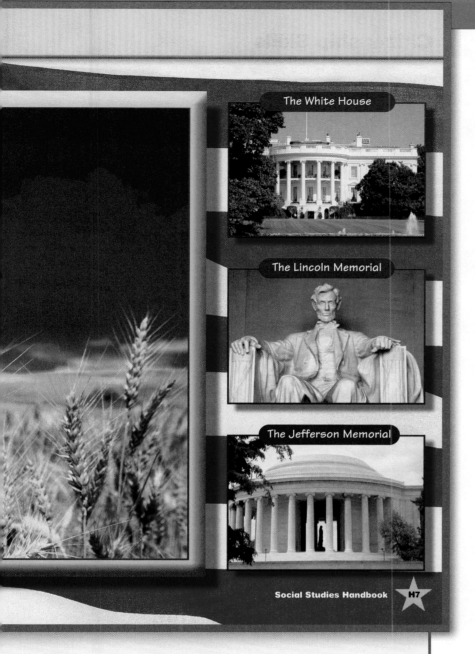

The White House

The Lincoln Memorial

The Jefferson Memorial

# Other Songs About the United States

- Ask children to think about other songs they may know of that celebrate the United States. Possible answers include "My Country 'Tis of Thee," "This Land Is Your Land," "You're a Grand Old Flag," "Yankee Doodle," and "The Star Spangled Banner."

- Choose one or more of these songs to recite or sing with your class. The words to all of the songs listed above appear in *Celebrate Freedom: Songs, Symbols, and Sayings of the United States* (Primary).

- Lead children in a discussion about what they think these songs say about our country. Explain any words or phrases children may not understand that are in any of the songs.

## SOCIAL STUDIES Background

**About the White House, Lincoln Memorial, and Jefferson Memorial**

- The White House, located at 1600 Pennsylvania Avenue in Washington, D.C., is the official home of the President of the United States.

- The 132-room mansion not only contains living quarters for the President's family but also offices where the President conducts business.

- The Lincoln Memorial is a massive marble monument in Washington, D.C., that honors Abraham Lincoln, the sixteenth President of the United States. It stands at the end of the National Mall.

- The Jefferson Memorial, also in Washington , D.C., is a beautiful monument to Thomas Jefferson, the third President of the United States. It was dedicated in 1943, the 200th anniversary of Jefferson's birth.

# The Pledge of Allegiance

## Saying the Pledge of Allegiance

- Recite the Pledge of Allegiance to the United States Flag. Explain any words or phrases children may not understand, such as *allegiance*, *to the Republic for which it stands*, and *indivisible*.

- On a second reading have children echo each line.

- Encourage children to be attentive and show their respect and thanks to the United States by standing, removing their hat, facing and looking at the flag, placing their right hand over their heart, and avoiding fidgeting.

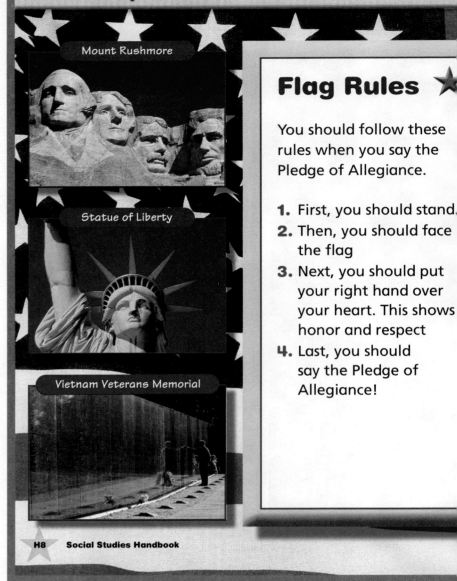

### Citizenship Skills

Mount Rushmore

Statue of Liberty

Vietnam Veterans Memorial

## Flag Rules ★

You should follow these rules when you say the Pledge of Allegiance.

1. First, you should stand.
2. Then, you should face the flag
3. Next, you should put your right hand over your heart. This shows honor and respect
4. Last, you should say the Pledge of Allegiance!

**H8** Social Studies Handbook

# Practice and Extend

SOCIAL STUDIES
**Background**

**The United States Flag**

On June 14, 1777, the Continental Congress passed the first Flag Act. It said that the flag would be made of up thirteen alternating red and white stripes and thirteen white stars on a blue field. The stars were to represent a new constellation—a group of new states that were united into one nation.

In the United States flag, the color red stands for courage, white stands for goodness, and blue stands for justice.

Some nicknames for the United States flag are Old Glory, the Stars and Stripes, and the Star-Spangled Banner.

# The Pledge of Allegiance

pledge allegiance to the Flag of the United States
f America, and to the Republic for which it stands,
ne Nation under God, indivisible, with liberty and
ustice for all.

## FYI SOCIAL STUDIES Background

### About Mount Rushmore, the Statue of Liberty, and The Vietnam Veterans Memorial

- Mount Rushmore is in the Black Hills of South Dakota. The faces of four United States presidents are carved into rock high on the mountain: George Washington, Thomas Jefferson, Theodore Roosevelt, and Abraham Lincoln. Each face is 60 feet high.

- The Statue of Liberty is in New York Harbor. At 152 feet tall, it is one of the largest statues in the world. The torch is held high to light the way for freedom and give hope to people coming to the United States.

- The Vietnam Veterans Memorial is in Washington, D.C. It honors the men and women who served in the war in Vietnam. In consists of the Wall of Names, the Three Servicemen Statue, and the Vietnam Women's Memorial.

# Taking Care of Our Flag

Point to the American flag in the classroom. Explain to children that this flag is a symbol of our country.

- Tell children that the number of stripes stands for the number of states when the country first began. Have children count the stripes with you.
- Tell children there are fifty stars—one star for each of the fifty states.

Tell children the following rules about displaying the flag:

- No other flag should be placed above the American flag.
- The flag should be displayed during school days in or near every school.
- When a flag passes in a parade, you should stand and put your hand over your heart.

# Think Like a Historian

## Objectives

- Define archaeology and archaeologist.

- Explain how artifacts help historians understand what life is like, both in the past and today.

## 1 Introduce and Motivate

- Have children look around the classroom. Ask them to make a list of the items they see. Write the list on the board. Next, ask them to predict what will happen to some of these items when they are old and worn out.

- Explain that "trash" can tell us how people of the past lived. Finding pieces of a desk, chair, crayon, jacket, or other items will help future historians understand what their school was like.

- Archaeology uncovers the things people left behind. Tell children that a special type of historian, known as an archaeologist, carefully digs in the ground to discover artifacts left by people who lived there long ago.

## 2 Teach and Discuss

- **Photograph of archaeological work.** This student is doing the work of an archaeologist. This student is using a trowel (a small scraping tool), dustpan, and bucket to carefully dig up artifacts from a historic site. Artifacts can be quite old, and many are broken. Ask children why they think archaeologists must be very careful when they excavate.

- **Artifacts are primary sources.** Explain to children that objects can tell a lot about a time period or the people who used the objects.

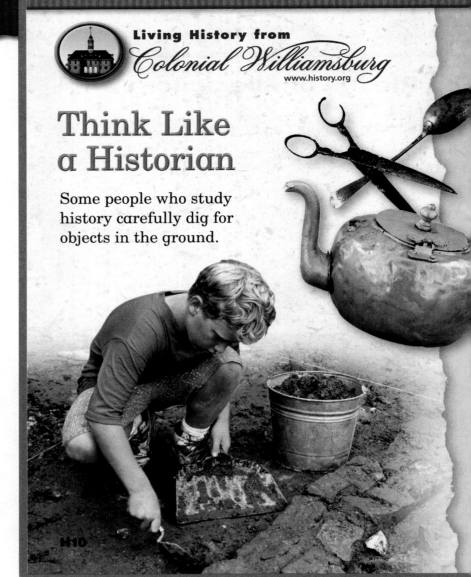

Living History from *Colonial Williamsburg*
www.history.org

# Think Like a Historian

Some people who study history carefully dig for objects in the ground.

H10

# Practice and Extend

## FYI SOCIAL STUDIES Background

### Archaeologists
*by Dr. William E. White, Colonial Williamsburg Historian*

- Children may be familiar with how we have learned about dinosaurs. Scientists called paleontologists learn about them by digging up their fossilized bones. Similarly, archaeologists learn about how people lived in the past by studying their artifacts.

- Many people do not leave written documents for us to investigate, so we must find a different way to learn about their lives. Archaeologists retrieve from the ground the artifacts that people left behind.

- Archaeologists discover all kinds of personal items like shoes, buttons, buckles, spoons, ceramics, and glass. These items can tell us how people lived their daily lives. Sometimes we even find bones, seeds, and pollen in trash pits that tell us what people ate long ago.

Many things they find are broken. This plate is broken. It must be put back together to see what it looks like.

What did this plate look like when it was new? Draw a picture. Show what it may have looked like.

**H11**

**CURRICULUM CONNECTION**
## Art

### Artifacts

- Remind children that historians learn about people of the past by studying the everyday items they used and left behind.
- Review with children the list they created of classroom items.
- Have children draw a picture of one of those items. Have them share their drawings and describe what the artifact could tell others about what school is like today.

- **Spoon, scissors, and copper teakettle** These are the kinds of artifacts archaeologists might uncover at the site of a home from long ago. They were made in England in the mid to late 1700s. Ask children to identify these three artifacts. They are much like items we still use today.

- **Broken plate** Most archaeological artifacts are found in pieces. Objects that are broken into many pieces can be very difficult to recognize. Often, archaeologists must put all the pieces of an object together—much like a puzzle—before they can identify what it is and how it was used in the past. Ask children what they think this artifact is. Explain that this plate is like one Colonial Williamsburg archaeologists found.

## 3 Close and Assess

- Review with children the artifacts shown on this spread. Discuss what they tell us about people from long ago. Help children describe the decorative elements they see in the broken plate and discuss how those elements are arranged.

- Ask children to draw a picture of what the plate might have looked like before it was broken.

# Gather and Report Information

## Find the Facts

- Have children identify the pictures on this page. Read the introductory text to children as they follow along. Then read aloud the six questions. Ask children to answer the questions using what they know today.

- Explain that research helps us learn about things that are new to us. Some scientists look at objects they find in the ground and ask questions like these to help them learn about people and places long ago.

# Find the Facts

Suppose a scientist in the future found these objects buried in the ground. Scientists ask questions to learn more about things. Look at some of the questions they ask. How would you answer these questions?

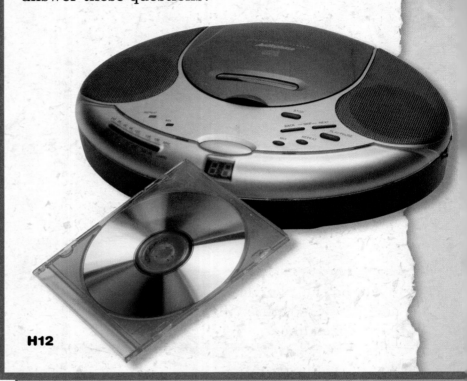

**H12**

# Practice and Extend

## FAST FACTS

### Archaelogical Finds

- On August 12, 1990, fossil hunter Sue Hendrickson discovered bones from a Tyrannosaurus Rex on the Cheyenne River Sioux Indian Reservation near Faith, South Dakota. The dinosaur is estimated to have been 42 feet long, 13 feet high, and have weighed 600 pounds. It was named Sue in her honor. The skeleton was mounted and was put on display at the Field Museum in Chicago in May 2000.

- Arrow and spear points known as Clovis Points, are among the oldest tools discovered in North America, and have often been found with the remains of ice age animals. These points were discovered in the Southwestern part of the United States near Clovis, New Mexico. They are said to be from people living as long ago as 9000 B.C. The points were gathered from sources hundreds of miles away from the sites where they were found, indicating that their makers traveled long distances while following herds of game.

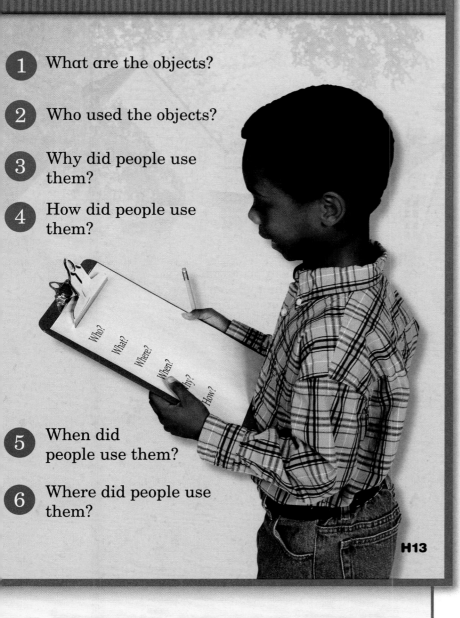

1. What are the objects?

2. Who used the objects?

3. Why did people use them?

4. How did people use them?

5. When did people use them?

6. Where did people use them?

**H13**

1. **What are the objects?** A CD player and a CD.

2. **Who used the objects?** The objects were used by people.

3. **Why did people use them?** People used them to listen to music.

4. **How did people use them?** Possible answer: The CD player had to be connected to a power source—an electrical outlet or batteries.

5. **When did people use them?** Possible answer: People used them any time they wanted to listen to music.

6. **Where did people use them?** Possible answer: People used them at home, at parties, at the beach, and so on. They could be carried from place to place.

**CURRICULUM CONNECTION**
## Art

**Research in the Future**

- Have children draw a picture of an item in their home that a scientist might find many years from now. If necessary, provide examples such as clock radio, telephone, computer, or skateboard.
- Ask them to write or dictate answers to the questions Who?, What?, Where?, When?, Why?, and How?
- Have children share their drawings with the class.

## Use Different Resources

If possible, take children as a group to the school or community library. Show them the reference section. Identify examples of encyclopedias, dictionaries and atlases. Allow children time to look through examples of each type of reference material. Discuss each one. Be sure children understand that encyclopedias come in a set. Point out the letter or letters on the covers and spine of the encyclopedias. Tell children that information on words that begin with the letter or letters on the cover are inside that book.

Brainstorm different topics with children. Write their answers on the board. Ask which encyclopedia they would look in to find out more about each topic. Underline the first letter of each topic as answers are correctly given.

- **What order are the topics in an encyclopedia listed?** Alphabetical
  **Main Idea and Details**

- **What letter would we look under to find out more about Virginia?** The letter "V"
  **Recall and Retell**

- **What is the next letter we should look at to try and find the word Virginia in the "V" encyclopedia?** The letter "i" **Infer**

## Use Different Resources

There are many different resources you can use to get information. Colonial Williamsburg is in Virginia. Suppose you want to learn more about the state of Virginia.

### Encyclopedia

An encyclopedia has information about many topics. The topics are in alphabetical order. You can find out more about Virginia by looking under "V" in the encyclopedia.

**H14**

## Practice and Extend

**CURRICULUM CONNECTION**
**Writing**

### Research a Topic

- Have children chose a topic they would like to learn more about.
- Ask them to use the resources they learned about to write a short report on the topic.
- Tell children they can include pictures and maps in their reports.
- Have volunteers share their reports with the class.

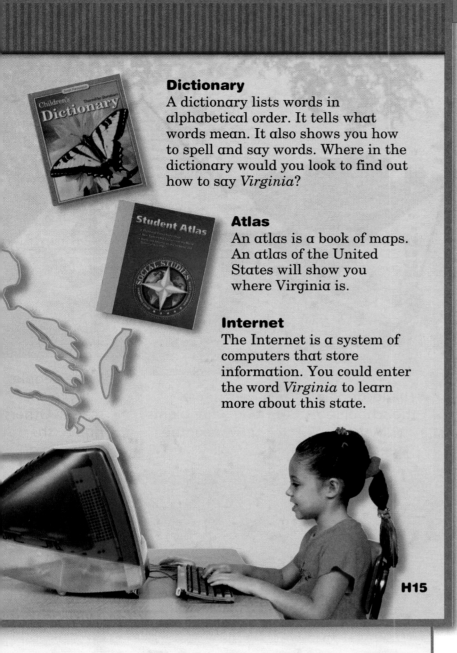

### Dictionary

A dictionary lists words in alphabetical order. It tells what words mean. It also shows you how to spell and say words. Where in the dictionary would you look to find out how to say *Virginia*?

### Atlas

An atlas is a book of maps. An atlas of the United States will show you where Virginia is.

### Internet

The Internet is a system of computers that store information. You could enter the word *Virginia* to learn more about this state.

H15

- **What order are the topics in a dictionary listed?** Alphabetical **Main Idea and Details**
- **Look at a dictionary. What information does a dictionary give you about each word?** What a word means, how to spell the word, how to say the word **Main Idea and Details**
- **Which resource would you look in if you wanted to look at a map of Virginia?** An atlas **Main Idea and Details**
- **With which resource are you also using technology?** The Internet **Main Idea and Details**

### WEB SITE
## Technology

**Safety on the Internet**

- Tell children that they should never to give out personal information, such as their name, home address, phone number, age, race, family income, school name or location, or friends' names without permission.
- Tell children that they should never share their password with anybody, including their friends.
- Warn children never to arrange to meet somebody they meet online without first talking with a parent or teacher.
- Children should understand that they do not have to respond to every message they get over the Internet. They should never respond to messages that make them feel uncomfortable. They should ignore the message and tell a teacher, parent, or older trusted adult right away.
- Make sure children understand that people they meet online are not always who they say they are, and online information is not private.

# The Five Themes of Geography

From "*Guidelines for Geographic Education: Elementary and Secondary Skills*," prepared by the Joint Committee on Geographic Education of the National Council for Geographic Education and the Association of American Geographers

## Location

Explain to children that *location* is the place where you find something. You may wish to have children use the Big Book Atlas to complete the following.

- Explain to children their school is in a community, and their community is in a city. Help children find the exact or approximate location of their city on a map of their state.
- Have children locate their state on a map of the United States.

## Place

*Place* is what makes one location different from another. Place can be described by telling about people or things at a location. Sometimes it is helpful to locate a place by describing how near or far it is to another place.

**1 Where are the trees, grass, and other plants?** They are near the school.
**Analyze Pictures**

## Movement

*Movement* is going from one place to another. It includes ways people travel.

**2 How have buses and cars made it easier for some children to go to school?** Possible answer: Children who live so far away from school that they can't walk can now ride to school.
**Make Inferences**

### Five Things to Think About

Geography is the study of Earth. This study sometimes looks at the Earth in five different ways. These ways are the five themes of geography. Each theme is a way of thinking about an area. Look at the examples for this school.

**Location**

200 Melrose Street

The location of the school is at 200 Melrose Street.

**Place**

Trees, grass, and other plants grow near the school. **1**

**Movement**

Some people walk to the school. Others ride to the school in a bus or a car.

H16 Social Studies Handbook

# Practice and Extend

**FYI** SOCIAL STUDIES
**Background**

**The Essential Elements of Geography**
From the National Council for Geographic Education

- **The World in Spatial Terms** Geography studies the spatial relationships between people, places, and environments.
- **Places and Regions** The identities of individuals and cultures can be found in particular places and regions.
- **Physical Systems** Physical processes shape Earth's surface and create, sustain, and change ecosystems.
- **Humans Systems** Human activities help shape Earth's surface.
- **Environment and Society** The physical environment is modified by human activities. Human activities are also influenced by Earth.
- **The Uses of Geography** Knowledge of geography enables people to understand the relationships between people, places, and environments over time.

### Places and People Change Each Other

People put swings and a slide here. Now children can play outside. ③

### Region

This school is in a part of the United States that is near the center of the country. ④

Social Studies Handbook H17

## Drama

**Traveling to School by Bus**

- Have children dramatize going to school by bus.
- Have children play the roles of bus driver, parents accompanying children to a bus stop, and children boarding the bus.
- The bus driver winds his or her way around the classroom picking up children, who follow behind. Meanwhile, the parents return to their seats.
- The final destination of the bus is the teacher's desk, where children, one-by-one, get out of the bus and return to their seats.

## Places and People Change Each Other

*People* can make places different. For example, people cut down trees, build houses, and farm land. *Places* can make people different. For example, people who live in cold climates must dress warmly.

③ **What might the school yard have looked like before people put swings and a slide there?** Possible answer: Rocks and grass might have been there. Make Inferences

## Region

A *region* is a large area that is different from other large areas. A region can be described by features such as landforms and climate.

④ **What do the states in this region have in common?** They are in the center of the country. Apply Information

## Additional Resources

The following resources can be used throughout Grade 1 to teach and reinforce geography skills.

- Primary Big Book Atlas
- Outline Maps
- Desk Maps
- Map Resources CD-ROM

# Map and Globe Skills Review

## Talk About the Pictures

- Help children to understand that certain areas have common characteristics and can be called regions.

- Have children look at the pictures. Discuss with children whether there are forests, plains, mountains, or oceans near where they live. Define any terms that may be unfamiliar to children, such as *plains.* Ask children if they have ever visited any of the types of regions that are not nearby.

---

### Some Regions on Earth

The Earth is made up of land and water. Some of the pictures below show different kinds of land. One picture shows water. Earth has forests, plains, mountains, and oceans.

The forest has many kinds of trees. Owls, squirrels, and deer live in the forest.

You might see tall grasses growing on the plains. Horses, rabbits, and foxes live here.

 **H18** Social Studies Handbook

---

## Practice and Extend

 **FYI** SOCIAL STUDIES **Background**

**Fast Facts**

- At 14,433 feet, Mt. Elbert is the highest peak in the U.S. portion of the Rocky Mountains.

- The Pacific Ocean covers about 28% of the global surface—larger than the total land area of the world.

- The Atlantic Ocean is the second largest of the world's five oceans (after the Pacific Ocean, but larger than the Indian Ocean, Southern Ocean, and Arctic Ocean).

- In the United States the Plains include parts of North Dakota, South Dakota, Montana, Wyoming, Colorado, Nebraska, Kansas, Oklahoma, New Mexico, and Texas.

Many parts of our country have very tall mountains. Moose, bears, and big horn sheep live in the mountains.

Some parts of our country are near the ocean. Many kinds of plants and animals live underwater.

Social Studies Handbook **H19**

**AUDIO CD**
**Technology**

Play the CD, *Songs and Music*, to listen to "This Land is Your Land."

# Geographical Regions of the United States

- Explain to students that the United States is divided into five regions: Northeast, Southeast, Midwest, Southwest and West.

- Use a large map to point out each region and the states that make up each region.

- Help children locate their state on the map and identify the region of the country the state is in.

- Point out one or two special features in each region of the United States. For example; Niagara Falls in the Northeast, the Appalachian Mountains in the Southeast; the Great Lakes in the Midwest; the Grand Canyon in the Southwest; and the Sonoran desert in the West.

# Map and Globe Skills Review

## Talk About the Picture of Earth

- Have children tell whether they see more land or water on this picture of Earth.
- Explain to children that the white area at the top of the Earth is frozen water.

### From Earth to a Globe

Here is a picture that looks down at our Earth. It is a picture taken from space. Earth looks round like a ball.

The smooth blue parts of Earth are water. The other parts with green and brown on them are land. It is very exciting to see Earth this way.

Right now you are down there somewhere on the land.

 **Social Studies Handbook**

## Practice and Extend

**FYI** SOCIAL STUDIES **Background**

### About Globes

- One of the first globes was made by Martin Behaim in Germany in 1492.
- Most globes are 22 inches in diameter. Some globes are so big that you can stand inside them.
- At the Dynamic Earth Globe at the American Museum of Natural History in New York, visitors seated below the globe are able to watch a special film that makes it appear that they're seeing Earth rotating from outer space.

**Vocabulary**

globe
Earth
model

The **globe** on this page looks like the picture of **Earth.** A globe is a round **model** of Earth. You can put it on a table. You can turn it and see all around it. You can study it in your class.

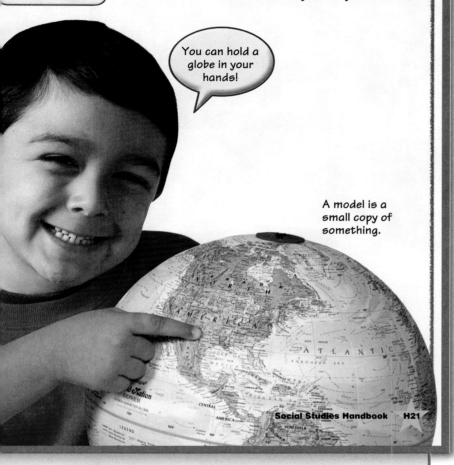

You can hold a globe in your hands!

A model is a small copy of something.

Social Studies Handbook  H21

## CURRICULUM CONNECTION
## Math

**Measure Distances**

Have children use linked paper clips to measure the shortest distance between two points on the globe.

- Europe to North America
- Africa to North America
- Explain to children that actual distances could be measured in miles or kilometers.

# Use a Globe

- Discuss with children that a model is a small copy of something. Ask for examples of models. Then ask children to identify the similarities and differences between actual Earth pictured on p. H20 and the globe pictured on p. H21.

- Tell children that a continent is a very large body of land. Point out North America and South America on the picture of the globe. Ask children which continent the boy in the picture is pointing to (North America). Tell children that the United States is part of North America.

- Help children locate the United States on a globe. Then ask them to locate their state.

### SOCIAL STUDIES STRAND
### Geography

**Features of Places**

Use a map or globe to talk with children about the similarities and differences among geographic locations, regions, and environments in different parts of the world in terms of the four spatial elements of location (point), transportation and communication routes (line), regions (areas), and lakes filled with water (volume).

## Vocabulary

**globe:** a small round model of Earth

**Earth:** the whole world where people live

**model:** a small copy of something

# Map and Globe Skills Review

## Talk About the Picture

Read p. H22 to children.

- Ask children whether the photograph of the area was taken from below, the side, or above. (above)

- Ask children if the area in the photograph is a local community, state, or nation. (local community)

- Have children identify things in the picture that were made by people. (houses, streets)

- Ask children if they think this is an area where people live or work. (live) Why? (It has many houses and no stores.)

Vocabulary

map

### From a Picture to a Map

Maybe you do not want to study the whole Earth. Maybe you want to look down only at the area where you live. Your area might look something like th

**H22** Social Studies Handbook

# Practice and Extend

## FYI SOCIAL STUDIES Background

### Taking Pictures of Earth from Above

- The primary task in creating a map is to accurately represent an area on a much smaller surface.

- To make a map of Earth, the size and shape of landforms and bodies of water must be carefully measured. Photographs of areas can greatly help in making these measurements.

- Airplanes are commonly used to take pictures of large areas of Earth. They can provide information more accurately and easily than ground measurements, especially when the land is rough and the climate extreme.

- Satellites and spacecraft are used to take photographs of Earth from space.

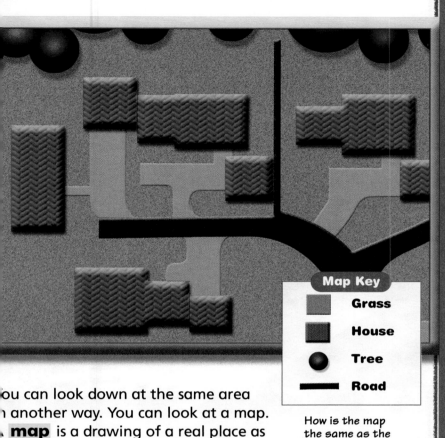

**Map Key**

■ Grass

■ House

● Tree

▬ Road

ou can look down at the same area
n another way. You can look at a map.
**map** is a drawing of a real place as
is seen from above. A map of the
ame part of town might look like this.

How is the map
the same as the
picture? How is
the map different
from the picture?

# Talk About the Map

- Ask children how the map on p. H23 is similar to the picture on p. H22. (They both show the same area, are much smaller than the real area, and are flat.)

- Ask children how the map is different from the picture. (The map is a drawing of the area. The picture is an actual photograph of the area.)

Tell children that the shapes on the map stand for something else.

- Have children point to the different shapes on the map. Ask them what the shapes stand for. (grass, house, tree, road)

- Have children compare a map to a globe. (A map is on a page. It is flat. A globe is a round model of Earth.)

## Vocabulary

**map:** a drawing of a real place as seen from above

**CURRICULUM CONNECTION**
## Science

**Climate, Weather, and Clothing**

- Have children discuss what kinds of clothing they wear to school at different times of the year, and how this is related to changes in the weather for different seasons.

- Also, have them discuss how their clothing would be different if they lived in a region that had a climate quite a bit different from the one where they live.

# Map and Globe Skills Review

## Talk About the Picture

Read p. H24 to children.

- Ask children to identify things they recognize in the picture. (The school, children on the sidewalk, the school bus.)
- Ask children to compare the school in the picture to their own school. What is the same? What is different?
- Have children tell what they think the inside of the school would look like. (There would be classrooms, a gym, a cafeteria, a playground, and so on.)

### Look at a Picture of a School

Look at this picture of a school. You can see the walls and the roof of the school.

H24   Social Studies Handbook

# Practice and Extend

## ESL  EXTEND LANGUAGE
## ESL Support

**Make a Map** Draw a map of the classroom, using shapes and colors to identify the location of places in the classroom. Point to places on the map. Have children repeat the name of each place.

**Beginning** Have children copy the map. Then have them point to the shapes and name what they stand for.

**Intermediate** Have children copy the map and name the shapes. Ask them to write a title for the map: "Classroom Map." Then have them label the "top," "bottom," "left side," and "right side" of the map.

**Advanced** Have children do the activities listed above. Work together to include a map key to explain the shapes used. Say the name of various places on the map (student's desk, teacher's desk, door, window, bookcase, flag) and ask students to point to each one on the map and in the classroom.

## Read a Map of a School

Here is a map that lets you look down inside the same school without the roof. This map shows some of the rooms in the school. Can you point to the cafeteria? What room is the music room next to?

**CURRICULUM CONNECTION**
## Art

**Create and Use Classroom, School, Community, and State Maps**

- Help children create a map of the classroom, including the location of the entrance and the place where they are sitting. Have children trace the way from the entrance to the place where they are sitting.

- Help children create a map of the hallways between the school entrance and classroom entrance. Ask them to trace the way from the entrance to their classroom.

- Help children create a map of the community showing their school and nearby streets. Have children trace the way they travel along a nearby street to the school entrance.

- Give children a map of their state. Help children locate and label their town or city on the map.

# Talk About the Map

- Ask children to look at the map on p. H25. Explain that this map lets you look down at the inside of the school without the roof. This type of map helps you understand where different rooms in the school are located.

- Ask children to name the rooms they can see in the school. (Classrooms, cafeteria, gymnasium, music room, computer lab, offices.)

- Have children tell where the computer lab is located. (Across the hall from the cafeteria.) Ask them to tell you how many classrooms they can see (Two.)

- Have children name some places in their own school that they would include on a map of the school. (Possible answers: Library, Art Room, Principal's Office, Auditorium, and so on.)

# Map and Globe Skills Review

## Use Directions

Explain to children that a map can be used for directions. Directions can tell you where to go.

- To activate prior knowledge, ask children to tell about when a map was used for directions at a zoo, park, shopping mall, or some other place.
- Ask children for directions to the school entrance and other school locations.

Tell children to look at the map of a zoo on p. H26.

- Ask children what animal is farthest away from the elephants. (snakes)
- Ask children what animal is between the lions and the snakes. (turtles)

## Answers

**1.** Giraffes

**2.** Lions

### Use Directions

A map helps you know where things are. Things can be near or far away. They can be between or behind other things. Look at this map of a zoo.

What animal is near the snakes

What animal is between the lions and elephants? What animal is farthest away from the monkeys?

H26    Social Studies Handbook

## Practice and Extend

**CURRICULUM CONNECTION**
### Drama

**Giving Directions**

Have children describe the location of self and objects using directions words such as *near, far away from, in front of, next to, between,* and *behind.* First model each activity.

- Have children describe their location relative to the classroom bulletin board.
- List classroom objects. Have children describe the location of the objects relative to the classroom bulletin board.
- Ask children to pretend that have just entered school through the main entrance. Have them describe their location relative to the school bulletin board.

# Vocabulary Routines

**The following examples of reading and vocabulary development strategies can be used to instruct students about unit vocabulary.**

## BEFORE READING

### Related Word Study

Vocabulary: school, group, flag, country, rule

**Meaningful Sentence Posters**  Use the five unit vocabulary words to create meaningful sentences with children. Write each word on a separate sheet of paper or posterboard. Explain the meaning of each word and write the meaning on the posterboard. Then have children develop meaningful sentences for each word and share them with the class. Write down their sentences on the posterboard and tape the posterboards to a word wall or another area of the room designated for vocabulary. Children can look at the posters throughout the lessons to help them remember what each word means.

*Let's look at the word* **rule**. *A rule tells us what to do and what not to do. Let me write that down. Who can think of a sentence with the word* **rule** *in it? One school rule is keep your hands to yourself. If you do not follow a school rule, then you will get in trouble. At home, our mealtime rule is do not talk with your mouth full.*

> **RULE**
>
> **A rule tells us what to do and what not to do.**

## DURING READING

### Context Clues

**Apply That Word**  At the end of each page, stop briefly and encourage children to think about how a new word relates to something they have seen or done in their own lives. By applying the vocabulary word, children increase their chances of recalling the word and retaining its meaning. You can use this technique with any of the unit vocabulary, as shown in the example at right:

*When you stand with your friends at recess, you could say "I like to talk with my* **group** *of friends at recess." When you put a rubber band around a bunch of pencils, you could say "I put the pencils in a* **group**." *What other sentences could you make with the word* **group**?

*A* **group** *of us are going to the park after school.*

*I like to sit under that* **group** *of trees.*

## AFTER READING

### Individual Word Study

**Word Wizard**  Use this routine to encourage children to look and listen for their vocabulary words outside of the classroom. Award a point for each example a child shares with the class. You may wish to tally points on an individual or a group basis.

*What vocabulary words did you see or hear?*

(I saw pictures of flags around the world in a book. Each country has a different flag. I remembered that *country* and *flag* were two of the words we read about.)

*That is correct. I will give you two points for finding those words at home.*

# ★ Unit 1 ★

# Teaching with Leveled Readers

**This series of readers focuses on rules in the home, school, and community.**

**Below Level**

**On Level**

**Above Level**

## LEVELED READER VOCABULARY ACTIVITY

- Have children preview the vocabulary words at the beginning of the reader.

- As children read, have them find the vocabulary words in the text.

- After reading, have children explain the connection between the words *rule* and *law*.

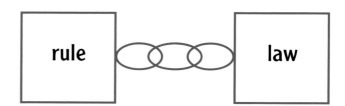

## CONNECTIONS TO THE LESSON

Unit 1, Lesson 3: Rules We Follow

## CONNECTIONS TO TODAY

- Have children read the lesson. Then provide the leveled readers to enhance their understanding of rules they know about in their school and community.

- **Points for Discussion:**
    1. Have children discuss why we have rules.

    2. Children can also discuss some of the rules in their families.

# Time for School

# Unit 1 Planning Guide
## Time for School

**Begin with a Song** pp. 2–3　　**Vocabulary Preview** pp. 4–5

**Reading Social Studies, Use Picture Clues** pp. 6–7

| Lesson Titles | Pacing | Main Ideas |
|---|---|---|
| **Lesson 1** **Getting to Know Andrew** pp. 8–9 <br><br> **Biography: Carl Stotz** pp. 10–11 <br><br> *Colonial Williamsburg* **Families Long Ago** pp. 12–13 | 2 days | • A person can belong to many groups. <br> • Carl Stotz founded Little League so that children could enjoy playing baseball. <br> • Families long ago enjoyed many of the same activities as families today. |
| **Lesson 2** **Home and School** pp. 14–17 <br><br> **Citizen Heroes:** **Courage** **Ruby Bridges Hall** pp. 18–19 <br> **Chart and Graph Skills: Read a Calendar** pp. 20–21 | 3 days | • A typical school day includes routines, one of which is pledging allegiance to the flag. <br> • Ruby Bridges Hall showed courage by attending a school in which she was—for her first year there— the only African American student. <br> • A calendar is a special kind of chart that shows days, weeks, months, and years. |
| **Lesson 3** **Rules We Follow** pp. 22–25 <br><br> **Thinking Skills: Problem on the Playground** pp. 26–27 | 2 days | • It is important to know the rules at school and at home—and to follow those rules. <br> • People such as principals and teachers help us to understand the rules. <br> • Solving a problem involves following certain steps: name the problem, investigate it, list solutions, choose and execute a good one, and evaluate the results. |
| **Lesson 4** **Learning About My School** pp. 28–31 <br><br> **Biography: Mary McLeod Bethune** pp. 32–33 <br> **Then and Now: Things We Use** pp. 34–35 | 3 days | • Schools, like other things, change over time. <br> • Mary McLeod Bethune, an educator and public speaker, started a school for African American girls. <br> • Tools children use at school have changed over time. |

✓ **End with a Poem** pp. 36–37　　✓ **Unit 1 Review** pp. 38–41　　✓ **Unit 1 Project** p. 42

✓ = Assessment Options

| Vocabulary | Resources | Meeting Individual Needs |
|---|---|---|
| **school**<br>**group** | • Workbook, pp. 3–4<br>• Vocabulary Cards: school, group<br>• Every Student Learns Guide,<br>  pp. 2–5 | • Leveled Practice, TE p. 13a |
| **flag**<br>**country** | • Workbook, pp. 5–6<br>• Vocabulary Cards: flag, country<br>• Every Student Learns Guide,<br>  pp. 6–9<br>• Transparency 10 | • ESL Support, TE p. 15<br>• Leveled Practice,<br>  TE pp. 16, 21a |
| **rule** | • Workbook, pp. 7–8<br>• Vocabulary Card: rule<br>• Every Student Learns Guide,<br>  pp. 10–13<br>• Transparencies 11, 12 | • ESL Support, TE p. 23<br>• Leveled Practice,<br>  TE p. 27a |
| | • Workbook, p. 9<br>• Every Student Learns Guide,<br>  pp. 14–17 | • ESL Support, TE p. 29<br>• Leveled Practice,<br>  TE pp. 35, 35a |

# Providing More Depth

## Additional Resources

- Trade Books
- Family Activities
- Vocabulary Workbook and Cards
- Social Studies Plus!
- Daily Activity Bank
- Read Alouds and Primary Sources
- Big Book Atlas
- Student Atlas
- Outline Maps
- Desk Maps

## Technology

- Video Field Trips
- Songs and Music
- Digital Learning CD-ROM Powered by KnowledgeBox
- AudioText
- MindPoint® Quiz Show CD-ROM
- ExamView® Test Bank CD-ROM
- Colonial Williamsburg Primary Sources CD-ROM
- Teacher Resources CD-ROM
- Map Resources CD-ROM
- SFSuccessNet: Online Student Edition, Online Teacher Edition, Online Planner
- **www.sfsocialstudies.com**
  (Biographies, news, references, maps, and activities)

 *To establish guidelines for your children's safe and responsible use of the Internet, use the Scott Foresman Internet Guide.*

**Additional Internet Links**

To find out more about:
- Colonial Williamsburg, visit **www.history.org**

# Unit 1 Objectives

**Beginning of Unit 1**

- Learn why children attend school. (pp. 2–3)

- Determine the meanings of words. (pp. 4–5)

- Obtain information about a topic using pictures. (pp. 6–7)

**Lesson 1**
**Getting to Know Andrew**
pp. 8–9

- Understand that people belong to many different groups.

- Obtain information about a topic using pictures.

- Identify contributions of historical figures who have influenced the community, state, and nation. (pp. 10–11)

- Learn about families 200 years ago by using a variety of visual sources, such as artifacts and photographs. (pp. 12–13)

- Describe the kinds of activities families from long ago did together and compare them with family activities today. (pp. 12–13)

**Lesson 2**
**Home and School**
pp. 14–17

- Explain how selected symbols reflect an American love of individualism and freedom.

- Explain how routines are part of our daily life at home and at school.

- Identify characteristics of good citizenship, such as a belief in equality. (pp. 18–19)

- Read and create a calendar. (pp. 20–21)

- Obtain information about a topic using visual sources, such as graphics and pictures. (pp. 20–21)

**Lesson 3**
**Rules We Follow**
pp. 22–25

- Give examples of rules.

- Identify the responsibilities of authority figures in the school and home.

- Explain the need for rules and laws in the home, school, and community.

- Use a problem-solving process. (pp. 26–27)

**Lesson 4**
**Learning About My School**
pp. 28–31

- Obtain information about a topic using a variety of oral sources, such as interviews.

- Compare past and present.

- Identify characteristics of good citizenship, such as belief in equality. (pp. 32–33)

- Identify the contributions of historical figures in the period of history since 1880. (pp. 32–33)

- Recognize that things change over time. (pp. 34–35)

**End of Unit 1**

- Obtain information about a topic using literature. (pp. 36–37)

# Assessment Options

## ✓ Formal Assessment

- **What did you learn?** PE/TE pp. 9, 17, 25, 31, 41
- **Unit Review,** PE/TE pp. 38–41
- **Unit 1 Test,** Assessment Book pp. 1–4
- **ExamView® CD-ROM**

## ✓ Informal Assessment

- **Teacher's Edition Questions,** throughout Lessons and Features
- **Close and Assess,** TE pp. 9, 11, 13, 17, 19, 21, 25, 27, 31, 33, 35, 37
- **Try it!** PE/TE pp. 7, 27
- **Think and Share,** PE/TE pp. 9, 11, 17, 25, 31, 33, 41
- **Courage in Action,** PE/TE p. 19
- **Hands-on History,** PE/TE p. 35

### Ongoing Assessment

**Ongoing Assessment** is found throughout the Teacher's Edition lessons using an **If...then** model.

**If =** students' observable behavior,

**then =** reteaching and enrichment suggestions

## ✓ Portfolio Assessment

- **Portfolio Assessment,** TE pp. 1
- **Leveled Practice,** TE pp. 4, 13a, 16, 21a, 27a, 35, 35a
- **Workbook Pages,** pp. 1–11
- **Unit Review: Skills on Your Own,** PE/TE p. 40
- **Curriculum Connection: Writing,** TE pp. 13a, 21a, 27a, 33

## ✓ Performance Assessment

- **Hands-on Unit Project** (Unit 1 Performance Assessment), PE/TE pp. 1, 42
- **Internet Activity,** PE p. 42
- **Unit Review: Think and Share,** PE/TE p. 41
- **Scoring Guides,** TE pp. 36a, 39, 40, 42

## Test Talk

### Test-Taking Strategies

**Understand the Question**

- **Locate Key Words in the Question,** TE p. 41
- **Locate Key Words in the Text,** TE p. 11

**Understand the Answer**

- **Choose the Right Answer**
- **Use Information from the Text,** TE p. 19
- **Use Information from Graphics,** TE p. 21
- **Write Your Answer,** TE p. 31

*For additional practice, use the Test Talk Practice Book.*

### Featured Strategy

**Locate Key Words in the Question**

Children will:

- Find the key words in the question.
- Turn the key words into a statement that begins "I need to find out...."

**PE/TE** p. 41

# Curriculum Connections
## Integrating Your Day

The lessons, skills, and features of Unit 1 provide many opportunities to make connections between social studies and other areas of the elementary curriculum.

### Reading

**Biographies,** TE p. 11

**Reading Skill—Use Picture Clues,** TE pp. 8, 28

**Reading Skill—Put Things in Order,** TE p. 14

**Learn a Calendar Rhyme,** TE p. 20

**Reading Skill—Classify/Categorize,** TE p. 22

### Writing

**Make a Picture Glossary,** TE p. 5

**Make a Book,** TE p. 13a

**My Country, My Flag,** TE p. 21a

**Rules on Rules,** TE p. 27a

**Sharing Time,** TE p. 33

### Math

**School "Counts,"** TE p. 7

**Special Days,** TE p. 21a

**Tools,** TE p. 35a

### Social Studies

### Literature

**The Story of Ruby Bridges,** TE p. 19

**Books About School,** TE p. 37

**Read About School,** PE/TE p. 41

### Science

**Snack Survey,** TE p. 16

**Reducing Trash,** TE p. 26

### Music/Drama

**Games We Play,** TE p. 13a

**"This Is the Way,"** TE p. 36

### Art

**This Is How We Work and Play!** TE p. 3

**Things I Like,** TE p. 13a

 Look for this symbol throughout the Teacher's Edition to find **Curriculum Connections.**

# Professional Development

## Teaching Social Studies to Young Children

**by Sara Miranda Sanchez**
Albuquerque Public Schools

Early childhood pedagogy has long recognized that young children under the age of eight do not learn isolated facts with much success; neither are they passive learners. We know that allowing children to address academic goals that represent specific knowledge and skills in interactive, child-centered experiences will promote greater depth of learning. Yet, a common struggle in the primary classroom is finding the balance between covering predetermined content and developing multifaceted critical thinkers and learners.

My most successful practices set up experiences for children to be active participants in their own learning. The key is to find the experiences that meet the learning needs of all children. With a classroom of children each coming to school from unique situations and varying experiences, my teacher role was to create a learning environment to facilitate learning at multiple levels.

*The following activities in the Teacher's Edition are designed to meet children's individual needs by suggesting variations at three levels of difficulty.*

- *Explore the School*, p. 4
- *Find Pictures of Groups*, p. 13a
- *The United States*, p. 16
- *Hooray for Me!* p. 21a
- *Wall Mural*, p. 27a
- *Guess the Time*, p. 35
- *Then or Now*, p. 35a

## ESL Support

**by Jim Cummins, Ph. D.**
University of Toronto

### Activate Prior Knowledge/ Build Background

*In Unit 1, you can use the following fundamental strategy to help ESL students expand their language abilities.*

There is general agreement among cognitive psychologists that we learn by integrating new input into our existing cognitive structures. Our prior experience provides the foundation for interpreting new information. No learner is a blank slate. In reading, for example, we construct meaning by bringing our prior knowledge of language and of the world to the text. For example, a child who knows a lot about baseball will find it much easier to understand a story about baseball than a child who has very little prior knowledge about the game. The same holds true for social studies. The more a child already knows about a particular topic in the text, the more of the text he/she is likely to understand. And, the more of the text a child understands, the more new knowledge he/she can acquire.

*The following example in the Teacher's Edition will help you to activate students' prior knowledge and build background for the concepts developed in the lesson.*

- *Finding Clues* on p. 6 helps English Language Learners learn how to use picture clues.

# Read Aloud

## The Wheels on the Bus

The wheels on the bus go round and round,
Round and round, round and round,
The wheels on the bus go round and round,
As off to school we go.

The driver on the bus says buckle up,
Buckle up, buckle up,
The driver on the bus says buckle up,
As off to school we go.

The children on the bus sing a song,
Sing a song, sing a song,
The children on the bus sing a song,
As off to school we go.

The wheels on the bus go round and round,
Round and round, round and round,
The wheels on the bus go round and round,
As off to school we go.

**Build Background**
- Ask children how they get to school each day.
- Ask children to tell about rules they obey while coming to school.
- Ask children what they learn in school.

**Read Alouds and Primary Sources**
*Read Alouds and Primary Sources* contains additional selections to be used with Unit 1.

# Bibliography

*Froggy Goes to School,* by Jonathan London and Frank Remkiewicz (Illustrator), (Puffin, ISBN 0-14-056247-8, 1998) **Easy**

*My First Day of School,* by Patrick K. Hallinan (Hambleton-Hill; ISBN 1-57102-154-X, 2000) **Easy**

*My Teacher Sleeps in School,* by Leatie Weiss and Ellen Weiss (Illustrator), (Econo-Clad Books, ISBN 0-808-57413-2, 1999) **Easy**

*Owen,* by Kevin Henkes (Greenwillow, ISBN 0-688-11449-0, 1993) **Easy** *Caldecott Honor Book, 1994*

*Double Trouble in Walla Walla,* by Andrew Clements and Sal Murdocca (Illustrator), (Millbrook Press, ISBN 0-7613-0275-1, 1997) **On-Level**

*Lilly's Purple Plastic Purse,* by Kevin Henkes (Greenwillow, ISBN 0-688-12897-1, 1996) **On-Level** *ALA Notable Book*

*No Good in Art,* by Miriam Cohen and Lillian Hoban (Illustrator), (Morrow, ISBN 0-688-84234-8, 1980) **On-Level**

*Rex and Lilly Schooltime,* by Laurene Krasny Brown and Marc Brown (Illustrator), (Little Brown, ISBN 0-316-10920-7, 1997) **On-Level**

*Marianthe's Story: Painted Words, Spoken Memories,* by Aliki (Greenwillow, ISBN 0-688-15661-4, 1998) **Challenge**

*More Than Anything Else,* by Marie Bradby and Chris Soentpiet (Illustrator), (Orchard Books, ISBN 0-531-09464-2, 1995) **Challenge**

*Nobody's Mother Is in Second Grade,* by Robin Pulver and G. Brian Karas (Illustrator), (Dial Books for Young Readers, ISBN 0-8037-1210-3, 1992) **Challenge**

*Virgie Goes to School with Us Boys,* by Elizabeth Fitzgerald Howard and E. B. Lewis (Illustrator), (Simon & Schuster, ISBN 0-689-80076-2, 2000) **Challenge** *ALA Notable Book*

*Bringing History Home,* by M. Gail Hickey (Allyn & Bacon, ISBN 0-205-28169-9, 1998) **Teacher Reference**

*Hands Around the World,* by Susan Milord (Williamson, ISBN 0-913-58965-9, 1992) **Teacher Reference**

Look for this symbol throughout the Teacher's Edition to find **Award-Winning Selections**. Additional book references are suggested throughout this unit.

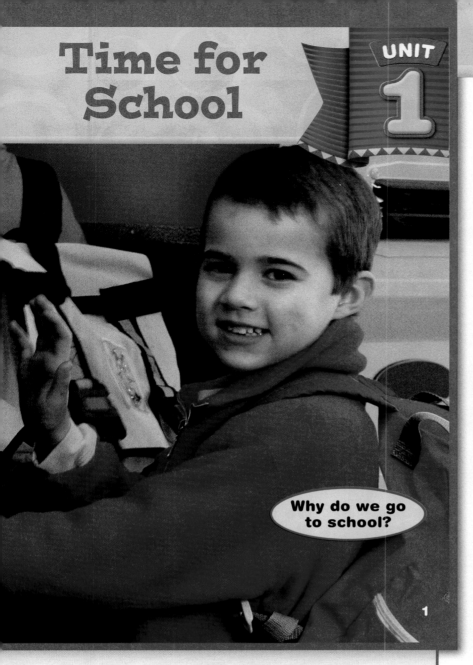

# Time for School

Why do we go to school?

1

UNIT 1

# Time for School

## Unit Overview

This unit introduces children to aspects of life at school, such as daily routines, rules, school history, and individuals who have contributed to education.

## Introduce Andrew

Read the unit title and then introduce the featured child for this unit as a first-grader named Andrew. Talk about where Andrew is going and why.

## Unit Question

- Ask children the question on this page.

- Initiate a discussion of what children hope to learn at school. Encourage them to talk about things that might help them to learn, such as a quiet place, trying hard, asking questions, practicing self-control, and working with others.

- To activate prior knowledge, make a list on chart paper of children's responses to the unit question: Why do we go to school?

✓ **Portfolio Assessment** Keep the list for the Portfolio Assessment at the end of the unit.

# Practice and Extend

## Hands-on Unit Project

### ✓ Unit 1 Performance Assessment

- The Unit 1 Project, *Follow Me!* found on p. 42, is an ongoing performance assessment project to enrich children's learning throughout the unit.

- This project, which has children making a model of a video camera and then giving a video tour of their school, may be started now or at any time during this unit of study.

- A performance assessment scoring guide is located on p. 42.

# We Go to School

## Objective
- Learn why children attend school.

## Resources
- *Songs and Music* CD "We Go to School"
- Poster 1
- Social Studies Plus!

# Introduce the Song

**Preview** Tell children that they will be singing a song about school. Focus on the picture of Andrew, and review where Andrew is going.

**Warm Up** To activate prior knowledge, use the list generated during the Portfolio Assessment activity (p. 1). Ask each child to tell what he or she most wants to learn at school this year.

# Sing the Song

- Have children sing the song "We Go to School."
- Have children pantomime the activities named in the song.
- Have children act out other things they want to learn to do at school.
- Ask children to help rewrite the third sentence of the song to reflect their own answers to the question: Why do we go to school? Then sing the song with the new lines.

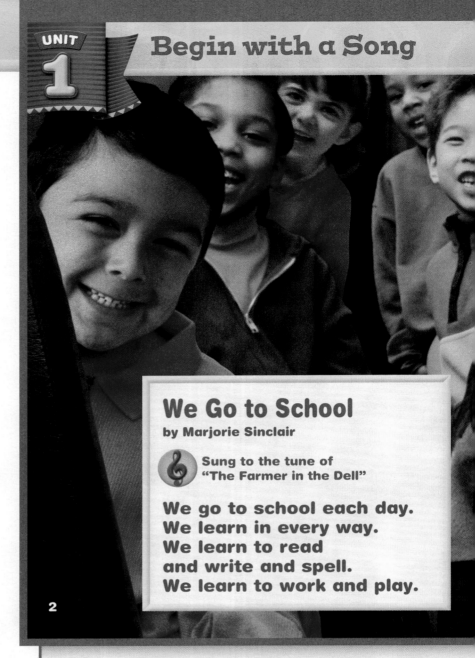

**We Go to School**
by Marjorie Sinclair

Sung to the tune of
"The Farmer in the Dell"

We go to school each day.
We learn in every way.
We learn to read
and write and spell.
We learn to work and play.

2

# Practice and Extend

## FAST FACTS

**Learning Long Ago**

You may want to mention a few of the schoolbooks that American children used long ago.

- To learn to read, they used "McGuffey's Readers," which taught patriotism as well as reading.
- To learn spelling, children used Noah Webster's "Blue-Backed Speller."

If possible, share with children an example of an old textbook, such as a McGuffey Reader.

 **AUDIO CD**
## Technology

Play the CD, *Songs and Music,* to listen to "We Go to School."

## Talk About the Photograph

Direct attention to the photograph on these two pages. Point out that the children in the picture are on a school bus. Ask children if any of them take a bus to school. Then point out Andrew in the photo.

**1 Why do you think Andrew looks happy?** He may be excited about going to school; he may be eager to meet new friends and learn to do new things. **Make Inferences**

**2 Who do you think the other children on the bus are?** Possible answers: Andrew's classmates, children who go to Andrew's school. **Make Inferences**

**CURRICULUM CONNECTION**
## Art

**This Is How We Work and Play!**

- Direct children's attention to the last sentence of the song. Ask them to name ways they learn to work and play in school.

- Have children draw a picture to illustrate their favorite work or play activity. Help them write captions for their pictures.

- Provide time for children to share their drawings with the class.

## Objective

• Determine the meanings of words.

## Resources

• Workbook, p. 1

• Vocabulary Cards

• Poster 2

## Introduce the Vocabulary

Read aloud and spell each vocabulary word as you point to it and the photograph illustrating it. Ask children to repeat each word and its spelling. Have volunteers give the meanings of the words. Then have children find several examples of the vocabulary words in the illustration. Write these examples on the board.

| Vocabulary Word | Illustrated Examples |
| --- | --- |
| school | school building, music school |
| group | ball team, children in classrooms |
| flag | flag outside school, flags in second-floor classrooms |
| country | two United States maps in second-floor classrooms |
| rule | crossing guards with stop signs, rules posted on bulletin board in second-floor left classroom |

⭐ **SOCIAL STUDIES STRAND**
**Citizenship**

**Prejudice Reduction** Listed below are some basic ideas of citizenship for young children. Direct your discussion of the illustration toward the development of these concepts.

• playing fairly

• exhibiting good sportsmanship

• helping others

• love of country

• treating others with respect

• rules to keep us safe

• taking responsibility for one's actions

• identifying compassion as a trait of a good citizen

school

group

flag

4

## Practice and Extend

❄ **MEETING INDIVIDUAL NEEDS**
**Leveled Practice**

### Explore the School

Invite children to explore the school shown on pp. 4–5 with you.

**Easy** Begin outside the school, and name things you see. Each time you name a vocabulary word, have children repeat it after you. Continue to explore inside the school with children. **Reteach**

**On-Level** Have children take turns guiding a "new student" around the school. Encourage them to use vocabulary words to describe what they see. **Extend**

**Challenge** Invite children to describe something in the picture—without naming it. Have others try to name the item being described. **Enrich**

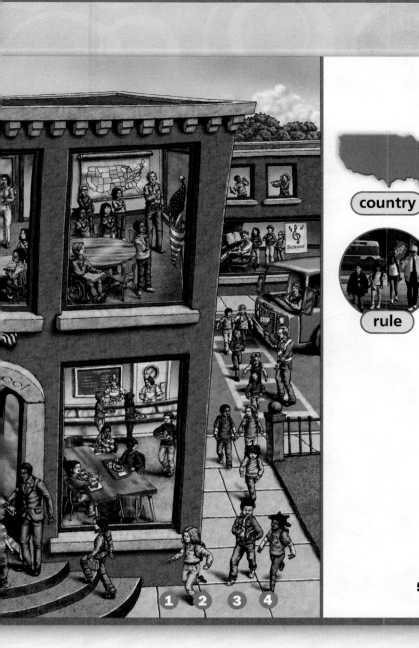

country

rule

**5**

① ② ③ ④

**CURRICULUM CONNECTION**
**Writing**

**Make a Picture Glossary**

Children can add the vocabulary for Unit 1 to "My Word Book." Words may be entered at the beginning of the unit or added as they are introduced in the specific lessons.

**WEB SITE**
**Technology**

You can look up vocabulary words online. Click on *Social Studies Library* and select the dictionary at **www.sfsocialstudies.com**.

**Workbook, p. 1**

Draw a picture for each word. **Drawings will vary.**

| school | group |
|--------|-------|
| flag | rule STOP |
| country | |

Directions: Read the words and draw pictures to illustrate them. Cut out the boxes to use as word cards.  Home Activity: Look through magazines with your child to find a picture that illustrates each word.

Workbook  Vocabulary Preview **1**

**Also on Teacher Resources CD-ROM.**

# Talk About the Picture

Point out that the picture shows several aspects of life at school. Then, to help children relate the picture to their own experiences, ask questions such as: *How close to the board are you? How far is the teacher's desk from the bookcase? Which way would you walk to go to the cafeteria? How close is the principal's office to the front door?*

① **What country do you think this school is in? How do you know?** Children may assume that the school is in the United States because the setting seems familiar. Some children may use the picture clues of the United States flags and the United States maps. **Draw Conclusions**

② **What are the children in the classrooms doing?** In one classroom, children are working at tables and putting a map puzzle together. In another classroom, children are pledging allegiance to the flag of the United States. **Analyze Pictures**

# Look Ahead

Tell children that they will learn more about each of the vocabulary words as they study Unit 1.

You may want to revisit the picture with children to review the concepts and vocabulary in the unit.

③ **What do you think would happen if children didn't follow the rules of the crossing guard?** Children might get hurt crossing the street. **Hypothesize**

④ **What do you think the children pledging the flag are saying?** The Pledge of Allegiance **Draw Conclusions**

# Andrew at School

## Use Picture Clues

### Objective
Obtain information about a topic using pictures.

### Vocabulary
**school** a place where children learn (p. 6)

### Resource
• Workbook, p. 2

### About the Unit Target Skill
• The target reading skill for this unit is Use Picture Clues.

• Children are introduced to the unit target skill here and are given an opportunity to practice it.

• Further opportunities to use picture clues are found throughout Unit 1.

## 1 Introduce and Motivate

**Preview** Display the Vocabulary Card **school**, and ask children to name their school. Share the meaning of *school* as a place where people learn. Then, to determine if children understand the concept of using picture clues, show 2–3 photos of yourself or of others doing activities in various settings. Ask children to tell you what each picture shows. Help them identify who is in the picture and what the actions are. You might ask: *Where was the photo taken? What is this person doing? Is he/she having fun?*

**Warm Up** To activate prior knowledge, show children a picture book with which they are familiar. Encourage them to point out picture clues that help tell the story.

---

# Andrew at School

## Use Picture Clues

Hi. My name is Andrew. I am in first grade at school. **School** is the place where I learn. Look at the pictures. Then tell about my busy day.

6

## Practice and Extend

**ESL** **BUILD BACKGROUND**
## ESL Support

**Finding Clues** Draw a picture of a child next to a house. Include a sun and flowers. Ask children: *Is it daytime or night? How do you know?* Write the word *clue* on the board. Then point to the sun in the picture. Explain that the sun is a picture clue telling that it is daytime.

**Beginning** Ask children to point to various objects in the picture as you narrate. For example: *It's morning. How do we know? There's a sun. Point to the sun.*

**Intermediate** As you look at the picture, ask questions that elicit one-word answers or phrases. For example: *Is this the sun or the moon?*

**Advanced** Ask children to describe what they see. Point to various items in the picture and ask questions to elicit more language.

---

**6** Unit 1 • Time for School

You can learn a lot from pictures. Pictures even help you learn about words. Where do I eat my lunch? What is the name of the place where I go to get a book?

**Cafeteria**

**Library**

**Try it!**

Make a picture book. Draw pictures to show what you do at **school**. Give the book to your partner. Have your partner get clues from your pictures to tell about your day.

**7**

**Workbook, p. 2**

Use Picture Clues

Circle where each child is going.

Draw where each child is going. Drawings will vary.

Also on Teacher
Resources CD-ROM.

## 2 Teach and Discuss

Read p. 6 and point out the pictures on pp. 6–7. Have children identify Andrew and tell what each picture shows him doing.

Read p. 7, pausing after each question. Ask children to point to the picture that shows where Andrew eats lunch. Point out the picture caption, and read the word *Cafeteria* for children. Ask if that's what they call the place where they eat lunch. Ask children to find the picture that shows where Andrew goes to get a book. Point out the picture caption, and read the word *Library* for children.

**Ongoing Assessment**

**If...** children do not understand how to use picture clues,

**then...** have them choose their favorite picture book and tell the story by looking only at the pictures. Explain that they used picture clues to tell the story.

Tell children that looking for clues in pictures can help them better understand what they read.

## 3 Close and Assess

**Try it!**

Review with children what they do each day (get ready for school, go to school, do class work, have lunch, play, and so on). Have each child select 4–5 such activities to illustrate. Help children staple sheets of drawing paper together to make a book. Tell children to draw one activity on each page. As children share their books with partners, they can use picture clues to describe events in each other's days.

# Workbook Support

Use the following Workbook pages to support content and skills development as you teach Unit 1. You can also view and print Workbook pages from the Teacher Resources CD-ROM.

## Workbook, p. 1

Draw a picture for each word. **Drawings will vary.**   *Use with Pages 4–5.*

| school | group |
| --- | --- |
| flag | rule |
| country | |

**Directions:** Read the words and draw pictures to illustrate them. Cut out the boxes to use as word cards.

**Home Activity:** Look through magazines with your child to find a picture that illustrates each word.

### Use with Pupil Edition, p. 5

## Workbook, p. 2

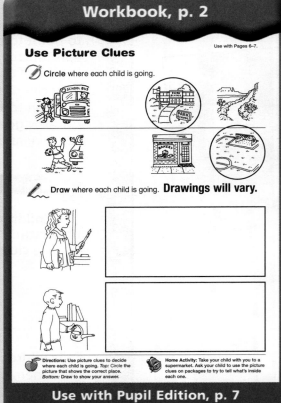

### Use Picture Clues   *Use with Pages 6–7.*

Circle where each child is going.

Draw where each child is going. **Drawings will vary.**

**Directions:** Use picture clues to decide where each child is going. *Top:* Circle the picture that shows the correct place. *Bottom:* Draw to show your answer.

**Home Activity:** Take your child with you to a supermarket. Ask your child to use the picture clues on packages to try to tell what's inside each one.

### Use with Pupil Edition, p. 7

## Workbook, p. 3

### Getting to Know Andrew   *Use with Pages 8–9.*

Color two pictures that show groups. **Color pictures 1 and 3.**

Draw a picture of a group. **Drawings will vary.**

**Directions:** *Top:* Color the two pictures that show groups. *Bottom:* Draw a picture of a group.

**Home Activity:** Ask your child to help you find pictures of groups at play or at work. Have your child describe what the people are doing.

### Use with Pupil Edition, p. 9

## Workbook, p. 4

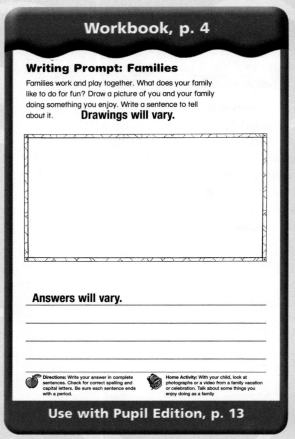

### Writing Prompt: Families

Families work and play together. What does your family like to do for fun? Draw a picture of you and your family doing something you enjoy. Write a sentence to tell about it.   **Drawings will vary.**

**Answers will vary.**

**Directions:** Write your answer in complete sentences. Check for correct spelling and capital letters. Be sure each sentence ends with a period.

**Home Activity:** With your child, look at photographs or a video from a family vacation or celebration. Talk about some things you enjoy doing as a family.

### Use with Pupil Edition, p. 13

## Workbook, p. 5

### Home and School   *Use with Pages 14–17.*

Color pictures that show things you do. **Answers will vary.**

Draw what you like to do at school. **Drawings will vary.**

**Directions:** *Top:* Look at the pictures. Color those that show things you do at school. *Bottom:* Draw a picture of something you like to do at school.

**Home Activity:** Ask your child to tell you about his/her school day. You might have your child draw a picture of an activity that he/she enjoyed especially.

### Use with Pupil Edition, p. 17

## Workbook, p. 6

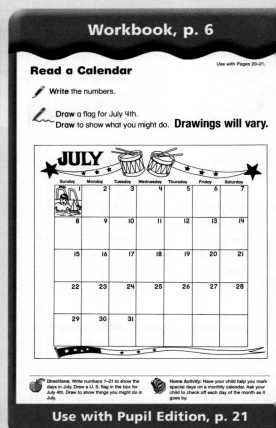

### Read a Calendar   *Use with Pages 20–21.*

Write the numbers.

Draw a flag for July 4th.
Draw to show what you might do. **Drawings will vary.**

**JULY**

| Sunday | Monday | Tuesday | Wednesday | Thursday | Friday | Saturday |
| --- | --- | --- | --- | --- | --- | --- |
| 1 | 2 | 3 | 4 | 5 | 6 | 7 |
| 8 | 9 | 10 | 11 | 12 | 13 | 14 |
| 15 | 16 | 17 | 18 | 19 | 20 | 21 |
| 22 | 23 | 24 | 25 | 26 | 27 | 28 |
| 29 | 30 | 31 | | | | |

**Directions:** Write numbers 1–31 to show the days in July. Draw a U.S. flag in the box for July 4th. Draw to show things you might do in July.

**Home Activity:** Have your child help you mark special days on a monthly calendar. Ask your child to check off each day of the month as it goes by.

### Use with Pupil Edition, p. 21

# Workbook Support

## Workbook, p. 7

### Rules We Follow

Use with Pages 22–25.

Circle any animal that is NOT following rules.

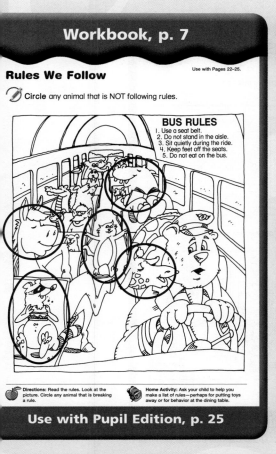

**BUS RULES**
1. Use a seat belt.
2. Do not stand in the aisle.
3. Sit quietly during the ride.
4. Keep feet off the seats.
5. Do not eat on the bus.

**Directions:** Read the rules. Look at the picture. Circle any animal that is breaking a rule.

**Home Activity:** Ask your child to help you make a list of rules—perhaps for putting toys away or for behavior at the dining table.

**Use with Pupil Edition, p. 25**

## Workbook, p. 8

### Cleaning Up!

Use with Pages 26–27.

Circle the problem in this picture.

Check each step as you do it.

Step 1   Name the problem.  _____
Step 2   Find out more about the problem.  _____
Step 3   List ways to solve the problem.  _____
Step 4   Talk about the best way to solve the problem.  _____
Step 5   Solve the problem.  _____
Step 6   How well is the problem solved?  _____

**Directions:** Work with a partner. Look at the picture. Then follow the steps to solve the problem. Check off each step as you do it.

**Home Activity:** Ask your child to think of a problem, or suggest one that you and your child can solve together. Use the steps in the problem-solving process.

**Use with Pupil Edition, p. 27**

## Workbook, p. 9

### Learning About My School

Use with Pages 28–31.

Color the picture from long ago. **Color picture 2.**

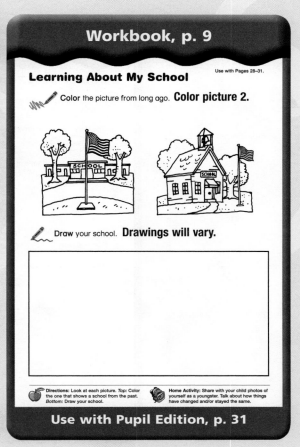

Draw your school. **Drawings will vary.**

**Directions:** Look at each picture. *Top:* Color the one that shows a school from the past. *Bottom:* Draw your school.

**Home Activity:** Share with your child photos of yourself as a youngster. Talk about how things have changed and/or stayed the same.

**Use with Pupil Edition, p. 31**

## Workbook, p. 10

Draw lines to match.

Use with Unit 1.

school
flag
country
rules

Draw a picture of a group. **Drawings will vary.**

**Directions:** *Top:* Read the words, and then match each word with a picture at the right. *Bottom:* Draw a picture that shows a group.

**Home Activity:** While traveling by bus or car, point out to your child some rules that drivers must follow.

**Use with Unit 1**

## Workbook, p. 11

**UNIT 1 Project   Follow Me!**

DISCOVERY CHANNEL SCHOOL

**Choose** a place in your school.

Draw a picture of what happens there. **Drawings will vary.**

Write the name of the place. **Answers will vary.**

Write about your picture. _____

**Directions:** *Top:* Draw a picture of something that happens in the place you've chosen. *Bottom:* Write the name of the place you've chosen. Then write to tell about your picture.

**Home Activity:** Invite your child to tell you about the picture he or she has drawn for this project. Ask leading questions, as needed.

**Use with Pupil Edition, p. 41**

# Assessment Support

 Use these Assessment Book pages and the ExamView® CD-ROM to assess content and skills in Unit 1. You can also view and print Assessment Book pages from the Teacher Resources CD-ROM.

## Assessment Book, p. 1

### Unit 1: Content Test

🖊 **Circle** a word to finish each sentence.

1. The United States of America is a ____.
   (country)     school

2. I learn to read and write at ____.
   (school)     flag

3. My family is a ____.
   flag     (group)

4. My teacher makes ____ for the class.
   country     (rules)

5. There are stars and stripes on the ____.
   (flag)     rules

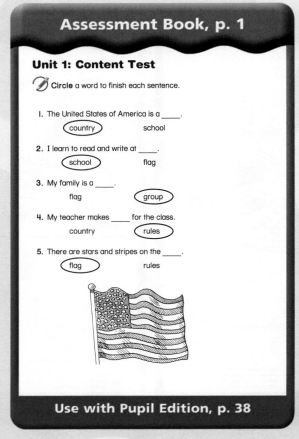

**Use with Pupil Edition, p. 38**

## Assessment Book, p. 2

✏ **Draw** pictures of two groups you belong to.

**Drawings will vary.**

🖊 **Circle** people who help you follow school rules.

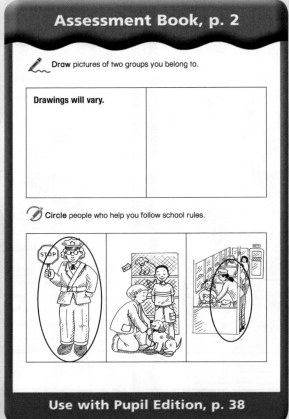

**Use with Pupil Edition, p. 38**

## Assessment Book, p. 3

### Unit 1: Skills Test

🖊 **Circle** a clue that tells what time of day it is.

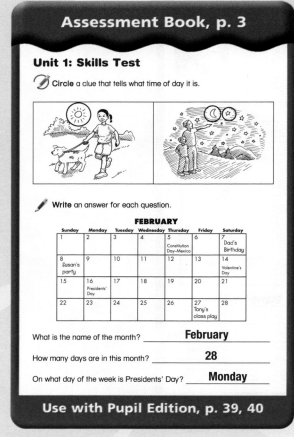

✏ **Write** an answer for each question.

**FEBRUARY**

| Sunday | Monday | Tuesday | Wednesday | Thursday | Friday | Saturday |
|---|---|---|---|---|---|---|
| 1 | 2 | 3 | 4 | 5 Constitution Day–Mexico | 6 | 7 Dad's Birthday |
| 8 Susan's party | 9 | 10 | 11 | 12 | 13 | 14 Valentine's Day |
| 15 | 16 Presidents' Day | 17 | 18 | 19 | 20 | 21 |
| 22 | 23 | 24 | 25 | 26 | 27 Tony's class play | 28 |

What is the name of the month? __**February**__

How many days are in this month? __**28**__

On what day of the week is Presidents' Day? __**Monday**__

**Use with Pupil Edition, p. 39, 40**

## Assessment Book, p. 4

🖊 **Circle** the picture that shows a group.

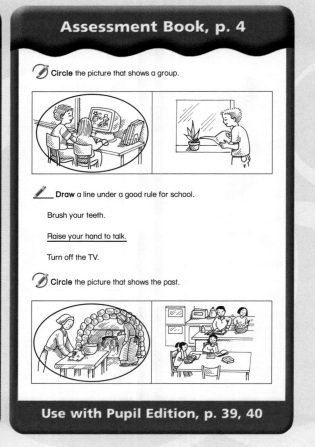

✏ **Draw** a line under a good rule for school.

Brush your teeth.

<u>Raise your hand to talk.</u>

Turn off the TV.

🖊 **Circle** the picture that shows the past.

**Use with Pupil Edition, p. 39, 40**

# Lesson ① Overview

| | | |
|---|---|---|
| **Getting to Know Andrew**<br>pages 8–9 | Children will learn the meaning of the word *group* and explore the concept that people belong to many different groups. They will identify main ideas and obtain information from oral, visual, and print sources. |  **Time** 20 minutes<br>**Resources**<br>• Workbook, p. 3<br>• Vocabulary Card group<br>• Every Student Learns Guide, pp. 2–5 |
| **Meet Carl Stotz**<br>pages 10–11 | Children will identify contributions of figures who have influenced the community, state, and nation. |  **Time** 15–20 minutes |
| *Colonial Williamsburg*<br>**Families Long Ago**<br>pages 12–13 | Children will learn about some activities that families long ago enjoyed doing together, and how they compare to activities families enjoy today. |  **Time** 15–20 minutes<br>**Resource**<br>• Workbook, p. 4 |

# Build Background

## Activity

### Getting to Know You

 **Time** 15–20 minutes

Ask each child to draw a picture that tells something about himself or herself. Help children put their initials, but not their names, on their pictures.

Use clothespins to suspend children's pictures from a length of twine. Then have children use their pictures to get to know each other better. Point to a picture, and ask if children can figure out who the artist is from the picture. If children don't quickly identify the artist, have him or her tell what the picture shows—and why it's important to the child.

**If time is short,** children can take turns introducing themselves to classmates and telling something they like or like to do.

## Read Aloud

### Groups
**by Peri Jones**

My pals and I
Like to play.
We bike or blade
Most every day.

We're quite a group—
Jed, Jan, and me—
Even though
We're only three.

My dad and I
Do things, too.
A group can be
Just us two.

## Lesson 1

# Getting to Know Andrew

### Objectives

- Understand that people belong to many different groups.
- Obtain information about a topic using pictures.

### Vocabulary

**group** a set of people or things (p. 9)

**QUICK Teaching Plan**

*If time is short,* have children look at the pictures and brainstorm a list of groups.

- Have each child draw a quick sketch of a group to which he or she belongs.

## 1 Introduce and Motivate

**Preview** Display the Vocabulary Card **group**, and ask children to name the group to which they *all* belong. (Children might name their room, class, or school.) Share the meaning of *group* as a "set of people or things." Have children locate the term as they preview the lesson.

**Warm Up** To activate prior knowledge, explain to children the difference between doing something alone and as a part of a group. Then ask children to name some interests or hobbies they have and whether they practice their interest and hobbies alone or with friends. Children may enjoy acting out games and/or activities that they and their friends do together.

---

## Lesson 1

# Getting to Know Andrew

I have so much to tell you! Look at my pictures. They will help you learn about me. Many of my friends like the same things.

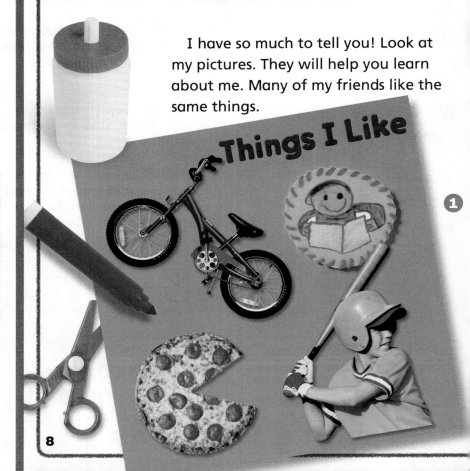

Things I Like

**8**

**1**

## Practice and Extend

### READING/VOCABULARY
**Use Picture Clues**

*Target Skill*

**Look!** Tell children that they can learn a lot about Andrew by looking at the pictures on these pages.

- For each picture on p. 8, have children point to a picture and name the item shown to complete this sentence: *Andrew likes _____.*
- For the pictures on p. 9, have children complete this sentence: *Two groups that Andrew belongs to are _____ and _____.*

### WEB SITE
**Technology**

You can look up vocabulary words online. Click on *Social Studies Library* and select the dictionary at **www.sfsocialstudies.com**.

I belong to many groups. A **group** is made up of people or things. People in a group can do things together. Look at the pictures of me in different groups.

My Team     My Family

## What did you learn

1. Name three things that Andrew likes.

2. Look at the pictures of groups. Tell about each **group.**

3. **Think and Share** Name other groups. Tell who is in each group.

9

**Possible Misconceptions**

- Help children see that groups can and do change. Show this by having children form groups (as for a game) and then form other groups (as for center activities).

- Discuss how people in a group must act responsibly, divide up tasks, and work together to accomplish a goal.

**Workbook, p. 3**

Getting to Know Andrew

Color two pictures that show groups. **Color pictures 1 and 3.**

Draw a picture of a group. **Drawings will vary.**

**Also on Teacher Resources CD-ROM.**

**ESL** **ESL Support**

*For ESL support, use Every Student Learns Guide, pp. 2–5.*

## 2 Teach and Discuss

Page 8

Point out that Andrew made the poster shown on p. 8. Ask children to name the things that he likes.

**1 What things that Andrew likes do you like? What different things do you like?** Answers will vary but might include: alike—pizza, reading; different—bike, baseball. **Compare and Contrast**

Explain to children the difference between fact and opinion statements. Have them practice making fact and opinion statements about Andrew or themselves.

Page 9

Help children find Andrew in each of the photographs. Then read the page with them.

**2 What groups does Andrew belong to?** A ball team, a family **Analyze Pictures**

Children may think that families only include people who live together. Tell children that families can also include relatives such as grandparents, aunts, uncles, and cousins. Explain that some family members, even parents and siblings, may live in different homes.

**3 What groups do you belong to?** Answers will vary but may include a class, a team, a family, and so on. **Apply Information**

## 3 Close and Assess

Have children brainstorm a class list of groups they belong to. Encourage children to think of groups both inside and outside school.

## ✓ What did you learn

1. Answers should include one or more of the things shown.

2. Answers should include name of group and who is in the group.

3. **Think and Share** Answers will vary but should include type of group and group members.

# Carl Stotz

## Objective
• Identify contributions of historical figures who have influenced the community, state, and nation.

# 1 Introduce and Motivate

**Preview** Ask children to name games or sports they enjoy playing or watching. Use their suggestions to make a word web. Write *games and sports* in the center cell.

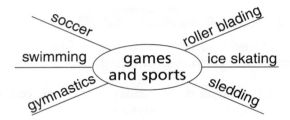

soccer
swimming
gymnastics
games and sports
roller blading
ice skating
sledding

**Warm Up** To activate prior knowledge, ask children which of these activities they participate in—and which they like to watch. Ask if there is an activity they would like to do but are not old enough to do yet. Mark these on the web with an asterisk, or star.

Have children look at the pictures on pp. 10–11. Identify the man as Carl Stotz, and ask children what they think he is doing. Ask children who play on teams to name the people who coach those teams.

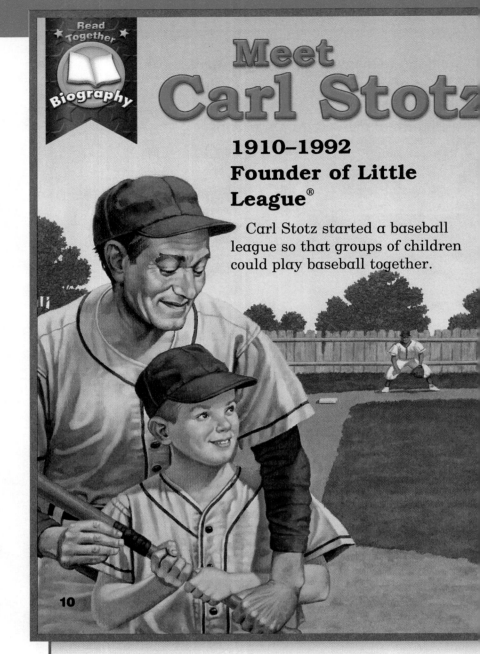

## Meet Carl Stotz

**1910–1992**
**Founder of Little League®**

Carl Stotz started a baseball league so that groups of children could play baseball together.

10

# Practice and Extend

## FYI SOCIAL STUDIES Background

**About Carl Stotz**

• Carl Stotz, who worked by day as a clerk, founded Little League® Baseball. He was also the league's first commissioner.

• The first Little League game was played on June 6, 1939, in Williamsport. In that game, Lundy Lumber beat Lycoming Dairy 23–8.

• Williamsport is the permanent home of the annual Little League Baseball World Series.

## WEB SITE Technology

You may help children find out more about Carl Stotz by clicking on *Meet the People* at **www.sfsocialstudies.com**.

# Families Long Ago

## Objectives

- Learn about families 200 years ago by using a variety of visual sources, such as artifacts and photographs.

- Describe the kinds of activities families from long ago did together and compare them with family activities today.

## 1 Introduce and Motivate

- Review the types of things families do together.

- Explain to children that 200 years ago life was very different from today, but families back then did many of the same things together that modern families do together, including work and play.

- As a class, make a list of the things families do together.

## 2 Teach and Discuss

### C SOCIAL STUDIES STRAND
### Culture

- **Working: Photograph of a family working** In this photograph an interpreter portraying a Native American mother teaches her two young children how to prepare a deer hide. Hides were used for clothing, shelter, and to make tools. Children in the 1700s were expected to help with daily chores. Ask children to discuss the types of chores they help with around the house.

# Families Long Ago

Families from long ago did many things together.

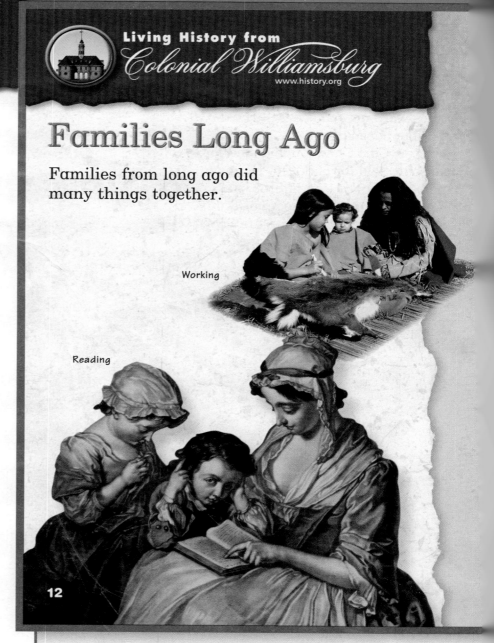

Working

Reading

12

## Practice and Extend

### FYI SOCIAL STUDIES
### Background

**Family Life**
*by Dr. William E. White, Colonial Williamsburg Historian*

- Long ago, families worked together, played together, and learned together just like families do today. History shows us that families have always been important to American culture, nurturing and educating our children through work and play.

- Children were expected to help with daily chores and other household tasks like stacking and bringing in firewood, preparing some foods, hauling water, weeding gardens, and tending animals.

- Most families did not have much free time. They worked hard to tend their farm or business, however, there was always time for children to play. Parents recognized play as an important form of education for their children.

Carl played baseball as a boy. The games were not fun. The field was very big. The bats were too heavy. Rules were not followed. Carl wanted to make baseball fun.

Later, Carl Stotz made a smaller baseball field for children. He made the bats smaller and lighter. He made rules for Little League. Today, many children from around the world enjoy playing in Little League!

The first Little League game was played in Williamsport, Pennsylvania.

Carl Stotz with one of the first Little League teams

### Think and Share

How did Carl Stotz make baseball fun for children to play?

For more information, go online to *Meet the People* at **www.sfsocialstudies.com**.

11

---

**CURRICULUM CONNECTION**
## Reading

### Biographies

Display examples of picture-book biographies of historical figures from your school library.

- Tell children that a biography is the true story of someone's life.
- Point out the covers on the books, and read aloud the titles. Point out that the title usually tells who the biography is about.
- Have partners select a book, look through it, and use picture clues to get a sense of subject's story.
- Ask children to select a biography for you to read aloud to them. As you share the book, point out how picture clues help readers understand a story. Also use the book to identify similarities and differences in daily life in the past and present.

---

## 2 Teach and Discuss

Read the biography together. Help children locate Pennsylvania on a map of the United States. Tell them that the Little League Baseball World Series is still held every year in Williamsport, PA.

### Test Talk

**Locate Key Words in the Text**

**1 Why didn't Carl Stotz think it was fun to play baseball?** Answers include the field was too big, the bats were too heavy, and rules were not followed. After children respond, help them find details in the first paragraph on p. 11 to support their answers. **Cause and Effect**

**2 What changes did Carl Stotz make in the game?** He made the field smaller and the bats smaller and lighter. He made rules for young players. **Apply Information**

## 3 Close and Assess

### Think and Share

Using their own words, children should be able to tell three ways in which Carl Stotz made baseball fun for children. (He made the playing field smaller; he made bats smaller and lighter; he made new rules.)

Eating

Cooking

Playing

Draw a picture of something families do together today.

**13**

- In 1744, when he was a young man, George Washington copied down 110 rules for good behavior. You can see all of the rules by visiting the Colonial Williamsburg website at www.history.org. Paraphrase the rules for children. Examples: 1st—Show respect to others. 5th—Turn your head and put your hand in front of your face when you cough, sneeze, or yawn. 14th—Don't turn your back on others.

- Discuss these rules with children. Do the rules still apply today for girls and boys with good manners?

- Ask children to make a list of rules for their classroom.

**Workbook, p. 4**

Use with Pages 12–13.
**Writing Prompt: Families**
Families work and play together. What does your family like to do for fun? Draw a picture of you and your family doing something you enjoy. Write a sentence to tell about it.
**Drawings will vary.**

Answers will vary.

**Also on Teacher Resources CD-ROM.**

- **Reading: Print—"Children like tender Oziers..."** This engraving was made in England in 1756. Ask children to describe what is happening in this picture. In the 1700s there were few formal schools for young children. Children often learned to read at home. Discuss with children the kinds of books they like to read.

- **Eating: Print—"A Journeyman Parson with a Bare Existence"** is an engraving made in England in 1760. It shows a family eating dinner together. Two hundred years ago the mid-day meal, served about 2:00 p.m., was the main meal of the day and a time for the family to gather together. Ask children to describe some of the conversations they have when they eat with family or friends.

- **Cooking: Photograph of a family preparing food** This photograph depicts an African-American mother and her two daughters preparing food. Children, as young as age 5 or 6 years old, helped with household chores. Daughters helped with the daily kitchen chores. Families today also spend time preparing and cooking food each day. Ask children to discuss how they help with food preparation and cooking at home.

- **Playing: Photograph of a family enjoying leisure time** This photograph portrays an eighteenth-century family enjoying some leisure time. Ask children to identify the family members. The adults are drinking tea. You might notice that both children are wearing dresses. Even boys wore dresses until they were about 6 years old. Have children identify the toys. Ask children if they enjoy similar kinds of toys.

## 3 Close and Assess

- Ask children to review the kinds of activities they see illustrated by these images of families from long ago.

- Ask children to explain how the activities are the same as today and how they are different.

- Choosing one of the activities shown on the spread, have children make a drawing of a family doing the same activity today. Their drawings could also include a one-word caption.

# Lesson 1 Wrap-Up

## MEETING INDIVIDUAL NEEDS
## Leveled Practice

**Find Pictures of Groups**

Ask children to cut out magazine pictures that show people in identifiable groups. Use the pictures to make a classroom bulletin board.

**Easy** Have each child tell about one group. **Reteach**

**On-Level** Help children make labels (*a family, a soccer team, a book club,* and so on) to attach to the different groups. **Extend**

**Challenge** Help children write captions for the pictures. Each caption should tell something about what the people in the group are doing. **Enrich**

## Hands-on Activities

 **CURRICULUM CONNECTION**
### Writing/Vocabulary

# Make a Book

**Objective** Define and illustrate the word *group*.

**Resources** Vocabulary Card: **group**

**Materials** stiff paper, drawing paper, crayons, pencils, yarn, scissors, two-hole punch

**Learning Style** Visual

**Individual**

**Time** 20–25 minutes

1. Using stiff paper, have children write *My Word Book* and their names.

2. Have children write the letters *Gg* at the top of a page, followed by *group*. Children then draw pictures of groups.

3. Punch holes in the pages. Tie their pages with yarn.

Gg
group

 **CURRICULUM CONNECTION**
### Art

# Things I Like

**Objective** Share interests with others; obtain information using visual sources.

**Materials** drawing paper, crayons, glue, scissors, old magazines

**Learning Style** Visual/Verbal

**Individual**

**Time** 20 minutes

1. Have children make posters to tell about themselves.

2. Tell children to write *Things I Like* at the top of a sheet of drawing paper.

3. Have children cut out three or four pictures of things they like and paste their pictures onto their posters.

4. As children display their posters, they should ask: "What can you learn about me from my pictures?"

 **CURRICULUM CONNECTION**
### Music/Drama

# Games We Play

**Objective** Role-play how people interact in groups; obtain information using oral sources.

**Learning Style** Verbal/Visual

**Group**

**Time** 15–20 minutes

1. Have small groups take turns showing how to play a favorite singing game, such as "Farmer in the Dell" or "London Bridge."

2. After children play a game, have them invite a classmate who doesn't know the game to join them. Children can explain the rules of the game to the newcomer.

# Lesson ② Overview

**Home and School**
pages 14–17

Children will learn the meanings for the words *flag* and *country*, and explain how selected symbols reflect an American love of individualism and freedom.

🕐 Time 20 minutes
**Resources**
- Workbook, p. 5
- Vocabulary Cards **flag** **country**
- Every Student Learns Guide, pp. 6–9

**Ruby Bridges Hall**
pages 18–19

Children will identify characteristics of good citizenship, such as a belief in equality.

🕐 Time 15 minutes

**Read a Calendar**
pages 20–21

Children will explore the concept that calendars show the passing of time and identify special days. They will read and create a calendar.

🕐 Time 15–20 minutes
**Resource**
- Workbook, p. 6

# Build Background

## Activity

### The Way We Do It

🕐 **Time** 15–20 minutes

Create an oversized two-column chart, with the title "The Way We Do It." Label one column *School* and the other *Home*. Then have children draw pictures and/or describe in words how they do one thing every day at school and one thing every day at home.

**If time is short,** have children contribute their ideas orally as you list them on the chart.

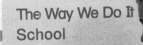

## Read Aloud

### My Busy Day

by Jane Holland

I make my bed so it's nice and flat.
I clean my room and feed the cat.
I brush my teeth, I use my comb.
These are things I do at home.

I see my friends, we all play tag.
I stand in class and salute the flag.
I work and play and follow each rule.
These are things I do at school.

# Lesson 2 Home and School

## Objectives

- Explain how selected symbols reflect an American love of individualism and freedom.

- Explain how routines are part of our daily life at home and at school.

## Vocabulary

**flag** a symbol that stands for a country or state (p. 16)

**country** land where a group of people live (p. 16)

## QUICK Teaching Plan

*If time is short,* have children stand, put their hands over their hearts, and recite the Pledge of Allegiance.

- Ask why we put our hands over our hearts when we say the Pledge.

# 1 Introduce and Motivate

**Preview** Display the Vocabulary Cards for **flag** and **country**. Ask children to point out any flags on display in your room. Ask if they know the name of the country in which they live. Have children locate the words *flag* and *country* as they preview the lesson. Ask volunteers to tell the meaning of the word *loyalty*. Discuss this idea, then explain that *allegiance* means "loyalty, especially to one's country or government." Also tell them that *pledge* means "promise."

**Warm Up** To activate prior knowledge, ask children to tell what they do before they come to school each day. Ask what they do once they get to school. Have a child pantomime an early-morning activity; have other children try to name the activity. Then face the American flag and place your hand over your heart. Ask children if they know what you are about to do and why.

# Lesson 2 Home and School

Every morning I eat breakfast. Then I brush my teeth and make my bed. What do you do every morning?

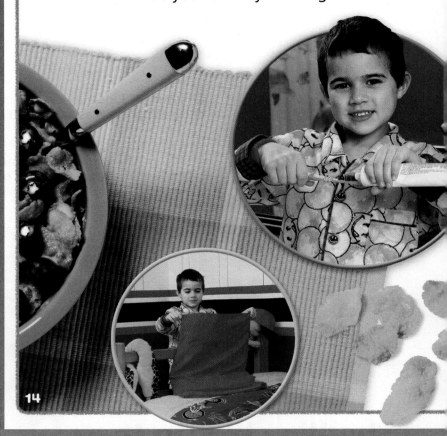

14

# Practice and Extend

## READING SKILL
## Put Things in Order

**Draw to Order**

- Tell children that activities at home and school are often done in a certain order. For example, at school they may say the Pledge of Allegiance first, and then listen to school announcements.

- Discuss the order of things that children do from the time they wake up until the time they leave for school.

- Have children draw three pictures of things they do each morning before going to school.

- Have children number their pictures *1, 2, 3* to show the order in which they are done.

My class at school does the same things every morning. We hang up  our coats and put our snacks away. Then we sit in our seats.

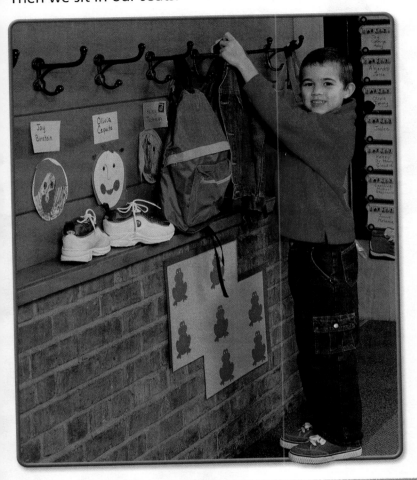

15

## 2 Teach and Discuss

### Page 14

Ask a volunteer to identify Andrew in the pictures. Have children tell what Andrew is doing. Then read p. 14 with children.

**① What does Andrew do first in the morning?** Eats breakfast **Does he brush his teeth before or after he eats breakfast?** After Sequence

**② What else do you think Andrew does each morning?** Answers will vary but should include such tasks as gathering materials for school, feeding pets, and so on. Make Inferences

### Page 15

**③ What does Andrew's class do every morning?** Hang up coats, put snacks away, sit down Main Idea and Details

**④ What does your class do each morning at school?** Possible answers: Put coats/snacks away, take attendance, say Pledge of Allegiance Apply Information

## ESL ACCESS CONTENT ESL Support

**Analyze Pictures** The pictures in Lesson 2 show tasks that form part of Andrew's routine at home and school.

**Beginning** Model pointing to each picture while telling each thing that Andrew does. Then have children point to the pictures and name the activity.

**Intermediate** Pantomime some of the activities pictured and invite children to name them. Ask children to take turns acting out classroom routines for others to identify.

**Advanced** Have children point out routines Andrew does that your class does also. Have children dictate a list of routines in your class. Use the chart on p. 17 as a model.

*For additional ESL support, use Every Student Learns Guide pp. 6-9.*

Lesson

**2**

continued

---

### Page 16

Have children recite the Pledge of Allegiance. Explain to children that the Pledge also honors people who have sacrificed to keep our country free. Then read pp. 16–17.

**Pledge of Allegiance**
I pledge allegiance to the flag of the United States of America and to the Republic for which it stands, one Nation, under God, indivisible, with liberty and justice for all.

⑤ **Why do we put our hands over our hearts when we say the Pledge of Allegiance?** To honor the flag; to show respect for our flag and country **Draw Conclusions**

 **SOCIAL STUDIES STRAND**
**Citizenship**

**Prejudice Reduction** Tell children that when we say the pledge, we are promising to be loyal to the United States. Explain that *indivisible* means "cannot be divided." Discuss the meaning of the words *liberty* and *justice*. Explain that all citizens are guaranteed liberty and justice. The flag represents these things.

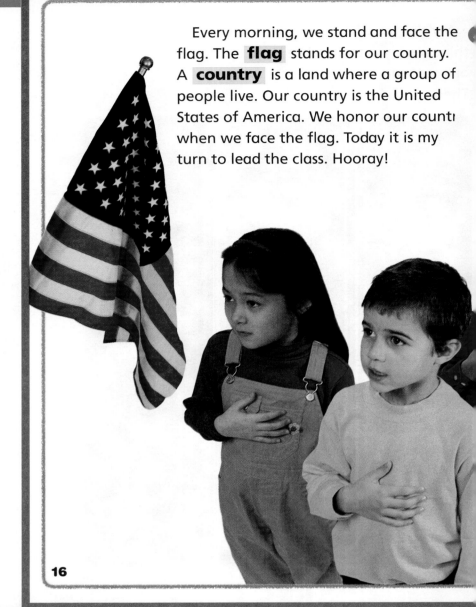

Every morning, we stand and face the flag. The **flag** stands for our country. A **country** is a land where a group of people live. Our country is the United States of America. We honor our country when we face the flag. Today it is my turn to lead the class. Hooray!

16

---

# Practice and Extend

 **CURRICULUM CONNECTION**
**Science**

**Snack Survey**

• Ask children to tell about snacks they often have in school. Include snacks provided by the school, and use sensitivity if children get food assistance.

• Help children categorize the foods: cereals, fruits and vegetables, breads, dairy, and meats.

**WEB SITE**
**Technology**

You can look up vocabulary words online. Click on *Social Studies Library* and select the dictionary at **www.sfsocialstudies.com**.

 **MEETING INDIVIDUAL NEEDS**
**Leveled Practice**

**The United States**

Show children the United States on a wall map or globe.

**Easy** Trace your finger along the borders of the United States, and ask children to do the same. Emphasize that everything inside these lines is part of the United States. **Reteach**

**On-Level** Help children identify the country to the north of the United States as Canada, and the country to the south as Mexico. Ask children to trace the lines that separate the United States from Canada and Mexico. **Extend**

**Challenge** Help children locate Alaska and Hawaii. Explain how these two states are separated from the rest of the United States. Alaska is separated by Canada; Hawaii, by the Pacific Ocean. **Enrich**

## Our Day

Say the Pledge of Allegiance.
Read the calendar.
Work on the computer.
Read a story.
Go outside.

Look at the other things we will do today. We will have a very busy day at school!

### What did you learn

1. What does Andrew do each morning at home? What does he do each morning at school?

2. Why does Andrew's class stand and face the **flag** each day?

3. **Think and Share** Make a list of things that you do each morning. Tell what you do at home. Tell what you do at school.

17

**6** **Which activity on the "Our Day" list do you think will take the most time?** Children may suggest that working on the computer, reading a story, and going outside will take longer than saying the Pledge of Allegiance and reading the calendar. **Evaluate**

**7** **Which activity on the "Our Day" list do you think would be the most fun? Why?** Accept all reasonable answers. **Point of View**

## 3 Close and Assess

Have each child draw one thing he/she did at home and one thing he/she did at school today. Have children compare and contrast their pictures.

### ✓ What did you learn

1. At home, he eats breakfast, brushes his teeth, and makes his bed. At school, he hangs up his coat, puts away his snack, takes his seat, says the Pledge of Allegiance.

2. They face the flag to honor it as they say the Pledge of Allegiance.

3. **Think and Share** Answers should reflect typical morning activities for a first grader.

## SOCIAL STUDIES STRAND
## Science/Technology

**Using the Computer**

- Talk with children about ways in which they will use a computer in school this year. If possible, have them help you compose an e-mail message to send to a nearby classroom.

- Discuss ways in which people communicated before they had computers. Ask a volunteer to deliver the same message by hand.

- Encourage children to ask family members about how computers have changed the way they work.

### Workbook, p. 5

**Home and School**

Color pictures that show things you do. **Answers will vary.**

Draw what you like to do at school. **Drawings will vary.**

**Also on Teacher Resources CD-ROM.**

## Ruby Bridges Hall

### Objective

• Identify characteristics of good citizenship, such as a belief in equality.

## 1 Introduce and Motivate

**Preview** Ask children what they think the word *courage* means. Have volunteers share stories of things they have done themselves or seen others do that took courage. Help children understand that having courage usually means doing something you know should be done, even if it scares you.

**Warm Up** To activate prior knowledge, ask children why they go to school. Ask children how they would feel if they weren't allowed to go to school.

Introduce Ruby Bridges Hall. Point out the photo of Ruby as a child. Tell children that they will learn why Ruby Bridges Hall is a citizen hero.

## 2 Teach and Discuss

Orient children to where Ruby went to school by reviewing the small map and caption on p. 18. Use a wall map to show children where New Orleans is in relation to your state. Then read the text on p. 18 with children.

**❶ How do you think Ruby felt about being the only African American child in her whole school?** Possible answer: She may have felt lonely or frightened. **Make Inferences**

**❷ Why did some people not want Ruby to go to their school?** She was African American. **Cause and Effect**

**❸ How did Ruby show she had courage or that she was brave?** Children should recognize that Ruby kept going to school every day. **Make Inferences**

# CITIZEN HEROES

## Ruby Bridges Hall

Ruby went to school in New Orleans, Louisiana.

Ruby was six years old when she began first grade. She was the only African American child in her whole school. African American children had never been allowed to go to that school before. At that time, people were often kept apart because of the color of their skin. Many people in the town did not want Ruby to go to their school. She was very brave. Being brave means having courage.

Ruby as a child

Mrs. Henry an Ruby Bridges

**18**

## Practice and Extend

**SOCIAL STUDIES Background**

### About Separate Schools

• Segregation by race was an accepted practice in American schools for almost 200 years. African American children and white children, with few exceptions, did not attend the same schools.

• In 1954, in a landmark decision known as *Brown* v. *Board of Education of Topeka*, the United States Supreme Court ruled that public schools could not separate children by race.

• While many communities moved to integrate the public schools, others resisted. In 1957 Federal troops were used to protect African American students at Central High School in Little Rock, Arkansas.

BUILDING CITIZENSHIP
Caring
Respect
Responsibility
Fairness
Honesty
★ Courage

Ruby's teacher was named Mrs. Henry. Other children would not come into Mrs. Henry's classroom. Ruby was Mrs. Henry's only student for most of the year.

Ruby and her family knew this was wrong. The courage of one little African American girl made a difference. When Ruby was in second grade, more African American children went to Ruby's school.

Now Ruby Bridges Hall is grown up. She wrote a book about what happened to her. Many people want to read about Ruby Bridges Hall.

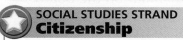
★ Courage in Action ★

What is one way to show that you are brave, or that you have courage?

CURRICULUM CONNECTION
Literature

**The Story of Ruby Bridges**

- Share with children this biography by Robert Coles (Scholastic; ISBN: 0-590-57281-4). Pause occasionally, asking children to tell how they think Ruby must have felt. Ask how they would have felt, if they had been Ruby Bridges.

- Afterwards, you may also want to read aloud selected passages from *Through My Eyes* by Ruby Bridges (Scholastic; ISBN 0-590-18923-9). Help children compare and contrast the two accounts.

❹ **Why was Ruby the only child in Mrs. Henry's class?** Other children would not come into Mrs. Henry's room. They might not have understood the importance of treating people equally. **Draw Conclusions**

**Test Talk**

**Use Information from the Text**

❺ **How was Ruby's second year at school better than her first year?** She wasn't the only African American at the school. Also, she began to make some friends. Point out the paragraph that begins "In second grade." Help children understand that second grade was Ruby's second year at school. Have them find details in this paragraph that support their answers. **Compare and Contrast**

★ SOCIAL STUDIES STRAND
**Citizenship**

**Prejudice Reduction** Point out that both Ruby and Mrs. Henry showed great courage as citizens. Both believed that all children should have the same education. They believed in justice and equality. Both acted bravely when they stood up for what they believed. Ask children to name real people or story characters who have acted bravely and stood up for their beliefs.

# ③ Close and Assess

★ **Courage in Action** ★

Read the question and have children discuss possible answers. Responses may include: standing up for a friend, making a phone call in an emergency, and so on.

# Read a Calendar

## Objectives
- Read and create a calendar.
- Obtain information about a topic using visual sources, such as graphics and pictures.

## Vocabulary
**calendar** a chart that show the days, weeks, and months of the year (p. 20)

# 1 Introduce and Motivate

**Preview** Write the word *calendar* on the board. Read the word, and ask children to point out any calendars on display in your classroom. Have children locate the term as they preview the lesson.

**Warm Up** To activate prior knowledge, ask children to tell what day of the week it is. Ask if anyone knows the *date*. Write the date on the board, including the year, and help children read it. Then guide children in locating the date on the classroom calendar. Confirm the name of the day of the week by pointing it out on the calendar.

### Page 20

Read the introduction. Before children respond to the questions below the calendar, have them point to September 1 and name the day of the week on which it falls. Repeat for a few other dates. Then have children answer the bulleted questions.

**1 What holiday is on September 1?** Labor Day. Labor day is a day we honor people who work. **Interpret Charts**

**2 What holiday is on September 17?** Citizenship Day **Interpret Charts**

### ★ SOCIAL STUDIES STRAND
**Citizenship**

Tell children that Citizenship Day honors citizens who have reached voting age. It is celebrated on September 17 because that is the date on which the U.S. Constitution was signed.

---

# Read a Calendar

Every day Andrew's class reads the calendar. A **calendar** is a chart that shows the days, weeks, and months of the year. A calendar helps us remember important days.

**September**

| Sunday | Monday | Tuesday | Wednesday | Thursday | Friday | Saturday |
|---|---|---|---|---|---|---|
| | 1 Labor Day | 2 | 3 | 4 | 5 | 6 |
| 7 | 8 | 9 | 10 | 11 | 12 | 13 |
| 14 | 15 | 16 | 17 Citizenship Day | 18 | 19 | 20 Mom's Birthday |
| 21 | 22 First Day of Fall | 23 | 24 | 25 | 26 | 27 |
| 28 | 29 | 30 | | | | |

- The name of the month is at the top of the calendar. What month is it?
- Each square is one day. How many days are on this calendar?
- Look at the box that has the number 1 in it. Why is that day important?

20

# Practice and Extend

###  CURRICULUM CONNECTION
**Reading**

**Learn a Calendar Rhyme**

- Tell children that every four years an extra day is added to February, giving it 29 days instead of 28.
- Display the following rhyme, and have children recite it with you.

> 30 days has September,
> April, June, and November.
> All the rest have 31,
> All the rest, that is, but one.
> February has 28!
> Except in Leap Year, that's the time
> When February has 29!

Andrew likes the month of February best. This calendar shows special days in February.

## February

| Sunday | Monday | Tuesday | Wednesday | Thursday | Friday | Saturday |
|--------|--------|---------|-----------|----------|--------|----------|
|        |        |         |           | 1        | 2 *Groundhog Day* | 3 |
| 4      | 5      | 6       | 7         | 8        | 9      | 10       |
| 11     | 12 *Lincoln's Birthday* | 13 | 14 *Valentine's Day* | 15 | 16 | 17 |
| 18     | 19 *Presidents' Day* | 20 | 21 | 22 *Washington's Birthday* | 23 | 24 |
| 25 *Andrew's Birthday* | 26 | 27 | 28 |  |  |  |

## What did you learn

1. What is one reason we use a **calendar**?

2. Why do you think that Andrew likes the month of February the best?

3. **On Your Own** Make a calendar for this month. Label the important days. Why are these days important?

21

③ **What season of the year begins toward the end of September?** Fall or autumn
Interpret Charts

---
**Page 21**
---

Read p. 21. Point out that Andrew's birthday is in February. Then ask:

④ **Which Presidents' birthdays do we also celebrate in February?** Lincoln's and Washington's birthdays **Interpret Charts**

## Test Talk

**Use Information from Graphics**

⑤ **How is the calendar for February different from the one for September?** It has fewer days. It shows different special days. Be sure children understand that they need to use *both* calendars to answer the question. **Compare and Contrast**

## 3 Close and Assess

Encourage children to bring in samples of different kinds of calendars. If possible, show them examples of appointment books, desk calendars, and so on. Guide children in finding today's date on each calendar.

## ✓ What did you learn

1. Possible answer: We use a calendar to help us remember important days.

2. Possible answer: His birthday is in February.

3. **On Your Own** Calendars should show the current month with days and dates labeled. They should also show the important days in the month. Children should be able to explain why the days are important.

# Lesson ② Wrap-Up

## MEETING INDIVIDUAL NEEDS
## Leveled Practice

### Hooray for Me!
Have each child draw pictures of two things he/she has learned at school so far this year. Have children take turns displaying their pictures.

**Easy** Ask a volunteer to put his/her pictures in order to show what was learned first. Name the two activities shown. Have all children in the group repeat. **Reteach**

**On-Level** Have children order their pictures and then tell what they learned *first* and *next*. **Extend**

**Challenge** Have children order their pictures and identify the activities. Then have them dictate captions for you to write under each picture. **Enrich**

## Hands-on Activities

### CURRICULUM CONNECTION
### Writing/Vocabulary

## My Country, My Flag

**Objective** Demonstrate an understanding of the words *flag* and *country*.

**Resources** Vocabulary Cards: **flag, country**

**Materials** crayons, drawing paper

**Learning Style** Visual/Verbal

**Individual**

**Time** 10–15 minutes

1. Write the following on the board:
The United States is our ___.
Our ___ is red, white, and blue.

2. Display the Vocabulary Cards, and have children use the words to complete the sentences.

3. Have children copy the sentences and draw pictures to illustrate them.

4. Have children add the new words to their "My Word Book."

### CURRICULUM CONNECTION
### Math

## Special Days

**Objective** Make a calendar for a given month.

**Materials** calendar for current month, blank calendar grids, markers or crayons, self-stick notes

**Learning Style** Visual/Kinesthetic

**Group**

**Time** 15–20 minutes

1. Help children use the classroom calendar to identify important days (holidays) in this month.

2. Invite children to draw pictures on self-stick notes to represent the holidays they have identified.

3. Have children copy the dates onto a blank calendar and then attach their pictures in appropriate places.

**February**

| Sunday | Monday | Tuesday | Wednesday | Thursday | Friday | Saturday |
|--------|--------|---------|-----------|----------|--------|----------|
| 1 | 2 | 3 | 4 | 5 | 6 | 7 |
| 8 | 9 | 10 | 11 | 12 | 13 | ♥ |
| 15 | 16 | 17 | 18 | 19 | 20 | 21 |
| 22 | 23 | 24 | 25 | 26 | 27 | 28 |

### SOCIAL STUDIES STRAND
### Citizenship

## Citizen Heroes

**Objective** Identify good citizenship qualities in people they know. (Prejudice Reduction)

**Materials** markers, bulletin board, paper

**Learning Style** Verbal

**Individual**

**Time** 10–15 minutes

1. Have each child identify someone who shows good citizenship.

2. Give children paper and markers. Invite them to make a border of words, such as "kind to new children," describing the good citizenship.

3. Ask children to draw pictures of their citizenship heroes inside the word borders.

4. Post all the heroes on the bulletin board.

# Lesson ③ Overview

**Rules We Follow**
pages 22–25

Children will learn the meaning of the word *rules* and some reasons why rules are necessary. They will also identify authority figures who help people follow the rules.

🕐 Time 20–30 minutes

**Resources**
- Workbook, p. 7
- Vocabulary Card **rules**
- Every Student Learns Guide, pp. 10–13

**Problem on the Playground**
pages 26–27

Children will learn how to use problem-solving strategies, such as those needed to keep the schoolyard clean.

🕐 Time 15 minutes

**Resource**
- Workbook, p. 8

# Build Background

## Activity

### Rules of the Game

🕐 **Time** 15–20 minutes

Ask children to name their favorite game or sport. Write children's suggestions on the board. Then, have children make a drawing showing something about their favorite game or sport. Have a sports section of a newspaper or magazine available for reference. Ask children if there are rules for playing their game or sport.

**If time is short,** ask children to explain some of the rules in a game such as tag, jacks, or baseball.

## Read Aloud

### The Rules

#### by Ben Farhi

I can cross a busy street
If a grown-up is around.
This rule keeps me safe
  and sound.

I wait my turn when we play,
And so does everyone.
This rule makes our play more fun!

## Lesson 3 Rules We Follow

### Objectives

- Give examples of rules.

- Identify the responsibilities of authority figures in the school and home.

- Explain the need for rules and laws in the home, school, and community.

### Vocabulary

**rule** what we can do and what we should not do (p. 22)

**QUICK Teaching Plan**

*If time is short,* have children choose one picture from pp. 22–23 and tell what would happen if people didn't follow this rule.

## 1 Introduce and Motivate

**Preview** Display the Vocabulary Card **rule** and invite children to help you write a definition for it. Ask children to tell you why they think people make rules. Then ask who helps us follow the rules at home, at school, and in the community.

**Warm Up** To activate prior knowledge, direct children's attention to any posted lists of class or school rules. Have volunteers read these rules aloud.

Discuss the meaning of *privacy* with students. Remind them there are times when they should not disturb others, and that there are times when they do not want to be disturbed. For example, going into a family member's room without permission. Have volunteers share other examples. Point out that an official document of the United States called the *Constitution* allows everyone privacy. Remind students that the consequences of privacy can be both beneficial and costly.

## Lesson 3 Rules We Follow

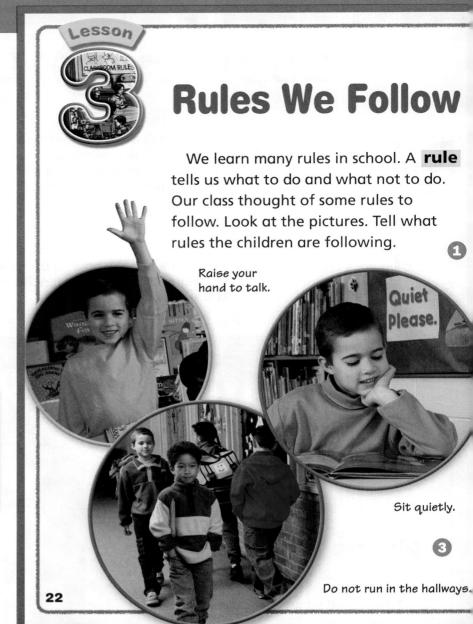

We learn many rules in school. A **rule** tells us what to do and what not to do. Our class thought of some rules to follow. Look at the pictures. Tell what rules the children are following.

❶

Raise your hand to talk.

Quiet Please.

Sit quietly.

❸

22

Do not run in the hallways.

## Practice and Extend

What other rules do you follow at school? What are some rules you follow at home?

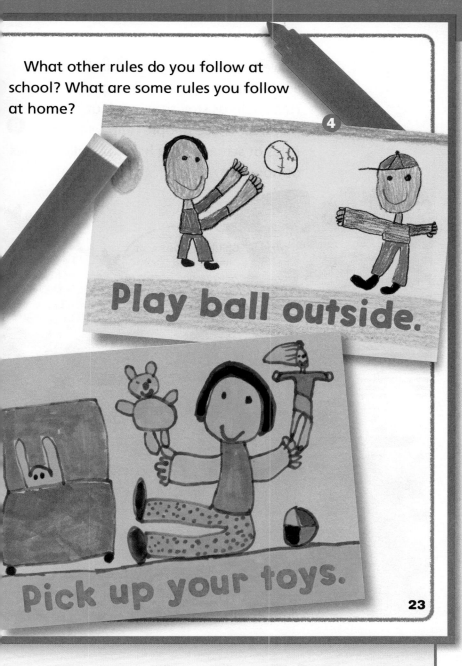

Play ball outside.

Pick up your toys.

23

## 2 Teach and Discuss

Page 22

Have children describe the rules Andrew is following.

**1** **Which of these rules do you have in your class?** Children will most likely suggest that all three are rules in their school. **Compare and Contrast**

**2** **Why is raising your hand to talk a good rule?** Possible answers: So everyone doesn't talk at once, so everyone gets a turn **Evaluate**

**3** **What could happen if there wasn't a rule for walking in the halls?** Children could run into each other and get hurt. **Predict**

Page 23

Explain to children that families, schools, and communities in other countries may have different rules.

**4** **Do you think there should be a rule for playing ball outside? Why or why not?** Children may realize the danger of breaking things with balls, but some may think that ball play can be done safely in a basement or with an adult. **Point of View**

**SOCIAL STUDIES STRAND**
**Citizenship**

Tell children that adults have rules too. They follow rules in many places, including places they work and places they shop. Ask children to think of times they've seen their parents or other adults work or shop. What are some rules they must follow at these times? Possible answers: Stop at red lights, get to places on time, pay for the things bought, wait one's turn, follow rules at work, obey people in authority, and so on.

**ESL** **EXTEND LANGUAGE**
**ESL Support**

**Add a Rule** Review the rules already in place in your classroom. Then have children add their own rules to the list.

**Beginning** Invite children to pantomime the rule they would like to add to the list. Write a rule for children that reflects their pantomime.

**Intermediate** Pair children to develop a rule. Have them draw the rule and then write a brief caption, such as "No hitting."

**Advanced** Invite children to write their rules in both English and their home language. Ask them to explain why each rule is important.

*For additional ESL support, use Every Student Learns Guide, pp. 10–13.*

**Lesson 3**

continued

### Page 24

Have children identify the people (a bus driver and a crossing guard) shown in the photo. Discuss what rules they might help us follow.

**5 How are rules at home and school alike? How are they different?** Possible answers: Listening to parents and teachers, cleaning up after work or play time, sharing with classmates and family members. **Compare and Contrast**

**6 Who else helps you follow rules at school? at home?** Possible answers: Teacher aides, school custodian, cafeteria workers, guards, parents, babysitters, other family members
**Apply Information**

**Ongoing Assessment**

**If...** children cannot name people who help them follow school rules,

**then...** remind them of people who work or help out at your school.

**ST** SOCIAL STUDIES STRAND
**Science/Technology**

Point out that people use technology to help keep themselves and others safe. For example, the bus driver may have a radio, cell phone, or locating device in the bus. This enables the driver to call for help or to get information about road problems. Ask children how people they know use technology when they travel.

**7 What can Andrew do to make sure he understands the rules?** He can listen carefully, ask questions to make sure he understands the rules, and ask for help in following the rules.
**Apply Information**

**24** Unit 1 • Time for School

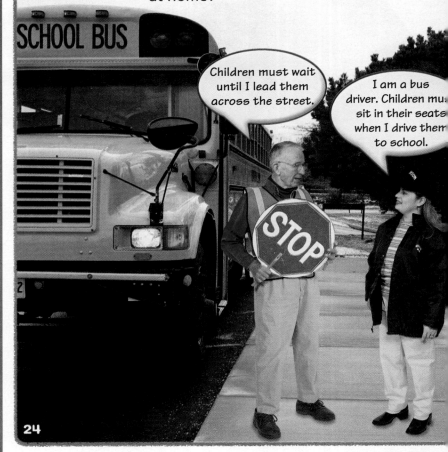

We have rules at school and at home. Some rules help us work together. Some rules help us stay safe. Look at the pictures. These people help us follow **6** rules at school. Who helps us follow rules at home?

Children must wait until I lead them across the street.

I am a bus driver. Children mu sit in their seats when I drive them to school.

24

## Practice and Extend

**FYI** SOCIAL STUDIES
**Background**

### Playing by the Rules

- Some children may think that rules spoil their fun. Ask if a game such as soccer would be more or less fun if it had no rules. Help children conclude that rules not only help a game go smoothly but also make it more fun to play.

- Young children may notice that rules sometimes vary, depending on one's age. Point out that a six-year-old may need to hold an adult's hand to cross a street, while a twelve-year-old can probably safely cross alone.

- Help children conclude that rules not only make a game fair for everyone that plays, but make it more fun to play. Remind them that good sportsmanship means enjoying a game whether you win or lose.

- Point out that parents and other adults are responsible for setting rules and for making sure that rules are followed. A parent makes rules about when it's time for bed. Teachers make rules about how to behave in school. A police officer helps people follow traffic rules.

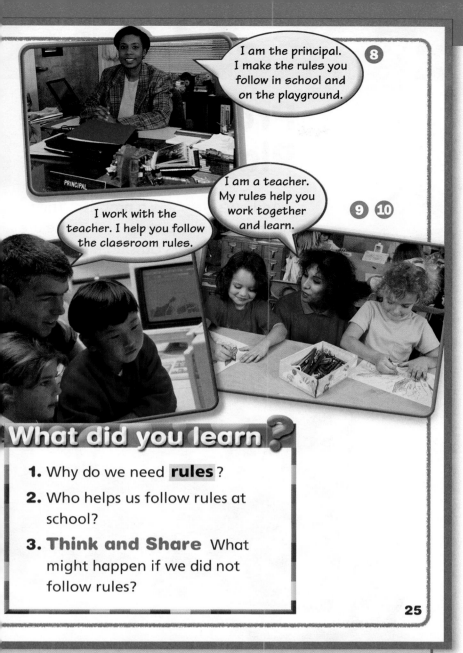

I am the principal. I make the rules you follow in school and on the playground. **8**

I am a teacher. My rules help you work together and learn. **9 10**

I work with the teacher. I help you follow the classroom rules.

## What did you learn?

1. Why do we need **rules**?

2. Who helps us follow rules at school?

3. **Think and Share** What might happen if we did not follow rules?

25

## Workbook, p. 7

**Also on Teacher Resources CD-ROM.**

Discuss with children reasons for having rules at home and at school, such as to solve a problem or to be fair. Have children identify the people shown on p. 25 and tell how each person helps us follow rules.

**8 What are some rules a principal might ask children to follow?** Answers should reflect children's knowledge of school-wide rules such as for conduct in the auditorium, the cafeteria, on the playground, and in hallways. **Apply Information**

**9 How might grown-ups in Andrew's classroom help him follow the rules?** Possible answers: by posting the rules, by explaining them, by reminding him of the rules if he breaks one, by having a consequence for breaking rules **Hypothesize**

**10 How do you feel about the rules you have to follow at home and school?** Children may express sadness, anger, and/or pride in being able to follow rules or understanding the need for rules. **Express Ideas**

## 3 Close and Assess

To check children's understanding of rules, have them work in small teams to identify the three rules they think are most important at home, school, and in the community. After the groups exchange ideas, take a poll to choose three "high priority" rules for the class. Write these three rules on chart paper, and save for use in the Lesson 3 Wrap-Up.

## ✓ What did you learn?

1. We need rules to keep us safe and to help us work together.

2. Answers may include teachers, principals, aides, crossing guards, and bus drivers.

3. **Think and Share** Possible answers: People could get hurt, people might not be able to learn or do the jobs they need to do, people couldn't find things when they needed them.

# Problem on the Playground

## Objective

- Use a problem-solving process.

# 1 Introduce and Motivate

**Preview** Ask children to tell what they think a problem is. Then have them explain what they think it means to solve a problem.

**Warm Up** To activate prior knowledge, ask children to name some problems the class has solved in the last few days. If necessary, prompt children with an example, such as the class's group effort to find a missing book.

# 2 Teach and Discuss

### Page 26

Discuss the photo with children. Ask what they think the problem is on this playground. (trash on the ground)

**❶ What is the first step the children use to solve the problem?** They name the problem. **Sequence**

**❷ Why do you think it is so important to start by naming the problem?** Possible answer: You need to understand what the problem is before you can pick the best way to solve it. **Solve Problems**

**❸ What can Andrew and his friends do to find out more about their problem?** Possible answers: Look at the trash to see where it comes from, find out where on the playground there is trash, notice whether the trash is worse at certain times of day **Solve Problems**

# Problem on the Playground

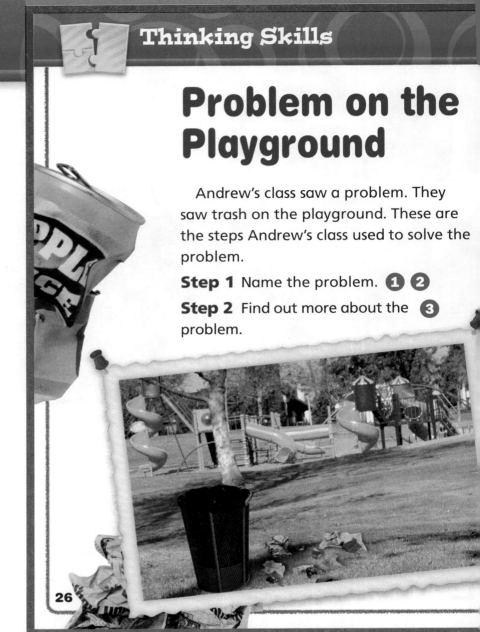

Andrew's class saw a problem. They saw trash on the playground. These are the steps Andrew's class used to solve the problem.

**Step 1** Name the problem. ❶ ❷

**Step 2** Find out more about the ❸ problem.

26

## Practice and Extend

**CURRICULUM CONNECTION**
### Science

**Reducing Trash**

- Tell children that each person in the United States produces more than four pounds of trash a day. Explain that this enormous amount of trash is a threat to our environment.

- Encourage children to examine a sample of classroom trash. Use proper precautions, such as wearing latex gloves.

- Ask children if they think some of the trash could have been recycled or reused. Work with children to generate a list of ideas for reducing trash.

**Step 3** List ways to solve the problem.

**Step 4** Is one way more useful than another? Talk about the best way to solve the problem. **4**

**Step 5** Solve the problem.

**Step 6** How well is the problem solved?

Now we have a nice, clean playground! **5**

## Try it!

1. What problem did Andrew's class see?

2. What steps did Andrew's class take to solve the problem?

3. **On Your Own** Think of a problem. Tell how you would solve it. Use the steps Andrew's class used.

27

### Problem Solving

Select one of the problems children identified during their walk through school and review it with the class. Help children use the following process to solve the problem.

1. Identify a problem.

2. Gather information.

3. List and consider options.

4. Consider advantages and disadvantages.

5. Choose and implement a decision.

6. Evaluate the effectiveness of the solution.

**Workbook, p. 8**

Cleaning Up!

Circle the problem in this picture.

Check each step as you do it.

| Step 1 | Name the problem. | |
| Step 2 | Find out more about the problem. | |
| Step 3 | List ways to solve the problem. | |
| Step 4 | Talk about the best way to solve the problem. | |
| Step 5 | Solve the problem. | |
| Step 6 | How well is the problem solved? | |

**Also on Teacher Resources CD-ROM.**

Have children recount the steps Andrew and his class take to solve their problem. Remind them to keep the steps in order.

**4 How does talking about the best way to solve a problem help?** People can share ideas for how to solve the problem. This helps everyone see which ideas work and which do not.
**Make Inferences**

**GEOGRAPHY**
**People and Places Change Each Other**

**5 How do Andrew and his friends solve their problem?** They clean up the playground. They put trash in a trash can and items for recycling in a recycling bin. **Analyze Pictures**

## 3 Close and Assess

Give children clipboards, paper, and pencils. Lead the class on a tour of the school and its grounds. Each time a child spots a problem, tell all the children to record it. When you return to the classroom, have children suggest ways each problem can be solved.

## Try it!

1. They saw trash on the playground.

2. First they named the problem. Then they learned more about the problem. Next they listed ways to solve the problem. Then they talked about the best way to solve the problem. Next they put their ideas into action. Finally, they thought about how well they had solved the problem.

3. **On Your Own** Problems should be clearly named. Solutions should include the general goal, as well as each of the six problem-solving steps from the lesson.

# Lesson ③ Wrap-Up

## MEETING INDIVIDUAL NEEDS
## Leveled Practice

### Wall Mural
Have children draw or find pictures of people who make and enforce the rules in the home, school, and community. Use the pictures to create a wall mural.

**Easy** Have children identify each authority figure and give an example of a rule that the person might help them follow. **Reteach**

**On-Level** Next to each picture, children can write *safety* or *working together* to tell the kind of rules the pictured person makes. **Extend**

**Challenge** Have children make handouts to introduce others to the people shown. Handouts should tell the kind of rules each person makes and why those rules are important. **Enrich**

## Hands-on Activities

### CURRICULUM CONNECTION
### Writing/Vocabulary

## Rules on Rules

**Objective** Define and illustrate the word *rule*.

**Resources** Vocabulary Card: **rule**
**Materials** ruled chart paper
**Learning Style** Verbal/Visual
**Individual**
⏱ **Time** 15–20 minutes

1. Using chart paper, write the word *RULES* in a vertical column.

2. For each letter, ask children to suggest a classroom rule beginning with the letter. For *R*, they may say: *Running in halls—NO!*

3. Continue for each letter. Then display the completed chart in the classroom.

| **R** unning in the halls – *NO!* |
|---|
| **U** |
| **L** |
| **E** |
| **S** |

4. Have children add *rule* to their "My Word Book."

### SOCIAL STUDIES STRAND
### Government

## Rule-Making

**Objective** Understand the rules made by the school principal.

**Learning Style** Verbal
**Group**
⏱ **Time** 15–20 minutes

1. Invite the school principal to visit the class for a discussion about rule-making.

2. Help children prepare questions to ask the principal about the rules he or she makes. Children might ask: *What do you think is the most important rule? Which rule gets broken the most?*

3. After the interview, have children describe what the principal's job is. Talk with them about where people such as the principal get their authority.

• What is the most important school rule?

• Which rule gets broken the most?

### SOCIAL STUDIES STRAND
### Citizenship

## Our Rules

**Objective** Express a rule through a simple drawing.

**Materials** chart paper
**Learning Style** Verbal
**Group**
⏱ **Time** 10–15 minutes

1. Review with children any rules you have already established for your classroom.

2. Brainstorm with children other rules that might be added to your list. Alternatively, have children create and adopt a set of rules for a specific area of your room, such as the classroom library.

| **OUR RUL** |
|---|
| 1. Sign the book o |
| 2. Take care of t |
| 3. |

3. Have children draw a picture of one of the rules they have added to the list.

# Lesson 4 Overview

| | | |
|---|---|---|
| **Learning About My School**<br>pages 28–31 | Through an interview, children will learn how a school has changed and reasons for the changes. They will learn to distinguish between past, present, and future. | ⏱ Time 20–30 minutes<br>**Resources**<br>• Workbook, p. 9<br>• Every Student Learns Guide, pp. 14–17 |
| **Mary McLeod Bethune**<br>pages 32–33 | Children will learn about Mary McLeod Bethune and how her efforts brought about important changes in education. | ⏱ Time 15 minutes |
| **Things We Use**<br>pages 34–35 | Children will learn how to use visual sources, such as pictures, to compare and contrast objects from different time periods. | ⏱ Time 15 minutes |

# Build Background

### Activity

## Time Capsules

⏱ **Time** 20–30 minutes

Ask children to imagine that they are trying to describe their school to people in the future. Have them work in groups of three or four to create time capsules. Give each group a large envelope to decorate and label "_____ School in the year 200_." Have each child draw a picture and/or dictate a sentence telling one thing about the school. Place each group's entries in its envelope and exchange the envelopes. Ask children if they were surprised to learn what other groups thought.

**If time is short,** make one time capsule for the whole class. Use slips of paper you complete from children's oral suggestions.

Our School in 2003

### Read Aloud

## School History

### by Steve Lopez

Before I was born, I'm sure as can be

Other children walked these halls— just like me

What did they learn? What did they wear?

Did their teacher sit in my teacher's chair?

It's fun to think about this little mystery.

My school has seen a lot of things. It has a history.

# Lesson 4
# Learning About My School

## Objectives

- Obtain information about a topic using a variety of oral sources, such as interviews.

- Compare past and present.

### QUICK Teaching Plan

*If time is short,* have children use the photos on p. 29 to compare and contrast Andrew's school then and now.

## 1 Introduce and Motivate

**Preview** As you preview the lesson, point out the interview and scrapbook formats. Ask children if they keep family pictures in a scrapbook. Explain that scrapbooks are one way to preserve memories of events from the past. Tell children that in this lesson, Andrew learns about some pictures by asking questions. Explain that learning information by asking questions is called an interview. Encourage children to ask you questions about your school. Then tell them they just interviewed you!

**Warm Up** To activate prior knowledge, take children on a quick tour of their school. Ask children to describe different parts of the school.

## 2 Teach and Discuss

### Page 28

Tell children that in this lesson, Andrew is talking with Mr. Jones, the principal of his school.

**1** **What are Andrew and Mr. Jones doing?**
Looking at an old scrapbook **Analyze Pictures**

---

# Lesson 4
# Learning About My School

**Andrew** Our school is so big!

**Mr. Jones** Yes, it is. Let me tell you a story about our school.

28

## Practice and Extend

**READING/VOCABULARY**
**Use Picture Clues**

*Target Skill*

### Photo Clues

- Direct children's attention to the two photos on p. 29. Ask them to describe the photos.

- Ask children to describe how the photos look the same and different. Answers might include that one photo is in color and one is a black-and-white photo. Both photos show a building and people.

- Tell children that they can learn a lot by looking for clues about when something happened in pictures and photographs.

**Mr. Jones** Look at these pictures. They give clues about how our school has changed.

**Andrew** Long ago, our school was in a small building. Why?

④ ⑤

29

**❷ Is the school in a bigger or smaller building now than it used to be?** A bigger building **Apply Information**

**❸ Why might Andrew's school have been in a smaller building many years ago?** Possible answers: Not as many children lived in the neighborhood then; perhaps they didn't need as many classrooms. **Hypothesize**

**❹ Which picture shows how the school looked in the *past*?** The top picture **Analyze Pictures**

✓ **Ongoing Assessment**

| **If...** children cannot identify the historical picture, | **then...** point out the visual clues that suggest it is from the past. |
|---|---|

**❺ What other ways are the schools in the two pictures different?** Possible answers: One is brick; one is wood; one has a bus in front; the people are dressed differently. **Compare and Contrast**

**SOCIAL STUDIES STRAND**
**Geography**

Tell children that schools vary not just from past to present but also from place to place. Schools reflect the culture of the people who build them and the geography of places where they are found. In cold climates, schools are often brick buildings; in hotter climates, they are often long, low, and open.

**Dialogue** Explain that Mr. Jones and Andrew are having a conversation about the school. Reread pp. 28–29. Change your voice for the two characters, and point to each as you read their lines.

**Beginning** Ask children to point to Andrew and then to his lines. Repeat for Mr. Jones. Ask children to point to the old school and then to the new school.

**Intermediate** Ask simple questions about the page. For example, *Is this the school now? Is it big or small?*

**Advanced** Simplify part of the dialogue, and ask two children to act out a short exchange. For example:
**Andrew:** *Our school is big!*

**Mr. Jones:** *Yes, it is. Let me tell you a story about our school.*

*For additional ESL support, use Every Student Learns Guide, pp. 14–17.*

**Lesson 4**
continued

## Page 30

Have children tell what they see in the photos.

**6** **How are the children in the two pictures the same? How are they different?** Possible answers: They are about the same age; their clothes are different. **Compare and Contrast**

**7** **How are the classrooms different?** Children's responses may indicate that the classroom of the past looks very plain compared with the one from the present. **Compare and Contrast**

**8** **What do you think a classroom of the future might look like?** Possible answers: children in very different clothing, robots in the classroom, the classroom looking like a spaceship **Hypothesize**

**Mr. Jones** Fewer people lived in this area in the past. We did not have as many children coming to our school then.

**Mr. Jones** Many people have moved here. Now we have more children. We had to build a bigger school.

30

# Practice and Extend

**SOCIAL STUDIES**
**History**

**"Then-and-Now" Reports**

Help children find out what your own school looked like in the past.

- If your building is quite old, invite a member of your local historical society to share pictures of your school as it looked in the past.
- If your building is relatively new, try to obtain pictures that show it during construction.
- Guide children in writing short "Then-and-Now" reports about your school.

**MEETING INDIVIDUAL NEEDS**
**Learning Styles**

**Making Room** Have children demonstrate and explain how Andrew's school has changed.

**Kinesthetic** Designate several distinct areas in the room as "classrooms." Start with just a few children in each "classroom." As the "school" gets bigger, put more children into each "classroom." As the "classrooms" get crowded, add a new "classroom" and redistribute the children to show the effect.

**Auditory** Divide children into "Then" and "Now" groups. Have the groups take turns saying something they learned about Andrew's school from their time period.

**Andrew** The old school used to be small. Now our school is much bigger. I wonder if my ❾ school will get even bigger in the future!

## What did you learn ?

1. **Use the pictures** to tell how Andrew's school changed.

2. Why did Andrew's school change in size?

3. **Think and Share** Why might your school change in the future? List ways your school might change.

31

❾ **What would happen if more and more children started going to Andrew's school?** Possible answers: The school would need more classrooms, class sizes might get bigger, and so on. **Hypothesize**

# 3 Close and Assess

To check what children have learned in this lesson, do the following activity.

• Have each child ask an older family member to tell about something that is different now from the way it was when that person was young. If possible, have children bring in visual materials that show the changes.

• Have children take turns telling what they learned.

## ✓ What did you learn ?

1. Answers may include that his school has gotten bigger and there are more children in each class.

2. More children attend the school.

**Test Talk**

**Write Your Answer**
3. **Think and Share** Answers will vary but may include that it will get bigger and have more students. Before children share their lists, they should ask themselves, "Do the ideas on my list make sense?"

# Mary McLeod Bethune

## Objectives

- Identify characteristics of good citizenship, such as belief in equality.
- Identify the contributions of historical figures in the period of history since 1880.

# 1 Introduce and Motivate

**Preview** On the board, begin a word web with *Education* in the center cell. In the outer cells, write *People, Places,* and *Tools.*

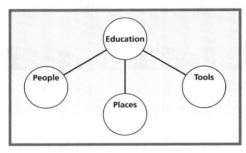

Tell children that people go to school to learn—or to get an education. Write the word *educator* under *People.* Explain that an educator is a person who helps others learn. Ask children to help fill in the word web.

**Warm Up** To activate prior knowledge, remind children of Ruby Bridges Hall and ask them to tell about her experience when she went to school. Tell children that they are going to read about another woman and the things she did for education.

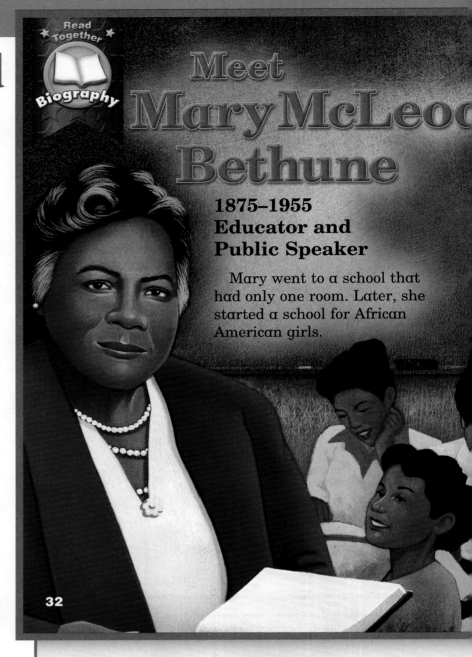

## Meet Mary McLeod Bethune

**1875–1955**
**Educator and Public Speaker**

Mary went to a school that had only one room. Later, she started a school for African American girls.

32

# Practice and Extend

**FYI** **SOCIAL STUDIES**
**Background**

### About Mary McLeod Bethune

- After finally getting some education in the one-room school, Bethune went on to learn at a seminary and at the Moody Bible Institute in Chicago.
- Bethune represented African American women as president of organizations such as the National Association of Colored Women and by founding the National Council of Negro Women.
- In 1936, she became the first African American woman to head a federal agency. President Franklin D. Roosevelt had appointed her director of the Division of Negro Affairs of the National Youth Administration. She also served Presidents Coolidge and Truman, providing her expertise about minority affairs and education.

When Mary was a girl, she wanted to learn how to read. Mary could not go to school because there were no schools for African Americans. No one in her family had ever been to school.

When Mary was about nine, she started going to a tiny, one room school. She came home and taught her family what she learned.

When Mary McLeod Bethune became an adult, she started her own school for African American girls. She spoke to groups all around the country. She wanted to help other African Americans. She helped people understand how important it is to have good schools.

Mary McLeod Bethune was born in Mayesville, South Carolina.

Mary McLeod Bethune and a group of students

### Think and Share

How did Mary McLeod Bethune help others?

For more information, go online to *Meet the People* at **www.sfsocialstudies.com.**

33

## 2 Teach and Discuss

Read the biography for children. Remind children that there used to be separate schools for African American children.

**1 Why didn't Mary McLeod Bethune go to school when she was a little girl?** There were no schools for African Americans **Cause and Effect**

**2 How old was Mary when she finally started school?** Nine **Main Idea and Details**

**3 Why do you think Mary wanted to teach her family the things she learned at school?** Children may suggest that Mary was very excited to be learning and wanted to share her knowledge. **Make Inferences**

### Ongoing Assessment

| **If...** children have difficulty understanding why Mary wanted to teach her family and others, | **then...** ask them what they tell their family members or friends when something very exciting happens to them. |

**4 What did Mary McLeod Bethune do to help African American children?** She started a school for African American girls. She showed people the importance of school. **Draw Conclusions**

## 3 Close and Assess

### Think and Share

Children may suggest that she helped African American children by starting a school and that she helped people understand the importance of good schools.

# Then and Now
## Living History

# Things We Use

## Objective
• Recognize that things change over time.

# 1 Introduce and Motivate

**Preview** Have children scan pp. 34–35 and name those things that are familiar to them. Then point out the Then and Now icon, and explain that this lesson is about things children used in school in the past and things they use now.

**Warm Up** To activate prior knowledge, ask children to list objects they use in school. Suggest that they look around the classroom and in their desks. Record children's ideas on the board.

# 2 Teach and Discuss

### Page 34

Help children identify any items pictured on p. 34 that may be unfamiliar to them, such as the metal lunch pail. Explain that these are items used in schools in the past.

**1 What do the pictures on p. 34 show?** Things children used in school in the past Analyze Pictures

**2 How do you think children used each of these things?** Possible answers: The pencil was used for writing; the pail, to carry lunch; the slate and chalk, for writing; the bookstrap, instead of a backpack; the scissors, for cutting. Make Inferences

**3 How do you or other children you know carry books to school today?** Possible answer: In a backpack Apply Information

# Then and Now
## Living History

# Things We Use

These pictures show some things children used at school in the past. What did they use then?

① ② ③

34

# Practice and Extend

### FAST FACTS

**School in History**

• In ancient Egypt, only boys had writing tools. At first they practiced writing on pieces of broken pottery. Then, once they were good at it, they were given a few sheets of paper called papyrus.

• For a long time, children had no books. They learned by listening to the teacher. Around the Fifteenth Century, children in Europe began to get books of Latin grammar.

• In the middle of the Nineteenth Century, Louis Braille developed a reading system for the blind. After that blind people could "read" their school books too.

Some things children use at school have changed. Look at the pictures. What do you use today?

## Hands-on History

Draw a picture of something you might use in a school of the future. Tell about it.

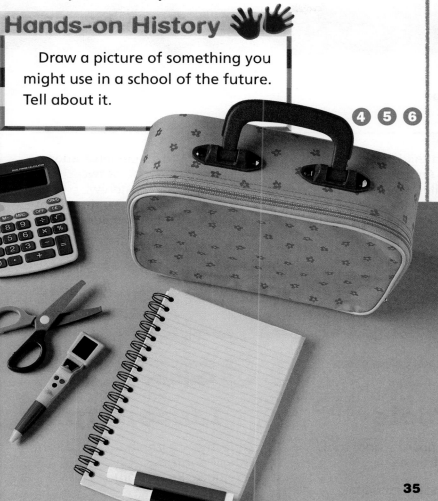

35

Have volunteers identify the school tools pictured on this page. Ask children which they use at school.

**4 How do children use the calculator? the notebook? the lunch box?** The calculator is for math; the notebook, for writing; the lunch box, for carrying food. **Analyze Pictures**

**5 How are things we use in school today different from those used in the past?** Possible answer: Today we can use calculators to do math, and we write on paper instead of on a slate. **Compare and Contrast**

**6 Why can the kinds of tools we use at school change?** Answers should reflect some understanding of changing times and technologies. **Cause and Effect**

## 3 Close and Assess

### Hands-on History

Have children brainstorm ideas for future school tools before they make their drawings. As a follow-up activity, have volunteers describe their future tools.

---

### MEETING INDIVIDUAL NEEDS
### Leveled Practice

**Guess the Time** Show children "Then and Now" photographs of your community, or of other subjects for which such photographs are available. Have children group the pictures into "Then" and "Now."

**Easy** Choose two pictures in which the time period is clearly different. Ask children leading questions, such as *Does this look like the town you live in today?* **Reteach**

**On-Level** Have children choose a picture and explain what picture clues they used to determine whether it was a "Then" or "Now" picture. **Extend**

**Challenge** Invite children to look at several pictures from the "Then" group. Ask them to suggest a possible time order for the pictures, using clues to decide which images come from farthest in the past. **Enrich**

# Lesson ④ Wrap-Up

 **MEETING INDIVIDUAL NEEDS**
## Leveled Practice

### Then or Now
Tell children that they will use objects (such as blocks) and/or pantomime to show how Andrew's school has changed.

**Easy** Have children show how Andrew's school has changed in size. As they point to objects or present pantomimes, other children can identify the time period by saying "Then" or "Now." **Reteach**

**On-Level** Remind children that there are reasons why Andrew's school has changed. Ask children to show a change—with objects or pantomime—and then tell what caused it. **Extend**

**Challenge** After their demonstration, children can dictate one or two sentences about how Andrew's school has changed. Then ask how the school might change if a lot of children moved from the area. **Enrich**

 ## Hands-on Activities

 **SOCIAL STUDIES STRAND**
### Economics

## Who Does What?

**Objective** Describe the jobs of teachers and other school workers.

**Learning Style** Verbal/Kinesthetic
**Group** 👧👦👧👦
🕐 **Time** 20–25 minutes

1. Name some familiar school staff, such as the gym teacher, art teacher, or principal.

2. Have volunteers role-play what each worker does. If necessary, prompt children with questions about the staff member's role at school.

3. Make a list on the board of teachers in your school and what they do.

 **CURRICULUM CONNECTION**
### Math

## Tools

**Objective** Compare school tools from different times.

**Materials** pencils and paper; calculators
**Learning Style** Kinesthetic
**Partners** 👧👦
🕐 **Time** 5–10 minutes

1. Give children a grade-level appropriate math problem such as 2 + 2 = ?.

2. Show one child in each pair how to use a calculator to compute the answer. Direct the other child to find the answer using pencil and paper. Then have children exchange roles.

3. Discuss how tools have made some school tasks go more quickly for children today.

 **SOCIAL STUDIES STRAND**
### Culture

## Listen Up!

**Objective** Learn about schools in other countries. (Prejudice Reduction)

**Learning Style** Auditory/Verbal
**Individual** 🧍
🕐 **Time** 20–25 minutes

1. Arrange for an older student who has attended school in another country to visit your class. Have the student share his or her experiences. Encourage the student to tell what things are the same in both places and what things are different.

2. After the visit, help children compose a class thank-you letter to the student. Children can dictate sentences that tell what they learned.

# Ending Unit 1

## End with a Poem
### pages 36–37

Children will listen to and talk about a poem—"School Today" by Herbert Thomas—that answers the question: "What do I do at school?"

## Unit 1 Review
### pages 38–41

Children will review unit vocabulary words and the unit skills of using picture clues, problem solving, and reading a calendar. Children will answer questions about what they learned in the unit. Children will learn about several books about going to school.

**Resources**
✓ • Workbook, p. 10
• Assessment Book, pp. 1-4

## Unit 1 Project
### page 42

Children will create and present a mock video tour of their school. They will also be directed to a Web site where they can learn more about schools.

**Resource**
• Workbook, p. 11

# Wrap-Up

## Activity

## School Days

Have children make accordion picture books of things they do at school. Cut sheets of 11" x 17" paper in half lengthwise. Then, holding the paper the long way, show children how make accordion folds so there are four panels.

- On the front, children should draw a picture of something they do in school in each panel.

- On the back, children should write their names and then copy and complete this sentence: *At school I learn to __.* Allow them to complete the sentence with words or pictures.

### Performance Assessment
You can use the activity on this page as a performance assessment.

✓ **Assessment Scoring Guide**

| Make an Accordion Book About School | |
|---|---|
| 6 | Draws four different, detailed school activities and writes a complete, legible, sentence for each one. |
| 5 | Draws four different school activities and writes a clear sentence for each one. |
| 4 | Draws four school related activities and completes the sentences appropriately. |
| 3 | Draws four activities but not all are clearly school-related. Completes the sentence appropriately. |
| 2 | Draws two or three school activities and attempts to complete the sentences |
| 1 | Draws one or two school activities and fails to complete sentences. |

If you require a 4-point rubric, adjust scoring guide accordingly.

# School Today

## Objective
• Obtain information about a topic using literature.

## 1 Introduce and Motivate

**Preview** Point to and read the title of the poem and the poet's name. Ask children what they think this poem is about. Suggest that they think about the title and look at the pictures for ideas.

Tell children that a poem is a kind of writing that often has rhyming words. Mention that this poem has many rhyming words.

**Warm Up** Ask children to name things they do at school each day. Ask them to tell about some things they have learned to do—and to suggest things they would like to learn before the end of the year.

## 2 Teach and Discuss

Explain to children that the poet is writing as if he were a child in school. Have children listen and look at the pictures as you read the poem.

**1** **What are some things these children do at school?** Possible answers: Sing, play with friends, learn to read, plant seeds **Main Idea and Details**

**2** **Do you do these same things at school?** Children may say that they do all or most of the things mentioned in the poem. **Compare and Contrast**

**3** **Do you think the children in the pictures like going to school? Why or why not?** Possible answer: Yes, because the poem is a happy one, and because the pictures show happy children **Make Inferences**

## School Today
### by Herbert Thomas

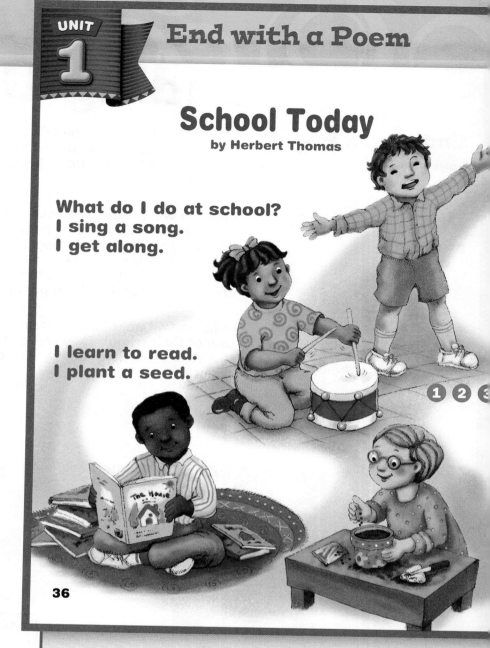

What do I do at school?
I sing a song.
I get along.

I learn to read.
I plant a seed.

**36**

# Practice and Extend

**CURRICULUM CONNECTION**
## Music

**"This Is the Way"**

• Teach children new words (and actions!) to the old singing game, "This Is the Way We Wash Our Clothes."

This is the way we read our books,

Read our books, read our books.

This is the way we read our books,

Each and every school day.

• Invite children to suggest their own words and actions for the words *read our books*. Use ideas from the poem on pp. 36–37, or draw from children's favorite class activities.

read a map.
sing and clap.

write and spell.
show and tell.

I stretch and bend.
I make a friend.
This is what I do at school!

37

- Divide the class into two groups. Read the first three lines of the poem. Have one group create a pantomime for the first action: *sing a song*. Have the other group create a pantomime for the second action: *get along*.

- Reread the lines, having groups perform their pantomimes at the appropriate times.

- Continue for the remaining lines of the poem.

- Discuss with children which parts of the school day they like most. Ask if their favorite parts are mentioned in the poem.

## CURRICULUM CONNECTION
### Literature

**Books About School**

Children might enjoy reading these books related to school.

***See You Tomorrow, Charles,*** by Miriam Cohen and Lillian Hoban (Illustrator), (Bantam Books, ISBN 0-440-41151-3, 1997) Charles is blind but he proves that he can take charge in certain situations. Easy

***When Jo Louis Won the Title,*** by Belinda Rochelle and Larry Johnson (Illustrator), (Houghton Mifflin, ISBN 0-395-81657-2, 1996) A young African American girl is afraid of being teased about her name—until her grandfather tells her the story behind that name. On-Level

***The Toll-Bridge Troll,*** by Patricia Rae Wolff and Kimberly Bulcken Root (Illustrator), (Voyager Picture Book, ISBN 0-15-202105-1, 2000) When the troll who lives under the bridge demands the customary toll, Trigg decides to outwit him by using riddles and logic. Challenge ALA Notable Book, 1996

# UNIT 1 Review

## Resources
- Assessment Book, pp. 1–4
- Workbook, p. 10: Vocabulary Review

# Vocabulary Review

1. school
2. flag
3. rule
4. country

 **Answers to Test Prep**

1. c. group
2. a. rule

---

# UNIT 1 Review

# Vocabulary Review

Match each word to its picture.

flag
school
rule
country

1.

2.

3.

4.

★ ★ ★ ★ ★ ★ ★ ★

**TEST PREP** Which word completes each sentence?

1. When you play on a team, you are part of a _____.
   **a.** rule          **b.** map
   **c.** group       **d.** country

2. We learn to work together and stay safe when we follow a _____.
   **a.** rule          **b.** flag
   **c.** map          **d.** country

38

---

# Practice and Extend

## Assessment Options

✓ **Unit 1 Assessment**
- Unit 1 Content Test: Use Assessment Book, pp. 1–2
- Unit 1 Skills Test: Use Assessment Book, pp. 3–4

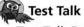 **Standardized Test Prep**
- Unit 1 tests contain standardized test formats.

✓ **Unit 1 Performance Assessment**
- See p. 42 for information about using the Unit 1 Project as a means of performance assessment.
- A scoring guide for the Unit 1 Project is provided in the teacher's notes on p. 42.

**Test Talk**
- Test Talk Practice Book

---

# Skills Review

## Use Picture Clues

Look at these pictures.
Tell what is happening.

★ ★ ★ ★ ★ ★ ★ ★

# Problem Solving

Your cafeteria is too noisy. Tell steps
you would take to solve the problem.

**39**

**Workbook, p. 10**

Draw lines to match.

school
flag
country
rules

Draw a picture of a group. **Drawings will vary.**

**Also on Teacher
Resources CD-ROM.**

---

# Skills Review

## Use Picture Clues

- A girl is swinging.
- A boy is playing with his pet.
- Children are saying the Pledge of Allegiance.

## ✓ Assessment Scoring Guide

| Picture Clues | |
|---|---|
| 6 | Uses precise details and complete sentences to describe the activity shown in each picture. Shows creativity in responses by offering additional details such as naming the children. |
| 5 | Uses precise details to describe the activity shown in each picture. Demonstrates a clear understanding of each activity, may provide additional details. |
| 4 | Describes each picture accurately. Clearly understands each activity. |
| 3 | Describes each picture adequately and shows understanding of the activity shown in the pictures. |
| 2 | Describes each picture with few details, but is unable to identify each activity shown in the pictures. |
| 1 | Unable to use picture clues to identify details or the activity shown in each picture. |

If you require a 4-point rubric, adjust scoring guide accordingly.

## Problem Solving

Answers will vary but should include steps
presented in a logical sequence according to the
process taught in Problem on the Playground.
Answers should identify the problem (the cafeteria
is too noisy) and then describe the child's efforts to
find out more about the problem, list ways to solve
the problem, review possible solutions, implement
the solutions, and review the impact of solutions.

## Review

continued

# Skills Review

## Read a Calendar

- 30
- November 11th
- Wednesday

## Skills on Your Own

- Children's calendars should be in the format shown for November and should include accurate labels for month and days of the week. Be sure to show children on which day the month they have chosen begins.

Use the following scoring guide.

### ✓ Assessment Scoring Guide

| Make a Calendar | |
|---|---|
| 6 | Shows an accurate calendar for the chosen month, including the correct number of days and two or more special days. |
| 5 | Shows an accurate calendar for the chosen month, including the correct number of days and at least one special day. |
| 4 | Shows an accurate calendar format, with the correct number of days. |
| 3 | Shows a calendar for the chosen month in a format with a few errors such as the incorrect number of days or incorrect order in days of the week. |
| 2 | Shows a calendar containing some errors in information or labeling. |
| 1 | Attempts to complete calendar but has difficulty numbering the days or naming days of the week. |

If you require a 4-point rubric, adjust scoring guide accordingly.

## Review

# Skills Review

## Read a Calendar

1. How many days are in this month?
2. When is Veterans Day?
3. What day of the week is November 16?

## Skills On Your Own

Draw a calendar of your favorite month. Mark the important days.

# Practice and Extend

### Revisit the Unit Question

✓ Unit 1 Portfolio Assessment

- Have children look back at the reasons for going to school that they suggested on p. 1.
- Ask children if they wish to add any new reasons to that list now.
- Have children explain each reason they have supplied, telling why it made going to school sensible.
- Ask children to help prioritize the list in order of importance. Use *1* for the most important reason, *2* for the next most important reason, and so on.
- Have children copy the list and add it to their Social Studies Portfolio.

# What did you learn?

1. Name two different groups.

2. What are two rules that help you work together? What are two rules that keep you safe?

3. Why is it important to follow rules?

4. **Think and Share** Think of rules for your class. Make a list of your rules. Share your rules with the class.

Test Talk

Look for key words in the question.

# Read About School

Look for books like these in the library.

41

# What did you learn?

1. Possible answers: Family, class, friends, team

2. Possible answers: To raise your hand before speaking, to sit quietly in class; to sit on the bus, to cross only when the guard tells you to

3. Answers may include to keep us safe, so we can work together.

4. **Think and Share** List of rules should show that children need to get along and respect others in a group situation.

Test Talk

**Locate Key Words in the Question**
Use Question 3 to model the strategy.

**Find the key words in the question.**
Remind children that a question beginning with *Why* is asking for a reason.

**Turn the question into a statement.**
Say: "It is important to follow rules because...."
Ask children to complete the statement.

# Read About School

Make books about school available to children. Have them read the books and tell about them.

*School from A to Z* by Bobbie Kalman (Crabtree Publishing, ISBN: 0-86505-418-5, 1999) Tells children's experiences in school, from *A* to *Z*.

*Yoko* by Rosemary Wells (Hyperion Press, ISBN: 0-7868-0395-9, 1998) When Yoko brings an unusual lunch to school, her teacher concocts a delicious plan to stop the teasing.

*Mary McLeod Bethune* by Eloise Greenfield (Harper Trophy, ISBN: 0-064-46168-8, 1994) This biography of the educator is simply told and beautifully illustrated.

## Unit 1 Project

# Follow Me!

## Objective
• Dramatize a video tour that describes different parts of the school and explains what happens in each part.

## Resource
• Workbook, p.11

## Materials
paper, crayons or colored markers, small boxes, paper towel tubes, other classroom objects that can be used to make a model video camera

## Follow This Procedure
• Have children use simple classroom materials to construct a model of a video camera.

• Review with children different places in and around your school, including classrooms, media center, cafeteria, and so on. Have each child choose a place.

• Explain that people who make videos first draw pictures before they begin filming. Tell children that these pictures are sometimes called storyboards. Have each child draw a picture of the place he or she has chosen.

• Divide the class into small groups. Put each group's pictures together so that they form a storyboard. Have children use their model cameras to present a video tour.

### ✓ Assessment Scoring Guide

| | Follow Me! |
|---|---|
| 6 | Uses elaborate details and precise language. |
| 5 | Uses several details and clear language. |
| 4 | Uses some details and acceptable language. |
| 3 | Attempts to include details and acceptable language. |
| 2 | Uses limited details, and vague or incomplete language. |
| 1 | Unable to provide details, and makes incorrect word choices. |

If you require a 4-point rubric, adjust scoring guide accordingly.

# 1 Project

## Follow Me!

**Give a video tour of your school.**

**1** **Think** about what some important places are in your school. What happens in each place?

**2** **Draw** a picture that shows what happens in one of the important places.

**3** **Make** a model of a video camera.

**4** **Use** your model camera to give a video tour. Describe the place you drew in your picture. Tell what visitors would need to know about your important place.

### Internet Activity

Go to www.sfsocialstudies.com/activities to learn more about schools.

42

# Practice and Extend

### Hands-on Unit Project

✓ **Performance Assessment**
• The Unit Project can also be used as a performance assessment activity.
• Use the scoring guide to assess each group's work.

### WEB SITE Technology

Children can launch the activity by clicking on *Grade 1, Unit 1* at **www.sfsocialstudies.com/activities.**

### Workbook, p. 11

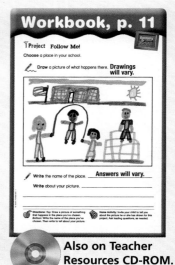

**Also on Teacher Resources CD-ROM.**

# Vocabulary Routines

The following examples of reading and vocabulary development strategies can be used to instruct students about unit vocabulary.

## BEFORE READING

### Individual Word Study

**Student-Friendly Definitions** Building student-friendly definitions helps children fully understand the meanings of new words. First, have children characterize the new word by asking why we use the word and what we think of when we hear the word. Be prepared to make suggestions or read a definition if children are unable to suggest enough information to create a useful definition. Next, have children generate a definition by helping them put it in their own words. You can use this routine with any of the unit vocabulary as shown in the example at right.

*Let's look at the word* **neighborhood.** *When do we use the word* **neighborhood?** *We use it when we talk about where people live and work and play together. What do you think of when you hear the word* **neighborhood?** (homes; streets; buildings; families; playgrounds) *So what is a good definition for* **neighborhood?** *It is a place where people live, work, and play. In the neighborhood, there are streets, homes, and other buildings. Neighborhoods can be big or small.*

neighborhood   —a place where people live, work, and play

                —they have homes, streets, buildings, families, playgrounds

## DURING READING

### Context Clues

**Questions, Reasons, and Examples** Read the lesson with children and pause at the end of each page. Review lesson vocabulary words covered on the page. Use pantomime when possible to help reinforce ideas. Ask a question about the word and give examples. Encourage children to respond to the examples and explain their reasoning, as shown at right.

*One of the words in our lesson is* **law.** *A law is a rule that people must obey.* Pantomime driving a car stopping at a stop light. *I always stop when the light is red. Why is it a law that drivers must stop at a red light?* (They have to wait their turn. If they go when the light is red, they might cause an accident and hurt someone.) *Which of these is a law—to clean up the toys in your room or to have to pay for a toy before you take it from the store?* (pay for a toy before you take it from the store, because it is against the law to steal) *You should clean up your toys, but it is not against the law to have a messy room.*

## AFTER READING

### Related Word Study

Vocabulary: neighborhood, community, law, leader, state, continent, ocean

**Possible Sentences** Use this routine with any vocabulary word after you have read the lesson with children. Point out the word and then use it in a sentence. Ask children if the sentence is possible or not. Have children explain their reasoning.

*One of our new words is* **continent.** *I want you to think about what* **continent** *means. Now I'm going to use* **continent** *in a sentence. I want you to tell me if my sentence makes sense or not:* **Florida is a continent.** *That sentence doesn't make sense, does it? Florida is a state, not a continent.*

# Teaching with Leveled Readers

**This series of readers focuses on how homes and communities have changed over the years.**

**Below Level**

**On Level**

**Above Level**

## LEVELED READER VOCABULARY ACTIVITY

- Preview with children the vocabulary word *community*.

- As children read, have them identify different characteristics of a community.

- After reading, have children draw a past and present picture of a community.

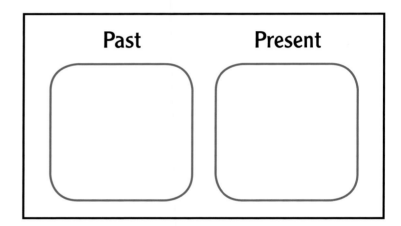

| Past | Present |
|------|---------|
|      |         |

## CONNECTIONS TO THE LESSON

Unit 2, Lesson 2: Different Kinds of Communities

## CONNECTIONS TO TODAY

- Have children read the lesson. Then provide the leveled readers to enhance their understanding of different types of communities and how a community today may be different from years ago.

- **Points for Discussion:**

    1. Have children discuss what makes their home or community special.

    2. Children can also discuss how their community might be different in the future.

# In My Community

# Unit 2 Planning Guide
## In My Community

**Begin with a Song** pp. 44–45    **Vocabulary Preview** pp. 46–47
**Reading Social Studies, Alike and Different** pp. 48–49

| Lesson Titles | Pacing | Main Ideas |
|---|---|---|
| **Lesson 1 Welcome to My Neighborhood** pp. 50–53 <br><br> Map and Globe Skills: Use a Map Key pp. 54–55 | 2 days | • A neighborhood is a place where people live, work, and play. <br> • Neighborhoods can be alike in some ways and different in other ways. <br> • A map key tells what the symbols used on a map stand for. |
| **Lesson 2 Different Kinds of Communities** pp. 56–57 <br><br> Then and Now: How a Community Changed pp. 58–59 <br> Map and Globe Skills: Use Four Directions pp. 60–61 | 2 days | • A neighborhood is part of a larger community. <br> • Cities, towns, and farms are kinds of communities. <br> • A community may change over time. <br> • A map includes cardinal directions: north, south, east, west. |
| **Lesson 3 Special Things We Do** pp. 62–65 <br><br> Chinese New Year pp. 66–67 <br> Citizen Heroes: **Fairness** Harriet Tubman pp. 68–69 | 3 days | • People in a community share many customs. <br> • Celebrations of the Chinese New Year are a custom from another country. <br> • Harriet Tubman helped many African Americans move to places where they could be free. |
| **Lesson 4 Community Laws and Leaders** pp. 70–71 <br><br> Biography: Jane Addams pp. 72–73 | 2 days | • People must obey the laws of a community. <br> • A mayor and other leaders work for the common good of the community. <br> • Jane Addams started Hull House to help the people of Chicago. |
| **Lesson 5 Where in the World Do I Live?** pp. 74–77 <br><br> Biography: Henry Flagler pp. 78–79 | 2 days | • The United States is a country made up of fifty states. <br> • The United States is on the continent of North America. <br> • A continent is a large piece of land; an ocean is a large body of salt water. <br> • Henry Flagler helped Florida grow by building hotels and expanding railroads. |

✓ **End with a Poem** pp. 80–81    ✓ **Unit 2 Review** pp. 82–85    ✓ **Unit 2 Project** p. 86

✓ = Assessment Options

| Vocabulary | Resources | Meeting Individual Needs |
|---|---|---|
| neighborhood | • Workbook, pp. 14–15<br>• Vocabulary Card: neighborhood<br>• Every Student Learns Guide, pp. 18–21<br>• Transparencies 13, 14 | • ESL Support, TE p. 52<br>• Leveled Practice, TE p. 55a |
| community | • Workbook, pp. 16–17<br>• Vocabulary Card: community<br>• Every Student Learns Guide, pp. 22–25<br>• Transparency 15 | • ESL Support, TE pp. 58, 61<br>• Leveled Practice, TE p. 61a |
|  | • Workbook, p. 18<br>• Every Student Learns Guide, pp. 26–29 | • ESL Support, TE p. 64<br>• Leveled Practice, TE p. 69a |
| law<br>leader | • Workbook, p. 19<br>• Vocabulary Cards: law, leader<br>• Every Student Learns Guide, pp. 30–33 | • Leveled Practice, TE pp. 73, 73a |
| state<br>continent<br>ocean | • Workbook, p. 20<br>• Vocabulary Cards: state, continent, ocean<br>• Every Student Learns Guide, pp. 34–37<br>• Transparencies 16, 17 | • ESL Support, TE p. 76<br>• Leveled Practice, TE p. 79a |

# Providing More Depth

## Additional Resources

- Trade Books
- Family Activities
- Vocabulary Workbook and Cards
- Social Studies Plus!
- Daily Activity Bank
- Read Alouds and Primary Sources
- Big Book Atlas
- Student Atlas
- Outline Maps
- Desk Maps

 **Technology**

- Video Field Trips
- Songs and Music
- Digital Learning CD-ROM Powered by KnowledgeBox
- AudioText
- MindPoint® Quiz Show CD-ROM
- ExamView® Test Bank CD-ROM
- Colonial Williamsburg Primary Sources CD-ROM
- Teacher Resources CD-ROM
- Map Resources CD-ROM
- SFSuccessNet: Online Student Edition, Online Teacher Edition, Online Planner
- **www.sfsocialstudies.com** (Biographies, news, references, maps, and activities)

 *To establish guidelines for your children's safe and responsible use of the Internet, use the Scott Foresman Internet Guide.*

**Additional Internet Links**

To find out more about:

- your own community, visit the web site for your village, town or city
- Henry Flagler, visit **www.flaglermuseum.us**

# Unit 2 Objectives

**Beginning of Unit 2**

- Obtain information using oral sources, such as conversations, interviews, and music. (pp. 44–45)

- Determine the meanings of words. (pp. 46–47)

- Compare and contrast by telling about likenesses and differences. (pp. 48–49)

- Identify and describe the human characteristics of places, such as types of houses. (pp. 48–49)

- Express ideas orally, based on knowledge and experiences. (pp. 48–49)

**Lesson 1**
**Welcome to My Neighborhood**
pp. 50–53

- Identify buildings in relation to the school and neighborhood.

- Recognize that communities include people who have diverse ethnic origins, customs, and traditions and who make contributions to their communities.

- Create and use simple maps to identify the location of places in the classroom. (pp. 54–55)

- Construct a map using basic map symbols. (pp. 54–55)

**Lesson 2**
**Different Kinds of Communities**
pp. 56–57

- Explain similarities and differences between life in city, town, suburban, and farm communities.

- Distinguish among past, present, and future and identify changes in the community. (pp. 58–59)

- Locate places using the four cardinal directions. (pp. 60–61)

**Lesson 3**
**Special Things We Do**
pp. 62–65

- Describe various customs and traditions and explain their importance.

- Obtain information about a topic using a variety of sources, such as interviews.

- Describe selected customs.

- Describe community celebrations. (pp. 66–67)

- Describe various customs of families. (pp. 66–67)

- Obtain information about a topic using a variety of visual sources, such as pictures. (pp. 66–67)

- Identify characteristics of good citizenship, such as belief in equality. (pp. 68–69)

**Lesson 4**
**Community Laws and Leaders**
pp. 70-71

- Explain the need for laws in the community.

- Identify responsibilities of authority figures in the community.

- Describe the role of public officials including mayor.

- Identify contributions of historical figures in the period of history since **1880.** (pp. 72–73)

**Lesson 5**
**Where in the World Do I Live?**
pp. 74–77

- Locate places of significance on maps.

- Identify contributions of historical figures in the period of history since **1880.** (pp. 78–79)

**End of Unit 2**
pp. 80–81

- Obtain information about a topic using a variety of visual sources, such as pictures and literature.

- Identify main ideas from oral, visual, and print sources.

# Assessment Options

## ✓ Formal Assessment

- **What did you learn?** PE/TE pp. 53, 57, 65, 71, 77
- **Unit Review,** PE/TE pp. 82–85
- **Unit 2 Test,** Assessment Book pp. 5–8
- **ExamView® CD-ROM**

## ✓ Informal Assessment

- **Teacher's Edition Questions,** throughout Lessons and Features
- **Close and Assess,** TE pp. 49, 53, 55, 57, 59, 61, 65, 67, 69, 71, 73, 77, 79, 81
- **Try it!** PE/TE pp. 49, 55, 61
- **Think and Share,** PE/TE pp. 53, 57, 65, 71, 73, 77, 79
- **Fairness in Action,** PE/TE p. 69
- **Hands-on History,** PE/TE p. 59

### Ongoing Assessment

**Ongoing Assessment** is found throughout the Teacher's Edition lessons using an **If…then** model.

| | |
|---|---|
| **If** = students' observable behavior, | **then** = reteaching and enrichment suggestions |

## ✓ Portfolio Assessment

- **Portfolio Assessment,** TE p. 43
- **Leveled Practice,** TE pp. 43, 55a, 61a, 69a, 73, 73a, 79a
- **Workbook,** pp. 12–22
- **Unit Review: Skills on Your Own,** PE/TE p. 84
- **Curriculum Connection: Writing,** TE pp. 45, 55a, 69a, 73a

## ✓ Performance Assessment

- **Hands-on Unit Project** (Unit 2 Performance Assessment), PE/TE pp. 43, 86
- **Internet Activity,** PE p. 86
- **Scoring Guides,** TE pp. 80a, 83, 84, 86

## Test Talk

### Test-Taking Strategies

**Understand the Question**

- **Locate Key Words in the Question,** TE p. 52
- **Locate Key Words in the Text,** TE p. 85

**Understand the Answer**

- **Choose the Right Answer,** *Test Talk Practice Book*
- **Use Information from the Text,** TE p. 67
- **Use Information from Graphics,** TE p. 47
- **Write Your Answer,** TE p. 53

*For additional practice, use the Test Talk Practice Book.*

### Featured Strategy

**Locate Key Words in the Text**

Children will:

- Make sure that they understand the key words in the question.
- Find key words in the text that match key words in the question.

**PE/TE** p. 85

# Curriculum Connections
## Integrating Your Day

The lessons, skills, and features of Unit 2 provide many opportunities to make connections between social studies and other areas of the elementary curriculum.

## Social Studies

### Reading

*Reading Skill—Compare and Contrast (Alike and Different),* TE p. 50

*Creating Symbols,* TE p. 54

*Reading Skill—Make Word Webs (Alike and Different),* TE p. 56

*Reading Skill—Common Customs (Alike and Different),* TE p. 62

*Reading Skill—Telling Why,* TE p. 70

*Reading Skill—Venn Diagram (Alike and Different),* TE p. 74

*Name Game,* TE p. 79a

### Writing

*Interview,* TE p. 45

*Add to "My Word Book,"* TE p. 55a

*Customs,* TE p. 69a

*Class Letter,* TE p. 73a

### Math

*Simon Says,* TE p. 61a

### Literature

*Read My New York,* TE p. 57

*Smoky Night,* TE p. 59

*City, Country,* TE p. 61a

*Routes,* TE p. 79a

*Books About Communities,* TE p. 81

*Read About Communities,* PE/TE p. 85

### Science

*Climate and Homes* TE p. 49

*Draw to Show Weather Changes,* TE p. 60

*Where's North?* TE p. 61a

### Music/Drama

*Plan a Street,* TE p. 55a

*Sing Out!* TE p. 69a

### Art

*Draw Your Community,* TE p. 47

*Design a Street Sign,* TE p. 51

*Make a "Customs" Calendar,* TE p. 64

*Make a State Puzzle,* TE p. 75

 Look for this symbol throughout the Teacher's Edition to find **Curriculum Connections.**

# Professional Development

## Reading the Social Studies Textbook

**by Candy Dawson Boyd, Ph.D.**
St. Mary's College of California

The pedagogical and learning demands of reading social studies text with both understanding and engagement has daunted elementary teachers for too long. It is important to devote real time to the teaching of social studies, with the textbook as a core part of the active curriculum.

A critical first step is for the teacher to carefully explore both the Teacher's Edition and Pupil's Edition in the social studies textbook series. A perusal of the table of contents offers the structure of content in the form of units and lessons. Examining how individual components are structured at the lesson, special feature, unit, and overall textbook levels aids in assessing the reading strategies and skills readers need. Critical questions to ask include: How are lessons organized? Is vocabulary labeled in clear ways? Are illustrations and photographs presented where they need to be to serve as support for the reader? Are visuals presented in a way that informs the reader without being overwhelming? Are there a variety of clear, focused maps? The answers to these questions will impact how easily the reader will be able to engage text. Below are some ways Scott Foresman *Social Studies* structures its program to help students read with understanding and engagement.

*Every unit has a **Vocabulary Preview** that introduces unit vocabulary and relates each word to a photograph. Students then are asked to find in an illustration examples that relate to each vocabulary word.*

*Every unit has a **Reading Social Studies** feature that highlights a target reading skill. Students are then encouraged to apply that strategy throughout the unit.*

***Map and Globe Skills** features are found in many lessons. This allows students to connect visually to the content of the lesson while using map skills.*

## ESL Support

**by Jim Cummins, Ph. D.**
University of Toronto

In order to understand how to extend students' grasp of academic language and how to use language powerfully, it is important to distinguish the following three very different aspects of proficiency in a language:

***Conversational fluency*** is the ability to carry on a conversation in familiar face-to-face situations.

***Discrete language skills*** reflect specific phonological, literacy, and grammatical knowledge that students acquire as a result of direct instruction and both formal and informal practice (e.g., reading).

***Academic language proficiency*** includes knowledge of the less frequent vocabulary of English as well as the ability to interpret and produce increasingly complex written language.

The learning of discrete language skills does not generalize automatically to academic language proficiency. ESL students who can "read" English fluently may have only a very limited understanding of the words they can decode. The development of reading comprehension ability in the content areas, and academic language proficiency generally, requires very different forms of instruction than the forms that are successful in teaching discrete language skills.

*The following examples in the Teacher's Edition will help you to enable ESL students to extend language:*

- ***Telling About Neighborhoods*** *on p. 52 helps English Language Learners learn and use words that describe neighborhoods.*

- ***Work with New Words*** *on p. 58 has children work with words used to talk about past, present, and future events.*

- ***A Spinning Game*** *on p. 76 involves children in playing a game that uses vocabulary relating to maps and globes.*

# Read Aloud

## Where I Live
### by Lou Myers

I live in a house
That's painted white.
It's cozy; it's small;
For me, just right.

I live on a street
With lots of trees.
I like my neighbors
And they like me.

I live in a town
That's not very old.
It was once a farm—
Or so I am told.

**Build Background**
- Ask children to tell about the places where they live.
- Ask children if they would like to live in the place described in the poem. Encourage them to give reasons for their answers.

**Read Alouds and Primary Sources**
*Read Alouds and Primary Sources* contains additional selections to be used with Unit 2.

# Bibliography

**Carpenters,** by Vicky Franchino (Compass Point Books, ISBN 0-756-50006-0, 2000) **Easy**

**Fire Fighters,** by Lucia Raatma (Compass Point Books, ISBN 0-756-50009-5, 2000) **Easy**

**Letter Carriers,** by Alice K. Flanagan (Compass Point Books, ISBN 0-756-50010-9, 2000) **Easy**

**Mayors,** by Alice K. Flanagan (Compass Point Books, ISBN 0-756-50064-8, 2001) **Easy**

**My Town,** by Rebecca Treays (EDC, ISBN 0-746-03079-7, 1998) **Easy**
**Notable Social Studies Book**

**Police Officers,** by Alice K. Flanagan (Compass Point Books, ISBN 0-756-50011-7, 2000) **Easy**

**Aurora Means Dawn,** by Scott Russell Sanders and Jill Kastner (illustrator), (Aladdin, ISBN 0-689-81907-2, 1998) **On-Level**

**Little House, The,** by Virginia Lee Burton (Turtleback, ISBN 0-606-01531-0, 1969) **Caldecott Medal, 1943** **On-Level**

**Philharmonic Gets Dressed, The,** by Karla Kuskin (HarperCollins, ISBN 0-06-443124-X, 1986) **On-Level**

**Raising Yoder's Barn,** by Jane Yolen and Bernie Fuchs (illustrator), (Little Brown, ISBN 0-316-96887-0, 1998) **On-Level**

**Uptown,** by Bryan Collier (Henry Holt, ISBN 0-805-05721-8, 2000) **On-Level** **Coretta Scott King Award**

**Journey, The,** by Sarah Stewart and David Small (illustrator), (Farrar Straus & Giroux, ISBN 0-374-33905-8, 2001) **Challenge**

**New Coat for Anna, A,** by Harriet Ziefert and Anita Lobel (illustrator), (Econo-Clad Books, ISBN 0-833-51245-5, 1999) **Challenge**

**Urban Roosts: Where Birds Nest in the City,** by Barbara Bash (Little Brown, ISBN 0-316-08312-7, 1992) **Challenge**

**Window,** by Jeannie Baker (Greenwillow, ISBN 0-688-08918-6, 1991) **Challenge**

**Discovery Channel School Videos**
**Two Children, Two Cultures.** Get a taste of two cultures of the world. Meet Koumba from the Congo, Africa, and Yeye from Shanghai, China; 25 minutes/2 segments.

Look for this symbol throughout the Teacher's Edition to find **Award-Winning Selections**. Additional book references are suggested throughout this unit.

# In My Community

# In My Community

## Unit Overview

This unit introduces children to aspects of life in a community and helps children learn about their relationship to home, neighborhood, community, and state.

## Introduce Kim

Read the unit title and then introduce the featured child for this unit as a first grader named Kim. Talk about what Kim might like best about her community.

## Unit Question

- Ask children the questions on this page.

- Initiate a discussion of what children like about their own community.

- To activate prior knowledge, make a list on the board of what children like about their own community.

✓ **Portfolio Assessment**  Keep a copy of this list for the Portfolio Assessment at the end of the unit on p. 84.

**What do you like best about where you live? Why?**

43

# Practice and Extend

## Hands-on Unit Project

✓ **Unit 2 Performance Assessment**

- The Unit 2 Project, News for All, found on p. 86, is an ongoing performance assessment project to enrich children's learning throughout the unit.

- This project, which has children make a poster and give a news report about a community event, may be started now or at any time during this unit of study.

- A performance assessment scoring guide is on p. 86.

# This Is My Community

## Objective

- Obtain information using oral sources, such as conversations, interviews, and music.

## Resources

- *Songs and Music* CD "This Is My Community"
- Poster 3
- Social Studies Plus!

## Introduce the Song

**Preview** Tell children that they will be singing a song about a community. Focus attention on the urban aspects of Kim's community.

**Warm Up** To activate prior knowledge, refer to the list of things children like about their community. Ask if they think other communities also have these things. Ask them to share what they know about other communities. This will help you evaluate children's knowledge of communities.

## Sing the Song

- Have children sing the song "This Is My Community."
- Ask children what they think Kim's day is like—based on the words of the song.
- Invite children to tell what they learned about Kim's community from singing the song.

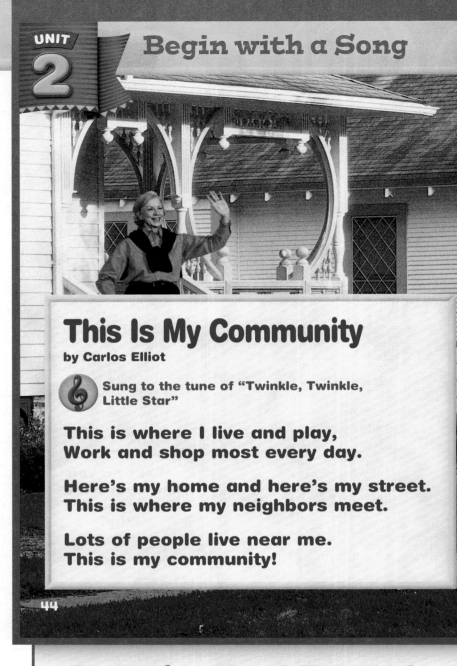

# This Is My Community
by Carlos Elliot

Sung to the tune of "Twinkle, Twinkle, Little Star"

This is where I live and play,
Work and shop most every day.

Here's my home and here's my street.
This is where my neighbors meet.

Lots of people live near me.
This is my community!

44

# Practice and Extend

**FYI** SOCIAL STUDIES
**Background**

**Possible Misconceptions**

Children living in suburban or rural areas may be surprised to learn that urban families can often walk to shops and offices. Conversely, children living in cities may not know that suburban and rural families often have to drive to stores and places of business. Discuss such differences among suburban, rural, and urban areas.

AUDIO CD
**Technology**

Play the CD, *Songs and Music*, to listen to "This Is My Community."

## Talk About the Picture

Direct children's attention to the picture. Ask them to name some things in Kim's community.

**① The song says that Kim lives and plays in her community. What else does she do there?** She works and shops. **Main Idea and Details**

**② What does the picture show Kim doing?** Walking her dog **Analyze Pictures**

**③ Who do you think the woman in the picture is? How do you know?** She is Kim's neighbor. The song says that neighbors meet on Kim's street. **Make Inferences**

**CURRICULUM CONNECTION**
## Writing

**Interview**

- Have each child ask an older person about the community in which he or she grew up.
- Have children draw pictures to show the communities their interviewees tell them about. Children can write or dictate captions for their pictures.
- Have children show their drawings and share what they have learned with classmates.

## Objective

• Determine the meanings of words.

## Resources

• Workbook, p. 12

• Vocabulary Cards

• Poster 4

## Introduce the Vocabulary

Read aloud and point to each vocabulary word and the photograph illustrating it. Have volunteers give the meanings of the words. Then have children find examples of vocabulary words in the illustration. Write these examples on the board:

| Vocabulary Word | Illustrated Examples |
| --- | --- |
| neighborhood | school neighborhood |
| community | city (tall buildings in distance) |
| law | street signs (one way, no parking), traffic lights |
| leader | governor, mayor |
| state | Florida map, Virginia map |
| continent | South America (on globe) |
| ocean | pictures (on billboard and in window) on globe |

In addition, for *leader*, identify local and state leaders, as well as the leaders of our country.

 **SOCIAL STUDIES STRAND**
## Geography

Listed below are some basic principles of geography for young children. Direct your discussion of the illustration toward the development of these concepts.

• similarities and differences
• neighborhood features
• ways people use maps to locate places
• role of location and physical surroundings in people's lives
• ways communities change over time
• four cardinal directions
• community customs and celebrations

**neighborhood**

**community**

**law**

**leader**

**46**

# Practice and Extend

## MEETING INDIVIDUAL NEEDS
## Leveled Practice

### Here Comes the Welcome Wagon!

Ask children to imagine that they are newcomers to this community—and that you are the welcoming committee. Tell children that you will show them around.

**Easy** Guide children into finding illustrations of each vocabulary word. Have children repeat the vocabulary words as you point to the illustrations. **Reteach**

**On-Level** Have children use picture clues to tell you more about the people and places illustrated. Encourage children to use the vocabulary words in their descriptions. **Extend**

**Challenge** Have children select a location in the picture (such as the travel agency or city hall) and have them find the addresses for these things in their community. If necessary, show them how to use the phone book. Then discuss what happens in these places. **Enrich**

state

continent

ocean

47

## Workbook, p. 12

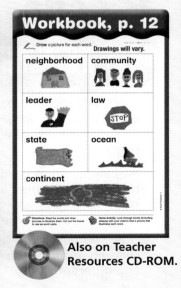

Draw a picture for each word.

**Drawings will vary.**

| neighborhood | community |
| leader | law |
| state | ocean |
| continent | |

**Also on Teacher Resources CD-ROM.**

# Talk About the Illustration

Allow children time to study the illustration. Encourage children to talk about what the other people in the picture are doing.

 **Test Talk**

**Use Information from Graphics**

**1 Which signs are telling people what to do?**
Possible answers: One Way sign tells drivers that cars can only go in one direction. The sign with a circle and a bar over the letter *P* means "No Parking." Traffic lights tell drivers when to stop and go. Tell children to use details from the picture to support their answers. **Analyze Pictures**

**2 Ask children what special event is happening in the picture. How can they tell?**
Possible answer: The leader of the state, Governor Smith, is visiting. There is a welcome sign and decorations. **Analyze Pictures**

# Look Ahead

Tell children that they will learn more about each of these words as they study Unit 2.

You may want to revisit the picture with children to review the concepts and vocabulary in the unit.

**3 How is a community like a neighborhood? How is a community different from a neighborhood?** Both are places where people live and work. A community is bigger than a neighborhood. A community has many neighborhoods. **Compare and Contrast**

# Where Kim Lives

## Target Skill Alike and Different

### Objectives

- Compare and contrast by telling about likenesses and differences.

- Identify and describe the human characteristics of places such as types of houses.

- Express ideas orally, based on knowledge and experiences.

### Resource

- Workbook, p. 13

### About the Unit Target Skill

- The target reading skill for this unit is Alike and Different. Children are introduced to the unit target skill here and are given an opportunity to practice it.

- Further opportunities to practice comparing and contrasting are found throughout Unit 2.

# 1 Introduce and Motivate

**Preview** Display two balls of different sizes and colors. Ask children to tell how the two objects are alike. (Both are balls; both are round spheres.) Then ask them to tell how they are different. (in size, in color) Write *alike* and *different* on the board. Relate *alike* to "same" and *different* to "not the same."

**Warm Up** To activate prior knowledge, remind children about the story of Andrew's school from Mr. Jones's scrapbook (Unit 1). Ask children to tell one thing about the school from long ago; for example, "It was small." Then ask them to tell if the school is still like that now. (No, it is much bigger now.)

# Where Kim Lives

## Target Skill Alike and Different

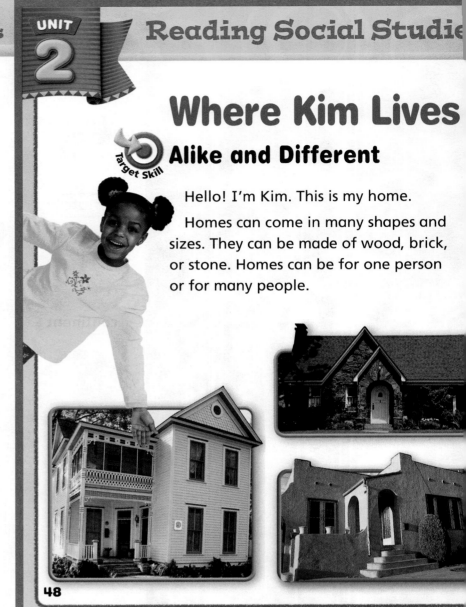

Hello! I'm Kim. This is my home.

Homes can come in many shapes and sizes. They can be made of wood, brick, or stone. Homes can be for one person or for many people.

**48**

# Practice and Extend

### ESL ACCESS CONTENT
### ESL Support

**Work with New Words** Discuss the meanings of the words *alike* and *different*. Have children write the words on cards and then draw pictures that remind them of the English meanings.

**Beginning** Show children two similar picture books. Have children display their *alike* or *different* cards to respond to statements you make, such as: *Both are storybooks.* (alike) *The stories are not the same.* (different)

**Intermediate** Show a pair of similar items, and have children prompt each other to tell how the items are alike and different.

**Advanced** Have children locate their own paired items, hold up their cards, and explain how the items are alike or different.

Homes can look alike. **Alike** means how things are the same. Homes can also look different from each other. **Different** means how things are not the same. Look at these pictures. How are the homes alike? How are they different?

Draw pictures of two homes. Tell how they are **alike** and **different**.

49

**Workbook, p. 13**

**Alike and Different**

Circle two houses that are alike.

Color these houses so they are different. **Answers will vary.** Color the cars so they are different, too.

**Also on Teacher Resources CD-ROM.**

# 2 Teach and Discuss

Read p. 48 and have children look at the pictures on pp. 48–49. Ask children to point out Kim's house. Then have them describe each of the other homes pictured.

Read p. 49 and focus on the terms *alike* and *different.* Ask children to tell one way in which the pictured homes are all alike. Then ask them to tell how the homes are different. Explain that homes have many characteristics in common because they are built for humans. Ask children why they think all the homes have windows. Discuss what this tells us about what people need. Ask why they all have doors.

Explain that we can use the word *compare* to tell how things are alike and the word *contrast* to tell how things are different.

## ✓ Ongoing Assessment

**If...** children do not understand how to use the words *alike* and *different* to compare and contrast,

**then...** display two identical items, and tell how they are alike. Then replace one with a similar but not identical item. Discuss how the two items are alike but also different.

# 3 Close and Assess

## Try it!

Tell children that they may draw any kind of homes they like. Use the pictures on pp. 48–49 to review some possible choices. Children's drawings should show two homes. Their oral statements should include at least one point of comparison and one point of contrast.

# Workbook Support

Use the following Workbook pages to support content and skills development as you teach Unit 2. You can also view and print Workbook pages from the Teacher Resources CD-ROM.

## Workbook, p. 12

Draw a picture for each word.
Use with Pages 46-47.

**Drawings will vary.**

| neighborhood | community |
| leader | law |
| state | ocean |
| continent | |

**Directions:** Read the words and draw pictures to illustrate them. Cut out the boxes to use as word cards.

**Home Activity:** Look through books (including atlases) with your child to find a picture that illustrates each word.

**Use with Pupil Edition, p. 47**

## Workbook, p. 13

### Alike and Different
Use with Pages 48-49.

Circle two houses that are alike.

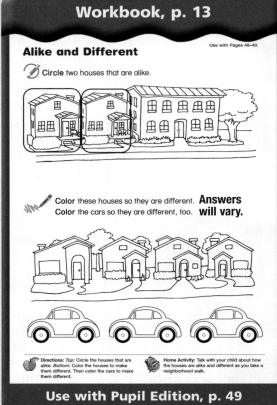

Color these houses so they are different. **Answers**
Color the cars so they are different, too. **will vary.**

**Directions:** *Top:* Circle the houses that are alike. *Bottom:* Color the houses to make them different. Then color the cars to make them different.

**Home Activity:** Talk with your child about how the houses are alike and different as you take a neighborhood walk.

**Use with Pupil Edition, p. 49**

## Workbook, p. 14

### Welcome to My Neighborhood
Use with Pages 50-53.

Cut out the boxes at the bottom.
Paste three of them where they belong.

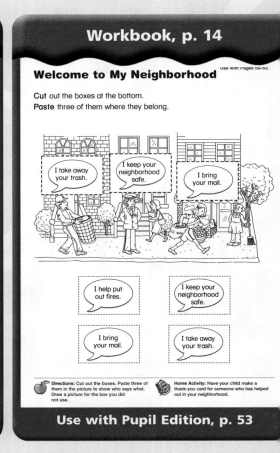

I take away your trash.
I keep your neighborhood safe.
I bring your mail.

I help put out fires.
I keep your neighborhood safe.
I bring your mail.
I take away your trash.

**Directions:** Cut out the boxes. Paste three of them in the picture to show who says what. Draw a picture for the box you did not use.

**Home Activity:** Have your child make a thank-you card for someone who has helped out in your neighborhood.

**Use with Pupil Edition, p. 53**

## Workbook, p. 15

### Use a Map Key
Use with Pages 54-55.

Look at the map key.

Draw symbols on the map to show where things are.

**Answers will vary.**

Map Key
🏠 house
🏫 school
🌳 tree
— street

Oak Street
School Lane

**Directions:** Make your own map of a neighborhood around a school. Use the symbols in the map key to show trees, houses, and a school.

**Home Activity:** Help your child make a simple map of your street or block. Include a map key.

**Use with Pupil Edition, p. 55**

## Workbook, p. 16

### Different Kinds of Communities
Use with Pages 56-57.

Write *city*, *town*, or *farm*.

Color the picture that shows a community like yours.
**Answers will vary.**

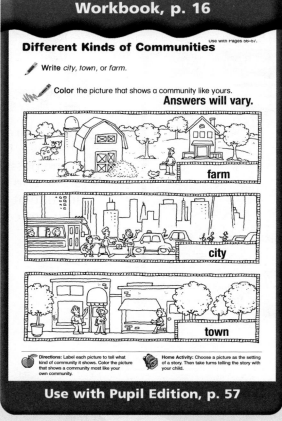

farm

city

town

**Directions:** Label each picture to tell what kind of community it shows. Color the picture that shows a community most like your own community.

**Home Activity:** Choose a picture as the setting of a story. Then take turns telling the story with your child.

**Use with Pupil Edition, p. 57**

## Workbook, p. 17

### Use Four Directions
Use with Pages 60-61.

Draw the route Pat should take.

Dear Pat,
Start at the school.
Go north on James Road.
Go east on Main Street.
Stop at the park.
Meet me there.
Dad

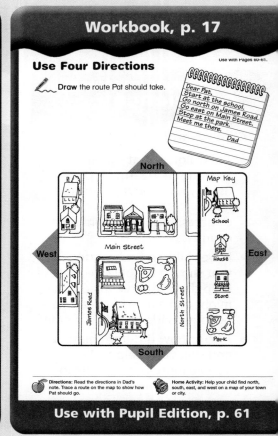

North
West
East
South

Map Key
School
House
Store
Park

Main Street
James Road
North Street

**Directions:** Read the directions in Dad's note. Trace a route on the map to show how Pat should go.

**Home Activity:** Help your child find north, south, east, and west on a map of your town or city.

**Use with Pupil Edition, p. 61**

# Workbook Support

## Workbook, p. 18

### Special Things We Do

Use with Pages 62–65.

*Draw* to show what you might do on July 4th. **Drawings will vary.**

**Directions:** Draw a picture to show how you would like to celebrate the 4th of July, Independence Day.

**Home Activity:** Tell your child about a family custom or tradition you celebrated when you were growing up.

**Use with Pupil Edition, p. 65**

## Workbook, p. 19

### Community Laws and Leaders

Use with Pages 70–71.

*Circle* the picture that goes with the sentence.

It is safe to cross.

Keep our park clean.

Walk your dog on a leash.

**Directions:** Read each sentence. Circle the picture that shows who is obeying the law.

**Home Activity:** Point out signs in your own community that tell people what they may and may not do.

**Use with Pupil Edition, p. 71**

## Workbook, p. 20

### Where in the World Do I Live?

Use with Pages 74–77.

*Color* your state red.
*Color* states that touch your state blue.

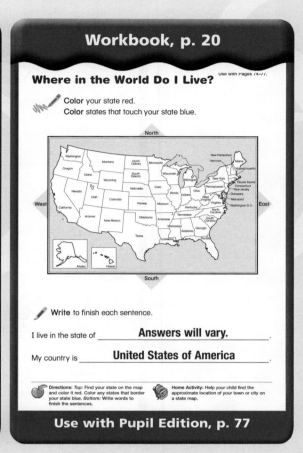

*Write* to finish each sentence.

I live in the state of _____ **Answers will vary.**

My country is _____ **United States of America**

**Directions:** Top: Find your state on the map and color it red. Color any states that border your state blue. Bottom: Write words to finish the sentences.

**Home Activity:** Help your child find the approximate location of your town or city on a state map.

**Use with Pupil Edition, p. 77**

## Workbook, p. 21

*Draw* lines to match.

state

law

leader

continent

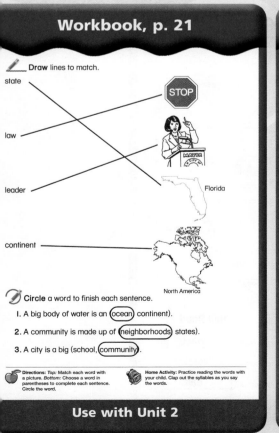

STOP

MAYOR

Florida

North America

*Circle* a word to finish each sentence.

1. A big body of water is an (ocean) continent).

2. A community is made up of (neighborhoods) states).

3. A city is a big (school, (community)).

**Directions:** Top: Match each word with a picture. Bottom: Choose a word in parentheses to complete each sentence. Circle the word.

**Home Activity:** Practice reading the words with your child. Clap out the syllables as you say the words.

**Use with Unit 2**

## Workbook, p. 22

### 2 Project  News for All

*Draw* a picture of an event in your community. **Drawings will vary.**

*Write* the name of the event. **Answers will vary.**

*Write* what happens at the event. _____

**Directions:** Top: Choose your community event, and then draw a picture of it. Bottom: Write to tell what the event is and what happens at it.

**Home Activity:** Talk with your child about a recent community event, such as a block party or a holiday celebration. Discuss how such events bring people together.

**Use with Pupil Edition, p. 86**

# Assessment Support

 Use these Assessment Book pages and the ExamView® CD-ROM to assess content and skills in Unit 2. You can also view and print Assessment Book pages from the Teacher Resources CD-ROM.

## Assessment Book, p. 5

**Unit 2: Content Test**

✏ **Circle** a word to finish each sentence.

1. North America is a ____.
   law     (continent)

2. Many neighborhoods make up my ____.
   (community)     ocean

3. A mayor is one kind of ____.
   state     (leader)

4. Atlantic is the name of a big ____.
   law     (ocean)

⭐ **TEST PREP** Which word completes each sentence?

1. Littering is against the ____.
   a. leader     (b.) law
   c. ocean     d. state

2. Florida is a ____.
   a. leader     b. lake
   c. continent     (d.) state

**Use with Pupil Edition, p. 82**

## Assessment Book, p. 6

✏ **Draw** one person who helps in your neighborhood.
**Draw** a leader in your community. **Drawings will vary.**

✏ **Circle** a word to complete each sentence.

1. A town community is not as big as a ____.
   (city)     farm

2. Going to a parade on July 4th is a ____.
   law     (custom)

3. The United States is part of ____.
   Florida     (North America)

**Use with Pupil Edition, p. 82**

## Assessment Book, p. 7

**Unit 2: Skills Test**

✏ **Color** the two houses that are alike.

✏ **Color** the school red.
**Color** the park green.
**Color** the lake blue.

**Use with Pupil Edition, pp. 84, 85**

## Assessment Book, p. 8

🔍 **Look** at the map.

✏ **Write** an answer for each question.

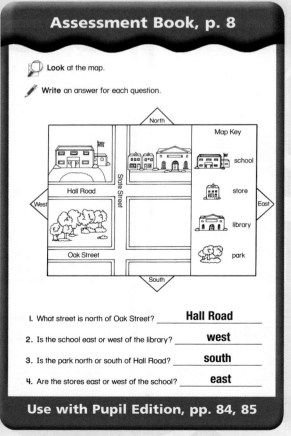

1. What street is north of Oak Street? **Hall Road**

2. Is the school east or west of the library? **west**

3. Is the park north or south of Hall Road? **south**

4. Are the stores east or west of the school? **east**

**Use with Pupil Edition, pp. 84, 85**

# Lesson ① Overview

## Welcome to My Neighborhood
pages 50–53

Children will learn the meaning of the word *neighborhood*. They will explore features of a neighborhood and learn how to use a street address to locate places.

**Time 20–30 minutes**

**Resources**
- Workbook, p. 14
- Vocabulary Card **neighborhood**
- Every Student Learns Guide, pp. 18–21

## Use a Map Key
pages 54–55

Children will learn to use map keys, including those containing symbols.

**Time 15–20 minutes**

**Resource**
- Workbook, p. 15

# Build Background

## Activity

### Welcome!

 **Time 15–20 minutes**

Have children draw pictures either of their homes or their schools. Give each child a strip of paper with the name of his/her street or the name of the school's street on it. Have children paste the labels onto the backs of their pictures.

As children share their work, have them tell the name of the street on which their homes or school is located. Children who live on the same street might line up to show their pictures—and neighborhoods.

**If time is short,** ask children to tell the name of the street on which they live or on which the school is located. Write the street names on the board.

## Read Aloud

### Hi, Neighbor!

**by Peri Jones**

I live in a house
On a nice quiet street.
My neighbors say HI!
Whenever we meet.

They come to my home
And I go to theirs.
We sit and we talk—
Have done so for years.

# Lesson 1

# Welcome to My Neighborhood

## Objectives

- Identify buildings in relation to the school and neighborhood.

- Recognize that communities include people who have diverse ethnic origins, customs, and traditions and who make contributions to their communities.

## Vocabulary

**neighborhood** a place where people live, work, and play (p. 52)

### QUICK Teaching Plan

*If time is short,* have children look at the pictures and then tell:

- how their own neighborhoods are like Kim's and

- how their own neighborhoods are different from Kim's.

# 1 Introduce and Motivate

**Preview** Display the Vocabulary Card **neighborhood**. Pronounce the word, and spell it aloud for children. Share its meaning as "a place where people live, work, and play." Have children locate the term as they preview the lesson.

**Warm Up** To activate prior knowledge, ask children to tell briefly about some of their own neighbors. If necessary, point out that neighbors are the people who live nearby. Then have children tell how neighbors help each other.

# Lesson 1

# Welcome to My Neighborhood

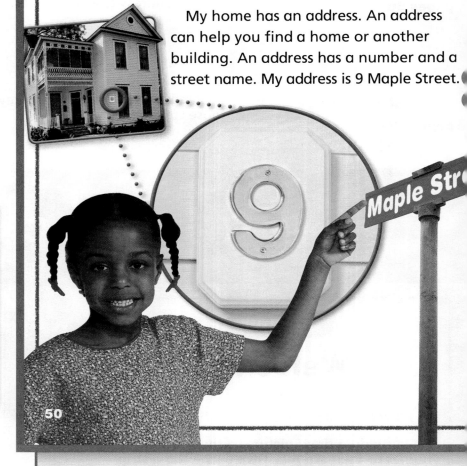

My home has an address. An address can help you find a home or another building. An address has a number and a street name. My address is 9 Maple Street.

50

# Practice and Extend

**READING/VOCABULARY**
## Alike and Different

**Compare and Contrast** Remind children that they can use the word *alike* to tell how things are the same and *different* to tell how things are not the same.

- After children finish p. 53, make a chart like the one shown below.

- Have children look at the two neighborhoods shown on p. 52. Guide them in finding ways in which the neighborhoods are alike and different.

- Ask volunteers to tell some ways in which the neighborhoods are alike and different.

| Alike | Different |
|-------|-----------|
|       |           |
|       |           |
|       |           |

Look on the map. Find my home. Now find my school. What is the address of my school?

**Pine Street**

**Blue Street**

**Maple Street**

③
④

51

**CURRICULUM CONNECTION**
## Art

**Design a Street Sign**

- Point out the street sign Kim is pointing to on p. 50.
- Ask children to make a street sign that tells the address of Kim's school.
- Provide strips cut from index cards. Have children write the street name on their strip.
- Give children pencils or dowels and tape. Show them how to tape their sign strip onto the pencil.

**WEB SITE**
## Technology

You can look up vocabulary words online. Click on *Social Studies Library* and select the dictionary at **www.sfsocialstudies.com**.

---

# 2 Teach and Discuss

**Page 50**

Identify Kim in the photograph. Ask what Kim is doing.

❶ **What is the name of Kim's street? What is the number of her house on Maple Street?** Maple Street; nine **Recall and Retell**

❷ **Why do you think most addresses have a street name and a number?** Possible answer: So people can find the specific house they are looking for **Draw Conclusions**

**Page 51**

Point out the map of Kim's neighborhood. Help children find Kim's home and school.

**Themes of Geography: Location**

❸ **Tell how Kim uses street names to find her home on the map.** She looks for Maple Street, which is the name of her street. **Interpret Maps**

❹ **Find Kim's house on the map. Is the school near her house? Explain.** Yes, the school is on the next block. **Interpret Maps**

**Lesson**

**1**

continued

---

**Page 52**

Have children compare and contrast the two photographs on p. 52.

**Test Talk**

**Locate Key Words in the Question**

**5** **How is a big neighborhood different from a small neighborhood?** Call attention to the key words *different from* in the question. Remind children that they need to tell how the two neighborhoods are *not* the same. Elicit that a big neighborhood has more buildings, more traffic, more people, and more noise.
**Compare and Contrast**

**6** **How are people in these neighborhoods alike?** Possible answer: They are doing things in their communities; they are helping to make their communities nice places in which to live.
**Compare and Contrast**

**7** **How can people in a neighborhood help each other?** Possible answer: Police officers help keep people safe. Shop owners sell the things people need. **Make Inferences**

---

My home and school are part of my neighborhood. A **neighborhood** is a place where people live, work, and play.

Neighborhoods can be big or small. They can be noisy or quiet. They can have many buildings or just a few buildings.

Tell how these neighborhoods are alike and different.

**5** **6**

52

---

# Practice and Extend

**ESL**  **EXTEND LANGUAGE**
# ESL Support

**Telling About Neighborhoods** Use the neighborhood pictures in Lesson 1 to help children learn new words about things found in neighborhoods.

**Beginning** Point to such things as stores, buildings, and people. Name items in the pictures as you point to them. Have children repeat the names.

**Intermediate** Help children name the various items in the neighborhood pictures. Ask if they have those same things in their neighborhoods. Encourage them to answer in sentences: *I have ___ in my neighborhood.*

**Advanced** After talking about the pictures, ask children to draw pictures of their own neighborhoods. Have them take turns telling each other about their neighborhoods.

*For additional ESL support, use Every Student Learns Guide, pp. 18–21.*

Meet some people who work in my neighborhood.

ick up the trash.

My mom works in a shop.

**8 9**

I deliver the mail.

## What did you learn

1. What is a **neighborhood?**

2. Name three kinds of work people can do in a neighborhood.

3. **Think and Share** Write about your neighborhood. Tell how it is **alike** and **different** from the neighborhoods shown in the pictures.

53

**Page 53**

Point out Kim, the trash collector, and the mail carrier.

**8 How does the mail carrier help the people in Kim's neighborhood?** He brings them their mail. **Make Inferences**

**9 How does a mail carrier know where to take each letter?** He or she looks at the address on the envelope and takes the letter to that address. **Make Inferences**

## Close and Assess

Have children describe their own school neighborhood. Tell them to include the school's address and to describe the buildings near the school. Ask where they live in relation to the school.

### ✓ What did you learn

1. It's a place where people live, work, and play.

2. Possible answers: Sell things in a store, collect trash, deliver mail

**Test Talk**

**Write Your Answer**
Ask children to reread their answers to make sure they are correct.

3. **Think and Share** Answers might include more buildings, more people, the same workers.

---

**FYI** SOCIAL STUDIES
**Background**

**Why People Move**

- Mention that people move from place to place for a variety of reasons. Explain that sometimes families move to new neighborhoods, cities, or states. Discuss reasons people decide to move: to be near family or friends, new jobs, etc.

- Tell children that some people move from faraway countries to the United States. People do this for the same reasons listed above: to be near family or friends, new jobs, etc. Discuss reasons it might be difficult to move to the United States from another country.

**Workbook, p. 14**

**Welcome to My Neighborhood**

Cut out the boxes at the bottom.
Paste three of them where they belong.

**Also on Teacher Resources CD-ROM.**

# Use a Map Key

## Objectives

- Create and use simple maps to identify the location of places in the classroom.
- Construct a map using basic map symbols.

## Vocabulary

**symbol** a picture that stands for a real thing (p. 54)

**map key** a set of pictures and words that tell what the symbols on a map mean (p. 55)

# 1 Introduce and Motivate

**Preview** Write the vocabulary words on the board, and share the definitions with children. Then point to the map key on p. 55, and identify it for children. Tell children that a map key is sometimes called a map legend.

**Warm Up** To activate prior knowledge, remind children that a map is a drawing that shows what a real place looks like from above. Then remind them of symbols they use in math, such as the plus sign and the equals sign. Then display two simple drawings: one of a can of soup and the other of a box of cereal. Tell children to imagine they are at a supermarket and these pictures are hung at the beginning of two different aisles. Ask: *Which sign would you look for if you wanted to buy soup? Which would you look for if you wanted to buy cereal?* Explain that the pictures are symbols because they stand for something else that is real.

# Use a Map Key

Some maps use pictures to stand for real things. A picture that stands for a real thing is called a **symbol.** On this map, the 🌳 stands for a tree.

Rose Street

54

# Practice and Extend

**CURRICULUM CONNECTION**
**Reading**

**Creating Symbols**

- Have children take turns pointing to different areas of the classroom, such as learning centers, and describing each area.

- Point out any signs you have put up to name special areas. Help children read the signs. Then tell children you need their help in adding some picture symbols to show what the different areas are for.

- Assign each child a partner and an area. Ask the pair to design a picture symbol for it. If necessary, brainstorm ideas: a picture of a book for the classroom library, a pencil for the writing center, a paintbrush for the art center.

- Have partners work together to create pictorial symbols. Post these in the appropriate areas.

This is a map of the park near Kim's home. The map has a map key. A **map key** tells what the symbols ❶ on the map mean.

## Map Key

🗑 trash can

🛝 swingset ❷

drinking fountain

🪑 park bench

🌳 tree

▭ street

## Try it!

1. Why are **symbols** on a map important?

2. What is next to the 🗑 in the park?

3. **On Your Own** Draw a map and **map key** of your classroom. Show how you go from your desk to your teacher's desk.

55

### SOCIAL STUDIES STRAND
### Geography

- Have each child draw a map of the street on which he or she lives. Give children colored paper to cut out shapes for homes, shops, and other buildings on the street. Then ask children to put their cut-outs on the drawings in the place they think each belongs.

- Have children make a map key for their maps. Remind them to put both pictures and words in their map keys.

## Workbook, p. 15

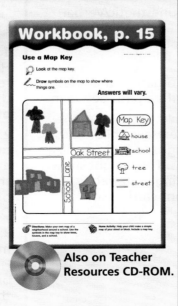

**Also on Teacher Resources CD-ROM.**

# ❷ Teach and Discuss

Pages 54-55

Read pp. 54–55 with children. Then have them point to the map key on p. 55. Tell them that a map key is also known as a map legend. Most maps have map keys, or legends, that include symbols that represent objects.

❶ **What is the purpose of a map key?** It tells what the symbols on a map mean. **Main Idea and Details**

❷ **What play equipment does this park have? How do you know?** It has a swingset. The map key shows the symbol for swingset. That same symbol appears on the map. **Interpret Maps**

# ❸ Close and Assess

## Try it!

1. They show where to find things and places.

2. The park bench

3. **On Your Own** Maps will vary but should include a map key and features of the classroom, such as children's desks, teacher's desk, board, and perhaps doors or windows. Maps should show the correct route to the teacher's desk.

#  Lesson ① Wrap-Up

 **MEETING INDIVIDUAL NEEDS**
## Leveled Practice

###  Comparing and Contrasting Neighborhoods

Have each child draw pictures of two familiar neighborhoods. Suggest that children choose from among these neighborhoods: their own, a friend's, the school, Kim's.

**Easy** Direct children to put their two pictures side by side for study. Each child can then tell one way in which the two neighborhoods are alike and one way in which they are different. **Reteach**

**On-Level** Have children add one street name and an address for one building in each of their pictures. Then have children tell classmates how the neighborhoods they have drawn are alike and different. **Extend**

**Challenge** Encourage children to write captions for their pictures. Each caption should define the neighborhood and tell some of its features. Children can then use their captions to tell how the neighborhoods are alike and different. **Enrich**

 ## Hands-on Activities

 **CURRICULUM CONNECTION**
### Writing/Vocabulary

## Add to "My Word Book"

**Objective** Define and illustrate the words *neighborhood, symbol,* and *map key.*

**Resources** Vocabulary Cards **neighborhood, symbol, map key**

**Materials** crayons, pencils

**Learning Style** Visual

**Individual**

 **Time** 20–25 minutes

**1.** Display the Vocabulary Card for *neighborhood.* Direct children to find the "N" page in their Word Books and have them write *neighborhood* in a word space.

**2.** Have children draw pictures to illustrate the word. Also encourage them to write a sentence using the word.

**3.** Follow a similar procedure for *symbol* and *map key.* Children may want to draw simple map keys to illustrate the latter.

 **CURRICULUM CONNECTION**
### Drama

## Plan a Street

**Objective** Create a make-believe neighborhood.

**Materials** classroom desks, paper, crayons or markers, tape, any classroom costume or role-play objects

**Learning Style** Kinesthetic/Verbal

**Group** 🧒🧒🧒🧒

**Time** 15–30 minutes

**1.** Help children organize their desks into two rows with a path between.

**2.** Direct each child to develop one desk into a home. Have children use props or make signs to individualize their desk-homes. They might show its color or building material, or decorate its "front yard" with flowers, or use classroom props to show typical activities.

**3.** Invite children to take you on a tour of their "neighborhood."

 **SOCIAL STUDIES STRAND**
### Geography

## Make a Map

**Objective** Make a map of a familiar area, using map symbols.

**Materials** large sheets of construction paper, pencils, crayons

**Learning Style** Visual/Kinesthetic

**Group** 🧒🧒🧒🧒

**Time** 15–30 minutes

**1.** Visit the playground with children. Have them dictate a list of its features for you to record. Also have them make rough sketches of a map of the area.

**2.** Back in the classroom, guide children in making a map key that includes the important features of the playground. Display the key.

**3.** Have children make maps of the playground. Have them copy the key onto construction paper. Then have them draw a map, referring to their sketches and using items from the key to locate features.

 jungle gym

swing

sliding board

# Lesson ② Overview

| | | |
|---|---|---|
| **Different Kinds of Communities**<br>pages 56–57 | Children will learn the meaning of the word *community* and explore ways in which a community is different from a neighborhood. |  **Time** 20 minutes<br>**Resources**<br>• Workbook, p. 16<br>• Vocabulary Card **community**<br>• Every Student Learns Guide, pp. 22–25 |
| **How a Community Changed**<br>pages 58–59 | Children will use pictures to learn how communities can change over time. |  **Time** 15–20 minutes |
| **Use Four Directions**<br>pages 60–61 | Children will learn the meanings of the four cardinal directions and practice using them to locate places on a map. |  **Time** 15–20 minutes<br>**Resource**<br>• Workbook, p. 17 |

# Build Background

## Activity

### Picture Places

 **Time** 20–25 minutes

Provide children with magazines. Have them cut out pictures that show where people live or work. Encourage them to find a variety of such places—large and small, busy and quiet, near and far, from long ago or from today.

Ask children to sort pictures into "places we work" or "places we live." Have children mount the pictures on construction paper and save them for later use. (As children learn more about communities, they can put the pictures into groups and bind the pages to make books.)

**If time is short,** show children pictures of different communities and ask them to describe these places.

## Read Aloud

### Points of View

#### by Mara McDuff

I love the city!
It's big and it's bold.
But country is better—
Or so I am told.

I love the country.
It's quiet, it's green.
Best place in the world
That I've ever seen!

I love my town.
It's neat, it's clean.
Not city or country
But right in between.

## Lesson 2
# Different Kinds of Communities

### Objective
- Explain similarities and differences between life in city, town, suburban, and farm communities.

### Vocabulary
**community** a group of people and the place where they live (p. 56)

## QUICK Teaching Plan

*If time is short,* brainstorm with children ways in which communities can be alike yet different.

- Use the photographs on pp. 56–57 to help children identify features of a city, a suburb, a town, and a farm community.

## 1 Introduce and Motivate

**Preview** Display the Vocabulary Card **community**, read the word, and ask children what they think it means. Then share the meaning of the word, pointing out that many neighborhoods together make up a community.

**Warm Up** To activate prior knowledge, ask children to name schoolmates NOT in your class. Elicit times and places that children see these schoolmates, such as on the bus or playground. Explain that your class is like a neighborhood—you see the people in it a lot—but that the whole school is like a community—you might see the people in it only sometimes.

## 2 Teach and Discuss

### Page 56

Discuss with children the city community pictured on p. 56. Point out the things made by people: buildings, roads, and so on. Tell children that we call these things *human features.*

**56** Unit 2 • In My Community

---

## Lesson 2
# Different Kinds of Communities

*I live in a big city.*

My neighborhood is part of a community. A **community** is a group of people and the place where they live. A community is bigger than a neighborhood. Many ❶ different neighborhoods can be part of a community.

A city is a big community. Many people live and work in the city.

**56**

# Practice and Extend

### READING/VOCABULARY
## Alike and Different

**Make Word Webs**

- On the board, begin a word web:

- Have children identify details in the photo on p. 56. Ask them to suggest words to add under *city.*

- Follow a similar procedure for *suburb, town* and *farm.* Then have children use the completed web to compare and contrast the communities.

### WEB SITE
## Technology

You can look up vocabulary words online. Click on *Social Studies Library* and select the dictionary at **www.sfsocialstudies.com.**

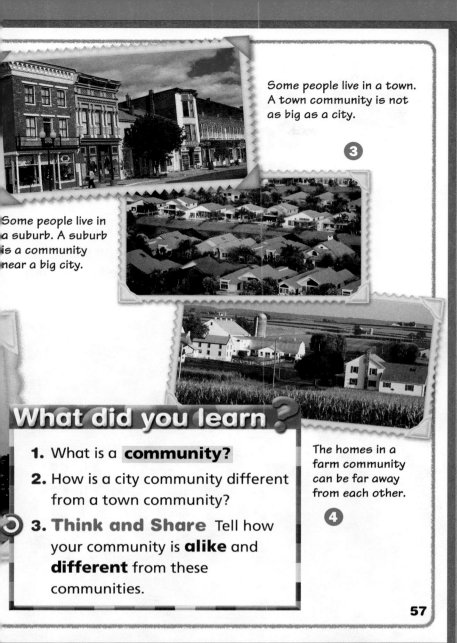

Some people live in a town. A town community is not as big as a city.

**3**

*Some people live in a suburb. A suburb is a community near a big city.*

*The homes in a farm community can be far away from each other.*

**4**

## What did you learn

1. What is a **community**?

2. How is a city community different from a town community?

3. **Think and Share** Tell how your community is **alike** and **different** from these communities.

57

**CURRICULUM CONNECTION**
**Literature**

**Read** *My New York*

- Use *My New York,* by Kathy Jakobsen (Little Brown, 1993; ISBN 0-316-45653-5), to explore different neighborhoods found in a big city.

- Contrast the last scene, which shows a farm community, with the city community.

- Note that the World Trade Center appears on the fly-leaf map and in two pictures. You may want to talk about the tragic events of September 11, 2001, with children. See also pages TR1–TR2.

**Workbook, p. 16**

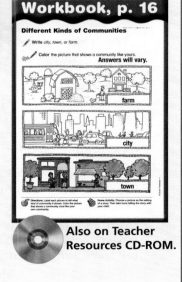

**Different Kinds of Communities**

Write city, town, or farm.

Color the picture that shows a community like yours.
**Answers will vary.**

farm

city

town

*Directions: Label each picture to tell what kind of community it shows. Color the picture that shows a community most like your own.*  *Home Activity: Choose a picture as the setting of a story. Then take turns telling the story with your child.*

**Also on Teacher Resources CD-ROM.**

---

**1** **How is a community different from a neighborhood?** It is bigger. It has several neighborhoods. **Compare and Contrast**

**2** **Look at the photo on p. 56. How would you describe a city community?** Possible answer: It's big and busy; there are many people and tall buildings. **Analyze Pictures**

---

**Page 57**

**3** **How are a suburb and a town like a city?** Each community has people, homes, shops, and other buildings. **Compare and Contrast**

**4** **How is a town different from a farm community?** The homes and buildings are closer together in a town. **Compare and Contrast**

**ST** SOCIAL STUDIES STRAND
**Technology**

Today, technology helps people from different communities stay in touch. For example, people can communicate by telephone or by e-mail. They can learn about people in other places through radio, television, and the Internet. Talk about how these advances in technology have changed the way people communicate and do business.

## **3** Close and Assess

Begin a three-column chart of kinds of communities: city, town, farm. Ask children to suggest words for you to write in each column.

## ✓ What did you learn

1. A community is a group of people and the place where they live. It contains several neighborhoods.

2. A city community is bigger. It has more people and more buildings.

3. **Think and Share** Children should identify at least one similarity and one difference.

# How a Community Changed

**Living History**

## Objective

- Distinguish among past, present, and future and identify changes in the community.

# 1 Introduce and Motivate

**Preview** Tell children that most things—including communities—don't stay the same forever; they *change*. *Change* means to make or become different. Ask children how they have changed since they were babies.

**Warm Up** To activate prior knowledge, write *past, present,* and *future* as column headings. Display pictures of a log cabin, a modern apartment house, and a space station. Use the words *past, present,* and *future* as you talk about the pictures with children.

# 2 Teach and Discuss

### Page 58

Review ways to get clues from pictures, and then ask children to study the photograph on p. 58. Be sure they understand that it shows the past.

**1 What did Kim's community look like in the past?** Possible answers: Buildings were not very tall; there were not many cars. **Analyze Pictures**

**H** **SOCIAL STUDIES STRAND**
**History**

Tell children that all communities change over time. Show children past and present pictures of your own community. (Copies can often be obtained from a local historical society or library.) After talking about the pictures and the changes they show, help children put the pictures in an order that shows changes over time.

# How a Community Changed

**Living History**

This picture shows what Kim's community looked like in the past. Her community has changed since then.

58

# Practice and Extend

**ESL** **ESL SUPPORT**
**Extend Language**

**Work with New Words** Review the meaning of *past, present, and future*. Have children write each word on a card and then a word in their home language to remind them of the English meaning. Display pictures showing past, present, and future communities.

**Beginning** Have children match a card to each picture. Say something about each picture, using phrases such as *in the past, long ago; today, now;* and *in the future.*

**Intermediate** Follow the procedure for Beginning, but have children use the terms *past, present,* and *future* to tell something about each picture.

**Advanced** Have children sort the pictures according to whether they show a community from the past, the present, or the future. Have children label the group of pictures and then share their ideas about them.

This is Kim's community today. More people live and work in her community now. The community has more homes and stores. Look how it has changed.

## Hands-on History

Think about how a community might change. Draw three pictures of a community. Label them *past*, *today*, and *future*.

**59**

### CURRICULUM CONNECTION
## Literature

**Smoky Night**

- To help children deal with disasters that may change a community, read aloud the 1995 Caldecott Medal winner *Smoky Night* by Eve Bunting (Harcourt, ISBN 0-15-269954-6, 1994). In the story, Daniel and his mother witness a riot, after which their apartment building catches fire.

- After reading, discuss what Daniel learned about the importance of getting along with others regardless of race or background. Ask children to comment on Daniel's suggestion that the cats belonging to him and to Mrs. Kim were enemies only because they didn't know each other well enough. Invite predictions about how the story characters will treat each other in the future.

- For activities to help children deal with fear and loss, see pp. TR1–TR2.

Have volunteers describe the people and buildings in the photograph of modern-day Miami.

**2 How has Kim's community changed since the past? Look at the pictures for clues.** Possible answers: More people live and work there. There are many tall buildings now.
↪ Compare and Contrast

**3 Why do you think there are more shops in Kim's community now than long ago?** Possible answer: More people live there now and need to buy things. **Make Inferences**

**4 What is one way that change might hurt a community?** Answers might relate to crowding or pollution. **Predict**

### Themes of Geography: Places and People Change Each Other

**5 What has changed in your community?** Possible answer: More people have moved in, and more houses have been built; new stores have opened; there is more traffic and less open space. **Apply Information**

## 3 Close and Assess

### Hands-on History

Review the meaning of the words *past*, *present*, and *future*. After children draw their pictures, have them cut the pictures apart. They can then exchange sets of pictures with partners. Tell partners to put the pictures in an order that shows first (yesterday or past), next (today or present), and last (tomorrow or future).

# Use Four Directions

## Objective

- Locate places using the four cardinal directions.

## Vocabulary

**directions** things on a map that tell which way to go (p. 60)

# 1 Introduce and Motivate

**Preview** Write the vocabulary word on the board, and read the word for children. Explain that on a map, directions tell which way to go: north, south, east, or west. Point out where north is in your classroom. Post a sign saying *north* on this wall (or in this area). Do the same for south, east, and west.

**Warm Up** To activate prior knowledge, have children identify the *north, south, east,* and *west* signs in your classroom. Ask a volunteer to walk toward the north sign. Explain that he or she is moving north. Repeat with other volunteers and directions. Then add the abbreviations *N, S, E,* and *W* to the signs. Tell children that we sometimes use just the letters to stand for the directions.

# 2 Teach and Discuss

### Page 60

Have children look at the map and find the labels *North, South, East,* and *West.*

**1** **Which direction is at the top of the map?** North **Where is south?** At the bottom; opposite north Interpret Maps

**2** **Looking at the map, which direction is opposite east?** West Interpret Maps

**3** **Is the post office east or west of Pine Street?** West Interpret Maps

**60** Unit 2 • In My Community

---

# Use Four Directions

Kim uses the directions on a map to find places in her community. **Directions** tell her which way to go. North, south, east, and west are the four main directions.

**1** **2** **3** **4**

## Practice and Extend

**CURRICULUM CONNECTION**
**Science**

**Draw to Show Weather Changes**

- Point out the United States on a map. Be sure the map has directional arrows. Explain that in the United States, the weather usually gets colder the farther north you travel.

- Point to Miami on the map. Mention that in January, the temperature here is usually around 70°F, so people may need to wear light jackets. Point to Chicago. Explain that this city is farther north. Since the January temperature is usually around 20°F, people need to wear much warmer clothing.

- Tell children to imagine that the north end of your classroom is colder than the south end. Have them draw pictures to show how people might dress in the north end or the south end of your room. Post the pictures in the appropriate parts of the room.

Put your finger on Pine Street. Move your finger toward the arrow that points south. You are moving south. Now move your finger toward the arrow that points north. Which direction are you moving? When you face north, east is on your right. What direction is on your left?

## Try it!

1. Is the park north or south of Main Street?

2. Find the fire station. What **direction** would you go to get to the bank?

3. **On Your Own** Stand by your desk. Face north. Tell where things are in your classroom and school. Use the words *north, south, east,* and *west.*

**61**

**SOCIAL STUDIES STRAND**
## Geography

Explain to students that many maps have a symbol called a *compass rose* that is used to identify the four directions. Draw a simple compass rose for students on the board, or point to the compass rose on a classroom map. Point out that the map on page 60 identifies the four directions in a different way. Show children a globe. Remind students that a globe stands for the earth, and that the earth is divided into four hemispheres using the equator and the prime meridian. Explain that on a globe, north is at the top, and south is at the bottom. Have children take turns putting their fingers on the equator and moving north or south as you give them directions.

### Page 60

**4** **In which directions does Main Street go?**
East and west **Interpret Maps**

### Ongoing Assessment

| **If...** children cannot correctly identify directions on the map, | **then...** reconstruct the map in the classroom by labeling desks as the buildings. Orient the three-dimensional model of the map to your posted direction markings. Then have children walk the routes discussed in the lesson questions. |

## 3 Close and Assess

## Try it!

1. South

2. West

3. **On Your Own** Children should use the words *north, south, east,* and *west* as they describe where things are in the classroom and the school.

### ESL BUILD BACKGROUND ESL Support

**Locating Places** Hide several objects. Tell children that you will give directions for finding the objects.

**Beginning** Give children explicit clues, such as: *It is under the reading table.* Have children try to find the objects.

**Intermediate** Describe where you have hidden one object. Have children take turns trying to identify the place.

**Advanced** Use directional words to provide clues, for example: *It is two steps north of my desk.*

### Workbook, p. 17

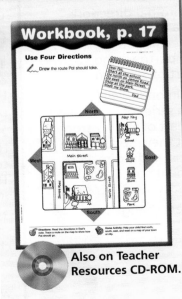

**Use Four Directions**

Draw the route Pat should take.

Also on Teacher Resources CD-ROM.

# Lesson ② Wrap-Up

 ## MEETING INDIVIDUAL NEEDS
## Leveled Practice

###  Compare and Contrast Community Pictures

Provide children with a selection of picture books that shows different communities. Have them browse through the books.

**Easy** Present two pictures to children and ask questions such as: *Which of these communities is bigger? Which is a farm community? Which community is more like your community?* **Reteach**

**On-Level** Remind children of what they learned about their own community during the lesson. Then, as you show them pictures from the books, ask them to tell how each community is similar to and different from their own community. **Extend**

**Challenge** Have children find pictures in the books that show communities from the past. Challenge them to put a few books in order, according to whether their pictures show past, present, or future. **Enrich**

 ## Hands-on Activities

 **CURRICULUM CONNECTION**
**Literature/Vocabulary**

## City, Country

**Objective** Compare and contrast two communities.

**Materials** *City Mouse—Country Mouse* and *Two More Mouse Tales from Aesop* by John C. Wallner (illustrator) (Scholastic, ISBN 0-590-41155-1, 1987) crayons, drawing paper

**Learning Style** Auditory/Kinesthetic

**Partners** 

**Time** 20–25 minutes

1. Share the illustrations as you read. Talk about how the artist depicts the two communities.

2. Have partners draw the story settings. One child can draw the city scenes; the other, the country.

3. Have partners present their work and tell how the two communities are alike and different.

4. Remind children to add the words *community* and *directions* to their Word Books.

 **SOCIAL STUDIES STRAND**
**Geography**

## Simon Says

**Objective** Use cardinal directions to locate places in the classroom.

**Learning Style** Auditory/Kinesthetic

**Partners**

**Time** 10–15 minutes

1. Review the cardinal directions posted in the classroom. Then position pairs of children randomly in the room. Have partners choose who will play the part of Simon first.

2. Explain that Simon's role is to give his/her partner a series of directions to get to another part of the classroom. Tell children that they must include a number (for steps) and a direction word. Remind them how Simon speaks: "Simon says: Go 3 steps north."

3. Have partners change roles.

 **CURRICULUM CONNECTION**
**Science**

## Where's North?

**Objective** Observe how a compass helps one find cardinal directions.

**Materials** a compass

**Learning Style** Visual

**Group** 

**Time** 20–25 minutes

1. Display a compass. Allow children to experiment with it. Have them note that the needle points north.

2. Take children outdoors. Have them use the compass to find north. Then help them locate south, east, and west.

3. Change your position several times, and have children take turns using the compass to find north. Ask them to explain how to find south—with or without the compass.

# Lesson ③ Overview

| | | |
|---|---|---|
| **Special Things We Do**<br>pages 62–65 | Children will learn about the special customs that people from different cultures share. | ⏱ Time 20–30 minutes<br>**Resources**<br>• Workbook, p. 18<br>• Every Student Learns Guide, pp. 26–29 |
| **Chinese New Year**<br>pages 66–67 | Children will learn how to use visual sources, such as pictures, to gather information about the custom of Chinese New Year. | ⏱ Time 15–20 minutes |
| **Harriet Tubman**<br>pages 68–69 | Children will learn how Harriet Tubman led some African Americans to freedom. | ⏱ Time 15–20 minutes |

# Build Background

## Activity

### Celebrate a Custom

⏱ **Time** 20–25 minutes

Beforehand, cut a large star from cardboard and cover it with gold foil paper.

Tell children that you have a custom you'd like to share with them. Explain that every time there is perfect attendance in your class, you like to celebrate by hanging the star on your door. Show children the star. Brainstorm ideas for another way to celebrate perfect attendance.

List children's ideas on the board, and have children vote to choose just one.

The next time you do have perfect attendance, remind children of the custom—and proceed to celebrate.

**If time is short,** have children tell about ways they like to celebrate special days or events.

## Read Aloud

### Flag Song
by Susan Drake

Our flag shines bright and true,
Waving red, white, and blue,
Looking so grand.

Protecting all who come,
Welcoming everyone,
To our homeland.

# Lesson 3

# Special Things We Do

## Objectives

- Describe various customs and traditions and explain their importance.
- Obtain information about a topic using a variety of oral sources, such as conversations.
- Describe selected customs.

## QUICK Teaching Plan

*If time is short,* guide children in making a list of customs they already know.

- Then refer children to the pictures in the lesson for ideas about some common customs associated with special days.

# 1 Introduce and Motivate

**Preview** Tell children that a custom is an old or popular way of doing things. Give an example, such as having a cake on one's birthday. Explain that customs are part of tradition. Tradition is the combination of beliefs and customs we get from our family, religion, or culture. Tell children that some traditions can help make families closer. Some traditions help us remember our heritage. Traditions and celebrations are important because they help us celebrate who we are. Explain to children the importance of *multiculturalism,* or the practice of equally valuing all cultures and groups. Ask children why they think having a diverse population of people benefits the United States.

**Warm Up** To activate prior knowledge, ask what children do with their families on holidays or on special days, such as birthdays. Invite children to share information about favorite foods, decorations, or activities. Ask them why they think everyone enjoys special occasions. Encourage children to ask questions about any customs mentioned that are unfamiliar to them.

**62** Unit 2 • In My Community

---

# Lesson 3

# Special Things We Do

People in my community share different customs. A custom is the way people usually do something. My picture book shows special customs we have.

We have a picnic on Independence Day. It is our country's birthday.

**1 2 3**

We give a basket of fruit to new neighbors. Welcome to our neighborhood!

62

# Practice and Extend

## Target Skill
### READING/VOCABULARY
## Alike and Different

### Common Customs

- Help children compare and contrast the customs pictured on pp. 62–63. Ask which pictures show something Kim does only once a year. Ask which picture shows something Kim and her family may do whenever a new family moves into the neighborhood.
- Ask children if they have any of these same customs. Chart their responses, as follows:

|  | Independence Day | Mother's Day | To welcome neighbors |
|---|---|---|---|
| Kim |  |  |  |
| Us |  |  |  |

- Follow a similar procedure to compare and contrast the customs pictured on pp. 64–65.

I make my mother a special gift every Mother's Day.

63

SOCIAL STUDIES
## Background

**About Mother's Day**

- In 1872, Julia Ward Howe (who wrote the words to *Battle Hymn of the Republic*) suggested the idea of Mother's Day, which she saw as a day dedicated to peace.
- In 1907, Ana Jarvis began a campaign to establish a national Mother's Day. By 1911, Mother's Day was celebrated in almost every state.
- In 1914, President Woodrow Wilson made Mother's Day a national holiday.
- Mother's Day in the United States falls on the second Sunday in May.
- Wearing a carnation is a tradition associated with Mother's Day.

# 2 Teach and Discuss

## Page 62

After reading p. 62, point out that many of the pictures in this lesson show pages from Kim's scrapbook.

**1 Why is Kim wearing red, white, and blue to celebrate Independence Day?** Possible answer: She is wearing the colors of our country's flag; those colors are symbols of our country. **Make Inferences**

**2 What does Kim do on Independence Day?** Go on a picnic **Main Idea and Details**

**3 How do you celebrate Independence Day?** Possible answers: Go to a parade; have a picnic; watch fireworks **Apply Information**

**4 What does Kim's family do when new neighbors move in? Why?** Give them a basket of fruit to welcome them **Cause and Effect**

## Page 63

**5 How does Kim celebrate Mother's Day?** She gives her mother a card and some flowers. **Analyze Pictures**

**6 In some countries, people celebrate Children's Day. Would you like such a day? What would you do?** Most children will probably agree that Children's Day is a great idea; accept all reasonable responses to the second part of the question. **Express Ideas**

**Lesson 3**

continued

Page 64

Discuss what Kim's scrapbook picture on p. 64 shows. Emphasize that people can share in the customs of their friends.

**7 How do Kim's friends celebrate Chinese New Year?** They go to a parade. **Recall and Retell**

**8 How else do people celebrate the beginning of a new year?** Possible answers: They go to First Night celebrations; they watch parades and football on TV on New Year's Day. **Apply Information**

**C SOCIAL STUDIES STRAND**
**Culture**

**Prejudice Reduction** Point out that families in a community can have different beliefs, traditions, and customs that come from their religious beliefs, their ethnicity, or their cultures. Have volunteers share examples of such customs, beliefs, or traditions (such as Kwanzaa, Hanukkah, Lent, and Christmas) and explain their importance. Discuss ways in which customs may be alike—even if they come from different cultures.

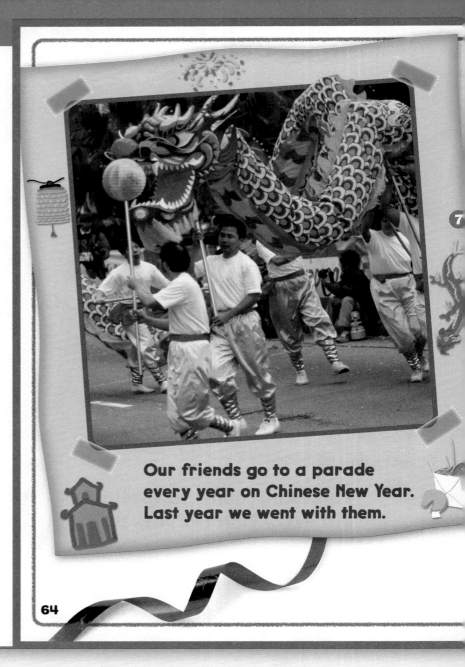

Our friends go to a parade every year on Chinese New Year. Last year we went with them.

64

# Practice and Extend

**CURRICULUM CONNECTION**
**Art**

### Make a "Customs" Calendar

- Give each child a blank calendar for the current month. Remind them of what they learned about calendars in Unit 1. Have them number the days of the month.

- Brainstorm a list of special days for the month. Include events celebrated by the class, by children's families, and by the community—as well as state and national holidays. Have children share their knowledge of the holidays or customs identified.

- Read about a few unfamiliar holidays for the current month from a children's encyclopedia.

- Distribute self-stick notes. Have children draw pictures to show the holidays you've learned about. Stick them onto the calendar grid.

**ESL BUILD BACKGROUND**
**ESL Support**

**Using Pictures** Provide several pictures that show typical American holidays and the customs associated with them.

**Beginning** Ask children to name holidays in their home language. When possible, link these holidays to American holidays by pointing to any appropriate pictures.

**Intermediate** Have children look at the pictures and point out customs with which they are familiar. Encourage them to ask questions about customs they don't recognize. Provide answers, or have others in the class do so.

**Advanced** Follow a procedure similar to that suggested for Intermediate. Then give children a calendar showing pictorial representations of common holidays. Talk about when each holiday occurs—and about any that may be coming up.

*For additional ESL Support, use Every Student Learns Guide, pp. 26–29.*

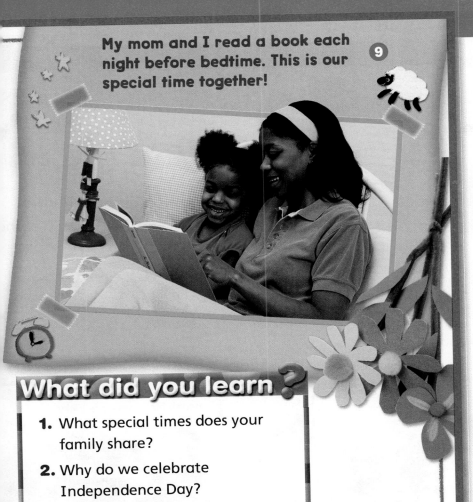

My mom and I read a book each night before bedtime. This is our special time together! **9**

## What did you learn?

1. What special times does your family share?

2. Why do we celebrate Independence Day?

3. **Think and Share** Draw a picture of one way to celebrate a special day. Tell what is happening in your picture.

65

**Workbook, p. 18**

Special Things We Do

Draw to show what you might do on July 4th. Drawings will vary.

Also on Teacher Resources CD-ROM.

Explain that customs can be any special activities that people do again and again.

**9 Is the time Kim spends with her mom each night a custom? Tell why.** Possible answer: Yes, it is a custom because they spend this time together every night, doing the same thing.
**Main Idea and Details**

## 3 Close and Assess

Have children work with partners to brainstorm a special custom the class could begin. Tell each pair to agree on one suggestion. Then have each child draw a picture and write a sentence about the idea.

## ✓ What did you learn?

1. Answers will vary but may include birthday celebrations, religious or cultural traditions, and/or any activities family members do together on a regular basis.

2. It is the birthday of the United States.

3. **Think and Share** Children should identify the special days celebrated in their pictures; they should also tell what they do on those days, and why the days are important to them.

# Chinese New Year

## Objectives

- Describe community celebrations.

- Describe various customs of families.

- Obtain information about a topic using a variety of visual sources, such as pictures.

## 1 Introduce and Motivate

**Preview** Discuss with children the fact that many communities in their state include people of different ethnic origins. Many of these people come from different places around the world. Remind children of the picture of Chinese New Year in Kim's scrapbook (p. 64). Then read the title of this lesson, and have children look at the pictures on pp. 66-67. Ask if they would like to take part in a Chinese New Year celebration.

**Warm Up** To activate prior knowledge, ask children to tell about any New Year celebrations they have taken part in.

Read the introduction with children. Ask if they agree with Man Po that Chinese New Year is a colorful celebration. Ask what they think makes it so colorful.

## 2 Teach and Discuss

Have children point to the photos as you read the captions. Allow time for them to respond to the pictures.

**❶ Find the message that Man Po has written. How is Chinese writing different from writing in English?** Chinese writing uses characters that look like little pictures; English writing uses letters of the alphabet. **Compare and Contrast**

**❷ What will Man Po find in the envelope to help her get rich?** She'll find money in it. **Draw Conclusions**

---

 C E L E B R A T I O N S

# Chinese New Year

Man Po is nine years old and lives in China. She likes Chinese New Year. It is one of the world's most colorful celebrations.

Thousands of people watch the floats in the New Year parade.

Tangerines with leaves are often called the lucky fruits of the New Year.

This float is sometimes in the New Year parade.

Some Chinese believe that peach blossoms are lucky.

Some people think a kumquat tree brings good luck.

66

## Practice and Extend

 **FYI** SOCIAL STUDIES **Background**

### About Chinese New Year

- The Chinese calendar year begins sometime between the end of January and the middle of February.

- Each year of the calendar gets an animal name, chosen from a series of 12 animals. For example, the year 2002: the year of the horse; the year 2003: the year of the sheep.

- Chinese New Year celebrations last for about three days. To get ready for the new year, families give their homes a thorough cleaning. They may paint their doors and windows a bright red.

- Two dances are important to the celebration of Chinese New Year, the Lion Dance and the Dragon Dance. Specially trained dancers performing in costume do each dance. Some believe that these dances bring good luck.

"My outfit is made of silk. It is very beautiful."

**1** "I have written words in Chinese that wish a person riches."

**2** On New Years morning, Chinese children get money in red envelopes.

Law Pak Ko

**4** One of Man Po's favorite foods is Law Pak Ko, a cake with shrimps.

**3** Red is the main color for clothes and decorations at New Year. It is a color of happiness.

67

## Test Talk

**Use Information from the Text**

**3** **Why does Man Po wear red on Chinese New Year?** Red is a color of happiness; it's a color that many Chinese people wear on this day. Ask children to listen as you reread the question. Ask if they have given the right information from the text.
**Make Inferences**

**4** **What is one food that people enjoy on Chinese New Year?** A cake with shrimps
**Analyze Pictures**

# 3 Close and Assess

- Ask children what part of the Chinese New Year celebration they would enjoy most. Encourage them to give reasons for their choices.

- Tell children that Man Po has written *Kung Hei Fat Choy* in Chinese. Have them practice saying it with you in Chinese. (/kŭng hā fǎt choi/) Ask what else people say to wish others a happy new year.

## C SOCIAL STUDIES STRAND
## Culture

**Chinese New Year Celebration**

- Explain that Chinese New Year marks the beginning of a new year and is also a religious holiday.

- Suggest that the class plan its own Chinese New Year celebration.

- Provide additional details about the holiday, such as its being about cleaning your house for good luck in the new year.

- Plan how to decorate the classroom. Have children make masks from paper bags.

- Invite children to put on their masks and have a parade.

# CITIZEN HEROES

## Harriet Tubman

### Objective
- Identify characteristics of good citizenship, such as a belief in equality.

## 1 Introduce and Motivate

**Preview** Ask for volunteers to share any experiences they may have had about moving to a new community. Ask children to compare their former and new communities. How are they alike? How are they different? If children have not had this experience, or to extend the discussion, ask them to list reasons that people might have for moving to a new community.

**Warm Up** To activate prior knowledge, ask children what they think the word *fairness* means. Have volunteers describe ways to treat people fairly. Ask children why they think it is important to treat all people fairly.

Introduce Harriet Tubman. Explain that she lived in our country long ago. Point out the illustration of Harriet Tubman. Tell children that they will learn why Harriet Tubman is a citizen hero.

## 2 Teach and Discuss

**1 What did Harriet Tubman work hard to do?** Harriet Tubman worked hard so African Americans could be treated fairly. **Recall and Retell**

**2 What do you think "to be treated fairly" means?** Possible answer: The rules are the same for everyone; what goes for one, goes for everyone. **Generalize**

**3 What was the Underground Railroad?** A special path in the woods that helped African Americans move to places where they could be free. **Recall and Retell**

# CITIZEN HEROES

# Harriet Tubman

Harriet Tubman was born in Dorchester County, Maryland.

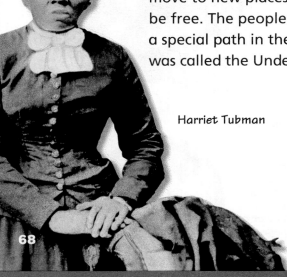
Harriet Tubman

Some customs and ways of life have changed from long ago. Harriet Tubman lived in our country when some African Americans were not free. She wanted fair treatment for everyone.

Harriet Tubman worked hard so people could be treated fairly. She helped many African Americans move to new places where they could be free. The people she helped followed a special path in the woods. The path was called the Underground Railroad.

68

## Practice and Extend

 **SOCIAL STUDIES Background**

### About Harriet Tubman

- Harriet Tubman was born in 1820 in Dorchester County, Maryland.
- She married John Tubman, a free African American, when she was 25 years old.
- Her family did not agree with her plans to escape to the North, so Harriet traveled alone.
- In 1897 her bravery won her the silver medal bestowed by Queen Victoria.

Caring
Respect
Responsibility
Fairness
Honesty
Courage

Harriet Tubman was a very brave woman. Today we remember her as a leader who believed in fairness and freedom for African Americans.

House on the Underground Railroad

## ★ Fairness in Action ★

What can you and your classmates do to be sure everyone is treated fairly?

**69**

## Problem Solving

### Use a Problem-Solving Process

- Present this problem-solving scenario: *A boy from another country has just joined our class. Some children in the class are being mean to the boy. They are not treating him fairly.*

  1. Identify a problem.
  2. Gather information.
  3. List and consider options.
  4. Consider advantages and disadvantages.
  5. Choose and implement a solution.
  6. Evaluate the effectiveness of a solution.

- For each step in the process, have children discuss what to do to solve the problem.

  After children have worked through the process, ask them to compare their solutions to the one that Vira and her friends decided upon.

④ **Do you agree that Harriet Tubman a brave woman?** Possible answer: Yes, because she helped many African Americans find freedom, usually at night when it was dark. **Point of View**

⑤ **What can you tell people about Harriet Tubman?** Answers will vary but should reflect children's understanding of treating people fairly. **Apply Information**

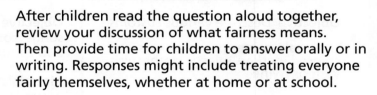

### SOCIAL STUDIES STRAND
### Citizenship

Point out that Harriet Tubman showed she was a good citizen by working to get fair treatment for all African Americans. Explain to students that it took courage for Harriet Tubman to help African Americans follow the Underground Railroad to freedom. Ask children to tell about ways in which they can show courage.

## 3 Close and Assess

### ★ Fairness in Action ★

After children read the question aloud together, review your discussion of what fairness means. Then provide time for children to answer orally or in writing. Responses might include treating everyone fairly themselves, whether at home or at school.

# Lesson ③ Wrap-Up

## MEETING INDIVIDUAL NEEDS
## Leveled Practice

### Make a Scrapbook

Guide children in making a scrapbook of familiar customs. To prepare, have children bring in photos from home or draw their own pictures.

**Easy** Ask each child to choose a picture and then tell about the custom it shows. After children talk about the pictures, have them dictate a title for each one. **Reteach**

**On-Level** Have children work in pairs to develop captions for their pictures. Partners should discuss what the picture shows and then write or dictate a sentence describing it. Ask how the customs shown in various pictures are alike and different. **Extend**

**Challenge** Have children help you organize the scrapbook. Lead them in choosing appropriate categories—for example, birthdays—for the pictures. Then ask them to write or dictate a short description of the category. **Enrich**

## Hands-on Activities

 **CURRICULUM CONNECTION**
## Writing/Vocabulary

## Customs

**Objective** Describe various *customs*.

**Materials** poster paper, pencils, colored markers, plastic clothespins, yarn or twine

**Learning Style** Verbal/Visual

**Group** 👤👤👤👤

⏱ **Time** 10–15 minutes

1. Have children work in groups to choose a custom from among those they learned about in the lesson.

2. Have groups make posters to tell others about their chosen customs. As children are working, help them write short captions that tell what each custom is and why it is important.

3. Using plastic clothespins, hang children's posters so that they stretch out across the room.

 **CURRICULUM CONNECTION**
## Music/Drama

## Sing Out!

**Objective** Learn and perform songs from different countries and cultures.

**Materials** Book of songs from around the world, such as *Wee Sing Around the World* by Pamela Conn Beall and Susan Hagen Nipp (Penguin Putnam, ISBN 0-8431-3740-1,1994); world map

**Learning Style** Auditory

**Group** 👤👤👤👤

⏱ **Time** 25–30 minutes

1. Tell children that the songs people sing can be customs too. Explain they will now learn some songs sung by children from around the world.

2. Sing (or play) one of the songs for children. Name the country the song comes from. Then, using a world map, locate the country for children.

3. Follow a similar procedure with several other songs. Invite children to choose a few songs they wish to learn. The whole class might learn all the songs. Or, small groups of children can learn different songs.

4. Provide children with outline maps that show where the songs they have learned come from. Children can color the maps and display them as they sing.

5. Invite parents and/or another class to come to your "sing out." Introduce each song before children sing it—or have a child act as narrator.

# Lesson ④ Overview

| | | |
|---|---|---|
| **Community Laws and Leaders**<br>**pages 70–71** | Children will learn the meaning of the words *law* and *leader* and about the responsibilities of community leaders. They will also learn about the importance of community laws.  |  **Time** 20 minutes<br>**Resources**<br>• Workbook, p. 19<br>• Vocabulary Cards law , leader<br>• Transparency 15<br>• Every Student Learns Guide, pp. 30–33 |
| **Meet Jane Addams**<br>**pages 72–73** | Children will identify the contributions of Jane Addams, a historical figure who influenced the nation and demonstrated good citizenship. | **Time** 15–20 minutes |

# Build Background

## Activity

### Choose a Rule

 **Time** 15–20 minutes

Ask each child to draw a picture or pantomime to tell about a rule from home or school. Direct children to choose rules that they have to follow often. As children share their rules, ask them who they think made each rule—and why it might be important to follow it.

**If time is short,** ask children to name some school rules and to tell why each rule is important.

## Read Aloud

### Signs
#### by D. G. Chester

Look around and you will see
Signs that help you and me.

At the corner there's a sign
For cars to stop at the line.

There's a light to help you know
When to wait and when to go.

Heed the signs. Do what they say.
It's the law! You must obey.

# Lesson 4 Community Laws and Leaders

## Objectives

- Explain the need for laws in the community.
- Identify the responsibilities of authority figures in the community.
- Describe the role of public officials including the mayor.

## Vocabulary

**law** a rule that people must obey (p. 70)

**leader** someone who helps people decide what to do (p. 71)

### QUICK Teaching Plan

*If time is short,* identify Officer Taylor and Mayor Garza and read the sentences in their speech balloons.

- Have children tell one thing each person pictured does to help the community.

## 1 Introduce and Motivate

**Preview** Display the Vocabulary Cards **law** and **leader**. Ask children what they think each word means. Share the meaning for each word and use it in a sentence: *People must obey each law of our state. The President of the United States is the leader of our country.*

**Warm Up** To activate prior knowledge, ask children if they can name people at school who make rules or who are leaders. Mention that you made rules for the classroom, but that the principal makes rules for the school, since he/she is the leader of the school. Then say that when leaders of a community or nation make rules, they are called laws.

---

# Lesson 4 Community Laws and Leaders

*I am Officer Taylor. I make sure you follow laws.*

A **law** is a rule that people must obey. Laws help keep us safe. They also help keep communities clean. ❶ ❷

Look at these signs. They show different laws. Kim has all these signs in her community. Which laws keep people safe? Which law keeps the community clean?

NO SWIMMING

STOP

70

---

## Practice and Extend

### READING SKILL
### Cause and Effect

**Telling Why**

- Discuss the laws suggested by the signs on p. 70. Have children tell why these laws are important. Ask what might happen if people didn't obey them.
- Display Transparency 15. Tell children to first draw a picture that shows someone breaking one of the laws from p. 70. Then have them draw a picture to show the result.

### WEB SITE
### Technology

You can look up vocabulary words online. Click on *Social Studies Library* and select the dictionary at **www.sfsocialstudies.com**.

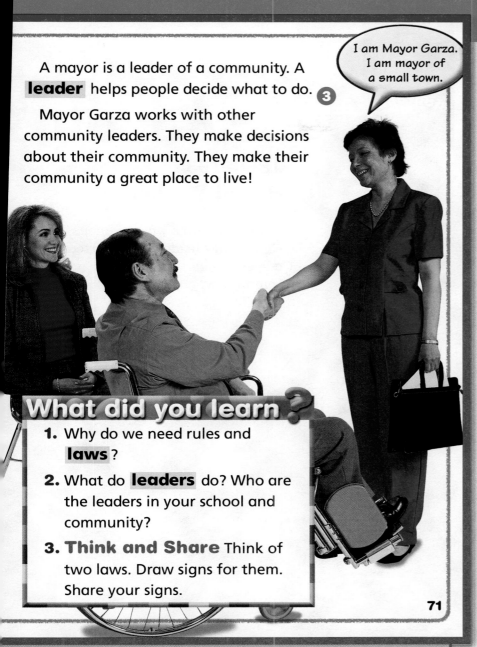

A mayor is a leader of a community. A **leader** helps people decide what to do. ③

I am Mayor Garza. I am mayor of a small town.

Mayor Garza works with other community leaders. They make decisions about their community. They make their community a great place to live!

## What did you learn

1. Why do we need rules and **laws**?

2. What do **leaders** do? Who are the leaders in your school and community?

3. **Think and Share** Think of two laws. Draw signs for them. Share your signs.

**71**

### Decision Making

**Use a Decision-Making Process**

- Say: *Suppose you are the class leader. You want to make it easier for children to see the teacher. You want to change how the desks are arranged in the classroom. What is the best way to put the desks?*

- Children should use the decision-making process to decide what arrangement best achieves their goal.

- For each step in the process, have children discuss what to consider as they make their decision. You can refer to the steps listed here. To guide children, read aloud the steps as they are listed on p. H5.

**Workbook, p. 19**

**Community Laws and Leaders**

Also on Teacher Resources CD-ROM.

1. Identify a situation that requires a decision.
2. Gather information.
3. Identify options.
4. Predict consequences.
5. Take action to implement a decision.
6. Evaluate the decision.

## 2 Teach and Discuss

Page 70

After reading p. 70, direct children's attention to the signs.

**❶ What is the job of a police officer like Officer Taylor?** A police officer's job is to make sure people obey laws. **Generalize**

**❷ What are some laws that Officer Taylor wants you to follow?** Stop at stop signs, don't litter, no swimming **Analyze Pictures**

Page 71

**❸ Why do communities need leaders?** Possible answers: To make the community a good place to live, to make decisions about how the community should be run **Generalize**

## 3 Close and Assess

✓ What did you learn

Name the mayor and/or other leaders in your community. Ask children what they think these leaders do.

1. To keep our communities safe and clean and to help people get along with each other

2. Leaders make decisions for the community. The school principal is a school leader and a mayor is a community leader.

3. **Think and Share** Possible answers: Octagon with the word "stop" in it, circle with a bar through a person walking

# Jane Addams

## Objectives

- Identify contributions of historical figures in the period of history since 1880.
- Identify historic figures who have exemplified good citizenship.

## 1 Introduce and Motivate

**Preview** Point out the term *social worker* in the lesson subtitle. Tell children that a social worker helps people in many different ways. Point out that in this lesson, children will learn about one social worker and the ways she helped people in her community.

**Warm Up** To activate prior knowledge, invite children to suggest some ways that people at school help them. Prompt children by naming staff members, such as school nurse, school social worker or psychologist, playground supervisors, office staff, cafeteria staff. List these on the board.

Have children look at the pictures on pp. 72–73. Identify the woman as Jane Addams, and ask children what they think she is doing.

## 2 Teach and Discuss

Read the biography together. Tell children that Jane Addams was a leader of the settlement house movement. Explain that settlement houses are centers to which people who need help can go.

**1 Why did Jane Addams start Hull House?** So people in the community would have a place to go for help Main Idea and Details

**2 What is one way you could help people in your community?** Possible answers: Give food to hungry people, give clothes to people who need them, keep lonely older people company
Solve Problems

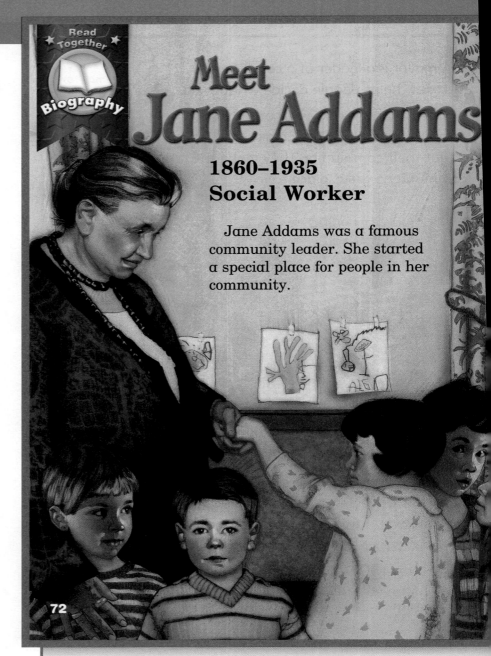

# Meet Jane Addams

### 1860–1935 Social Worker

Jane Addams was a famous community leader. She started a special place for people in her community.

72

# Practice and Extend

### SOCIAL STUDIES Background

#### About Jane Addams and Hull House

- Jane Addams fought for the rights of poor women and children. She set up a nursery at Hull House, so women had access to child care.
- Addams believed in justice and equality. She helped create playgrounds that *all* children could use.
- Alfred Nobel wanted to honor people who worked for the good of humanity. Jane Addams won the Nobel Peace Prize as a result of her work for the common good of her community.

### WEB SITE Technology

You may help children find out more about Jane Addams by clicking on *Meet the People* at **www.sfsocialstudies.com**.

When she was growing up, Jane learned how important it was to help others. As an adult, Jane Addams and a friend took over a big, empty house in Chicago, Illinois. They called it Hull House.

Jane Addams was born in Cedarville, Illinois.

Hull House became a place where people in the community could go to get help. Some people went to Hull House because they were sick. Others went because they had questions about the law. Some ❶ people needed care for their children. People also went there to take classes. Hull House had a community kitchen, playground, and nursery.

In 1931, Jane Addams was the first American woman to win an ❷ ❸ important prize called the Nobel Peace Prize.

Hull House Museum

### Think and Share

How did Jane Addams help people in the community?

For more information, go online to *Meet the People* at **www.sfsocialstudies.com.**

73

❸ **Why was winning the Nobel Peace Prize such an honor for Jane Addams?** She was the first American woman to win the prize.
**Make Inferences**

⭐ **SOCIAL STUDIES STRAND**
**Citizenship**

**Prejudice Reduction** Explain that Jane Addams showed she was a good citizen by helping poor immigrants help themselves. By providing child care and schooling, Jane Addams gave these people the tools they needed to make their own lives better. By teaching them English and an understanding of American laws, she helped them speak for themselves and try to get fair treatment. Ask children if they think Jane Addams deserved the prize she won, and if so, why.

# 3 Close and Assess

## Think and Share

Have children review the lesson pictures and text before they answer. Answers should suggest that Jane Addams provided a place where people could go to learn or to get help—because they were sick, because they had questions about the law, because they needed care for their children.

**MEETING INDIVIDUAL NEEDS**
**Leveled Practice**

### Make a Collage

Help children make a list of things Jane Addams did to help others. Tell children that they will use this list as they make a collage celebrating her work.

**Easy** Have children draw pictures to illustrate the items on the list. **Reteach**

**On-Level** Have children refer to the list to write sentences about the work of Jane Addams. Provide index cards and have children write one sentence on each card. **Extend**

**Challenge** Help children brainstorm a list of words and phrases that describe a good citizen. Have children write the words and phrases on colored index cards. **Enrich**

Have groups of children arrange the pictures and cards on poster board and paste them in position. Display the collages.

# Lesson ④ Wrap-Up

 **MEETING INDIVIDUAL NEEDS**
## Leveled Practice

### Make a Web
Lead children in making a concept web about community leadership. Place the words *community leader* in the center cell.

**Easy** Have children draw pictures showing things that community leaders do. Ask them to put their pictures on the outer cells of the web. Tell children they may include pictures of Jane Addams or other community leaders they know about. **Reteach**

**On-Level** Have children brainstorm additional ways leaders help a community. Add more cells to the web. Then have children add their pictures. Ask how the leader is helping his/her community. **Extend**

**Challenge** Review earlier lessons about the qualities of a good citizen. Then have children choose one picture from the expanded web. Ask them to tell how the community leader pictured is a good citizen. **Enrich**

 ## Hands-on Activities

 **CURRICULUM CONNECTION**
## Writing/Vocabulary

### Class Letter

**Objectives** Use lesson vocabulary; explain the need for leadership and laws.

**Resources** Vocabulary Cards **law, leader**

**Materials** lined paper, pencils

**Learning Style** Verbal

**Group**

🕐 **Time** 10–15 minutes

**1.** Show children the Vocabulary Cards *law* and *leader*. Review the meaning of these words.

**2.** Invite children to write a class letter to a school or community leader.

**3.** Discuss laws identified in Lesson 4 or others children know. Have them choose a few laws they feel are important and dictate sentences telling why the laws are good for the community.

**4.** Remind children to add *law* and *leader* to their Word Books.

 **SOCIAL STUDIES STRAND**
## Citizenship

### Help Hints

**Objective** Interview to learn about the roles of public officials.

**Learning Style** Verbal

**Group** 👤👤👤👤

🕐 **Time** 20–30 minutes

**1.** Invite the mayor or other leader in your community to visit the classroom. Prepare the guest by providing a list of probable questions.

> 1) What is your job?
>
> 2) How did you get elected?
>
> 3) What is a problem in our community?

**2.** Tell children about the visit, and ask them to help you make a list of questions to ask the leader.

**3.** After the guest tells about his or her role in the community, have children take turns asking their questions.

 **SOCIAL STUDIES STRAND**
## Government

### Mayor for a Day

**Objectives** Act out the roles of public officials, including a mayor; demonstrate the importance of voting to make choices about leaders.

**Learning Style** Kinesthetic/Verbal

**Group** 👤👤👤👤

🕐 **Time** 15 minutes

**1.** Provide a "mayor" costume, such as a special hat or coat.

**2.** Ask a child with good leadership qualities to start out as classroom mayor (or have children vote to select a mayor). Tell children that this job will rotate.

**3.** Have other children play the role of classroom council leaders. Together, the mayor and the leaders can think of problems in the classroom—and can then suggest ways to solve these problems.

# Lesson ⑤ Overview

## Where in the World Do I Live?
pages 74–77

Children will learn the meaning of the words *state*, *continent*, and *ocean* and how a community fits into a state, a country, and a continent. They will also learn how to find continents on a world map.

 **Time** 20–30 minutes

**Resources**
- Workbook, p. 20
- Vocabulary Cards state , continent , ocean
- Transparency 13
- Every Student Learns Guide, pp. 34–37

## Meet Henry Flagler
pages 78–79

Children will identify the contributions of Henry Flagler, a historical figure who influenced the State of Florida.

 **Time** 15–20 minutes

# Build Background

## Activity

### Map It!

 **Time** 20–30 minutes

Display several maps in the classroom. Include maps of the United States, North America, and the world.

Direct children to the appropriate map, and show them how to trace their state, the United States of America, and the continent of North America. Have them cut out the shapes they traced. Then ask children if they can tell in which cutouts their community belongs.

**If time is short,** ask children if they know what state or country their community is in.

## Read Aloud

### Our Round Earth

**by Mae Carroll**

Our Earth is round
Like a ball.
Our Earth is big
But I am small.

Our Earth has land,
Called continents,
And water too,
Called oceans,
hence—

If you could fly
To the moon
You'd see a ball
With lots of blue.

## Lesson 5

# Where in the World Do I Live?

## Objective
• Locate places of significance on maps.

## Vocabulary
**state** a part of a country (p. 75)

**continent** a very large piece of land (p. 76)

**ocean** a very large body of salt water (p. 76)

### QUICK Teaching Plan

*If time is short,* help children use the map on p. 75 to locate their state.

• Have them use the map on pp. 76–77 to identify large bodies of land and water.

• Read the captions for the world map. Point out the United States and North America.

## 1 Introduce and Motivate

**Preview** Display the Vocabulary Card **state**, **continent**, and **ocean**. Ask children what they think each word means. Share the meaning of each word. Ask children to name their state and country. Then have children look at the map on p. 75 as you point out the two oceans that border the contiguous United States.

**Warm Up** To activate prior knowledge, ask if children have traveled to other states. List the states children name on the board; then point them out on a map of the United States. (If children name countries or cities, list these on a separate section of the board.)

---

## Lesson 5

# Where in the World Do I Live?

Here is my community. My community is a city called Miami. I live in the state of Florida. A **state** is part of a country.

## Practice and Extend

### Target Skill
**READING/VOCABULARY**
## Alike and Different

**Venn Diagram** Remind children that thinking about how things are alike and different can help us understand those things better. After they finish reading p. 76, help them complete a Venn diagram to compare and contrast a continent with an ocean. Use Transparency 13.

| continent | | ocean |
|---|---|---|
| • piece of land | • part of the earth | • body of salt water |
| • one of seven | • large in size | • one of four |

Have children use the completed diagram to tell how continents and oceans are alike and different.

The United States of America is my country. We have fifty states in the United States. What is the name of your state? Find it on the map.

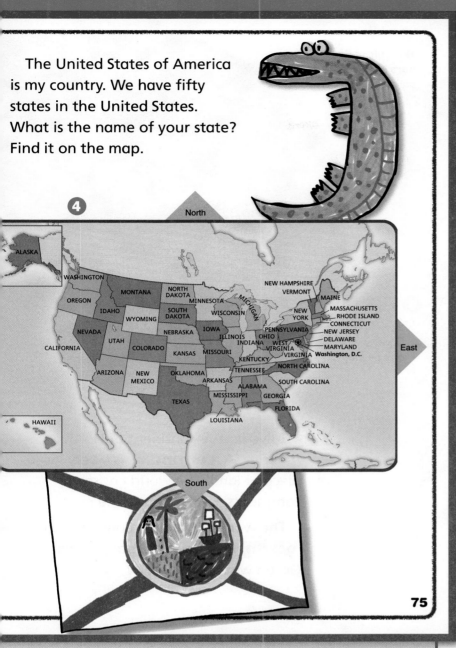

④ North

ALASKA

WASHINGTON
OREGON
MONTANA
NORTH DAKOTA
MINNESOTA
IDAHO
SOUTH DAKOTA
WISCONSIN
MICHIGAN
NEW HAMPSHIRE
VERMONT
MAINE
WYOMING
NEW YORK
MASSACHUSETTS
RHODE ISLAND
CONNECTICUT
NEVADA
NEBRASKA
IOWA
ILLINOIS
INDIANA
OHIO
PENNSYLVANIA
NEW JERSEY
DELAWARE
MARYLAND
CALIFORNIA
UTAH
COLORADO
KANSAS
MISSOURI
WEST VIRGINIA
VIRGINIA Washington, D.C.
KENTUCKY
ARIZONA
NEW MEXICO
OKLAHOMA
ARKANSAS
TENNESSEE
NORTH CAROLINA
SOUTH CAROLINA
ALABAMA
GEORGIA
TEXAS
MISSISSIPPI
FLORIDA
LOUISIANA

East

HAWAII

South

75

CURRICULUM CONNECTION
Art

**Make a State Puzzle**

- Provide each child with an outline map of your state. Have children note the shape of their state.
- Have children paste the outline onto oaktag and then color and cut it out.
- Next, have children cut their state into four or five "puzzle" pieces.
- Have partners trade puzzle pieces and try to put them back together to make the shape of your state.

WEB SITE
Technology

You can look up the vocabulary words online. Click on *Social Studies Library* and select the dictionary at **www.sfsocialstudies.com**.

# 2 Teach and Discuss

Page 74

Explain that in this lesson, Kim tells us about her community—and where in the world it is. Point out that children can use the information Kim shares to learn more about their own community.

❶ **What does the picture Kim is pointing to show?** The city of Miami Make Inferences

❷ **How is Kim's community like your community? How is it different?** Possible answers: Kim lives in a city, but I live in a town. Her city is bigger, and buildings are taller and closer together than those in my town.
Compare and Contrast

Page 75

Point out that the map shows the whole United States. Locate the United States on a globe before reading the page. Point out Alaska and Hawaii, explaining that these two states do not touch the other states.

❸ **What is the name of Kim's state?** Florida
Recall and Retell

❹ **What other states touch your state?** Answers will vary, depending on where children live. Interpret Maps

## Themes of Geography: Location

Have children locate the cardinal directions on the map. Ask which direction—north, south, east, or west—best describes the location of their state in the United States. Explain that we sometimes call a state such as Florida a southern state.

**Lesson**

**5**

continued

## Page 76

Explain that the map on pp. 76–77 shows the whole world. Help children locate the United States on this map. Point out a few physical features, such as the Florida peninsula, that might help children find the United States on any world map.

**5** **What continent is the United States a part of? How do you know?** The caption by the map says that it is part of North America. Interpret Maps

### SOCIAL STUDIES STRAND
### Geography

Mention that the United States is just one country on the continent of North America. Point out the location of Mexico, and explain that it is also in North America. Follow a similar procedure for Canada.

**6** **How can you tell land from water on a map?** Water is blue in color. Interpret Maps

**7** **What are the names of the world's four oceans?** Atlantic, Pacific, Arctic, Indian
Interpret Maps

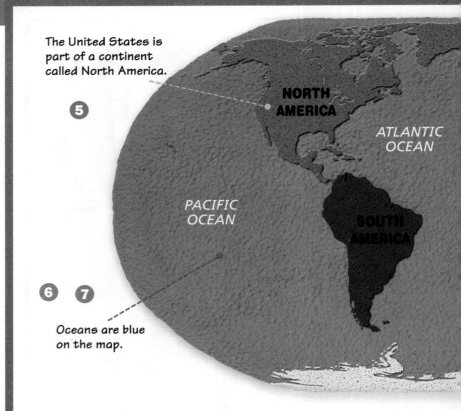

The United States is part of a continent called North America.

**5**

NORTH AMERICA

ATLANTIC OCEAN

PACIFIC OCEAN

SOUTH AMERICA

**6** **7**

Oceans are blue on the map.

I live on the continent of North America. A **continent** is a very large piece of land. The world has seven continents. Find them on the map.

The world has four oceans too. An **ocean** is a very large body of water. Ocean water is very salty.

76

# Practice and Extend

### ESL EXTEND LANGUAGE
### ESL Support

**A Spinning Game** Invite children to practice using words that relate to maps by playing a game.

**Beginning** Place your finger lightly on the globe, and then spin it around. When the globe stops spinning, ask children if you are on land or on water.

**Intermediate** Follow a similar procedure as for Beginning. Have children tell whether you have touched an ocean or a continent. Name the ocean or continent.

**Advanced** Follow a similar procedure as for Beginning, but have children try to name the continent or the ocean on which your finger lands. Allow them to use their home language first, if need be. Then provide the English name, and have children repeat it.
*For additional ESL Support, use Every Student Learns Guide, pp. 34–37.*

## FAST FACTS

You may want to share these facts about the continents with children.

- Asia is the largest continent. Australia is the smallest.
- Antarctica is the coldest continent. It is covered with ice, much of which extends out into the waters around Antarctica.
- The Sahara Desert in Africa is almost as big as the United States.
- Australia is the only continent that is also a country. The country is also called Australia.
- Europe is part of the same piece of land as the continent of Asia. Some people call the two continents by one name: *Eurasia.*

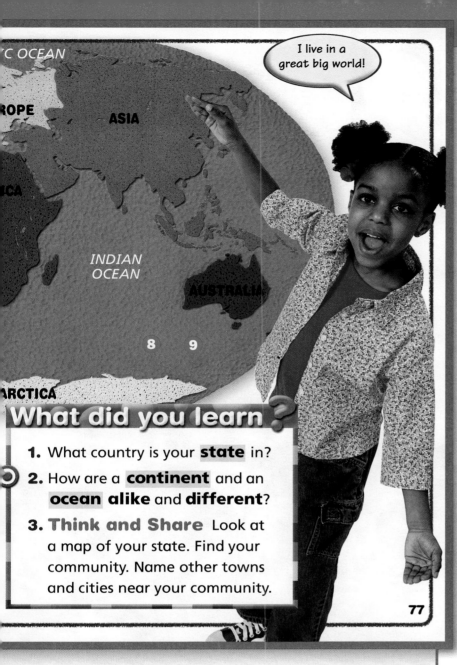

I live in a great big world!

ASIA

INDIAN OCEAN

AUSTRALIA

8   9

ARCTICA

## What did you learn ?

1. What country is your **state** in?

2. How are a **continent** and an **ocean alike** and **different**?

3. **Think and Share** Look at a map of your state. Find your community. Name other towns and cities near your community.

77

### WEB SITE Technology

You may help children find out more about your state by going online. Click on *Atlas* at **www.sfsocialstudies.com.**

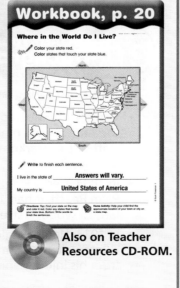

**Workbook, p. 20**

Where in the World Do I Live?

■ Color your state red.
■ Color states that touch your state blue.

North

West                        East

South

✏ **Write** to finish each sentence.

I live in the state of _____ **Answers will vary.**

My country is _____ **United States of America**

**Also on Teacher Resources CD-ROM.**

Help children find the approximate locations of their home states on the world map.

**8** **Do you live near an ocean? If so, which one?** Answers will vary, depending on where children live. **Interpret Maps**

**9** **What are the names of the seven continents?** North America, South America, Europe, Asia, Africa, Australia, Antarctica. **Recall and Retell**

### $ SOCIAL STUDIES STRAND Economics

Point out the continent of Europe on the map. Tell children that the United States trades goods with many other countries—including countries in Europe. Ask them to trace a route on the map from the United States to Europe. Ask what ocean the goods need to cross to get to Europe. Follow a similar procedure for Asia.

## 3 Close and Assess

Trace and cut out two states, including your own. Ask children to point out which outline is your state. Repeat this activity with two country outlines, including the United States.

### ✓ What did you learn ?

1. The United States of America

2. Both a continent and ocean are very big. A continent is a piece of land. An ocean is a body of salt water.

3. **Think and Share** Children should be able to locate their community and name at least two nearby communities.

# Henry Flagler

## Objective

- Identify contributions of historical figures in the period of history since 1880.

# 1 Introduce and Motivate

**Preview** Review with children the different types of transportation people use to move from place to place. For example: bicycles, cars, buses, trains, and airplanes. Discuss with children the advantages and disadvantages of each type of transportation. Ask them to think about ways changes in transportation have made it easier for people to get places that were once considered far away.

**Warm Up** To activate prior knowledge, ask children to recall the name of the city in which Kim lives. If necessary, show them the picture of Miami on p. 74. Explain that Henry Flagler made it easier for people to travel to many places in Florida, including Miami.

Have children preview the pictures on pp. 78–79. Identify Henry Flagler. Point out the pictures of the train on p. 78 and the hotel on p. 79. Ask children to predict why Henry Flagler was important to the state of Florida.

## Meet Henry Flagler

### 1830–1913 Businessman and Builder

Henry Flagler helped Florida become an important part of the United States.

78

# Practice and Extend

## FYI SOCIAL STUDIES Background

### About Henry Flagler

- Henry's first job at age fourteen paid $5 per month. By the time he was nineteen, he was promoted to the sales staff of L.G. Harkness and Company at a salary of $400 per month.

- In 1894, Henry Flagler built the Royal Poinciana Hotel in Palm Beach. It had 1150 rooms, and was at that time the largest wooden structure in the world.

- In 1913, Henry Flagler fell down a flight of stairs at Whitewall, his Palm Beach estate. He never recovered from his injuries and died that same year at the age of 84.

## WEB SITE Technology

You may help children learn more about Henry Flagler by clicking on *Meet the People* at **www.sfsocialstudies.com**.

Young Henry got his first job when he was fourteen years old. He worked very hard. Soon, Henry Flagler and other businessmen started the Standard Oil Company. **1**

Henry Flagler moved to Florida. At that time if people came to visit Florida, there were not many places to stay  Before long, Henry Flagler **2** built a hotel in St. Augustine.

Later, Henry Flagler bought a railroad. His railroad soon went to many cities throughout Florida. Henry Flagler built many big, beautiful hotels in these cities.

Henry Flagler's railroad and hotels made it possible for many people to visit Florida. This helped the state to grow and become an important part of the **3** United States.

Henry Flagler was born in Hopewell, New York.

*Ponce de Leon Hotel*

### Think and Share

What are two ways Henry Flagler helped Florida?

For more information, go online to *Meet the People* at **www.sfsocialstudies.com.**

79

---

## SOCIAL STUDIES STRAND
## Geography

- Locate Florida on a map of the United States. Point out the cities of St. Augustine, West Palm Beach, Miami, and Key West.

- Explain to students that it took about twenty years for Henry Flagler's railroad, the Florida East Coast Railway, to reach all the way from St. Augustine to Key West.

- Point out that the early citizens of what is now Miami wanted their city to be named "Flagler" to honor all the work that Henry Flagler did to help the city grow. Henry Flagler declined, and asked that the city keep its old Indian name, "Miami."

- Ask children to share details of trips they may have taken in their state or to other states. Have them discuss experiences traveling in cars, airplanes, trains, or other forms of transportation.

---

## 2 Teach and Discuss

Tell children that Henry Flagler was important to helping the state of Florida to grow.

**1 What was the name of the company that Henry Flagler helped to start?** The Standard Oil Company. **Recall and Retell**

### H SOCIAL STUDIES STRAND
### History

Henry Flagler's railroads, along with an effort to develop farmland in southern Florida, had an impact on the citrus industry in the late nineteenth century. The railroads made it possible to pick oranges in south Florida; put them on a train heading north; and allow people in other states to enjoy them in less than a week.

**2 Why did Henry Flagler decide to build the Ponce de Leon hotel?** He wanted people that were visiting Florida to have places to stay. **Make Inferences**

**3 Why were Henry Flagler's railroads and hotels important to the state of Florida?** The railroads were important because they helped people travel to different cities in Florida. The hotels were important because people visiting Florida had places to stay in the cities the railroads went through. **Recall and Retell**

## 3 Close and Assess

### Think and Share
Possible answers: Henry Flager helped Florida by building railroads and hotels. These types of changes allowed more people to visit Florida, and the state was able to grow.

# Lesson ⑤ Wrap-Up

## MEETING INDIVIDUAL NEEDS
## Leveled Practice

### State Shapes
Guide children in getting to know the shape of their state. Using a wall map, trace the shape of three states, including your own state, and duplicate for children.

**Easy** Have children find your state on a wall map. Then display three of the state shapes, and have children point out which of the three is their state. Ask what clues children used to decide which state was theirs. **Reteach**

**On-Level** Distribute all three state shapes to children. Have them identify their own state, cut it out, and label it. Then have them refer to a wall map of the United States to identify the other two states. **Extend**

**Challenge** Give children all three state shapes, and have them cut them out and label them. Then guide children in writing clues to your own state. Help children write their clues on index cards. Others in the class can then try to match the cards with their states. **Enrich**

## Hands-on Activities

 **CURRICULUM CONNECTION**
**Reading/Vocabulary**

# Name Game

**Objective** Use lesson vocabulary.

**Resources** Vocabulary Cards **state, continent, ocean**

**Materials** index cards, pencil, scissors, glue

**Learning Style** Verbal/Kinesthetic

**Partners** 👥

🕐 **Time** 20–25 minutes

1. Prepare simple word clues for each vocabulary word: *state, continent, ocean*. For *continent*, you might say: *There are seven of me*. Write the clues on index cards.

2. Give pairs of children a few index cards. Have them discuss the clues and try to guess the words.

3. Once children guess the words, have them cut out magazine pictures or draw their own pictures to illustrate each index card.

4. Remind children to add the lesson vocabulary to their Word Book.

There are seven of me.

 **CURRICULUM CONNECTION**
**Literature**

# Routes

**Objective** Locate places and trace a route on a map or globe.

**Materials** *How to Make an Apple Pie and See the World,* by Marjorie Priceman (Alfred A. Knopf, ISBN 0-673-61098-5, 1994), world map

**Learning Style** Verbal/Visual

**Group** 👥👥

🕐 **Time** 20–25 minutes

1. Display the map at the beginning of the book. Have children compare it with the map on pp. 76–77.

2. Read the story aloud, sharing the pictures. As the storyteller arrives in each new place, locate it on a wall map. Have children point to the corresponding location on the map on pp. 76–77.

3. Finally, help children trace the storyteller's route.

4. Children may enjoy making up their own travel stories for the missing ice cream.

 **SOCIAL STUDIES STRAND**
**History**

# What's in a Name?

**Objective** Use oral sources to learn how a community got its name.

**Learning Style** Verbal/Kinesthetic **Individual** 🧍

🕐 **Time** 20–25 minutes

1. Help children brainstorm possible explanations for the name of your community. For example, it might be named for a geographical feature, such as a river or mountain.

2. If your community is named for a person, provide children with information about this person.

3. Have each child draw a community logo. Logos should include the name of the community, decorated with drawings that explain the name of the community or its history.

Deep River

# Ending Unit 2

**End with a Poem**
pages 80–81

Children will listen to and talk about a poem—"One Great Big Community" by Toni Barkley—that tells about a child and where his home fits into the world.

**Unit 2 Review**
pages 82–85

Children will review unit vocabulary words and the unit skills of identifying alike and different, using a map key, and using four directions. Children will answer questions about what they learned in the unit. Children will learn about several books about communities and geography.

**Resources**
- Workbook, p. 21
- Assessment Book, pp. 5–8

**Unit 2 Project**
page 86

Children will create posters and give news reports about community events. They will also be directed to a Web site where they can learn more about communities.

**Resource**
- Workbook, p. 22

# Wrap-Up

**Activity**

## Helping My Community

Have children make trading cards to show how people help care for their own neighborhoods and communities.

- On the cards, children can write descriptions or draw pictures to show ways in which people help other people in their own communities. Brainstorm ideas with them, such as: by being leaders, by helping to keep places clean, and by caring for sick people.
- On each card, have children add a small picture of a child if the activity is one in which children can participate.

**Performance Assessment**
You can use the activity on this page as a performance assessment.

✓ **Assessment Scoring Guide**

| Make Trading Cards About Helping Communities | |
|---|---|
| 6 | Descriptions are very clear and complete, with many details. |
| 5 | Descriptions are clear and include details. |
| 4 | Descriptions are good, with some details. |
| 3 | Descriptions are adequate with an attempt to provide details. May be incomplete. |
| 2 | Descriptions show gaps in information and few details. Support may be inadequate. |
| 1 | Descriptions provide little or inaccurate information and few or vague details. |

If you require a 4-point rubric, adjust scoring guide accordingly.

# One Great Big Community

## Objectives

- Obtain information about a topic using a variety of visual sources, such as pictures and literature.

- Identify main ideas from oral, visual, and print sources.

## 1 Introduce and Motivate

**Preview** Point to and read the title; then identify the author of the poem. Ask children what they think the poem is about. Suggest that they think about the title and look at the picture before they answer.

**Warm Up** Remind children of the song with which they began this unit. You may want to turn to p. 44 and sing the song with children once again.

## 2 Teach and Discuss

Explain that a poem is a kind of writing that often has rhyming words. Read the poem aloud, and then have children read it with you.

**1 What are some ways to describe the boy's house?** Answers might include very tall and just the right size. **Recall and Retell**

**2 What things do you see in the boy's neighborhood?** Different houses, trees, hills **Analyze Pictures**

**3 How is the boy's neighborhood different from his community?** His neighborhood is smaller than his community. **Compare and Contrast**

## One Great Big Community
### by Toni Barkley

Here is my home.
It's very tall.
It's just the right size
To fit us all.

Here is my neighborhood
All around me.
It's part of a bigger
Community.

80

# Practice and Extend

### SOCIAL STUDIES STRAND
### Economics

**Community Connections**

- Talk with children about the many communities to which the boy in the poem—and they—belong. Help children list these: home, neighborhood, community, state, country, world.

- Point out that all these communities can connect to one another in many ways. One way is that people travel across town, to other states, and even around the world for fun and for work. They take things with them. They also bring things back to their homes with them.

- Explain to children that the things they wear, eat, and use often come from the different communities they listed above. Tell children that in Unit 3 they will learn more about the ways people depend on many communities to get what they need and want.

Here is my state.
It's one of fifty.
It's part of my country.
It's very nifty!

Here is my world.
It's special, you see.
It's the perfect home
For you and me!

④

81

Page 81

Explain to children that the word *nifty* means "attractive or stylish." Point out the state silhouette and help children identify the state shown.

④ **Name two very big communities in which the boy lives.** Possible answers: His state, his country, the world **Main Idea and Details**

# 3 Close and Assess

- Organize children in six groups: home, neighborhood, community, state, country, world. Divide up a set of nesting boxes or cups, giving each group an ascending size box or cup.

- Have groups read the lines of the poem related to their assigned community. As they read, help children assemble the stack of boxes or cups. Demonstrate how each fits into the next biggest size box or cup.

- Reread the poem again as a group. Ask children what they think the title means now. Explain that the boy sees the world as a huge community in which there are other communities of smaller and smaller size, all the way down to his own home.

## CURRICULUM CONNECTION
## Reading

**Books About Communities**

Children might enjoy reading these books.

*Officer Buckle and Gloria*, by Peggy Rathmann (Putnam, ISBN 0-399-22616-8, 1995) A police officer and a very special dog team up to present school safety programs. **Easy** *Caldecott Medal 1996*

*Me on the Map*, by Joan Sweeney and Annette Cable (illustrator), (Dragonfly, ISBN: 0-517-88557-3, 1998) In a game children love to play, a girl describes herself and her surroundings in ever-widening circles. **On-Level**

*Miss Rumphius*, by Barbara Cooney (Viking, ISBN 0-140-50539-3, 1985) A gentle story about a world traveler who made her own part of the world more beautiful for later generations. **Challenge** *Notable Social Studies Book.*

# UNIT 2 Review

## Resources

- Assessment Book, pp. 5–8
- Workbook, p. 21: Vocabulary Review

## Vocabulary Review

1. neighborhood
2. leader
3. state
4. continent
5. ocean

### TEST PREP Answers to Test Prep

1. law
2. community

---

# UNIT 2 Review

## Vocabulary Review

Tell which word completes each sentence.

neighborhood
continent
ocean
leader
state

1. People live, work, and play in a _____.
2. A mayor is a community _____.
3. Florida is a _____.
4. A very large piece of land is a _____.
5. A very large body of salt water is called an _____.

★ ★ ★ ★ ★ ★ ★ ★

### TEST PREP Which word completes the sentence?

1. A rule you must obey is a _____.

   **a.** law          **b.** state

   **c.** leader       **d.** community

2. A city is a big _____.

   **a.** neighborhood   **b.** continent

   **c.** ocean          **d.** community

82

---

# Practice and Extend

## Assessment Options

### ✓ Unit 2 Assessment

- Unit 2 Content Test: Use Assessment Book, pp. 5–6

- Unit 2 Skills Test: Use Assessment Book, pp. 7–8

#### TEST PREP Standardized Test Prep

- Unit 2 tests contain standardized test formats.

### ✓ Unit 2 Performance Assessment

- See p. 86 for information about using the Unit 2 Project as a means of performance assessment.

- A scoring guide for the Unit 2 Project is provided in the teacher's notes on p. 86.

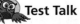 **Test Talk**

- Test Talk Practice Book

# Skills Review

## ⊙ Alike and Different

Tell or write about how laws can be **alike** and **different**.

## Use a Map Key

1. What does 🏫 stand for?

2. How many symbols are on the map key?

3. Draw a symbol for something on the map that is not in the map key.

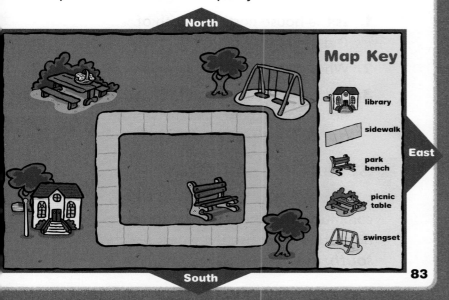

North

Map Key

🏠 library

▭ sidewalk

🪑 park bench

🛋 picnic table

🎠 swingset

East

South

83

**WEB SITE Technology**

For more information, you can select the dictionary or encyclopedia from *Social Studies Library* at **www.sfsocialstudies.com**.

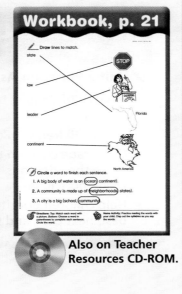

**Workbook, p. 21**

Also on Teacher Resources CD-ROM.

# Skills Review

## ⊙ Alike and Different
*Target Skill*

- Possible answer: Some laws help keep us safe. Other laws help keep our community clean. All laws must be obeyed by people who live in a community.

Use the following scoring guide.

### ✓ Assessment Scoring Guide

| Compare and Contrast Laws | |
|---|---|
| 6 | Explains that laws are alike in that all laws must be obeyed. Explains that laws are different in that some laws keep people safe while others help keep the community clean; gives several example of each kind of law. |
| 5 | Explains that laws are alike in that laws must be obeyed. Explains that laws are different in that some laws keep people safe while others help keep the community clean; gives one example of each kind of law. |
| 4 | Explains that laws are alike in that all laws must be obeyed. Explains how laws are different but gives an example of only one kind of law, not both. |
| 3 | Explains that all laws must be obeyed. Explains how laws are different but does not give an example of either kind of law. |
| 2 | Explains that all laws must be obeyed. Is able to give some examples of laws but is unable to tell how they differ. |
| 1 | Explains that all laws must be obeyed. Is unable to give examples. |

If you require a 4-point rubric, adjust scoring guide accordingly.

## Use a Map Key

1. Library

2. 5

3. Children should draw a symbol for a tree.

# Review

continued

# Skills Review

## Use Four Directions

1. North

2. The park

3. I would go west on Old Street and south on New Street.

## Skills on Your Own

- Children's maps should include cardinal directions and a map key, as well as symbols showing their homes and school. They should use cardinal direction words to tell how to get from their home to school.

Use the following scoring guide.

### ✓ Assessment Scoring Guide

| | Make a Map |
|---|---|
| 6 | Map includes home and school, and other places, as well as cardinal directions and a map key. Child provides detailed explanation of how to get from home to school, using direction words *north, south, east, west*. |
| 5 | Map includes home and school, as well as cardinal directions and a map key. Child is able to tell how to get from home to school using direction words *north, south, east, west*. |
| 4 | Map includes home and school as well as cardinal directions and a map key. Child is able to tell how to get from home to school, bit may use direction words incorrectly. |
| 3 | Map includes home and school but is lacking either cardinal directions or a map key. Child is able to tell how to get from home to school but does not use direction words. |
| 2 | Map includes home and school but lacks both cardinal directions and a map key. Child is unable to tell how to get from home to school. |
| 1 | Map includes only one of the four required features. |

If you require a 4-point rubric, adjust scoring guide accordingly.

**84** Unit 2 • In My Community

# Review

## Skills Review

### Use Four Directions

1. Is the house north or south of Old Street?

2. What place is west of New Street?

3. Tell how you would go from the house to the park. Use the words *north, south, east,* or *west.*

## Skills On Your Own

Draw a map and map key of your community. Tell how you would go from home to school. Use the words *north, south, east,* and *west.*

84

# Practice and Extend

## Revisit the Unit Question

### ✓ Unit 2 Portfolio Assessment

- Have children look back at the list that they suggested on p. 43.

- Ask if children would like to add to that list now.

- Encourage children to tell what has prompted them to make the additions. Did the lessons in the unit give them more ideas?

- Help children prioritize the list to show what they like best, next best, and so on.

# What did you learn?

1. Why is it important to know your home address?

2. How can you live in a community and state at the same time?

**Test Talk**

Find key words in the text.

3. Name two ways a community might change over time.

4. **Write and Share** Write about a mayor and a principal. Tell how these leaders are **alike** and **different.**

# Read About Communities

Look for books like these in the library.

85

# What did you learn?

1. Answers will vary but may include so you can tell people where you live.

2. A community is part of a state. A state is made up of many communities.

3. Possible answers: A community might get bigger in size and have more people or it might get smaller and have fewer people.

4. **Write and Share** Children may suggest that a principal is a school leader and a mayor is a community leader.

**Test Talk**

**Locate Key Words in the Text**
Use Question 2 of What did you learn? to model the Test Talk strategy.

**Decide where you will look for the answer.**
Have children make notes about details from the text that answer the question.

**Use information from the text.**
Have children check their notes and then ask themselves, "Do I have the right information?"

*For additional practice, use the Test Talk Practice Book.*

# Read About Communities

Invite children to read one or more of these books:

*Where I Live,* by Christopher Wormell (Dial, ISBN 0-8037-2056-4,1996) This book introduces fourteen animals in their natural habitats.

*As the Roadrunner Runs: A First Book of Maps,* by Gail Hartman (Bradbury, ISBN 0-02-743092-8, 1994) A lizard, a jackrabbit, a roadrunner, a deer, and a mule roam the Southwest.

*A Home Album,* by Peter and Connie Roop (Heineman, ISBN 1-57572-602-5, 1998) This book traces patterns of continuity and change in homes people live in.

# News for All

## Objective

- Identify, describe, and communicate information about an event in the community.

## Resource

- Workbook, p. 22

## Materials

poster board, crayons or markers, construction paper, fabric cords, balls

## Follow This Procedure

- Discuss how reporters relate news about local and world events, weather, and other topics.

- Explain that reporters ask questions, especially *who*, *what*, *where*, *when*, and *why*. Write these words on the board.

- Discuss with children some of the current events in the community. Explain that they will act as news reporters covering one of those events. Assign children to work in groups to report *who*, *what*, *where*, *when*, and *why*.

- Have children create a poster about the event and then give a news report about it.

✓ **Assessment Scoring Guide**

| | News for All |
|---|---|
| 6 | Demonstrates a solid understanding of how to present information about an event with several specific details. |
| 5 | Demonstrates a good understanding of how to present information about an event with some specific details. |
| 4 | Demonstrates a fair understanding of how to present information about an event with an attempt to provide details. |
| 3 | Demonstrates a fair understanding of how to present information about an event but does not identify specific details. |
| 2 | Has difficulty expressing an understanding of how to present information about an event with specific details. |
| 1 | Is unable to communicate an understanding about an event and/or provide few if any specific details. |

If you require a 4-point rubric, adjust scoring guide accordingly.

## News for All

**TV news reporters tell us what goes on in the world. You can report what goes on in your community.**

**1 Choose** an event that happened or might happen in your community.

**2 Make** a poster about the event. At the bottom of your poster, write words that describe what is happening.

**3 Give** a news report about the event. Tell what happened and who was there. Tell when and where the event happened. Tell why it is news.

**Internet Activity**

Go to www.sfsocialstudies.com/activities to learn more about communities.

86

# Practice and Extend

 **Hands-on Unit Project**

✓ **Performance Assessment**

- The Unit Project can also be used as a performance assessment activity.

- Use the scoring guide to assess each group's work.

**WEB SITE Technology**

Children can launch the activity by clicking on *Grade 1, Unit 2* at **www.sfsocialstudies.com/ activities.**

## Workbook, p. 22

Name _____
Use with Page 86.

**2 Project** News for All

✎ Draw a picture of an event in your community. **Drawings will vary.**

Write the name of the event ___ **Answers will vary.**

Write what happens at the event ___

22 Discovery Channel Project                Workbook

**Also on Teacher Resources CD-ROM.**

# Vocabulary Routines

**The following examples of reading and vocabulary development strategies can be used to instruct students about unit vocabulary.**

## BEFORE READING

### Individual Word Study

**Venn Diagram** This routine helps children connect background knowledge to vocabulary. Ask children what they already know about the word. For the word *job*, for example, create a Venn diagram for jobs children do at school and jobs children do at home. Have children brainstorm different jobs they do. Ask where each job should go in the diagram. Write the words in the diagram. Point out that jobs children do both at school and at home belong in both circles.

*Let's talk about the kinds of jobs you do at school and home. What kind of job do you only do at school?* (safety patrol; clean erasers) *What kind of job do you only do at home?* (wash dishes; walk dog) *Can you think of jobs that you do both at school and at home? What are they?* (sweep floor; put things away).

Jobs at School    Jobs at Home

clean erasers | sweep floors | wash dishes
safety patrol | put things away | walk dog

## DURING READING

### Context Clues

**Reciprocal Teaching** Use reciprocal teaching to help children learn and retain content area vocabulary. As you read the lessons with children, have them stop reading at the end of the page. Ask children to generate a question and encourage them to use vocabulary words in their questions. Have other children attempt to provide answers. Answer questions children cannot answer.

*Let's stop so you can ask some questions about what we have just read. Who would like to ask a question about **needs** and **wants**?* (How is a *want* different from a *need*? I want a toy but I do not have to have it. I must have food so food is a need.)

## AFTER READING

### Related Word Study

Vocabulary: tools, goods, service, volunteer

**Choose and Say It** Use this routine to reinforce vocabulary by presenting situations and having children make choices. Say a vocabulary word, then make several statements, some of which are examples, and some of which are not. Have children repeat the vocabulary word after they hear you give a correct example. By repeating the words, children are able to interact with the target word. Have children explain their reasoning.

*Think about the word **volunteer**. If any of the things I say might be examples of a person who is a volunteer, say "Volunteer." If not, don't say anything.*

*Someone is paid to fix a window.*

*Someone helps clean up the park for free. (volunteer).*

*Someone plays the violin in a concert but does not get paid for it. (volunteer)*

*Someone receives money to work in a factory.*

# Teaching with Leveled Readers

**This series of readers focuses on jobs and the tools needed to do those jobs.**

**Below Level**

**On Level**

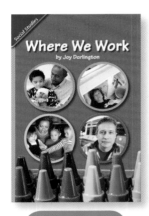

**Above Level**

## LEVELED READER VOCABULARY ACTIVITY

- Have children preview the vocabulary words *jobs* and *tools*.

- As children read, have them choose one of the jobs discussed in the book.

- After reading, have children write or draw a list of tools needed for the job they chose.

Job: _____

Tools:

## CONNECTIONS TO THE LESSON

Unit 3, Lesson 4: Welcome to Job Day!

## CONNECTIONS TO TODAY

- Have children read the lesson. Then provide the leveled readers to enhance their understanding of different jobs in the community.

- **Points for Discussion:**
    1. Have children discuss the different jobs at a school.
    2. Children can also discuss what types of jobs are available in their community.

# Work! Work! Work!

# Unit 3 Planning Guide
## Work! Work! Work!

**Begin with a Song** pp. 88–89    **Vocabulary Preview** pp. 90–91

**Reading Social Studies, Sequence** pp. 92–93

| Lesson Titles | Pacing | Main Ideas |
|---|---|---|
| **Lesson 1** **Ben's Jobs** pp. 94–97 <br><br> Chart and Graph Skills: Use a Chart pp. 98–99 | 2 days | • Children do jobs at home and at school. <br> • A chart is a way to show things using words and pictures. |
| **Lesson 2** **Needs and Wants** <br><br> pp. 100–101 <br><br> Then and Now: Changing Toys pp. 102–103 | 2 days | • Families have needs and wants. <br> • Some types of toys have changed over time. |
| **Lesson 3** **Spending and Saving** <br><br> pp. 104–105 <br><br> Here and There: Money Around the World pp. 106–107 | 2 days | • People who earn money must make choices about spending and saving. <br> • People all over the world spend and save money. |
| **Lesson 4** **Welcome to Job Day!** pp. 108–111 <br><br> Citizen Heroes: **Caring** Kid's Kitchen pp. 112–113 <br> Biography: Clara Barton pp. 114–115 | 3 days | • Workers provide goods and services. <br> • Some volunteers show they care by helping people in their communities. <br> • Clara Barton started the American Red Cross, a volunteer group that helps many people. |
| **Lesson 5** **Interview with a Farmer** pp. 116–119 <br><br> Map and Globe Skills: Follow a Route pp. 120–121 <br> Biography: George Washington Carver pp. 122–123 | 3 days | • A farmer provides goods by growing the food we buy at the store. <br> • We can use a map to find out how to get from one place to another. <br> • George Washington Carver taught farmers how to grow peanuts and found ways to make many other products from peanuts. |
| **Lesson 6** **From Place to Place** <br><br> pp. 124–125 <br><br> [DK] Transportation pp. 126–127 | 2 days | • Transportation moves people and goods from place to place. <br> • Different kinds of trucks help people do different jobs. |

✔ **End with a Poem** pp. 128–129    ✔ **Unit 3 Review** pp. 130–133    ✔ **Unit 3 Project** p. 134

✔ = Assessment Options

| Vocabulary | Resources | Meeting Individual Needs |
|---|---|---|
| **job** | • Workbook, pp. 25–26<br>• Transparencies 9, 19<br>• Vocabulary Card: job<br>• Every Student Learns Guide, pp. 38–41 | • ESL Support, TE p. 96<br>• Leveled Practice, TE p. 99a |
| **needs**<br>**wants** | • Workbook, p. 27<br>• Vocabulary Cards: needs, wants<br>• Every Student Learns Guide, pp. 42–45 | • ESL Support, TE p. 101<br>• Leveled Practice, TE p. 103a |
| | • Workbook, p. 28<br>• Every Student Learns Guide, pp. 46–49<br>• Transparency 20 | • ESL Support, TE p. 105<br>• Leveled Practice, TE p. 107a |
| **tools**<br>**goods**<br>**service**<br>**volunteer** | • Workbook, p. 29<br>• Vocabulary Cards: tools, goods, service, volunteer<br>• Every Student Learns Guide, pp. 50–53 | • ESL Support, TE p. 110<br>• Leveled Practice, TE p. 115a |
| | • Workbook, pp. 30–31<br>• Transparencies 9, 21<br>• Every Student Learns Guide, pp. 54–57 | • ESL Support, TE p. 118<br>• Leveled Practice, TE p. 123a |
| **transportation** | • Workbook, p. 32<br>• Vocabulary Card: transportation<br>• Every Student Learns Guide, pp. 58–61 | • ESL Support, TE p. 126<br>• Leveled Practice, TE p. 127a |

# Providing More Depth

## Additional Resources

- Trade Books
- Family Activities
- Vocabulary Workbook and Cards
- Social Studies Plus!
- Daily Activity Bank
- Read Alouds and Primary Sources
- Big Book Atlas
- Student Atlas
- Outline Maps
- Desk Maps

 **Technology**

- Video Field Trips
- Songs and Music
- Digital Learning CD-ROM Powered by KnowledgeBox
- AudioText
- MindPoint® Quiz Show CD-ROM
- ExamView® Test Bank CD-ROM
- Colonial Williamsburg Primary Sources CD-ROM
- Teacher Resources CD-ROM
- Map Resources CD-ROM
- SFSuccessNet: Online Student Edition, Online Teacher Edition, Online Planner
- **www.sfsocialstudies.com** (Biographies, news, references, maps, and activities)

 *To establish guidelines for your children's safe and responsible use of the Internet, use the Scott Foresman Internet Guide.*

**Additional Internet Links**

To find out more about:

- being a smart consumer, visit **www.zillions.org**
- trains visit the California State Railroad Museum at **www.csrmf.org**

# Unit 3 Objectives

## Beginning of Unit 3

- **List the different jobs that many people do.** (pp. 88–89)
- **Determine the meanings of words.** (pp. 90–91)
- **Recognize words that help tell order.** (pp. 92–93)
- **Analyze pictures and text to identify sequence.** (pp. 92–93)
- **Sequence information.** (pp. 92–93)

## Lesson 1
### Ben's Jobs
pp. 94–97

- **Describe the requirements of various jobs and the characteristics of a job well-performed.**
- **Express ideas orally based on knowledge and experiences.**
- **Sequence information.**
- **Obtain information about a topic using visual sources, such as graphics and pictures.** (pp. 98–99)
- **Recognize a chart, its parts, and its function.** (pp. 98–99)
- **Read and understand a chart.** (pp. 98–99)

## Lesson 2
### Needs and Wants
pp. 100–101

- **Describe ways that families meet basic human needs.**
- **Distinguish between wants and needs.**
- **Explain how people fulfill needs and wants.**
- **Distinguish among past, present, and future.** (pp. 102–103)
- **Compare and contrast toys from the past and today.** (pp. 102–103)

## Lesson 3
### Spending and Saving
pp. 104–105

- **Identify examples of people wanting more than they can have.**
- **Explain why wanting more than they can have requires that people make choices.**
- **Identify examples of choices families make when buying goods and services.**
- **Obtain information about a topic using visual sources, such as pictures and maps.** (pp. 106–107)

## Lesson 4
### Welcome to Job Day!
pp. 108–111

- **Identify examples of goods and services in the home, school, and community.**
- **Describe the requirements of various jobs and the characteristics of a job well-performed.**
- **Describe how specialized jobs contribute to the production of goods and services.**
- **Describe characteristics of good citizenship, as exemplified by ordinary people.** (pp. 112–113)
- **Identify characteristics of good citizenship, such as responsibility for the common good.** (pp. 112–113)
- **Explain that people can both give and receive care.** (pp. 112–113)
- **Identify contributions of historical figures who have influenced the nation.** (pp. 114–115)
- **Identify historic figures, such as Clara Barton, who have exemplified good citizenship.** (pp. 114–115)

## Lesson 5
### Interview with a Farmer
pp. 116–119

- **Describe how specialized jobs contribute to the production of goods and services.**
- **Obtain information about a topic using a variety of oral sources, such as interviews.**
- **Identify the role of markets in the exchange of goods and services.**
- **Sequence information.**
- **Use a simple map to identify the location of places.** (pp. 120–121)
- **Locate places of significance on maps.** (pp. 120–121)
- **Identify a historic figure who has exhibited a love of individualism and inventiveness.** (pp. 122–123)
- **Identify contributions of historical figures in the period of history since 1880.** (pp. 122–123)

## Lesson 6
### From Place to Place
pp. 124–125

- **Identify the role of transportation in the exchange of goods.**
- **Describe how technology has changed transportation.**
- **Obtain information about a topic using a variety of visual sources, such as pictures and graphics.** (pp. 126–127)
- **Identify ways people exchange goods and services.** (pp. 126–127)

## End of Unit 3

- **Obtain information about a topic using a variety of visual sources, such as pictures and literature.** (p. 128–129)
- **Describe the requirements of a job.** (p. 134)

# Assessment Options

## ✓ Formal Assessment

- **What did you learn?** PE/TE pp. 97, 101, 105, 111, 119, 125, 133
- **Unit Review,** PE/TE pp. 130–133
- **Unit 3 Test,** Assessment Book pp. 9–12
- **ExamView® CD-ROM**

## ✓ Informal Assessment

- **Teacher's Edition Questions,** throughout Lessons and Features
- **Close and Assess,** TE pp. 93, 97, 99, 101, 103, 105, 107, 111, 113, 115, 119, 121, 123, 125, 127, 129
- **Try it!** PE/TE pp. 93, 99, 121
- **Think and Share,** PE/TE pp. 97, 101, 105, 111, 115, 119, 123, 125
- **Caring in Action,** PE/TE p. 113
- **Hands-on History,** PE/TE p. 103

### Ongoing Assessment

**Ongoing Assessment** is found throughout the Teacher's Edition lessons using an **If…then** model.

**If** = students' observable behavior,      **then** = reteaching and enrichment suggestions

## ✓ Portfolio Assessment

- **Portfolio Assessment,** TE pp. 87, 132
- **Leveled Practice,** TE pp. 90, 99a, 103a, 107a, 115a, 123a, 127a
- **Workbook,** pp. 23–34
- **Unit Review: Skills on Your Own,** PE/TE p. 132
- **Curriculum Connection: Writing,** TE pp. 99a, 103, 103a, 115, 115a, 127a

## ✓ Performance Assessment

- **Hands-on Unit Project** (Unit 3 Performance Assessment), PE/TE pp. 87, 130, 134
- **Internet Activity,** PE p. 134
- **Scoring Guides,** TE pp. 131, 132, 134

## Test Talk

### Test-Taking Strategies

**Understand the Question**

- **Locate Key Words in the Question,** TE p. 95
- **Locate Key Words in the Text,** TE p. 102

**Understand the Answer**

- **Choose the Right Answer,** TE p. 130
- **Use Information from the Text,** TE p. 107
- **Use Information from Graphics,** TE p. 91
- **Write Your Answer,** TE p. 93

*For additional practice, use the Test Talk Practice Book.*

### Featured Strategy

**Choose the Right Answer**

Children will:

– Narrow the answer choices and rule out choices they know are wrong.
– Choose the right answer.

**PE/TE** p. 130

# Curriculum Connections
## Integrating Your Day

The lessons, skills, and features of Unit 3 provide many opportunities to make connections between social studies and other areas of the elementary curriculum.

### Reading

**Make a Picture Glossary,** TE p. 91

**Reading Skill—Put Things in Order (Sequence),** PE/TE pp. 92–93, 94, 116–119

**Add to My Word Book,** TE p. 99a

**Reading Skill—Compare and Contrast,** TE p. 100

**Reading Skill—Categorize,** TE p. 104

**Reading Skill—Main Idea and Details,** TE p. 108

**I Spy a Job,** TE p. 115a

**What a Plot!** TE p. 123a

**Reading Skill—Analyze Pictures,** TE p. 124

**Rhyming Words,** TE p. 128

### Math

**Measure to Make Lemonade,** TE p. 93

**Ordinal Numbers,** TE p. 98

**A Wish List,** TE p. 103a

**Count Pennies,** TE p. 107

**From Most to Least,** TE p. 107a

### Writing

**Job Coupons,** TE p. 99a

**Naming Toys,** TE p. 103

**Give Thanks,** TE p. 103a

**Book of Homes,** TE p. 103a

**Helping Someone,** TE p. 115

**Who's Working?** TE p. 115a

**A Poem,** TE p. 127a

### Social Studies

### Literature

**Read a Story,** TE p. 111

**All Aboard,** TE p. 127a

**Books About Work,** TE p. 129

**Read About Work,** PE/TE p. 133

### Science

**What a Plant Needs,** TE p. 117

**How Wheels Work,** TE p. 127

### Music/Drama

**Write Other Song Versions,** p. 89

**Sing a Song,** TE p. 96

**Who Am I?** TE p. 99a

**Perform a Skit,** TE p. 113

**What's My Line?** TE p. 115a

**Dramatize an Interview,** TE p. 118

### Art

**Hands on the Job,** TE p. 94a

**What Will You Pack?** TE p. 100a

**How Will You Go?** TE p. 124a

 Look for this symbol throughout the Teacher's Edition to find **Curriculum Connections.**

# Professional Development

## Teaching Curriculum Goals and Standards

**by Dr. M. Gail Hickey**
Indiana University/Purdue University

Effective social studies learning experiences must be defensible in light of national and state level curriculum standards. The National Council for Social Studies (NCSS) identified ten thematic strands in social studies. Below are several ways to incorporate two such strands as you teach *Scott Foresman Social Studies*.

### Strand: Production, Distribution, and Consumption

- Students dealing with economic concepts and issues need to understand and answer questions such as: What goods are to be made? What services are to be done? How do goods and services reach the people who need them?

- *Have children study the pictures and captions found on pp. 108–109 in Lesson 4 and pp. 118–119 in Lesson 5. Make sure that children understand the similarities and differences between goods and services. Have children describe how the people shown make or produce goods or provide services to others.*

### Strand: Global Connections

- Connections across the globe are becoming increasingly important. The theme of global connections typically appears in units dealing with geography, culture, and economics.

- *The Here and There feature "Money Around the World" (pp. 106–107) shows a world map and pictures of coins to create students' awareness that people all over the world spend and save money.*

## ESL Support

**by Jim Cummins, Ph.D.**
University of Toronto

The social studies concepts students are learning are also linguistic concepts. The language of a Social Studies text will likely be challenging for ESL students to learn.

### Access Content

One way to make the input comprehensible for ESL students is to modify how we present the content. We do this through extensive use of visuals such as graphic organizers, photographs, drawings, and so on. Other ways to help ESL students understand meaning are through paraphrasing the language and by use of examples and demonstrations that connect with students' prior knowledge.

*The following examples in the Teacher's Edition will help you to enable ESL students to access the content:*

- *"**Analyze Pictures**" on p. 96 helps English Language Learners learn and use job words. This will aid in their understanding of various jobs and their requirements.*

- *"**Using Graphic Organizers**" on p. 118 has children use graphic organizers to put things in order to show steps in a process. This activity will reinforce the use of the words* first, next, *and* last, *as well as help children understand the processes of growing peanuts and sending them to market.*

# Read Aloud

## Allowance
**by Aiko Saubi**

My mom gives me allowance
For doing all my chores.
I can spend my money
When she takes me to the store.

But I don't spend all my money
I put half of it away,
Mom calls it my savings
For a very special day.

**Build Background**
- Ask children to tell about any jobs they have had in which they earned money.
- Ask children how they might save money they have earned.

**Read Alouds and Primary Sources**
*Read Alouds and Primary Sources* contains additional selections to be used with Unit 3.

# Bibliography

*My Town,* by Rebecca Treays (EDC, ISBN 0-746-03079-7, 1998) **Easy** Notable Social Studies Book, 1999

*Sam and the Lucky Money,* by Karen Chinn (Lee and Low, ISBN 1-880-00013-X, 1995) **Easy**

*3 Pigs Garage,* by Peter Lippman (Workman Publishing International Ltd., ISBN 0-7611-1361-4, 1998) **Easy**

*Trucks That Build,* by Lars Klove (Simon & Schuster, ISBN 0-68-98176-22, 1999) **Easy**

*Buzby,* by Julia Hoban and John Himmelman (illustrator), (Harper Audio, ISBN 0-694-70044-4, 1996) **On-Level**

*Jamal's Busy Day,* by Wade Hudson and George Ford (illustrator), (Just Us Books, ISBN 0-940975-21-1, 1991) **On-Level**

*Night Worker, The,* by Katie Banks and Georg Hallensleben (illustrator), (Farrar Straus & Giroux, ISBN 0-374-35520-7, 2000) **On-Level** *2001 Charlotte Zolotow Award, An ALA Notable Children's Book*

*Tight Times,* by Barbara Shook Hazen and Trina Shart Hyman (illustrator), (Viking, ISBN 0-14-0504427-7, 1983) **On-Level**

*Animal Rescue: The Best Job There Is,* by Susan E. Goodman (Simon & Schuster, ISBN 0-689-81794-0, 2000) **Challenge**

*Boy Who Loved to Draw, Benjamin West, The* by Barbara Brenner (Houghton Mifflin, ISBN 0-395-85050-0, 1999) **Challenge** *Notable Social Studies Trade Book, 2000*

*Magic School Bus Gets Programmed,* by Joanna Cole (Scholastic Books, ISBN 0-590-187-37, 1999) **Challenge**

*Steven Caney's Kids' America,* by Steven Caney (Workman, ISBN 0-911-10480-1, 1978) **Teacher Reference**

*Discovery Channel School Videos Technology at Work.* Take a look at how the forces of technology, from television to computers to satellites, affect our world—and the universe; 2 videos. 49 minutes/9 segments.

Look for this symbol throughout the Teacher's Edition to find **Award-Winning Selections**. Additional book references are suggested throughout this unit.

# Work! Work! Work!

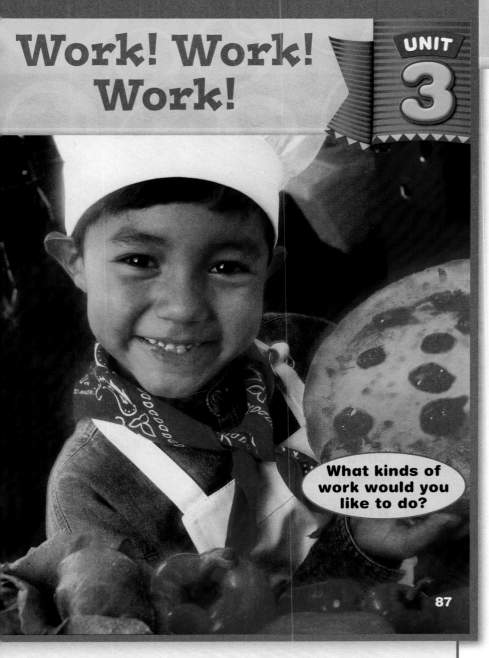

What kinds of work would you like to do?

87

# Work! Work! Work!

## Unit Overview

This unit introduces children to the concepts of jobs at home and at school and explores basic economic concepts relating to how people work to fulfill their economic needs and wants.

## Introduce Ben

Read the unit title and then introduce the featured child for this unit as a first-grader named Ben. Talk about what kind of work Ben might like to do.

## Unit Question

- Ask children the question on this page.

- Initiate a discussion of the kinds of work children would like to do when they are grown up.

- To activate prior knowledge, list on the board the jobs children name.

✓ **Portfolio Assessment** Keep a copy of this list for the Portfolio Assessment at the end of the unit on p. 132.

# Practice and Extend

## Hands-on Unit Project

✓ **Unit 3 Performance Assessment**

The Unit 3 Project, *Jobs in Your Community*, on p. 134, is an ongoing performance assessment project to enrich children's learning throughout the unit.

- This project, which has children making a puppet and giving an interview, may be started now or at any time during this unit of study.

- A performance assessment scoring guide is located on p. 134.

Unit 3 • Work! Work! Work! **87**

UNIT
3

# Lots of Jobs

## Objective
• List the different jobs that many people do.

## Resources
• *Songs and Music* CD "Lots of Jobs"
• Poster 5
• Social Studies Plus!

## Introduce the Song

**Preview** Tell children that they will be singing a song about jobs. Focus attention on the picture of Ben and review what job Ben would like to do. (Be a cook; own a pizza shop)

**Warm Up** To activate prior knowledge, invite children to name a place of work for each worker on the list generated on p. 87. Remind children that people can work at home or at places outside the home, such as an office, a factory, a store, or a restaurant. Ask volunteers to identify and describe what the workers at each of these places do to earn a living.

## Sing the Song

• Have children sing the song "Lots of Jobs."
• Have children act out the jobs named in the song.
• You may want to have children act out other jobs from the list.

UNIT
3

# Lots of Jobs
by Latrice Butler

 Sung to the tune of "Skip to My Lou"

Baker, teacher, doctor, too.

Lots of jobs I'd like to do.

Care for animals in the zoo.

What kinds of work would you do?

88

# Practice and Extend

**FYI** SOCIAL STUDIES
**Background**

**Possible Misconceptions**

To avoid stereotypes in occupational roles, you might encourage children to use names like homemaker for housewife, firefighter for fireman, police officer for policeman, salesperson for salesman, and so on.

 AUDIO CD
**Technology**

Play the CD, *Songs and Music*, to listen to "Lots of Jobs."

Ben's Pizza

① ②

## Talk About the Photograph

Direct children's attention to the photograph on these two pages. Talk with children about how this photograph differs from the one on p. 87.

**① What does this photograph show that we did not see when we met Ben on the last page?** Answers may include a restaurant with an outside dining area and Ben in restaurant whites instead of an apron. **Compare and Contrast**

**② What clues tell you that the photograph shows a restaurant?** Answers may include the name "Ben's Pizza," the utensils shown in the restaurant's sign, or the outside dining area. **Interpret Pictures**

**CURRICULUM CONNECTION**
## Music

**Write Other Song Versions**

- Write the song "Lots of Jobs" on the board, as follows.

  **Lots of Jobs**

  _____, _____, _____, too.
  Lots of jobs I'd like to do.
  _____.
  What kinds of work would you do?

- Work with children to create their own personal version of the song "Lots of Jobs" by rewriting the first and third sentences.

- Point out that the last word in the third line should rhyme with *too* and *do.*

- Sing the new versions of the song. Children may illustrate the jobs shown in the new verses of the song.

## Objective

• Determine the meanings of words.

## Resources

• Workbook, p. 23

• Vocabulary Cards

• Poster 6

## Introduce the Vocabulary

Read aloud and point to each vocabulary word and the photograph illustrating it. Have volunteers give the meanings of the words. Then have children find several examples of vocabulary words in the illustration. Write these examples on the board:

| Vocabulary Word | Illustrated Examples |
|---|---|
| job | boy carrying trash, adults working |
| needs | home, groceries |
| wants | bike, toy |
| tools | wrench, jackhammer, rake |
| goods | fruits, vegetables, cars |
| service | paper delivery, road workers |
| volunteer | crossing guard |
| transportation | bus, trucks, cars |

($) **SOCIAL STUDIES STRAND**
**Economics**

Listed below are some basic principles of economics for young children. Direct your discussion of the illustration toward the development of these concepts:

• needs and wants

• goods and services

• types of jobs

• choices people make and opportunity costs

• ways people exchange goods and services

• ways people use money

• role of stores in the exchange of goods and services

• people producing and consuming goods and services

job

needs

wants

tools

90

## Practice and Extend

**MEETING INDIVIDUAL NEEDS**
**Leveled Practice**

**Take a Tour**

Invite children to take a tour through the community in the illustration.

**Easy**  Explain that you will be their tour guide. Begin at one end of a specific street and describe in detail all the buildings, people, signs, vehicles and other things along the way. Have children repeat the vocabulary words as you guide them from one end of the street to the other. **Reteach**

**On-Level**  Have children take turns leading a tour through the community, using vocabulary words to describe what they see. **Extend**

**Challenge**  Invite children to describe something in the community using some of the vocabulary words. Have others guess what is being described. **Enrich**

goods

service

volunteer

transportation

91

## Talk About the Illustration

Allow children time to study the illustration. The picture shows a community with many kinds of workers and stores. Encourage children to talk about what various workers in the illustration are doing.

**Test Talk**

**Use Information from Graphics**

**1** **How are people using tools?** Possible answers: digging up the street, cooking, painting. Tell students to use details from the picture to support their answers. **Apply Information**

**2** **How are volunteers helping people?** As volunteer hospital workers, firefighters, and crossing guards **Apply Information**

## Look Ahead

Tell children that they will learn more about each of these words as they study Unit 3.

You may want to revisit the picture with children to review the concepts and vocabulary in the unit.

**3** **How are the types of transportation shown in the picture alike and different?** Possible answers: All shown have wheels; some carry many people, and some carry few. **Compare and Contrast**

**4** **What do you think would happen if these people didn't do their jobs?** Possible answers: Someone might get hurt; you could not buy what you need and want. **Predict**

### CURRICULUM CONNECTION
## Reading

### Make a Picture Glossary

Children can add the vocabulary for Unit 3 to "My Word Book." Words may be entered at the beginning of the unit or added as they are introduced.

### WEB SITE
## Technology

You can look up vocabulary words online. Click on *Social Studies Library* and select the dictionary at **www.sfsocialstudies.com.**

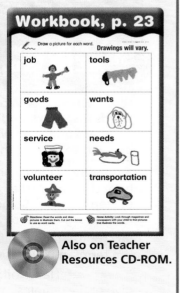
## Workbook, p. 23

Draw a picture for each word.    Drawings will vary.

| job | tools |
| --- | --- |
| goods | wants |
| service | needs |
| volunteer | transportation |

**Also on Teacher Resources CD-ROM.**

# Ben at Work

## 🎯 Put Things in Order
**(Sequence)**

### Objectives
- Recognize words that help tell order.
- Analyze pictures and text to identify sequence.
- 🎯 Sequence information.

### Resources
- Workbook, p. 24
- Transparency 18

### About the Unit Target Skill
- The target reading skill for this unit is Put Things in Order.
- Children are introduced to the unit target skill here and are given an opportunity to practice it.
- Further opportunities to put things in order are found throughout Unit 3.

## 1 Introduce and Motivate

**Preview** To determine if children understand the concept of putting things in order, or sequencing, ask children to tell when they do things in a certain order. Possible answers may include their routines for getting ready for school or going home from school. Write the word *order* on the board and explain that the word means "to tell when things happen."

**Warm Up** To activate prior knowledge, direct children's attention to today's class schedule. Ask a volunteer to name three activities the class will do before lunch. Record their responses in complete sentences as they are given. Have children arrange the activities in order to tell about the morning at school.

---

# Ben at Work

## 🎯 Put Things in Order

Hi! I'm Ben. Someday I want to own a pizza shop.

Saturday I had a lemonade stand. These pictures show the order in which things happened. Use your own words to tell what I did.

**First**          **Next**

92

## Practice and Extend

### ESL — ACCESS CONTENT — ESL Support

**Work with New Words** Discuss the meaning of the words *first, next,* and *last.* Have children write each word on a card and then write a word in their home language below it to remind them of the English meaning.

**Beginning** Display pictures that show time order and have children display the appropriate card for each event or step pictured. Some children may benefit from numbering the cards *1–3.*

**Intermediate** As children become more proficient using the terms, mix the events or steps and repeat.

**Advanced** Have children work in pairs. Ask one child to give oral examples of time order and the other to hold up the appropriate card. Then have them reverse roles.

Did you use words like **first, next,** and **last?** Those words tell the order in which things happened.

**First,** I made the lemonade.

**Next,** I set up my stand.

**Last,** I sold a cup to my friend.

Look for **first, next,** and **last** as you learn more about people at work.

**Last**

## Try it!

 Tell or write about how Ben could make a pizza. Use the words **first, next,** and **last.** Draw pictures to show the order in which things happen.

93

### CURRICULUM CONNECTION
## Math

**Measure to Make Lemonade**

Help children to measure the ingredients and then make lemonade. Direct children to stir the following ingredients together until dissolved: 5 cups cold water, 2/3 cup granulated sugar, 1 cup lemon juice. Then help children pour the lemonade over ice.

### Workbook, p. 24

**Put Things in Order**

Write *1, 2,* and *3* to show the order.

| | | |
|---|---|---|
| 3 | 1 | 2 |

Write *first, next,* and *last* to show the order.

| | | |
|---|---|---|
| first | last | next |

**Directions:** Top: Show the order in which things happen by writing 1, 2, and 3. Bottom: Write first, next, and last to show the order.  **Home Activity:** Share a comic strip with your child. Then cut apart the boxes, mix them up, and help your child put them back in order.

Also on Teacher Resources CD-ROM.

## 2 Teach and Discuss

Read p. 92 and have children examine the three pictures on pp. 92–93. Invite three volunteers to tell what Ben is doing in each picture.

Read p. 93 and focus on the terms *first, next, last.* Point out that these words help connect parts of the story. Reread the story while children focus on the pictures. Point out that there may be more than one way to order some of the steps (for example, Ben could set up the lemonade stand first and make the lemonade next).

### ✓ Ongoing Assessment

**If...** children do not understand that the words *first, next,* and *last* tell order,

**then...** list *first, next, last* on the board and write *1* next to *first, 2* next to *next,* and *3* next to *last.*

Tell children that putting things in order when we read helps us understand when things happened.

## 3 Close and Assess

## Try it!

### Test Talk

**Write Your Answer**

Review with children the steps in making a pizza. Be sure they are familiar with pizza and know its ingredients. Children's stories and drawings should correctly show the order for making a pizza and correctly use the words *first, next,* and *last.* Have partners read each other's written answers and look at each other's pictures. Partners can check that the steps are in order. Then they can talk about what would happen if the order of the steps was changed.

# Workbook Support

 Use the following Workbook pages to support content and skills development as you teach Unit 3. You can also view and print Workbook pages from the Teacher Resources CD-ROM.

## Workbook, p. 23

Use with Pages 90–91.

Draw a picture for each word. **Drawings will vary.**

| job | tools |
| goods | wants |
| service | needs |
| volunteer | transportation |

**Directions:** Read the words and draw pictures to illustrate them. Cut out the boxes to use as word cards.

**Home Activity:** Look through magazines and newspapers with your child to find pictures that illustrate the words.

**Use with Pupil Edition, p. 91**

## Workbook, p. 24

Use with Pages 92–93.

### Put Things in Order

Write *1*, *2*, and *3* to show the order.

Write *first*, *next*, and *last* to show the order.

first    last    next

**Directions:** *Top:* Show the order in which things happen by writing *1, 2,* and *3*. *Bottom:* Write *first, next,* and *last* to show the order.

**Home Activity:** Share a comic strip with your child. Then cut apart the boxes, mix them up, and help your child put them back in order.

**Use with Pupil Edition, p. 93**

## Workbook, p. 25

Use with Pages 94–97.

### Ben's Jobs

Draw a job you do at home. **Drawings will vary.**

Draw a job you do at school.

**Directions:** Draw pictures to show jobs you do at home and at school. Then tell about each job—and how well you do it.

**Home Activity:** Assign your child a job, such as setting the table. Make a job chart to keep a record of your child's performance for a week.

**Use with Pupil Edition, p. 97**

## Workbook, p. 26

Use with Pages 98–99.

### Use a Chart

Write the helpers' names on the chart.

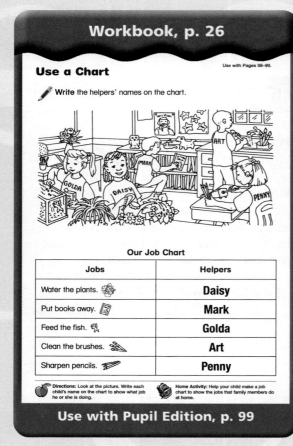

#### Our Job Chart

| Jobs | Helpers |
| --- | --- |
| Water the plants. | Daisy |
| Put books away. | Mark |
| Feed the fish. | Golda |
| Clean the brushes. | Art |
| Sharpen pencils. | Penny |

**Directions:** Look at the picture. Write each child's name on the chart to show what job he or she is doing.

**Home Activity:** Help your child make a job chart to show the jobs that family members do at home.

**Use with Pupil Edition, p. 99**

## Workbook, p. 27

Use with Pages 100–101.

### Needs and Wants

Circle things you need to stay alive.

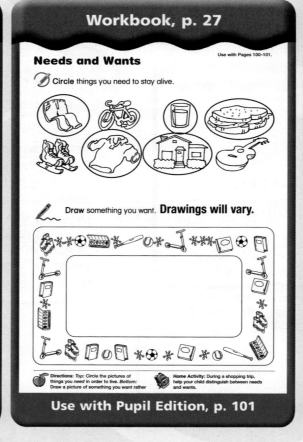

Draw something you want. **Drawings will vary.**

**Directions:** *Top:* Circle the pictures of things you *need* in order to live. *Bottom:* Draw a picture of something you *want* rather

**Home Activity:** During a shopping trip, help your child distinguish between needs and wants.

**Use with Pupil Edition, p. 101**

## Workbook, p. 28

Use with Pages 104–105.

### Spending and Saving

Write what each person can buy.

Kyla has 25¢.
She can buy a **banana**

Juan has 50¢.
He can buy a **pen**

Circle what you might buy for 75¢.

**Directions:** *Top:* Look at each picture. Complete the sentence to tell what each person can buy. *Bottom:* Circle things in the picture that you might buy, if you had 75 cents.

**Home Activity:** Point out the prices of different items bought at a supermarket. Ask your child what he or she could buy for a given amount of money.

**Use with Pupil Edition, p. 105**

# Workbook Support

## Workbook, p. 29

### Welcome to Job Day!

Use with Pages 108–111.

Circle people who have service jobs.

Draw a job you might like to have. **Drawings will vary.**

Directions: *Top:* Circle pictures of workers who provide services. *Bottom:* Draw a job you might like to do.

Home Activity: Point out to your child examples of people who provide services in your community.

**Use with Pupil Edition, p. 111**

## Workbook, p. 30

### Interview with a Farmer

Use with Pages 116–119.

Draw lines to match the pictures.

Directions: The pictures on the left show goods being made. The pictures on the right show goods being sold or used. Draw lines to match the pictures.

Home Activity: Talk with your child about jobs held by various family members. Point out how the jobs contribute to the production of goods or services.

**Use with Pupil Edition, p. 119**

## Workbook, p. 31

### Follow a Route

Follow the route that the pizza van takes.

Circle *yes* or *no* for each sentence.

1. The van goes east on Main Street. (yes) no
2. The van goes south on Dan Street. (yes) no
3. The van goes west on Low Street. yes (no)
4. The van goes south on Oak Hill. yes (no)

Directions: Follow the van's route on the map. Read each sentence, and circle *yes* or *no*. Then draw another route on the map to show how else the van might go.

Home Activity: Have your child draw another route on the map to show how the van might get from the pizzeria to the school.

**Use with Pupil Edition, p. 121**

## Workbook, p. 32

### From Place to Place

Use with Pages 124–125.

Make a chart to show then and now.
Cut out the pictures.
Paste them on the chart.

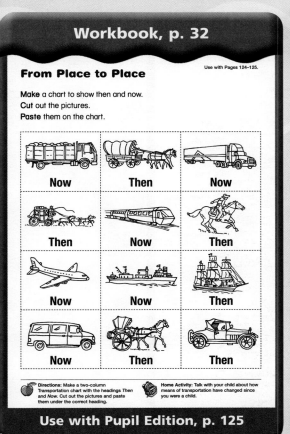

Directions: Make a two-column Transportation chart with the headings *Then* and *Now.* Cut out the pictures and paste them under the correct heading.

Home Activity: Talk with your child about how means of transportation have changed since you were a child.

**Use with Pupil Edition, p. 125**

## Workbook, p. 33

Use with Unit 3.

Circle the word that belongs on the line.

1. A teacher's job is a ___ job.
   (service)     goods

2. People who work for free are ___.
   wants     (volunteers)

3. A farmer's job is to grow ___.
   tools     (goods)

4. Food and clothes are both ___.
   (needs)     transportation

5. New toys are ___, not needs.
   tools     (wants)

Draw a picture of a job you do.
Draw a picture of a tool you use. **Drawings will vary.**

Directions: *Top:* Circle the word that is correct in each sentence. *Bottom:* Draw a picture of a job you do and a tool you use.

Home Activity: Help your child find pictures that show different means of transportation. Talk about what is being transported.

**Use with Unit 3.**

## Workbook, p. 34

### 3 Project   Jobs in Your Community

Draw a picture of a worker in your community. **Drawings will vary.**

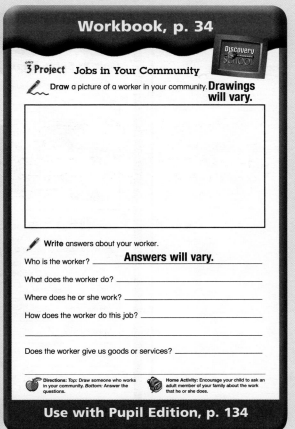

Write answers about your worker.

Who is the worker? ___ **Answers will vary.**

What does the worker do? ___

Where does he or she work? ___

How does the worker do this job? ___

Does the worker give us goods or services? ___

Directions: *Top:* Draw someone who works in your community. *Bottom:* Answer the questions.

Home Activity: Encourage your child to ask an adult member of your family about the work that he or she does.

**Use with Pupil Edition, p. 134**

Unit 3 • Workbook Support  **93b**

# Assessment Support

Use these Assessment Book pages and ExamView® Test Bank CD-ROM to assess content and skills in Chapter 2 and Unit 1. You can also view and print Assessment Book pages from the Teacher Resources CD-ROM.

## Assessment Book, p. 9

### Unit 3: Content Test

✎ **Circle** a word to finish each sentence.

1. Food, water, and clothing are ____.
   (needs)    jobs    volunteers

2. Toys, games, and TV are ____.
   needs    tools    (wants)

3. Hammers and nails are a builder's ____.
   (tools)    service    transportation

4. Cars, trucks, and vans are kinds of ____.
   needs    jobs    (transportation)

⭐ **TEST PREP** Which word completes each sentence?

1. A person who works for free is a ____.
   a. job    (b.) volunteer
   c. service    d. transportation

2. Things that are grown or made are ____.
   (a.) goods    b. wants
   c. needs    d. tools

**Use with Pupil Edition, p. 130**

## Assessment Book, p. 10

✎ **Draw** someone making or growing goods.
**Draw** someone doing a service job. **Drawings will vary.**

| Goods | Services |
|-------|----------|
|       |          |

✎ **Draw** a line under the answer to each question.

1. Which is a need?    toys    <u>food</u>

2. What is your job at school?    <u>to learn</u>    to eat

3. What can you do with money?    cook it    <u>save it</u>

4. Who grows the food we eat?    <u>farmers</u>    teachers

5. Which is a kind of transportation?    a house    <u>a truck</u>

**Use with Pupil Edition, p. 130**

## Assessment Book, p. 11

### Unit 3: Skills Test

✎ **Write** first, next, and last to show the order.

**first**    **last**    **next**

✎ **Write** names of people at home.

#### Jobs at Home

| Jobs | Helpers |
|------|---------|
| Set the table. | **Names will vary.** |
| Make the beds. | |
| Cook dinner. | |

**Use with Pupil Edition, pp. 131–132**

## Assessment Book, p. 12

Trace Lee's route on the map.

✎ **Write** words to complete the sentences.

1. Lee starts at the ____**school**____.

2. Lee goes ____**east**____ on School Street.

3. Lee goes ____**south**____ on Main Street.

4. Lee goes ____**east**____ on Library Lane.

**Use with Pupil Edition, pp. 131–132**

# Lesson ① Overview

## Ben's Jobs
**pages 94–97**

Children will learn the meaning of the word *job* and explore the kinds of jobs that children perform at home and at school.

 **Time 20–30 minutes**

**Resources**
- Workbook, p. 25
- Vocabulary Card **job**
- Transparency 9
- Every Student Learns Guide, pp. 38–41

## Use a Chart
**pages 98–99**

Children will learn how to use charts, such as jobs charts.

 **Time 15–20 minutes**

**Resource**
- Workbook, p. 26

# Build Background

## Activity

### Hands on the Job

 **Time 15–20 minutes**

Create a "Hands on the Job" chart similar to the one shown. Have children trace their hands on two different colors of paper. Children then write or draw one thing they do to help at home on one hand and a way they help at school on the other hand.

**If time is short,** have children suggest ways they help at home and at school. You can then write their ideas inside the large hand outlines.

## Read Aloud

### Little Helper

**by Andy Parker**

I run for Daddy's slippers.
I wheel the baby out.
I find my Grandma's glasses.
You never see me pout.
I help when Mommy's busy.
I am always kind and glad.
I am the kindest
 little helper
A family
 ever had.

Lesson

# Ben's Jobs

## Objectives

- Describe the requirements of various jobs and the characteristics of a job well-performed.
- Express ideas orally based on knowledge and experiences.
- Sequence information.

## Vocabulary

**job** the work people do (p. 94)

### QUICK Teaching Plan

*If time is short,* have children look at the pictures and brainstorm a list of jobs at home.

- Have them brainstorm a list of jobs at school.

## 1 Introduce and Motivate

**Preview** Display the Vocabulary Card **job** and ask children what a job is. Then share its meaning as "the work people do." Have children locate the term as they preview the lesson.

**Warm Up** To activate prior knowledge, ask children to give examples of work they do at home. Then ask children to suppose they are visiting Ben's family. Have them name jobs they might see people in the family doing. Invite volunteers to take turns selecting one of the jobs and acting it out for the class.

---

Lesson

# Ben's Jobs

**①  ②** I do lots of jobs to help at home. A **job** is the work people do. **First,** I put away my toys all by myself.

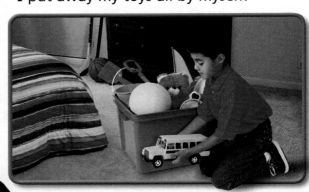

**Next,** I feed our dog. My whole family takes turns caring for Rusty.

94

## Practice and Extend

**READING/VOCABULARY**
### Put Things in Order

**Sequence** Tell children that this lesson includes words to help them tell order.

- After they read pp. 94–97, give children a copy of Transparency 9.
- Have them complete it to show what Ben did first, next, and last at home.
- Ask volunteers to share their answers with the class.

First   Next   Last

---

**Last,** my family and I work together to make dinner. I like to help cook. When the work is done, we all eat. I like that part the best!

95

Page 94

# 2 Teach and Discuss

Page 94

Identify Ben in the photographs. Invite volunteers to name the jobs Ben is doing. Point out that Ben is doing each job by himself.

**1 What jobs can you do by yourself?** Answers will vary but should reflect jobs children can perform individually. **Apply Information**

## Test Talk

**Locate Key Words in the Question**

**2 Compare two jobs that you can do.** Tell children that the word *compare* means to tell how two or more things are alike. Encourage children to tell about two jobs—and to tell what is the same about those jobs. **Compare and Contrast**

Page 95

Point out the members of Ben's family. Discuss the jobs involved in making dinner.

**3 Tell how Ben knows when he has done a job well.** Possible answers: The toys are all put away; the dog is no longer hungry; the dinner is delicious. **Make Inferences**

**4 Why might family members work together to do some jobs?** Possible answers: to get jobs done more quickly, to make things fair for everyone, to spend time together, or to make more time for fun **Make Inferences**

**5 What other jobs might Ben's family do together?** Answers will vary but should reflect jobs performed by two or more people. **Make Inferences**

## SOCIAL STUDIES Background

**Possible Misconceptions**

- Children may think that work performed at home has less value than work performed outside of the home.
- Work performed at home can include such activities as child care and housework, as well as work done for an outside employer.
- Discuss how work done at home is important.
- Explain to children that when they are expected to take care of something, or do a job, it becomes a responsibility. For example, it is Ben's responsibility to feed the dog.

## WEB SITE Technology

You can look up vocabulary words online. Click on *Social Studies Library* and select the dictionary at www.sfsocialstudies.com.

**Lesson 1** continued

## Page 96

Have children name the school jobs shown in the drawing.

**6** **What is your big job in school?** To learn
Apply Information

**7** **How might you be rewarded for a job well done at school?** Answers may include feeling proud, getting a sticker on a paper, getting a tally on a chart, or getting praise. Apply Information

**$ SOCIAL STUDIES STRAND**
**Economics**

Point out that going to school is similar to grown-ups going to work or working at home. Invite volunteers to discuss jobs done by adults.

**8** **Your job is to go to school and learn. Why is this such an important job?** Possible answers: to prepare for work as an adult, to understand things about the world, to learn how things work, to learn how to cooperate with others Make Inferences

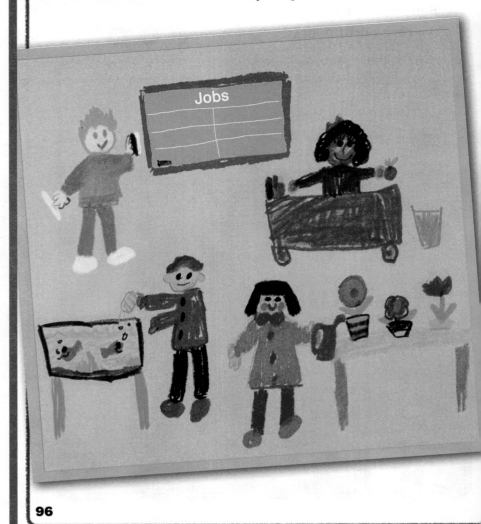

**6 7 8** I have jobs at school. My big job is to learn. That is your job at school too.

96

# Practice and Extend

**ESL** **ACCESS CONTENT**
**ESL Support**

**Analyze Pictures** The pictures in Lesson 1 show jobs children can do at home and at school.

**Beginning** Model pointing to each picture while telling about each job. Have children point to the pictures and repeat the job words.

**Intermediate** Demonstrate the jobs pictured and invite children to identify them. Invite children to take turns performing jobs for others to identify.

**Advanced** Invite children to draw a picture on an index card about jobs they do at home. Mix the cards. Have children take turns picking a card and dictating a sentence describing how to do the job.

*For additional ESL support, use Every Student Learns Guide, pp. 38–41.*

 **CURRICULUM CONNECTION**
**Music**

**Sing a Song**

Using lesson vocabulary words in songs not only reinforces the word and its meaning, but also helps reach children with other learning styles and talents. Have children take turns acting out a school job for others to guess. Children might pretend to pass out papers, hold the flag, or do other school tasks. Other related song adaptations could be "This Is a Job I Do at Home "or "This Is a Job I'd Like to Do."

Sing to the tune of
*This Is the Way We Go to School*

**This Is a Job**
**I Do at School**

This is a job I do at school,
Do at school,
Do at school.
This is a job I do at school.
Guess what it could be.

Today I have a special job. I get to feed our hamster. What are your special jobs at school?

  **9** **10** **11**

## What did you learn ?

1. What is a **job**? Why are jobs in your classroom important?

2. How are jobs at home and at school the same? How are they different?

3. **Think and Share** Tell or write about a job you do well. Use the words **first, next,** and **last** in your story.

97

Discuss the special school job in the photograph.

**9** **What things does Ben need to know to do his special job?** Possible answers: He needs to know how often to feed the hamster and where the hamster food is kept. **Make Inferences**

**Ongoing Assessment**

| **If...** children do not understand why Ben's job is special, | **then...** explain that a special job is a job you don't get to do every day. |

**10** **What special jobs might you do in art class?** Answers will vary but may include handing out or putting away art supplies. **Apply Information**

**11** **Tell how you might know when someone else has done a job well.** Possible answer: It is done completely, neatly, and on time. **Make Inferences**

## 3 Close and Assess

Have children brainstorm a list of all the special jobs they do. Encourage children to name jobs both inside and outside school. Then have children talk to a partner about what is required for them to do in their favorite special job and how they know when they did the job well.

## What did you learn ?

1. A job is the work someone does. Classroom jobs are important because they help make things run smoothly—so everyone can learn.

2. Answers will vary but should reflect jobs of children and the similarities and differences between those done at home and at school.

3. **Think and Share** Answers should explain the steps in the job.

# Use a Chart

## Objectives

- Obtain information about a topic using visual sources, such as graphics and pictures.

- Recognize a chart, its parts, and its function.

- Read and understand a chart.

## Vocabulary

**chart** a way to show things using words and pictures (p. 98)

# 1 Introduce and Motivate

**Preview** Ask children to say what they think a chart is. Tell children that a chart is a special way to show information. Mention that a chart often uses both words and pictures.

**Warm Up** To activate prior knowledge, have children identify any charts displayed in your classroom, such as the class schedule, a calendar, and so on. Explain that learning how to read a chart will help them understand a different way to get organized information.

# 2 Teach and Discuss

Read the introduction. Prior to reading the chart and discussing its parts, ask children to identify their left and right hands.

**1** **What does the right side of the chart show?** Helpers Interpret Charts

**2** **How many helpers are there on the chart?** Three Interpret Charts

**3** **What job will Sam do? How do you know?** He will clean the board; his name is next to that job. Interpret Charts

---

# Use a Chart

A **chart** is a way to show things using words and pictures. This chart shows some special jobs children do in school.

**1** **2** **3**

| Jobs at School | | |
|---|---|---|
| **Jobs** | | **Helpers** |
|  | Feed hamster. | Ben |
| | Water plants. | Mary |
| | Clean board. | Sam |

- The title tells what the chart is about. What is this chart about?

- The left side of the chart lists the jobs.

- Look at the name next to the first job. Which helper feeds the hamster?

**98**

---

# Practice and Extend

**CURRICULUM CONNECTION**
**Math**

### Ordinal Numbers

- The lesson requires children to find the first job on the "Jobs at School" chart. Children less familiar with ordinal numbers will benefit from a quick review.

- To make discussion of charts easier, prepare and label rows of classroom charts with the number and the ordinal word cards.

third    first

3rd    1st

---

Ben and his sister Rita have jobs at home. This chart shows the jobs they do. Use the chart to answer the questions.

## Jobs at Home

| Jobs | Helper |
|---|---|
|  Set table. | Ben |
| Clear table. | Rita |
| Walk dog. | Ben |
| Feed dog. | Rita |

④

### Try it!

1. Who clears the table?

2. Who walks the dog?

3. **On Your Own** Make a **chart** to show the jobs your family does at home.

99

④ **Look at the chart on p. 99. Why do you think Ben and Rita made this chart?** So that each would know what job to do **Make Inferences**

## 3 Close and Assess

To increase awareness of charts, have children go on a "chart hunt." As you go through the day, have children try to find charts in the classroom, halls, and in books. Keep a tally of how many charts are found. Have each child tell a partner what one of the charts shows.

### Try it!

1. Rita clears the table.

2. Ben walks the dog.

3. **On Your Own** Charts will vary but should reflect jobs of family members.

**Workbook, p. 26**

**Also on Teacher Resources CD-ROM.**

# Lesson ① Wrap-Up

**MEETING INDIVIDUAL NEEDS**
## Leveled Practice

### Find Pictures of Jobs
Ask children to draw or cut out magazine pictures that show people doing work.

**Easy** Use the pictures to make a classroom poster. Have each child tell about one of the jobs on the poster. **Reteach**

**On-Level** Use the pictures to make a classroom poster. Draw a word web on the board. Ask children to choose a picture from the poster for the topic of the web. Have children fill in the web with words that relate to the job. **Extend**

**Challenge** Use the pictures to make a classroom poster. Have children write and illustrate a story about one of the jobs pictured on the poster. Volunteers may share their stories with the class. **Enrich**

## Hands-on Activities

 **CURRICULUM CONNECTION**
### Reading

## Add to "My Word Book"

**Objective** Define and illustrate the word *job*.

**Resources** Vocabulary Card **job**
**Materials** crayons, pencils
**Learning Style** Visual
**Individual**
**Time** 10–15 minutes

1. Display the Vocabulary Card. Direct children to find the "J" page in their word book and have them write the word *job* in a word space.

2. Have children draw a picture to illustrate the word and write a sentence below or next to the picture using the word.

 **CURRICULUM CONNECTION**
### Drama

## Who Am I?

**Objective** Recognize jobs done at home.

**Materials** chart paper, marker
**Learning Style** Visual/Verbal/ Kinesthetic
**Group**
**Time** 15–30 minutes

1. Help children make a class list of jobs people do at home.

2. Invite volunteers to select a job and act it out for the class.

3. The other children can use the list to figure out which job is being done.

Jobs at Home
Cook
Clean
Wash the car
Feed the cat
Take out trash
Make the bed

 **CURRICULUM CONNECTION**
### Writing

## Job Coupons

**Objective** Demonstrate how doing a job helps others.

**Materials** paper, crayons
**Learning Style** Visual
**Group**
**Time** 10–15 minutes

1. Children will make a job coupon to see how their work benefits others. Provide children with half-sheets of drawing paper. Draw a sample coupon on the board for children to copy.

2. Tell children to write or draw a job on the line that they do not do at home but could do. The job should give another family member or caregiver a break.

# Lesson ② Overview

**Needs and Wants**
pages 100–101

Children will learn meanings of the words *needs* and *wants*. They will identify basic human needs and contrast needs with wants.

⏱ Time 20 minutes

**Resources**
- Workbook, p. 27
- Vocabulary Cards needs , wants
- Every Student Learns Guide, pp. 42–45

**Changing Toys**
pages 102–103

Children will learn how to use visual sources, such as charts, to compare and contrast.

⏱ Time 15–20 minutes

# Build Background

## Activity

## What Will You Pack?

⏱ **Time** 15–20 minutes

Ask children to suppose that they're going on a trip together. Have each child draw a picture of one thing to take. Then "pack" the pictures in a class shoe box.

Suggest a situation that reflects a need, such as: "I'm so thirsty! Did anyone pack a drink?" Select a volunteer to check the box to see if it contains a drink. Next, suggest a situation that reflects a want, such as: "I want to write in my journal. Did anyone pack a pencil?"

**If time is short,** have children suggest things they would pack for a trip. Ask the questions suggested above.

## Read Aloud

## What Do I Need?

### by Michael Brown

What do I need? Only these three:

Food to eat that's good for me.

Clothes to keep my body warm.

A home to keep me safe from harm.

That's all? you ask. Nothing more?

Just your love—and that makes four.

# Lesson 2 Needs and Wants

## Objectives

- Describe ways that families meet basic human needs.
- Distinguish between wants and needs.
- Explain how people fulfill needs and wants.

## Vocabulary

**needs** things we must have to live (p. 100)

**wants** things we would like to have (p. 101)

### QUICK Teaching Plan

*If time is short,* guide children in making a two-column list of needs and wants.

## 1 Introduce and Motivate

**Preview** Display the Vocabulary Cards **needs** and **wants**. Ask children what they think each word means. Then share the meaning of each word.

**Warm Up** To activate prior knowledge, ask children which they need: food or toys. Ask children to guess the things inside Ben's box. Ask them to group, or categorize, what they think is in Ben's box as a need or a want.

## 2 Teach and Discuss

#### Page 100

Point out that Ben is continuing to tell his story.

**1 What are some similarities in the ways families might meet their needs?** Possible answers: Many parents cook, provide a home, work to earn money to buy things that meet needs, and so on. **Draw Conclusions**

---

# Lesson 2 Needs and Wants

My family gives me many things I need. **Needs** are the things we must have to live. The pictures show some needs people have.

We need food and water to help us stay well and grow.

We need clothes to keep us warm.

We need a place to live.

**100**

## Practice and Extend

### READING SKILL
### Compare and Contrast

Tell children that this lesson talks about two kinds of things that are important to people. Ask children to read pp. 100–101. Then have them fold a piece of paper in half. Ask them to write the word *Needs* at the top of one half and the word *Wants* at the top of the other half. Tell them to draw or write about things people need to live and things people want under the correct headings.

### WEB SITE
### Technology

You can look up vocabulary words online. Click on *Social Studies Library* and select the dictionary at **www.sfsocialstudies.com.**

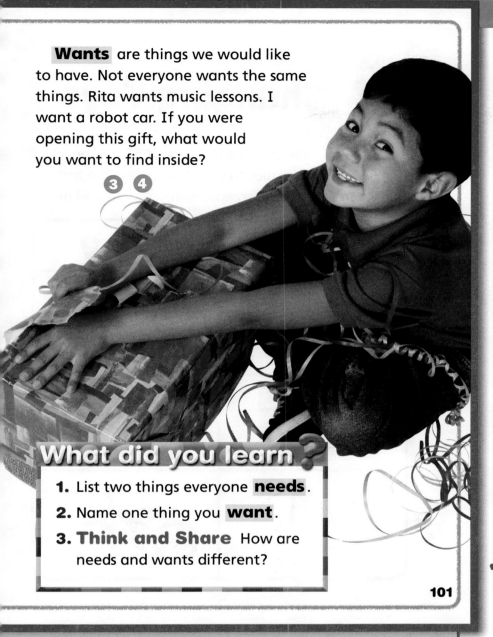

**Wants** are things we would like to have. Not everyone wants the same things. Rita wants music lessons. I want a robot car. If you were opening this gift, what would you want to find inside?

**3** **4**

## What did you learn ?

1. List two things everyone **needs**.

2. Name one thing you **want**.

3. **Think and Share** How are needs and wants different?

**101**

**Workbook, p. 27**

**Needs and Wants**

Circle things you need to stay alive.

Draw something you want. **Drawings will vary.**

Directions: Top: Circle the pictures of things you need in order to live. Bottom: Draw a picture of something you want rather than need.

Home Activity: During a shopping trip, help your child distinguish between needs and wants.

**Also on Teacher Resources CD-ROM.**

**2** **What are some differences in the ways families might meet their needs?** Possible answers: cooking different foods; living in different kinds of homes; growing foods that others might buy
**Make Inferences**

**Page 101**

**3** **What do you think Ben's gift is?** It may be the robot car Ben wants. **Draw Conclusions**

**4** **What are some ways people get the things they need and want?** Answers might indicate that parents or guardians usually provide for the needs and many of the wants children have or that people work to earn money to buy goods and services. **Make Inferences**

## 3 Close and Assess

Begin a two-column chart of needs and wants. Ask children to suggest items to place in each column. Then have each child tell a partner about one need and one want.

## ✓ What did you learn ?

1. Answers should include two of the following: clothes, food, water, a place to live.

2. Children may suggest such things as toys, participation in activities, books, games, and pets.

3. **Think and Share** Needs are the same for everyone. Needs are things you must have in order to stay alive. Wants are not the same for everyone. Wants are things a person would like to have but can live without.

**Then and Now**
Living History

# Changing Toys

## Objectives

- Distinguish among past, present, and future.
- Compare and contrast toys from the past and today.

## 1 Introduce and Motivate

**Preview** Ask children for different meanings of the word *change*. Explain that on pp. 102–103, *change* means that things do not stay the same. Have volunteers name some toys they play with and discuss whether they think toys have always been the same.

**Warm Up** To activate prior knowledge, review the difference between wants and needs with children, making sure they recognize toys as "wants." Also, have children brainstorm words people use when they talk about the past (*yesterday, last week,* etc.) and the present (*now, today,* etc.).

## 2 Teach and Discuss

### Page 102

Review the parts of a chart by having volunteers identify the two columns and their headings.

**Test Talk**

### Locate Key Words in the Text

**1 What does the chart show?** Have children point to the words at the top of the chart on p. 102. Explain that the words *Then* and *Now* are key words that will help them answer the question. Elicit that the chart shows toys *Then* and *Now*.
**Main Idea and Details**

---

**Then and Now**
Living History

# Changing Toys

Ben wants a robot car. Children have always played with toys. These are toys that children have wanted then and now.

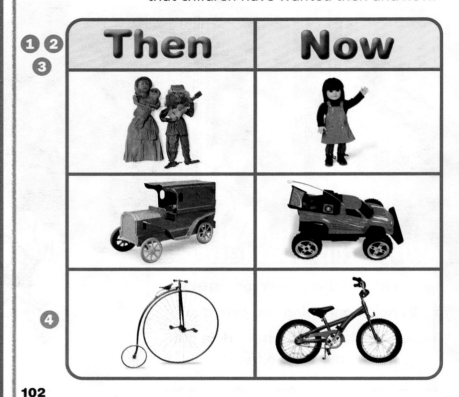

| **Then** | **Now** |
|----------|---------|

102

# Practice and Extend

**FYI** SOCIAL STUDIES **Background**

### About Toys in History

- Until the middle 1880s, most toys were made by families at home. Native American and colonial toys were usually made from local resources.
- Large-scale manufacturing of toys dates from after the Civil War. Toys made in Europe dominated the American market until World War I.
- One of the most popular toys of all time is the teddy bear, which was named for Theodore (Teddy) Roosevelt. The first one was made in 1903.
- Today the federal government regulates the safety of toys.

Where on the chart would you put these toys?

**5** **6**

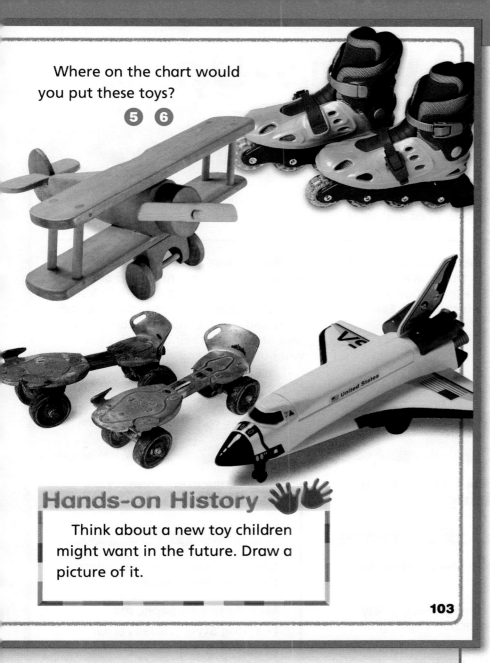

**Hands-on History** 👐

Think about a new toy children might want in the future. Draw a picture of it.

103

---

**CURRICULUM CONNECTION**
**Writing**

**Naming Toys**

- List the names of the class's favorite toys on the board.
- Ask each child to choose one toy and to rename it based on what it does or how it works.
- Have children write one or two sentences explaining why they chose the new name.

---

**2** **Which word on the chart tells that you are looking at toys from long ago?** *Then* Analyze Information

**3** **What word on the chart means the same as *today*?** *Now* Analyze Pictures

**4** **In what ways are the bicycles from THEN and NOW alike?** Possible answers: Both have pedals, two wheels, a seat, and handlebars. **Compare and Contrast**

**Page 103**

Have volunteers identify the toys on this page and explain how they are alike and different. Then have children tell where on the chart each belongs.

**5** **Why do toys and other things change?** Answers should reflect understanding of changing wants and technologies. **Draw Conclusions**

**6** **How do people learn about changes in toys?** Possible answers: Television and print advertisements, word of mouth, and so on **Make Inferences**

**3 Close and Assess**

**Hands-on History** 👐

Have the class brainstorm possible future toys before they make their drawings. Make a bulletin board labeled "Toys of the Future" with their drawings.

# Lesson ② Wrap-Up

## MEETING INDIVIDUAL NEEDS
## Leveled Practice

### Find Pictures of Needs and Wants
Have children cut out magazine pictures that show things they need and want.

**Easy** Have children sort the magazine pictures into two groups: one for needs and another for wants. This can be done by having children put the pictures into boxes—one labeled *needs*, and the other labeled *wants*. **Reteach**

**On-Level** Ask each child to choose a picture, identify the item as a need or a want, and then explain how it is—or is not—necessary for survival. **Extend**

**Challenge** Have each child select one picture that shows a need and one picture that shows a want. Write a story about a character who has the selected need and want. Children's stories should say how their characters get what they need and want. **Enrich**

## Hands-on Activities

### CURRICULUM CONNECTION
### Writing/Vocabulary

## Give Thanks

**Objective** Demonstrate an understanding of the words *needs* and *wants*.

**Resources** Vocabulary Cards: **needs, wants**

**Materials** crayons or markers, construction paper

**Learning Style** Visual/Verbal

**Individual** 👤

🕐 **Time** 20–25 minutes

*Dear Mom,*

*Thanks for giving me a great home!*

*I need that!*

*Love,*
*Joey*

1. Write the following sentence frames on the board:

Thanks for giving me ___.
I needed that!

Thanks for giving me___.
I wanted one!

2. Have children complete the sentence frames to make thank-you cards for people who gave them things.

3. Remind children to add their new words to the Word Book.

### CURRICULUM CONNECTION
### Writing

## Book of Homes

**Objective** Describe different kinds of homes.

**Materials** old magazines, safety scissors, construction paper, glue

**Learning Style** Visual/Verbal/Kinesthetic

**Individual** 👤

🕐 **Time** 20–30 minutes

1. Ask children to find and cut out pictures that show different kinds of homes people live in.

2. Have children glue their pictures onto construction paper.

3. Ask children to write or dictate sentences that describe the homes.

4. Bind the pages together to make a book.

### CURRICULUM CONNECTION
### Math

## A Wish List

**Objective** Compare and contrast things people want.

**Materials** chart paper, marker

**Learning Style** Visual/Verbal

**Group** 👥👥

🕐 **Time** 15–20 minutes

1. Have each child make a list to show three things he or she would like to have. (You may want to help children think of non-material wants, such as more play time.)

2. As a group, compare and contrast the items on the lists.

3. If time permits, make a graph to show the results. Have children use the graph to rank items as chosen most often, chosen least often, and so on.

*bike*
*wagon*
*soccer ball*
*play time*

# Lesson ③ Overview

| **Spending and Saving**<br>pages 104–105 | Children will learn how money is used to buy things people need or want. They will also learn the importance of saving money for future use. |  Time 20 minutes<br>**Resources**<br>• Workbook, p. 28<br>• Every Student Learns Guide, pp. 46–49 |
| --- | --- | --- |
| **Money Around the World**<br>pages 106–107 | Children will use a map to learn about coins from around the world. | Time 15–20 minutes |

# Build Background

## What Will You Buy?

 **Time** 15–20 minutes

Tell children that before there was money, people used to trade things. They would trade something they already had for something they didn't have.

Set up a "trading post" or "swap shop" where children can pretend to exchange something they have for something they want or need. Be sure children's names are on the items so they can be returned to their owners at the end of the activity.

**If time is short,** have children dictate a short list of things they might like to buy for the classroom. Then, for each item, ask what other item they would trade in exchange for the desired item.

*Trading Post*

## The Rainy Day

### by Andrea Johnston

A nickel from Mom,
A quarter from Dad.
Two dimes from Gramps,
That's all that he had.

I've got fifty cents.
I've counted it twice.
I can go shopping
For something nice.

Or I could save up
For a rainy day.
But look! It's raining!
Hip-hip-hooray!

# Lesson 3 Spending and Saving

## Objectives

- Identify examples of people wanting more than they can have.

- Explain why wanting more than they can have requires that people make choices.

- Identify examples of choices families make when buying goods and services.

### QUICK Teaching Plan

**If time is short,** ask which of the pictures on p. 104 show things that cost 70 cents or less.

## 1 Introduce and Motivate

**Preview** Have children point to each item shown in the pictures and name the price.

**Warm Up** To activate prior knowledge, have children pass real coins around and tell what they would do with the money, if it was theirs to spend.

## 2 Teach and Discuss

### Page 104

Remind children that on pp. 92–93, they read about Ben's lemonade stand.

**1 Which things shown on p. 104 can Ben buy with 70 cents or less?** Pen, apple
**Draw Conclusions**

**2 What is an example of a person wanting more than he or she can have?** Possible answers: A person wanted a book but did not have enough money; a family wanted to go to the movies and dinner but had only enough money to do one thing. **Make Inferences**

## Lesson 3 Spending and Saving

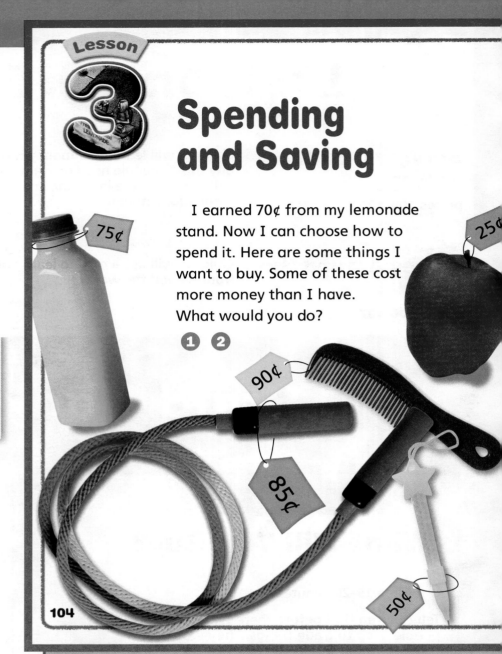

I earned 70¢ from my lemonade stand. Now I can choose how to spend it. Here are some things I want to buy. Some of these cost more money than I have. What would you do?

1 2

75¢    25¢    90¢    85¢    50¢

104

## Practice and Extend

### READING SKILL
### Categorize

**Sorting Things**

- Ask children to describe the objects pictured on p. 104. Encourage children to tell about price, shape, texture, and how each item is used. Have children point to the juice. Ask if there is another food item. (apple)

- Ask children to sort the items by price. Which things have a price of 50¢ or less? (pen, apple) Which things have a price of more than 50¢? (jump rope, juice, comb)

- Have children think of other ways to sort the objects, such as by color. Then have them name their groups.

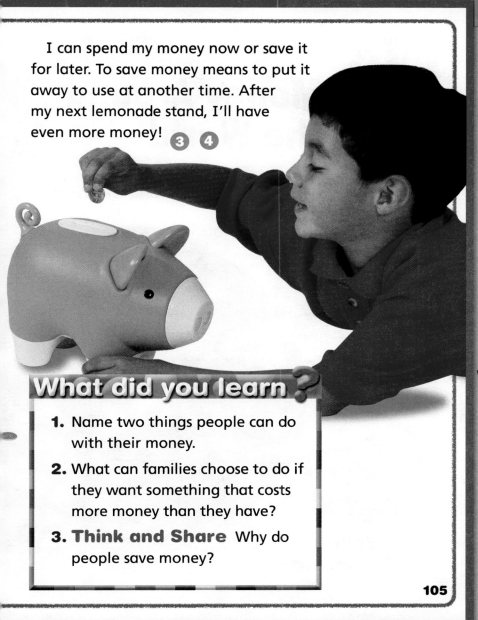

I can spend my money now or save it for later. To save money means to put it away to use at another time. After my next lemonade stand, I'll have even more money! ③ ④

## What did you learn

1. Name two things people can do with their money.

2. What can families choose to do if they want something that costs more money than they have?

3. **Think and Share** Why do people save money?

105

**ESL BUILD BACKGROUND ESL Support**

**Using Coins** Display samples of U.S. coins, such as pennies, nickels, dimes, and quarters.

**Beginning** Help children point to the coins as you name them. Say: *This is a penny*, and so on.

**Intermediate** Have children name the coins and state how much each coin is worth.

**Advanced** Have children dramatize using coins to buy something. Children can talk about their exchanges.

*For additional ESL Support, use Every Student Learns Guide, pp. 46–49.*

### Workbook, p. 28

**Spending and Saving**

Also on Teacher Resources CD-ROM.

---

Explain that cost is something a person gives up when they decide to do something. In this case, paying the money to buy something the person needs or wants. A benefit satisfies a want. The benefit for buying something is that it now belongs to us. Point out to children that most people cannot have everything they want. Lead a discussion about the need for people to make choices.

③ **What are some examples of choices families make when buying things?** Possible answers: Choosing different kinds and price ranges of foods and other products Analyze Information

**✓ Ongoing Assessment**

| **If...** children have difficulty thinking of examples of choices, | **then...** have them dramatize going to a market. Display items that could be purchased. |

### Decision making

④ **What would you do if you were Ben and you wanted to buy the comb?** Possible answers: Save the 70 cents and wait until I earn 20 cents more; buy something that costs less now and wait until I have 90 cents before I buy the comb. **Make Decisions**

## 3 Close and Assess

Have children tell what they would buy or how they would save if they were in Ben's place.

### ✓ What did you learn

1. People can save or spend their money.

2. Families can choose to save their money until they have enough to buy the item, or they can choose to buy something else that costs less.

3. **Think and Share** People save money so they can buy things they need or want at a later time.

## HERE AND THERE
Our World

# Money Around the World

## Objective
• Obtain information about a topic using visual sources, such as pictures and maps.

# 1 Introduce and Motivate

**Preview** Ask if children have ever seen coins or paper money from another country. If you have any foreign coins, share them with children.

**Warm Up** To activate prior knowledge, hold up a penny and ask what it is worth. (one cent) Pass a few pennies around so children can examine them. Challenge children to find the words *United States of America* on the pennies. Then have children name other coins used in the United States. Point out that we use both coins and paper bills as money.

# 2 Teach and Discuss

### Pages 106–107

Help children identify the continents shown on the world map. Then name the coins pictured on pp. 106–107: dollar, boliviano, zloty, yen, dollar, pound. As you name each one, have children use their fingers to follow the dashed leader line to the country from which the coin comes.

**1** **What do these pages show?** Different kinds of money used around the world
**Main Idea and Details**

**2** **In what country do people use bolivianos as money?** Bolivia **Analyze Pictures**

**3** **Where is Bolivia? How do you know?** It's in South America; the dashed line goes from the words *Bolivia/Boliviano* to *South America*.
**Analyze Pictures**

## HERE AND THERE
Our World

# Money Around the World

People all over the world spend and save money.

**1** **2** **3**

**United States Dollar**

**Bolivia Boliviano**

NORTH AMERICA

ATLANTIC OCEAN

PACIFIC OCEAN

SOUTH AMERICA

106

# Practice and Extend

## FYI  SOCIAL STUDIES  Background

### About Money

• Before there was a system of money, people used the barter system to trade by exchanging one kind of goods for other goods. In some places, people still barter.

• In the past, people used beads, salt, shells, and stones as money. They also used metals such as copper, gold, and silver.

• Paper money was first used in China.

• One place people can save money is in a bank. When money is put into a bank account is is called a "deposit." When money is taken out of the account it is called a "withdrawal."

Poland
**Zloty**

Japan
**Yen** ④

⑤

Australia
**Dollar**

Egypt
**Pound**

EUROPE
ASIA
AFRICA
INDIAN OCEAN
AUSTRALIA
ANTARCTICA
CTIC OCEAN

For more information, go online to the *Atlas* at **www.sfsocialstudies.com.**

107

④ **If you were traveling in Japan, what money might you use?** Yen **Analyze Pictures**

Ⓒ **SOCIAL STUDIES STRAND**
**Culture**

In the past, many cultures in Africa and the Pacific used shells as money. Some Native American cultures used pieces of shell rubbed smooth and strung together like beads. Other cultures have used nails and sheep as money. Show children objects or pictures of objects that have been used as money in other cultures. Children can dramatize paying for a book with one of the objects presented.

**Test Talk**

**Use Information from the Text**

⑤ **Which two countries use dollars?** Have students jot their answers on a slip of paper. Reread the question and have children check to be sure they have written the words *United States* and *Australia*. **Compare and Contrast**

## ③ Close and Assess

Ⓖ **SOCIAL STUDIES STRAND**
**Geography**

Have children plan a trip around the world. Have them tell where they would go and what kind of money they would need. Remind them to refer to the coins and bills and the places pictured on the map on pp. 106–107.

# Lesson ③ Wrap-Up

## MEETING INDIVIDUAL NEEDS
## Leveled Practice

### Using Pictures to Shop for Food
Have children cut out newspaper pictures and prices of grocery items.

**Easy** Have children sort through the grocery pictures. Have children choose the items they would need to buy. **Reteach**

**On-Level** Make a classroom poster with the food pictures and use these prices: 55¢, 50¢, 40¢, 33¢, and 20¢. Designate children to be "shoppers." They choose cards that tell how much money they can spend. Each shopper then decides which items he or she can afford to buy. **Extend**

**Challenge** Have children work with partners. One partner chooses two items from the poster. He or she "purchases" one of the items, then tells the partner which coins were used to make the purchase. The partner must guess which item was chosen, based on the coin combination. **Enrich**

## Hands-on Activities

 **SOCIAL STUDIES STRAND**
**Economics**

## Choosing One of Three

**Objective** Give reasons for making choices.

**Materials** mail-order catalogs, scissors

**Learning Style** Visual/Verbal/Kinesthetic

**Group** 👦👦👦👦
🕐 **Time** 15–20 minutes

1. Have each child cut out three items that he or she would like to have (want).

2. Tell children that they must now eliminate two of the three items they have chosen.

3. Have each child display his/her final choice and give a reason for its selection.

 **SOCIAL STUDIES STRAND**
**Economics**

## Piggy-Bank Fun

**Objective** Make a plan for saving money.

**Materials** disposable cups (with lids), tape, colored markers and other arts/crafts materials

**Learning Style** Kinesthetic

**Individual** 👦
🕐 **Time** 25–30 minutes

1. Give each child a cup, into which you've cut a slot, and a lid.

2. Have children tape down the lids and then decorate the cups. They might create animal shapes, using construction paper, pipe cleaners, and so on.

3. Ask each child to formulate a plan for saving, such as putting away a penny each week.

4. Have children take their banks home so they can put their plans into practice.

 **CURRICULUM CONNECTION**
**Math**

## From Most to Least

**Objective** Collect data to solve a problem.

**Materials** mail-order catalogs, scissors, glue, play money

**Learning Style** Verbal/Visual

**Partner** 👦👦
🕐 **Time** 15–20 minutes

1. Have partners choose and cut out several pictures of things they might wish for. Tell children to be sure to include the price of each.

2. Have children arrange and glue down the items in order, from most to least expensive.

3. Give pairs play money (including paper bills). Have children buy items from each other with play money.

# Lesson 4 Overview

| Welcome to Job Day!<br>pages 108–111 | Children will learn about a variety of jobs in which people provide goods and services. They will explore volunteerism and the importance of all jobs. |  Time 20 minutes<br>Resources<br>• Workbook, p. 29<br>• Vocabulary Cards tools goods service volunteer<br>• Every Student Learns Guide, pp. 50–53 |
| --- | --- | --- |
| Kid's Kitchen<br>pages 112–113 | Children will learn about volunteer work performed by children. | Time 15–20 minutes |
| Meet Clara Barton<br>pages 114–115 | Children will identify the contributions of Clara Barton, a person who exemplified good citizenship. They will use a map to locate Barton's birthplace. | Time 15–20 minutes |

# Build Background

## Activity

### Guess My Job

 Time 10–15 minutes

Ask a volunteer to think of a job he or she might like to have as an adult. Have other children ask questions that will help them guess what the job is.

If time is short, show several pictures of people at work. Have children tell what kind of job is shown in each picture.

## Read Aloud

### When I Grow Up

by Jennifer Cline

When I grow up, I'd like to be
A sailor who goes out to sea.
Or maybe I won't choose to roam.
I'll raise a family, stay at home.

When I grow up, I could teach,
Or be a lifeguard at the beach.
Or drive a truck or moving van,
Or play my trumpet in a band.

When I grow up, I'd be thrilled
Houses, bridges, and towns to build!
There are so many jobs to do.
What's the very best job for you?

# Lesson 4
# Welcome to Job Day!

## Objectives

- Identify examples of goods and services in the home, school, and community.

- Describe the requirements of various jobs and the characteristics of a job well-performed.

- Describe how specialized jobs contribute to the production of goods and services.

## Vocabulary

**tools** things people use to help them do work (p. 108)

**goods** things that are grown or made (p. 108)

**service** a job people do to help others (p. 109)

**volunteer** a person who works for free (p. 110)

## QUICK Teaching Plan

*If time is short,* have children look at the pictures and brainstorm a list of jobs.

- Ask children what goods or services the jobs might provide.

## 1 Introduce and Motivate

**Preview** Display the Vocabulary Card **tools, goods, service,** and **volunteer**. Ask children what they think each word means. Share the meaning of each word and use it in a sentence for children. Point out that goods satisfy people's needs and wants.

**Warm Up** To activate prior knowledge, ask children to name some jobs they might like to do when they grow up. Then ask children to suppose that they have accompanied one of the workers pictured in the lesson to his or her job. Ask volunteers to tell about their day at work.

## Lesson 4
## Welcome to Job Day!

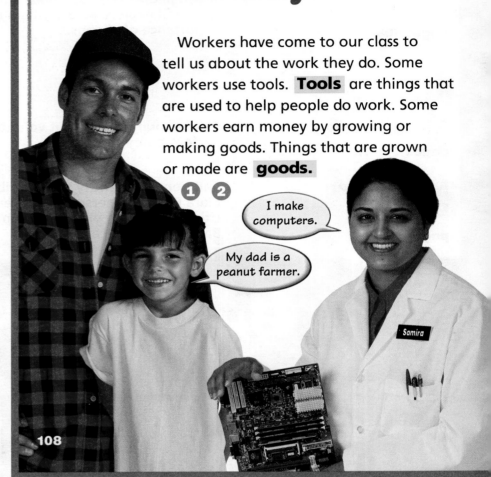

Workers have come to our class to tell us about the work they do. Some workers use tools. **Tools** are things that are used to help people do work. Some workers earn money by growing or making goods. Things that are grown or made are **goods.**

**1** **2**

> I make computers.

> My dad is a peanut farmer.

Samira

108

# Practice and Extend

## READING SKILL
## Main Idea and Details

### All About Job Day

- Have children read Lesson 4. Then have them draw pictures or write sentences that tell what Job Day is all about.

- Invite volunteers to share their drawings and sentences with the class.

## WEB SITE
## Technology

You can look up vocabulary words by going online. Click on *Social Studies Library* and select the dictionary at **www.sfsocialstudies.com.**

Some workers earn money by having service jobs. A **service** is a job people do to help others. It helps people meet their wants and needs. Do you know someone who has a service job? What does the person do?

My dad is a plumber. He fixes broken pipes.

I help children learn. I am a teacher.

109

**SOCIAL STUDIES**
**Background**

**About Different Kinds of Jobs/Labor Day**

- According to the U.S. Census Bureau, the majority of jobs in the United States are in manufacturing and retail. Other major job categories are health services, educational services, and financial services.

- One hundred years ago, most U.S. workers were farmers. Today, farming is near the bottom of the list, followed only by public utilities, entertainment, miscellaneous personal services, and mining.

- Americans honor all working people on Labor Day. Labor Day is observed the first Monday in September. The first Labor Day parade was held in 1882 in New York City. Labor Day became a holiday in 1894. Labor Day is also observed in Canada and certain other countries.

# 2 Teach and Discuss

Page 108

Have children identify the workers pictured on pp. 108–109. Read aloud the words in the speech balloons.

**1 What goods do the workers on this page provide?** The peanut farmer grows peanuts. The woman in the white coat makes computers. **Interpret Pictures**

**2 What are some examples of goods you use in your home? your school? your community?** Answers will vary but may include for home: appliances, clothes; for school: books, pens, computer; for community: playground equipment, water fountain. **Apply Information**

Page 109

**3 How might the plumber and the teacher know they have done a good job?** The pipes would no longer be broken and leak. Children in the teacher's class would learn many things. **Draw Conclusions**

**4 What are other examples of services you might use in your home? your school? your community?** Answers will vary but may include for home: painter, carpenter; for school: principal, cafeteria worker, teacher aide; for community: doctor, check-out clerk, or any other service job. **Apply Information**

**5 Was the lemonade Ben sold at his lemonade stand a good or a service? How do you know?** A good, because he made it. **Apply Information**

Lesson 4 continued

Discuss what the adults shown on the page do to help other people. Point out that some volunteers have paid jobs in addition to the work they do for free. They do volunteer work in their spare time.

**6** **How do these workers help others meet their needs?** They volunteer in a place that provides food, clothing, and shelter.
**Interpret Pictures**

**7** **Are there any volunteers in your school? What do they do?** Answers will vary but may include parents, older siblings, guardians and community members who help in the classroom, on the playground, on class trips, and so on.
**Apply Information**

Help children identify the workers doing specialized jobs pictured on p. 111.

**8** **Which job pictured provides goods? Which jobs provide services?** The baker provides goods; the musician and doctor provide services.
**Use Picture Clues**

**Ongoing Assessment**

| **If...** children do not know if what a particular worker provides is a good or a service, | **then...** remind them that goods are what workers make or grow and services are what workers do to help others. |

**G** **SOCIAL STUDIES STRAND**
**Government**

Explain to children that the government also provides services to the community. The local, state, and federal governments employ service workers.

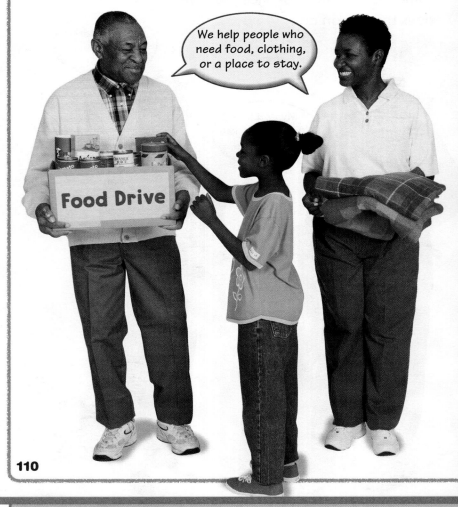

Some people do not earn money for their work. They are volunteers. A **volunteer** works for free. Volunteers help others.

We help people who need food, clothing, or a place to stay.

Food Drive

110

# Practice and Extend

**ESL** **ACCESS CONTENT**
**ESL Support**

**Using Pictures** Show children pictures of modern-day soup kitchens or other places people can go for help in the community.

**Beginning** Ask children to point to the pictures as they repeat the names of jobs of the workers pictured on pp. 108–111. Then show other job pictures and help children brainstorm a list of other jobs.

**Intermediate** Have children follow along as you read the sentences in speech balloons on pp. 108–110. Then have children name the workers pictured on p. 111 and dictate sentences the workers might say.

**Advanced** After children identify the workers pictured in the book, they can find pictures of other workers and use them to talk about the jobs these people do and the goods or services they provide.

*For additional ESL support, use Every Student Learns Guide, pp. 50–53.*

There are many kinds of jobs. Which would you choose? All kinds of work are important! How do all these workers help us?

## What did you learn

1. What are some **services** that help us?

2. How do **volunteers** help people?

3. **Think and Share** Name three **goods** you use every day. How do you use them?

## Close and Assess

Have children draw and write to show the kinds of jobs they would like to have as adults. Then have them tell partners about those jobs. Partners can make a list of the jobs. Ask children to tell whether the jobs involve providing goods or services. Help children see how some jobs, which may be specialized, contribute to the production of goods or services.

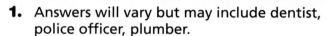

## ✓ What did you learn

1. Answers will vary but may include dentist, police officer, plumber.

2. Volunteers help people by doing things for them for free.

3. **Think and Share** Answers will vary but may include such things as books, pencils, hairbrushes, dishes, foods, and so on. Children should tell how each item is used.

**SOCIAL STUDIES STRAND**
**Economics**

Explain to children that people often advertise goods and services through different forms of communication—in the newspaper, on the radio, and on television.

**CURRICULUM CONNECTION**
**Literature**

**Read a Story**

- Read aloud *The Dream Jar* by Bonnie Pryor (Morrow, ISBN 0-688-13062-3, 1996). In this story, which is set in New York City in the early 1900s, each family member works hard to contribute to the family's dream of owning a store.

- After reading, talk about the job each family member did— and how well he or she did it.

- Guide children in comparing and contrasting the jobs people did long ago with those that people do today.

**Workbook, p. 29**

**Welcome to Job Day!**

Circle people who have service jobs.

Draw a job you might like to have. **Drawings will vary.**

**Also on Teacher Resources CD-ROM.**

# CITIZEN HEROES

## Kid's Kitchen

### Objectives

- Understand characteristics of good citizenship as exemplified by ordinary people.

- Identify characteristics of good citizenship, such as responsibility for the common good.

- Understand that people can both give and receive care.

## 1 Introduce and Motivate

**Preview** Encourage children to recall the definition of *volunteer* that they read in the previous lesson. Have them suggest some things they think volunteers could do.

**Warm Up** To activate prior knowledge, ask children what the word *caring* means to them. Help children to understand that caring may include concern, or interest in others, liking or loving another, or providing for or helping another.

Introduce the featured child, Sagen. Tell children that they will learn reasons why Sagen is a citizen hero.

## 2 Teach and Discuss

Read p. 112, including the caption for the map. You may wish to add to children's geography awareness by having them locate Georgia on your classroom map.

**1 Who does Kid's Kitchen help?** Families in need of food **Analyze Information**

---

# CITIZEN HEROES

Kid's Kitchen is in Warner Robins, Georgia.

## Kid's Kitchen

When Sagen was in second grade, she saw something interesting on TV. It was about helping her community. She decided to be a volunteer.

**1** Sagen started a group called Kid's Kitchen. The group gives lunch to families in need. It is open one day a week.

Sagen

112

## Practice and Extend

**FYI** SOCIAL STUDIES **Background**

### About Kid's Kitchen

- With help from the director of a local soup kitchen, Sagen planned menus and solicited money and donations of food for Kid's Kitchen.

- Kid's Kitchen is open every Wednesday during the summer. It is run completely by 8- to 12-year-olds.

- Sagen received the Spirit of Community Award for 2000. She also was commended by the Georgia Senate for her work as a Georgia Youth Volunteer.

BUILDING
CITIZENSHIP
Caring

Respect
Responsibility
Fairness
Honesty
Courage

Many children volunteer. They make hundreds of sandwiches each week. Some people take home leftovers for dinner. ❷ ❸

"When I tell someone about Kid's ❹ Kitchen, I hope it will inspire them to do something in their town," says Sagen.

★ **Caring in Action** ★

What can you do to show you care for someone?

❷ **Why might a volunteer be considered a good citizen?** Possible answer: He or she helps people for free. **Draw Conclusions**

🧩 **Problem Solving**

❸ **What should the children working at Kid's Kitchen do if they need to make more sandwiches in a week than they usually do?** Possible answers: Find more volunteers to work; get more ingredients for sandwiches **Solve Problems**

❹ **What has Sagen done that is a good example of caring?** Answers may include that she started Kid's Kitchen and that the group helps people by making lunch for them. **Main Idea and Details**

★ **SOCIAL STUDIES STRAND Citizenship**

**Prejudice Reduction** Point out that Sagen showed that she is a caring citizen by starting a group that gives food to families in need. Ask children to say names of people they know who are caring citizens and how those citizens show they care about others. Answers may include a parent or a school worker.

# ③ Close and Assess

★ **Caring in Action** ★

Read the question and have children discuss possible answers. Responses may include giving a family member a hug or kiss, helping another person in some way, making a card for someone, saying a kind word to another, and so on.

**CURRICULUM CONNECTION Drama**

**Perform a Skit**

- Work with pairs or small groups of children to create and perform short skits showing examples of caring.
- Suggest that some children pantomime their actions while others share their examples orally.
- For both kinds of skits, have children pay close attention to facial expressions and body language.

# Clara Barton

**Biography**

## Objectives

- Identify contributions of historical figures who have influenced the nation.

- Identify historic figures such as Clara Barton who have exemplified good citizenship.

## 1 Introduce and Motivate

**Preview** Begin a word web with *volunteer* in the center circle. Remind children that a volunteer helps other people but does not get paid.

**Warm Up** To activate prior knowledge, ask children to suggest some things they can do to help other people. Record their suggestions on the word web.

Have children look at the pictures on pp. 114–115. Identify the woman as Clara Barton, and ask children what they think she is doing. Point out the red cross on page 115. Ask children if they have ever seen this symbol before, and if so, where.

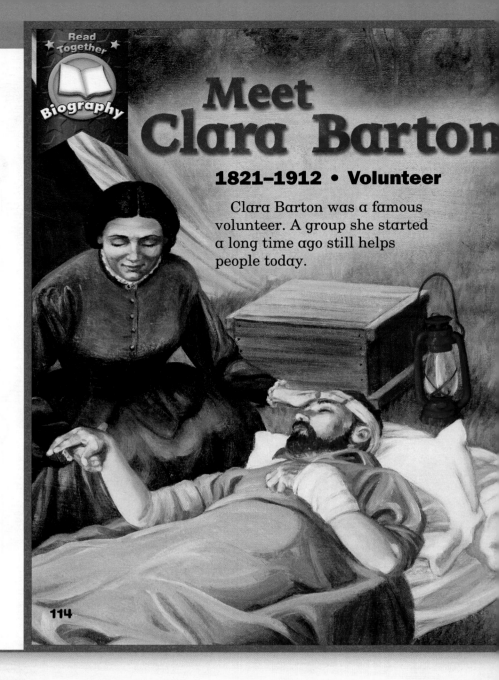

**Biography**

# Meet Clara Barton

### 1821–1912 • Volunteer

Clara Barton was a famous volunteer. A group she started a long time ago still helps people today.

114

# Practice and Extend

**SOCIAL STUDIES**
## Background

### About Clara Barton

- Although most famous for founding the American Red Cross, Clara Barton was also a teacher, a patent office clerk, a nurse, a writer, and a lecturer.

- During the Civil War, Barton became known as the "Angel of the Battlefield." Although not a trained nurse, she carried supplies to and nursed the wounded. After the war, she helped search for missing soldiers.

- In 1869, Barton went to Switzerland, where she learned of the International Committee of the Red Cross. After returning to the United States, she tried to interest others in the work of the Red Cross. Her work led to the establishment of the American branch in 1881.

**WEB SITE**
## Technology

You may help children find out more about Clara Barton by clicking on *Meet the People* at **www.sfsocialstudies.com**.

Clara Barton worked hard to help people. When she was just a girl, she helped take care of her brother. He was sick for about two years!

Clara Barton was born in Oxford, Massachusetts.

During the Civil War, Clara Barton was a volunteer. She helped soldiers who were hurt. She handed out bandages and medicine. Her work saved many lives. **2**

After the war, Clara Barton wanted to keep on helping people. She started the American Red Cross. Today the Red Cross gives food, clothing, and shelter to people who need help all over the world. **3** **4**

American Red Cross

Clara Barton made a red cross from a ribbon she wore.

### Think and Share

Tell two ways Clara Barton helped people.

For more information, go online to *Meet the People* at **www.sfsocialstudies.com**.

115

## CURRICULUM CONNECTION
## Writing

**Helping Someone**

Ask children to listen to this story:

**In 1884, there was a terrible flood. The waters of the Mississippi and Ohio Rivers poured out over the land. Many people lost their homes. Clara Barton wanted to help these people, and so did six children from Pennsylvania.**

**The children decided to put on a play. They charged admission—and earned $50.00! They sent this money to Clara Barton to help a homeless family. Here's what the children wrote in a letter to Clara Barton: "Sometime again when you want money for your good work, call on—the Little Six."**

Ask children to draw a picture of something they could do to help someone. Then have children dictate or write a sentence telling about their picture.

## 2 Teach and Discuss

Read the biography together. Tell children that the Civil War was fought in the United States and that the two sides were the North and the South.

**1 How did Clara Barton learn to help people?** When she was a girl, she took care of her sick brother for about two years. **Cause and Effect**

**2 Clara Barton helped soldiers who were on different sides during the Civil War. What kind of a citizen do you think she was?** She was kind and caring. The side of the war the soldiers were on didn't matter to her. **Draw Conclusions**

**3 What made Clara Barton a famous volunteer?** She started the group called the American Red Cross. The American Red Cross still helps people today. **Main Idea and Details**

**4 When might people need the help of the Red Cross?** When bad weather or war causes people to need food, clothing, or shelter **Make Inferences**

## 3 Close and Assess

### Think and Share

She cared for her sick brother; she brought bandages and medicine to wounded Civil War soldiers; she helped save lives; she started the American Red Cross.

# Lesson ④ Wrap-Up

## MEETING INDIVIDUAL NEEDS
## Leveled Practice

**Make a Chart**

Guide children in making a jobs chart with the column headings *Goods* and *Services*.

**Easy** Have children look in magazines for pictures showing different jobs. Ask them to place the pictures into the goods column or the services column. **Reteach**

**On-Level** Have children brainstorm other workers who grow/make goods or provide services. Add these workers to the appropriate column in the chart. Ask volunteers to tell the duties of each job and how the workers would know if they did their job well. **Extend**

**Challenge** Have partners choose one worker from each column of the chart. Ask them to write or dictate brief descriptions of the workers' jobs. Encourage them to tell about job requirements including the amount of schooling and on-the-job training. **Enrich**

## Hands-on Activities

### CURRICULUM CONNECTION
### Reading/Vocabulary

## I Spy a Job

**Objective** Demonstrate an understanding of lesson vocabulary.

**Materials** Pupil Book, pp. 90–91

**Learning Style** Visual/Verbal

**Partners**

 **Time** 15–20 minutes

1. Have one partner give clues about a worker on pp. 90–91. If the worker is, for example, the paperboy, clues might be: *I spy someone with a service job. This person helps by delivering something.*

2. Children take turns spying workers. Encourage children to use lesson vocabulary.

3. Remind children to add the lesson vocabulary in their Word Book.

### CURRICULUM CONNECTION
### Writing

## Who's Working?

**Objective** Describe jobs and their requirements.

**Materials** paper, scissors, arts/crafts materials

**Learning Style** Visual/Verbal/Kinesthetic

**Partners**

 **Time** 20–30 minutes

1. Cut out paper-doll outlines of people. You might want to have children work with partners and trace around each other's bodies. Children can dress and/or decorate the paper dolls to correspond to the jobs people do. Encourage them to include any tools that the workers may use.

2. Have children dictate sentences telling what each worker does and what skills they think the worker might need. Children can write these sentences on their paper dolls.

### CURRICULUM CONNECTION
### Drama

## What's My Line?

**Objective** Identify certain jobs.

**Materials** old magazines, scissors, glue, index cards

**Learning Style** Visual/Kinesthetic

**Group**

**Time** 20–25 minutes

1. Ask children to find and cut out as many pictures of workers as they can find. Children should glue each picture onto an index card.

2. Ask the children to pantomime what the workers do. Others in the class try to guess the job.

# Lesson 5 Overview

| | | |
|---|---|---|
| **Interview with a Farmer**<br>pages 116–119 | Through an interview, children will learn about the work of a farmer. They will also discover how farm produce gets to the market. |  **Time** 20–30 minutes<br>**Resources**<br>• Workbook, p. 30<br>• Transparency 9<br>• Every Student Learns Guide, pp. 54–57 |
| **Follow a Route**<br>pages 120–121 | Children will learn how to follow a route on a map. | **Time** 20–35 minutes<br>**Resource**<br>• Workbook, p. 31 |
| **Meet George Washington Carver**<br>pages 122–123 | Children will identify the contributions of George Washington Carver, a historical figure who has influenced the nation. | **Time** 15 minutes |

# Build Background

## Activity

### What Foods Do You Like?

 **Time** 15–20 minutes

Ask each child to find and cut out a picture of a favorite food. As children display their foods, ask where they think the food came from—and how it got to them.

**If time is short,** ask children to name a food. Ask children where they think the food came from—and how it got to them.

## Read Aloud

### Oats, Peas, Beans, and Barley Grow

Oats, peas, beans, and barley grow;
Oats, peas, beans, and barley grow.
Can you or I or anyone know
How oats, peas, beans, and barley grow?

Thus the farmer sows his seed,
Stands erect, and takes his ease.
He stamps his foot and claps his hands
And turns around to view his lands.

## Lesson 5

# Interview with a Farmer

### Objectives

- Describe how specialized jobs contribute to the production of goods and services.
- Obtain information about a topic using a variety of oral sources, such as interviews.
- Identify the role of markets in the exchange of goods and services.
- ➲ Sequence information.

## QUICK Teaching Plan

**If time is short,** have children use the photos on pp. 117–118 to summarize the steps in growing and marketing peanuts.

- Have children make a graphic organizer summarizing the three steps shown for growing peanuts. Then have them do the same for marketing peanuts.

## 1 Introduce and Motivate

**Preview** Ask children to tell what they think a farmer does. Remind children that a farmer earns money from his or her job. A farmer can use the money to buy goods and services. Then ask children to suppose they were talking with a farmer. What questions would they ask to learn more about a farmer's job?

**Warm Up** To activate prior knowledge, ask children to think about the steps in their school day. Brainstorm three school activities. Then discuss with children how to put the activities in the order that they do them.

---

## Lesson 5

# Interview with a Farmer

| Mr. Ford | I grow peanuts. |
| Ben | I love peanuts! How do you grow them? |
| Mr. Ford | It takes a lot of work to grow peanuts. |

**116**

---

## Practice and Extend

### Target Skill

**READING/VOCABULARY**
## Put Things in Order

**Sequence** In this lesson, children will use words to understand the order in which things happen.

- After children read pp. 116–117, display Transparency 9. Help them complete it to show what Mr. Ford does first, next, and last.
- You may want to use the transparency again after reading p. 118.
- Ask for volunteers to tell what Mr. Ford does first, next, and last.

---

**Mr. Ford**

**First,** I plant the ② ③ peanuts. They start to grow.

**Next,** I take care of them as they grow. ④

**Last,** I pull them up. ⑤

117

**Page 116**

Remind children that Mr. Ford is a farmer they saw in Lesson 4. Point out that Lesson 5 is an interview, or a meeting of people to talk something over or ask questions. Ben is interviewing Mr. Ford about his job.

① **Look at the shell that Mr. Ford is holding. What is inside the shell?** The peanuts **Make Inferences**

② **A farmer needs to know many special things to do his or her job. What are some things farmers do to produce peanuts?** A farmer plants the peanuts, cares for them, then digs them up. **Make Inferences**

**Page 117**

③ **What is the first thing Mr. Ford does?** He plants the peanuts. **Sequence**

④ **What does he do next?** He takes care of them as they grow. **Sequence**

⑤ **What does Mr. Ford do last?** He pulls them up with his tractor. **Sequence**

($) **SOCIAL STUDIES STRAND Economics**

Explain that someone who makes or grows things or who provides a service is called a **producer**, and that some who buys and uses food, clothing, or anything grown or made by someone else is called a **consumer**. Ask students for examples of people who are producers. (Possible answers: farmer, carpenter, plumber, electrician, etc.)

**CURRICULUM CONNECTION Science**

**What a Plant Needs**

- Help children identify the things a plant needs in order to grow. (soil, water, sunlight)

- Have children investigate by placing one seedling in a sunny window and watering it regularly. Place another in a dark corner and withhold water. After a few days, compare the plants. Compare again after a week.

- Alternatively, have children make three drawings to show stages in a plant's growth from seedling to mature plant. Have children label their pictures with terms such as *roots, stem, leaves*.

**Lesson 5 continued**

Page 118

**6** **Are the peanuts roasted before or after they are taken to the factory?** After
⤶ Sequence

**Ongoing Assessment**

**If...** children do not understand that the peanuts are roasted after they are taken to the factory,

**then...** have children copy the sentences beginning with *First* and *Next* and number them *1* and *2*. Then have them reread the sentences.

**7** **What is the last thing that workers do with the peanuts?** They put them into bags and send them to stores. ⤶ Sequence

**8** **What do you think workers in stores do after they receive the peanuts?** Possible answers: They put the peanuts in bins where shoppers can see them; they put up a sign showing the price of the peanuts; they sell the peanuts to people who want to eat peanuts. **Make Inferences**

---

**Ben** How do peanuts get from the farm to me?

**Mr. Ford**

**First,** a truck takes the peanuts to the factory.

**Next,** they are dried, cleaned, and roasted.
**6**

**Last,** they are put into bags and sent to the stores. **7** **8**

118

---

# Practice and Extend

**ESL** ACCESS CONTENT
## ESL Support

**Using Graphic Organizers** Make drawings of the steps of growing peanuts and the steps of peanuts going to market. Cut out the drawings, and then mix them up.

**Beginning** Have children arrange the drawings of growing peanuts in the proper order to form a graphic organizer. Have children say *first, next,* and *last* as they point to the pictured steps.

**Intermediate** Have children put all six steps in order. Have children describe what is happening in each step.

**Advanced** Have children use a sequence graphic organizer to write the six steps. They can also make their own graphic organizer showing the steps in a process familiar to them, such as making a sandwich.

*For additional ESL support, use Every Student Learns Guide, pp. 54–57.*

CURRICULUM CONNECTION
## Drama

**Dramatize an Interview**

- Have children work in small groups to dramatize the interview with Mr. Ford. Two children can read aloud the lines of Ben and Mr. Ford.

- Others can act out through pantomime the steps in growing the peanuts and getting them to market to be sold.

- Encourage the readers to pause after each step so that those doing the pantomime can elaborate on the actions.

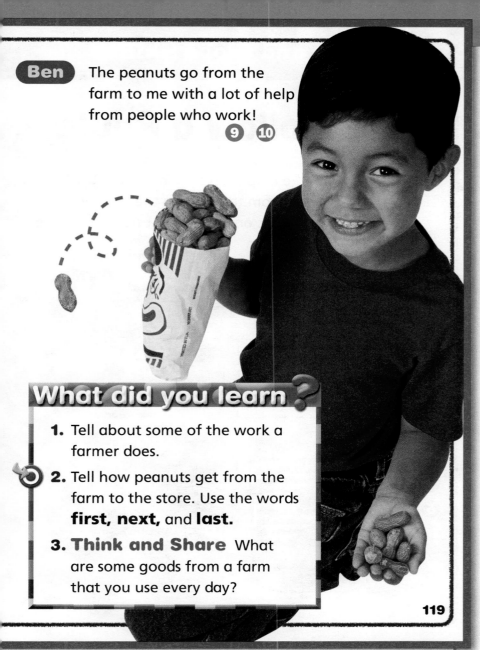

**Ben** The peanuts go from the farm to me with a lot of help from people who work! **9** **10**

## What did you learn

1. Tell about some of the work a farmer does.

2. Tell how peanuts get from the farm to the store. Use the words **first, next,** and **last.**

3. **Think and Share** What are some goods from a farm that you use every day?

119

## FAST FACTS

• The part of the peanut plant that we eat grows in a pod under the ground.

• The first peanut butter was made by South Americans 3,000 years ago, when they ground peanuts into a paste and mixed it with cocoa.

• The first peanut farmers in the United States grew peanuts only for feeding their turkeys, chickens, and pigs.

**Workbook, p. 30**

**Interview with a Farmer**

*Draw lines to match the pictures.*

**Also on Teacher Resources CD-ROM.**

Before reading p. 119, point out to children that the store pays the factory for the peanuts, and that the factory pays Mr. Ford. Ask children where they think Ben got the bag of peanuts he is holding in the photo on p. 119. Elicit that he probably bought them at a store or a food stand.

**9** **The peanuts you see here are still in their shells. How else can you buy peanuts?** Answers will vary, but may include jars or cans of peanuts without shells, as peanut butter, as peanut oil. **Main Idea and Details**

**10** **Which do you think is harder: growing peanuts or getting them to market?** Answers may vary but children should note that both processes probably take a lot of work. **Evaluate**

## 3 Close and Assess

Have children fold a sheet of drawing paper into thirds. On the front side of the paper, have children write a sentence in each section about the three steps in growing peanuts. On the back, have them do the same for the steps in marketing the peanuts.

## ✓ What did you learn

1. Answers will vary, but may include planting crops, caring for them, and harvesting them.

2. First, a truck takes them to a factory. Next, the peanuts are cleaned and roasted. Last, they are bagged and sent to stores.

3. **Think and Share** Answers will vary, but may include such things as fruits, vegetables, dairy products, and grains.

# Follow a Route

## Objectives

- Use a simple map to identify the location of places.
- Locate places of significance on maps.

## Vocabulary

**route** one way to get from one place to another (p. 120)

# 1 Introduce and Motivate

**Preview** Write the word *route* on the board, and ask children what they think it means. Then share the definition of the word.

**Warm Up** To activate prior knowledge, discuss the routes children take to get from one place to another. Begin by describing the route you take to get from one part of the classroom to another. Ask several volunteers to do the same. Then talk about the route you would take to get to the principal's office. Ask children to tell what route they would take to get to another classroom.

# Follow a Route

1 The map shows the route the truck takes from the farm to the factory. A **route** is one way to get from one place to another.

120

# Practice and Extend

**SOCIAL STUDIES STRAND**
**Geography**

**Giving Directions**

- Assign each child a partner.
- Have one partner give oral directions for getting from one place on the map to another. The other partner traces the route with his or her finger.
- Partners reverse roles to retrace the route for the return trip.

Look at the map. Tell what building is just north of the truck. What does the arrow show? Where does the route begin? Follow the route with your finger.

## Map Key

Farm

Store

Factory    East

School

House

- - -➤    Truck Route

### Try it!

1. What does the  stand for? How do you know?

2. What direction does the truck go on each street?

3. **On Your Own** Make a map and a map key of your school. Tell what **route** you would take to get from your classroom to the office.

**121**

## ② Teach and Discuss

**Pages 120–121**

Have children use the map key to locate the farm and the factory. Then have them find the truck on the map. Explain that it is the truck with Mr. Ford's peanuts.

**①** **What do the lines with arrows show?** The route the truck takes from the farm to the factory **Interpret Maps**

**②** **What street does the truck take first?** Red Street **Interpret Maps**

**③** **At the end of Red Street, the truck makes a turn. Onto what street does it turn?** Brown Road **Interpret Maps**

**④** **Where does the truck go last?** The factory **Interpret Maps**

**⑤** **Is there another route the truck could take? Would that route be shorter or longer?** Accept other possible routes, including entering Green Street from the farm. **Analyze Information**

## ③ Close and Assess

### Try it!

1. It stands for the store. It matches the symbol on the map key.

2. North on Red Street, east on Brown Road, north on Green Street, east on North Street

3. **On Your Own** Children's maps will vary but should include a route from the classroom to the office.

# George Washington Carver

## Objectives
- Identify a historic figure who has exhibited a love of individualism and inventiveness.
- Identify contributions of historical figures in the period of history since 1880.

# 1 Introduce and Motivate

**Preview** Hold up a jar of glue, a piece of paper, a rubber ball, and a plastic cup. Have children name the products. Write the names on the lines of a word web. Leave the center circle blank.

Write *peanut* in the center of the word web. Explain that peanuts can be used to make all of the things named on the web.

Tell children that many other products can be made using peanuts as one of the ingredients. Name and add these products to the web: cheese, shaving cream, cooking oil, flour, mayonnaise, bleach, ink, and shoe polish.

**Warm Up** Point to each word on the web and ask children to tell if they use or eat any of the products.

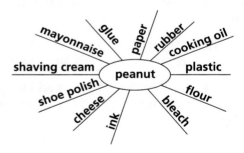

**Caution!** Because some children may be allergic to peanuts, do not bring peanuts into the classroom. Peanut allergies are very serious and can be life-threatening.

Have children preview the pictures on pp. 122–123. Invite children to describe what they see.

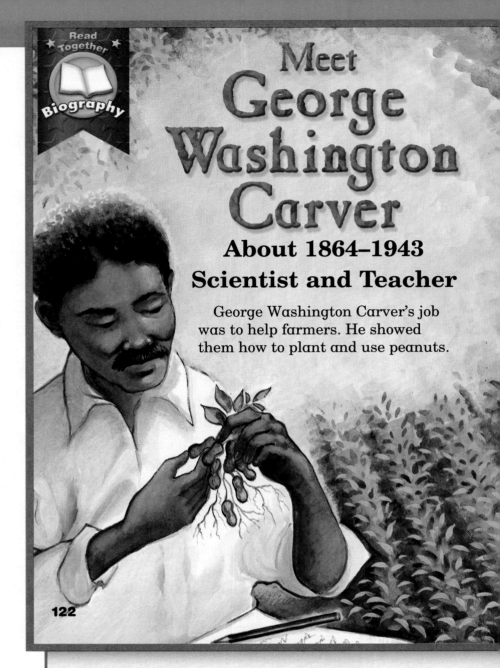

## Meet George Washington Carver

**About 1864–1943**

**Scientist and Teacher**

George Washington Carver's job was to help farmers. He showed them how to plant and use peanuts.

122

# Practice and Extend

**SOCIAL STUDIES Background**

### About George Washington Carver

- George Washington Carver was born into slavery near Diamond Grove, Missouri. Due to the lack of detailed records, the exact year of his birth is uncertain.
- Carver studied agricultural science at Iowa State Agricultural College, where he received a bachelor's degree in agricultural science in 1894 and a master of science degree in 1896.
- George Washington Carver developed a system of crop rotation and discovered hundreds of products that could be made from peanuts, soybeans, and sweet potatoes. Carver taught at Tuskegee Institute in Alabama for most of his life.
- In his later years, George Washington Carver gave 1864 as the date of his birth.

As a young boy, George liked plants. Later, he went to school to learn about plants and farming. He became a teacher to help farmers. **1**

George Washington Carver was born in Diamond Grove, Missouri.

George Washington Carver taught farmers how to grow peanuts. He knew that peanut plants help to make the soil healthy so other crops can grow. He also made many new things from peanuts. You may even use some of the things he learned to make. Did you know that soap, candy, and paint can be made from peanuts? **3**

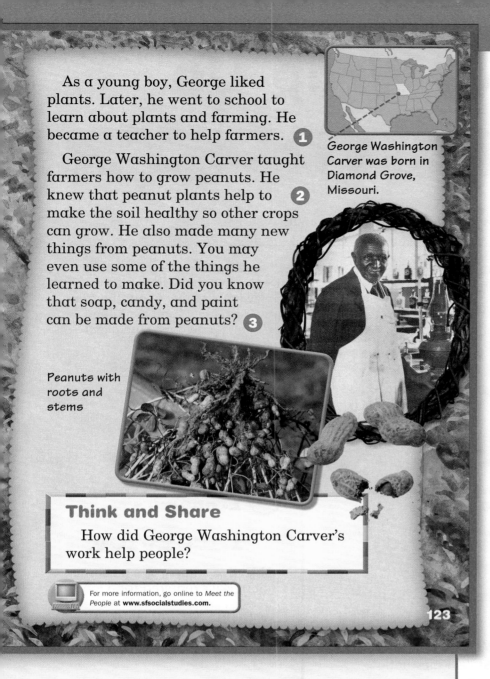

Peanuts with roots and stems

### Think and Share

How did George Washington Carver's work help people?

For more information, go online to *Meet the People* at **www.sfsocialstudies.com**.

123

## WEB SITE Technology

You may help children find out more about George Washington Carver by clicking on *Meet the People* at **www.sfsocialstudies.com**.

# 2 Teach and Discuss

Read the biography together. Tell children that when George Washington Carver was a child, his nickname was "the plant doctor."

**1** **What did George Washington Carver do before he became a teacher?** He went to school to learn about plants and farming. Sequence

**2** **How did George Washington Carver help farmers?** He helped them grow peanuts. Growing peanuts made their soil healthy. Cause and Effect

**3** **Which goods made from peanuts have you used?** Answers may include soap, milk, paint, candy, peanut butter, and so on. Apply Information

# 3 Close and Assess

### Think and Share

He taught farmers how to grow peanuts. He also made many new things from peanuts so the farmers had a market for their peanuts.

# Lesson ⑤ Wrap-Up

**MEETING INDIVIDUAL NEEDS**
## Leveled Practice

### Draw Sequential Pictures
Have children draw pictures of the steps in growing peanuts and marketing the peanuts.

**Easy** Have children pantomime some of the steps in growing peanuts and getting them to market. Classmates can try to guess which of the steps described in their pictures is being acted out. **Reteach**

**On-Level** Remind children that Mr. Ford thinks growing peanuts is hard work. Ask children to point to their drawing and tell why they think each step pictured might be hard work. **Extend**

**Challenge** Have children work with partners. Have them dramatize interviewing a farmer about the steps in growing peanuts and marketing them. The "farmer" may use pictures as visual aids. **Enrich**

## Hands-on Activities

 **CURRICULUM CONNECTION**
### Reading

## What a Plot!

**Objective** Recognize story plot.

**Materials** *The Little Red Hen (Makes a Pizza),* by Philemon Sturges (Dutton, ISBN 0-525-45953-7, 1999)

**Learning Style** Visual/Verbal

**Group**

🕐 **Time** 20 minutes

**1.** Share the pictures as you read the story to children.

**2.** Help children identify the story problem. Elicit that when the hen wanted to make a pizza, she got no help from the duck, the dog, or the cat.

**3.** Ask how the hen solved her problem. Elicit that she did all the work herself.

**4.** Invite children to tell how the story ends. If they know the original tale, have them contrast the story endings. (In this version, the hen shares the pizza and the animals agree to wash the dishes.)

 **SOCIAL STUDIES STRAND**
### Geography

## Placemat Maps

**Objective** Follow a route.

**Materials** old placemats, markers, blocks, toy cars

**Learning Style** Kinesthetic

**Partners**

🕐 **Time** 15–20 minutes

**1.** Draw simple map outlines on several old placemats. Have children add buildings with blocks or other small objects. Children can "drive" small-sized cars around their maps.

**2.** Ask children to draw copies of their maps and show the routes they "drove."

 **SOCIAL STUDIES STRAND**
### Economics

## Interview

**Objective** Interview a person about skills required for a job.

**Learning Style** Verbal
**Individual** 🧍

🕐 **Time** 20–25 minutes

**1.** Have each child interview a family member or a neighbor about his or her job.

**2.** Encourage children to ask how the person being interviewed prepared for his or her job. Did they need to learn special skills? Where did they learn those skills?

**3.** Children can give oral reports to share what they learned about the job of the person they interviewed.

# Lesson 6 Overview

**From Place to Place**
pages 124–125

Children will explore different modes of transportation and how transportation is used to move goods. They will also learn how technology has changed transportation.

⏱ **Time** 20 minutes

**Resources**
- Workbook, p. 32
- Vocabulary Card
  **transportation**
- Every Student Learns Guide, pp. 58–61

**Big Wheels**
pages 126–127

Children will use pictures to learn how different types of transportation help people do jobs.

⏱ **Time** 15–20 minutes

# Build Background

---

**Activity**

## How Will You Go?

⏱ **Time** 15–20 minutes

Ask children to draw pictures to show how they get to school each day. When children are finished, have them hold up their pictures and identify the modes of transportation used. Make a pictogram to show the results.

**If time is short,** have children tell how they get to school. Ask if they walk, come by car, ride on the school bus, or get there some other way.

---

**Read Aloud**

## Getting There

**by Janet Carroll**

To get to school, I ride the bus.
Gramps comes by car to visit us.

Subways run below the ground
So city folks can get around.

Trucks move on roads; trains, on rails.
Sailors need wind to blow their sails.

Jet planes travel through the air.
They fly so fast—from here to there.

But when I go next door to play,
I use my skates—they're quite OK.

# Lesson 6
# From Place to Place

## Objectives
- Identify the role of transportation in the exchange of goods.
- Describe how technology has changed transportation.

## Vocabulary
**transportation** things that move people and goods from place to place (p. 124)

### QUICK Teaching Plan

*If time is short,* brainstorm with children a list of vehicles that move people and goods.

- Use pp. 124–125 to explore with children different means of transportation.

## 1 Introduce and Motivate

**Preview** Display the Vocabulary Card **transportation** and ask children what they think it means. Then share its meaning. Have children locate the word as they preview the lesson.

**Warm Up** To activate prior knowledge, ask children to tell ways in which they get from place to place, other than by walking. Ask children to suppose they want to visit a friend who lives across the country. How can they get there? Then ask children to suppose they want to visit a friend who lives across the ocean. How could they get there?

---

# Lesson 6
# From Place to Place

Mr. Ford drives a tractor and a truck on his farm. The tractor and truck are his transportation. **Transportation** moves people and goods from place to place.

Sometimes Ben travels by bike or car. What kinds of transportation do you use?

**1**

124

## Practice and Extend

### READING SKILL
### Analyze Pictures

**Look Again!**

- Ask children to describe the photographs around the edge of these pages.
- Have children point to each kind of transportation in the drawing that matches a photograph.
- Ask how photographs and drawings are the same. (They can picture the same objects.) Ask how they are different. (Photographs show real objects; drawings can show real or imagined objects.)

### WEB SITE
### Technology

You can look up vocabulary words online. Click on *Social Studies Library* and select the dictionary at **www.sfsocialstudies.com**.

Some kinds of transportation move a lot of goods at one time. A truck can carry goods all over the country. An airplane can take goods across an ocean. What other kinds of transportation move goods from one place to another? **2** **3**

## What did you learn

1. Why do people use **transportation**?

2. What kinds of transportation does your community have?

3. **Think and Share** How is transportation for people and goods the same?

125

**Workbook, p. 32**

From Place to Place

Make a chart to show then and now.
Cut out the pictures.
Paste them on the chart.

| | | |
|---|---|---|
| Now | Then | Now |
| Then | Now | Then |
| Now | Now | Then |
| Now | Then | Then |

**Also on Teacher Resources CD-ROM.**

## 2 Teach and Discuss

Pages 124–125

Challenge children to see how many kinds of transportation they can name on pp. 124–125.

**1** **What are some ways people can move from place to place in a big city?** Possible answers: taxis, buses, and trains **Analyze Pictures**

Tell children that goods are moved across the country as well as to other countries around the world.

**2** **Which pictures show ways to move goods?** The trucks, the boat, perhaps the jet **Analyze Pictures**

**H** SOCIAL STUDIES STRAND **History**

Transportation has changed as technology has improved. These changes have affected people's daily lives. Remind children that before there were cars, people walked from place to place and rode in horse-drawn vehicles. After cars came along, drive-through restaurants changed the way people went out to eat. Ask children to recall old pictures they have seen of bikes, cars, trucks, or planes. Discuss how various means of transportation have changed, how those changes have affected people's daily lives, and the advantages and disadvantages of different types of transportation.

**3** **Why is it important to move peanuts from farms to stores?** So they can be sold **Draw Conclusions**

## 3 Close and Assess

### ✓ What did you learn

1. To move people and goods from place to place

2. Answers will vary but should reflect how location and surroundings affect transportation.

3. **Think and Share** Both people and goods are moved from place to place.

# Big Wheels

## Objectives

- Obtain information about a topic using a variety of visual sources, such as pictures and graphics.

- Identify ways people exchange goods and services.

## 1 Introduce and Motivate

**Preview** Ask children what they think the phrase *Big Wheels* means. Tell them that in this lesson, *Big Wheels* is another way of saying *trucks*. Have children locate the title *Big Wheels* as they preview the lesson.

**Warm Up** To activate prior knowledge, ask children what kinds of transportation they talked about in Lesson 6. Ask which kinds had wheels. (cars, buses, trucks, and so on) Tell children that they will now take a closer look at some trucks with big wheels.

Read the introduction with children. Ask them to try to guess what kinds of jobs these trucks do.

## 2 Teach and Discuss

Point out the two pictures of a concrete truck. Using the larger picture, have children identify the mixing drum and the hood.

**1 Look at the smaller picture. What is coming out of the back of the truck?** Accept reasonable answers, including concrete or cement.
*Analyze Pictures*

**2 Why do people need concrete?** To make sidewalks, streets, foundations for houses, and so on
*Make Inferences*

**3 What do you think happens in the mixing drum?** As the drum turns, the contents move around and around. This keeps the concrete well mixed; it also prevents it from hardening too soon.
*Make Inferences*

---

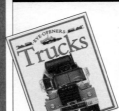

DK     TRANSPORTATION

# Big Wheels

Look at some types of transportation. What jobs do these trucks help people do?

concrete truck

hood

① ②     ③ mixing drum

tank

wheels

126

## Practice and Extend

FYI **SOCIAL STUDIES
Background**

### About Trucks

- Concrete is a mixture of cement, sand, gravel, and water.
- The larger the truck and the heavier its load, the more tires it requires. The additional tires help distribute the weight of the load more evenly. The tires also help protect the road surface.
- Sitting up high in the cab helps the truck driver to see long distances. However, if the hood of the truck sticks out, the driver can't see what is directly in front.

ESL **ACCESS CONTENT
ESL Support**

*For additional ESL support, use Every Student Learns Guide, pp. 58–61.*

delivery truck

④

⑤ cab

tow truck

⑥ ⑦

crane arm

hook

tanker truck

⑧

bumper

**127**

Next, have children focus on the two pictures of a delivery truck on p. 127. Remind children that trucks are a type of transportation that can move a lot of goods at one time.

④ **What does a delivery truck do?** It takes goods to stores and to people who need the goods. **Make Inferences**

⑤ **What is the part where the driver sits called?** The cab **Main Idea and Details**

Next, children should look at the pictures of a tow truck. Have children point to the crane arm and the hook in the larger picture.

⑥ **What is a tow truck used for?** To pull cars or trucks from one place to another **Make Inferences**

⑦ **Does a tow truck give people a good or a service?** A service **Analyze Information**

Finally, focus on the two pictures of the tanker truck. Explain that a tanker truck delivers fuel, and that the gas used to run cars is a fuel.

⑧ **How do you think fuel gets from the tank into the containers underground?** It goes through the big hose attached to the tank. **Analyze Pictures**

# 3 Close and Assess

- Ask children to point out where the driver sits in each truck. Have them compare the fronts of the trucks by naming the truck with a flat front (delivery truck), and the trucks with fronts that stick out (concrete mixer, tow truck, tanker truck).

- Have children look at the wheels on the trucks. Talk about why the tanker truck has more wheels than the other trucks.

- Ask children to tell how different kinds of trucks provide goods and services.

**CURRICULUM CONNECTION**
## Science

### How Wheels Work

Mention that wheels on a truck are attached to an axle. Explain that a wheel and axle is a simple machine. A wheel and axle is made of a rod, or axle, attached to the center of a wheel. The wheel turns around the axle. A wheel and axle moves or turns an object. Have children work in small groups to observe the workings of these wheel-and-axle tools.

- doorknob
- screwdriver
- egg-beater
- pencil sharpener
- pepper mill

# Lesson ⑥ Wrap-Up

## MEETING INDIVIDUAL NEEDS
## Leveled Practice

### Find Transportation Pictures
Ask children to cut out magazine or newspaper pictures that show different means of transportation.

**Easy** Divide a bulletin board into three sections: **Air, Land, Water.** Have children categorize and display the pictures in the appropriate sections. **Reteach**

**On-Level** Have each child choose a picture and paste it on a sheet of paper. Then have each student dictate or write sentences telling how that means of transportation moves people and/or goods. **Extend**

**Challenge** Have children find information on and then draw examples of vehicles used long ago. Children can use the pictures to make "Now and Then" posters to compare and contrast various means of transportation from the past and present. **Enrich**

## Hands-on Activities

 CURRICULUM CONNECTION
### Writing/Vocabulary

## A Poem

**Objective** Write a poem using lesson vocabulary.

**Materials** chart paper, markers
**Learning Style** Visual/Verbal
**Group**
⏱ **Time** 15–30 minutes

**1.** Create a word web around the word *transportation* and the phrases *on land, on water,* and *in the air.*

**2.** Ask children to pick a favorite mode of transportation. Write the word vertically, one letter under the other, on chart paper. Help children create a poem for the mode of transportation by suggesting a word or phrase for each letter.

**3.** Remind children to add their word *transportation* to the Word Book.

 CURRICULUM CONNECTION
### Literature

## All Aboard

**Objectives** Describe how trains move people; compare/contrast trains then and now.

**Materials** *Window Music,* by Anastasia Suen (Penguin, ISBN 0-14-056093-9, 1998)

**Learning Style** Auditory/Visual
**Group**
⏱ **Time** 10–15 minutes

**1.** Read the book aloud, displaying the pictures. Have children note how the scenery changes as the train moves.

**2.** Ask children to find pictures of modern trains. Compare them with the train shown in the book. Talk about how technology has changed the way trains look and run.

**3.** Reread the story, inviting children to join in.

 SOCIAL STUDIES STRAND
### Economics

## Trucks That Work

**Objective** Demonstrate how trucks help people.

**Materials** toy and/or model trucks
**Learning Style** Visual/Verbal/ Kinesthetic
**Group**
⏱ **Time** 10–15 minutes

**1.** Ask children who have toy or model trucks at home to bring them to school.

**2.** Have the owners demonstrate how the trucks work. Encourage them to tell what the trucks help people do.

**3.** Ask children to look for real trucks that do some of these same things in their own communities.

# Ending Unit 3

## End with a Poem
pages 128–129

Children will listen to and talk about a poem, "Work Day" by Kate Greenwood, that tells about a child who goes to work with her mother.

## Unit 3 Review
pages 130–133

Children will review unit vocabulary words and the unit skills of put things in order, follow a route, and use a chart. They will answer questions about what they learned in the unit. Children will also learn about several books relating to jobs and work.

### Resources
- Workbook, p. 33
- ✓ Assessment Book, pp. 9–12

## Unit 3 Project
page 134

Children will learn how to make a community worker puppet. They will also be directed to a Web site where they can learn more about people at work.

### Resource
- Workbook, p. 34

# Wrap-Up

### Activity

## My Book About Work

Have each child make a small book by folding two sheets of plain paper in half. The front page should carry the title, *My Book About Work.*

- On the inside pages, ask children to write descriptions or draw pictures showing work they do now including schoolwork, chores at home, and so on.

- The last page should be devoted to the kind of work they would like to do as adults. Encourage children to include volunteer work.

**Performance Assessment**
You can use the activity on this page as a performance assessment.

If you require a 4-point rubric, adjust scoring guide accordingly.

### ✓ Assessment Scoring Guide

| Make a "My Neighborhood" Poster | |
|---|---|
| 6 | Descriptions and goals are complete and detailed. |
| 5 | Descriptions and goals are clear and complete. |
| 4 | Descriptions and goals are clear and complete, and include some details. |
| 3 | Descriptions and goals contain gaps in information and few details. |
| 2 | Descriptions and goals provide little information or details. |
| 1 | Descriptions and goals are unclear or unfocused and may not relate to the topic. |

# Work Day

## Objective
- Obtain information about a topic using a variety of visual sources, such as pictures and literature.

## 1 Introduce and Motivate

**Preview** Point to and read the title, then identify the author of the poem. From the title and art, ask children what the poem could be about. Write their responses on the board and review them after the reading.

Explain that a poem is a kind of writing that often has rhyming words.

**Warm Up** To activate knowledge, ask children if they have ever visited a place of work of someone they know. Encourage them to tell what they saw and did there.

## 2 Teach and Discuss

Invite children to listen as you read the poem. Encourage them to picture in their minds the actions of the poem.

**1 In what kind of place do you think the mother works?** Possible answer: An office
Make Inferences

**2 What do you think the child might have done at work?** Possible answers: Played with her doll or other toys she brought from home; played with office supplies, such as paper and pencils
Make Inferences

Have children listen for rhyming words at the ends of the phrases as you read the poem aloud again.

## Work Day
by Kate Greenwood

My mom and I
went to work today.

Well, she went to work
and I went to play.

She met with people
and talked on the phone.

I wonder what I'll do **1** **2**
when I'm all grown.

128

# Practice and Extend

CURRICULUM CONNECTION
## Reading

**Rhyming Words**

Direct small groups of children to locate and write pairs of rhyming words from the poem—*today* and *play, phone* and *grown.* Encourage them to add other rhyming words to each pair. Upon completion, each group can share their groups of words.

# 3 Close and Assess

- Divide children into two groups.

- Have children do a choral reading of the selection, with each group reading alternate stanzas.

- After children have read the poem aloud, invite them to share what they like most about the poem.

## CURRICULUM CONNECTION
## Reading

### Books About Work

Children might enjoy reading these books related to work.

*Career Day,* by Anne F. Rockwell (HarperCollins Children's Book Group, ISBN 0-06-027565-0, 2000). In this picture book, children in a class introduce parents and grandparents who demonstrate their occupation. **Easy**

*Worksong,* by Gary Paulsen (Harcourt Brace, ISBN 0-15-200980-9, 1997) The rhyming text and visuals in this book celebrate the world of work. **On-Level**

*Mama & Papa Have a Store,* by Amelia Lau Carling (Dial Books for Young Readers, ISBN 0-8037-2044-0, 1998) A young Chinese girl describes a typical day in her parents' general store in Guatemala City. **Challenge** *Pura Belpré Honor, 2000*

## Resources

- Assessment Book, pp. 9–12
- Workbook, p. 33: Vocabulary Review

# Vocabulary Review

1. needs
2. job
3. service
4. volunteer
5. transportation
6. goods

**TEST PREP** **Answers to Test Prep**

1. wants
2. tools

### Test Talk

Use Question 1 to model the Test Talk strategy.

**Narrow the answer choices.**
Tell children to read each answer choice carefully. Children should rule out any choice that they know is wrong.

**Choose the right answer.**
After children make their answer choice, tell them to check their answer by comparing it to the text.

*For additional practice, use the Test Talk Practice Book.*

---

# Vocabulary Review

Tell which word completes each sentence.

> transportation
> job
> service
> goods
> volunteer
> needs

1. Food and clothing and a place to live are _____.
2. Work that people do is a _____.
3. A job workers do to help others is a _____.
4. A person who works for free is a _____.
5. A plane is one type of _____.
6. Things that are grown or made are _____.

★ ★ ★ ★ ★ ★ ★ ★

 **TEST PREP** Which word completes each sentence?

**Test Talk**

Rule out answers you know are wrong.

1. Things we would like to have are _____.
   **a.** goods     **b.** transportation
   **c.** tools     **d.** wants

2. Pliers and a hammer used by a carpenter are called _____.
   **a.** service     **b.** transportation
   **c.** tools     **d.** wants

**130**

---

# Practice and Extend

## Assessment Options

✓ **Unit 3 Assessment**

- Unit 3 Content Test:
  Use Assessment Book, pp. 9–10

- Unit 3 Skills Test:
  Use Assessment Book, pp. 11–12

**TEST PREP** **Standardized Test Prep**

- Unit 3 tests contain standardized test formats.

✓ **Unit 3 Performance Assessment**

- See p. 134 for information about using the Unit 3 Project as a means of performance assessment.

- A scoring guide for the Unit 3 Project is provided in the teacher's notes on p. 134.

**Test Talk**

- Test Talk Practice Book

# Skills Review

## Put Things in Order

Write about a job you want to do some day. Tell what you would do **first, next,** and **last.**

★ ★ ★ ★ ★ ★ ★ ★ ★

## Follow a Route

1. What buildings are east of the store?

2. Follow the route with your finger. Where does Pat's route begin?

3. Tell what direction Pat goes on each street.

131

**Workbook, p. 33**

**Also on Teacher Resources CD-ROM.**

---

# Skills Review

## Put Things in Order

- Children's answers should show an understanding of the concept of jobs. Children's answers should include correct use of the words *first, next,* and *last.*

Use the following scoring guide.

✓ **Assessment Scoring Guide**

| | Write About Sequence Related to a Job |
|---|---|
| 6 | Describes a job with precise details, uses complete sentences, and uses the words *first, next,* and *last* correctly. |
| 5 | Describes a job with many precise details, using the words *first, next,* and *last* correctly. |
| 4 | Describes a job with adequate details, using the words *first, next,* and *last* correctly. |
| 3 | Describes a job with few clear details, using two of the words *first, next,* and *last* correctly. |
| 2 | Describes a job with few or no details, using one or none of the words *first, next,* and *last* correctly. |
| 1 | Has difficulty describing a job, provides almost no details, unable to use the words *first, next,* and *last* correctly. |

If you require a 4-point rubric, adjust scoring guide accordingly.

## Follow a Route

1. A house and the post office

2. At the post office

3. West on Steve Lane, south on Oak Road

# Skills Review

## Use a Chart

1. Four
2. Lisa
3. Sara

## Skills On Your Own

- Children's charts should be in the correct format and accurately reflect class jobs.

Use the following scoring guide.

✓ **Assessment Scoring Guide**

| | Make a Chart |
|---|---|
| 6 | Shows precise class jobs in an easy-to-read, correct chart format with few if any spelling errors. |
| 5 | Shows precise class jobs information in an easy-to-read, correct chart format. |
| 4 | Shows accurate class jobs information in a correct chart format. |
| 3 | Shows class jobs information with a few errors in a format that is similar to a chart. |
| 2 | Shows class jobs information with many errors in a format that is not a chart. |
| 1 | Is able to describe class jobs but has a great deal of difficulty understanding a chart format. |

If you require a 4-point rubric, adjust scoring guide accordingly.

# Skills Review

## Use a Chart

Use the chart to answer the questions.

1. How many tools does the chart show?
2. Who used a ruler?
3. Who used a pencil?

| Tools We Used Today | |
|---|---|
| **Tools** | **People** |
| Pencil | Sara |
| Computer | Tony |
| Brush | Ryan |
| Ruler | Lisa |

## Skills On Your Own

Make a chart of some jobs in your class. Write a title for your chart. Write the jobs on the left. Write the names of the helpers next to the jobs they do.

### Jobs in Our Class

| | | |
|---|---|---|
| | Hand out tools. | Anna |
| | Be line leader. | Maria |
| | Clean board. | Henry |
| | Hand out milk. | Mark |

# Practice and Extend

## Revisit the Unit Question

✓ **Unit 3 Portfolio Assessment**

- Have children look back at the list of jobs they made on p. 87.
- Have children list details about the job they would like to have.
- Ask children to underline the details they learned about jobs from studying this unit.
- Ask children to draw a picture of a job they would like to do when they are grown.
- Have children write two sentences about the job.
- Have children add their lists, drawings, and sentences to their Social Studies Portfolio.

# What did you learn?

1. Why do people work?

2. How are goods different from services?

3. Name some jobs. Tell what good or service each job provides.

4. **Write and Share**
   Write what you could do if you wanted to buy a toy that costs more money than you have.

## Read About Work

Look for books like these in the library.

# What did you learn?

1. People work to earn money, to help people, and because they like what they do.

2. Goods are things people grow or make; services are jobs people do to help others.

3. Possible answers include: Doctors help keep people well and salespeople sell different goods.

4. **Write and Share**  Children's answers should reflect understanding of the concept that wanting more than one can have requires that people make choices.

## Read About Work

You might want to have these or other books about work available in the classroom. Invite children to read one or more of the books and write a short book report or tell why they liked the book.

*Cowboy Bunnies,* by Christine Loomis (Putnam, ISBN 0-399-22625-7, 1997) The bunnies in this book are indeed cowboys who "Start at sunup/Work all day/Roping cows/Tossing hay." **Easy**

*Dancin' in the Kitchen,* by Wendy Gelsanliter and Frank Christian (Putnam, ISBN 0-399-23035-1, 1998) Three generations of a family help to prepare a meal—while dancing to the music on the radio. **On-Level**

*A Weed Is a Flower: The Life of George Washington Carver,* by Aliki (Aladdin, ISBN 0-671-66490-5, 1988) This inspiring biography includes dramatic action—and makes for good class read-aloud. **Challenge**

# Unit 3 Project

# Jobs in Your Community

## Objective
- Describe the requirements of a job.

## Resource
- Workbook, p. 34

## Materials
paper bags, scissors, paper, crayons, glue

## Follow This Procedure
- Review different kinds of workers in the community. Discuss any special clothes they wear, tools they use, and how they provide goods or services.
- Tell children they will be making a worker puppet and then interviewing each other's puppets.
- Reproduce patterns of arms, hats, special tools, and clothing, on construction paper.
- Have children color, cut, and glue the pieces onto the bag.
- Explain to children that they're going to act as the worker and give an interview about the worker's job.

✓ **Assessment Scoring Guide**

| Jobs in Your Community | |
|---|---|
| 6 | Detailed description of jobs and exchanging goods or services. Answers questions clearly and completely. |
| 5 | Good descriptions. Answers questions clearly and completely. |
| 4 | Adequate descriptions. Answers most questions clearly and completely. |
| 3 | Adequate descriptions. Answers to questions contain gaps in information. |
| 2 | Weak descriptions. Answers most questions with confusing information and few details. |
| 1 | Attempts to describe jobs and exchanging goods or services. Has difficulty answering questions and providing details. |

If you require a 4-point rubric, adjust scoring guide accordingly.

## UNIT 3 Project

### Jobs in Your Community

**Make a community worker puppet. Give an interview about your community worker's job.**

**1** Choose a kind of worker in your community.

**2** Make a puppet of your worker. Show any special clothes or tools.

**3** Tell how your worker gives us goods or services.

**4** Answer questions from your classmates about your worker's job.

### Internet Activity

Go to www.sfsocialstudies.com/activities to learn more about people at work.

**134**

# Practice and Extend

## Hands-on Unit Project

✓ **Performance Assessment**
- The Unit Project can also be used as a performance assessment activity.
- Use the scoring guide to assess each group's work.

## WEB SITE Technology

Children can launch the activity by clicking on *Grade 1, Unit 3* at **www.sfsocialstudies.com/ activities.**

### Workbook, p. 34

**3 Project** Jobs in Your Community

Draw a picture of a worker in your community. **Drawings will vary.**

Write answers about your worker.

Who is the worker? **Answers will vary.**

What does the worker do? _____

Where does he or she work? _____

How does the worker do this job? _____

Does the worker give us goods or services? _____

**Also on Teacher Resources CD-ROM.**

# Vocabulary Routines

The following examples of reading and vocabulary development strategies can be used to instruct students about unit vocabulary.

## BEFORE READING

### Related Word Study

Vocabulary: mountain, plain, lake, river

**Semantic Feature Analysis** You can make a semantic feature analysis chart like the one below to show children how concepts are similar to and different from one another. As you read the word in each row, have children explain why each example belongs (+) or does not belong (-) in a particular column. If possible, show pictures illustrating each word.

*Let's look at the word* **mountain**. *What is a mountain? A mountain is the highest kind of land. It is much bigger than a hill. Our first column says "made of land." Is a mountain made of land? Yes, so we will put a + in this column. Our next column says "made of water." Is a mountain made of water? No, so we will put a – in the column. The third and fourth columns say "Pointed" and "Flat". Is a mountain pointed or is it flat? A mountain is pointed, not flat, so we will put a + in the third column and a – in the last column.*

| Kind of Land and Water | | | | |
|---|---|---|---|---|
| | **Made of land** | **Made of water** | **Pointed** | **Flat** |
| **mountain** | + | - | + | - |
| **plain** | + | - | - | + |
| **lake** | - | + | - | + |
| **river** | - | + | - | + |

## DURING READING

### Context Clues

**Idea Completions** Many children will use a word in a sentence without knowing what the word means. For example, "A natural resource is important" does not demonstrate that a child knows what a natural resource is. You can use the idea completions routine to provide children with sentence stems to build context for vocabulary words. This routine works well with many unit vocabulary words, as shown at right.

*We've been reading about Earth and its resources. Let's talk about a natural resource. Listen closely so you can finish the sentence. It is important that we do not use up land, air, water, and other natural resources because . . . (we cannot make more of them once we use them up)*

## AFTER READING

### Individual Word Study

**Picture Dictionary** Pass out sheets of paper with a different vocabulary word written on each sheet. Have children copy over their words and then draw pictures that tell about the word's meaning. Have children present their vocabulary words to the class.

*Look at the paper I just gave you and read the vocabulary word on it. Write the word over, to practice it. Think about what the word means and how you can show what it means. Then draw a picture that illustrates your word. When you are finished, you can tell the class about your word.*

# Teaching with Leveled Readers

**This series of readers focuses on how maps and globes are alike and different.**

**Below Level**

**On Level**

**Above Level**

## LEVELED READER VOCABULARY ACTIVITY

- Preview with children the vocabulary words at the beginning of the reader.
- Have children predict what they will read about.
- After reading, have pairs of children fill in a Venn diagram about the similarities and differences of maps and globes.

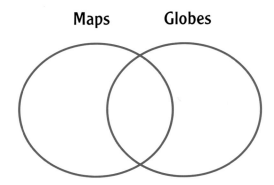

Maps    Globes

## CONNECTIONS TO THE LESSON

Unit 4, Lesson 2: Looking at Our Land and Water

## CONNECTIONS TO TODAY

- Have children read the lesson. Then provide the leveled readers to enhance their understanding of how people use maps and globes to gain information.
- **Points for Discussion:**
    1. Have children discuss how they can tell water from land on a map or globe.
    2. Children can also discuss what else they might find on a map or globe.

# Our Earth, Our Resources

# Unit 4 Planning Guide
## Our Earth, Our Resources

**Begin with a Song** pp. 136–137   **Vocabulary Preview** pp. 138–139

**Reading Social Studies, Find the Main Idea** pp. 140–141

| Lesson Titles | Pacing | Main Ideas |
|---|---|---|
| **Lesson 1 Different Kinds of Weather** pp. 142–145<br><br>**Chart and Graph Skills: Read a Time Line** pp. 146–147<br><br>*Colonial Williamsburg* **Weather and Seasons Long Ago** pp. 148–149 | 2 days | • Weather can vary from day to day and from place to place; weather affects what we wear and what we do.<br>• A time line is a graphic organizer used to show the order in which things happen.<br>• The changes in seasons affected the everyday life and work of people who lived long ago. |
| **Lesson 2 Looking at Our Land and Water** pp. 150–153<br><br>**Map and Globe Skills: Locate Land and Water** pp. 154–155 | 2 days | • Earth has different kinds of land (such as mountains, hills, and plains) and water (such as oceans, lakes, and rivers).<br>• A globe is a round model of Earth; like a map, it shows landforms and bodies of water. |
| **Lesson 3 Our Earth's Resources** pp. 156–159<br><br>**Citizen Heroes: Responsibility Tree Musketeers** pp. 160–161<br>**Read Together Biography: Elvia Niebla** pp. 162–163 | 3 days | • Among Earth's natural resources are land, water, air, trees, oil, and gas. It is important to conserve our natural resources.<br>• Tree Musketeers helps take care of Earth.<br>• Elvia Niebla, a Mexican American, is a scientist who studies forests and works for their conservation. |
| **Lesson 4 Interview About Farm History** pp. 164–167<br><br>**Biography: Sacagawea** pp. 168–169 | 2 days | • A visit to "Living History Farms" is one way to learn about the history of an area—and how farming has changed over the years.<br>• Sacagawea was a Shoshone who guided explorers Lewis and Clark during their search for a water route to the Pacific Ocean. |
| **Lesson 5 Caring for Our Resources** pp. 170–173<br><br>**Here and There: Endangered Animals** pp. 174–175 | 2 days | • To conserve our natural resources, people can observe the 3 *R*s: reduce, reuse, and recycle.<br>• When people care for Earth, they also help endangered animals, such as giant pandas and tigers. |

✔ **End with a Legend** pp. 176–177  ✔ **Unit 4 Review** pp. 178–181  ✔ **Unit 4 Project** p. 182

✔ = Assessment Options

| Vocabulary | Resources | Meeting Individual Needs |
|---|---|---|
| **weather** | • Workbook, pp. 37–39<br>• Vocabulary Card: weather<br>• Every Student Learns Guide, pp. 62–65<br>• Transparency 22 | • ESL Support, TE p. 144<br>• Leveled Practice, TE p. 149a |
| **mountain**<br>**plain**<br>**lake**<br>**river** | • Workbook, pp. 40–41<br>• Vocabulary Cards: mountain, plain, lake, river<br>• Every Student Learns Guide, pp. 66–69<br>• Transparency 23 | • ESL Support, TE pp. 151, 154<br>• Leveled Practice, TE p. 155a |
| **natural resource** | • Workbook, p. 42<br>• Vocabulary Card: natural resource<br>• Every Student Learns Guide, pp. 70–73 | • ESL Support, TE pp. 157, 162<br>• Leveled Practice, TE p. 163a |
| **history** | • Workbook p. 43<br>• Vocabulary Card: history<br>• Every Student Learns Guide, pp. 74–77 | • ESL Support, TE p. 166<br>• Leveled Practice, TE p. 169a |
| | • Workbook p. 44<br>• Every Student Learns Guide, pp. 78–81<br>• Transparency 24 | • ESL Support, TE p. 171<br>• Leveled Practice, TE p. 175a |

# Providing More Depth

## Additional Resources

- Trade Books
- Family Activities
- Vocabulary Workbook and Cards
- Social Studies Plus!
- Daily Activity Bank
- Read Alouds and Primary Sources
- Big Book Atlas
- Student Atlas
- Outline Maps
- Desk Maps

 **Technology**

- Video Field Trips
- Songs and Music
- Digital Learning CD-ROM Powered by KnowledgeBox
- AudioText
- MindPoint® Quiz Show CD-ROM
- ExamView® Test Bank CD-ROM
- Colonial Williamsburg Primary Sources CD-ROM
- Teacher Resources CD-ROM
- Map Resources CD-ROM
- SFSuccessNet: Online Student Edition, Online Teacher Edition, Online Planner
- **www.sfsocialstudies.com** (Biographies, news, references, maps, and activities)

 *To establish guidelines for your children's safe and responsible use of the Internet, use the Scott Foresman Internet Guide.*

**Additional Internet Links**

To find out more about:
- Tree Musketeers, visit **Info@TreeMusketeers.org**
- Living History Farms, visit **http://www.lhf.org**

# Unit 4 Objectives

## Beginning of Unit 4

- **Obtain information about a topic using a variety of oral sources such as music.** (pp. 136–137)
- **Use pictures to obtain information.** (pp. 138–139)
- **Determine the meanings of words.** (pp. 138–139)
- **Identify main ideas from print sources.** (pp. 140–141)

## Lesson 1
### What Is the Weather Today?
pp. 142–145

- **Identify and describe the physical characteristics of places, such as weather and climate.**
- **Describe how climate affects the way people live, including their clothing and recreation.**
- **Use vocabulary related to chronology, including *yesterday, today,* and *tomorrow.***
- **Distinguish among past, present, and future.** (pp. 146–147)
- **Create a time line.** (pp. 146–147)
- **Create visual and written material including time lines.** (pp. 146–147)

- **Interpret information presented in picture time lines to show sequence of events.** (pp. 146–147)
- **Learn how the seasons of the year affected everyday life and work long ago.** (pp. 148–149)
- **Compare work in the eighteenth century to work today.** (pp. 148–149)

## Lesson 2
### Looking at Our Land and Water
pp. 150–151

- **Identify and describe the physical characteristics of places such as landforms and bodies of water.**
- **Describe how location and physical surroundings affect the way people live, including their recreation.**
- **Identify a globe as a model of the Earth.** (pp. 154–155)
- **Distinguish between land and water on globes and maps.** (pp. 154–155)
- **Relate locations on globes to locations on the Earth.** (pp. 154–155)

## Lesson 3
### Our Earth's Resources
pp. 156–159

- **Identify and describe the physical characteristics of places such as their natural resources.**
- **Identify examples of and uses for natural resources in the community, state, and nation.**

- **Identify characteristics of good citizenship such as responsibility for the common good.** (pp. 160–163)
- **Identify ordinary people who exemplify good citizenship.** (pp. 160–161)

## Lesson 4
### Interview About Farm History
pp. 164–167

- **Distinguish among past, present, and future.**
- **Identify examples of and uses for natural resources.**
- **Identify contributions of historical figures who have influenced the nation.** (pp. 168–169)

## Lesson 5
### Caring for Our Resources
pp. 170–173

- **Identify ways that natural resources can be used and reused.**
- **Obtain information about a topic using maps and pictures.** (pp. 174–175)
- **Identify ways that protecting natural resources helps animals.** (pp. 174–175)
- **Respond to important problems with the Earth's natural resources.** (pp. 174–175)

## End of Unit 4
pp. 176–177

- **Retell stories from selected folktales and legends.**

# Assessment Options

## ✓ Formal Assessment

- **What did you learn?** PE/TE pp. 145, 153, 159, 167, 173, 181
- **Unit Review,** PE/TE pp. 178–181
- **Unit 4 Test,** Assessment Book pp. 13–16
- **ExamView CD-ROM**

## ✓ Informal Assessment

- **Teacher's Edition Questions,** throughout Lessons and Features
- **Close and Assess,** TE pp. 141, 145, 147, 149, 153, 155, 159, 161, 163, 167, 169, 173, 175, 177
- **Try it!** PE/TE pp. 141, 147, 155
- **Think and Share,** PE/TE pp. 145, 153, 159, 163, 167, 173
- **Responsibility in Action,** PE/TE p. 161

### Ongoing Assessment

**Ongoing Assessment** is found throughout the Teacher's Edition lessons using an **If…then** model.

**If** = students' observable behavior,

**then** = reteaching and enrichment suggestions

## ✓ Portfolio Assessment

- **Portfolio Assessment,** TE pp. 180
- **Leveled Practice,** TE pp. 138, 149a, 155a, 163a, 169a, 175a
- **Workbook,** pp. 35–46
- **Unit Review: Skills on Your Own,** PE/TE p. 180
- **Curriculum Connection: Writing,** TE pp. 136, 149a, 155a, 163a, 169a, 175a

## ✓ Performance Assessment

- **Hands-on Unit Project** (Unit 4 Performance Assessment), PE/TE pp. 135, 182
- **Internet Activity,** PE p. 182
- **Hands-on Unit Project,** PE/TE p. 182
- **Scoring Guides,** TE pp. 176a, 179, 180, 182

 **Test Talk**

## Test-Taking Strategies

**Understand the Question**
- **Locate Key Words in the Question,** TE p. 152
- **Locate Key Words in the Text,** TE p. 172

**Understand the Answer**
- **Choose the Right Answer,** Test Talk Practice Book
- **Use Information from the Text,** TE p. 144
- **Use Information from Graphics,** TE p. 166
- **Write Your Answer,** TE p. 161

*For additional practice, use the Test Talk Practice Book.*

## Featured Strategy

**Use Information from the Text**

Children will:

– Decide where they will look for the answer and make notes about details from the text.

– Use information from the text, then look back at the question and the text to make sure they have the right answer.

**PE/TE** p. 179, **TE** p. 144

# Curriculum Connections
## Integrating Your Day

The lessons, skills, and features of Unit 4 provide many opportunities to make connections between social studies and other areas of the elementary curriculum.

## Reading

**Reading Skill—Find the Main Idea,** PE/TE pp. 140–141, TE p. 142

**Reading Skill—Time Lines,** TE p. 147

**Reading Skill—Alike and Different,** TE p. 150

**Reading Skill—Find the Main Idea,** TE pp. 156, 170

**Reading Skill—Sequence,** TE p. 164

**Books About Things That Grow,** TE p. 176

## Writing

**Office Recycling Can,** TE p. 136

**Weather Word Puzzle,** TE p. 149a

**Where Am I?** TE p. 155a

**Poster,** TE p. 163a

**Farm Contest,** TE p. 169a

**Save Animals,** TE p. 175a

## Math

**Water, Water, Everywhere,** TE p. 163a

## Social Studies

## Literature

**A Prairie Boy's Winter,** TE p. 148

**Blue Whales,** TE p. 175a

**Books About Caring for Earth and About People Around the World,** TE p. 181

## Science

**Planting Trees,** TE p. 141

**Weather Prediction Chart,** TE p. 143

**Make a Weather Time Line,** TE p. 146

**Between a Rock and a Soft Place,** TE p. 163

**Trees, Above and Below,** TE p. 163a

**Research an Endangered Animal,** TE p. 175

## Music/Drama

**Living Time Lines,** TE p. 149a

**Take a Tour,** TE p. 169

**Mugs,** TE p. 175a

**Jill and Johnny Appleseed's Dance,** TE p. 177

## Art

**Make a Globe,** TE p. 155

**Build It!** TE p. 155a

 Look for this symbol throughout the Teacher's Edition to find **Curriculum Connections.**

# Professional Development

## The Place of Literature in a Social Studies Program

**by Dr. Valerie Ooka Pang**
San Diego University

Children's literature is one of the most important tools we, as teachers, can use in social studies education. Literature brings the hope and joy of life into the classroom. It celebrates the human spirit. Literature also describes the human condition. Well-written books can demonstrate how people from diverse communities work together to create a more compassionate and just society. Literature can also show the struggle of many individuals who have fought against oppressive practices and triumphed. It also provides children with the opportunity to look at life from many different people's perspectives.

*This unit provides several opportunities to incorporate children's literature into* Scott Foresman Social Studies.

- *For Lesson 1, read the hilarious spoof* Cloudy With a Chance of Meatballs *by Judi Barrett.*

- *For Lesson 2, read* Three Days on a River in a Red Canoe *by Vera B. Williams.*

- *For Lesson 3, read the Caldecott winner* The Gardener *by Sarah Stewart, illustrated by David Small.*

- *For Lesson 4, read* Aliki's Corn Is Maize: The Gift of the Indians, *as well as the biography of Sacagawea recommended on TE p. 169a.*

- *For Lesson 5, read the nonfiction book* Recycle! *by Gail Gibbons.*

## ESL Support

**by Jim Cummins, Ph. D.**
University of Toronto

Inviting students to contribute what they already know to the class discussion communicates to students that the cultural and linguistic knowledge they are bringing into the classroom is important. It also enables teachers to get to know their students much better than if students are confined to more passive roles in the classroom.

### Strategies for Activating Prior Knowledge and Building Background Knowledge

Teachers can use a variety of strategies to activate students' prior knowledge. Some of the most useful strategies are:.

- *Brainstorming/discussion as a whole class, in small groups, or in pairs*

- *Visuals in texts such as posters, photographs, etc., can be used to stimulate discussion about aspects of their meaning*

- *Direct experiences such as taking a walk around the neighborhood of the school or going on a field trip followed by a group language experience narrative.*

*The following examples in the Teacher's Edition will help you to activate ESL students' prior knowledge and to build background for the content of the lesson.*

- *Relate to Personal Experience on p. 140 encourages children to identify things they have seen that are named in the unit song.*

- *Using Pictures on p. 151 helps English language learners compare and contrast the physical characteristics of the plains to where they live.*

- *The Grand Tour of the Classroom on p. 157 asks children to identify things in their classroom made from natural resources, such as a pencil, jump rope, or paper bag.*

# Read Aloud

## Water
### By Hilda Conkling

The world turns softly

Not to spill its lakes and rivers.

The water is held in its arms

And the sky is held in the water.

What is water,

That pours silver,

And can hold the sky?

**Build Background**
- Ask children to show on a globe how the world "turns softly."
- Ask children to tell about reflections they have seen in water.

**Read Alouds and Primary Sources**
*Read Alouds and Primary Sources* contains additional selections to be used with Unit 4.

# Bibliography

*I Celebrate Nature,* by Diane Iverson (Dawn Publications, ISBN 1-883-22000-9, 1995) **Easy** *Notable Social Studies Book*

*I Took a Walk,* by Henry Cole (Greenwillow, ISBN 0-688-15115-9, 1998) **Easy**

*Morning, Noon, and Night,* by Jean Craighead George and Wendell Minor (Illustrator) (Harpercollins, ISBN 0-060-23628-0, 1999) **Easy**

*Backyard,* by Donald M. Silver and Patricia J. Wynne (Illustrator) (McGraw-Hill, ISBN 0-070-57930-X, 1997) Encourages children to explore their own backyards for interesting sights, sounds, and smells from the ground up. **On-Level**

*Birdsong,* by Audrey Wood and Robert Florczak (Illustrator) (Voyager, ISBN 0-152-02419-0, 2001) Children interact with birds in the wild, listening to their songs and viewing their habitats. **On-Level** *Notable Social Studies Book*

*Where Once There Was a Wood,* by Denise Fleming (Henry Holt, ISBN 0-805-06482-6, 2000) Celebrates the natural world that existed before a housing development appeared. **On-Level** *Notable Social Studies Book*

*Turtle Bay,* by Saviour Pirotta and Nilesh Mistry (Illustrator) (Farrar Straus & Giroux, ISBN 0-374-37888-6,1997) A boy learns about caring for Japanese sea turtles. **Challenge** *Notable Social Studies Book*

*Where Does the Garbage Go?* by Paul Showers, Randy and Paul Chewning (Illustrators) (Harpercollins, ISBN 0-064-45114-3, 1994) **Challenge**

*Mapmaking with Children: Sense of Place Education for the Elementary Years,* by David Sobel (Heinemann, ISBN 0-325-00042-5, 1998) **Teacher Reference**

**Discovery Channel School Videos**
*Dynamic Earth.* Meet Nature in a really bad mood. Learn about tidal waves, hurricanes, tornadoes, and lightning; 52 minutes/4 segments.

*Invention: Recycling.* Learn about how people create new ways to reuse materials and how this recycling helps save our environment; 27 minutes.

Look for this symbol throughout the Teacher's Edition to find **Award-Winning Selections**. Additional book references are suggested throughout this unit.

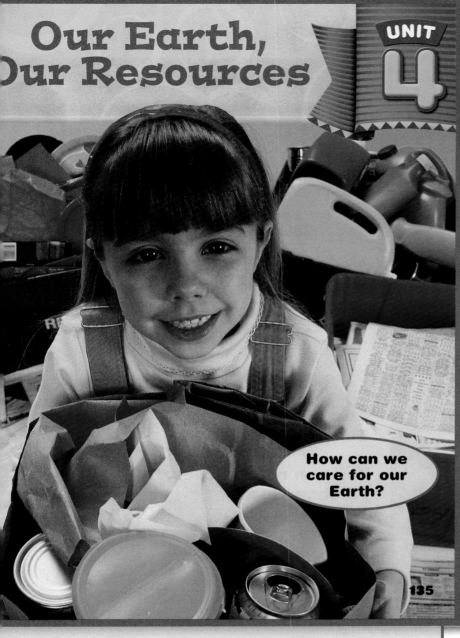

# Our Earth, Our Resources

# Our Earth, Our Resources

## Unit Overview

This unit introduces children to our Earth and its resources, and identifies and describes physical characteristics of places such as landforms, bodies of water, and weather.

## Introduce Debby

Read the unit title and then introduce the featured child for this unit as a first-grader named Debby. Talk about how Debby might take care of Earth.

## Unit Question

- Ask children the question on this page "How can we care for our Earth?"

- Initiate a discussion of ways people can care for Earth.

- To activate prior knowledge, make a list on the board of ways children name to care for Earth.

✔ **Portfolio Assessment** Keep a copy of this list for the Portfolio Assessment at the end of the unit on p. 180.

> How can we care for our Earth?

135

# Practice and Extend

## Hands-on Unit Project

✔ **Unit 4 Performance Assessment**

The Unit 4 Project, *Weather Report*, found on p. 182, is an ongoing performance assessment project to enrich children's learning throughout the unit.

- This project, which has children giving a television weather report, may be started now or at any time during this unit of study.

- A performance assessment scoring guide is located on p. 182.

# Show You Care

## Objective

- Obtain information about a topic using a variety of oral sources such as music.

## Resources

- *Songs and Music* CD "Show You Care"
- Poster 7
- Social Studies Plus!

# Introduce the Song

**Preview** Tell children that they will be singing a song about caring for our Earth. Point out that the song suggests ways for people to show they care in their daily life.

**Warm Up** To activate prior knowledge, discuss with children ways to care for our Earth at home, school, and recreational locations, such as a park or beach.

# Sing the Song

- Have children sing the song "Show You Care."

- Have children mime the ways to care described in the song.

- Have children mime other ways to care for our Earth.

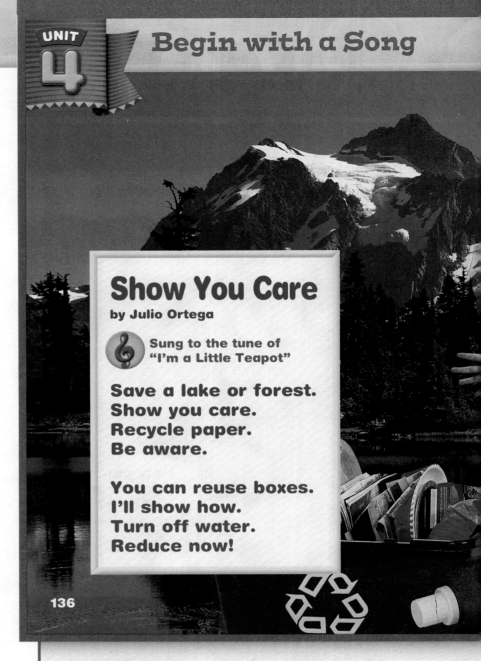

## Show You Care
by Julio Ortega

Sung to the tune of
"I'm a Little Teapot"

Save a lake or forest.
Show you care.
Recycle paper.
Be aware.

You can reuse boxes.
I'll show how.
Turn off water.
Reduce now!

136

# Practice and Extend

**CURRICULUM CONNECTION**
## Writing

**Office Recycling Can**

Explain to children that many offices have recycling cans for white paper only.

- Have children write *Recycle These* and *Not These* across the top of a sheet of paper.
- As you read the following to children, tell them to write down the papers under the appropriate headings: white photocopy paper, food wrappers, white paper for letters, newspapers, magazines.

**AUDIO CD**
## Technology

Play the CD, *Songs and Music*, to listen to "Show You Care."

# Talk About the Picture

Focus attention on the picture of Debby. Ask children to tell what is in the foreground (recycling bins) and the background (sky, mountains, trees, lake).

**① What things are in the recycling bins?**
Possible answers include plastic bottles, aluminum cans, paper plates, magazines, and cardboard boxes.
**Interpret Pictures**

**② Describe the landform and body of water.**
Answers will vary but may include a snow-capped mountain and a wide lake with still water.
**Interpret Pictures**

**SOCIAL STUDIES**
**Background**

**Possible Misconceptions**

Children may not understand the connection between recycling paper and saving the trees shown in the picture. Explain that trees and forests are valuable not only for their beauty and recreational use but also for their wood. Tell children that recycling paper helps protect these trees from people who might want to cut them down for wood.

## Vocabulary Preview

### Objectives
● Determine the meanings of words.
● Use pictures to obtain information.

### Resources
● Workbook, p. 35
● Vocabulary Cards
● Poster 8

### Introduce the Vocabulary

Read aloud and point to each vocabulary word and the photograph illustrating it. Have volunteers give the meanings of the words. Then have children find examples of geography vocabulary words in the picture in the following locations: the exhibit of landforms and bodies of water within the national park; the rest of the park; and beyond the park. Then have children find examples of history in the park.

| Vocabulary Word | Illustrated Examples |
| --- | --- |
| weather | partly cloudy, mildly windy, cool |
| mountain | exhibit of mountain, base of mountain, sign |
| plain | exhibit of plain, sign |
| lake | exhibit of lake, sign |
| river | exhibit of river, river |
| natural resource | air, trees, water, land |
| history | house, bridge, canoe |

⭐ **Social Studies Strand**
**Geography**

Listed below are some basic principles of geography for children. Direct most of your discussion of the picture toward the development of these concepts.

● kinds of weather

● kinds of landforms

● kinds of bodies of water

● kinds of natural resources

● uses of natural resources

Then explain that history is the story of people and places from the past. Direct the rest of your discussion toward the development of this concept.

weather

mountain

plain

138

## Practice and Extend

❄ **MEETING INDIVIDUAL NEEDS**
**Leveled Practice**

**Visit a National Park**

Invite children to visit the national park in the picture.
**Easy** Have children lead a tour through the exhibit of landforms and bodies of water, using vocabulary words.
**Reteach**
**On-Level** Have children lead a tour through the park and beyond, describing things that show the weather, such as the cloud shows it's partly cloudy, the kite shows it's mildly windy, the sweaters, long-sleeved shirts, and long pants show it's cool. **Extend**
**Challenge** Have children lead a tour through the park, describing things that might have been made in the past, such as the house, bridge, canoe, and fence. Ask children to describe how these things might be made in the present. **Enrich**

lake

river

natural resource

history

## Talk About the Picture

Allow children time to study the picture. The picture shows a national park with both physical and human characteristics of the environment. Encourage children to identify and describe both of these characteristics.

**1** **Look at the sky. What is the weather?** Cloudy **Analyze Pictures**

**2** **What body of water is nearest the "Enter" sign?** River **Analyze Pictures**

**3** **What things in the picture were made by people?** Answers will vary but may include the house, the bridge, the boat, and the fences. **Make Inferences**

## Look Ahead

Tell children they will learn more about each of the vocabulary words as they study Unit 4.

You may want to revisit the picture with children to review the concepts and vocabulary in the unit.

**4** **Look at the sign. What three activities might you do in the national park?** See plants on the plains, climb Bear Mountain, and hike in the woods. **Analyze Information**

### WEB SITE
## Technology

You can look up vocabulary words online. Click on *Social Studies Library* and select the dictionary at **www.sfsocialstudies.com.**

**Workbook, p. 35**

Draw a picture for each word. **Drawings will vary.**

| natural resource | mountain |
| history | lake |
| weather | plain |
| river | |

Also on Teacher Resources CD-ROM.

# Celebrate the Earth

## Find the Main Idea

### Objective
Identify main ideas from print sources.

### Resource
• Workbook, p. 36

### About the Unit Target Skill
• The target reading skill for this unit is Find the Main Idea.

• Children are introduced to the unit target skill here and are given an opportunity to practice it.

• Further opportunities to find the main idea are found throughout Unit 4.

# 1 Introduce and Motivate

**Preview** To determine if children understand how to find the main idea, write the following on the board: *Then they visit other flowers. The butterflies stop at a flower to drink the nectar. Nectar is a sweet liquid found in many flowers.* Ask a volunteer to rearrange the sentences and tell the main idea in his or her own words. (Possible answer: Butterflies drink nectar from flowers.) Then write the words *main idea* on the board and explain that the main idea is the most important idea.

**Warm Up** To activate prior knowledge, direct children's attention to the unit song on p. 136. Ask children what the song is about. Record their responses on the board. Discuss with children which response best describes the main idea. (Show you care about Earth.)

# Celebrate the Earth

## Find the Main Idea

Hi! My name is Debby. My class wrote a story for the school newspaper. Every story tells about something. What the story tells about is called the **main idea.** Read our story. Find the **main idea.**

## Butterfly Garden

Our class will take care of our Earth. We will plant a butterfly garden. We will plant flowers that butterflies like. We hope to have many butterfly visitors soon.

140

# Practice and Extend

**ESL** **ACTIVATE PRIOR KNOWLEDGE**
**ESL Support**

**Relate to Personal Experience** Remind children that the main idea of the song is *Show you care about Earth.* Have children draw pictures of three things they've seen that are named in the song. (Tree, forest, paper, or water)

**Beginning** Have children tell about their drawings.

**Intermediate** Have children identify their drawings by writing labels for them.

**Advanced** Have children write directions under their drawings telling how to show you care.

(Possible directions: "Recycle paper," "Reuse boxes," and "Turn off water.")

The **main idea** is in the first sentence of our newspaper story. The other sentences tell how my class will take care of the Earth.

You can use your own words to tell what a story is about. What is our newspaper story all about? It is about one way to take care of the Earth!

## Try it!

Write a story about something you like to do. Then write one sentence that tells the **main idea** of your story.

141

## CURRICULUM CONNECTION
### Science

**Planting Trees**

- Tell children that another way people can care for Earth is to plant trees.
- Explain to children that topsoil can be washed away by rain if grass, flowers, and trees do not hold it in place.
- Have children make drawings of grass, flowers, and trees above the ground and their roots under the ground.
- Remind students that grass has the smallest roots and trees have the biggest roots.

### Workbook, p. 36

**Find the Main Idea**

Cut out the headlines at the bottom of the page.
Paste the right headlines over the stories.

| Ms. Snow's class plants sunflowers. | Snowball visits first-grade class. |

Ms. Snow's class planted sunflower seeds. We dug holes in the ground. We put in the seeds. We watered them. We put up signs so people wouldn't walk on our plants. We can't wait for them to grow!

Nan brought her white guinea pig to class. Nan told us how she takes care of her pet. She feeds him sunflower seeds! We asked how Snowball got his name. Nan said that he curls into a ball to sleep.

| Ms. Snow's class plants sunflowers. | Snowball visits first-grade class. | Ms. Snow's class goes to the zoo. |

**Directions:** Read each news story. Then cut out the headlines at the bottom of the page. Decide which headline tells the main idea of each story. Paste the headlines in place.

**Home Activity:** Share a few newspaper headlines with your child. Talk about what the content of the news stories might be.

**Also on Teacher Resources CD-ROM.**

## 2 Teach and Discuss

Page 140

Read p. 140 and ask children to define *main idea*. (What a story tells about)

Page 140

**What sentences in the newspaper story support the main idea?** We will plant a butterfly garden. We will plant flowers that butterflies like. We hope to have many butterfly visitors soon. **Main Idea and Details**

### ✓ Ongoing Assessment

**If...** children think that a main idea can only be identified from print sources,

**then...** tell them that sometimes a main idea can be identified from oral and visual sources as well.

## 3 Close and Assess

### Try it!

The sentences about the story will vary but should summarize the story.

# Workbook Support

 Use the following Workbook pages to support content and skills development as you teach Unit 4. You can also view and print Workbook pages from the Teacher Resources CD-ROM.

## Workbook, p. 35

Use with Pupil Edition, p. 139.

## Workbook, p. 36

Use with Pupil Edition, p. 141.

## Workbook, p. 37

Use with Pupil Edition, p. 145.

## Workbook, p. 38

Use with Pupil Edition, p. 147.

## Workbook, p. 39

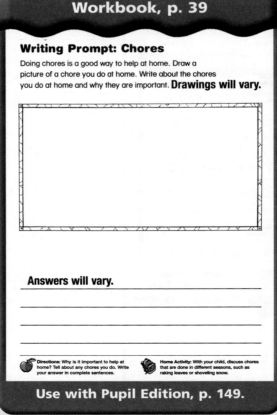

Use with Pupil Edition, p. 149.

## Workbook, p. 40

Use with Pupil Edition, p. 153.

# Workbook Support

## Workbook, p. 41

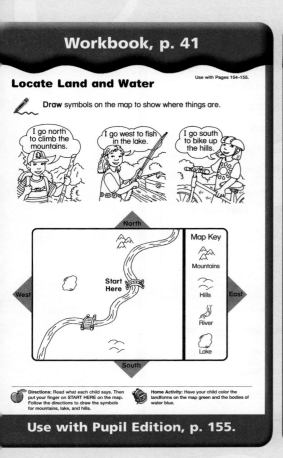

**Locate Land and Water**

Use with Pages 154–155.

Draw symbols on the map to show where things are.

*I go north to climb the mountains.*

*I go west to fish in the lake.*

*I go south to bike up the hills.*

Map Key
- Mountains
- Hills
- River
- Lake

North
West
East
South

Start Here

**Directions:** Read what each child says. Then put your finger on START HERE on the map. Follow the directions to draw the symbols for mountains, lake, and hills.

**Home Activity:** Have your child color the landforms on the map green and the bodies of water blue.

**Use with Pupil Edition, p. 155.**

## Workbook, p. 42

**Our Earth's Resources**

Use with Pages 156–159.

Draw a line to match each natural resource with a use.

water

soil

trees

oil and gas

Write an ending for the sentence.

I can take care of our natural resources by ___ **Possible answer:** **not wasting paper**

**Directions:** *Top:* Match each natural resource with a picture to show how it can be used by people. *Bottom:* Write to tell what you can do to help take care of our natural resources.

**Home Activity:** Help your child make a list of things in your home that come from trees.

**Use with Pupil Edition, p.159.**

## Workbook, p. 43

**Interview About Farm History**

Use with Pages 164–167.

Write *then* or *now* to tell about each picture.

**now**       **then**       **now**

**now (or) then**       **then**

Draw a job you might like to do on a farm. **Drawings will vary.**

**Directions:** *Top:* Decide if the picture shows the past or the present. Write *then* if it shows the past; write *now* if it shows the present. *Bottom:* Draw a job you might like to do on a farm.

**Home Activity:** Tell your child about a way in which machines have changed the way you do work.

**Use with Pupil Edition, p. 167.**

## Workbook, p. 44

**Caring for Our Resources**

Use with Pages–170–173.

Write *reduce*, *reuse*, or *recycle* by each picture.

*We brought our own bags!*       **reuse**

*Let's turn off the water.*       **reduce**

*We used to throw cans away!*       **recycle**

Write an ending for this sentence.

I can **reuse** by ___ **Answers will vary.**

**Directions:** Label each picture to tell whether it shows that people know how to *reduce*, *reuse*, or *recycle*. Then write to tell how you

**Home Activity:** Develop a plan with your child to reduce, reuse, and recycle. Try to get the whole family involved!

**Use with Pupil Edition, p. 173.**

## Workbook, p. 45

Write words to complete the sentences.

Use with Unit 4.

| | | |
|---|---|---|
| natural resource | lake | mountain |
| river | plain | weather |
| history | | |

1. In summer, we like to swim in the ___ **lake** .

2. You can see far from the top of the ___ **mountain** .

3. Water is a ___ **natural resource** we use for drinking.

4. We can't play outside in bad ___ **weather** .

5. I read a book about the ___ **history** of our flag.

6. A large piece of flat land is a ___ **plain** .

7. The water in a ___ **river** m oves toward a lake or the ocean.

**Directions:** Write a word or phrase to complete each sentence. Choose from the words and phrases in the box.

**Home Activity:** Help your child find pictures of various water and land features. Discuss which ones are found where you live.

**Use with Unit 4.**

## Workbook, p. 46

**4 Project   Weather Report**

Draw a picture of one kind of weather. **Drawings will vary.**

Write answers about the weather.

What kind of weather is it?       **Answers will vary.**

What are the children wearing?

What are the children doing?

**Directions:** *Top:* Draw one kind of weather. Include children. *Bottom:* Answer the questions.

**Home Activity:** Invite your child to describe what kind of clothes children wear and what children do in different kinds of weather.

**Use with Pupil Edition, p. 182.**

# Assessment Support

 Use these Assessment Book pages and the ExamView® CD-ROM to assess content and skills in Unit 4. You can also view and print Assessment Book pages from the Teacher Resources CD-ROM.

## Assessment Book, p. 13

### Unit 4: Content Test

Circle a word to finish each sentence.

1. A hill is not so high as a ____.
   lake        (mountain)

2. An ocean is much bigger than a ____.
   natural resource    (lake)

3. Air, water, and soil are examples of ____.
   endangered    (natural resources)

4. Tigers and blue whales are ____ animals.
   weather    (endangered)

**TEST PREP** Which word completes the sentence?

1. For days now, the ____ has been rainy.
   (a.) weather        b. natural resource
   c. history          d. river

2. That book tells the ____ of our state.
   a. mountain        (b.) history
   c. plain           d. lake

**Use with Pupil Edition, p. 178.**

## Assessment Book, p. 14

Write how you use each natural resource. **Sample answers.**

air _____ **to breathe** _____

water _____ **to drink** _____

soil _____ **to grow crops** _____

gas _____ **to drive cars** _____

Draw how you can help save a natural resource.

**Drawings will vary.**

Draw a line under the answer to each question.

1. Which is a large body of salt water?    pond    <u>ocean</u>    hill

2. Which do we get from trees?    oil    corn    <u>paper</u>

3. Who were the first farmers in Iowa?    Seneca    <u>Ioway</u>    Shoshone

4. What can you recycle at school?    <u>cans</u>    water    paint

**Use with Pupil Edition, p. 178.**

## Assessment Book, p. 15

### Unit 4: Skills Test

Look at the picture and read the story.

Jim wants to save trees. He doesn't take paper he doesn't need. When he writes, he writes on both sides. He uses the recycling bin to throw paper away. That way, the paper can be made into something for Jim to use again.

Draw a line under the main idea of the story.

Jim hikes in the woods.

<u>Jim wants to save trees.</u>

Jim is a good writer.

Draw to show what you did each day. **Drawings will vary.**

| Saturday | Sunday | Monday |
|---|---|---|
|  |  |  |

**Use with Pupil Edition, pp. 179–180.**

## Assessment Book, p. 16

Draw symbols on the map key.
Then use the key to make a map.

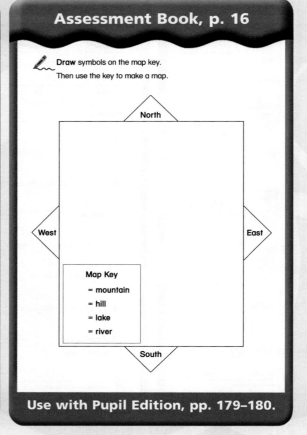

North

West        East

Map Key
= mountain
= hill
= lake
= river

South

**Use with Pupil Edition, pp. 179–180.**

**141c** Unit 4 • Our Earth, Our Resources

# Lesson 1 Overview

## Different Kinds of Weather
pages 142–145

Children will learn how weather affects their lives, and explore how weather is different in different locations.

 Time 20–30 minutes

Resources
- Workbook, p. 37
- Vocabulary Card weather
- Every Student Learns Guide, pp. 62–65

## Read a Time Line
pages 146–147

Children will learn how to read a time line.

 Time 15–20 minutes

Resource
- Workbook, p. 38

## Colonial Williamsburg
## Weather and Seasons Long Ago
pages 148–149

Children will learn how the seasons of the year affected everyday life and work long ago.

 Time 15–20 minutes

Resource
- Workbook, p. 39

# Build Background

## Activity

## What's the Weather?

 Time 15–20 minutes

Make a "What's the Weather?" poster similar to the one shown. Ask children what kind of day today is—is it sunny, cloudy, or windy? Is it cold, warm, or hot? Have children draw pictures of things affected by the weather. Children can add their pictures to the poster.

**If time is short,** ask children questions about today's weather. Sketch details on the poster reflecting children's answers.

"What's the Weather?"

## Read Aloud

## Fun in the Sun

### By Linda Popov

Today the sun will shine,
And fun outdoors will rule!
I love to play in the sun.
But I'm no fool.
When the air is too hot
I swim in a pool
And eat in the shade
Where it's cool.

# Lesson 1

## Different Kinds of Weather

### Objectives

- Identify and describe the physical characteristics of places, such as weather and climate.
- Describe how climate affects the way people live, including their clothing and recreation.
- Use vocabulary related to chronology, including *yesterday, today,* and *tomorrow.*

### Vocabulary

**weather** the way it is outside at a certain place and time (p. 142)

## QUICK Teaching Plan

*If time is short,* have children look at the pictures and describe the weather.

- Have children describe the weather outside.
- Have children describe activities they could do outside in this weather.

## 1 Introduce and Motivate

**Preview** Display the Vocabulary Card **weather** and say the word. Tell children that weather can be described using words such as *wet* or *dry*, *hot* or *cold, clear* or *cloudy, calm* or *windy.* Explain that weather can change from day to day. *Climate,* in contrast, is the kind of weather a place has. For example, the climate in southern Texas is usually very warm in summer, and less warm in winter.

**Warm Up** To activate prior knowledge, have children measure and record the outside temperature with a thermometer. Repeat this activity later in the day. Ask children how the temperature changed.

**142** Unit 4 • Our Earth, Our Resources

---

# Lesson 1

## Different Kinds of Weather

Today is hot.

Tomorrow my class is going to plant a butterfly garden. I can hardly wait! I hope the weather is nice. The **weather** ② is how it is outside at a certain place and time. I am going to check the weather report to see what tomorrow will be like.

①

Yesterday was warm and partly cloudy.

**142**

## Practice and Extend

### Target Skill
**READING/VOCABULARY**
**Find the Main Idea**

Tell children that this activity provides a main idea and asks them to give information that tells about this main idea.

- Ask children to write "I Wear Warm Things in Very Cold Weather" in the center oval of a spider map. Explain that this is the main idea.
- Then explain that what they wear in cold weather provides more information about the main idea.
- Ask children to brainstorm a list of clothing they wear in cold weather.
- Ask children to draw what they wear in cold weather in the ovals at the end of the spider legs.

If tomorrow is sunny, we can plant.

If tomorrow is rainy, we can draw.

3 4

143

### Page 142

Tell children that the first picture shows Debby yesterday. Read the caption. Tell them that the second picture shows her today. Read the speech bubble. Explain that weather words such as *warm, cloudy, hot, rainy,* and *sunny* can be used to describe the physical characteristics of places.

**1 How do you know yesterday's weather was partly cloudy?** The sky seen outside the window has clouds. **Analyze Pictures**

**2 What might you wear on a hot day?** Answers will vary but should include clothing appropriate for hot weather. **Analyze Pictures/Draw Conclusions**

### Page 143

**3 What are Debby and her father doing in the picture?** They are trying to find out tomorrow's weather. **Analyze Pictures**

**4 What will Debby's class do tomorrow in the sunny weather?** The class will help plant a butterfly garden. **Apply Information**

### SOCIAL STUDIES STRAND
### S|T Science/Technology

Point out that Debby and her father are learning about tomorrow's weather by reading the newspaper. Ask children what other sources they can use to obtain information about a topic such as tomorrow's weather. (Possible answers: Internet, radio, and television)
**Make Inferences/Apply Information**

### CURRICULUM CONNECTION
### Science

**Weather Prediction Chart**

- Have children predict tomorrow morning's weather.
- First draw a 3-column chart on the board with *Today's Weather, Weather Prediction,* and *Actual Weather* as the heads. Then have children fold a piece of paper and copy the chart.
- Ask them to fill in the first two columns today, and the third column tomorrow, using such words as *hot, warm, cool,* or *cold; sunny* or *cloudy; clear* or *rainy.*

### WEB SITE
### Technology

You can look up vocabulary words online. Click on *Social Studies Library* and select the dictionary at **www.sfsocialstudies.com.**

### Page 144

**5** **Why does Debby wonder about the weather in Michigan?** Her pen-pal class is there.
**Make Inferences**

Explain to children that an e-mail can be sent from one computer to another computer far away. Point out that the picture of children planting flowers is part of the e-mail.

### Test Talk

**Use Information from the Text**

**6** **According to the e-mail, what will the weather be tomorrow in California?** Hot and sunny. Have children reread the text to make sure they have the right answer. **Apply Information**

**7** **Where does Debby's pen-pal class live? How do you know?** The pen-pal class lives in Michigan. They signed their e-mail "Your pals in Michigan," and there is a map pointing out Detroit, Michigan. **Main Idea and Details**

### Page 145

Discuss the e-mail, text, and illustrations on p. 145. Point out that this e-mail letter answers the e-mail on p. 144.

 **GEOGRAPHY THEMES**
**Place**

**8** **What ways can you play in a place where it snows?** Answers will vary, but may include build a snowman, sled, and ski. **Make Inferences**

**9** **Decision Making** If it was cold outside, would you stay inside or go out to play? Answers will vary, but should include such considerations as clothing, temperature, and availability of playmates.

---

I live in California. My class has a pen-pal class in Michigan. Our teacher helps us e-mail them. I wonder if the weather will be warm in Michigan tomorro

San Diego, California

Hi everyone,
Tomorrow we will plant lots of brightly colored flowers. It will be hot and sunny. Some of us will ride our bikes to school. What is the weather like where you live?

Your pen pals in California **5** **6**

144

## Practice and Extend

**ESL** **EXTEND LANGUAGE**
## ESL Support

**Matching Words with Pictures** Have children draw pictures of a favorite warm-weather activity. These may include riding a bicycle, flying a kite, having a picnic, or swimming in the ocean.

**Beginning** Have children use home-language words to describe the activity. For each home-language word they use, provide the English translation.

**Intermediate** Have children complete the following sentence: "In my picture I am _____."

**Advanced** Have children write a one-sentence description of the activity.

*For additional support, use Every Student Learns Guide, pp. 62–65.*

Dear California pen pals,
The weather here is cold today. Yesterday was cold too. Tomorrow is supposed to be cold again. We will play in the snow at recess.

Have fun,
Your pals in Michigan ❼❽❾

Detroit, Michigan

## What did you learn?

1. How does the **weather** help you decide what to do?

2. What is the **main idea** of the letter from the class in Michigan?

3. **Think and Share** Write the words *yesterday, today,* and *tomorrow.* Draw a picture of the weather for each day. Write a sentence about each picture.

**145**

**Workbook, p. 37**

Different Kinds of Weather

Draw your neighborhood in the winter. **Drawings will vary.**

Draw your neighborhood in the summer.

Write what you do in the summer.
**Answers will vary.**

**Also on Teacher Resources CD-ROM.**

---

SOCIAL STUDIES STRAND
## Geography

Remind children that climate is the kind of weather a place has. Ask them what the climate is during the summer and winter where they live. Suggest that they use such words as *usually, often,* and *mostly* as well as *hot* and *cold, moist* and *dry,* and *clear* and *cloudy.* Have children use the Internet to research the summer and winter climates in northern Michigan and southern California. Then ask children how the summer and winter climates in these places affect people's decisions about clothing and activities.

Explain to children that different regions of the country experience extreme weather, such as blizzards, tornadoes, and hurricanes. In 2005, Hurricanes Katrina and Rita forced thousands of families to leave their homes near the Gulf Coast.

## 3 Close and Assess

Have children listen to a weather report on the radio. Remind them that knowing what the weather will be can help them make decisions about what to do and what to wear.

### ✓ What did you learn?

1. Answers will vary. Possible answers: Knowing what the weather will be can help people decide what to wear, what to do, and where to go.

2. The weather is cold in Michigan.

3. **Think and Share** The drawings under *yesterday* and *today* should accurately show the weather for those days. Answers for the sentence will vary but should describe the weather.

# Read a Time Line

## Objectives

- Distinguish among past, present, and future.

- Create a time line.

- Create visual and written material including time lines.

- Interpret information presented in picture time lines to show sequence of events.

## Vocabulary

**time line** A line that shows the order in which things happened (p. 146)

## 1 Introduce and Motivate

**Preview** Tell children what a **time line** is and point to the time line on pp. 146–147 as an example. Explain that this time line shows how the weather changes over five days.

**Warm Up** To activate prior knowledge, have children discuss steps they take to prepare for going to school. Tell them that creating a time line for these events can help them more easily explain to people how they prepare for school.

# Read a Time Line

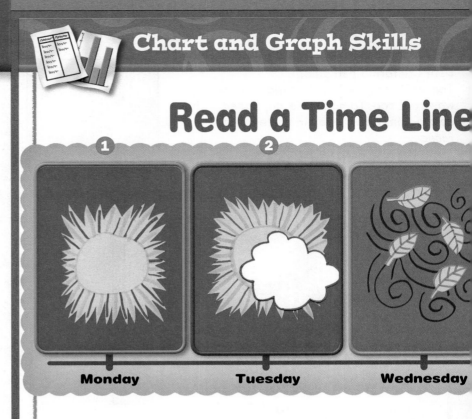

| ① Monday | ② Tuesday | Wednesday |
|----------|-----------|-----------|

Debby and her class wanted to show how the weather might change during one school week. They made a time line. A **time line** shows the order in which things happen. Look at the time line. Tell how the weather changed from day to day.

146

## Practice and Extend

**CURRICULUM CONNECTION**
**Science**

### Make a Weather Time Line

- Help children record how windy it is on a time line using the words *high, medium,* and *low.* Have children hold a ruler with an attached piece of fabric outside the window. Explain that the windier the day, the more the fabric will move.

- Have children use this method to record how windy it is on a time line for five days.

**WEB SITE**
**Technology**

You can look up the vocabulary term by going online. Click on *Social Studies Library* and select the dictionary at **www.sfsocialstudies.com.**

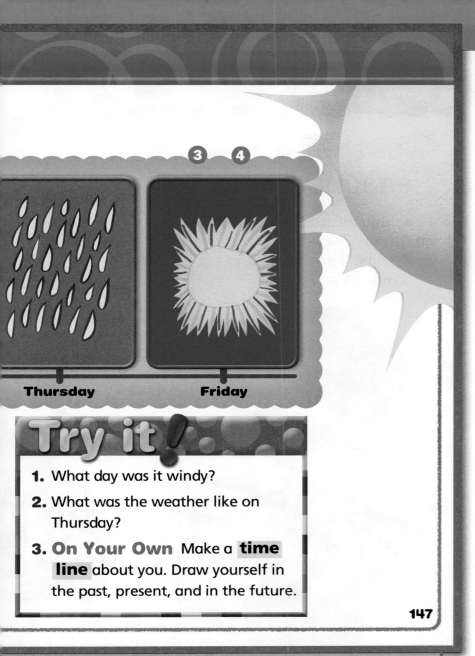

**3** **4**

Thursday          Friday

## Try it!

1. What day was it windy?

2. What was the weather like on Thursday?

3. **On Your Own** Make a **time line** about you. Draw yourself in the past, present, and in the future.

147

### READING SKILL
## Time Lines

- Have children create a time line with pictures that show what they did yesterday and today and what they will do tomorrow.

- Have children exchange time lines with a partner.

- Direct children to describe what their partner did yesterday and today and will do tomorrow. Tell them to use the words *yesterday, today,* and *tomorrow* in their descriptions. Explain that yesterday is about the past, today is about the present, and tomorrow is about the future.

### Workbook, p. 38

**Read a Time Line**

Draw to show what you did or will do. **Drawings will vary.**

Yesterday          Today          Tomorrow

**Also on Teacher Resources CD-ROM.**

## 2 Teach and Discuss

Page 146

**1** **What is the first day on the time line?**
Monday **Interpret Time Lines**

**2** **What was the weather like on Tuesday? How can you tell?** It was cloudy.
The sky has clouds. **Interpret Time Lines/Make Inferences/Analyze Pictures**

Page 147

**3** **Suppose it is Friday. Tell what the weather is *today*. Then tell what the weather was *yesterday*.** Today it is sunny. Yesterday it was rainy.
**Interpret Time Lines**

**4** **How was the weather on Monday and Friday alike?** Both days were sunny.
**Compare and Contrast/Interpret Time Lines**

## 3 Close and Assess

## Try it!

1. It was windy on Wednesday.

2. It was rainy.

3. **On Your Own** Time lines will vary but should include three pictures, labels of children's ages, and depictions of themselves that reflect the past, present, and future.

# Weather and Seasons Long Ago

## Objectives

- Learn how the seasons of the year affected everyday life and work long ago.

- Compare work in the eighteenth century to work today.

## 1 Introduce and Motivate

- Explain to children that two hundred years ago most people were farmers.

- Discuss with children the types of activities that take place in farm communities (plowing, planting, weeding, and harvesting).

- Explain to children that a long time ago most farm work was done by hand. The work also changed according to the season.

## 2 Teach and Discuss

**ST SOCIAL STUDIES STRAND**
**Science • Technology**

- **Gathering firewood** Ask children to identify what this young man is carrying. Explain that there was no electricity in the eighteenth century. Instead, people used firewood to heat their homes and cook food. The daily chore of gathering and bringing wood into the home was frequently given to children.

- **Milking a cow** Many farm families owned cows. Ask children if they know of any food products that come from cows. Cattle are used to provide dairy products such as milk, cream, butter, and cheese. In the 1700s, the chore of feeding and milking cows everyday was often given to children.

# Weather and Seasons Long Ago

Long ago most children lived on farms. They did chores every day. They worked in all kinds of weather.

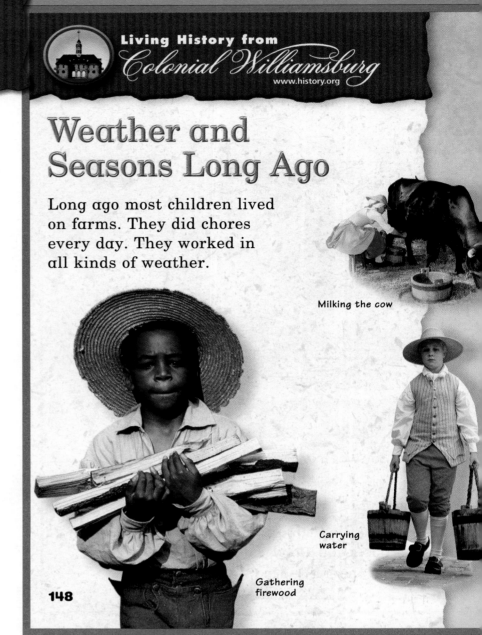

Milking the cow

Carrying water

Gathering firewood

**148**

# Practice and Extend

**FYI SOCIAL STUDIES**
**Background**

### Chores
*by Dr. William E. White, Colonial Williamsburg Historian*

- In the 1700s most Americans were farmers. They planted crops every spring and hoped for good weather. Each season had its special jobs and chores. Children helped plant and tend the crops. They also helped with the harvest.

- Today we heat and cool our buildings to control the climate as the seasons change, but early Americans were cold in the winter and hot in the summer. Most families used wood to cook and to heat their houses. Children helped cut and split firewood in the spring and summer. During the autumn and winter, children carried firewood into the house each day and tended the fireplace to keep the house warm.

- There were few schools in colonial America. Most children were taught at home. Young ladies learned how to run a household. Young men learned about farming and the raising of animals.

## Each Season Had Special Chores

**Spring**
Farmers plowed the fields and planted in the warm and rainy spring.

**Summer**
In the hot summer they took care of the garden and pulled the weeds.

**Winter**
The cold winter days were spent working indoors.

**Autumn**
It was time to harvest when autumn came.

What kind of chores do you do at home? Are they different in every season?

149

- **Carrying water** Another chore for children was to carry water into the household from streams and wells. Ask children what they think this water was used for. Large quantities of water had to be carried into the house each day for drinking, cooking, and cleaning.

- **Spring** This picture shows a 1700s farmer using oxen to plow his field. Farmers prepared the fields and planted crops each spring. Ask children if their family has a garden or house plants. What types of plants do they grow?

- **Summer** In this picture children are weeding the family garden. Summer is the growing season. Fruits and vegetables need to be constantly watered and weeded. Ask children to discuss what chores they do during summer.

- **Autumn** This picture shows a man harvesting some potatoes. Fall is the end of the growing season and field crops that have been growing since spring are ready for harvest. It takes a lot of people to harvest crops. Everyone, including children, helped with the work. Ask children if they have special chores in autumn.

- **Winter** In this picture a father teaches his son how to make a basket—an ideal indoor task during the cold winter months. Eighteenth-century families spent much of their time indoors doing such things as repairing tools, making household items such as baskets, and sewing or mending clothes. Ask children what kinds of activities they enjoy in the winter and how the weather affects their daily lives.

## 3 Close and Assess

- Review each of the seasons and remind children how weather changes with each season.

- Ask children to fold a piece of paper twice to create four equal sections. Have them write one season in each section at the top.

- Using the four sections, have children draw a picture and label the activities they do in each of the four seasons.

## CURRICULUM CONNECTION
## Writing

### Chores at Home

- Ask children if they help with chores at home. Make a list of the different types of chores children currently help with or would like to help with.

- Have children make four-page booklets to take home. On each page, they should draw and/or write about a chore they can help with at home.

- Have them take their booklets home to share with their families.

### Workbook, p. 39

**Writing Prompt: Chores**

Doing chores is a good way to help at home. Draw a picture of a chore you do at home. Write about the chores you do at home and why they are important. **Drawings will vary.**

Answers will vary.

*Directions:* Why is it important to help at home? Tell about any chores you do. Write your answer in complete sentences.

**Home Activity:** With your child, discuss chores that are done in different seasons, such as raking leaves or shoveling snow.

Workbook    Writing Prompt **39**

**Also on Teacher Resources CD-ROM.**

# Lesson ① Wrap-Up

 **MEETING INDIVIDUAL NEEDS**
## Leveled Practice

### Find Weather Pictures
Provide children with magazines and ask them to cut out pictures showing people in different kinds of weather.

**Easy** Ask children to sort the pictures into categories such as "sunny," "rainy," "cold," or "hot." Prompt them with pictures from each stack to describe what people are doing. **Reteach**

**On-Level** Have children choose a picture and tell a story about the people in it. Stories should describe the weather and how it has affected what people are wearing and doing. **Extend**

**Challenge** Direct children to choose pictures that reflect the local weather yesterday and today. Have them label the pictures in correct time order. Invite children to tell the class about the pictures, using the words *yesterday* and *today*. **Enrich**

## Hands-on Activities

 **CURRICULUM CONNECTION**
### Writing/Vocabulary

## Weather Word Puzzles

**Objective** Demonstrate an understanding of new vocabulary; use weather words to fit shapes.

**Resources** Vocabulary Card: **weather**

**Materials** crayons

**Learning Style** Verbal-Linguistic

**Individual**
⏱ **Time** 10–15 minutes

1. Hand out weather word puzzles, using the words *cloud, rainy,* and *wind*.

2. Have children write the weather word from the box in the shape that fits.

3. Remind children to add the vocabulary word *weather* to their "My Word Book."

 **SOCIAL STUDIES STRAND**
### Geography

## Storm Warning

**Objective** Create a class weather report.

**Materials** poster board, crayons

**Learning Style** Verbal-Linguistic

**Group** 👥👥👥👥
⏱ **Time** 15–20 minutes

1. Help children pretend to predict tomorrow's weather—a big storm—by dramatizing a television weather report.

2. Help children create a large weather map of the local region. Then have children stand next to the map and describe the approaching storm. Have them include suggestions for what people should wear.

3. Invite children to take turns delivering the weather report "in the studio" and "on location."

 **CURRICULUM CONNECTION**
### Drama

## Living Time Lines

**Objective** Create and dramatize a family time line.

**Materials** paper, pencils, crayons

**Learning Style** Bodily-Kinesthetic

**Partners**
⏱ **Time** 15–30 minutes

1. Have children draw a time line using the words "past," "present," and "future." Ask them to draw pictures of their families traveling to a place (past), learning about a place (present), and leaving the place (future).

2. Invite partners or small groups to dramatize their time lines.

# Lesson ❷ Overview

## Looking at Our Land and Water
pages 150–153

Children will learn about different landforms including mountains, hills, and plains. They will explore bodies of water, such as oceans, lakes, and rivers.

 Time 20–30 minutes

**Resources**
- Workbook p. 40
- Vocabulary Cards
  mountain  plain
  lake  river
- Every Student Learns Guide, pp. 66–69

## Locate Land and Water
pages 154–155

Children will learn how to recognize land and water on a globe and a map.

Time 15–20 minutes

**Resource**
- Workbook, p. 41

# Build Background

## Activity

## Matching Pictures

Have children cut out a magazine photograph of a mountain, plain, hill, lake, river, or ocean. Then have children paste the photograph on paper.

Have children identify the land and water features in their photograph. Write the landform or body of water on an index card.

Invite children to select a card at random and show it to the class. Ask children to tell which photograph the card describes.

**If time is short,** show children some pictures of different landforms and bodies of water and ask them to describe each one.

## Read Aloud

## Favorite Places
### by Seth Coleman

In winter the mountain
Is covered with snow.
If you like to ski,
That's where to go.

In winter the lake
Is a sheet of ice.
If you like to skate,
The lake is quite nice.

But me—I like summer,
It's sunny; it's hot.
I go to the ocean;
That's *my* favorite spot!

### Lesson

# 2 Looking at Our Land and Water

## Objectives

- Identify and describe the physical characteristics of places such as landforms and bodies of water.

- Describe how location and physical surroundings affect the way people live, including their recreation.

## Vocabulary

**mountain** the highest kind of land (p. 150)

**plain** a large piece of land that is mostly flat (p. 151)

**lake** a body of water with land totally or almost totally around it (p. 152)

**river** a long body of water that usually moves toward a lake or an ocean (p. 153)

## QUICK Teaching Plan

*If time is short,* guide children in drawing different landforms and bodies of water.

- Use the pictures on pp. 150–153 to prompt children's drawings.

# 1 Introduce and Motivate

**Preview** Have children preview the illustrations on pp. 150–153. Then display the Vocabulary Cards **mountain**, **plain**, **lake**, and **river**. Ask children to tell what each word means. Tell children they will learn about some other kinds of land and water in this lesson.

**Warm Up** To activate prior knowledge, ask children which is bigger, an ocean or a lake and a mountain or a hill. Invite them to name activities they could do at these places.

### Lesson

# 2 Looking at Our Land and Water

Places on the Earth can have different kinds of weather. They can have different kinds of land and water too. We can do many things on land and in the water. My class is saving pictures of different kinds of land and water. ①

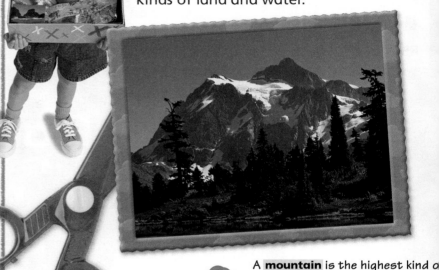

② A **mountain** is the highest kind of land. It can snow and get very cold at the top of a mountain.

**150**

# Practice and Extend

### READING SKILL
## Alike and Different

- Have children point to and describe the different landforms and bodies of water in the photographs on pp. 150–153.

- Name pairs of landforms or bodies of water. Have children use comparison words *bigger, smaller, taller,* and *flatter* to compare the relationship between the two.

### WEB SITE
## Technology

You can look up vocabulary words online. Click on *Social Studies Library* and select the dictionary at **www.sfsocialstudies.com**.

A hill is land that is higher than the land around it. A hill is not as high as a mountain. Hills have rounded tops.

A **plain** is a large piece of land. A plain is mostly flat. Plains are good for growing different kinds of food.

151

Page 150

Have children read the paragraph. Then have a volunteer read the caption aloud as you point to the mountains and snow in the picture.

**1 What is the main idea of the paragraph?** Places on Earth can have different kinds of land and water. **Main Idea and Details**

✓ **Ongoing Assessment**

| **If...** children think that the main idea is always the first sentence of a paragraph, | **then...** remind them that sometimes the main idea may be elsewhere in the paragraph. |
|---|---|

**2 What kind of weather might you find on a mountain?** It can be cold and snowy. **Recall and Retell**

Page 151

Have children describe the landforms in the two pictures.

$ **SOCIAL STUDIES STRAND**
**Economics**

Point out to students that the work people do may depend on the region in which they live. Tell them plains are good for farming because it is easy to plant and grow things there. Farmers can more easily use tractors and other machines on flat land than on hills. Ask children what kind of job people might do in the mountains. (Possible answers: Ski instructor or guide)

**Lesson 2** continued

**Page 152**

**3** **A beach is often next to an ocean. What can you do at the beach?** Possible answers: Dig a hole in the sand, look for shells, play catch.
**Apply Information**

**Test Talk**

**Locate Key Words in the Question**

**4** **How are a lake and an ocean alike? How are they different?** Answers may include: Alike: Oceans and lakes are both made up of water and are good for swimming and fishing. Different: Oceans are much bigger than lakes. Oceans have salt water. Most lakes have fresh water. Tell children that a key word such as *alike* tells them to look for similarities and a key word such as *different* tells them to look for contrast. **Compare and Contrast**

Explain to children that some features of Earth are human-made, such as a reservoir. Have children compare a natural lake to an artificial lake.

**GEOGRAPHY THEMES**
**Region**

Point out that a **region** is a large land area that has special features. These special features make a region different from other areas. Explain that our country can be divided into five regions: the Western Region, the Southwest Region, the Midwest Region, the Southeast Region, and the Northeast Region. Look at a map of the United States. Ask children to identify regions in which they would find mountains, hills, plains, oceans, or lakes. Be sure to discuss other features of each region. Have volunteers tell which region different states are in, including their own state.

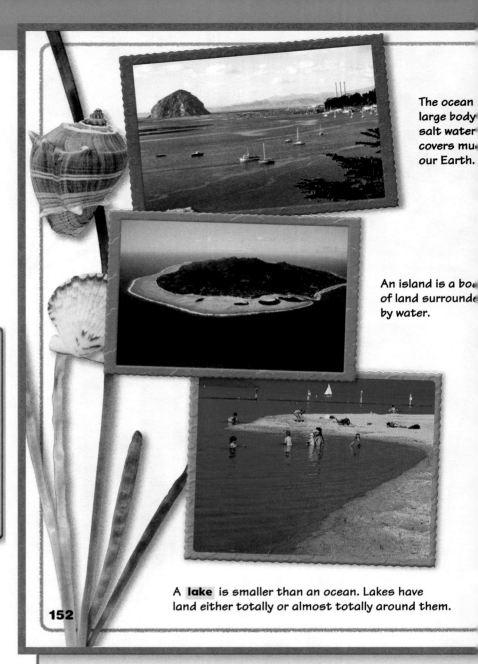

The ocean large body salt water covers mu our Earth.

An island is a bo of land surrounde by water.

A **lake** is smaller than an ocean. Lakes have land either totally or almost totally around them.

152

# Practice and Extend

**FYI**  **SOCIAL STUDIES**
**Background**

**About Oceans**

- Remind children that there are four oceans: the Atlantic, Pacific, Indian, and Arctic. Help children locate these oceans on a map or globe.
- Explain that the four oceans flow into each other.
- Point out that the Pacific Ocean is the largest ocean, and the Arctic Ocean is the smallest.
- Point out that the Pacific Ocean is also the deepest ocean. It is deeper than the tallest mountain is tall.
- Show children gulfs, bays, or seas that form as oceans meet the land. Explain that they are still part of an ocean.

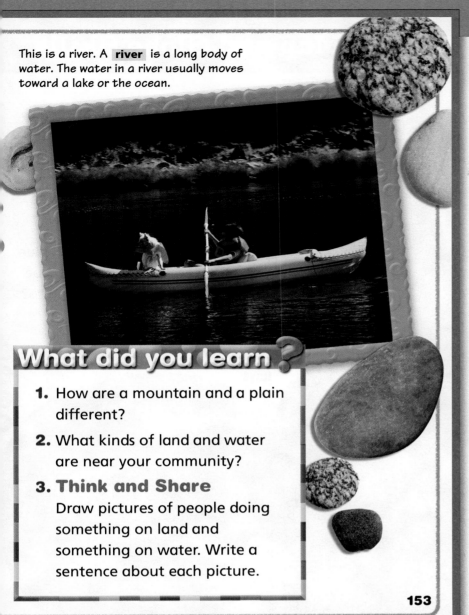

This is a river. A **river** is a long body of water. The water in a river usually moves toward a lake or the ocean.

## What did you learn ?

1. How are a mountain and a plain different?

2. What kinds of land and water are near your community?

3. **Think and Share**
   Draw pictures of people doing something on land and something on water. Write a sentence about each picture.

153

Discuss the illustration with children.

**5** **How is the water in a river different from the water in most lakes?** Answers may include: In a river, the water usually moves toward a lake, ocean, or another river. In most lakes, the water is totally or almost totally surrounded by land. **Compare and Contrast**

**6** **What kinds of activities could you do in a river?** Possible answers: Swimming, boating, fishing, and rafting **Apply Information**

# 3 Close and Assess

Ask children to name some things they could do at each of the places shown in the lesson. Then invite volunteers to tell which place they would most like to visit and why.

## ✓ What did you learn ?

1. A mountain is a very high kind of land. A plain is a flat area of land.

2. Children should correctly identify any nearby mountains, hills, plains, river, lakes, or oceans.

3. **Think and Share** The activities shown in the drawings and described in the sentence should be appropriate to the land and water depicted in the drawings.

**Workbook, p. 40**

Looking at Our Land and Water

Write a label for each postcard.

| lake | river | hill | ocean | plain |

hill

ocean

plain

lake

river

Color the postcards.
Use green for landforms.
Use blue for bodies of water.

**Also on Teacher Resources CD-ROM.**

Unit 4 • Lesson 2 **153**

# Locate Land and Water

## Objectives

- Identify a globe as a model of Earth.
- Distinguish between land and water on globes and maps.
- Relate locations on globes to locations on Earth.

## 1 Introduce and Motivate

**Preview** Point out that the word *locate* in the lesson title means *find*. Direct children's attention to the globe and tell them that this is what the Earth looks like from space.

**Warm Up** To activate prior knowledge, show children a globe. Have them find land and water. Remind them that a continent (such as Europe, North America, Africa, or Asia) is a very large body of land; most continents have countries on them (the continent Australia has only one country, and Antartica has no countries, although it's used by several countries as a scientific research center); and a state (such as California or Florida) is part of a country.

## 2 Teach and Discuss

| Page 154 |
|---|

Read the introduction. Prior to finding locations on the globe, explain to children that a globe is a round model of Earth.

### ✓ Ongoing Assessment

| If... children do not understand that a globe is a model of Earth, | then... explain that a model is a small copy of something. Compare other models (such as a dollhouse or a model train) to the things they represent. |
|---|---|

## Map and Globe Skills

# Locate Land and Water

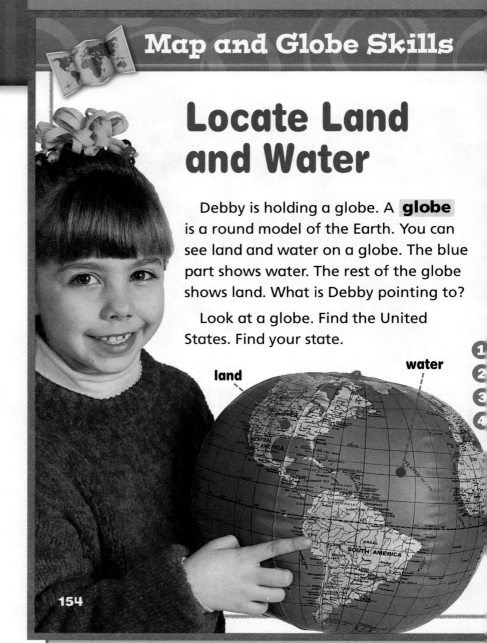

Debby is holding a globe. A **globe** is a round model of the Earth. You can see land and water on a globe. The blue part shows water. The rest of the globe shows land. What is Debby pointing to?

Look at a globe. Find the United States. Find your state.

land        water

154

## Practice and Extend

**ESL** **ACCESS CONTENT**
**ESL Support**

**Using a Globe** Have children plan a trip to Mexico from their home community. Ask what direction they would travel. Model pointing north, south, east, and west on the globe.

**Beginning** Show children the route from their home community to Mexico, saying the cardinal directions. Have children repeat the directions.

**Intermediate** Have children trace the route from their home community to Mexico, saying the directions.

**Advanced** Have children trace a round trip from their home community to Mexico and back, saying the directions.

What kinds of land and water do you see on the map?

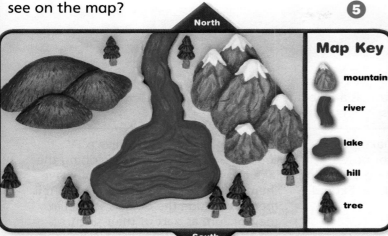

**5**

North

**Map Key**

🏔 **mountain**

〰 **river**

◖ **lake**

⬮ **hill**

🌲 **tree**

East

South

## Try it!

1. What does a **globe** show? How is it like the Earth?

2. Is the river east or west of the hills?

3. **On Your Own** Look at a map of your state. Name the different kinds of land and water there.

For more information, go online to *Atlas* at www.sfsocialstudies.com.

**155**

**CURRICULUM CONNECTION**
**Art**

**Make a Globe**

- Give children a blown-up balloon, tape, and a paper cut-out of North America and South America.
- Then help them tape the continent cut-out to their "globe."

**WEB SITE**
**Technology**

You may help children find out more by clicking on *Atlas* at www.sfsocialstudies.com.

**Workbook, p. 41**

Locate Land and Water

Also on Teacher Resources CD-ROM.

---

Show children a globe. Briefly discuss the continents. Then help children find the locations in the questions below.

**❶ Where is the continent of North America on the globe?** Children should correctly identify North America. **Interpret Globes**

**❷ Where is the United States on the globe?** Children should correctly locate the United States. **Interpret Globes**

**❸ Where is your state on the globe?** Children should correctly find the approximate location of their state. **Interpret Globes**

Children may notice the line running around the middle of the globe. Explain that this line is called the equator, and it divides Earth into two parts.

**❹ Where is your local community on the globe?** Children should correctly find the approximate location of their local community. **Interpret Globes**

**Page 155**

Discuss each symbol on the map key with children. Then ask them to identify the landforms and bodies of water on the map. Point out the direction tabs.

**❺ Look at the map. Are the mountains to the east or west of the river and lake?** East **Interpret Maps**

## 3 Close and Assess

## Try it!

1. The globe shows the land and water on Earth. Both Earth and a globe are shaped like a ball.

2. The river is east of the hills.

3. **On Your Own** Children should accurately identify land and water in the state.

# Lesson ② Wrap-Up

Use with pages 150–155

## MEETING INDIVIDUAL NEEDS
## Leveled Practice

**Draw Pictures of Land and Water**
Ask children to draw pictures of a lake including objects in the lake, such as a sailboat, ducks, and a tiny island, and around the lake, such as houses and trees.

**Easy** Have children identify the objects in and around the lake. **Reteach**

**On-Level** Have children make their picture into a vacation spot poster. Have them create an inviting title using a made-up name for the lake. **Extend**

**Challenge** Have children give a TV commercial for the lake, describing the lake as an inviting vacation spot. Have them make up a name for the lake. Tell them to include the objects shown in their picture as part of their pitch. **Enrich**

## Hands-on Activities

### CURRICULUM CONNECTION
### Writing/Vocabulary

## Where Am I?

**Objective** Demonstrate the meaning of the words *mountain* and *lake*.

**Resources** Vocabulary Cards: **mountain, lake**

**Materials** pencils, paper

**Learning Style** Verbal

**Partners**

 **Time** 10–15 minutes

1. Have partners write features of a mountain or lake.

2. Invite partners to prompt each other with "clues" from their list, asking "Where am I?"

3. Partners should provide clues until the location is recognized.

4. Remind partners to add the vocabulary words *mountain, plain, lake,* and *river* to their "My Word Book."

### CURRICULUM CONNECTION
### Art

## Build It!

**Objective** Make a landform model to identify and describe physical characteristics of places.

**Materials** modeling clay, water, plastic lunch trays

**Learning Style** Visual/Kinesthetic

**Group**

 **Time** 20–25 minutes

1. Have groups use modeling clay on a tray to create a landform model of a river flowing into a lake.

2. Groups may add water to their model.

### SOCIAL STUDIES STRAND
### Geography

## Spinning Globes

**Objective** Use cardinal directions to locate places on a globe.

**Materials** classroom globe

**Learning Style** Visual/Kinesthetic

**Partners**

 **Time** 10–15 minutes

1. Have a partner slowly spin the globe. Then have the partner stop the spinning by placing a finger on the globe. This spot is the starting place.

2. Then have the other partner trace the most direct route from the starting place to the United States to the home region to the approximate location of the home state, saying the direction of the route (north, south, east, west).

3. Have partners change roles. Repeat the game until all partners have had a turn.

# Lesson ③ Overview

| | | |
|---|---|---|
| **Our Earth's Resources**<br>pages 156–159 | Children will learn the meaning of the term *natural resource* and identify the use of a natural resource and the reason for protecting it. |  **Time** 20–30 minutes<br>**Resources**<br>• Workbook p. 42<br>• Vocabulary Card  natural resource <br>• Every Student Learns Guide, pp. 70–73 |
| **Tree Musketeers**<br>pages 160–161 | Children will learn about volunteers who plant trees. | 🕐 **Time** 15–20 minutes |
| **Elvia Niebla**<br>pages 162–163 | Children will learn about the contributions Elvia Niebla, a scientist, has made to protect forests. | 🕐 **Time** 15–20 minutes |

# Build Background

## Activity

## Where Does It Come From?

 **Time** 15–20 minutes

Invite children, one by one, to hold up small items that belong to them, such as an apple, pencil, barrette, coin, or mitten. Ask children to tell what they think each item is made of. Prompt them by asking, *Is it made of wood? of plastic?*

**If time is short,** show children classroom objects. Ask them what each item is made of and whether it comes from something from the Earth or is something created by humans.

## Read Aloud

## Nature's Gifts
### By Mike Paterno

We all need the land,
Even you, dude.
For it's in the soil
We grow our food.

We all need water,
Cool and clean.
We all need fresh air
So we can breathe.

These gifts of Nature,
May come free,
But they need care, dude,
From you and me.

# Lesson 3 Our Earth's Resources

## Objectives
- Identify and describe the physical characteristics of places such as natural resources.
- Identify examples of and uses for natural resources in the community, state, and nation.

## Vocabulary
**natural resource** a useful thing that comes from nature (p. 156)

### QUICK Teaching Plan

*If time is short,* guide children in brainstorming examples of natural resources and ways people use them. Refer children to the web on p. 157 to help them get started.

## 1 Introduce and Motivate

**Preview** Display the Vocabulary Card **natural resource** and explain that a natural resource is a useful thing that comes from nature. Ask children for examples.

**Warm Up** To activate prior knowledge, ask children to recall some of the things they identified as needs and wants in Unit 3. Discuss what these things are made of and where they come from. Point out that many of the things we need and want come directly from nature or are made from things in nature. Examples include air, water, food, and shelter.

---

# Lesson 3 Our Earth's Resources

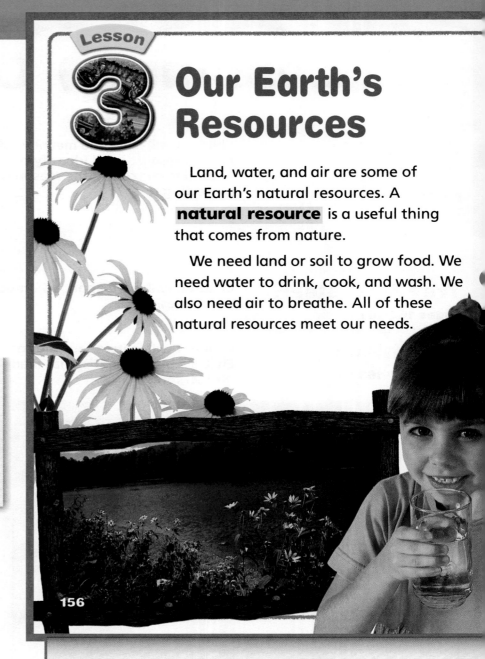

Land, water, and air are some of our Earth's natural resources. A **natural resource** is a useful thing that comes from nature.

We need land or soil to grow food. We need water to drink, cook, and wash. We also need air to breathe. All of these natural resources meet our needs.

156

## Practice and Extend

### READING/VOCABULARY
### Find the Main Idea

- Tell children that sometimes the main idea of a paragraph is in the last sentence. Read the second paragraph aloud. Note that the final sentence (*All of these natural resources meet our needs.*) is the main idea.
- Point out that the other sentences are details that give examples of ways natural resources meet our needs.
- Ask a volunteer to read the paragraph on p. 157 aloud and find the main idea sentence. (*Trees are another natural resource.*)

### WEB SITE
### Technology

You can look up vocabulary words online. Click on *Social Studies Library* and select the dictionary at **www.sfsocialstudies.com.**

Trees are another natural resource. Many different things can come from trees. People cut trees into lumber to build homes. They also use the fruits and nuts that grow on trees for food. Look at the pictures. What other things can come from a tree?

**2**
**3**

fruits

nuts

furniture

wooden blocks

paper **157**

# 2 Teach and Discuss

**Page 156**

Have children identify the natural resources in the picture. (water, trees, air, soil)

**1 What can the natural resources be used for?** Possible answers: Water can be used for drinking or swimming. Air is used for breathing. Soil can be used to grow vegetables.

**$ SOCIAL STUDIES STRAND**
**Economics**

Explain to children that many cities in the United States were settled near rivers in order to help the exchange of goods. Many things to be bought and sold were more easily transported by water than land. List several cities along rivers, including ones in your state. Have children locate them on a map. Point out the nearby river.

**Page 157**

**2 What are some natural resources in your community?** Answers will vary but may include coal, rivers, trees, and lakes. **Apply Information**

**3 How would you make a chair from a tree?** Answers will vary but should include cutting down the tree, making lumber, cutting the lumber into smaller pieces, and fitting the pieces together. **Make Inferences**

**Lesson 3**

continued

### Page 158

Explain to children that the picture in the circle shows an oil well getting oil from the ground.

**4 What are some ways you use oil or gas at home?** Possible answers: To heat the house and water, to cook, to make the car go
**Apply Information**

✓ **Ongoing Assessment**

| **If...** children do not understand that gasoline is needed to make a car move, | **then...** tell them gasoline in a car is like food in a human: it provides the energy to move. |

**5 Remember the kinds of transportation you learned about in Unit 3. What do you think happens to cars, trucks, airplanes, and trains when they don't have gasoline?** They won't go. **Cause and Effect**

**$ SOCIAL STUDIES STRAND**
**Economics**

**Scarcity:** Tell children that sometimes natural resources begin to run out. This is called **scarcity**. Scarcity means there is not enough of something to meet all of people's wants and needs. Some examples of natural resources that may become scarce are oil, wood and gasoline. Tell students to think about things that are made of wood like paper and furniture. Ask them to think about what it would be like to run out of natural resources.

**158** Unit 4 • Our Earth, Our Resources

Oil and gas are also natural resources. They come from under the ground. They
**4** are used to heat our homes and other buildings. Some oil is made into gasoline for cars, buses, trucks, trains,
**5** and airplanes.

*Oil wells get oil from the ground.*

158

## Practice and Extend

### FAST FACTS

Lesson 3 discusses national parks. Provide these facts about America's national parks.

- National parks are places where natural resources, sometimes special ones, are protected so people can enjoy them.
- The U.S. National Park System includes 350 park lands of various sizes and kinds.
- Yellowstone National Park, in Wyoming, Montana, and Idaho, created in 1872, was the first national park in the world.
- Through John Muir's efforts, Congress declared Yosemite, in California, a national park in 1890.
- To protect the natural resources in national parks, laws limit the kinds of activities people can do. Usually hunting, mining, or cutting down trees is not allowed. People can fish for their own use.

It is important to take care of our natural resources. My class wrote a report about John Muir. He wanted to help save our Earth's natural resources.

## John Muir

John Muir thought natural resources were very important. He loved nature. He wrote about natural resources. He helped start many national parks. ⑥

## What did you learn

1. Name three ways **natural resources** meet our needs.

2. What is the **main idea** of the report on John Muir?

3. **Think and Share** Think about a pencil. Draw a picture of it. Name the natural resources that it came from.

**159**

⑥ **Why did John Muir work to create national parks—so that people could make things from natural resources, or so that people could enjoy natural resources?** So that people could enjoy natural resources **Make Inferences**

**SOCIAL STUDIES STRAND**
**Citizenship**

Point out to students that John Muir was a good citizen because he wanted to establish national parks, not just for himself but for everyone. Ask children how people enjoy national parks. (Possible answer: People hike, camp, fish, and just observe the beauty of mountains, valleys, waterfalls, and trees.)

## ③ Close and Assess

Have children brainstorm a list of the uses of water. (Answers may include washing, cooking, drinking, swimming, and sailing.)

## ✓ What did you learn

1. Answers will vary, but may include air for breathing; soil for growing crops; trees for making lumber.

2. John Muir thought natural resources were very important.

3. **Think and Share** Children should identify trees as one of the natural resources from which pencils are made. Extend the discussion by explaining to children that human resources are people and the work that they do. Review the types of jobs discussed in Unit 3.

**SOCIAL STUDIES**
**Background**

**About John Muir**

• John Muir's family came to America from Scotland when he was 11. They settled on a farm in Wisconsin. Help children find Wisconsin on a map of the United States.

• Muir's love of nature began when he was a boy.

• In 1892, Muir founded the Sierra Club, a conservation organization. The Sierra Club still works to care for Earth's natural resources.

**Workbook, p. 42**

**Our Earth's Resources**

Draw a line to match each natural resource with a use.

water

soil

trees

oil and gas

Write an ending for the sentence.

I can take care of our natural resources by **Possible answer: not wasting paper**

**Also on Teacher Resources CD-ROM.**

# CITIZEN HEROES

## Tree Musketeers

### Objectives

- Identify characteristics of good citizenship such as responsibility for the common good.

- Identify ordinary people who exemplify good citizenship.

## 1 Introduce and Motivate

**Preview** Tell children that the name *Tree Musketeers* is a play on words based on the title of a famous story called *The Three Musketeers*. A long time ago, musketeers were soldiers who protected the king. The Tree Musketeers group protects trees.

**Warm Up** To activate prior knowledge about good citizenship, discuss with children why they should not pick flowers in the park. Guide them to understand that the flowers are for everyone.

Introduce the featured child, Tara. Tell children that they will learn reasons why Tara and her fellow Tree Musketeers are citizen heroes.

## 2 Teach and Discuss

### Page 160

**1 What step did Tara take to help take care of Earth?** Possible answer: She helped start a group called Tree Musketeers. **Analyze Information**

**2 Why does Tara Church ask volunteers to help plant trees?** Possible answer: The more people who help, the more trees get planted. **Draw Conclusions**

# CITIZEN HEROES

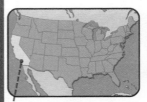

Tree Musketeers is in El Segundo, California.

# Tree Musketeers

Tara

When Tara was eight years old, she wanted to help take care of the Earth. Tara and a group of children planted a tree in their community.

Tara helped start a group called Tree Musketeers. Tree Musketeers has many volunteers. They take responsibility for helping the Earth. One thing they do is ask people to plant trees. Over one million trees have been planted because of Tara and Tree Musketeers!

Tree Musketeers

**160**

## Practice and Extend

**FYI** SOCIAL STUDIES **Background**

### About Tree Musketeers

- Tree Musketeers has a goal called 1-2-3. It wants one million groves of trees planted by two million children during three million hours.

- In addition to its tree-planting work, Tree Musketeers organizes volunteer efforts such as recycling programs and volunteer training.

- Tree Musketeers sends out Youth How-To Kits to teach children about forestry and recycling. You can find information about Tree Musketeers at **Info@ TreeMusketeers.org.**

BUILDING
CITIZENSHIP

Caring
Respect
★ **Responsibility**
Fairness
Honesty
Courage

Tara and Tree Musketeers have been given many awards for their work. One year, their group was given the President's Volunteer Action Award.

Today, Tara Church is a young adult. She talks to young people about doing volunteer work. Tara Church thinks that volunteering is the best way to make a difference.

**3**

**4** Tree Musketeers planting

### ★ Responsibility in Action ★

How can you be more responsible in the way you use natural resources?

### SOCIAL STUDIES STRAND
## Citizenship

**What Can You Do?**

- Point out that Tara Church is a good citizen not just for planting trees herself, but for encouraging others to plant trees.
- Discuss with children reasons Tara Church might give for volunteering. (Possible answers: It makes you feel good about yourself; it makes the world a better place to live.)
- Invite adults from the community to discuss volunteering appropriate for young children.
- Ask children what kinds of volunteering might interest them, now or in the future.

**3** **How has Tara shown that she feels a responsibility for all people?** Possible answers: She wants to protect the earth for everyone. She wants to plant trees that everyone can enjoy. **Analyze Information**

**Test Talk**

**Write Your Answer**

**4** **What is one of the things that Tree Musketeers volunteers do to help Earth? Write your answer.** They ask people to plants trees. Ask children to reread their answer to make sure it is correct. **Analyze Information**

Review the list of citizenship traits in the upper right corner. Tell children that Tara Church has been a good citizen because she took responsibility not only for herself but for others. Ask children for examples of people who take responsibility for others in the home or community.

## **3** Close and Assess

### ★ Responsibility in Action ★

Read the question and have children discuss answers. Responses might include: Putting trash in receptacles, turning off lights before leaving a room, and recycling.

# Elvia Niebla

## Objective

- Identify characteristics of good citizenship such as responsibility for the common good.

## 1 Introduce and Motivate

**Preview** Direct children's attention to the lesson title. Pronounce the name Elvia Niebla's name (EHL vee uh    nee EH bluh) for children and have them repeat it after you. Then tell children that Elvia Niebla is a scientist who studies forests. Ask children what a forest is *(a lot of trees in a large area)*.

**Warm Up** To activate prior knowledge, ask children if they have ever visited a forest. Ask them to describe what it was like.

## Meet Elvia Niebla

**1945–**
**Scientist**

Elvia Niebla is a scientist who studies forests.

162

## Practice and Extend

### EXTEND LANGUAGE ESL SUPPORT

**Work with Related Words** Have children create a flowchart with the base word *science* at the top. Explain that *science* is the process of gathering knowledge based on observed facts and tested truths; a *scientist* is a person who is specially trained in a field of science; and *scientific* means having to do with science.

**Beginning** Have children complete the chart with words on pp. 162–163 that are related to the word *science*.

**Intermediate** Have children complete the flowchart with words on pp. 162–163 that are related to the word *science*. Have them write the sentences containing these words.

**Advanced** Have children complete the chart with words on pp. 162–163 that are related to the word *science*. Challenge them to write their own sentences using *science, scientist,* and *scientific*.

Elvia was born in Mexico. When she was six years old, her family moved to Arizona. As a child, Elvia liked science. Later, Elvia Niebla went to school to learn more about trees and soil. She learned how some things might harm these natural resources. She also studied ways to protect trees and soil.

Elvia Niebla has helped write rules to protect soil. She leads scientific studies about how different materials and changes in weather can affect the soil. She knows that keeping our air and water clean can also help our forests. Elvia Niebla believes that people need to work together to protect our natural resources.

Elvia Niebla was born in Nogales, Mexico.

### Think and Share

How does Elvia Niebla help take care of forests?

For more information, go online to *Meet the People* at **www.sfsocialstudies.com**.

**163**

# 2 Teach and Discuss

Pages 162–163

Read the biography together. Point out Elvia Niebla in the pictures on pp. 162–163.

**1 What did Elvia Niebla learn in school about trees and soil?** She learned how some actions might harm trees and soil and ways to protect them. **Analyze Information**

**G SOCIAL STUDIES STRAND**
**Government**

Point out that Elvia Niebla helped write rules to protect soil and forest plants for the Environmental Protection Agency (EPA), a part of the U.S. government. This rule helps prevent people and corporations from allowing harmful chemicals to enter soil where food is grown.

**2 How do rules keeping the air and water clean help forests?** Possible answer: Dirty air and water are harmful to trees.
**Make Inferences/Cause and Effect**

**Ongoing Assessment**

**If...** children cannot connect clean air and water to healthy forests,

**then...** explain that trees, like all living things, need clean water and clean air to live.

# 3 Close and Assess

### Think and Share

Children's answers should identify ways that Elvia Niebla's work has helped forests. (Answers may include: She has helped write rules to protect soil. She has helped scientists learn ways that changes in weather and different materials affect the soil.)

**CURRICULUM CONNECTION**
**Science**

**Between a Rock and a Soft Place**

- Ask children if they have ever turned over a rock in the soil. Tell children to describe the living and nonliving things that they might find under a rock. (bugs, pieces of rock, twigs, leaves)
- Have children draw living and nonliving things they might find under a rock.

**WEB SITE**
**Technology**

You may help children find our more about Elvia Niebla by clicking on *Meet the People* at **www.sfsocialstudies.com**.

Use with pages 156–163

# Lesson ③ Wrap-Up

 **MEETING INDIVIDUAL NEEDS**
## Leveled Practice

### There's a Tree in the Living Room
Work with children to make a list of things commonly found in the home that come from trees.

**Easy** Have children draw pictures of things in the home that come from trees. **Reteach**

**On-Level** Have children make a list of things commonly found in the home that come from trees. **Extend**

**Challenge** Have children write the names of things surrounding a home that come from trees. Possibilities include a fence, porch, and a dog house. **Enrich**

## Hands-on Activities

 **CURRICULUM CONNECTION**
### Writing/Vocabulary

## Poster

**Objective** Demonstrate an understanding of the term *natural resource*.

**Resources** Vocabulary Card: **natural resource**

**Materials** poster paper, markers

**Learning Style** Verbal/Visual

**Individual**

🕐 **Time** 10–15 minutes

**1.** Write the following on the board:

Protect _____. We need this natural resource for _____.

**2.** Have children copy and complete the sentences. Then have them illustrate their poster.

**3.** Remind children to add *natural resource* to their Word Book.

 **CURRICULUM CONNECTION**
### Science

## Trees, Above and Below

**Objective** To draw a tree.

**Learning Style** Spatial

**Individual**

🕐 **Time** 15–20 minutes

**1.** Have children draw a tree.

**2.** Have children label the roots, stem, and leaves of the tree.

**3.** Remind children that even though the roots are under ground, they are an important part of the tree because they take in water.

 **CURRICULUM CONNECTION**
### Math

## Water, Water Everywhere

**Objective** To identify the uses of water in school.

**Learning Style** Logical-Mathematical

**Partners**

🕐 **Time** 15–20 minutes

**1.** Have partner teams make a list of uses of water in school, such as cleaning the floor, watering plants, filling up the fish tank, and drinking from fountains.

**2.** With a specific ten-minute time limit, have teams tour the classroom and immediate hallway for uses of water. Tell teams to record and number the examples they found.

**3.** Chart each teams' results on a simple bar graph.

# Lesson ④ Overview

| | | |
|---|---|---|
| **Interview About Farm History**<br>pages 164–167 | Through an interview, children will learn about farms in history and how farming has changed over time. | 🕐 Time 20–30 minutes<br>**Resources** <br>• Workbook p. 43<br>• Vocabulary Card history<br>• Every Student Learns Guide, pp. 74–77 |
| **Sacagawea**<br>pages 168–169 | Children will identify the contributions of Sacagawea, a Shoshone Indian who helped explorers long ago. | 🕐 Time 15–20 minutes |

# Build Background

## Activity

## Farming Now and Then

🕐 **Time** 15–20 minutes

Show children pictures of oxen performing heavy work on a farm long ago. Explain that a pair of oxen were joined by a yoke—a wooden bar with bows at the ends that fitted around the oxen's necks. Have children draw pictures of oxen helping a farmer.

**If time is short,** ask children to describe how people grow vegetable gardens.

## Read Aloud

## Old MacDonald
**traditional song**

Old MacDonald had a farm,
E-I-E-I-O!

And on that farm he grew some corn, E-I-E-I-O!

With one row here, and one row there,

Here a row, there a row, everywhere a row to hoe.

Old MacDonald had a farm,
E-I-E-I-O!

# Lesson 4 Interview About Farm History

## Objectives
- Distinguish among past, present, and future.
- Identify examples of and uses for natural resources.

## Vocabulary
**history** telling the story of people and places from the past (p. 164)

### QUICK Teaching Plan

*If time is short,* have children use the time line on p. 166 to summarize the ways farming has changed over time.

- Children can write a sentence describing each picture in the time line. The three sentences will form their summaries.

# 1 Introduce and Motivate

**Preview** Discuss the lesson title with children and then display the Vocabulary Card **history**. Share the definition above. In order to help children understand the concept of different times in history, explain that the time when their grandparents were children is farther in the past than the time when their parents were children. Explain that the present is now, when they themselves are children. Then explain that in the future they will be grown-ups.

**Warm Up** To activate prior knowledge, remind children of Unit 3, Lesson 5 "Interview with a Farmer." Review the interview format and the things children learned about farm work. Then ask children to name three things that might be grown on a farm.

---

# Lesson 4 Interview About Farm History

My family visits friends in Iowa. Our friends live on a farm. One day, we went to a place called "Living History Farms." **History** tells the story of people and places from the past. History also tells about things that happened in the past.

Who were the first farmers in Iowa?

164

# Practice and Extend

### READING SKILL
## Sequence

- In order to have children understand how events are linked by time, draw on the board a Linear String graphic organizer with three boxes. Label box one "Eat Dinner," box two "Read Book," and box three "Go to Bed."
- Have children describe these events orally.
- Then have children draw pictures of these events in three boxes.

### WEB SITE
## Technology

You can look up vocabulary words online. Click on *Social Studies Library* and select the dictionary at **www.sfsocialstudies.com**.

**Mrs. Waters** The first farmers in Iowa were Native ④
Americans. Native Americans called
the Ioway probably farmed the land
we are standing on right now!

**Debby** What did the Ioway grow?

**Mrs. Waters** They grew many things including
corn, beans, pumpkins, and squash.

165

**SOCIAL STUDIES**
**Background**

**Water Supply**

- Ask children what things plants need to grow. (soil,
  water, sunlight)
- Remind children of when they planted a seedling and
  watered it regularly. (Unit 3, Lesson 5, p. 117)
- Explain that some farmers in history depended on a
  nearby flooding river or rain for water. Other farmers
  built ditches or canals that directed water from a
  nearby river or lake to the farmer's field.

# 2 Teach and Discuss

**Page 164**

Tell children that Debby is talking to Mrs. Waters,
who works at Living History Farms. This is a place
that shows how people farmed in history.

❶ **What kind of land do you think is easiest
to farm—a mountain, hill, or plain?** Plain
**Why?** A plain is mostly flat. Make Inferences

❷ **What natural resource do you think Debby
will find on a farm?** Possible answers: Trees,
plants, and soil Make Inferences

❸ **What does Debby want to know the
history of?** She wants to know about the first
farmers in Iowa. Apply Information

**Page 165**

Point out the beginning of the interview format.
Explain that each lozenge carries the name of the
person speaking the words opposite it.

❹ **Who were the first farmers in Iowa?** Native
Americans called the Ioway Draw Conclusions

**Ongoing Assessment**

**If...** children are confused
about the names of the
Native Americans in Iowa,

**then...** explain that the
Ioway are also known as
the Iowa. *Iowa* tends to be
the legal term, *Ioway* the
cultural term. Traditional
members of the tribe
usually refer to themselves
as the Ioway.

**Lesson 4**

continued

**Page 166**

Have children describe and explain the time line on p. 166. Point out that the word *present* means *now* or *today*.

**5** **Why do you think oxen-power replaced man-power on the farm?** Possible answer: Oxen are big and strong. They can pull plows, logs, and other heavy things.
Make Inferences/Analyze Pictures

**Test Talk**

**Use Information from Graphics**

**6** **Which picture in the time line shows the oldest way to farm and the oldest date?** Children should indicate the drawing of people hoeing in 1700. Tell children to look at the time line again to find the oldest date.
Sequence/Interpret Time Lines

**7** **Tell what tool people use to farm in the present.** Tractor Analyze Pictures

**Mrs. Waters** Many other people came to live in Iowa after the Native Americans. Some of the people who came were also farmers.

**Debby** What were their farms like?

**Mrs. Waters** Farmers grew corn, potatoes, and other food on their farms. They had oxen. The animals helped them do heavy work around the farm.

This time line shows some ways farming has changed.

**6**     **7**

1700     1850     Present

166

# Practice and Extend

## ESL SUPPORT
## Build Background

**Understand Changes** Show children a picture of loggers using a chain saw. Discuss how the Ioway used hatchets to cut bark and branches from trees to make their lodges.

**Beginning** Have children pantomime cutting down a tree with a chain saw. Then have children pantomime Native Americans cutting down a tree with a hatchet.

**Intermediate** Have children complete the sentence frame: Long ago, people cut down a tree by using a _____. Now, people use a _____.

**Advanced** Have children complete the sentence frame above. Then ask them to describe the change.

*For additional ESL support, use Every Student Learns Guide, pp. 74–77.*

## FYI SOCIAL STUDIES
## Background

**First North Americans**

Remind children that the groups of people who first lived in North America are called either Native Americans or American Indians. Even among these people, preference for the terms is mixed. Some prefer to be called by their tribal name rather than either general term.

## WEB SITE
## Technology

You may help children learn more about Living History Farms by going online. Use **http://www.ioweb.com/lhf.**

**Mrs. Waters** Farming continued to change over time. Some farmers began to use horses **8** instead of oxen.

**Debby** Now farmers use more tools such as tractors to do farm work.

## What did you learn

1. Who were the first farmers in Iowa?

2. How has farming changed over time?

3. **Think and Share** Draw a farm from the past and the present. Tell what a farm might look like in the future.

167

**8** **Why might horses be better helpers on a farm than oxen?** Possible answers: Horses are faster and smarter. **Make Inferences**

## **3** Close and Assess

Have pairs of children prompt each other with clues about farming in different time periods. Children can respond by identifying the time period as "1700," "1850," or "Present."

## ✓ What did you learn

1. Native Americans called the Ioway were the first farmers in Iowa.

2. Today farmers use tools and animals to make their jobs easier.

3. **Think and Share** Children's drawings should show accurate details from historical and modern farms. Their writing should reflect the idea that new tools will probably make farming in the future even easier.

**SOCIAL STUDIES**
**Background**

**Farming**

- Explain to children that although farming has changed, in some ways it is still the same. Point out that the same basic natural resources—soil, sun, and water—are used to grow crops on all farms.

- Then point out that most crops on farms are seasonal. Seeds are planted in the spring and the crops are harvested in the fall.

**Workbook, p. 43**

Interview About Farm History

Also on Teacher Resources CD-ROM.

# Sacagawea

## Objective
• Identify contributions of historical figures who have influenced the nation.

## 1 Introduce and Motivate

**Preview** Have children look at the illustration. Tell them that Sacagawea led people across dangerous land and water long ago.

**Warm Up** To activate prior knowledge, ask children if they remember ever being guided across a dangerous street, rocks, or a stream. Ask children to describe the experience. Discuss with children the responsibilities of a guide.

## 2 Teach and Discuss

### Pages 168–169

Read the biography together. Tell children that Lewis and Clark were two men who were asked by the government to find a way from the middle of the United States to the Pacific Ocean using rivers and lakes, if possible. Show children this region on a map, using St. Louis as the starting point.

**① Why is Sacagawea important to our history?** Possible answer: She helped Lewis and Clark on their trip to the Pacific Ocean.
**Make Inferences**

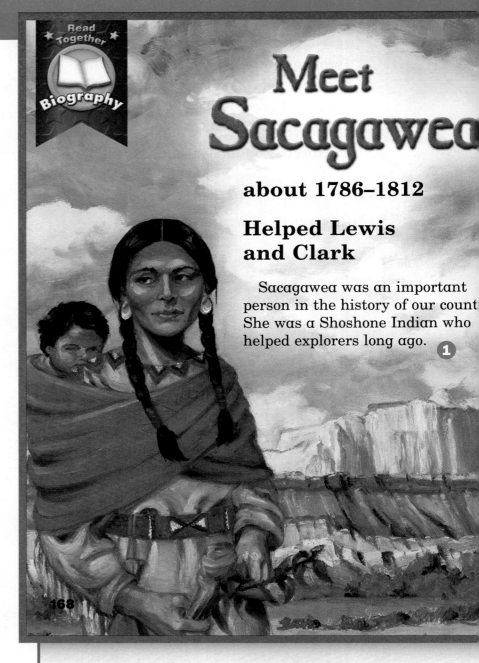

Read Together
**Biography**

# Meet Sacagawea

### about 1786–1812

### Helped Lewis and Clark

Sacagawea was an important person in the history of our count She was a Shoshone Indian who helped explorers long ago. ①

168

# Practice and Extend

**FYI** SOCIAL STUDIES
**Background**

### About Sacagawea

• Tell children that Sacagawea (sä cä′ gä we ä) was a Native American, a Shoshone. The date of her birth is uncertain. When she was born, her name was Boinaiv, which means "Grass Maiden." When the Hidatsa, who spoke another language, captured her, they changed her name to Sacagawea, which means "Bird Woman."

• Sacagawea's husband was from Canada. When Sacagawea and her husband guided Lewis and Clark, they brought along their newborn baby.

• Sacagawea helped the explorers to make friends with different Native American groups. These groups knew that war parties never traveled with women and children. When they saw Sacagawea and her baby, they knew that Lewis and Clark were friendly.

When Sacagawea was a young child, she was living in a Shoshone village in the Bitterroot Mountains in what is now Idaho. Then the Hidatsas took her to live and work in their village in what is now North Dakota.

Young Sacagawea lived in what is now Idaho.

In 1805 and 1806, a group of men was traveling across the United States. The leaders of the group were Meriwether Lewis and William Clark. They wanted to find a route to the Pacific Ocean.

Sacagawea helped Lewis and Clark on their journey. She showed them how to find food. The American Indians, or Native Americans, that Lewis and Clark met on their journey did not speak English. Sacagawea translated, or changed the words from one language to another. With the help of Sacagawea, Lewis and Clark reached the Pacific Ocean.

A picture of Sacagawea is on the one dollar gold coin.

Obverse © 1999 U.S. Mint. All rights reserved. Used with permission.

## Think and Share

What are two ways Sacagawea helped the explorers?

 For more information, go online to *Meet the People* at **www.sfsocialstudies.com**.

169

## CURRICULUM CONNECTION
### Drama

**Take a Tour**

- Have children take turns role-playing Sacagawea. They can "guide" groups of classmates around parts of the school.
- Encourage children who are role-playing the guide to point out different parts of the school and introduce the other children to people they meet.

### WEB SITE
### Technology

You may help children find out more about Sacagawea by clicking on *Meet the People* at **www.sfsocialstudies.com**.

---

**2 Where did Sacagawea live with the Shoshone? Point to the state on the classroom map.** Children should identify Idaho.
**Make Inferences/Interpret Maps**

### SOCIAL STUDIES STRAND
### C Culture

**Prejudice Reduction** Explain to children that Sacagawea experienced different cultures during her life. Among them were that of the Shoshone, the Hidatsa, and, after marrying her Canadian husband, Canadians. Ask children what it might be like to experience more than one culture. (Answers will vary but may include: exciting or confusing.)

**3 What direction did Lewis and Clark travel? How do you know?** They traveled west. The Pacific Ocean is west of mainland United States.
**Make Inferences**

**4 How did Sacagawea help Lewis and Clark communicate with the American Indians?** She translated. **Apply Information**

# 3 Close and Assess

## Think and Share

Possible answers: She helped them find food, and she translated for them.

# Lesson ④ Wrap-Up

 **MEETING INDIVIDUAL NEEDS**
## Leveled Practice

### Compare and Contrast Pictures

Have children draw two pictures showing ways that farmers in Iowa used natural resources in the past and use them now. Discuss ways these uses are alike and different.

**Easy** Direct children's attention to two features common in both drawings, such as soil in which plants grow. Ask them if farmers in both times used this resource. **Reteach**

**On-Level** Ask children to identify in their drawings ways that farmers in the present work differently from farmers in the past. Have children indicate the tools in their drawings that make farming today different from in the past. **Extend**

**Challenge** Have partners dramatize a conversation between farmers, one from the past and one from the present, in their drawings. Suggest to children that they talk about farming problems. **Enrich**

 ## Hands-on Activities

 **CURRICULUM CONNECTION**
### Writing/Vocabulary

## Farm Contest

**Objective** Demonstrate an understanding of the word *history*.

**Resources** Vocabulary Card: **history**

**Materials** drawings from "Compare and Contrast Pictures" activity

**Learning Style** Verbal/Visual

**Group**

⏱ **Time** 10–15 minutes

1. Place all the drawings from "Compare and Contrast Pictures" (above) in a bag.

2. Show drawings one at a time. Ask children if the drawings show a farm in history or a farm now. Ask how they know.

3. Remind children to add the vocabulary word *history* to their "My Word Book."

 **SOCIAL STUDIES STRAND**
### Geography

## Find the Way

**Objective** Follow a route from history.

**Materials** classroom map of the United States

**Learning Style** Spatial

**Individual** 👤

⏱ **Time** 15 minutes

1. Remind children that Lewis and Clark were looking for a way to reach the Pacific Ocean using rivers and lakes.

2. Show children examples of rivers and lakes on your classroom map. Help children find St. Louis. Then have children look at the western United States on the map. Tell them to find rivers and lakes that connect.

3. Ask children whether it is possible to reach the Pacific Ocean from St. Louis without leaving the United States and without traveling over land. (No, it is not.)

**H** **SOCIAL STUDIES STRAND**
### History

## Sacagawea

**Objective** Identify contributions of historical figures who have influenced the nation.

**Materials** paper, crayons

**Learning Style** Spatial

**Individual** 👤

⏱ **Time** 20–30 minutes

1. Read aloud parts of *A Picture Book of Sacagawea* by David A. Adler. Have children identify the settings. Then show the illustrations.

2. Have children respond to the story by drawing pictures of their favorite parts and labeling them.

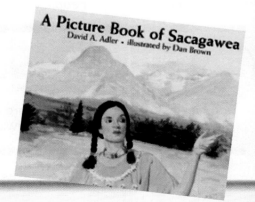

# Lesson ⑤ Overview

**Caring for Our Resources**
pages 170–173

Children will learn ways to conserve natural resources by reducing, reusing, and recycling.

 Time 20–30 minutes

**Resources**
- Workbook p. 44
- Every Student Learns Guide, pp. 78–81

**Endangered Animals**
pages 174–175

Children will learn that helping care for the Earth helps protect endangered animals.

 Time 15–20 minutes

# Build Background

## Activity

### Can You Use Less?

Time 15–20 minutes

Have children draw a picture of juice spilled from a glass. Then discuss with them the benefits of cleaning the liquid with a sponge rather than a paper towel. Have children include a sponge in their drawing. Ask them to caption the drawing "Save Paper/Wipe Up with a Sponge."

**If time is short,** invite children to name some ways that they use paper. Then ask them for ways to use less paper.

Save Paper!

Wipe Up with a Sponge

## Read Aloud

### Hurt No Living Thing

by Christina Rossetti

Hurt no living thing;
Ladybug, nor butterfly,
Nor moth with dusty wing,
Nor cricket chirping cheerily,
Nor grasshopper so light of leap,
Nor dancing gnat, nor beetle fat,
Nor harmless worms that creep.

# Lesson 5 — Caring for Our Resources

## Objective
- Identify ways that natural resources can be used and reused.

## QUICK Teaching Plan

*If time is short,* brainstorm with children about ways to conserve natural resources.

- Use the pictures and boxed text on pp. 170–173 to prompt children's thinking.

## 1 Introduce and Motivate

**Preview** Have children glance at the lesson pages. Explain that the words in the speech bubbles are the advice Debby and her classmates give others about reducing, reusing, and recycling natural resources. Then explain that the words in the boxed text are helpful hints about ways to reduce, reuse, and recycle.

**Warm Up** To activate prior knowledge, show children the recycling symbol on p. 172 and ask if anyone knows what it means. Ask children how plastic and glass can be recycled in the home. Then ask about recycling newspapers or magazines in the home.

# Lesson 5 — Caring for Our Resources

Reduce! Use less paper. This will help save a tree.

Sacagawea and Lewis and Clark traveled across many different kinds of land. The land is a natural resource. Our class is learning how to help save natural resources. We follow the 3 Rs—reduce, reuse, and recycle. ❶ ❷

## Practice and Extend

### READING/VOCABULARY — Find the Main Idea

- In this lesson children read lists with advice about reducing, reusing, and recycling natural resources.
- Tell children that the title of a list tells them what the list is about. It is the main idea. Each item below the title is a detail or an example.
- Ask a volunteer to read aloud the *Please Reduce!* list on page 171.

Reuse! Use something again.

## Please Reuse!

1. Reuse paper. Write on both sides.
2. Save bags and boxes. Reuse them.

## Please Reduce!

1. Walk instead of riding in a car. This will reduce the amount of gas and oil that is used.
2. Turn off the water faucet while you brush your teeth. This will reduce the amount of water you use.
3. Turn off the light when you leave a room. This will reduce the amount of electricity you use. **3**

171

# 2 Teach and Discuss

### Page 170

Have children describe the items around Debby. Point out that they are all paper products.

**1 What natural resource is used to make the things around Debby?** Trees
**Inferences/Cause and Effect**

#### Ongoing Assessment

| **If...** children cannot identify paper as coming from a natural resource, | **then...** tell them that paper is made, in part, from wood ground into a soft, wet mass. |

**2 Why does Debby call *reduce, reuse,* and *recycle* the 3 R's?** All three words start with the letter *R*. **Context Clues**

### Page 171

Review the Reading Skill about understanding lists on TE p. 170 with children.

**3 What is item 3 on the "Please Reduce!" list?** *Turn off the light when you leave a room. This will reduce the amount of electricity you use.*
**Analyze Text**

**$** **SOCIAL STUDIES STRAND**
## Economics

Point out to children that reducing electricity can save money. Most families pay for the use of electricity each month. The more electricity families use, the more they have to pay. Ask children for ways of reducing the use of electricity. (Answers will vary. Possible answers: Use the air conditioning only for sleeping and shut off the computer when it isn't in use.)

**Lesson**
**5**
continued

**Page 172**

Point out that in the picture, Debby's classmates are recycling.

**Test Talk**

**Locate Key Words in the Text**

**4 Where are the children putting the things they are recycling?** The children are putting things in recycling bins. Have children locate the key word *recycling* in the text that matches the key word *recycling* in the question. **Analyze Pictures**

**5 What is the boy recycling?** Used bottles and cans **Analyze Pictures**

**6 What are some things you can recycle?** Possible answers: Glass bottles, newspapers, magazines, and metal cans **Apply Information**

**Ongoing Assessment**

**If...** children cannot name items for recycling,    **then...** display some of the items above.

**G** SOCIAL STUDIES STRAND
**Government**

Explain to children that many communities have required or voluntary recycling programs. These programs set up a procedure for recycling plastic, glass, paper, and other materials. When trash is collected, the things for recycling are kept separate.

**Please Recycle!**
1. Collect things that you can recycle.
2. Put them into a recycling bin.

Recycle! The things you recycle can be made into new things.

4 5 6

172

# Practice and Extend

SOCIAL STUDIES STRAND
**Citizenship**

**School Recycling**

- Explain to children that all people in school can share a responsibility for recycling.
- Have children visit the administrative office staff to ask about recycling.
- Have children note any special bins or signs for recycling.
- Have custodial staff show children where recyclables are left to be picked up.

## We Recycle!

Paper
Cans
Plastic
Glass

Here is what our class recycles. What can you recycle at school? What can you recycle at home? **7** **8**

### What did you learn

1. How do you show that you care about the Earth when you reduce, reuse, and recycle?

2. What is the **main idea** of this lesson?

3. **Think and Share** In your journal, write how you can reduce, reuse, and recycle each day.

173

**7** **Why might you be considered a good citizen if you recycle?** Possible answer: It helps make sure that things made from natural resources are available for everybody. **Make Inferences**

**$ SOCIAL STUDIES STRAND**
### Economics

Tell children that some states have bottle deposit laws. Explain that this means that people pay a deposit or extra money for beverage containers. They get money back from a store when they return used bottles and cans. Ask children if they think this plan gets people to recycle beverage containers more often. Have children support their answers. (Possible answers: Yes. People have an incentive to recycle—they get money back. No. People like to do all their recycling in one place.)

**8** **Many cardboard juice containers have an aluminum foil lining. Do you think the containers can be recycled?** No—unless they are separated from the lining. **Apply Information**

## 3 Close and Assess

Start a word web on the board with "the 3 R's" in the center and three branches labeled "Recycle," "Reuse," and "Reduce." Have children take turns adding to the web with ideas from the lesson.

### ✓ What did you learn

1. You help keep Earth from running out of natural resources.

2. You should save natural resources by reducing, reusing, and recycling.

3. **Think and Share** Children's journal entry should identify reasonable examples of reducing, reusing, and recycling.

---

**FYI SOCIAL STUDIES**
### Background

#### Possible Misconceptions

Tell children that recyclables are used to make many common household items, such as plastic drink containers. Explain, however, that recyclables can also be used to make many surprising things:

- glass to make part of a mixture to cover roads

- plastic to make carpets; park benches; bridges for people to cross; and soft, warm jackets

### Workbook, p. 44

**Caring for Our Resources**

Write reduce, reuse, or recycle by each picture.

We brought our own bags!
reuse

Let's turn off the water.
reduce

We used to throw cans away!
recycle

Write an ending for this sentence.
I can reuse by _____ **Answers will vary.**

**Also on Teacher Resources CD-ROM.**

# Endangered Animals

## Objectives

- Obtain information about a topic using maps and pictures.
- Identify ways that protecting natural resources helps animals.
- Respond to important problems with the Earth's natural resources.

# 1 Introduce and Motivate

**Preview** Explain that when all of a group of animals, such as the giant panda and the mountain gorilla, are endangered, that means they are all in danger of becoming extinct. Then explain that *extinct* means "died out" or "no longer existing." Tell them that dinosaurs are extinct. Point out that once there were many giant pandas and mountain gorillas. Now there are only a few. Let children know that these endangered animals need to be protected so they do not become extinct.

**Warm Up** To activate prior knowledge, tell children that most animals are used to living in a certain kind of place. When that place is destroyed or even damaged, the animal may become endangered. Ask children what would happen to fish in the ocean if poisons were dumped in its waters.

# 2 Teach and Discuss

### Pages 174–175

Have children preview the map and pictures on pp. 174–175. Point out the animals shown in each circle.

# Endangered Animals

Helping the Earth helps animals too. Some animals are endangered.

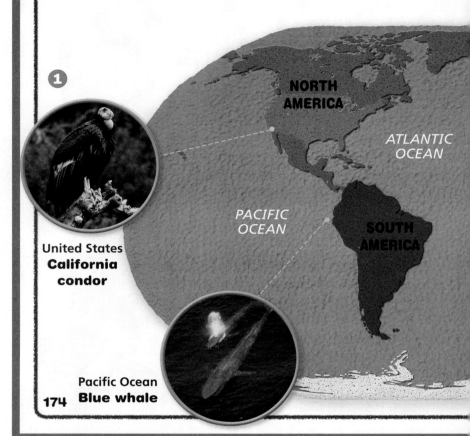

**1**

NORTH AMERICA

ATLANTIC OCEAN

PACIFIC OCEAN

SOUTH AMERICA

United States
**California condor**

Pacific Ocean
**Blue whale**

174

# Practice and Extend

**SOCIAL STUDIES Background**

### About Endangered Species

- The United States Interior Department can protect endangered plants and animals under the Endangered Species Act.
- Plants or animals listed under this act get strict protection. Many times this means protecting wildlife habitats from nearby development.
- In the United States, laws against poisoning or shooting endangered animals have helped prevent them from dying out. Some of these animals have grown in number since the laws were passed.
- Twenty nine different plants and animals, including the Miami blue butterfly and the Big Cypress fox squirrel were recently put on the Endangered Species list.

Endangered means that very few of these animals are living. Some day, some kinds of endangered animals might not be found on Earth any more. The pictures show some endangered animals.

For more information, go online to *the Atlas* at **www.sfsocialstudies.com**.

**2**

TIC OCEAN

ROPE

ASIA

ICA

INDIAN OCEAN

AUSTRALIA

ARCTICA

China
**Giant panda**

India
**Tiger**

Democratic Republic of the Congo
**Mountain gorilla**

175

## CURRICULUM CONNECTION
### Science

**Research an Endangered Animal**

- Provide books and articles about the five endangered animals pictured on pp. 174–175.
- Have children draw pictures of one of the animals. Have children write a caption telling something about the animal.

## WEB SITE
### Technology

You may help children find out more about places on these pages by clicking on *Atlas* at **www.sfsocialstudies.com**.

**1** **What kinds of animals are in the circles?**
Condor or bird, whale, panda, tiger, gorilla
**Analyze Pictures**

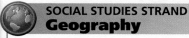
SOCIAL STUDIES STRAND
## Geography

Explain that the animals shown in the circles live in the general part of the world where the lines point to on the map. Ask children what continent the giant panda lives on. (Asia)

**Ongoing Assessment**

| **If...** children do not understand how to use the pictures and the map, | **then...** show them how to trace their finger along the dotted line from the giant panda to Asia. |

## Problem Solving

**2** **What might you do to let people know about endangered animals?** Possible answer: Gather information about endangered animals. List options such as making a poster or sending e-mail. Ask other children to help make a poster.
**Solve Problems**

# 3 Close and Assess

Discuss with children how helping the Earth helps animals too. Explain that some animals are endangered because the place where they naturally live is getting smaller.

# Lesson ⑤ Wrap-Up

 **MEETING INDIVIDUAL NEEDS**
## Leveled Practice

### Thrift Shop

Have children "set up" a thrift shop— a store where used clothes and miscellaneous items are sold to raise money for charity—on a bulletin board by "stocking" it with labeled drawings of clothing, toys, books, etc.

**Easy** Have children sort the items on the thrift shop bulletin board into categories, such as things to wear, to play with, and to read. **Reteach**

**On-Level** Have children price the items with sticky notes, and sell them to customers with play money. **Extend**

**Challenge** Have children record the purchases in a book and count up the "profits." Have children announce that the thrift shop "profits" will be donated to an organization that protects natural resources. **Enrich**

## Hands-on Activities

 **CURRICULUM CONNECTION**
### Writing/Vocabulary

## Save Animals

**Objective** Demonstrate an understanding of lesson vocabulary.

**Materials** poster board, crayons or markers

**Learning Style** Visual

**Individual** 👤

🕐 **Time** 20–25 minutes

1. Have children make a poster asking people to help save one of the endangered animals shown on pp. 174–175.

2. Have children include a title and a drawing on their poster.

3. Remind children to add the word *endangered* to their "My Word Book."

Save the Panda

 **CURRICULUM CONNECTION**
### Literature

## Blue Whales

**Objective** Read about blue whales and illustrate their size.

**Materials** picture book, paper, crayons

**Learning Style** Visual/Spatial

**Group** 👤👤👤👤

🕐 **Time** 15–30 minutes

1. Explain to children that blue whales are the largest mammals to live on Earth.

2. Read *Big Blue Whale*, an informational text, by Nicola Davies to the class. Show the illustrations as you read.

3. In order to help children comprehend the large size of the blue whale, have children draw a picture of an elephant, a human being, or a dog next to a blue whale.

**CURRICULUM CONNECTION**
### Drama

## Mugs

**Objective** Use role-playing to show how to reuse things.

**Learning Style** Kinesthetic

**Partners** 👤👤

🕐 **Time** 15–20 minutes

Invite children to think about all the paper that would be saved if adults asked to have their coffee put in their personal durable mug instead of a paper cup.

1. Organize children in pairs, one to play the adult, the other to play the child.

2. Help teams prepare short skits of the child offering a mug to the adult drinking coffee from a paper cup. The adult takes the mug and agrees that it's a good idea.

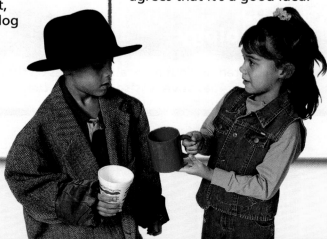

# Ending Unit 4

| | | |
|---|---|---|
| **End with a Legend**<br>pages 176–177 | Children will listen to and talk about a legend: "Johnny Appleseed." | |
| **Unit 4 Review**<br>pages 178–181 | Children will review unit vocabulary words and the unit skills of finding the main idea, reading a time line, and locating land and water on a globe and map. Children will answer questions about what they learned in the unit. Children will learn about several books about Earth. | **Resources**<br>• Workbook, p. 45<br>✓ • Assessment Book, pp. 13–16  |
| **Unit 4 Project**<br>page 182 | Children will present a weather report. They will also be directed to a Web site where they can learn more about the weather. | **Resource**<br>• Workbook, p. 46 |

# Wrap-Up

### Activity

## Postcard of a Place to Visit

Have children make a postcard about a beautiful location on Earth where they would like to visit. The location does not have to be named.

- On the front of the postcard, have children create a picture that includes a landform, body of water, or natural resource in the location. Have children write a caption describing the location.

- On the back of the postcard, ask children to write a short message telling about why they like the location.

**Performance Assessment**
You can use the activity on this page as a performance assessment.

### ✓ Assessment Scoring Guide

| Postcards of a Place to Visit | |
|---|---|
| **6** | Clear geographic features; writes accurate caption and strongly reasoned message. |
| **5** | Clear geographic features; accurate caption clear, complete message. |
| **4** | Clear geographic features; writes accurate caption, incomplete message. |
| **3** | Clear geographic features; vague caption, incomplete message. |
| **2** | Includes geographic features; incomplete message and caption, several errors. |
| **1** | Difficulty with geographic features; no captions, incomplete messages. |

If you require a 4 point rubric, adjust scoring guide accordingly.

# Johnny Appleseed

## Objective
• Retell stories from selected folktales and legends.

## 1 Introduce and Motivate

**Preview** Tell children that apple trees are very common in the United States. In fact, they are grown in all 50 states. Ask children if they have ever seen an apple tree or apple orchard. Tell children that a legend is a story that has come down from the past that many people have believed. Remind children that a legend, unlike history, is not entirely true. A legend usually starts with something or someone real and then exaggerates. In this case, there really was a John Chapman and he sold apple trees. But the story grew far beyond what the real John Chapman did. Tell children that the legend of Johnny Appleseed explains how apple trees spread.

**Warm Up** Point to the pictures of Johnny Appleseed on pp. 176–177. Ask children what he is holding in the picture on p. 176 (apple seeds), doing in the picture at the bottom of p. 177 (scattering apple seeds), and holding in the picture on the side of p. 177 (apples). Point out that he isn't wearing shoes.

# Johnny Appleseed

John Chapman lived many years ago. He planted so many apple seeds that people started calling him Johnny Appleseed. People have been telling stories about Johnny Appleseed for over 200 years.

Johnny grew up near an apple orchard. When he left home, he planted apple seeds wherever he went. Soon apple trees grew. Johnny Appleseed planted many apple orchards.

**176**

## Practice and Extend

### CURRICULUM CONNECTION
### Reading

**Books About Things That Grow**

Read children other stories about things that grow, such as *The Legend of the Bluebonnet* by Tomie dePaola (Putnam Publishing Group, ISBN 0-399-20937-9, 1986), a tale about the origin of the state flower of Texas, and *The Sunflower Garden* by Janice May Udry (available in libraries), a story about a Native American girl who started the first sunflower garden in her village. Have children retell the stories.

People started telling stories about Johnny Appleseed. Some people said Johnny was bitten by a rattlesnake. They said the bite did not hurt him because his feet were so tough! Other people said they saw Johnny playing with a family of bears.

Today, people still remember the legend of Johnny Appleseed. Some people even say they have seen him planting his apple seeds!

177

CURRICULUM CONNECTION
## Drama

### Jill and Johnny Appleseeds Dance

Have children retell the story of Johnny Appleseed in dance, accompanied by appropriate music, such as Aaron Copland's *Appalachian Spring*. Have several children—shoeless Jill and Johnny Appleseeds wearing wide-brim hats—dance around scattering confetti. The other children, who have been lying on the floor, slowly rise with their arms spread like branches, holding apples. The Jill and Johnny Appleseeds then dance around collecting the apples as they drop into their hat.

# 2 Teach and Discuss

Invite children to listen as you read the legend. Encourage them to picture in their minds the events.

**1 Why was Johnny Chapman given the name Johnny Appleseed?** Because he planted so many apple seeds Analyze Information

**2 What did Johnny grow up near?** An apple orchard Apply information

### ✓ Ongoing Assessment

| **If...** children do not understand what an orchard is, | **then...** explain that it is an area of land on which fruit trees are grown. |
| --- | --- |

### $ SOCIAL STUDIES STRAND Economics

About 100 varieties of apples are grown for sale in the United States. Thirty-six states grow apples for sale. Most apples are handpicked in the fall.

**3 Why was the snake able to bite Johnny Appleseed's foot?** Because he walked barefoot Analyze Pictures

**4 Why might Johnny Appleseed be considered a good citizen?** Answers will vary but may include that by planting apple seeds he gave greatly to others. Draw Conclusions

# 3 Close and Assess

Have children retell the story of Johnny Appleseed in their own words.

### Resources

- Assessment Book, pp. 14-17
- Workbook, p. 45: Vocabulary Review

# Vocabulary Review

**1.** natural resource

**2.** lake

**3.** river

**4.** mountain

 **TEST PREP** Answers to Test Prep

**1.** history

**2.** weather

# Vocabulary Review

Tell which word completes each sentence.

| natural resource |
| river |
| mountain |
| lake |

**1.** A useful thing that comes from the Earth is called a _____.

**2.** A body of water that has land around it is a _____.

**3.** A long body of water is called a _____.

**4.** The highest kind of land is a _____.

★ ★ ★ ★ ★ ★ ★ ★

 **TEST PREP** Which word completes the sentence?

**1.** A story about people and places of the past is called _____.

  **a.** weather      **b.** recycle

  **c.** history      **d.** natural resource

**2.** Sunny is one kind of _____.

  **a.** mountain      **b.** weather

  **c.** plain      **d.** natural resource

**178**

# Practice and Extend

## Assessment Options

✓ **Unit 4 Assessment**

- Unit 4 Content Test: Use Assessment Book, pp. 14-15

- Unit 4 Skills Test: Use Assessment Book, pp. 16-17

 **Standardized Test Prep**

- Unit 4 tests contain standardized test formats.

✓ **Unit 4 Performance Assessment**

- See p. 182 for information about using the Unit 4 Project as a means of performance assessment.

- A scoring guide for the Unit 4 Project is provided in the teacher's notes on p. 182.

**Test Talk**

- Test Talk Practice Book

# Skills Review

## Find the Main Idea

Read the following sentences.

> Debby recycles each day. She saves empty cans. She saves paper after she writes or draws on it. She saves the newspaper her family reads each day. Debby and her family take the cans and paper to the recycling center in town.

What is the main idea?

**a.** empty cans

**b.** going to town

**c.** recycling

**d.** saving paper

**Test Talk**

Look for details to support your answer.

## Locate Land and Water

Make a map and map key. Show land and water. Draw symbols on your map key. Label the symbols to show different types of land and water.

**179**

### WEB SITE Technology

For more information, you can select the dictionary or encyclopedia from *Social Studies Library* at **www.sfsocialstudies.com.**

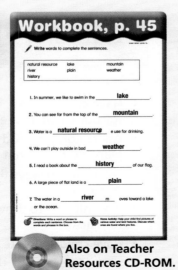

## Workbook, p. 45

Write words to complete the sentences.

| natural resource | lake | mountain |
| river | plain | weather |
| history | | |

1. In summer, we like to swim in the __lake__.

2. You can see for from the top of the __mountain__.

3. Water is a __natural resource__ e use for drinking.

4. We can't play outside in bad __weather__.

5. I read a book about the __history__ of our flag.

6. A large piece of flat land is a __plain__.

7. The water in a __river__ m oves toward a lake or the ocean.

Also on Teacher Resources CD-ROM.

---

# Skills Review

## Find the Main Idea

- Answer: c. recycling
- Remind children that the main idea is what the paragraph is about.
- Tell them that details support the main idea.

Use the following scoring guide.

### ✔ Assessment Scoring Guide

| | Find the Main Idea |
|---|---|
| 6 | Selects the main idea and summarizes paragraph. |
| 5 | Selects the main idea. |
| 4 | Selects an important supporting detail that is close to the main idea. |
| 3 | Selects an important supporting idea that is far from the main idea |
| 2 | Selects a detail that barely supports the main idea. |
| 1 | Has difficulty selecting a detail and understanding the main idea. |

If you require a 4-point rubric, adjust scoring guide accordingly.

## Locate Land and Water

Children's map key should contain symbols of land and water with labels; the map itself should contain the symbols in an arrangement that reasonably mirrors nature. Suggest that children create a map of a place in the community or beyond.

**Test Talk**

**Use Information from the Text**
Use the Skills Review question to model the Test Talk strategy.

**Decide where you will look for the answer.**
Have children make notes about details from the text that answer the question.

**Use information from the text.**
Have children check their notes, then ask themselves, "Do I have the right information?" Have children look back at the question and the text to make sure they have the right answer.

## Review

continued

# Skills Review

## Read a Time Line

**1.** 5

**2.** Thursday

**3.** Debby read a book.

## Skills on Your Own

- Children's time line should include a drawing of an activity for each day of the school week.

Use the following scoring guide.

### ✓ Assessment Scoring Guide

| Read a Time Line | |
|---|---|
| 6 | Makes 5 boxes, names and correctly spells the 5 school days, writes legibly, shows school activities. |
| 5 | Makes 5 boxes, names and correctly spells the 5 school days, shows school activities. |
| 4 | Makes 5 boxes, names and correctly spells the 5 school days, includes non-school activities. |
| 3 | Makes 5 boxes and names but incorrectly spells the 5 school days. |
| 2 | Makes 5 boxes but names non-school days. |
| 1 | Does not make all 5 days, unable to name more than two or three school days. |

If you require a 4-point rubric, adjust scoring guide accordingly.

## Review

# Study Skills

## Read a Time Line

Debby drew a time line showing what she did each day after school. Use the time line to answer the questions.

| Monday | Tuesday | Wednesday | Thursday | Friday |

**1.** How many days did Debby put in her time line?

**2.** Which day did Debby ride her bike?

**3.** What did Debby do on Tuesday?

## Skills On Your Own

Draw a time line of five things that happened in school this week. Write each day of the week. Draw pictures that show what happened on each day.

**180**

# Practice and Extend

## Revisit the Unit Question

### ✓ Unit 3 Portfolio Assessment

- Have children look back at the list of ways we can care for our Earth, made on p. 135.
- Ask children to add ways to care for Earth, such as planting trees, that they learned about in this unit.
- Ask children ways they would like to help take care of Earth.
- Ask children to draw a picture of themselves caring for Earth.
- Have children write a sentence describing their drawing.
- Have children add their list, drawing, and sentence to their Social Studies Portfolio.

# What did you learn?

1. Describe two kinds of weather.

2. What are some natural resources that you need to live?

3. Name three ways people can care for the Earth.

4. **Write and Share** Write about natural resources in your community. Put the **main idea** in your first sentence. Write other sentences that tell how you can use the natural resources.

## Read About Earth

Look for books like these in the library.

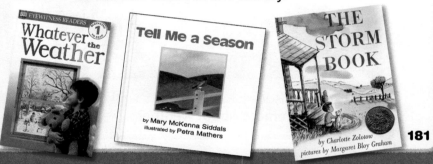

**181**

# What did you learn?

1. Answers will vary but may include sunny, rainy, and cold.

2. Answers will vary but may include land, water, air, trees, and oil.

3. Answers will vary but may include use less paper, plant trees, and reuse bags.

4. **Write and Share** Children's answers should accurately identify and describe natural resources in their community. The main idea should be in the first sentence. The supporting details should reflect ways to use natural resources.

## Read About Earth

You may want to have these books available in the classroom. Read the books aloud for children; then invite them to browse through the books. Encourage them to tell why these books are good ones to include in this unit. They may also wish to review the books for classmates.

*Whatever the Weather* by Karen Wallace (DK, ISBN 0-789-44750-9, 1999) Looking out a window, William watches the weather change with the seasons. Easy

*Tell Me a Season* by Mary McKenna Siddals (Clarion Books, ISBN 0-395-71021-9, 1997) This book presents the change of seasons by describing and showing the changes that occur in one house and its surroundings. On-Level

*The Storm Book* by Charlotte Zolotow (HarperTrophy, ISBN 0-064-43194-0, 1989) This book depicts a fierce summer storm. Challenge

**CURRICULUM CONNECTION**
**Literature**

**Books About Caring for Earth and About People Around the World**

You may want to read and discuss with children the following books about the ways to care for Earth and about people around the world.

*The Great Kapok Tree: A Tale of the Amazon Rain Forest* by Lynne Cherry (Voyager Picture Book, ISBN 0-152-02614-2, 2000).

*EcoArt!: Earth-Friendly Art & Craft Experiences for 3–9-Year-Olds* by Laurie Carlson (Williamson Publishing, ISBN 0-913-58968-3, 1992).

*Bob's Recycling Day* by Annie Auerbach (Simon Spotlight, ISBN: 0-689-84379-8, 2001).

*This Is the Way We Go to School* by Edith Baer (Scholastic Trade, ISBN 0-590-43162-5, 1992).

# Unit 4 Project

# Weather Report

## Objective
- Identify and describe different kinds of weather.

## Resource
- Workbook, p. 46

## Materials
construction paper, scissors, crayons, string, cotton balls, glue, and other art supplies

## Follow This Procedure
- Tell children that they are going to present a weather report to the class.

- Review with children the different kinds of weather.

- Have children work in groups of four or five. Tell them that one child in each group will be the weather reporter. The others will act out situations and show props appropriate for different kinds of weather.

- Have the children make props such as a sun for a sunny day, streamers for a windy day, an umbrella for a rainy day, or cotton for clouds. If possible, videotape the presentations.

- Direct each group to present a weather report.

✓ **Assessment Scoring Guide**

| Weather Report | |
|---|---|
| 6 | Describes one type of weather in great detail with accurate vocabulary, precise details, and excellent props. |
| 5 | Describes one type of weather with accurate vocabulary, precise details, and suitable props. |
| 4 | Describes one type of weather with mostly accurate vocabulary, some details, and suitable props. |
| 3 | Describes one type of weather with limited vocabulary, few details, and less elaborate props. |
| 2 | Describes one type of weather with limited details, incorrect vocabulary, and props. |
| 1 | Has difficulty describing weather, uses few details, incorrect vocabulary and props. |

If you require a 4-point rubric, adjust scoring guide accordingly.

# UNIT 4 Project

## Weather Report

**Create a weather television program of your own.**

**1** Choose one kind of weather.

**2** Make or draw something to show the weather you chose.

**3** Give a television weather report. Show the class what you made that tells about the weather.

**4** Ask students to tell you what they learned from your report.

**Internet Activity**

Go to www.sfsocialstudies.com/activities to learn more about weather.

182

# Practice and Extend

## Hands-on Unit Project

✓ **Performance Assessment**
- The Unit Project can also be used as a performance assessment activity.
- Use the scoring guide to assess each group's work.

## WEB SITE Technology

Children can launch the activity by clicking on *Grade 1, Unit 4* at **www.sfsocialstudies.com/ activities.**

**Workbook, p. 46**

4 Project  Weather Report

Draw a picture of one kind of weather.  Drawings will vary.

Write answers about the weather.

What kind of weather is it?  **Answers will vary.**

What are the children wearing?

What are the children doing?

**Also on Teacher Resources CD-ROM.**

# Vocabulary Routines

**The following examples of reading and vocabulary development strategies can be used to instruct students about unit vocabulary.**

## BEFORE READING

### Individual Word Study

**K-W-L** Use a K-W-L chart to build background for unit vocabulary words. Ask children what they already Know **(K)** about the word. This is particularly helpful in clearing up any misconceptions children might have about the meaning of a particular vocabulary word. Have children ask questions about What they would like to learn **(W)** about the word. Revisit the chart after reading and fill in what children have Learned **(L)** about the word.

*Let's look at the word* **holiday.** *What do you already know about holidays?* (They are special days we celebrate. There is no school or work on some holidays.) *What would you like to learn about holidays?* (Who decides which holidays people celebrate? Do other countries have the same holidays we have? Why do we have parades on some holidays?)

| K | W | L |
|---|---|---|
| Holidays are special days we celebrate. | Do other countries have the same holidays we have? | |

## DURING READING

### Context Clues

**Questioning the Author** Use the research-based routine of questioning the author to help children understand the vocabulary and text. As you read the lessons with children, choose places in the lessons to stop and discuss what the author is saying. Model the procedure for children by asking questions and paraphrasing important points. Then have children ask the questions and paraphrase the information.

*What new word does the author—the person who wrote the book—use? The author uses* **capital.** *Why does the author ask what our state's capital is?* (He or she thinks it is important.) *The author wants us to know where our state's leaders work. Why does the author say to look on the map?* (The map helps us find our state and helps us locate the state's capital.)

## AFTER READING

### Related Word Study

Vocabulary: freedom, colony, citizen, vote, capital

**Picture This** Assign pairs of children a vocabulary word. Read the words out loud to the class as you assign them. Have a collection of books and magazines that children can go through to find images that might be used to illustrate each word. Then have children share with the class what they have found to illustrate their words. One child of each pair can hold up the picture(s), while the other one explains how it relates to the word.

*I want you and your partner to read the assigned vocabulary word together. Talk about what the word means and find where it is used in the book. This will help you to remember why we have learned it. Then go through the books and magazines and find pictures that show something about what the word means. Once you have found pictures you like, we will share the pictures with the class, and you can tell us what the picture shows about your word's meaning.*

# Teaching with Leveled Readers

**This series of readers focuses on why the Fourth of July is an important day for people of the United States.**

**Below Level**

**On Level**

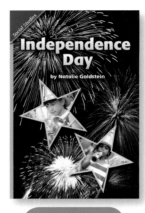

**Above Level**

## LEVELED READER VOCABULARY ACTIVITY

- Preview the vocabulary with children. Have each child choose one vocabulary word.

- As children read, have them take note of their word and its definition.

- After reading, have children draw a picture of their vocabulary word in the context of a Fourth of July celebration. Have them write their word at the bottom of the picture.

> Draw a picture of a Fourth of July celebration.
>
>
> Vocabulary word:

## CONNECTIONS TO THE LESSON

Unit 5, Lesson 3: The Colonies Become Free

## CONNECTIONS TO TODAY

- Have children read the lesson. Then provide the leveled readers to enhance their understanding of why our country continues to celebrate the Fourth of July today.

- **Points for Discussion:**
  1. Have children discuss why our country celebrates special days and events.

  2. Children can also discuss other national holidays, such as the birthdays of important people in our country's history.

# This Is Our Country

# Unit 5 Planning Guide

## This Is Our Country

**Begin with a Song** pp. 184–185    **Vocabulary Preview** pp. 186–187

**Reading Social Studies, Recall and Retell** pp. 188–189

| Lesson Titles | Pacing | Main Ideas |
|---|---|---|
| **Lesson 1 Native Americans** pp. 190–191 <br><br> **Chart and Graph Skills: Read a Diagram** pp. 192–193 <br> **Native American Objects** pp. 194–195 | 3 days | • The first people to live in North America were Native Americans. <br> • A diagram is a picture that shows the parts of something. <br> • Native Americans made many of the things they used. |
| **Lesson 2 Early Travelers to America** pp. 196–199 <br><br> **Map and Globe Skills: Use a History Map** pp. 200–201 | 2 days | • Christopher Columbus landed near North America in 1492. Later, the Pilgrims came from England to North America to be free. <br> • A history map shows places or routes from the past. |
| **Lesson 3 The Colonies Become Free** pp. 202–205 <br><br> **Biography: Benjamin Franklin** pp. 206–207 | 2 days | • The 13 colonies fought a war against England to be free. <br> • Benjamin Franklin helped the colonies become free. |
| **Lesson 4 Symbols in Our Country** pp. 208–209 <br><br> **Then and Now: Our Country's Flag** pp. 210–211 | 2 days | • Our national symbols include the Statue of Liberty, the bald eagle, and the Liberty Bell. <br> • Our flag, a symbol of freedom, has undergone many changes. |
| **Lesson 5 We Celebrate Holidays** pp. 212–215 <br><br> **Biography: Abraham Lincoln** pp. 216–217 | 2 days | • On national holidays, we honor important people or events in history. <br> • Abraham Lincoln, our 16th President, led our country during a war between the states. |
| **Lesson 6 Choosing Our Country's Leaders** pp. 218–221 <br><br> **Citizen Heroes: Honesty** **Eleanor Roosevelt** pp. 222–223 | 2 days | • Citizens of our country vote to choose their leaders. These leaders help make our laws. <br> • Eleanor Roosevelt worked for equal rights for all people. |

✓ **End with a Song** pp. 224–225    ✓ **Unit 5 Review** pp. 226–229    ✓ **Unit 5 Project** p. 230

✓ = Assessment Options

| Vocabulary | Resources | Meeting Individual Needs |
|---|---|---|
| | • Workbook, pp. 49–51<br>• Every Student Learns Guide, pp. 82–85<br>• Transparencies 25, 26 | • ESL Support, TE p. 192<br>• Leveled Practice, TE p. 195a |
| freedom | • Workbook, pp. 52–53<br>• Vocabulary Card: freedom<br>• Every Student Learns Guide, pp. 86–89<br>• Transparency 27 | • ESL Support, TE p. 198<br>• Leveled Practice, TE p. 201a |
| colony | • Workbook, p. 54<br>• Vocabulary Card: colony<br>• Every Student Learns Guide, pp. 90–93<br>• Transparency 28 | • ESL Support, TE p. 204<br>• Leveled Practice, TE p. 207a |
| | • Workbook, p. 55<br>• Every Student Learns Guide, pp. 94–97<br>• Transparencies 29, 30 | • ESL Support, TE p. 210<br>• Leveled Practice, TE p. 211a |
| holiday<br>President | • Workbook, p. 56<br>• Vocabulary Cards: holiday, President<br>• Every Student Learns Guide, pp. 98–101<br>• Transparencies 31, 32 | • ESL Support, TE p. 214<br>• Leveled Practice, TE p. 217a |
| citizen<br>vote<br>capital | • Workbook, p. 57<br>• Vocabulary Cards: citizen, vote, capital<br>• Every Student Learns Guide, pp. 102–105 | • ESL Support, TE p. 220<br>• Leveled Practice, TE p. 223a |

# Providing More Depth

## Additional Resources

- Trade Books
- Family Activities
- Vocabulary Workbook and Cards
- Social Studies Plus!
- Daily Activity Bank
- Read Alouds and Primary Sources
- Big Book Atlas
- Student Atlas
- Outline Maps
- Desk Maps

 **Technology**

- Video Field Trips
- Songs and Music
- Digital Learning CD-ROM Powered by KnowledgeBox
- AudioText
- MindPoint® Quiz Show CD-ROM
- ExamView® Test Bank CD-ROM
- Colonial Williamsburg Primary Sources CD-ROM
- Teacher Resources CD-ROM
- Map Resources CD-ROM
- SFSuccessNet: Online Student Edition, Online Teacher Edition, Online Planner
- **www.sfsocialstudies.com** (Biographies, news, references, maps, and activities)

 *To establish guidelines for your children's safe and responsible use of the Internet, use the Scott Foresman Internet Guide.*

**Additional Internet Links**

To find out more about:

- Pilgrims, visit **www.plimoth.org**

# Unit 5 Objectives

**Beginning of Unit 5**

- **Obtain information using oral sources, such as music.** (pp. 184–185)

- **Determine the meanings of words.** (pp. 186–187)

- **Recall and retell event or ideas.** (pp. 188–189)

- **Express ideas based on oral and written sources.** (pp. 188–189)

- **Describe various customs of families.** (pp. 188–189)

- **Describe ways that families meet basic needs.** (pp. 188–189)

**Lesson 1**
**Native Americans**
pp. 190–191

- **Obtain information about a topic using a variety of visual sources, such as maps.**

- **Describe similarities and differences in ways families meet basic needs.**

- **Obtain information about a topic using a variety of visual sources, such as diagrams.** (pp. 192–193)

- **Identify the human characteristics of types of houses.** (pp. 192–193)

- **Obtain information about a topic using a variety of visual sources, such as pictures and artifacts.** (pp. 194–195)

**Lesson 2**
**Early Travelers to America**
pp. 196–199

- **Describe the origins of selected holidays.**

- **Cite reasons for observing holidays.**

- **Obtain information abut a topic using a variety of visual sources, such as maps.** (pp. 200–201)

- **Use cardinal directions on a map.** (pp. 200–201)

**Lesson 3**
**The Colonies Become Free**
pp. 202–205

- **Describe the origin of selected holidays and celebrations such as Independence Day.**

- **Describe the events associated with Independence Day.**

- **Explain how selected celebrations reflect an American love of freedom.**

- **Identify contributions of historic figures such as George Washington.**

- **Identify contributions of historical figures who have influenced the nation.** (pp. 206–207)

- **Identify historic figures who exemplified good citizenship.** (pp. 206–207)

- **Identify historical figures who have exhibited a love of inventiveness.** (pp. 206–207)

**Lesson 4**
**Symbols in Our Country**
pp. 208–209

- **Identify the motto of the United States.**

- **Explain selected national and state patriotic symbols such as the Liberty Bell and the Eagle.**

- **Identify symbols that represent the United States and what it stands for.**

- **Recognize the symbols that honor and foster patriotism in the United States by identifying the bald eagle, Washington Monument, and Statue of Liberty.**

- **Obtain information about a topic using a variety of visual sources such as pictures and graphics.**

- **Explain selected national patriotic symbol such as the United States flag.** (pp. 210–211)

- **Distinguish between past and present.** (pp. 210–211)

- **Explain how selected symbols reflect an American love of freedom.** (pp. 210–211)

**Lesson 5**
**We Celebrate Holidays**
pp. 212–215

- **Describe the origins of selected holidays and celebrations of the nation, such as Martin Luther King, Jr. Day and Veterans Day.**

- **Cite reasons for observing special days and holidays.**

- **Describe the lives of people commemorated by Presidents' Day.**

- **Identify contributions of historical figures, such as Abraham Lincoln, who have influenced the nation.** (pp. 216–217)

- **Describe the lives of people commemorated by Presidents' Day.** (pp. 216–217)

**Lesson 6**
**Choosing Our Country's Leaders**
pp. 218–221

- **Identify leaders in the state and nation.**

- **Describe the roles of public officials, including governor and president.**

- **Locate Washington, D.C., and the capital of your state on a United States map.**

- **Identify historic figures, such as Eleanor Roosevelt, who have exemplified good citizenship.** (pp. 222–223)

- **Identify characteristics of good citizenship such as a belief in justice, truth, equality, and responsibility for the common good.** (pp. 222–223)

**End of Unit 5**
pp. 224–230

- **Identify anthems and mottoes of the United States and individual states.** (pp. 224–225)

- **Identifies a historic event and understands that events occur in a sequence.** (p. 230)

# Assessment Options

## ✓ Formal Assessment

- **What did you learn?** PE/TE pp. 191, 199, 205, 209, 215, 221, 229
- **Unit Review,** PE/TE pp. 226–229
- **Unit 5 Test,** Assessment Book, pp. 17–20
- **ExamView® CD-ROM**

## ✓ Informal Assessment

- **Teacher's Edition Questions,** throughout Lessons and Features
- **Close and Assess,** TE pp. 189, 191, 195, 199, 201, 205, 207, 209, 215, 217, 221, 223, 225
- **Try it!** PE/TE pp. 189, 193, 201
- **Think and Share,** PE/TE pp. 191, 199, 205, 207, 209, 215, 217, 221
- **Write and Share,** PE/TE p. 229
- **Honesty in Action,** PE/TE p. 223
- **Hands-on History,** PE/TE p. 211

### Ongoing Assessment

**Ongoing Assessment** is found throughout the Teacher's Edition lessons using an **If...then** model.

| **If** = students' observable behavior, | **then** = reteaching and enrichment suggestions |

## ✓ Portfolio Assessment

- **Portfolio Assessment,** TE pp. 183, 228
- **Leveled Practice,** TE pp. 195a, 201a, 207a, 211a, 217a, 223a
- **Workbook,** pp. 47–59
- **Unit Review: Skills on Your Own,** PE/TE p. 228
- **Curriculum Connection: Writing,** TE pp. 195a, 201a, 207a, 211a, 217a, 223, 223a

## ✓ Performance Assessment

- **Hands-on Unit Project** (Unit 5 Performance Assessment), PE/TE pp. 183, 228, 230
- **Internet Activity,** PE p. 230
- **Unit Review: Write and Share,** PE/TE p. 229
- **Scoring Guides,** TE pp. 224a, 227, 228, 230

## Test Talk

### Test-Taking Strategies

**Understand the Question**
- **Locate Key Words in the Question,** TE p. 214
- **Locate Key Words in the Text,** TE p. 199

**Understand the Answer**
- **Choose the Right Answer,** Test Talk Practice Book
- **Use Information from the Text,** TE p. 221
- **Use Information from Graphics,** TE pp. 193
- **Write Your Answer,** TE p. 203

*For additional practice, use the Test Talk Practice Book.*

### Featured Strategy

**Use Information from Graphics**

Children will:
- Understand the question and form a statement that begins "I need to find out..."
- Skim the graphics to find the right information to support their answer.

**PE/TE** p. 228, **TE** p. 193

# Curriculum Connections
## Integrating Your Day

The lessons, skills, and features of Unit 5 provide many opportunities to make connections between social studies and other areas of the elementary curriculum.

### Reading

**Make a Picture Glossary,** TE p. 187

**Reading Skill–Recall and Retell,** PE/TE pp. 188–189, TE p. 190, TE p. 208

**Native American Story,** TE p. 195a

**Reading Skill—Main Idea and Details,** TE p. 196

**Reading Skill—Categorize,** TE p. 202, TE p. 218

**One If by Land, Two If by Sea,** TE p. 207a

**Reading Skill—Analyze Pictures,** TE p. 212

### Writing

**Native American Objects,** TE p. 195a

**Making Words from Freedom,** TE p. 201a

**Far Away Places,** TE p. 207a

**Picturing Symbols,** TE p. 211a

**New Mottoes,** TE p. 211a

**Holiday Spirit,** TE p. 217a

**A Letter to Eleanor Roosevelt,** TE p. 223

**Stand Up and Be Counted,** TE p. 223a

**It's a Secret!** TE p. 223a

### Math

**Native American Design,** TE p. 194

**Compare Land Areas,** TE p. 200

**Arranging the Stars,** TE p. 211a

**Making Cents,** TE p. 217a

**Tallying the Votes,** TE p. 223a

## Social Studies

### Literature

**Read About Our Country,** TE p. 229

### Music/Drama

**I Love a Parade!** TE p. 185

**Traditional Tunes,** TE p. 195a

**Celebration at Plymouth,** TE p. 201a

**Signing the Declaration of Independence,** TE p. 207a

### Art

**My Home,** TE p. 190a

**Make a Diagram of the Classroom,** TE p. 192

**All Aboard!** TE p. 196a

**Sailing the Ocean Blue,** TE p. 201a

**Red, White, and Boom,** TE p. 202a

**Holidays,** TE p. 212a

**A Medal for Your Service,** TE p. 217a

**Vote for a Place,** TE p. 218a

**Welcome to America!** TE p. 224a

### Science

**Keeping Fit,** TE p. 189

**Cool Shades,** TE p. 207

 Look for this symbol throughout the Teacher's Edition to find **Curriculum Connections.**

# Professional Development

## Improving History Instruction in the Social Studies Classroom

### by Rita Geiger
Norman Oklahoma Public Schools

The two major concepts of social studies are *space* and *time*. Children develop these concepts slowly and systematically during the elementary school years. *Space* includes the immediate environment (such as home, school, neighborhood, and city), which children learn about through direct experience. The concept of space then extends to include the child's remote environment (that of the state, nation, and world), areas which are learned about largely through vicarious experiences. *Time* consists of the past, present, and future. Elementary children relate primarily to the present, and the effective elementary social studies teacher should focus mainly on present experiences in the immediate environment. However, the teacher can help children begin to understand the past, or "history," through a variety of strategies and activities.

*Here is how you can help children begin to understand the past as you teach* Scott Foresman Social Studies.

*Use the two Read Together Biographies (pp. 206–207 and pp. 216–217) to explore the lives of historical figures such as Benjamin Franklin and Abraham Lincoln.*

*To help children begin to understand spatial concepts, use the history map on pp. 200–201. To help them understand chronological relationships, use the time line in Then and Now: Our Country's Flag (pp. 210–211).*

## ESL Support

### by Jim Cummins, Ph. D.
University of Toronto

Language is central to the teaching of virtually every school subject. Social studies concepts are not just ideas that belong within the discipline of social studies; they are also *linguistic* concepts. The concept of *democracy*, for example, is both a linguistic concept and a concept that occupies a central space in the teaching of social studies.

One important strategy in making the language of social studies comprehensible to ESL students involves activating and building their background knowledge. The more background knowledge we have, the more of the text we can understand.

Another way to support, or scaffold, students' learning is by modifying the input itself. Here are just a few ways to modify the presentation of academic content so students can more effectively access the meaning:

- using visuals (pictures, photographs, real objects);
- acting out through gestures and pantomime;
- clarifying the language (paraphrasing ideas and explaining new concepts and words);
- making personal and cultural connections.

*The following examples in the Teacher's Edition will help you to enable ESL students to access content:*

*Focus on Meaning,* TE p. 188

*Questioning,* TE p. 192

*Telling About Cultural Traditions,* TE p. 198

*Understanding Bravery,* TE p. 204

*Interviewing and Retelling,* TE p. 210

*Telling About Holidays,* TE p. 214

*Interpret Maps,* TE p. 220

# Read Aloud

## Yankee Doodle

words by Dr. Richard Shuckburgh

Traditional Song

Yankee Doodle went to town,

A-riding on a pony,

He stuck a feather in his cap

And called it macaroni!

Yankee Doodle, keep it up,

Yankee Doodle dandy;

Mind the music and the step,

And with the girls be handy!

**Build Background**

• Tell children that the words to "Yankee Doodle" were set to the tune of an English folk song. Ask them if they know any traditional songs with new words.

**Read Alouds and Primary Sources**

*Read Alouds and Primary Sources* contains additional selections to be used with Unit 5.

# Bibliography

*Cheyenne Again,* by Eve Bunting and Irving Toddy (illustrator), (Clarion Books, ISBN 0-395-70364-6, 1995) **Easy**

*First Thanksgiving Feast, The,* by Joan Anderson and George Ancona (photographer), (Clarion Books, ISBN 0-395-51886-5, 1989) **Easy**

*Hooray for the Fourth of July,* by Wendy Watson (Houghton Mifflin, ISBN 0-618-04036-6, 2000) **Easy**

*I Have Heard of a Land,* by Joyce Carol Thomas and Floyd Cooper (illustrator), (HarperCollins, ISBN 0-06-443617-9, 2000) **Easy ALA Notable Book, Coretta Scott King Honor Book, Notable Social Studies Book**

*T Is for Texas,* by Anne Bustard (Voyageur, ISBN 0-896-58113-6, 1989) **Easy**

*To Be a Drum,* by Evelyn Coleman and Aminah Brenda Lynn Robinson (illustrator), (Albert Whitman, ISBN 0-807-58007-4, 2000) **Easy**

*Boston Coffee Party, The,* by Doreen Rappaport and Emily Arnold McCully (illustrator), (HarperTrophy, ISBN 0-064-44141-5, 1990) **On-Level**

*Sam the Minuteman,* by Nathaniel Benchley and Arnold Lobel (illustrator), (Harper Trophy, ISBN 0-064-44107-5, 1987) **On-Level**

*Star-Spangled Banner, The,* by Francis Scott Key and Peter Spier (illustrator), (Yearling Books, ISBN 0-440-40697-8, 1992) **On-Level**

*Flag We Love, The,* by Pam Muñoz Ryan and Ralph Masiello (illustrator), (Charlesbridge Publishing, ISBN 0-881-06844-6, 2000) **Challenge**

*Story of the Statue of Liberty, The,* by Betsy C. Maestro and Giulio Maestro (illustrator), (Mulberry Books, ISBN 0-688-08746-9, 1989) **Challenge**

*History Workshop: Reconstructing the Past with Elementary Students,* by Karen L. Jorgensen (Heinemann, ISBN 0-435-08900-5, 1993) **Teacher Reference**

*Discovery Channel School Videos Heroes of American History.* Get to know both early leaders, such as George Washington, and later heroes, such as Martin Luther King, Jr. 2 videos; 42 minutes/6 segments.

 Look for this symbol throughout the Teacher's Edition to find **Award-Winning Selections**. Additional book references are suggested throughout this unit.

# This Is Our Country

Why is our country's past important?

183

# This Is Our Country

## Unit Overview

In this unit children learn about people and events that have helped shape the history of the United States. They explore the origins of some of our national holidays and symbols, and they learn about the roles played by our leaders.

## Introduce James

Read the unit title and then introduce the featured child for this unit as a first-grader named James. Talk about what holiday James might be celebrating. Explain that many holidays help us remember people and events from our country's past.

## Unit Question

• Ask children the question on this page.

• Initiate a discussion of why our country's past is important.

• To activate prior knowledge, make a list on the board of children's ideas about why our country's past is important.

✓ **Portfolio Assessment** Keep a copy of this list for the Portfolio Assessment at the end of the unit on page 228.

# Practice and Extend

## Hands-on Unit Project

✓ **Unit 5 Performance Assessment**

• The Unit 5 Project, *History on Parade,* found on p. 230, is an ongoing performance assessment project to enrich children's learning throughout the unit.

• This project, which has children put on a history parade, may be started now or at any time during this unit of study.

• A performance assessment scoring guide is located on p. 230.

# Holidays Are Special Days

### Objective
- Obtain information using oral sources, such as music.

### Resources
- *Songs and Music* CD "Holidays Are Special Days"
- Poster 9
- Social Studies Plus!

## Introduce the Song

**Preview** Tell children that they will be singing a song about celebrating holidays. Focus attention on how the people in the picture are celebrating.

**Warm Up** To activate prior knowledge, ask children how their families celebrate special days, such as birthdays and anniversaries.

## Sing the Song

- Have children sing the song "Holidays Are Special Days."

- Ask children to name things mentioned in the song that families may do when they get together on special days. (share food, have parades, have a celebration).

- Invite children to name any great people of our nation that they may know about.

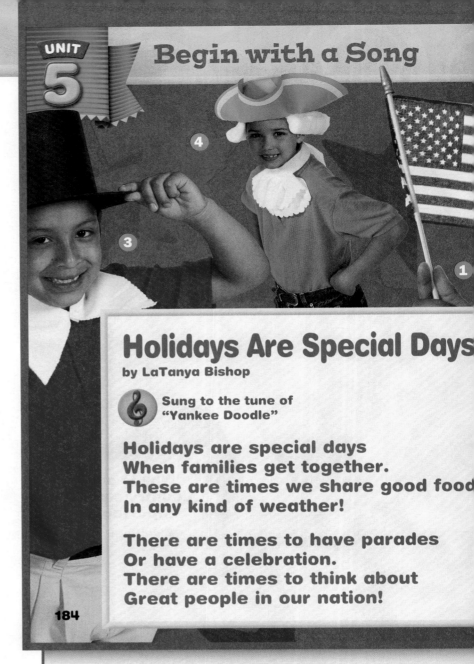

# Holidays Are Special Days
by LaTanya Bishop

Sung to the tune of "Yankee Doodle"

Holidays are special days
When families get together.
These are times we share good food
In any kind of weather!

There are times to have parades
Or have a celebration.
There are times to think about
Great people in our nation!

184

# Practice and Extend

**SOCIAL STUDIES**
**Background**

**Possible Misconceptions**

Children may not be aware that on some holidays we celebrate people and events in our nation's past. Tell children that on *their* birthdays, we celebrate the days on which they were born. Explain that on some holidays, we celebrate other people's birthdays. We also celebrate our *country's* birthday on July 4th.

**AUDIO CD**
**Technology**

Play the *Songs and Music* CD to listen to "Holidays Are Special Days."

# Talk About the Picture

Direct children's attention to the picture on these two pages. Ask children to name some things in the picture.

Point out to children that James is dressed like Uncle Sam. Uncle Sam stands for the United States government or people. Explain that most of the other children are dressed like people in our country's past.

**1 What is James holding?** The flag of the United States **Analyze Pictures**

Have children look at the girl and boy behind James on p. 185.

**2 Who are the girl and boy dressed like?** The girl is dressed like the Statue of Liberty. The boy is dressed like Abraham Lincoln.
**Interpret National Symbols/Analyze Pictures**

Have children look at the boy on the left on p. 184. Explain that he is dressed like some of the Pilgrims who came to North America long ago.

**3 What holiday do we celebrate that comes from the Pilgrims?** Thanksgiving
**Analyze Pictures**

Have children look at the boy on the right on p. 184. Explain that he is dressed like some of the people who fought for freedom against the English.

**4 What holiday do we celebrate that comes from the war against the English?**
Independence Day **Analyze Pictures**

CURRICULUM CONNECTION
## Music/Drama

**I Love a Parade!**

- Tell children that they are going to be in a class parade. Assign each child a partner, and have partners line up.
- Distribute any rhythm instruments that may be available.
- Have children play and sing "Holidays Are Special Days" as they parade around the classroom.
- If children already know the words to "Yankee Doodle," they can sing this song, too, as they march around the room. Suggest that children without instruments pantomime the actions of the song as they march.

## Objective
• Determine the meanings of words.

## Resources
• Workbook, p. 47

• Vocabulary Cards

• Poster 10

## Introduce the Vocabulary

Read aloud and point to each vocabulary word and the photograph illustrating it. Have volunteers give the meaning of the words. Then have children find several examples of vocabulary words in the illustration. Write these examples on the board.

| Vocabulary Word | Illustrated Examples |
|---|---|
| vote | mayoral candidate, vote signs on car, man with sign for mayor |
| President | presidential truck |
| citizen | citizen of year, citizen with placard |
| capital | Washington D.C., sign on truck, state capital travel poster on building |
| holiday | 4th of July banner, holiday sign in store window |
| freedom | symbols of freedom marchers, American flag on pole |
| colony | 13 colonies exhibit on truck |

⭐ SOCIAL STUDIES STRAND
## Citizenship

Listed below are some basic principles of history for young children. Direct your discussion of the illustration toward the development of these concepts.

• America in the past
• historic figures who shaped the nation
• historic figures who exemplify good citizenship
• origin of holidays that celebrate our nation and its leaders
• love of freedom
• patriotic symbolism of the flag
• voting
• role of public leaders
• places where laws are made

freedom

colony

holiday

President

186

# Practice and Extend

⭐ SOCIAL STUDIES STRAND
## Citizenship

**Let's Vote**

• Explain to children that in the United States, people choose Presidents by voting for them.
• Discuss Presidents Washington and Lincoln with children.
• Distribute blank ballots, and have children vote for which President is their favorite.
• Collect the ballots, and have children help you count the votes. Declare the winner.

🖥 WEB SITE
## Technology

You can look up vocabulary words online. Click on *Social Studies Library* and select the dictionary at www.sfsocialstudies.com.

citizen

vote

capital

**187**

## Talk About the Illustration

Allow children time to study the illustration. Encourage them to describe the parade from its front to its back.

**❶ What symbols of freedom are shown in the parade?** The Liberty Bell, the Statue of Liberty, the American flag, the bald eagle, and Uncle Sam **Analyze Pictures**

**❷ What holiday is being celebrated?** Fourth of July **Analyze Pictures**

## Look Ahead

Tell children that they will learn more about each of these words as they study Unit 5.

You may want to revisit the picture with children to review the concepts and vocabulary in the unit.

**❸ What Presidents are shown in the truck?** Abraham Lincoln and George Washington **Analyze Pictures**

**Workbook, p. 47**

Draw a picture for each word. **Drawings will vary.**

| vote | President |
| citizen | capital |
| holiday | freedom |
| colony | |

**Also on Teacher Resources CD-ROM.**

# James's Story

##  Recall and Retell

### Objectives

- Recall and retell events or ideas.
- Express ideas based on oral and written sources.
- Describe various customs of families.
- Describe ways that families meet basic needs.

### Resource

- Workbook, p. 48

### About the Unit Target Skill

- The target reading skill for this unit is Recall and Retell. Children are introduced to the unit target skill here and are given an opportunity to practice it.

# 1 Introduce and Motivate

**Preview** Assess whether children understand the concepts of recall and retell by asking them first to recall important things that happen in a familiar story and then to retell the story to a classmate. If necessary, explain that *recall* means "remember," and that *retell* means "tell again."

**Warm Up** To activate prior knowledge, review with children the legend of Johnny Appleseed (pp. 176–177). Then help children make a list of important events from the story. Demonstrate how to use the list to retell the story.

# James's Story

##  Recall and Retell

Hi! My name is James. I wrote a story about a Seminole Indian named Little Rabbit. Read my story to find out about Little Rabbit.

### Little Rabbit

Long ago there lived a boy named Little Rabbit. He liked to run races with his friends. He was very fast.

Little Rabbit was a Seminole. He lived in the Florida Everglades. Little Rabbit lived in a house called a chickee with his family. The family planted corn and other vegetables.

Little Rabbit loved to hear his grandfather tell stories. His favorite story was about a frog who could make it rain. Little Rabbit's grandfather taught him how to do the Green Corn Dance.

**188**

# Practice and Extend

## ESL ACCESS CONTENT ESL Support

**Focus on Meaning** Help children access the content of "Little Rabbit" by showing pictures of a chickee, corn, and other vegetables. Tell children that Seminole Indians lived in chickees.

**Beginning** Point to the picture of a chickee. Say chickee, and have children repeat after you. Repeat for the corn and other vegetables.

**Intermediate** Ask children to identify the items pictured. Ask what a chickee is used for (a home). Ask a volunteer to pantomime planting and picking vegetables.

**Advanced** Ask children to dictate captions for the pictures. Encourage them to tell how each item is used.

You **recall** when you think about something you have read or heard. You **retell** when you put it into your own words. Think about the story James wrote. Tell the story in your own words.

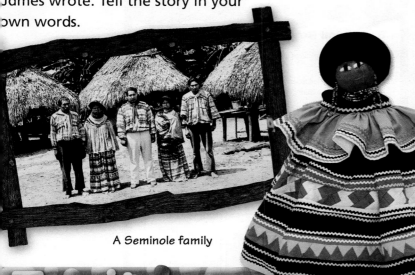

A Seminole family

A Seminole doll

## Try it!

↻ Draw three pictures that show something you **recall** about Little Rabbit. Use your pictures to **retell** the story in your own words.

**189**

Read pp. 188–189. Then tell children that they should first recall the important things in James's story. Read "Little Rabbit" again, asking children to follow along or to listen for important ideas. Then help them make a list of those ideas.

Little Rabbit was a fast runner.

He was a Seminole.

He lived with his family in a chickee.

His father taught him the Green Corn Dance.

Review the list with children. Have them use it to retell the story. Then cover the list, and ask a volunteer to retell the story.

### Ongoing Assessment

**If...** children have difficulty recalling important ideas,

**then...** suggest that they draw or write to make notes that will help them to remember.
Tell children that as they read in social studies, they should stop after each page or two and try to recall and retell the important ideas.

## 3 Close and Assess

## Try it!

↻ If you wish, remind children of the list of important events that you made after reading "Little Rabbit" so that they can refer to it as they draw their pictures. Have children work with partners to retell the story.

### CURRICULUM CONNECTION
### Science

**Keeping Fit**

- Point out to children that running is good exercise. Tell them that people can keep fit and healthy by eating the right foods and by getting exercise.

- Have children find pictures of different ways people exercise to keep fit. Display the pictures on a bulletin board.

- Ask children what ways they exercise. Make a list on the board.

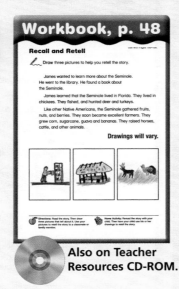

**Workbook, p. 48**

**Recall and Retell**

✎ Draw three pictures to help you retell the story.

James wanted to learn more about the Seminole. He went to the library. He found a book about the Seminole.

James learned that the Seminole lived in Florida. They lived in chickees. They fished, and hunted deer and turkeys.

Like other Native Americans, the Seminole gathered fruits, nuts, and berries. They soon became excellent farmers. They grew corn, sugarcane, guava and bananas. They raised horses, cattle, and other animals.

**Drawings will vary.**

**Also on Teacher Resources CD-ROM.**

# Workbook Support

Use the following Workbook pages to support content and skills development as you teach Unit 5. You can also view and print Workbook pages from the Teacher Resources CD-ROM.

## Workbook, p. 47

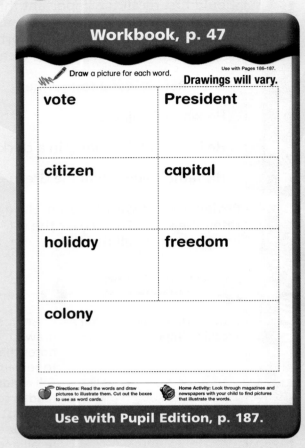

✎ Draw a picture for each word.

Use with Pages 186–187.

**Drawings will vary.**

| vote | President |
|------|-----------|
| citizen | capital |
| holiday | freedom |
| colony | |

🍎 **Directions:** Read the words and draw pictures to illustrate them. Cut out the boxes to use as word cards.

🧺 **Home Activity:** Look through magazines and newspapers with your child to find pictures that illustrate the words.

### Use with Pupil Edition, p. 187.

## Workbook, p. 48

### Recall and Retell

✎ Draw three pictures to help you retell the story.

James wanted to learn more about the Seminole. He went to the library. He found a book about the Seminole.

James learned that the Seminole lived in Florida. They lived in chickees. They fished, and hunted deer and turkeys.

Like other Native Americans, the Seminole gathered fruits, nuts, and berries. They soon became excellent farmers. They grew corn, sugarcane, guava and bananas. They raised horses, cattle, and other animals.

**Drawings will vary.**

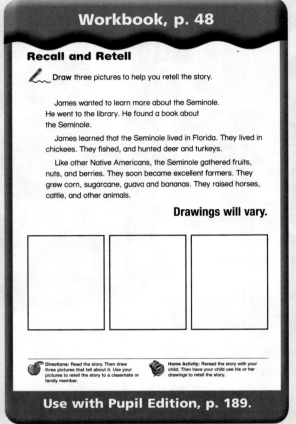

🍎 **Directions:** Read the story. Then draw three pictures that tell about it. Use your pictures to retell the story to a classmate or family member.

🧺 **Home Activity:** Reread the story with your child. Then have your child use his or her drawings to retell the story.

### Use with Pupil Edition, p. 189.

## Workbook, p. 49

### Native Americans

Use with Pages 190–191.

**Match** each picture with a sentence.

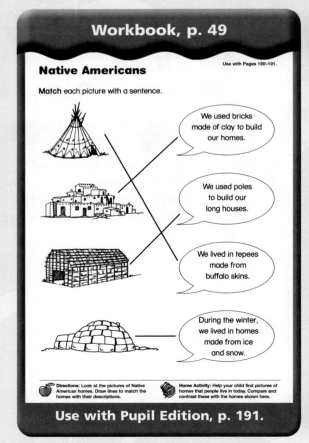

We used bricks made of clay to build our homes.

We used poles to build our long houses.

We lived in tepees made from buffalo skins.

During the winter, we lived in homes made from ice and snow.

🍎 **Directions:** Look at the pictures of Native American homes. Draw lines to match the homes with their descriptions.

🧺 **Home Activity:** Help your child find pictures of homes that people live in today. Compare and contrast these with the homes shown here.

### Use with Pupil Edition, p. 191.

## Workbook, p. 50

### Read a Diagram

Use with Pages 192–193.

👁 **Look** at the diagram.

✎ **Write** answers.

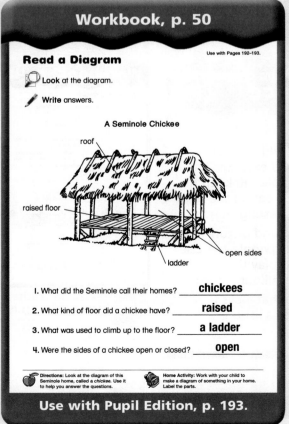

A Seminole Chickee

roof

raised floor

open sides

ladder

1. What did the Seminole call their homes? **chickees**

2. What kind of floor did a chickee have? **raised**

3. What was used to climb up to the floor? **a ladder**

4. Were the sides of a chickee open or closed? **open**

🍎 **Directions:** Look at the diagram of this Seminole home, called a chickee. Use it to help you answer the questions.

🧺 **Home Activity:** Work with your child to make a diagram of something in your home. Label the parts.

### Use with Pupil Edition, p. 193.

# Workbook Support

**Writing Prompt:** Native Americans made the clothes they wore and things they needed for work and play. Think about the things you use and wear today. How are they like the Native American objects you read about? How are they different? Draw a picture of a piece of Native American clothing and a piece of your own clothing. Write about ways they are similar and different.

### Drawings will vary.

| Native American Clothing | My Clothing |
|---|---|
|  |  |

**Answers will vary.**

**Directions:** Before you write, plan what you want to say. Include details to support your answer. Check for correct spelling, punctuation, and grammar.

**Home Activity:** Ask your child to tell you about the picture he or she has drawn. Talk about how both items in the picture might actually be made

**Use with Pupil Edition, p. 195.**

### Early Travelers to America

Use with Pages 196–199.

Draw to finish each picture. **Drawings will vary.**

Color the pictures.

**Columbus Day**

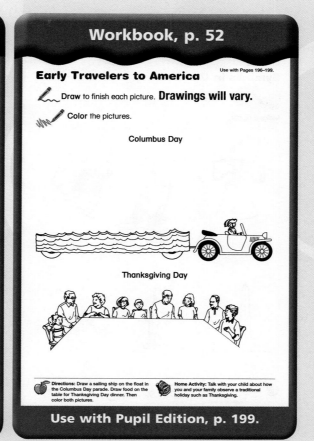

**Thanksgiving Day**

**Directions:** Draw a sailing ship on the float in the Columbus Day parade. Draw food on the table for Thanksgiving Day dinner. Then color both pictures.

**Home Activity:** Talk with your child about how you and your family observe a traditional holiday such as Thanksgiving.

**Use with Pupil Edition, p. 199.**

### Use a History Map

Use with Pages 200–201.

Draw the routes.

Color the land green and the water blue.

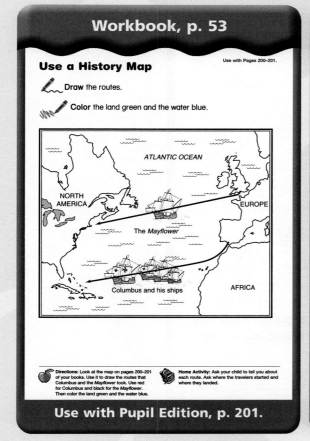

ATLANTIC OCEAN

NORTH AMERICA

EUROPE

The *Mayflower*

AFRICA

Columbus and his ships

**Directions:** Look at the map on pages 200–201 of your books. Use it to draw the routes that Columbus and the *Mayflower* took. Use red for Columbus and black for the *Mayflower*. Then color the land green and the water blue.

**Home Activity:** Ask your child to tell you about each route. Ask where the travelers started and where they landed.

**Use with Pupil Edition, p. 201.**

### The Colonies Become Free

Use with Pages 202–205.

Write words to finish the sentences.

| England | colonies | freedom | war | country |
|---|---|---|---|---|

1. There were thirteen __**colonies**__.

2. The colonies were ruled by __**England**__ and its king.

3. Many colonists wanted __**freedom**__ from England.

4. The colonies fought a __**war**__ with England.

5. The colonies won the war and became a __**country**__.

Write the name of a famous leader during the war.

**George Washington**

**Directions:** Use words from the box to complete the sentences. Then write the name of a famous leader during the war between England and the colonies.

**Home Activity:** Ask your child to tell you more about the person whose name he or she wrote at the bottom of the page.

**Use with Pupil Edition, p. 205.**

# Workbook Support

 Use the following Workbook pages to support content and skills development as you teach Unit 5. You can also view and print Workbook pages from the Teacher Resources CD-ROM.

## Workbook, p. 55

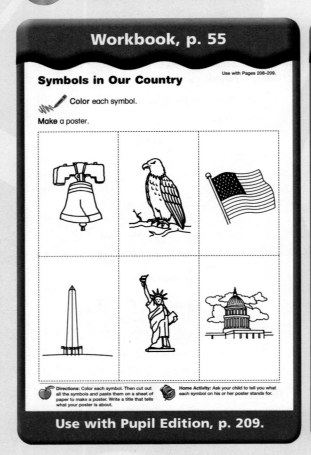

**Symbols in Our Country**

Use with Pages 208–209.

Color each symbol.

**Make** a poster.

**Directions:** Color each symbol. Then cut out all the symbols and paste them on a sheet of paper to make a poster. Write a title that tells what your poster is about.

**Home Activity:** Ask your child to tell you what each symbol on his or her poster stands for.

**Use with Pupil Edition, p. 209.**

## Workbook, p. 56

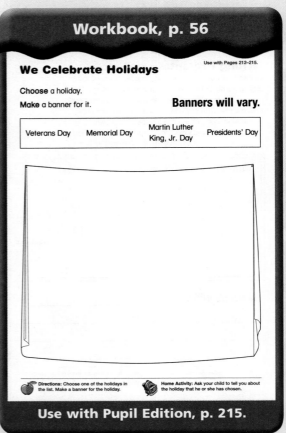

**We Celebrate Holidays**

Use with Pages 212–215.

**Choose** a holiday.

**Make** a banner for it.     **Banners will vary.**

| Veterans Day | Memorial Day | Martin Luther King, Jr. Day | Presidents' Day |
|---|---|---|---|

**Directions:** Choose one of the holidays in the list. Make a banner for the holiday.

**Home Activity:** Ask your child to tell you about the holiday that he or she has chosen.

**Use with Pupil Edition, p. 215.**

## Workbook, p. 57

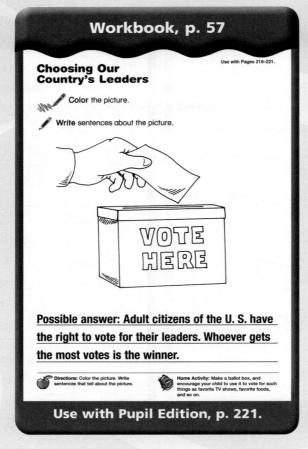

**Choosing Our Country's Leaders**

Use with Pages 218–221.

Color the picture.

Write sentences about the picture.

VOTE HERE

**Possible answer: Adult citizens of the U. S. have the right to vote for their leaders. Whoever gets the most votes is the winner.**

**Directions:** Color the picture. Write sentences that tell about the picture.

**Home Activity:** Make a ballot box, and encourage your child to use it to vote for such things as favorite TV shows, favorite foods, and so on.

**Use with Pupil Edition, p. 221.**

# Workbook Support

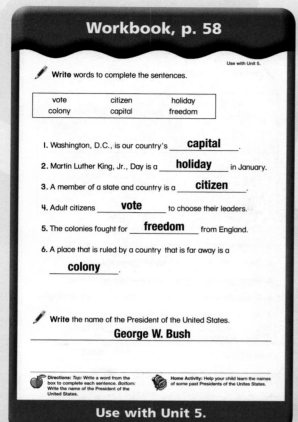

## Workbook, p. 58

Use with Unit 5.

✎ **Write** words to complete the sentences.

| vote | citizen | holiday |
|------|---------|---------|
| colony | capital | freedom |

1. Washington, D.C., is our country's __**capital**__ .

2. Martin Luther King, Jr., Day is a __**holiday**__ in January.

3. A member of a state and country is a __**citizen**__ .

4. Adult citizens __**vote**__ to choose their leaders.

5. The colonies fought for __**freedom**__ from England.

6. A place that is ruled by a country that is far away is a __**colony**__ .

✎ **Write** the name of the President of the United States.

**George W. Bush**

**Directions:** *Top:* Write a word from the box to complete each sentence. *Bottom:* Write the name of the President of the United States.

**Home Activity:** Help your child learn the names of some past Presidents of the Unites States.

**Use with Unit 5.**

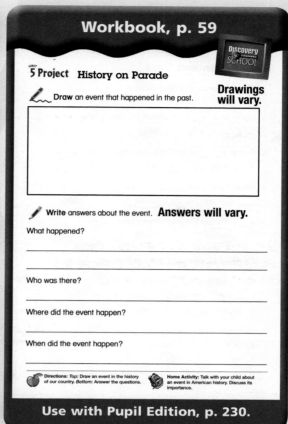

## Workbook, p. 59

DISCOVERY CHANNEL SCHOOL

**UNIT 5 Project   History on Parade**

✎ **Draw** an event that happened in the past.

**Drawings will vary.**

✎ **Write** answers about the event. **Answers will vary.**

What happened?

Who was there?

Where did the event happen?

When did the event happen?

**Directions:** *Top:* Draw an event in the history of our country. *Bottom:* Answer the questions.

**Home Activity:** Talk with your child about an event in American history. Discuss its importance.

**Use with Pupil Edition, p. 230.**

# Assessment Support

 Use these Assessment Book pages and the ExamView® CD-ROM to assess content and skills in Unit 5. You can also view and print Assessment Book pages from the Teacher Resources CD-ROM.

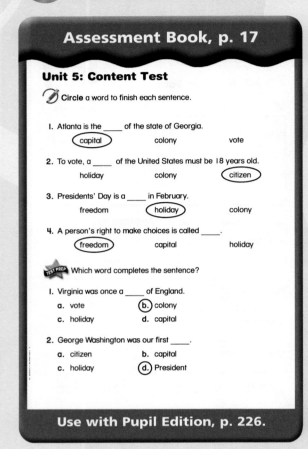

## Assessment Book, p. 17

### Unit 5: Content Test

Circle a word to finish each sentence.

1. Atlanta is the _____ of the state of Georgia.
   (capital)    colony    vote

2. To vote, a _____ of the United States must be 18 years old.
   holiday    colony    (citizen)

3. Presidents' Day is a _____ in February.
   freedom    (holiday)    colony

4. A person's right to make choices is called _____.
   (freedom)    capital    holiday

TEST PREP Which word completes the sentence?

1. Virginia was once a _____ of England.
   a. vote    (b.) colony
   c. holiday    d. capital

2. George Washington was our first _____.
   a. citizen    b. capital
   c. holiday    (d.) President

**Use with Pupil Edition, p. 226.**

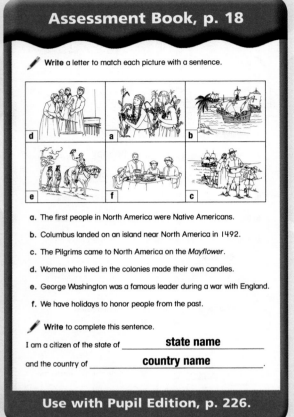

## Assessment Book, p. 18

Write a letter to match each picture with a sentence.

a. The first people in North America were Native Americans.

b. Columbus landed on an island near North America in 1492.

c. The Pilgrims came to North America on the *Mayflower*.

d. Women who lived in the colonies made their own candles.

e. George Washington was a famous leader during a war with England.

f. We have holidays to honor people from the past.

Write to complete this sentence.

I am a citizen of the state of _____ **state name** _____

and the country of _____ **country name** _____.

**Use with Pupil Edition, p. 226.**

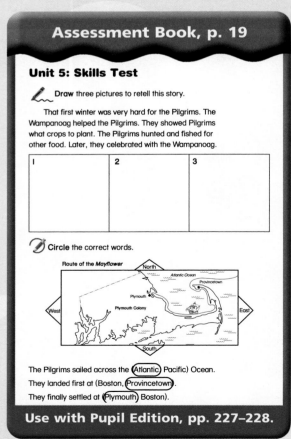

## Assessment Book, p. 19

### Unit 5: Skills Test

Draw three pictures to retell this story.

That first winter was very hard for the Pilgrims. The Wampanoag helped the Pilgrims. They showed Pilgrims what crops to plant. The Pilgrims hunted and fished for other food. Later, they celebrated with the Wampanoag.

| 1 | 2 | 3 |
|---|---|---|
|   |   |   |

Circle the correct words.

The Pilgrims sailed across the (Atlantic) Pacific) Ocean.
They landed first at (Boston, (Provincetown)).
They finally settled at ((Plymouth) Boston).

**Use with Pupil Edition, pp. 227–228.**

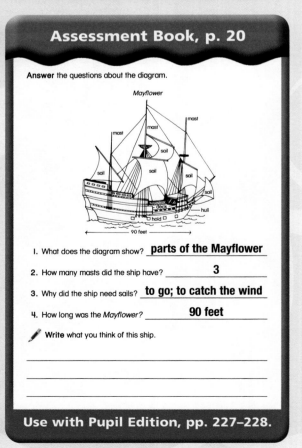

## Assessment Book, p. 20

Answer the questions about the diagram.

1. What does the diagram show?  **parts of the Mayflower**

2. How many masts did the ship have?  **3**

3. Why did the ship need sails?  **to go; to catch the wind**

4. How long was the *Mayflower*?  **90 feet**

Write what you think of this ship.

_____

_____

_____

**Use with Pupil Edition, pp. 227–228.**

# Lesson ① Overview

## Native Americans
pages 190–191

Children will learn about different groups of Native Americans and explore their diverse cultures and customs.

 **Time** 20 minutes

**Resources**
- Workbook, p. 49
- Every Student Learns Guide, pp. 82–85

## Read a Diagram
pages 192–193

Children will learn the meaning of the word *diagram* and gain knowledge about reading a diagram.

**Time** 15–20 minutes

**Resource**
- Workbook, p. 50

## Native American Objects
pages 194–195

Children will learn about clothing and other goods made by Native American groups.

**Time** 20 minutes

**Resource**
- Workbook, p. 51

# Build Background

## Activity

### My Home

 **Time** 15–20 minutes

Have children draw a picture of either the inside or outside of their home (for example, a house or apartment building). Invite students to label their picture "My Home." This activity will help children clarify similarities and differences between how they live and how Native Americans lived long ago.

**If time is short,** have children describe their home.

## Read Aloud

### People Then and Now
**by Vanessa Gates**

This much I know:
people long ago
were not like you and me,
I'm sure you'll agree.

They grew their own veggies
and lived in strange homes...
Wait a minute, if you please!
They needed food to eat
and a place to sleep.

Why I'm sure you'll agree
that's just like me!
This much I can say:
Long ago people
were like people today.

## Lesson 1

# Native Americans

## Objectives

- Obtain information about a topic using a variety of visual sources such as maps.
- Describe similarities and differences in ways families meet basic needs.

### QUICK Teaching Plan

*If time is short,* discuss the map with students. Explain that long ago, like today, Native American groups lived in different parts of the United States.

- Have children look at the pictures of the different kinds of homes. Then have them describe the differences.

## 1 Introduce and Motivate

**Preview** Tell children that they will learn where different Native American groups lived long ago, what kinds of homes they built, what they ate, and how they got food.

**Warm Up** To activate prior knowledge, ask children what they know about how Native Americans lived long ago. Ask them if they think Native Americans lived in houses like ours today. Ask them whether they think Native Americans bought food at a grocery store or dined at a restaurant.

## 2 Teach and Discuss

### Page 190

Identify James in the photograph. Invite volunteers to name the vegetables that James is holding (corn, squash).

Discuss with children the types of Native American homes shown. Explain that the Chinook lived in buildings called plank houses; the Pueblo lived in pueblos; the Lakota lived in tepees; the Wampanoag lived in wigwams.

**190** Unit 5 • This Is Our Country

---

## Lesson 1

# Native American

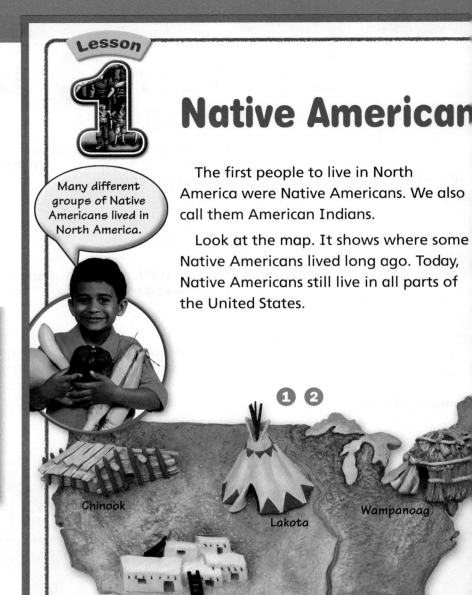

Many different groups of Native Americans lived in North America.

The first people to live in North America were Native Americans. We also call them American Indians.

Look at the map. It shows where some Native Americans lived long ago. Today, Native Americans still live in all parts of the United States.

1 2

Chinook

Lakota

Wampanoag

Pueblo

190

## Practice and Extend

### READING SKILL
### Recall and Retell

**Analyze Pictures** Tell children that they can use the pictures of Native American homes to help them recall and retell what they learned about Native Americans.

- Have children complete a word web by drawing the shapes of the Native American homes.

Some Native American groups hunted for their food. Other groups grew food such as corn, beans, and squash. Still others caught fish.

A Pueblo home

## What did you learn

1. Who were the first people to live in North America?

2. Tell how the Pueblo home is like the Lakota home. Tell how it is different.

3. **Think and Share** Draw pictures to show three things you **recall** about Native Americans. Use your pictures to **retell** what you learned in this lesson.

191

**1 Did the four groups of Native Americans live close to each other?** No. They lived in different parts of the United States. **Interpret Maps**

**2 How are Native American homes like our homes?** Answers may vary, but may include references to doors, windows, and roofs. **Compare and Contrast**

**3 What are some foods Native Americans ate?** Corn, beans, squash, fish **Recall and Retell**

**4 How did Native Americans get their food?** They hunted, fished, or grew food. **Recall and Retell**

## 3 Close and Assess

Have children form groups to discuss Native American homes. Then ask children to decide whether they would like to be Native Americans living long ago.

## ✓ What did you learn

1. Native Americans

2. Answers will vary but may include: Alike: Both have doors. Different: The Pueblo home has many doors. The Lakota home has one door.

3. **Think and Share** Answers should explain any three things students learned about any of the Native American groups.

SOCIAL STUDIES **Background**

**Native American Groups on the Map**

Tell children that the Native American groups identified on the map may have called themselves other names, and, like people today, many of them moved from place to place.

**Workbook, p. 49**

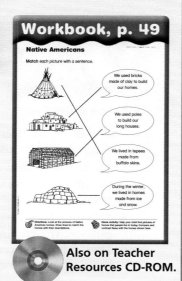

Native Americans

Match each picture with a sentence.

We used bricks made of clay to build our homes.

We used poles to build our long houses.

We lived in tepees made from buffalo skins.

During the winter, we lived in homes made from ice and snow.

**Also on Teacher Resources CD-ROM.**

# Read a Diagram

## Objectives

- Obtain information about a topic using a variety of visual sources such as diagrams.
- Identify the human characteristics of types of houses.

## Vocabulary

**diagram** a way to show the parts of something (p. 193)

# Introduce and Motivate

**Preview** Explain that a diagram is a drawing that explains something. Draw a diagram of a bicycle. Label the wheels, seat, pedals, and handlebars.

**Warm Up** To activate prior knowledge ask students to remember the kinds of homes some Native Americans built (tepees, pueblos, wigwams, and plank houses). Explain that they will look at a diagram of one type of home, an earth lodge. Explain that using a diagram will help them understand the parts of the earth lodge.

# Read a Diagram

Native Americans lived in different type of homes. One type of Native American home was called an earth lodge. The picture below shows an earth lodge. Native Americans made fires inside earth lodges to cook and to keep warm. Smoke from the fire left the lodge through a ho in the roof.

192

# Practice and Extend

### ESL ACCESS CONTENT
## ESL Support

**Questioning** Have children ask and answer questions about the diagrams in the book and on the board.

**Beginning** Ask questions about the diagram using the word *where*. Example: *Where are the wheels?* Have children point to the part you ask about.

**Intermediate** Ask children what and where questions about the diagrams. Examples: *What is a roof?* and *Where is the roof?* Have children point to the part and answer verbally.

**Advanced** Have children take turns asking each other *what* and *where* questions about the diagrams. Have one child ask a question and another child answer by both pointing to the part and answering verbally.

*For additional ESL Support, use Every Student Learns Guide, pp. 82–85.*

### CURRICULUM CONNECTION
## Art

**Make a Diagram of the Classroom**

- Explain to children that often somebody makes a diagram of a house before the house can be built.
- Hand out an outline of the classroom. Explain that it is an outline of the classroom from above as it is viewed from the ceiling.
- Point to the location of the teacher's desk on the outline. Tell children to draw a small rectangle there. Then have children make *X*s to indicate the location of the door and windows.
- Have children label the locations of the door, windows, and desk.

Look at this diagram of an earth lodge. A **diagram** shows the parts of something. Name the parts of the earth lodge you see on the diagram.

nce

roof

② hole in the roof

# Try it!

1. What does a **diagram** show?

2. What part did Native Americans use to enter the earth lodge?

3. **On Your Own** Make a diagram that shows a room in your home. Label each part.

**193**

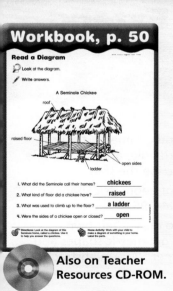
# ② Teach and Discuss

Read the introduction. Explain to children that today people might stay in a place called a lodge during special times of the year. For example, a family may vacation at a ski lodge in the winter. Have children look at the picture of the Native American earth lodge.

Point out the diagram. Explain to children that the picture shows both the inside and outside of an earth lodge.

❶ **What are three parts of an earth lodge?** An entrance, a roof, and a hole in the roof **Analyze pictures**

**Test Talk**

**Use Information from Graphics**
❷ **Why does the lodge have a hole in the roof?** It enables smoke from a fire to escape to the outside. Tell children to look at the diagram to figure out the right answer. **Make Inferences**

# ③ Close and Assess

Draw a diagram of a computer on the board with arrows pointing to the monitor, keyboard, and mouse. Have children name the parts. Then write them on the board.

## Try it!

1. The parts of something

2. The entrance

3. **On Your Own** Diagrams will vary but should reflect the parts of a room at home.

# Native American Objects

## Objective

- Obtain information about a topic using a variety of visual sources such as pictures and artifacts.

## Resource

Workbook, p. 51

# 1 Introduce and Motivate

**Preview** Ask if children have ever modeled with clay. Ask if they have ever done any weaving. Encourage those who have to tell what materials they used and what they made.

**Warm Up** To activate prior knowledge, remind children that in Lesson 1, they learned about several Native American groups. Review the names Pueblo, Lakota, Wampanoag, and Chinook. Have children refer back to p. 190 to talk about the homes different Native Americans made. Tell children that they will now look at some other everyday objects and clothing made by Native Americans.

Read the introductory paragraph with children. Point out that all the things shown on pp. 194–195 were made by Native Americans.

# 2 Teach and Discuss

Direct children's attention to the objects pictured on these two pages. You may want to begin with the large picture of the Ute child's coat and move through the other items. After reading each caption aloud for children, ask what materials they think were used to make the item. Also ask what the artifact may have been used for.

**1** **What do you think the pottery and the cornhusk bag were used for?** Possible answers: The pottery may have been used to hold water. The cornhusk bag may have been used to hold personal items. **Make Inferences**

---

# Native American Objects

This doll is dressed in traditional Dakota clothing.

Native Americans made the things they used and wore. **1** Many of these objects are still made and used today by Native Americans in our country.

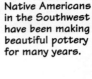

Colored beads forming a geometric design show the fine craftwork on this Ute child's coat.

Native Americans in the Southwest have been making beautiful pottery for many years.

The Penobscot are known for their deerskin moccasins which are often decorated with colorful beads.

**194**

---

# Practice and Extend

**CURRICULUM CONNECTION**
## Math

### Native American Design

- Show children samples of several geometric figures, including a circle, a square, a triangle, and a rectangle. Have children identify and describe the shapes.
- Ask children to find examples of geometric shapes on the artifacts pictured on pp. 194–195.
- Have children use the shapes to draw their own designs. Or, have them cut out geometric shapes and paste them on construction paper to form abstract collages.

The stick and ball game we now call Lacrosse was played by many Native American people.

②

These dolls are wearing the traditional clothing worn by Seminole women.

Tlingit women use wool from mountain goats to make dancing dresses for a special ceremony called a potlatch.
③

Many Native Americans used cradleboards to carry their babies safely from place to place.

Snowshoes allowed Cree children to move more easily on different sorts of terrain and snow.

The Pomo people made fine baskets and often decorated them with feathers. The basekets were woven by both men and women.

①

The Nez Perce are known for their cornhusk bags.

**195**

② **Look at the Seminole dolls. What do they tell you about the people who made them?**
Possible answer: The Seminole people liked to use beautiful, bright colors and patterns.
**Make Inferences**

③ **Why do you think the Native Americans decorated so many of the things they made?**
Possible answer: They wanted to make the items beautiful. **Make Inferences**

# 3 Close and Assess

- Ask each child to choose an artifact that he or she thinks is especially interesting or beautiful. Encourage children to explain their choices.

- Point out that all the artifacts shown on pp. 194–195 were made by hand. Ask children to name some household tools and appliances that their families use. Ask if children think these items were also made by hand.

- Point out that when the Native Americans made some of the things shown on pp. 194–195, people did not know about electricity. Ask how children think Native Americans did such things as get water and prepare food. Ask children to suggest other ways electricity has changed the ways people live.

**CURRICULUM CONNECTION**
**Art**

### Cave Paintings

- The objects on pp. 194–195 show one way in which daily life is reflected through art forms. Another example is how prehistoric people reflected their daily life through cave paintings.

- Discuss with children the idea behind cave paintings. Ask children to draw a picture showing something they do in every day. Have volunteers explain what their picture shows about their daily lives.

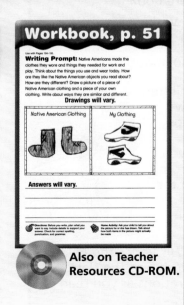

## Workbook, p. 51

Use with Pages 194–195.
**Writing Prompt:** Native Americans made the clothes they wore and things they needed for work and play. Think about the things you use and wear today. How are they like the Native American objects you read about? How are they different? Draw a picture of a piece of Native American clothing and a piece of your own clothing. Write about ways they are similar and different.
**Drawings will vary.**

| Native American Clothing | My Clothing |
|---|---|

**Answers will vary.**

**Also on Teacher Resources CD-ROM.**

# Lesson ① Wrap-Up

### ↪ Recall and Retell About Native Americans

Have children recall and retell what they learned about Native Americans.

**Easy** Have children draw a Native American home. Ask them to describe the home. **Reteach**

**On-Level** Have children draw a Native American home and make a label telling who lived there. **Extend**

**Challenge** Have children draw a Native American home and make labels telling the parts of the home and who lived there. **Enrich**

## Hands-on Activities

CURRICULUM CONNECTION
### Writing/Vocabulary

## Native American Objects

**Objective** Define and illustrate objects used by Native Americans.

**Materials** crayons
**Learning Style** Visual/Linguistic
**Individual** 👤
⏱ **Time** 10–15 minutes

1. Help children distinguish among the words *basket* (a container made of twigs, grasses, etc. woven together), *jar* (a container of stone, baked clay, etc. with a mouth), and *bowl* (a hollow, rounded dish).

2. Have them draw one of these objects. Suggest they include a decoration like one on pp. 194–195. Then have them label the object.

CURRICULUM CONNECTION
### Reading

## Native American Story

**Objective** Act out a Native American story.

**Materials** picture book
**Learning Style** Verbal/Linguistic
**Group** 👤👤👤👤
⏱ **Time** 15–30 minutes

1. Explain to children that many Native American groups have stories, or legends, that were passed down from earlier times to the present by parents to their children.

2. Read *How Jackrabbit Got His Very Long Ears* by Heather Irbinskas to the class. Show the illustrations as you read.

3. Have children act out important events of the story.

CURRICULUM CONNECTION
### Music

## Traditional Tunes

**Objective** Listen to traditional Native American songs.

**Materials** CD of Native American music

**Learning Style** Auditory/Verbal
**Group** 👤👤👤👤
⏱ **Time** 15–20 minutes

1. Play one of the Native American songs from the CD *Traditional Voices: Historic Recordings of Traditional Native American Music*. Tell children which Native American group created the song.

2. Play more songs from Native American groups and name the groups for children.

3. Ask children which song they liked best.

# Lesson ② Overview

## Early Travelers to America
pages 196–199

Children will gain knowledge about Christopher Columbus and the Pilgrims' life in America and learn the meaning of the word *freedom*.

 **Time** 20–30 minutes

**Resources**
- Workbook, p. 52
- Vocabulary Card freedom
- Every Student Learns Guide, pp. 86–89

## Use a History Map
pages 200–201

Children will learn how to use a map that shows historic routes.

 **Time** 15–20 minutes

**Resource**
- Workbook, p. 53

# Build Background

## Activity

### All Aboard!

 **Time** 20 minutes

Provide children with an outline of a ship on construction paper. Ask children to imagine that they are taking a long sea voyage to a new land. Ask them to draw what they would take with them.

**If time is short,** have children brainstorm things they would take with them. Ideas may include food, family, pets, games, or books.

## Activity

### America

**Samuel Francis Smith (1831)**

My country, 'tis of thee,
Sweet land of liberty,
Of thee I sing;
Land where my fathers died,
Land of the Pilgrims' pride,
From ev'ry mountain-side,
Let freedom ring!

# Lesson 2 Early Travelers to America

## Objectives
- Describe the origin of selected holidays.
- Cite reasons for observing holidays that originated prior to 1880.

## Vocabulary
**freedom** a person's right to make choices (p. 198)

### QUICK Teaching Plan

*If time is short,* discuss Columbus's voyage with children. Use the illustration to show the voyage. Explain the origin of Columbus Day.

- Explain that the Pilgrims came to this land in search of freedom. Tell how the Wampanoag helped the Pilgrims and how the Pilgrims and the Wampanoag celebrated their friendship.

## 1 Introduce and Motivate

**Preview** Display the Vocabulary Card **freedom**. Tell students that freedom means being allowed to choose things for yourself. Explain that many people come to the United States because they want more freedom. People have the freedom to elect public officials, express ideas in speech and in newspapers, meet together in groups, ask the government to correct a problem, and practice their religion. They can also choose the job they want to do and the place where they want to live. Ask children what it would be like to live in a country where people didn't have these freedoms.

**Warm Up** Ask children what they know about Christopher Columbus. Tell children that he traveled across the Atlantic Ocean by ship. Ask volunteers to tell about when they were on a boat or a ship.

Tell children that a holiday is a day for pleasure, enjoyment, and remembering. On holidays, most people don't have to work. Then ask children about Thanksgiving. Ask them what people do on this holiday. Then ask children if they know why we celebrate Thanksgiving.

**196** Unit 5 • This Is Our Country

---

# Lesson 2 Early Travelers to America

Christopher Columbus did not know about North America and the people who lived there. Long ago, Columbus sailed from Spain. Spain is a country in Europe. The king and queen of Spain told Columbus to go and find gold and other riches.

*These are the names of the ships that Columbus sailed on.*

North America

Santa Maria

196

## Practice and Extend

### READING SKILL
### Main Idea and Details

Tell children that pp. 196–197 are about Christopher Columbus's voyage to America. Ask children what information they learned about Christopher Columbus's voyage to America.

- Give children a copy of a web with a circle in the center and 3 spokes with circles on the end. Have them write *Columbus Sails to America* at the top of the page. Have them write *Columbus* in the center of the web.
- Have children complete the word web by writing one word of information about Christopher Columbus in each of three outer circles.

Columbus and his crew sailed for a long time. On October 12, 1492, they landed on an island near North America. The people who lived on this island were called the Taino. Columbus did not find gold. However, he did find people and a place that other people in Europe did not know about yet.

Every year, people remember the day Columbus landed on the island. The second Monday in October is Columbus Day.

Christopher Columbus

Nina

Pinta

Spain

197

## SOCIAL STUDIES
# Background

### About the Taino

- The Taino (TY noh) belonged to the Arawak group of American Indians.
- Although Columbus saw that some Taino were wearing gold ornaments, he did not find the source of the gold.

## WEB SITE
# Technology

You can look up vocabulary words online. Click on *Social Studies Library* and select the dictionary at **www.sfsocialstudies.com.**

# 2 Teach and Discuss

## Page 196

Tell children that Christopher Columbus lived a long time ago. Then read pp. 196–197 with children.

Identify James in the picture. Invite volunteers to tell the name of the ship that James is inside. (*Santa Maria*) Then have them name the other ships. Identify the body of water (the waves) as the Atlantic Ocean. Have children follow Columbus's voyage by pointing to Spain, the Atlantic Ocean, and North America. Tell children that Columbus returned to Europe to tell others about the New World. Have children trace his route back to Spain.

## Page 197

### GEOGRAPHY
## Movement

**1 Why did Christopher Columbus's voyage take a long time?** Answers may vary, but may include that Spain was across the Atlantic Ocean from North America and that long ago it took a long time to sail across the ocean. **Draw Conclusions**

**2 Did Christopher Columbus reach North America?** No. Christopher Columbus landed on a nearby island.
**Make Inferences**

**3 Even when October 12 is not on a Monday, why do you think Columbus Day is always celebrated on a Monday?** Celebrating on Monday enables people to extend their weekend. **Draw Conclusions**

**Lesson 2** continued

## Page 198

Ask children to point to the picture of the ship. Tell them that the name on the ship reads *Mayflower*.

**GEOGRAPHY**
**Movement**

**4 How did the Pilgrims get from England to North America?** They sailed on a ship called the *Mayflower*. **Recall and Retell**

**5 Why did the Pilgrims go to North America?** They wanted the freedom to practice their religion. **Apply Information**

### Ongoing Assessment

**If...** children believe that the Pilgrims were the first Europeans to arrive on the mainland United States in 1620,

**then...** explain that in 1513 the Spanish landed on the Florida coast near present-day St. Augustine, Florida.

The Mayflower

Later, a group of people we call Pilgrims left England to come to **4** North America. They sailed on a ship called the *Mayflower*.

The Pilgrims wanted their freedom. **Freedom** is a person's right to make choices. The Pilgrims wanted the freedom to practice **5** their own religion.

*The Pilgrims traveled far!*

North America

Mayflower

Engla

198

# Practice and Extend

## FAST FACTS

Columbus thought he had reached land close to India, called the East Indies. He called the people from the island *Indians*. This name was then used for all native people in North and South America.

- Nobody knows for certain where Columbus first landed. Most experts believe it was in the present-day Bahamas. He also landed on present-day Cuba and Hispaniola (Haiti and the Dominican Republic).
- Columbus was not the first European to reach North America. Led by Leif Ericson, the Vikings, from an area of Europe called Scandinavia, set sail from Greenland and landed in North America in 1001—about 500 years before Columbus.

## ESL — EXTEND LANGUAGE
## ESL Support

**Telling About Cultural Traditions** Have children tell about a holiday from their native culture during which they give thanks. If there is no comparable holiday to Thanksgiving, have children tell about another special day.

**Beginning** Have children use pictures, gestures, or a few words to tell about the holiday.

**Intermediate** Invite children to use words or sentences to tell about the holiday.

**Advanced** Encourage children to tell in sentences how and why people celebrate the holiday.

*For additional ESL Support, use Every Student Learns Guide, pp. 86–89.*

The Pilgrims built a village that they called Plymouth. Wampanoag Indians saved the Pilgrims by showing them how to grow corn and other plants. They also showed the Pilgrims how to fish.

The Pilgrims and the Wampanoag celebrated. They were thankful. Today, people have a special day to give thanks. We call the day Thanksgiving.

## What did you learn

1. Why do we have Columbus Day and Thanksgiving?

2. Why is **freedom** important?

3. **Think and Share** Draw a picture of how Thanksgiving was celebrated long ago and how you celebrate it today. Tell how the pictures are alike and different.

**199**

### Test Talk

**Locate Key Words in the Text**

**6** **What did the Wampanoag show the Pilgrims how to grow?** Corn and other plants Have children locate key words in the text that match key words in the question.
**Apply Information**

**7** **For what were the Pilgrims thankful?** Answers will vary but may include freedom, food, and friendly neighbors. **Draw Conclusions**

## 3 Close and Assess

Have children discuss with a partner what they know about Christopher Columbus and the Pilgrims.

### ✓ What did you learn

1. Answers will vary. These holidays remind us of the early settlers. They remind us of our freedom and why we should be thankful.

2. Answers will vary but may include: freedom is a person's right to make choices.

3. **Think and Share** To help children with their drawings, show children pictures of Pilgrims giving thanks and families in the present celebrating Thanksgiving. Suggest to children that they need only include two or three items (e.g., an ear of corn, a turkey, a Pilgrim's hat) in each drawing.

### SOCIAL STUDIES Background

**About the Pilgrims**

- The Pilgrims' voyage to the United States in 1620 lasted 65 days. They were headed for Virginia but a storm drove them north to Massachusetts. Because they arrived in the winter, life was hard. Many of them died.

- In the spring, two Wampanoag (WAH puh NOH ag) Indians, Samoset and Squanto, taught the Pilgrims to plant corn and other crops. As a result, the first harvest was bountiful.

**Workbook, p. 52**

Early Travelers to America

Draw to finish each picture. **Drawings will vary.**

Color the pictures.

Columbus Day

Thanksgiving Day

**Also on Teacher Resources CD-ROM.**

# Use a History Map

## Objectives

- Obtain information about a topic using a variety of visual sources such as maps.

- Use cardinal directions on a map.

## 1 Introduce and Motivate

**Preview** Ask children about the maps of the world they have seen. You may want to remind children of maps you have looked at as a class. Explain that they are going to look at a special kind of map called a history map. A history map shows places or things that happened in the past.

**Warm Up** To activate prior knowledge, ask children to remember the voyages of Christopher Columbus and the Pilgrims. Ask children to tell where Christopher Columbus's voyage started. (Spain) Ask children to tell the country from which the Pilgrims sailed. (England) Explain that the history map they will look at will show these places and the routes, or paths, that the ships took.

## 2 Teach and Discuss

Have children point to the part of the map that represents North America. Then have them point to England and Spain. Ask children to name the part of the map that is not land. (water) Ask them to tell how they know what parts of the map represent land. (They are labeled. They are a different color.) Have students trace with their finger the routes of the *Mayflower* and Columbus's ships.

**1 Did the Pilgrims land north or south of Columbus?** North **Interpret Maps**

# Use a History Map

A history map shows places or routes from the past. Look at this map.

**1** **2**

North

West  NORTH AMERICA

The Mayflower 1620

ATLANTIC OCEAN

Columbus and his ships 1492

South

200

# Practice and Extend

**CURRICULUM CONNECTION**
**Math**

**Compare Land Areas**

Have children compare the land size of countries and continents.

- Ask if Spain is larger than or smaller than Europe.
- Ask if North America is larger than or smaller than England.

Use your finger to follow the route
Columbus took. Then follow the route
the *Mayflower* took.

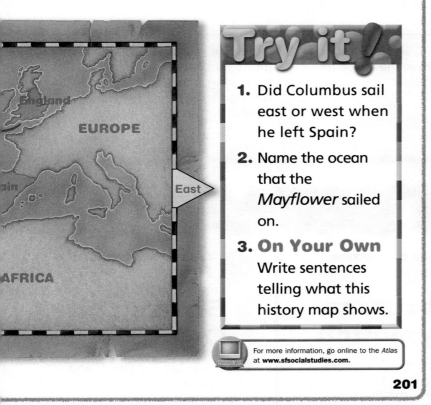

## Try it!

1. Did Columbus sail
   east or west when
   he left Spain?

2. Name the ocean
   that the
   *Mayflower* sailed
   on.

3. **On Your Own**
   Write sentences
   telling what this
   history map shows.

For more information, go online to the *Atlas*
at **www.sfsocialstudies.com.**

**201**

---

② **Did the Pilgrims sail from east to west or
from west to east?** East to west **Interpret Maps**

## 3 Close and Assess

Have children look at a globe to get a different
representation of the locations shown on the map.
Name the locations identified on the map and
have children find them on the globe. Then have
children trace from the area where Columbus
landed back to Spain.

### Try it!

1. Columbus sailed west after he left Spain.

2. The Mayflower sailed on the Atlantic Ocean.

3. **On Your Own** Sentences should tell
   about the people, places, and direction of the
   two voyages.

---

## WEB SITE Technology

You may help children find out
more by clicking on *Atlas* at
**www.sfsocialstudies.com.**

---

## Workbook, p. 53

**Use a History Map**

Draw the routes.

Color the land green and the water blue.

**Also on Teacher
Resources CD-ROM.**

# Lesson ② Wrap-Up

## MEETING INDIVIDUAL NEEDS
## Leveled Practice

### Understand Steps in Instructions

Read *Cranberry Thanksgiving* by Wende and Harry Devlin to children. Help children understand that baking cranberry bread is a process with steps. Explain that a recipe is a list of both ingredients and instructions.

**Easy** Read the recipe for cranberry bread in the book. Have children call out the step numbers in the recipe as you read. **Reteach**

**On-Level** Have children read out loud the set of directions in the recipe for cranberry bread. **Extend**

**Challenge** Have children describe how they could help an adult with the steps for baking cranberry bread (e.g., by stirring the batter or washing cranberries). **Enrich**

## Hands-on Activities

### CURRICULUM CONNECTION
### Writing/Vocabulary

## Making Words from Freedom

**Objective** Write words using the letters in *freedom*.

**Materials** paper, pencils

**Learning Style** Verbal-Linguistic

**Individual**

🕐 **Time** 10–15 minutes

1. Write the word *freedom* on the board. Remind children that the word *freedom* means a person's right to make choices.

| |
|---|
| freedom |
| do |
| free |
| me |
| red |

2. Challenge children to write words that they can make with the letters in the word *freedom*. (*deer, do, fed, feed, free, freed, me, more, of, or, ore, red, rod,* etc.)

3. Remind children to add the vocabulary word *freedom* to their "My Word Book."

### CURRICULUM CONNECTION
### Drama

## Celebration at Plymouth

**Objective** Dramatize the celebration between the Wampanoag and the Pilgrims.

**Materials** props, such as toy food

**Learning Style** Bodily/Kinesthetic Auditory/Verbal

**Group**

🕐 **Time** 20–30 minutes

1. Tell children that the Pilgrims and Wampanoag celebrated their friendship by playing games, running races, marching, and playing drums.

2. Have children dramatize a scene from the celebration, using actual or pretend items.

### CURRICULUM CONNECTION
### Art

## Sailing the Ocean Blue

**Objective** Learn a poem and illustrate it.

**Materials** Construction paper and crayons

**Learning Style** Musical/Visual

**Group**

🕐 **Time** 15–20 minutes

1. Write the following rhyme on the board. *In fourteen hundred ninety-two, Columbus sailed the ocean blue.*

2. Have children copy the words at the top of a piece of construction paper.

3. Say the rhyme aloud. Have children repeat it with you until they have it memorized.

4. Have children draw a picture on their paper to accompany the words. Display the pictures in the classroom.

# Lesson ③ Overview

**The Colonies Become Free**
pages 202–205

Children will gain knowledge about the colonies and how they became an independent nation and learn the meaning of the word *colony*.

🕐 Time 20–30 minutes
**Resources**
• Workbook, p. 54
• Vocabulary Card  colony
• Every Student Learns Guide, pp. 90–93

**Benjamin Franklin**
pages 206–207

Children will learn about Benjamin Franklin as a writer, inventor, and leader of America.

🕐 Time 15–20 minutes
**Resource**
• Workbook, p. 54

# Build Background

## Activity

### Red, White, and Boom

🕐 **Time** 20 minutes

Invite children to tell about the activities they do or see on Independence Day. Model the discussion by telling what events you attend, such as a picnic, parade, ball game, or fireworks display. Give each child a chance to speak. Then have children draw a picture of one of the activities.

**If time is short,** just have children discuss Independence Day activities.

## Read Aloud

### Time for Freedom

by Jason O'Donnell

More people followed the Pilgrims
To this land across the sea.

They came to live a better life
And for the chance to be free.

As time went on they knew
That freedom must be won.

They became a separate nation
After the long, brave fight was done.

## Lesson 3 The Colonies Become Free

### Objectives

- Describe the origins of selected holidays and celebrations such as Independence Day.

- Describe the events associated with Independence Day.

- Explain how selected celebrations reflect an American love of freedom.

- Identify historic figures such as Nathan Hale who have exemplified good citizenship.

- Identify contributions of historic figures such as George Washington.

### Vocabulary

**colony** a place that is ruled by a country far away (p. 202)

**QUICK Teaching Plan**

*If time is short,* discuss the origin of Independence Day when the colonies declared that they were independent of England.

## 1 Introduce and Motivate

**Preview** Display the Vocabulary Card **colony**. Tell children that many people came to America after the Pilgrims. They lived in areas called colonies that were ruled by England. Show children a map of the United States and point out the 13 states that were the 13 colonies (VA, NY, MA, CT, RI, NH, MD, NJ, NC, SC, PA, DE, and GA). Ask children how they think settlements in the colonies grew. (The colonists built homes, businesses, and farms. More colonists came. They had families. Some of the settlements expanded into towns and cities.)

**Warm Up** To activate prior knowledge, ask children what they know about George Washington. Children may know that he was the first President of the United States and that his face appears on the dollar bill and the state quarters. Explain that George Washington was a general in the army who helped lead the colonists in their fight for freedom from England's rule.

---

## Lesson 3 The Colonies Become Free

We learned that more people came to North America after the Pilgrims. They lived in places called colonies. A **colony** is a place that is ruled by a country that is far away. After a while, there were 13 colonies. These colonies were ruled by England and its king.

*Williamsburg was in the colony of Virginia.*

202

## Practice and Extend

### READING SKILL
### Categorize

**Sorting Power to Rule**

- After children have read pp. 202–203, give them a graphic organizer with three stacked boxes connected by lines.

- Ask children to arrange the following words in order of who or what has the most power to rule: *England, colonists, colonies.* Explain that power to rule is the right to do something or to tell other people what to do.

### WEB SITE
### Technology

You can look up vocabulary words online. Click on *Social Studies Library* and select the dictionary at **www.sfsocialstudies.com**.

Many colonists did not want to be ruled by England. They did not want to follow England's laws. They wanted to be free. On July 4, 1776, a group of leaders in the colonies agreed on an important paper called the Declaration of Independence. In the Declaration, they wrote that everyone had the right to be free. Today, we celebrate Independence Day on July 4.

203

# 2 Teach and Discuss

**Page 202**

Ask children what James is holding.

**C SOCIAL STUDIES STRAND**
## Culture

Tell children that in colonial times people used a quill for writing. A quill is a pen made from a large, stiff wing feather or tail feather of a bird.

**1 England was separated from its North American colonies by the Atlantic Ocean. Do you think England was close to America or far away?** Far away **Evaluate**

**2 How many original colonies were ruled by England?** Thirteen **Apply information**

**Page 203**

**Test Talk**

**Write Your Answer**
**3 What did many colonists want?** They wanted to be free. Ask children to reread their answer to make sure it is correct. **Apply Information**

**4 How did many leaders in the colonies clearly let everybody know that they wanted to be free?** They signed the Declaration of Independence. **Make Inferences**

**Lesson 3**
continued

**Page 204**

⑤ **How did George Washington help our country?** Answers will vary but may include that he led colonial soldiers in many battles against English soldiers. **Apply Information**

Explain to children that *to regret* is *to be sorry*.

⑥ **Why did Nathan Hale say he regretted that he could die only one time for his country?** Possible answer: This was his way of expressing how proud he was to die for his country. **Make Inferences**

**SOCIAL STUDIES STRAND**
**Citizenship**

Point out to children that Nathan Hale is a model of good citizenship. Explain that a good citizen thinks not only of his or her rights but the rights of others. Tell children that Nathan Hale so much believed in his cause—the right of all Americans to be free—that he volunteered to spy on English soldiers in New York. Unfortunately, he was caught by them and hanged. He was only 21 years old. His bravery, however, inspired the colonists in their war against England.

The colonies fought a war with England to be free. The war lasted many years. George Washington was a famous leader ⑤ in this war. He led many battles against English soldiers.

*Washington leading his sol...*

Nathan Hale was a teacher. He became a soldier in George Washington's army. He volunteered to spy on English soldiers. The English soldiers caught him. He said, "I only regret that I have but one life to lose for my country." He died in 1776.

*Nathan Hale*
*1755-1776*

204

# Practice and Extend

**EXTEND LANGUAGE**
**ESL Support**

**Understanding Bravery** To help children learn the meaning of the word *brave*, tell them that a brave person does the right thing even when it is hard or dangerous. Explain that Nathan Hale volunteered to go behind enemy lines to report on the movement of English soldiers. Have children draw a picture of many English soldiers represented by red stick figures with rifles, and Nathan Hale represented by a blue stick figure.

**Beginning** Ask children who is the brave colonist. Have them point to him.

**Intermediate** Have children write a title: "Nathan Hale Was Brave."

**Advanced** Have children write a title: "Nathan Hale Was Brave." Then ask them to tell why Nathan Hale was brave.

*For additional ESL Support, use Every Student Learns Guide, pp. 90–93.*

**SOCIAL STUDIES**
**Background**

**Loyalists**

- About 20 percent of the white population of the colonies opposed the War of Independence. These people were called "Loyalists." About 19,000 of them, armed by the English, even fought against fellow colonists in the war.

General George Washington and his soldiers helped the colonies win the war against England. After the war, the colonies became a country. The country was called the United States of America.

George Washington was a hero.

## What did you learn?

1. Why did many colonists want to be free?

2. Why do we celebrate Independence Day on July 4?

3. **Think and Share** Share with a classmate how each of you celebrates Independence Day. How are your celebrations alike? How are they different?

205

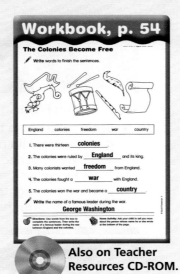

## FAST FACTS

- George Washington was President of the United States from 1789–1797.

- He is called the "Father of Our Country."

- His wife was named Martha. They had no children.

- He was an engineer before he became a soldier and a farmer after he was President.

### Workbook, p. 54

**The Colonies Become Free**

Write words to finish the sentences.

| England | colonies | freedom | war | country |

1. There were thirteen ___colonies___

2. The colonies were ruled by ___England___ and its king.

3. Many colonists wanted ___freedom___ from England.

4. The colonies fought a ___war___ with England.

5. The colonies won the war and became a ___country___

Write the name of a famous leader during the war.
___George Washington___

**Also on Teacher Resources CD-ROM.**

Tell children that the war against England was fought from 1775 to 1783. Tell them that it was almost eight years.

**7** **The war lasted longer than you have been alive. Do you think the American Revolution was a long war?** Answers will vary, but should reflect the concept of time. **Evaluate**

Explain that the war was very hard on the soldiers. They had to fight in harsh weather, such as snow and ice.

**8** **Why do you think the colonists were able to keep fighting for almost eight years?** They strongly believed that they should be separate from England. **Make Inferences**

**9** **What is the difference between a colony and a country?** Answers will vary but may include that a colony is a place far away from the country which controls it, and a country is a place in which people have their own government. **Compare and Contrast**

## 3 Close and Assess

Have children tell why the war against England was fought. Invite them to tell what they know about the Declaration of Independence. Then have pairs discuss one of the heroes they learned about.

## ✓ What did you learn?

1. They wanted to make rules for themselves.

2. Because that is the day leaders in the colonies agreed on the Declaration of Independence

3. **Think and Share** Children should give examples of activities they have participated in. Similarities and differences may include discussions of the people, food, and events.

# Benjamin Franklin

## Objectives

- Identify contributions of historical figures who have influenced the nation.
- Identify historic figures who exemplified good citizenship.
- Identify historical figures who have exhibited a love of inventiveness.

## 1 Introduce and Motivate

**Preview** Remind children that not all heroes are soldiers. Some, like Benjamin Franklin, are statespersons. A statesperson is somebody who is smart about the ways countries work. Tell children that Franklin needed glasses to read and to see in the distance. So he invented bifocals, special glasses for seeing both near and far.

**Warm Up** To activate prior knowledge, ask children to name some people they know who have helped their country. Have volunteers tell how the people named helped their country.

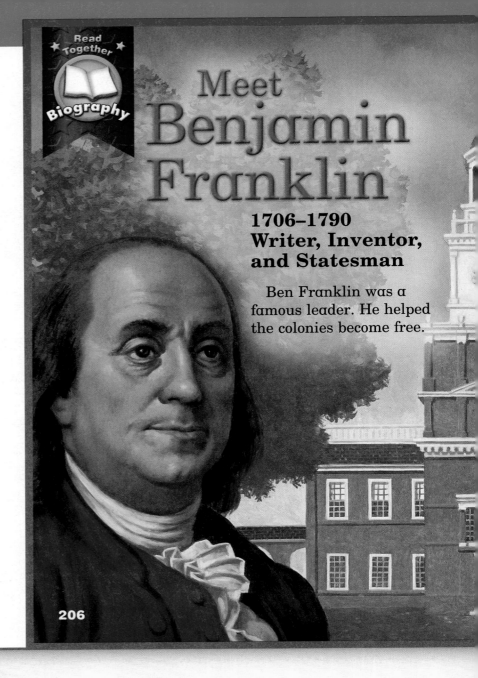

Read Together Biography

## Meet Benjamin Franklin

### 1706–1790
### Writer, Inventor, and Statesman

Ben Franklin was a famous leader. He helped the colonies become free.

206

# Practice and Extend

**FYI** SOCIAL STUDIES
**Background**

### Benjamin Franklin

- Born in Boston, Benjamin Franklin moved to Philadelphia, where he started a newspaper called the *Pennsylvania Gazette*. He wrote most of the articles for it. It was very successful and influential. He also printed books and pamphlets.
- When at 42 he became wealthy enough to retire from printing, his life was just beginning. He worked on his inventions; worked for public improvements, such as libraries and hospitals; and devoted himself to the concerns of our country.
- He was one of America's founding fathers.

## FAST FACTS

- Benjamin Franklin was the 15th of 17 children.
- Seeking to prove that lightning was an electrical current, Franklin performed a famous experiment in 1752. He attached a metal key to a kite, which he flew during a storm. Lightning passed through the key, proving that lightning was electricity. Caution children not to perform this experiment at home.

### WEB SITE
### Technology

You may help children find out more about Benjamin Franklin by clicking on *Meet the People* at **www.sfsocialstudies.com**.

Young Ben only went to school for about two years. However, he still wanted to learn. He learned math **1** by himself. He loved to read. When he became older, he bought his own newspaper. It became very popular.

Benjamin Franklin also wrote books. He wrote a book called *Poor Richard's Almanack.* It became **2** very famous.

Benjamin Franklin was an inventor too. He invented the rocking chair and a special type of eyeglasses. **3**

Benjamin Franklin wanted to help his country. He signed the Declaration of Independence. Later, he went to talk to the king of France. He asked the king to help the colonies become free. The king said he would. With France's help, America won its war against England.

Benjamin Franklin was born in Boston, Massachusetts.

### Think and Share

Why is Benjamin Franklin an important person in our country's history?

For more information, go online to *Meet the People* at www.sfsocialstudies.com.

207

---

**Cool Shades**

- Explain to children that people, animals, and plants need sunlight. Then explain that too much sun, however, can be harmful.

- Tell children that people around the world protect themselves from the sun in a variety of ways, from wearing wide-brim hats to carrying umbrellas. Tell children that sunglasses were invented to protect the eyes from the glare of the sun.

- Ask children to draw pictures of themselves wearing sunglasses with a bright sun overhead.

- Encourage children to fancifully decorate the sunglasses.

---

# 2 Teach and Discuss

**1 How do you think young Ben learned math all by himself?** Answers will vary but might include he read books that explained it. **Draw Conclusions**

Have children point to Boston on the map. Tell them that Boston was one of the first big cities in the United States. Then tell children that Benjamin Franklin moved to Philadelphia to start a printing business. Explain that an almanac is a book published each year that contains facts on many subjects.

Tell children that *Poor Richard's Almanack* included a collection of short sentences on the value of working hard, saving money, and leading a simple life. Many of the things Franklin wrote in the Almanac became famous. You may know his famous saying "Early to bed and early to rise, makes a man healthy, wealthy, and wise."

**2 Do you think *Poor Richard's Almanack* included advice about using time wisely or stories about talking animals?** Advice about using time wisely **Draw Conclusions**

**3 Why might Franklin have decided to make a special type of glasses and a rocking chair?** Answers might include: He could not see with the glasses he had; he wanted a chair that moved. **Generalize**

# 3 Close and Assess

Ask children to brainstorm aloud what they know about Ben Franklin. Then have them write a few sentences about him.

### Think and Share

He helped the colonists win freedom. He asked France for help in the war. He helped write the Declaration of Independence. He invented things we still use today.

# Lesson ③ Wrap-Up

 **MEETING INDIVIDUAL NEEDS**
## Leveled Practice

### The Stamp Act
Tell children that the English enacted a law—the Stamp Act—to raise money for England. This act forced the colonists to buy stamps to put on the newspapers they bought.

**Easy** Have children playing the English make stamps with 10 cents written on the front. **Reteach**

**On-Level** Have children playing the colonists buy a stamp with play coins. Have them glue the stamp on a newspaper. Ask them to count what it would cost to buy stamps for 5 days. **Extend**

**Challenge** Have children stand on a wooden box and make a speech against putting stamps on newspapers because the money goes to the English. Suggest that their argument include how much money the English make in one day from the stamps. **Enrich**

 ## Hands-on Activities

 **CURRICULUM CONNECTION**
### Writing/Vocabulary

## Far Away Places

**Objective** Demonstrate understanding of the lesson vocabulary.

**Resources** Vocabulary Card: **colony**

**Materials** crayons

**Learning Style** Visual

**Individual** 👤

🕐 **Time** 10–15 minutes

England – Colonies
Atlantic Ocean

1. Point out on a map the Atlantic Ocean, with the United States to the west and Europe to the east. Then point out the 13 American colonies and England.

2. Ask children to draw and label the ocean, the colonies, and England.

3. Remind children to add the vocabulary word *colony* to their "My Word Book."

 **CURRICULUM CONNECTION**
### Drama

## Signing the Declaration of Independence

**Objective** Dramatize the colonists signing the Declaration of Independence.

**Materials** props, including a piece of paper and a feather

**Learning Style** Verbal/Linguistic Bodily/Kinesthetic

**Group** 👤👤👤👤

🕐 **Time** 15–30 minutes

1. Have students act out the colonial leaders discussing why they want to be free.

2. Have children conduct a "signing" of the Declaration of Independence using a feather to sign their names to the bottom of the document.

**CURRICULUM CONNECTION**
### Reading

## One If by Land, Two If by Sea

**Objective** Read a book about the American Revolution.

**Materials** picture book

**Learning Style** Auditory/Verbal

**Group** 👤👤👤👤

🕐 **Time** 20–30 minutes

1. Read *The Midnight Ride of Paul Revere* by Longfellow, illustrated by Jeffrey Thompson, to the class. Tell children that this is the famous poem about Paul Revere, who rode a horse from Boston to Lexington, Massachusetts, warning people that the British were coming.

2. Use the illustrations to discuss the poem with students.

3. Ask students to tell about how Paul Revere exhibited good citizenship.

# Lesson ④ Overview

| | | |
|---|---|---|
| **Symbols in Our Country**<br>**pages 208–209** | Children will learn symbols in the United States and explore their meanings.  | ⏱ Time 10–15 minutes<br>**Resources**<br>• Workbook, p. 55<br>• Every Student Learns Guide, pp. 94–97 |
| **Our Country's Flag**<br>**pages 210–211** | Children will learn about the history and meaning of the United States flag. | ⏱ Time 10–15 minutes |

# Build Background

## Activity

## My Flag

 **Time** 20 minutes

Point out the American flag in the classroom. Tell children that it stands for the United States. Give children construction paper showing the outline of a wavy flag flowing from the top of a pole. Have children decorate the flag to represent themselves. Ask children to include what is important to them. Have children tell about their flag when they have finished.

**If time is short,** discuss with children what they would include in flags that stand for themselves.

## Read Aloud

## Monumental Riddle
### by Shawna Morrison

I remind people of a person

who could not tell a lie.

I'm a monument

that stretches way into the sky.

Well, to tell you the truth,

I'm only 555 feet, 5 and $\frac{1}{8}$ inches tall.

But I think that's still pretty high

all and all.

What am I?

[Washington Monument]

# Lesson 4 Symbols in Our Country

## Objectives

- Identify the motto of the United States.
- Explain selected national and state patriotic symbols such as the Liberty Bell and the eagle.
- Identify symbols that represent the United States and what it stands for.
- Obtain information about a topic using a variety of visual sources such as pictures and graphics.

### QUICK Teaching Plan

*If time is short,* point out each of the symbols and discuss the meaning and history of each.

## 1 Introduce and Motivate

**Preview** Have children look at the symbols in the lesson. Ask children whether they can identify any of them.

**Warm Up** To activate prior knowledge, ask children to name symbols and tell what they stand for, such as a heart (love). Tell children that our country and states also have symbols.

## 2 Teach and Discuss

### Page 208

As you discuss the symbols, be sure to point out that they are patriotic symbols: they honor those who helped build our country, and they foster appreciation for and loyalty to our nation and states. Symbols of our nation remind us to be patriotic. Explain that *patriotic* means "showing respect for and love of country."

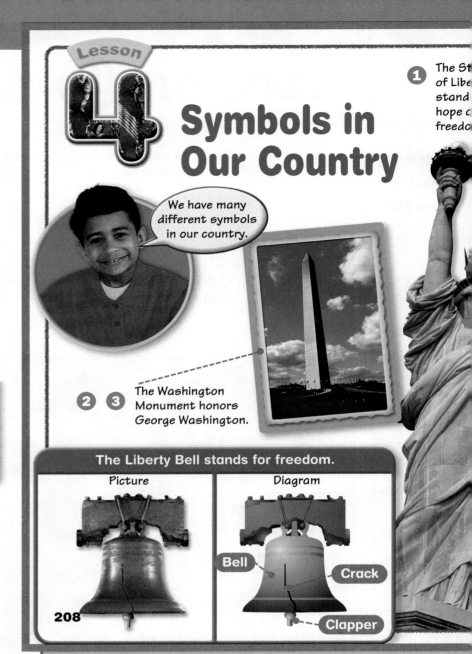

# Lesson 4 Symbols in Our Country

We have many different symbols in our country.

The Washington Monument honors George Washington.

The Liberty Bell stands for freedom.

Picture

Diagram

Bell

Crack

Clapper

208

The St of Libe stand hope c freedo

# Practice and Extend

### READING/VOCABULARY
### Recall and Retell

- After children have read pages 208–211, give children a copy of a web with a center circle and four outer circles.
- Have children write *Our Country's Symbols* in the center circle.
- Have them write the names of the country's symbols in the outer circles. (Statue of Liberty, bald eagle, Liberty Bell, Washington Monument)
- Ask children to tell what they know about each symbol.

The Capitol Building is in Washington, D.C. It is where the leaders of our country meet. **4**

Our country's motto is "In God We Trust." A motto is a saying that people try to live by. Our country's motto stands for freedom and trust.

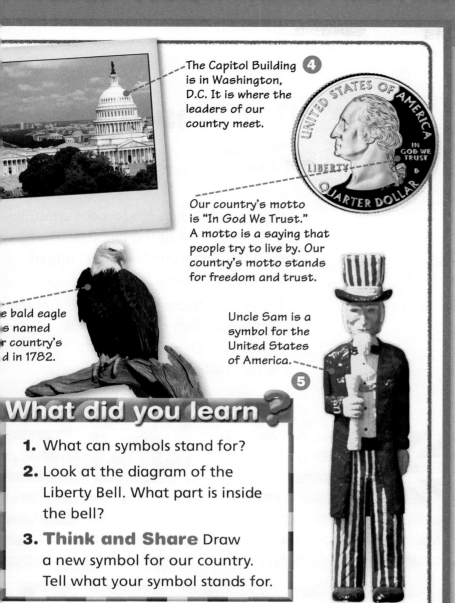

e bald eagle s named r country's d in 1782.

Uncle Sam is a symbol for the United States of America. **5**

## What did you learn ?

1. What can symbols stand for?

2. Look at the diagram of the Liberty Bell. What part is inside the bell?

3. **Think and Share** Draw a new symbol for our country. Tell what your symbol stands for.

**209**

**Workbook, p. 55**

Symbols in Our Country

Also on Teacher Resources CD-ROM.

**1** **Why do you think the Statue of Liberty stands for hope and freedom?** Possible answer: People coming to the United States want freedom and feel hopeful. **Draw Conclusions**

**2** **Why was a monument built for George Washington?** Answers will vary but may include: to honor him and to remind people of his great deeds. **Interpret**

**3** **Who would you like to see a monument built for?** Answers will vary but may include leaders, citizen heroes, family members, or friends. **Express Ideas**

**4** **Why do you think the Capitol building is important to our country?** Answers will vary but may include that it is a place where our government makes laws. **Draw Conclusions.**

**5** **Who is Uncle Sam?** Uncle Sam is a symbol for the United States of America. **Recall and Retell**

SOCIAL STUDIES STRAND
**Citizenship**

Ask children to identify the country's motto by pointing to it on the picture of the coin.

Tell children that our country also has special documents as symbols, such as the U.S. Constitution. It is the basis for the laws in our country.

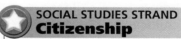

## 3 Close and Assess

Ask children to name some of the symbols of our country. Have them discuss with a partner what they know about these symbols.

## ✓ What did you learn ?

1. Answers will vary but may include states, countries, and ideas, such as hope and freedom.

2. The clapper

3. **Think and Share** Answers will vary but children's symbols should stand for an ideal for the whole country, such as freedom or peace.

**Living History**

# Our Country's Flag

## Objectives

- Explain selected national patriotic symbols such as the United States flag.

- Distinguish between past and present.

- Explain how selected symbols reflect an American love of freedom.

# 1 Introduce and Motivate

**Preview** Point to the American flag in the classroom. Explain to children that a flag is not only a piece of cloth with a pattern on it but also a symbol. This flag is a symbol of our country.

**Warm Up** Recite and explain the Pledge of Allegiance. On a second reading, have children echo each line. Encourage children to be attentive and show their respect and thanks to the United States by standing, removing their hat, facing and looking at the flag, placing their right hand over their heart, and avoiding fidgeting.

Ask children if they have ever been to a sporting event where fans sang the national anthem. Sing the first line. Explain that the same patriotic behavior is expected for singing the anthem.

# 2 Teach and Discuss

Have children point to each flag along the time line. Tell children that these were American flags at different times. Have them note the different numbers of stars and stripes and arrangements of stars. Tell children what the stars and stripes stand for. Explain that the flag changed as new states were added to the country.

Have children point to the large flag. Tell them that this is what the flag looks like today. Have children discuss the differences between the present American flag and those of the past.

**Living History**

# Our Country's Flag

Our country's flag is a famous symbol of freedom. Look at the pictures. They show some ways our flag has changed from the past to the present.

Today, the stripes stand for the number of states our country had when it became free. The 50 stars stand for each of our 50 states.

**①**

210                                1776                                        1795

# Practice and Extend

**ESL** **EXTEND LANGUAGE**
# ESL Support

**Interviewing and Retelling** Have children interview family members to find out about a symbol of their native country, such as a flag. Ask children to make a drawing of the symbol and explain what it stands for.

**Beginning** Have children tell about the symbol. Ask questions to prompt for information, such as *What does the flag look like? Where is the statue located?*

**Intermediate** Have children tell what the symbol looks like, and if it is not a flag, where it is located. If necessary, ask questions to clarify, such as *What does the bird on the flag stand for?*

**Advanced** Without prompting, have children tell what the symbol is and what it stands for.

*For additional ESL Support, use Every Student Learns Guide, pp. 94–97.*

Memorial Day and Veterans Day are two holidays. On these days, Americans honor the people who fought in our country's wars.

Memorial Day celebration

2

Veterans Day celebration

213

**SOCIAL STUDIES Background**

**About Memorial Day and Veterans Day**

- Memorial Day was first observed for soldiers killed in the Civil War.
- Most states observe Memorial Day on the last Monday in May.
- Memorial Day is marked by the laying of a wreath on the Tomb of the Unknown Soldier in Arlington National Cemetery (Virginia).
- Veterans Day was originally called Armistice Day and was set aside to celebrate the end of World War I. After the Korean War, it was designated as Veterans Day to honor soldiers of all U.S. wars.

# 2 Teach and Discuss

## Page 212

Point out the picture of the Independence Day celebration. Ask children what is shown in the sky. (fireworks)

**1 Why is a holiday a special day?** Answers will vary but may include that a holiday celebrates a person who influenced our country or an important event in our country's past. **Make Inferences**

## Page 213

Explain to children that a veteran is someone who was a soldier. Explain that on Veterans Day in the United States, we honor those soldiers—both living and dead—who served in times of war. Explain that on Memorial Day we honor veterans who lost their lives fighting for our country.

✓ **Ongoing Assessment**

| **If...** children do not understand what a holiday is, | **then...** write examples of national holidays on the board and discuss what each one celebrates. |

**2 What are some holidays that are not shown?** Answers will vary but may include Columbus Day, Kwanzaa, New Year's Day, and Thanksgiving. **Apply Information**

**C SOCIAL STUDIES STRAND Culture**

Explain to children that people in other countries also celebrate holidays. Work with children to locate Canada and Mexico on a map. Tell children that some holidays that people celebrate in Canada are *Family Day* (early February), *Canada Day* (July 1), *Remembrance Day* (November 11), and *Boxing Day* (December 26). Some holidays that people celebrate in Mexico are *Día de la Constitución* (February 5), *Carnival* (March 5), *Cinco de Mayo* (May 5), and *Las Posadas* (December 16).

**Page 214**

SOCIAL STUDIES STRAND
# History

Explain to children that once, in some states, African Americans had to sit at the back of the bus, were not allowed into restaurants for non-African Americans, and went to schools that were only for African Americans. In the 1950s and 1960s, Martin Luther King, Jr. led marches—sometimes at the risk to his life—to improve the lives of African Americans. His beautiful speeches inspired people from all backgrounds to work for change. He expressed a belief in equality for all people for the common good.

## Test Talk

### Locate Key Words in the Question

**3** **What did Martin Luther King, Jr. believe?** He believed that all people should be treated equally. Have children find the key words in the question. Children should finish the statement "I need to find out what Dr. King believed." **Apply Information**

Have children look at picture of Dr. King giving a speech. Discuss the custom of reading or listening to parts of his speeches on Martin Luther King, Jr. Day.

**4** **Why might people listen to a speech by Dr. King?** Possible answer: To help them become a better citizen. **Make Inferences**

SOCIAL STUDIES STRAND
# Citizenship

Discuss with children other Americans who have worked for the fair treatment of all people, such as Cesar Chavez. Chavez helped farm workers get fair pay and working conditions. His life and work are celebrated on March 31.

Martin Luther King, Jr. Day is in January. On this holiday, we honor Martin Luther King, Jr.

Dr. King believed that all people **3** should have the right to be treated fairly. He worked hard so that African Americans would be treated with **4** respect. He wanted all Americans to be treated the same. His birthday was on January 15.

214

# Practice and Extend

EXTEND LANGUAGE
## ESL Support

**Telling About Holidays** To help children practice and extend their vocabulary, have them tell about a holiday in their native culture, such as Chinese New Year. Ask children if they know of a holiday similar to Memorial Day or Presidents' Day. Children may need to get information from family members.

**Beginning** Have children name the holiday in their native language and give a translation, if they can.

**Intermediate** Have children name the holiday and tell how it is celebrated.

**Advanced** Have children tell everything they know about a holiday. They can describe the way it is celebrated and its origin.

*For additional ESL Support, use Every Student Learns Guide, pp. 98–101.*

We celebrate Presidents' Day in February. The **President** is our country's leader. We honor George Washington and Abraham Lincoln on this holiday. Both of these Presidents were born in February.

George Washington was our country's first President. We call him the "Father of our Country."

George Washington

Abraham Lincoln

## What did you learn

1. Why are Memorial Day and Veterans Day important **holidays** ?

2. Why do we celebrate Martin Luther King, Jr. Day?

3. **Write and Share** Tell why we celebrate holidays.

215

**About Martin Luther King, Jr.**

- Martin Luther King, Jr. was born in Atlanta, Georgia, on January 15, 1929.
- King worked with others to organize a bus boycott (1955–56) in Montgomery, Alabama, to protest racial segregation in public transportation.
- He was shot and killed on April 4, 1968.
- Since 1986, the third Monday in January has been designated a legal holiday for Martin Luther King, Jr.'s birthday.

**Workbook, p. 56**

**We Celebrate Holidays**

Choose a holiday.
Make a banner for it. **Banners will vary.**

| Veterans Day | Memorial Day | Martin Luther King, Jr. Day | Presidents' Day |

**Also on Teacher Resources CD-ROM.**

**5** **What do we call our country's leader?**
The President **Apply information**

Ask children to recall what they learned about George Washington. (He was born in Virginia. He was a leader in the war against the English to make the colonies free. He was our first President. We call him the "Father of our Country.")

**6** **Why do you think we honor George Washington and Abraham Lincoln?** Answers will vary but may include that they were great Presidents. **Express Ideas**

**7** **What good leaders do you know?** Answers will vary. Students may say a family member or coach. **Why is this person a good leader?** Answers will vary but might include that the person knows how to be in charge. **Express Ideas**

## 3 Close and Assess

Ask children to write the names of the holidays they learned about. Pair students and invite them to interview each other to find out how they celebrate different holidays.

## ✓ What did you learn

1. They honor people who fought in wars.

2. Answers will vary but may include that we honor him for speaking up so that all people would be treated fairly.

3. **Write and Share** We celebrate holidays to honor important people or to honor something important that happened in our country's history.

# Abraham Lincoln

## Objectives

- Identify contributions of historical figures such as Abraham Lincoln who have influenced the nation.

- Describe the lives of people commemorated by Presidents' Day.

# 1 Introduce and Motivate

**Preview** Ask children to look at the illustrations on pages 216–217. Invite students to share what they can tell about Abraham Lincoln from the pictures. (He had a beard. He wore a top hat. He lived in a log cabin.) With miniature toy logs, show children how a log cabin is built.

**Warm Up** Ask children to think about someone else they read about who had only a little schooling. (Ben Franklin) Invite children to discuss whether they think they could teach themselves to read, write, and do math or if they would need help at school.

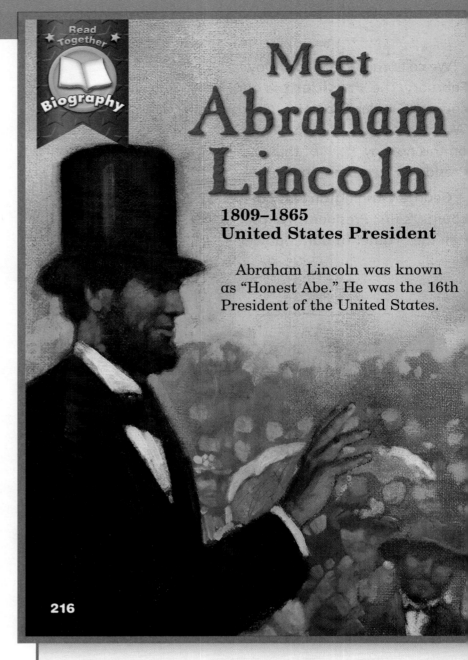

# Meet Abraham Lincoln

### 1809–1865
### United States President

Abraham Lincoln was known as "Honest Abe." He was the 16th President of the United States.

216

# Practice and Extend

### SOCIAL STUDIES
## Background

### About Abraham Lincoln

- Abraham Lincoln was born in a backwoods log cabin in Kentucky.

- His entire schooling amounted to no more than one year's attendance. However, he had a great love of learning. He walked miles just to borrow a book.

- During the Civil War he gave a famous speech, the "Gettysburg Address," to dedicate a battlefield.

- Although Lincoln played a large part in getting the Thirteenth Amendment, making slavery illegal, passed, he did not live to see it approved.

- Lincoln was shot and killed on April 14, 1865.

- Lincoln's face is one of four carved into Mount Rushmore, a 60-ft. high mountain and national monument in South Dakota.

Young Abe's family was very poor. He was not sent to school very often. However, he taught himself many different things. He liked to read books and tell stories. People liked listening to him. They thought he was a good speaker. Abraham Lincoln worked hard and became a lawyer. Later he became President of the United States.

Abraham Lincoln was the leader of our country during a war between the states. The states were fighting for many reasons. One reason was because some states wanted African Americans to be free. Other states did not. Abraham Lincoln worked to keep our country together. He helped free African Americans.

Abraham Lincoln was born near Hodgenville, Kentucky.

Lincoln's hat

Lincoln's home when he was a boy

### Think and Share

Why is Abraham Lincoln remembered as one of our greatest Presidents?

For more information, go online to *Meet the People* at www.sfsocialstudies.com.

217

---

---

## 2 Teach and Discuss

**1 If you could spend time teaching yourself something, what would it be?** Answers will vary but might include cooking, dancing, and things about dinosaurs. **Express Ideas**

**2 What do you think makes a good story-teller?** Answers will vary but may include someone who uses noises and voices or who tells funny stories, scary stories, and so on. **Express Ideas**

**H** SOCIAL STUDIES STRAND
### History

Explain that, before the Civil War, many African Americans were enslaved. Enslaved people are people who, like a house or land, a bicycle or a doll, are owned by another person. Although enslaved people were given shelter, clothes, food, and tools, they worked hard but received no pay. Sometimes they were treated cruelly, but the worst thing was that they were not free. Many people in northern states opposed slavery. Many people in southern states supported it. When many southern states withdrew from the United States, Lincoln led the war to keep the country together, and he helped end slavery.

**3 Why did the states fight in a war when Lincoln was President?** Answers will vary but may include that some states wanted African Americans to be free, and other states did not. **Generalize**

## 3 Close and Assess

Ask children to tell one good quality they think Lincoln had. Then have them write a sentence or two about his life.

### Think and Share

Answers will vary but may include that Lincoln worked to keep our country together and helped free African Americans.

# Lesson ⑤ Wrap-Up

## MEETING INDIVIDUAL NEEDS
## Leveled Practice

### Telling About a Holiday

Read books in the Holiday Histories series by Mir Tamim Ansary: *Memorial Day, Veterans Day, Martin Luther King Jr. Day,* and *Presidents' Day*. Have students choose one holiday to tell about.

**Easy** Have children draw a picture that shows people celebrating the holiday today. Have students tell about their picture. **Reteach**

**On-Level** Have children create a three-page picture book with captions of people celebrating the holiday. Help students do research on the Internet or at the library if they would like to learn more information. **Extend**

**Challenge** Have children direct a two-act play. The first act shows the origin of the holiday. The second act shows how people celebrate the holiday today. **Enrich**

## Hands-on Activities

 **CURRICULUM CONNECTION**
### Writing/Vocabulary

# Holiday Spirit

**Objective** Demonstrate understanding of the vocabulary words.

**Resources** Vocabulary Cards: **holiday, President**

**Materials** paper, pencils

**Learning Style** Verbal-Linguistic

**Individual** 👤

⏱ **Time** 10 minutes

1. Write the following holidays on the board: Independence Day, Thanksgiving, Columbus Day.

2. Ask children what each holiday is for (celebrates the signing of the Declaration of Independence, is a day of thanks, celebrates the day Columbus landed near North America).

Presidents

George Washington

Abraham Lincoln

George W. Bush

3. Remind children to add the vocabulary words *holiday* and *President* to their "My Word Book."

 **CURRICULUM CONNECTION**
### Art

# A Medal for Your Service

**Objective** Design a medal as a prize for someone.

**Materials** paper, crayons, ribbon, glue

**Learning Style** Visual

**Individual** 👤

⏱ **Time** 10–15 minutes

1. Have children look at the medals again in their textbook on page 213. Remind them that soldiers received the medals for acting bravely.

2. Invite children to design their own medal. Suggest that they can make rubbings from coins if they prefer. Help children paste their design to the ribbon.

3. Ask children to announce who they will award their medal to.

 **CURRICULUM CONNECTION**
### Math

# Making Cents

**Objective** Add the values of American coins.

**Materials** pennies and quarters

**Learning Style** Logical/Mathematical

**Pairs** 👥

⏱ **Time** 10 minutes

1. Give each pair of children 10 pennies and 1 quarter.

2. Present pairs with math problems using the faces that appear on the coins. Ask: *How many cents is one Washington and one Lincoln?* or, *Is one Washington greater than or less than one Lincoln?*

3. You may want to extend the lesson by adding nickels, explaining that the face on the nickel belongs to another President, Thomas Jefferson.

# Lesson 6 Overview

## Choosing Our Country's Leaders
pages 218–221

Children will learn how citizens vote for leaders. They will explore what state and country leaders do and where they work. They will also learn the meaning of the words *citizen*, *vote*, and *capital*.

⏱ Time 20–30 minutes

**Resources**
- Workbook, p. 57
- Vocabulary Cards citizen vote capital
- Every Student Learns Guide, pp. 102–105

## Eleanor Roosevelt
pages 222–223

Children will learn about Eleanor Roosevelt and explore her contributions to our country.

⏱ Time 15–20 minutes

# Build Background

## Activity

### Vote for a Place

⏱ **Time** 20 minutes

Tell children that people can vote not only for leaders but also for other choices, such as things to do or places to go. Have children suggest four places they would like to visit for a field trip, such as a zoo, science museum, or aquarium. List the places on the board. Name each place and ask children to raise their hand to vote for the place they would most like to visit. Remind children to vote only once. When the class has finished voting, add the votes and circle the place with the most votes. Then have children draw a picture of the place.

**If time is short,** talk with children about voting. Ask for examples of things they might vote on, such as student of the week or a field trip.

## Read Aloud

### Let's Take a Vote
**by Ravi Iyer**

Pancakes, blueberry muffins, eggs.
Make up your mind. Don't make me beg.
Milk and honey with fruit afloat.
We must decide on breakfast.
Let's take a vote.

Rabbit, dog, ferret, cat.
Lizard, snake, vampire bat.
What will our class pet be?
Take a vote and we shall see.

Baseball, kickball, soccer, tag. What game should we play? Give me a name.
Go down the list, raise your hands high.
Oh, no! Tell me that it's not a tie.

## Lesson 6 — Choosing Our Country's Leaders

### Objectives
- Identify leaders in the state and nation.
- Describe the roles of public officials including governor and president.
- Locate Washington, D.C. and the capital of your state on a United States map.

### Vocabulary
**citizen** a member of a state and country (p. 218)

**vote** a choice that gets counted (p. 218)

**capital** the city where important leaders of a state or country live and work (p. 220)

### QUICK Teaching Plan

**If time is short,** discuss what a citizen and voting are.

- Point out your state capital and Washington, D.C., on a map.

## 1 Introduce and Motivate

**Preview** Display the Vocabulary Card **citizen**. Discuss the definition. Then display the Vocabulary Card **vote**. Have children look at the pictures on pages 218–219. Explain that the man standing in the foreground on p. 218 is about to sign his name in preparation for voting, and James and his mother on p. 219 are surrounded by buttons and signs encouraging people to vote. Finally, display the Vocabulary Card **capital**. Discuss the definition. Invite a volunteer to tell the capital of your state.

**Warm Up** To activate prior knowledge, ask children to name the Presidents that they have learned about. (George Washington, Abraham Lincoln) Tell them that in the United States citizens vote for President. Then explain that voting is a fair way for a group to make a choice or a decision. Ask children if they have ever voted for a person or on a question that needed to be decided.

## Lesson 6 — Choosing Our Country's Leader

I am a citizen of the United States. A **citizen** is a member of a state and country. Adult citizens of the United States have the right to vote for their leaders. A **vote** is a choice that gets counted.

218

Mak Diffe

## Practice and Extend

### READING SKILL
### Categorize

- After children have read pp. 218–221, give them a two-column chart entitled "Government Leader." The chart has three rows entitled "Nation," "State," and "City."
- Tell children that they will be completing a "Government Leader" chart. Explain that a government leader is a person who has an important position in the national, state, or city government.
- Help children complete the chart.

Each citizen votes one time. When the voting is finished, each vote is counted. Whoever gets the most votes, wins.

# FAST FACTS

- In 1870, the Fifteenth Amendment to the Constitution was adopted to protect the voting rights of African Americans.
- In 1920, women won the right to vote when the Nineteenth Amendment was added to the Constitution.
- In 1924, Native Americans were declared citizens by Congress.
- The Civil Rights Act of 1965 finally brought an end to violations against the rights of African Americans to vote.

## WEB SITE
## Technology

You can look up vocabulary words online. Click on *Social Studies Library* and select the dictionary at **www.sfsocialstudies.com**.

# 2 Teach and Discuss

Explain that although citizens have the right to vote, they do not have to vote. That is why some buttons and signs encourage people to vote for a particular leader while others encourage people to simply vote.

### Page 218

**①  Why do people display posters to encourage people to vote?** Answers will vary but should reflect that people want to encourage other people to make a difference in their community, state, or nation.
**Draw Conclusions**

### Page 219

**②  Who are some leaders that citizens vote for?** Answers will vary but may include President, governor, and mayor. **Apply Information**

### Problem Solving

**③  What would you do if you were asked to vote for people you knew nothing about?** Possible answer: Get information about them in order to learn about their points of view.
**Solve Problems**

**Lesson 6 continued**

**Page 220**

Tell children that the picture shows the Georgia State Capitol, the building where the governor of Georgia works.

**④ Who works in the Georgia State Capitol besides the governor?** State leaders who make laws **Making Inferences**

**✓ Ongoing Assessment**

**If...** children do not understand how the governor and lawmakers work together,

**then...** explain that the lawmakers pass laws that regulate and guide daily life in Georgia and the governor puts the laws into action.

**Ⓖ SOCIAL STUDIES STRAND**
**Government**

Explain to children that government is a group of people in charge of a country, state, city, or other place. A governor governs—or leads—the state government. The primary responsibility of state government is to serve the needs of the people of the state.

Tell children that a democracy is a government that is run by the people.

Explain to children that a seal is a design stamped on a letter or document to show ownership or authority.

**⑤ What do you see in the scene on the seal of the state of Georgia?** A soldier, three columns, and the words "Wisdom, Justice, and Moderation." **Analyze Pictures**

---

Every state has a leader called a governor. Citizens of each state vote for their governor. The governor works with other state leaders to help make laws for their state.

Each state has a capital. A **capital** is the city where important leaders of a state or country live and work. What is your state's capital? Find it on a map. **⑤**

The governor of Georgia works in Atlanta.

**220**

## Practice and Extend

**ESL** **ACCESS CONTENT**
**ESL Support**

**Interpret Maps** Have children draw an outline of your state and make a small star to indicate the location of the capital.

**Beginning** Model pointing to the state and capital while identifying them. Have children point to the state and capital and repeat the words.

**Intermediate** Ask children to label the outline of the state and the star indicating the capital.

**Advanced** Ask children to label the outline of the state and the star indicating the capital. Then have children write a caption for their map: The governor of [your state] works in [your capital].

*For additional ESL Support, use Every Student Learns Guide, pp. 102–105.*

Our country also has a capital. It is called Washington, D.C. The President of the United States lives and works in our country's capital.

The President works with other leaders in our country to help make our country's laws. Citizens vote for President every four years in our country.

Washington D.C. is the capital of the United States.

## What did you learn

1. How does a person's **vote** help decide who will be leader?

2. Who is the leader of our state? Who is the leader of our country?

3. **Think and Share Recall** three things you learned about the President of the United States. **Retell** what you learned.

**221**

### SOCIAL STUDIES Background

**About the President of the United States**

- The President must be a natural-born citizen—somebody who is either born in the United States or born outside the United States to United States citizens.

- The President must be at least 35 years old.

- No person can be elected President more than twice.

- The President works with other leaders around the world.

**Workbook, p. 57**

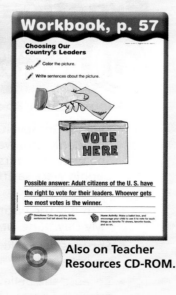

Choosing Our Country's Leaders

Color the picture.

Write sentences about the picture.

VOTE HERE

Possible answer: Adult citizens of the U. S. have the right to vote for their leaders. Whoever gets the most votes is the winner.

Also on Teacher Resources CD-ROM.

Explain to children that a bill—a plan for a new law—may originate with Congress or the President. Once the bill is approved by Congress, it goes to the President. Only when the President signs the bill does it become the law of the land.

### Test Talk

**Use Information from the Text**

6 **Why is the President of the United States an important person?** Answers will vary but may include that as the leader of the nation he helps make laws for the country. Have children find the details from the text to support their answer.
**Express Ideas**

Ask children to tell who the President of our country is. Have children locate Washington, D.C., on a map of the United States.

7 **After the President wins the election, how long does he or she keep the job?** Four years
**Apply Information**

## 3 Close and Assess

Ask children to tell why people vote. (to make choices) Pair children and have them discuss the importance of voting.

## ✓ What did you learn

1. Every vote counts. The person who gets the most votes becomes the leader.

2. Children should name the governor of your state and President by their names.

3. **Think and Share** Children's answers should reflect what they learned about the President of the United States.

## Eleanor Roosevelt

### Objectives

- Identify historic figures such as Eleanor Roosevelt who have exemplified good citizenship.

- Identify characteristics of good citizenship such as a belief in justice, truth, equality, and responsibility for the common good.

# 1 Introduce and Motivate

**Preview** Ask children to tell what the wife of the President of the United States is called. (First Lady) Tell children that they are going to learn about a woman who was First Lady a long time ago. Have children look at pictures of her.

**Warm Up** To activate prior knowledge, ask children what they learned about good citizens. Ask children what some of these good citizens did. Explain to children that Eleanor Roosevelt was a good citizen because she believed that people should be treated fairly. Ask children to name other people they learned about who wanted people to be treated fairly. (Martin Luther King, Jr., Abraham Lincoln)

Eleanor Roosevelt was born in New York City, New York.

# Eleanor Roosevelt

When Eleanor was young, she was very shy. When she grew older, she became more comfortable around people. She married a man named Franklin Roosevelt. He became our 32nd President.

Eleanor Roosevelt saw that there were problems in our country. She told people the truth about what she saw. She helped the poor. She worked hard to get equal rights for all people.

222

Young Eleanor

# Practice and Extend

## FYI SOCIAL STUDIES Background

### About Eleanor Roosevelt

- Eleanor Roosevelt helped her husband Franklin, the President, who was disabled by a disease called polio. She went on tours and reported back to him what people were saying and what condition the country was in. She became his "eyes and ears."

- Each day she wrote a newspaper column called "My Day." She wrote honestly in this column.

- She was particularly interested in helping people who were needy.

- Because she believed that all people should be treated fairly, she helped write the *Universal Declaration of Human Rights* in 1948. This document said that all people had a right not to be unfairly punished, unfairly hurt, or unfairly put in jail. The document was read by people all over the world.

The Autobiography of ELEANOR ROOSEVELT

Eleanor Roosevelt's own story including material from her memoirs, This Is My Story and On My Own

With a new Introduction by John Roosevelt Boettiger

BUILDING CITIZENSHIP
Caring
Respect
Responsibility
Fairness
Honesty
Courage

Eleanor Roosevelt wrote many books and newspaper articles. She was honest. She would say and write what she thought.

Eleanor Roosevelt traveled around the world many times. ② She visited many countries. She met many of the world's leaders.

⭐ **Honesty in Action** ⭐

How do you think Eleanor Roosevelt's honesty was helpful to others?

**223**

### CURRICULUM CONNECTION
## Writing

**A Letter to Eleanor Roosevelt**

- Tell children that Eleanor Roosevelt received many letters from children.
- Have children imagine that Eleanor Roosevelt is the First Lady. Have them write a letter pointing out a problem that needs her attention.
- Suggest that children begin the letter by telling Eleanor Roosevelt good things they have read about her.

## 2 Teach and Discuss

Tell children that Eleanor Roosevelt worked hard to get equal rights not only for people in America but around the world. Explain that equal rights are fair requests, like the right to speak freely.

❶ **How did Eleanor Roosevelt know that there were problems in our country?** Answers may vary but could include that she saw problems when she traveled or she read about them in newspapers or letters. **Hypothesize**

❷ **Why do you think Eleanor Roosevelt is a citizen hero?** She was honest. She helped poor people. She worked so that all people would be treated fairly. **Draw Conclusions**

## 3 Close and Assess

Ask children to tell about the life of Eleanor Roosevelt. Then have children write one sentence to tell why she was a good citizen.

⭐ **Honesty in Action** ⭐

She expressed her honest opinions and wrote about injustice. She helped the poor and worked for equal rights for all people.

# Lesson 6 Wrap-Up

 **MEETING INDIVIDUAL NEEDS**
## Leveled Practice

### Making Rules
Have children suggest rules for the class. Write their rules on the board. Have them vote for the very best rule.

**Easy** Have children suggest at least one rule. **Reteach**

**On-Level** Have children suggest rules. Then have them tell how the rules will help the class. **Extend**

**Challenge** Have two teams debate the rules, presenting different views. **Enrich**

## Hands-on Activities

 **CURRICULUM CONNECTION**
### Writing/Vocabulary

## Stand Up and Be Counted

**Objective** Demonstrate understanding of the vocabulary words.

**Resources** Vocabulary Cards: **vote, citizen, capital**

**Materials** cards

**Learning Style** Auditory/Verbal

**Group**

**Time** 10–15 minutes

1. Divide children into groups of four. Give each child in a group a card with a different vocabulary word.

2. Say the definition of one of the words. Ask children holding the word card that matches the definition to stand up and show their card. Repeat with the other two words.

3. Remind children to add the vocabulary words to their "My Word Book."

 **CURRICULUM CONNECTION**
### Math

## Tallying the Votes

**Objective** Count the number of votes candidates receive.

**Materials** tally sheets, pencils

**Learning Style** Mathematical/Logical

**Group**

**Time** 5–10 minutes

1. Fill in a tally sheet to look like the results of a vote for "Funniest Animal." Make the results close.

2. Hand out the filled-in tally sheets.

3. Have groups count the number of tally marks for each candidate.

4. The group that accurately counts up the tallies first is the winner.

5. Extend the exercise by adding new "votes" to the original tally.

 **CURRICULUM CONNECTION**
### Writing

## It's a Secret!

**Objective** Vote with secret ballots.

**Materials** paper, pencils, shoe box

**Learning Style** Visual

**Individual**

**Time** 10–15 minutes

1. Ask children for three suggestions for the fruit that should be served at a pretend picnic. Write the results on the board with small squares before the names. Have children copy the names and squares on paper ballots.

2. Have children make a check in the box of the fruit they choose. Tell them to fold their secret ballot and slip it into the shoe box slot. Tally the results on the board.

| | |
|---|---|
| apples | ☐ |
| bananas | ☐ |
| grapes | ☐ |

3. Have children draw a picture of the winner.

# Ending Unit 5

**End with a Song**
pages 224–225

Children will listen to and sing our national anthem: "The Star-Spangled Banner" by Francis Scott Key.

**Resource**
• *Songs and Music* CD

**Unit 5 Review**
pages 226–229

Children will review unit vocabulary words and the unit skills of recall and retell, using a history map and reading a diagram. Children will answer questions about what they learned in the unit. Children will learn about several books about the history of our country.

**Resources**
• Workbook, pp. 58–59
• Assessment Book, pp. 17–20

**Unit 5 Project**
page 230

Children will have a history parade. They will also be directed to a web site where they can learn more about our country's history.

# Wrap-Up

**Activity**

## Welcome to America!

Have children make posters to welcome visitors. Ask them to include at least one picture of what it's like to live in America and at least one national symbol, such as the Statue of Liberty.

• Have children cut out pictures from magazines or draw pictures themselves. They should arrange their pictures to form a collage and then paste them into place on large sheets of oaktag.

• Help children write titles for their posters. Remind them to spell all the words correctly, and to print neatly.

• Display children's posters prominently in your classroom.

**Performance Assessment**
You can use the activity on this page as a performance assessment.

✔ **Assessment Scoring Guide**

| Make a Poster About America | |
|---|---|
| **6** | Appropriate title, one or more pictures depicting life in America, and a National Symbol. Neat handwriting, no spelling errors. |
| **5** | Includes first 3 elements, legible handwriting, one or two spelling errors. |
| **4** | Includes first 3 elements, acceptable handwriting, some spelling errors. |
| **3** | Includes 2 of the elements, some errors in spelling. |
| **2** | Includes 2 of the elements, several spelling errors. |
| **1** | Includes only one of the required elements. |

If you prefer a 4-point rubric, adjust accordingly.

# The Star-Spangled Banner

## Objective

- Identify anthems and mottoes of the United States and individual states.

## Resource

- Transparency 33

# 1 Introduce and Motivate

**Preview** Point to and read the title of the song. Tell children that this song—"The Star-Spangled Banner"—is the national anthem of the United States. Read the songwriter's name and then ask children what they think the words *star-spangled banner* refer to. (the U.S. flag) Have children point to the flag in the picture. Tell children that states also have songs. For example, the state song of Georgia is "Georgia on My Mind," and the state song of Indiana is "On the Banks of the Wabash, Far Away." Discuss your state song.

**Warm Up** To activate prior knowledge, ask children when they have heard "The Star-Spangled Banner." Discuss reasons why the United States is called "the land of the free and the home of the brave."

# 2 Teach and Discuss

You may want to read the words to "The Star-Spangled Banner" with children before singing it. Explain any words or phrases children may not understand, such as *twilight's last gleaming* and *perilous fight*. (See Background below.)

**1** **Why do some people hold their hands over their hearts as they sing our national anthem?** To show their respect for the flag Hypothesize

**2** **Why do you think people stand when our national anthem is played or sung?** To show respect Hypothesize

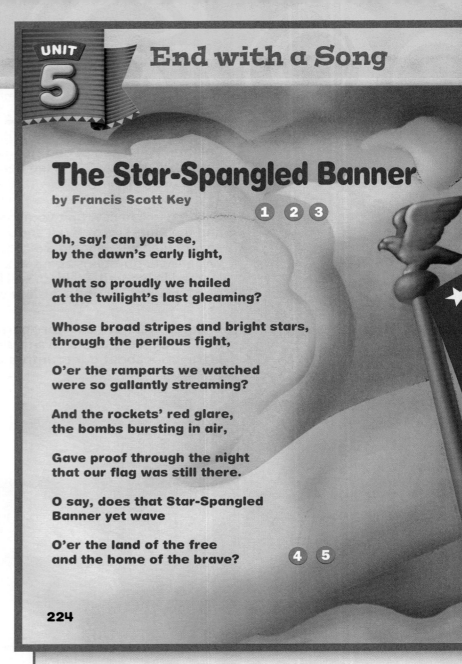

# The Star-Spangled Banner

by Francis Scott Key **1** **2** **3**

Oh, say! can you see,
by the dawn's early light,

What so proudly we hailed
at the twilight's last gleaming?

Whose broad stripes and bright stars,
through the perilous fight,

O'er the ramparts we watched
were so gallantly streaming?

And the rockets' red glare,
the bombs bursting in air,

Gave proof through the night
that our flag was still there.

O say, does that Star-Spangled
Banner yet wave

O'er the land of the free
and the home of the brave? **4** **5**

**224**

# Practice and Extend

**FYI** **SOCIAL STUDIES**
**Background**

**The Writing of the National Anthem**

- Francis Scott Key composed the words of the anthem during the War of 1812, which was fought between the United States and England. The melody was borrowed from another song: "To Anacreon in Heaven."

- Key wrote the song as he watched the bombardment of Fort McHenry from aboard a troop ship in Baltimore Harbor.

- The bombardment lasted all day and almost all night. At dawn, Key saw that the American flag was still flying at Fort McHenry. He was so moved that he pulled a letter or envelope from his pocket and used it to write the now-famous words.

- The anthem has four verses; only the first verse is shown here.

225

**3** **When have you heard • our national anthem played or sung?** Possible answer: Before a sporting event begins **Apply Information**

**4** **What is a motto?** Possible answer: A word or short sentence that tells what a nation, state, group, or person believes or stands for

⭐ SOCIAL STUDIES STRAND
**Citizenship**

Tell children that the official motto of the United States is *In God We Trust*. Write these words on the board, using all capital letters. Then distribute pennies or other U.S. coins to children. Ask them to find these same words on the coins. Ask children why they think these words appear on the coins.

Tell children that states also have mottoes. For example, the motto of Georgia is "Wisdom, Justice, and Moderation." and the motto of Indiana is "The Crossroads of America." Discuss your state motto and what it means.

**5** **Why do you think it is important for the United States to have a national anthem and a motto?** Possible answer: To have a song and a saying that sums up the beliefs and feelings most people share about their country

# 3 Close and Assess

- Have children stand and place their hands over their hearts as you sing the national anthem or play it on the *Songs and Music* CD.

- Display the words to the first verse of the national anthem on chart paper. Have children stand and sing the song along with you as you point to the words.

# UNIT 5 Review

## Resources

- Assessment Book, pp. 17–20
- Workbook, p. 58: Vocabulary Review

## Vocabulary Review

1. President
2. capital
3. vote
4. holiday

 **Answers to Test Prep**

1. c. freedom
2. a. citizen

---

# UNIT 5 Review

## Vocabulary Review

Match each word to a picture.

vote
holiday
President
capital

1.
2.
3.
4.

★ ★ ★ ★ ★ ★ ★ ★

 Which word completes the sentence?

1. The Pilgrims came to North America for _____.

   a. a holiday       b. riches
   c. freedom        d. gold

2. A member of a state and country is called a _____.

   a. citizen        b. capital
   c. holiday        d. vote

226

---

# Practice and Extend

## Assessment Options

✓ **Unit 5 Assessment**

- Unit 5 Content Test: Use Assessment Book, pp. 17–18

- Unit 5 Skills Test: Use Assessment Book, pp. 19–20

**Standardized Test Prep**

- Unit 5 tests contain standardized test formats.

✓ **Unit 5 Performance Assessment**

- See p. 230 for information about using the Unit 5 Project as a means of performance assessment.

- A scoring guide for the Unit 5 Project is provided in the teacher's notes on p. 230.

 **Test Talk**

- Test Talk Practice Book

---

# Skills Review

##  Recall and Retell

Make a list of what you learned about Nathan Hale. Read your list. Then put the list away. Try to **recall** what the list said and **retell** what you remember to a friend.

★ ★ ★ ★ ★ ★ ★ ★

## Use a History Map

Ben Franklin traveled to France in 1776. Look at the map to answer these questions.

**1.** Which direction did Ben Franklin travel to France?

**2.** What ocean did he travel across?

**3.** What continent is south of France?

227

### WEB SITE
### Technology

For more information, you can select the dictionary or encyclopedia from *Social Studies Library* at
**www.sfsocialstudies.com.**

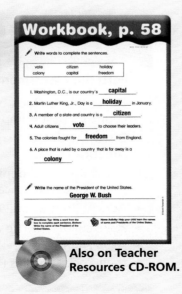
**Workbook, p. 58**

Also on Teacher Resources CD-ROM.

---

# Skills Review

## Recall and Retell

- Children's lists may include these facts:

  Nathan Hale was a teacher.

  He was a soldier in George Washington's army.

  He spied on the English but was caught.

  He is a hero who died for his country.

### ✓ Assessment Scoring Guide

| | Picture Clues |
|---|---|
| 6 | Recalls and tells 3–4 facts about Nathan Hale, especially those that relate to his heroism. Student speaks clearly and in complete sentences. |
| 5 | Recalls and tells 3–4 facts about Nathan Hale that relate to his heroism. Shows good use of language. |
| 4 | Recalls and tells 2–3 facts about Nathan Hale that relate to his heroism. Uses acceptable language. |
| 3 | Recalls and tells 1–2 facts about Nathan Hale that relate to his heroism. |
| 2 | Struggles to recall and tell 1–2 facts about Nathan Hale. One of these may relate to his heroism. |
| 1 | Recalls and tells a fact about Nathan Hal. Does not relate to his heroism. |

If you prefer a 4-point rubric, adjust accordingly.

## Using a History Map

**1.** east

**2.** Atlantic Ocean

**3.** Africa

## Review

continued

# Skills Review

## Read a Diagram

1. Torch

2. Crown

3. Lookout

**Test Talk**

**Use Information from Graphics**
Use Read a Diagram, Question 2, to model the Test Talk strategy.

**Understand the question.**
Children should ask themselves "What label points to the part on the statue's head?"

**Use information from graphics.**
Ask children to skim the diagram to find the right information to support their answer.

## Skills on Your Own

- Children's diagrams should include labels for all the parts and name the President: Abraham Lincoln.

- President Lincoln is on the front of the penny.

Use the following scoring guide.

### ✓ Assessment Scoring Guide

| | Draw a Diagram |
|---|---|
| 6 | Detailed diagram includes all the parts and President's full name. May offer additional information. |
| 5 | Includes most of the parts and President's name in full. |
| 4 | Includes some of the parts and President's name. |
| 3 | Includes only some of the parts or is missing President's name. |
| 2 | Includes some of the parts or President's name, but not both. |
| 1 | Lacking most of the parts and President's name. |

If you prefer a 4-point rubric, adjust accordingly.

## Review

# Study Skills
## Read a Diagram

Look at the diagram of the Statue of Liberty. Answer the questions.

**Test Talk**

Use the diagram to help you find the answer.

1. What is the highest part of the statue?

2. What part is on the statue's head?

3. Where can you stand to look down at the ground?

## Skills On Your Own

Draw a diagram of the front of a penny. Label the parts. What President of the United States is pictured on the penny?

Torch

Crown

Lo

228

# Practice and Extend

## Revisit the Unit Question

### ✓ Portfolio Assessment

- Have children look back at the list of reasons why our country's past is important, made on p. 183.

- Discuss with children the importance of freedom in America's past.

- Ask children to identify some of the historical events that express America's love of freedom.

- Ask children to draw a picture of our country's past.

- Have children write a sentence describing the drawing.

- Have children add their list, drawing, and sentence to their Social Studies Portfolio.

# What did you learn?

1. Tell what the United States flag and the Liberty Bell stand for.

2. Name three important Americans we honor with a holiday.

3. What does a governor do?

4. **Write and Share** Write about some of the reasons why you are proud to be an American or living in the United States.

# Read About Our Country

Look for books like these in the library.

229

**CURRICULUM CONNECTION**
**Literature**

**Books About Our Country's Past**

Children might enjoy reading these books about our country's past.

*Ox-Cart Man,* by Donald Hall and Barbara Cooney (illustrator) (Puffin, ISBN 0-140-50441-9, 1983) Follow the life of a farm family in the early days of our country. **Easy** Caldecott Medal, 1980

*Dakota Dugout,* by Ann Warren Turner and Ronald Himler (illustrator) (Aladdin, ISBN 0-689-71296-0, 1989) Describes life on the prairie for the pioneer families of the mid-19th century through the eyes of a woman who lived there. **On-Level** ALA Notable Book

*Peppe the Lamplighter,* by Elisa Bartone and Ted Lewin (illustrator) (Mulberry Books, ISBN 0-688-15469-7, 1997) A boy in New York's Little Italy is happy to find work lighting street lamps when the lamplighter returns to Italy. **Challenge** Caldecott Honor Book, 1994

# What did you learn?

1. Both the United States flag and the Liberty Bell stand for freedom.

2. Three important Americans we honor with a holiday are President George Washington, President Abraham Lincoln, and Martin Luther King, Jr.

3. A governor leads a state.

4. **Write and Share** Children's answers should reflect pride in the fact that the laws of the United States promote justice, truth, equality, and responsibility for the common good.

# Read About Our Country

You may want to have these books available in the classroom. Read the books aloud for children; then invite them to browse through the books. Encourage them to tell why these books are good ones to include in this unit. They may also wish to review the books for classmates.

*George, the Drummer Boy,* by Nathaniel Benchley and Don Bolognese (illustrator) (HarperCollins Children's Books, ISBN 0-060-20501-6, 1977) This book presents the beginning events of the American Revolution from an unusual viewpoint: that of an English drummer boy. The book not only provides information about the war from both sides but also in a personal way, which helps young readers become engaged. **Easy**

*Picture Book of Eleanor Roosevelt, A,* by David A. Adler and Robert Casilla (illustrator) (Holiday House, ISBN 0-823-40856-6, 1991) This book is a brief account of Eleanor Roosevelt's life told in simple sentences and colorful illustrations. It chronicles the unfolding of Roosevelt's strong-mindedness and presents her accomplishments. **On-Level**

*Across the Wide Dark Sea: The Mayflower Journey,* by Jean Van Leeuwen and Thomas B. Allen (illustrator) (Dial Books for Young Readers, ISBN 0-803-71166-2, 1995) This book tells the story of sailing to America and building a settlement. Told from the viewpoint of a young boy, it describes the Pilgrims' voyage, their first harsh winter, and the help they received from American Indians, and evokes the hopeful voyages of all immigrants to America. **Challenge**

# Unit 5 Project

# History on Parade

## Objective
- Identify a historic event and understand that events occur in a sequence.

## Resource
- Workbook, p. 59

## Materials
construction paper, posterboard, scissors, crayons, paint, glue, cotton balls

## Follow This Procedure
- Tell children that they are going to put on a history parade. Each child will make a drawing or object that shows something that happened in history. The event they show may be related to a person or a group of people.

- Explain that they will choose an event or a person and create a prop or costume; examples include a Pilgrim's hat for the first Thanksgiving; a ship for Christopher Columbus arriving in the New World; a drawing of an early U.S. flag.

- Direct children to make their props. Give each child an index card with the event's date. Help children determine the correct sequence. Once the props are completed, instruct children to line up in order and ask them to tell about their event.

- Hold a classroom parade. Consider holding the parade elsewhere in the school as well.

### ✓ Assessment Scoring Guide

| History on Parade | |
|---|---|
| 6 | Correct and very detailed description and illustration; correct sequence of all events. |
| 5 | Correct description and illustration; correct sequence of events. |
| 4 | Good description and illustration; correct sequence of events. |
| 3 | Acceptable description and illustration; correct sequence of most events. |
| 2 | Description contains some incorrect information, fair illustration; only a few events in correct sequence. |
| 1 | Incorrect description, does not create object that illustrates event, inaccurate sequence of events. |

If you prefer a 4-point rubric, adjust accordingly.

# UNIT 5 Project

## History on Parade

**Have a history parade.**

**1** **Choose** something that happened in the past.

**2** **Draw** or make an object that shows what happened.

**3** **Tell** what happened.

**4** **Line** up in order of when things happened. The first event should be first in line. The last event should be last. Walk around your classroom on parade.

### Internet Activity

Go to www.sfsocialstudies.com/activities to learn more about American history.

230

# Practice and Extend

## Hands-on Unit Project

✓**Performance Assessment**
- The Unit Project can also be used as a performance assessment activity.
- Use the scoring guide to assess each group's work.

## WEB SITE Technology

Children can launch the activity by clicking on *Grade 1, Unit 5* at **www.sfsocialstudies.com/ activities.**

### Workbook, p. 59

**5 Project** History on Parade

Drawings will vary.

Draw an event that happened in the past.

✐ Write answers about the event. **Answers will vary.**

What happened?

Who was there?

Where did the event happen?

When did the event happen?

*Directions:* Top: Draw an event in the history of our country. Bottom: Answer the questions. *Home Activity:* Talk with your child about an event in American history. Discuss its importance.

**Also on Teacher Resources CD-ROM**

# Vocabulary Routines

The following examples of reading and vocabulary development strategies can be used to instruct students about unit vocabulary.

## BEFORE READING

### Related Word Study

**Thinking of Synonyms** Use context clue sentences to help children figure out the meanings of vocabulary words. Make up a sentence that does not come from the text but that correctly uses a vocabulary word. Discuss the sentence with children. Encourage them to use their own words to tell what the sentence is about. Guide children to develop a synonym for the vocabulary word.

*One of our new vocabulary words is* **market.** *Listen to my sentence and see if you can figure out what* **market** *means:* **Mrs. Smith went to the market to buy some eggs, fruit, and vegetables.** *What is Mrs. Smith doing? She is buying some eggs, fruit, and vegetables. Where did she go? She went to a place called a market. Can you think of another name for a place where people go to buy food?* (a grocery store) *Good,* **grocery store** *is another name for* **market.**

## DURING READING

### Context Clues

Vocabulary: market, communicate, invention, inventor

**What Does It Mean?** Read the lesson with children and pause at the end of each page. Review lesson vocabulary words that children encountered on the page. Reread sentences on the page that contain vocabulary words. Ask children what each word means. Encourage children to restate the sentence in their own words.

*One of the words in our lesson is* **communicate.** *The sentence says:* **Telling stories and singing songs are two ways to communicate.** *What does* **communicate** *mean?* **Communicate** *means to let somebody know something. So we could say "Telling stories and singing songs are two ways to let somebody know something." Does that make sense?* (Yes)

## AFTER READING

### Individual Word Study

**Examples and Non-examples** Use this routine to help clarify examples and non-examples of vocabulary words. First, draw a circle on a large sheet of paper and write a vocabulary word in the center of it. Have a volunteer explain the meaning of the word. Then give examples and non-examples of the word and have children explain whether they are examples or not. Write the examples inside of the circle and the non-examples outside of the circle.

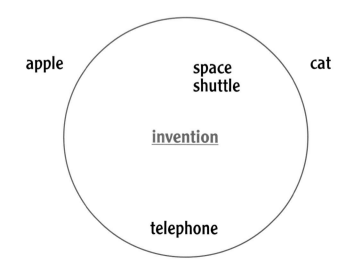

*Our first word is* **invention.** *Who can tell me what an invention is?* (An invention is something new. It never existed until a person made it.) *Is a computer an invention?* (Yes, somebody made it). *Is a telephone an invention?* (Yes, people never had phones a long time ago.) *Is a space shuttle an invention?* (Yes, space shuttles were invented so people could travel in space.) *Is an apple an invention?* (No, apples grow on trees.)

# Teaching with Leveled Readers

**This series of readers focuses on transportation and advancements in travel.**

**Below Level**

**On Level**

**Above Level**

## LEVELED READER VOCABULARY ACTIVITY

- Have children preview the vocabulary words at the beginning of the reader.

- As children read, have them pause as they come to a vocabulary word and repeat it softly to themselves.

- After reading, have children work in partners to brainstorm different inventions.

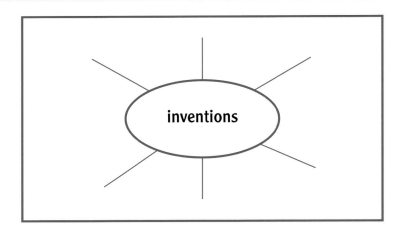

inventions

## CONNECTIONS TO THE LESSON

Unit 6, Lesson 4: How Travel Has Changed

## CONNECTIONS TO TODAY

- Have children read the lesson. Then provide the leveled readers to enhance their understanding of how travel has developed over the years to what it is today.

- **Points for Discussion:**
    1. Have children discuss how people in their family travel to different places.
    2. Children can also discuss how travel might change in the future.

Gate C23

Gate C24

10:23

231a

# Unit 6 Planning Guide

## Our Country, Our World

**Begin with a Song** pp. 232–233  **Vocabulary Preview** pp. 234–235

**Reading Social Studies, Predict** pp. 236–237

| Lesson Titles | Pacing | Main Ideas |
|---|---|---|
| **Lesson 1 Visiting the Market** pp. 238–239 <br><br> Gather Information pp. 240–241 | 2 days | • A market is a place where goods are sold and services are provided. <br> • Gathering information is one way to learn about the lives and accomplishments of people long ago. |
| **Lesson 2 How Things Have Changed** pp. 242–243 <br><br> Citizen Heroes: (Respect) Joseph Bruchac pp. 244–245 | 2 days | • Technological advances, such as computers and scanners, have changed the way people live and work. <br> • Joseph Bruchac, Native American writer, shows respect by recording the traditional stories told by elders. |
| **Lesson 3 Inventors and Inventions** pp. 246–249 <br><br> Telephones pp. 250–251 | 2 days | • Many inventions help people communicate. These include the printing press; the telephone, invented by Alexander Graham Bell; and the phonograph, invented by Thomas Alva Edison. <br> • The telephone has gone through many changes since it was first invented. |
| **Lesson 4 How Travel Has Changed** pp. 252–253 <br><br> Chart and Graph Skills: Read a Bar Graph pp. 254–255 <br><br> Biography: Mae Jemison pp. 256–257 | 3 days | • Land transportation has changed greatly over time. <br> • A bar graph helps people compare groups. <br> • Mae Jemison was the first African American woman to travel into space. |
| **Lesson 5 Life Around the World** pp. 258–261 <br><br> Biography: Laurence Yep pp. 262–263 <br> Here and There: It Is Time to Leave pp. 264–265 | 3 days | • Children around the world are alike and different. <br> • Laurence Yep, a Chinese American writer, writes about the Chinese American way of life. <br> • There are many sayings around the world for leave taking. |

✔ **End with a Folktale** pp. 266–267   ✔ **Unit 6 Review** pp. 268–271   ✔ **Unit 6 Project** p. 272

✔ = Assessment Options

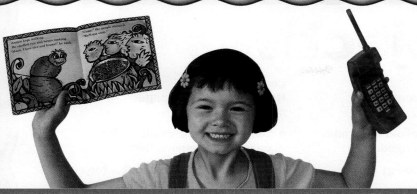

| Vocabulary | Resources | Meeting Individual Needs |
|---|---|---|
| market | • Workbook, pp. 62–63<br>• Vocabulary Card: market<br>• Every Student Learns Guide, pp. 106–109<br>• Transparency 34 | • ESL Support, TE p. 240<br>• Leveled Practice, TE p. 241a |
| | • Workbook, p. 64<br>• Every Student Learns Guide, pp. 110–113 | • ESL Support, TE p. 243<br>• Leveled Practice, TE p. 245a |
| communicate<br>invention<br>inventor | • Workbook, p. 65<br>• Vocabulary Cards: communicate, invention, inventor<br>• Every Student Learns Guide, pp. 114–117 | • ESL Support, TE p. 248<br>• Leveled Practice, TE p. 251a |
| | • Workbook, pp. 66–67<br>• Every Student Learns Guide, pp. 118–121<br>• Transparency 35 | • ESL Support, TE p. 257<br>• Leveled Practice, TE p. 257a |
| world | • Workbook, p. 68<br>• Vocabulary Card: world<br>• Every Student Learns Guide, pp. 122–125<br>• Transparency 36 | • ESL Support, TE p. 260<br>• Leveled Practice, TE p. 265a |

# Providing More Depth

## Additional Resources

- Trade Books
- Family Activities
- Vocabulary Workbook and Cards
- Social Studies Plus!
- Daily Activity Bank
- Read Alouds and Primary Sources
- Big Book Atlas
- Student Atlas
- Outline Maps
- Desk Maps

 **Technology**

- Video Field Trips
- Songs and Music
- Digital Learning CD-ROM Powered by KnowledgeBox
- AudioText
- MindPoint® Quiz Show CD-ROM
- ExamView® Test Bank CD-ROM
- Colonial Williamsburg Primary Sources CD-ROM
- Teacher Resources CD-ROM
- Map Resources CD-ROM
- SFSuccessNet: Online Student Edition, Online Teacher Edition, Online Planner
- **www.sfsocialstudies.com** (Biographies, news, references, maps, and activities)

 *To establish guidelines for your children's safe and responsible use of the Internet, use the Scott Foresman Internet Guide.*

**Additional Internet Links**

To find out more about:

- views of space from Earth, visit **www.nasa.gov**
- views of Earth's land features from space, visit **http://earth.jsc.nasa.gov**

# Unit 6 Objectives

## Beginning of Unit 6

- Obtain information about a topic using a variety of oral sources such as songs. (pp. 232–233)
- Determine the meanings of words.
- Obtain information about a topic using a variety of visual sources such as pictures. (pp. 234–235)
- Recognize words that help make a prediction.
- Analyze pictures and text to make a prediction.
- Make a prediction based on information given. (pp. 236–237)

## Lesson 1
### Visiting the Market
pp. 238–239

- Identify the role of markets in the exchange of goods and services.
- Gather information about the lives and accomplishments of selected men and women in the historical period before the Renaissance. (pp. 240–241)

## Lesson 2
### How Things Have Changed
pp. 242–243

- Describe how household tools and appliances have changed.
- Describe how technology has changed recreation.
- Describe how technology has changed the way people work.
- Identify people who exemplify good citizenship and exhibit a love of individualism. (pp. 244–245)

## Lesson 3
### Inventors and Inventions
pp. 246–249

- Describe how technology has changed communication.
- Identify historic figures such as Alexander Graham Bell and Thomas Edison who have exhibited a love of inventiveness.
- Obtain information about a topic using a variety of visual sources, such as pictures. (pp. 250–251)
- Describe how technology has changed communication. (pp. 250–251)

## Lesson 4
### How Travel Has Changed
pp. 252–253

- Describe how technology has changed transportation.
- Obtain information about a topic using a variety of visual sources, such as pictures. (pp. 254–255)
- Create visual and written material, including graphs. (pp. 254–255)
- Identify people who exhibit a love of individualism. (pp. 256–257)

## Lesson 5
### Life Around the World
pp. 258–261

- Compare housing, clothes, and foods from different parts of the world.
- Identify people who exhibit a love of individualism. (pp. 262–263)
- Show what people around the world say when they leave. (pp. 264–265)

## End of Unit 6

- Retell stories from selected folktales and legends such as Aesop's fables. (pp. 266–267)
- Create visual and written material including pictures, maps, time lines, and graphs. (pp. 270–271)
- Understand how machines benefit daily life. (p. 272)

# Assessment Options

## ✓ Formal Assessment

- **What did you learn?** PE/TE pp. 239, 243, 249, 253, 261
- **Unit Review,** PE/TE pp. 268–271
- **Unit 6 Test,** Assessment Book pp. 21–24
- **ExamView® CD-ROM**

## ✓ Informal Assessment

- **Teacher's Edition Questions,** throughout Lessons and Features
- **Close and Assess,** TE pp. 239, 243, 249, 253, 261
- **Try it!** PE/TE pp. 237, 241, 255,
- **Think and Share,** PE/TE pp. 243, 249, 253, 257, 261, 263
- **Respect in Action,** PE/TE p. 245

### Ongoing Assessment

**Ongoing Assessment** is found throughout the Teacher's Edition lessons using an **If…then** model.

| **If =** students' observable behavior, | **then =** reteaching and enrichment suggestions |

## ✓ Portfolio Assessment

- **Portfolio Assessment,** TE pp. 231, 270
- **Leveled Practice,** TE pp. 234, 241a, 245a, 251a, 257a, 265a
- **Workbook Pages,** pp. 60–70
- **Unit Review: Skills on Your Own,** PE/TE p. 270
- **Curriculum Connection: Writing,** TE pp. 241a, 245a, 251a, 257a, 265a

## ✓ Performance Assessment

- **Hands-on Unit Project** (Unit 6 Performance Assessment), PE/TE pp. 231, 268, 272
- **Internet Activity,** PE p. 272
- **Unit Review: Write and Share,** PE/TE p. 271
- **Scoring Guides,** TE pp. 266a, 269, 270, 272

## Test Talk

### Test-Taking Strategies

**Understand the Question**
- **Locate Key Words in the Question,** TE p. 259
- **Locate Key Words in the Text,** TE p. 244

**Understand the Answer**
- **Choose the Right Answer,** Test Talk Practice Book
- **Use Information from the Text,** TE p. 249
- **Use Information from Graphics,** TE p. 255
- **Write Your Answer,** TE pp. 241, 271

*For additional practice, use the Test Talk Practice Book.*

### Featured Strategy

**Write Your Answer**
Children will:
– Make sure their answer is correct.
– Make sure their answer is complete.
– Make sure their answer is focused.
**PE/TE** p. 271, **TE** p. 241

# Curriculum Connections
## Integrating Your Day

The lessons, skills, and features of Unit 6 provide many opportunities to make connections between social studies and other areas of the elementary curriculum.

### Reading

**Reading Skill—Predict,** PE/TE pp. 236–237, TE p. 238, TE p. 246

**To Market Again,** TE p. 241a

**Reading Skill—Categorize,** TE p. 242

**The Storyteller's Craft,** TE p. 245

**Things Change,** TE p. 245a

**Reading Skill—Sequence,** TE p. 252

**Reading Skill—Compare and Contrast,** TE p. 258

### Writing

**To Market Again, Rhyme Time,** TE p. 241a

**Computers of the Future,** TE p. 245a

**Related Words,** TE p. 251a

**A-Mazin'!** TE p. 257a

**Asia Puzzle,** TE p. 265a

### Math

**Calculating Telephone Numbers,** TE p. 251

**Measurement,** TE p. 254

## Social Studies

### Science

**Find Locations on a Globe,** TE p. 237

**Vote for Scientific Tools,** TE p. 241

**Zoom Rockets,** TE p. 257a

**Looking at the World,** TE p. 265a

### Literature

**Books by Laurence Yep,** TE p. 263

**Aesop's Fables,** TE p. 267

**Books About Our Country Our World,** TE p. 271

### Music/Drama

**Up, Up, and Away!** TE p. 233

**Singing at the Corner Grocery Store,** TE p. 241a

**Telephone Etiquette,** TE p. 250

**All Riiiight!** TE p. 251a

**Transportation Songs,** TE p. 257a

**The Sound of Music,** TE p. 265

### Art

**My Times,** TE p. 242a

**Bar Code,** TE p. 245a

**Business Cards,** TE p. 251a

**Modes of Transport,** TE p. 252a

 Look for this symbol throughout the Teacher's Edition to find **Curriculum Connections.**

# Professional Development

## Real World Knowledge and Authentic Assessment

**by James B. Kracht**
Texas A&M University

Curriculum, instruction, and assessment are the three critical elements of any teaching-learning system. Assessment provides information about how well students have achieved the goals set forth in the curriculum. Educators have devised a variety of new assessment tools that can help to reveal why students sometimes fail and whether or not students have mastered complex curriculum standards. These tools include alternative assessment, authentic assessment, portfolio, performance task, and rubric.

Throughout Unit 6, Scott Foresman Social Studies provides a variety of ways to assess children's learning. Examples include:

- *analytical questions throughout the lesson*
- *ongoing assessment features in lessons*
- *end of the unit performance, skills, and portfolio assessments, which include rubric assessment charts, pp. 266a–272*
- *Unit 6 Project, p. 272, "Future World," requires children to make a model of a machine people might use in the future, to create a commercial telling why the machine should be used, and to ask classmates for feedback. This task involves children in applying their knowledge (of how technology affects daily life) to produce a product and performance.*

## ESL Support

**by Jim Cummins, Ph. D.**
University of Toronto

Academic language proficiency does not automatically develop on the basis either of students' conversational fluency in English or their knowledge of discrete language skills taught by means of direct instruction in school. Students should be encouraged to become *language detectives* who investigate the mysteries of language. When we explore English and Spanish Social Studies vocabulary students who know Spanish or some other Romance language are given opportunities to shine in the classroom. They have prior knowledge in the form of their first language (L1) that is directly relevant to being a successful linguistic detective.

The following examples in the Teacher's Edition will help you to enable ESL children to extend language:

- **Focus on Meaning** on p. 236 helps English Language Learners learn that to predict is to *tell* what will happen *before* it happens.
- **Watching Television** on p. 243 has children performing activities which reinforce the meaning of *vision* in the word *television*.

# Read Aloud

## Ring Around the World
### by Annette Wynne

Ring around the world,
Taking hands together,
All across the temperate
And the torrid weather.

Past the royal palm trees,
By the ocean sand,
Make a ring around the world
Taking each other's hand.

In the valleys, on the hill,
Over the prairie spaces,
There's a ring around the world
Made of children's friendly faces.

**Build Background**
- Ask children to tell about family members who live or have lived in places outside the United States.
- Ask children about they ways they might communicate with people around the world.

**Read Alouds and Primary Sources**

*Read Alouds and Primary Sources* contains additional selections to be used with Unit 6.

# Bibliography

*Market Day: A Story Told with Folk Art,* by Lois Ehlert (Harcourt Brace, ISBN 0-152-02158-2, 2000) **Easy**

*On Market Street,* by Arnold Lobel and Anita Lobel (Illustrator) (Greenwillow, ISBN 0-688-80309-1, 1981) Alphabet book about a child who goes to Market Street to buy one item for each letter of the alphabet. Each merchant is made out of materials that he or she is selling. **Easy**

*Saturday Market,* by Patricia Grossman and Enrique O. Sanchez (Illustrator) (Lothrop Lee & Shepard, ISBN 0-688-12176-4, 1994) **Easy**

*Alexander Graham Bell: A Photo-Illustrated Biography,* by Greg Linder (Bridgestone Books, ISBN 0-736-80202-9, 1999) **On-Level**

*Great Ball Game: A Muskogee Story, The,* by Joseph Bruchac and Susan L. Roth (Illustrator) (Dial Books for Young Readers, ISBN 0-803-71539-0, 1994) **On-Level**

*I Spy a Freight Train: Transportation in Art,* by Lucy Micklethwait (Greenwillow, ISBN 0-688-14700-3, 1996) **On-Level**

*Market,* by Ted Lewin (Lothrop Lee & Shepard, ISBN 0-688-12161-6, 1996) **On-Level**

*Picture Book of Thomas Alva Edison, A,* by David A. Adler, John Wallner (Illustrator), Alexandra Wallner (Illustrator) (Holiday House, ISBN 0-823-41246-6, 1996) Book that chronicles the life of Thomas Alva Edison from the mishaps of his youth to his great accomplishments. **On-Level**

*Dragon Prince: A Chinese Beauty and the Beast Tale, The,* by Laurence Yep and Kam Mak (Illustrator) (HarperCollins Juvenile Books, ISBN 0-060-24381-3, 1997) **Challenge**

*Mae Jemison: The First African American Woman Astronaut,* by Liza N. Burby (Powerkids Press, ISBN 0-823-95027-1, 1998) **Challenge**

*Wake Up, World!: A Day in the Life of Children Around the World,* by Beatrice Hollyer (Henry Holt &Company, ISBN 0-805-06293-9, 1999) Book that chronicles a typical day in the life of children from eight countries around the world. **Challenge**

 *Discovery Channel School Videos* **Inventors and Inventions.** Explore how and why unique inventions were created, then meet some famous inventors; 2 videos. 60 minutes/7 segments.

 Look for this symbol throughout the Teacher's Edition to find **Award-Winning Selections**. Additional book references are found throughout this unit.

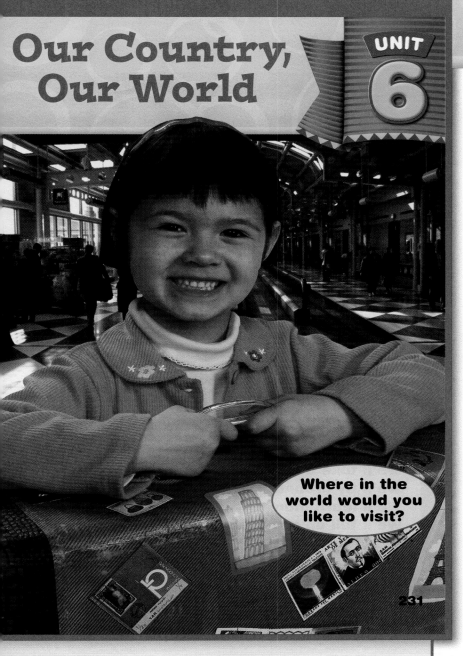

# Our Country, Our World

UNIT 6

**Where in the world would you like to visit?**

231

# Our Country, Our World

## Unit Overview
In this unit children learn about the market, decision-making, technology, and inventions. They also learn about life around the world.

## Introduce Kay

Read the unit title and then introduce the featured child for this unit as a first grader named Kay. Ask what is on the suitcase in the picture. (Airport stickers and tags from around the world)

## Unit Question
- Ask children the question on this page.
- Initiate a discussion of how children learned about the places they would like to visit.
- To activate prior knowledge, make a list on the board of places in the world where children would like to visit.
- ✓ **Portfolio Assessment**  Keep a copy of this list for the Portfolio Assessment at the end of the unit on page 270.

# Practice and Extend

### 👐 Hands-on Unit Project

✓ **Unit 6 Performance Assessment**

The Unit 6 Project, Future World, found on p. 272, is an ongoing performance assessment project to enrich children's learning throughout the unit.

- This project, which has children making a model and giving a commercial, may be started now or at any time during this unit of study.
- A performance assessment scoring guide is located on p. 272.

# Explore with Me!

## Objective

- Obtain information about a topic using a variety of oral sources such as songs.

## Resources

- *Songs and Music* CD "Explore with Me!"
- Poster 11
- Social Studies Plus!

## Introduce the Song

**Preview** Tell children that they will be singing a song about exploring the world. Show children photographs of places around the world. Ask if they can identify any of the places.

**Warm Up** To activate prior knowledge, ask children what they might experience if they traveled to a faraway place. (You try new foods, see new things, and meet new people.) Then ask what it is like to welcome somebody home from a trip.

## Sing the Song

- Have children sing the song "Explore with Me!"
- Ask children to identify the kinds of transportation named in the song.
- Ask children to tell about a place people have told them that they visited.

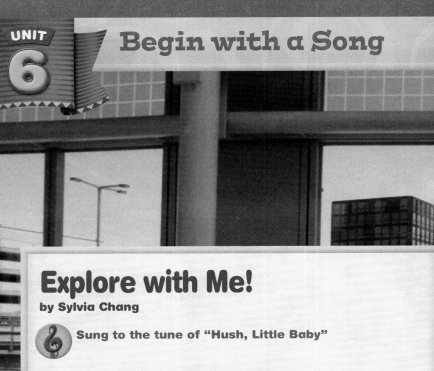

# Explore with Me!
by Sylvia Chang

 Sung to the tune of "Hush, Little Baby"

Travel the world. Explore with me.
There are so many things to do and see.
There are people we will meet.
There are new foods we will eat.

We'll take a boat, a bus, and train.
We'll fly around the world in a great big plane.
We'll learn many things we want to know.
We'll tell all about each place we go.

232

# Practice and Extend

**FYI** **SOCIAL STUDIES**
**Background**

**Possible Misconceptions**

Children may not be aware that people travel in different ways depending on where they are going. Tell children that if they are going to a nearby store, they might walk or take a bus. If they are going to another country, such as France or Japan, they might take a ship or an airplane.

**AUDIO CD**
**Technology**

Play the CD, *Songs and Music*, to listen to the song "Explore with Me!"

233

## Talk About the Picture

Direct children's attention to the picture on these two pages.

**❶ Where is Kay?** At an airport **What clues tell you where she is?** Answers may include the airplane and suitcases. Analyze Pictures

**❷ Who are the people in this picture?** They are members of Kay's family, her mother, her grandmother, and her grandfather. Analyze Pictures.

Have children compare this family to their own families. How are they alike and different? Invite students to think about how life might have been different for their parents or other adults when they were growing up. How was life different for grandparents, great-grandparents, or other older adults? Ask if they have seen pictures or heard stories about what life was like for them. Explain that the people in their families and the stories they tell are part of their family history.

---

### CURRICULUM CONNECTION
## Literature

- Children might enjoy hearing these stories that provide examples of ways to investigate and document a family history.

*Me and My Family Tree* by Joan Sweeney and Annette Cable (illustrator) (Random House, ISBN 0-517-70996-X, 2000). A young girl learns one way to document three generations of her family.

*The Keeping Quilt* by Patricia Polacco. (Simon & Schuster Children's, ISBN 0-671-64963-9, 2001). The story of a quilt passed down from mother to daughter over four generations.

## Objectives

- Determine the meanings of words.

- Obtain information about a topic using a variety of visual sources such as pictures.

## Resources

- Workbook, p. 60

- Vocabulary Cards

- Poster 12

## Introduce the Vocabulary

Read aloud and point to each vocabulary word and the photograph illustrating it. Have volunteers give the meanings of the words. Then have children find examples of culture vocabulary words in the picture. Write these examples on the board.

| Vocabulary Word | Illustrated Examples |
|---|---|
| market | food market, arts and crafts |
| communicate | boy talking on telephone, girl giving directions |
| invention | round machine with wheels, radio, telephone, computer, electric light bulb, automobile |
| inventor | Alexander Graham Bell, Thomas Alva Edison, Henry Ford, Amanda Jones |
| world | foods from many countries, "Food Market" banner |

**C** **SOCIAL STUDIES STRAND**
## Culture

Listed below are some basic principles of culture for young children. Direct most of your discussion of the picture towards the development of these concepts.

- different kinds of markets

- goods and services

- technology that has changed work, home, and recreation

- inventions that help people communicate

- changes in land transportation

- similarities and differences between people around the world

market

communicate

invention

234

## Practice and Extend

**MEETING INDIVIDUAL NEEDS**
## Leveled Practice

**Visit a School Fair**

Invite children to take a look at the areas with inventions and arts and crafts in the picture (p. 234).

**Easy** Randomly name some of the inventions and arts and crafts, identifying them as inventions or arts and crafts. Have children repeat the words after you. **Reteach**

**On-Level** Have one partner randomly name some of the inventions and arts and crafts and the other partner identify them as inventions or arts and crafts. Have partners reverse roles. **Extend**

**Challenge** Have children list some of the inventions and arts and crafts. Then have them compare and contrast the inventions and the drawings. (Alike: Children created them. Different: Many of the inventions are machines. They have a practical use. The drawings are things made to look beautiful.) **Enrich**

inventor

world

235

Workbook, p. 60

Draw a picture for each word. | Use with Pages 234-235.
**Drawings will vary.**

communicate | inventor

invention | market

world

**Directions:** Read the words and draw pictures to illustrate them. Cut out the boxes to use as word cards. | **Home Activity:** Look through newspapers with your child to find pictures that illustrate the words.

**Also on Teacher Resources CD-ROM.**

# Talk About the Picture

Allow children time to study the picture. The picture shows a school fair with food from around the world, an arts and crafts market, inventions, and ways to communicate. Encourage children to identify and describe these parts of the picture.

Have children look at the boy in the upper left on p. 234.

**1 How is the boy communicating?** By telephone **Analyze Pictures**

Have children look at the famous inventions on the table at the top of p. 234 and the posters of their inventors on the wall. Explain that the woman in the poster on the right is Amanda Jones. She invented the vacuum method of canning. Canning is a common method of food preservation in America. Part of the air is removed in the can in order to reduce the growth of bacteria.

**2 Who are the other inventors? Connect them to the inventions on the table.** Alexander Graham Bell (telephone), Thomas Alva Edison (electric light bulb), and Henry Ford (automobile) **Analyze Pictures**

## Look Ahead

Tell children they will learn more about each of the vocabulary words as they study Unit 6.

You may want to revisit the picture with children to review the concepts and vocabulary in the unit.

Have children look at the table on the lower left of p. 234 with things invented by children.

**3 Which invention is for transportation?** The round machine with wheels **Make Inferences**

Look at tables with foods from around the world on p. 235.

**4 What countries does the food come from?** Mali, China, Greece, and Mexico **Analyze Information**

# Kay's Grandparents

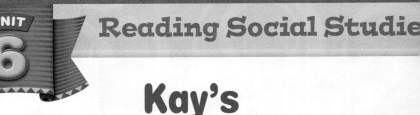

## Predict

### Objectives

- Recognize words that help make a prediction
- Analyze pictures and text to make a prediction.
- Make a prediction based on information given.

### Resource

- Workbook, p. 61

### About the Unit Target Skill

- The target reading skill for this unit is Predict.
- Children are introduced to the unit target skill here and are given an opportunity to practice it.
- Further opportunities to practice predicting are found throughout Unit 6.

# 1 Introduce and Motivate

**Preview** Assess whether children understand the concept of predicting by telling them *Tomorrow I will walk from my home to the grocery store. If it rains on the way, I will ….* Ask them to predict what you might do if it suddenly rains. (Run to the store, stand in a doorway, ask somebody for a ride, return home for an umbrella, etc.) Explain that to *predict* means to tell what you think may happen next.

**Warm Up** To activate prior knowledge, point to and identify the things from around the world shown on pp. 236–237. Then list them on the board. Tell children that they are going to vote for the thing they would most like to have. Ask them to write down what thing they predict will receive the most votes. Take a vote. Tally the results on the board. Have children display their predictions.

# Kay's Grandparents

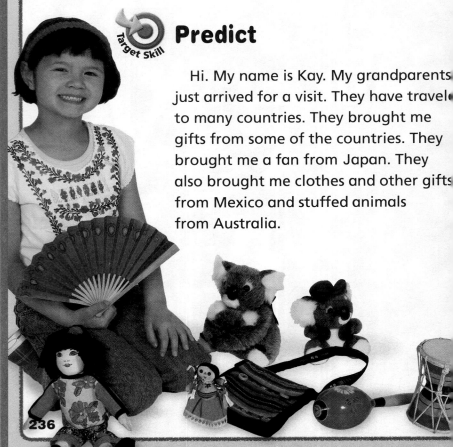

## Predict

Hi. My name is Kay. My grandparents just arrived for a visit. They have travele to many countries. They brought me gifts from some of the countries. They brought me a fan from Japan. They also brought me clothes and other gifts from Mexico and stuffed animals from Australia.

236

# Practice and Extend

**ESL** **EXTEND LANGUAGE**
**ESL Support**

**Focus on Meaning** Discuss the meaning of the word *predict* with children. Explain that to *predict* is to <u>tell</u> what will happen <u>before</u> it happens. Tell children that they can check the accuracy of their prediction in the future.

**Beginning** Have children draw a picture of what the weather might be tomorrow, and orally complete the sentence *I predict* ___ to tell what the weather might be.

**Intermediate** Have children draw a picture of what the weather might be tomorrow and write a caption that completes the sentence *I predict* ___.

**Advanced** Have children make a "Tomorrow's Weather" chart with two heads: "What I Predict" and "What Actually Happened." Have them fill in the first column daily for a week, completing the sentence *I predict* ___. Then have them fill in the second column the following day.

Now I want to give my grandparents a gift. I can draw a picture for them. I can make a card. I can give them flowers.

It is time to predict. **Predict** means to tell what you think will happen next. What do you think I will give my grandparents?

I decided to draw them a picture of myself. They said they liked it very much. Did I do what you thought I would do?

## Try it !

The sky is very dark and cloudy. **Predict** what kind of weather you might have.

237

---

### SOCIAL STUDIES STRAND
### Geography

**Find Locations on a Globe**

Revisit the meaning of cardinal directions.

Have children find the United States, Japan, Mexico, Canada, and Australia on a globe. First have them locate their home state in the United States. Then have them locate the other countries by tracing the route and saying aloud the cardinal directions.

### Workbook, p. 61

**Predict**

Write what you predict will happen.

Juan and his family are in Mexico City. They are visiting Juan's grandparents. This is the first time that Juan has been in Mexico.

His grandfather has taken Juan to Chapultepec Park. It is the biggest park in Mexico City! There is a zoo in the park.

What will Juan do?

**Juan will go to the zoo.**

Juan has fun at the park. His grandfather has a good time too. Juan asks if he can buy something to take home. He wants to remember this day!

What will Juan buy?

**Juan will buy a balloon.**

**Also on Teacher Resources CD-ROM.**

---

## 2 Teach and Discuss

Look at the picture on p. 236.

Discuss with children some of the gifts Kay's grandparents gave her. Then discuss the different things Kay can give her grandparents. Talk about the picture Kay made for her grandparents.

## 3 Close and Assess

### Try it !

Have children draw pictures of their prediction. You may first want to discuss with them what often happens after a sky turns dark and cloudy. (It rains.)

# Workbook Support

 Use the following Workbook pages to support content and skills development as you teach Unit 6. You can also view and print Workbook pages from the Teacher Resources CD-ROM.

## Workbook, p. 60

Use with Pages 234–235.

✏️ Draw a picture for each word. **Drawings will vary.**

| communicate | inventor |
|---|---|
| invention | market |
| world | |

**Directions:** Read the words and draw pictures to illustrate them. Cut out the boxes to use as word cards.

**Home Activity:** Look through newspapers with your child to find pictures that illustrate the words.

**Use with Pupil Edition, p. 235.**

## Workbook, p. 61

Use with Pages 236–237.

### Predict

✏️ Write what you predict will happen.

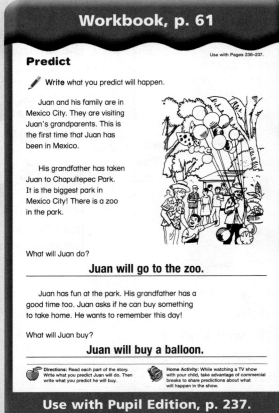

Juan and his family are in Mexico City. They are visiting Juan's grandparents. This is the first time that Juan has been in Mexico.

His grandfather has taken Juan to Chapultepec Park. It is the biggest park in Mexico City! There is a zoo in the park.

What will Juan do?

**Juan will go to the zoo.**

Juan has fun at the park. His grandfather has a good time too. Juan asks if he can buy something to take home. He wants to remember this day!

What will Juan buy?

**Juan will buy a balloon.**

**Directions:** Read each part of the story. Write what you predict Juan will do. Then write what you predict he will buy.

**Home Activity:** While watching a TV show with your child, take advantage of commercial breaks to share predictions about what will happen in the show.

**Use with Pupil Edition, p. 237.**

## Workbook, p. 62

Use with Pages 238–239.

### Visiting the Market

✏️ Draw stars by 3 goods. **Stars will vary.**

🔵 Circle people who provide services.

🖍️ Color people who use the goods. **Color all people.**

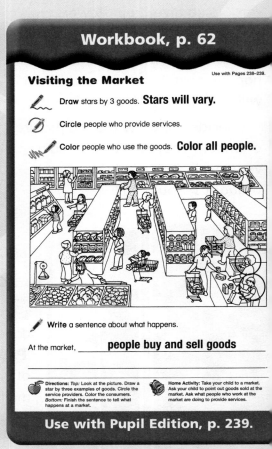

✏️ Write a sentence about what happens.

At the market, **people buy and sell goods**

**Directions:** Top: Look at the picture. Draw a star by three examples of goods. Circle the service providers. Color the consumers. Bottom: Finish the sentence to tell what happens at a market.

**Home Activity:** Take your child to a market. Ask your child to point out goods sold at the market. Ask what people who work at the market are doing to provide services.

**Use with Pupil Edition, p. 239.**

## Workbook, p. 63

Use with Pages 240–241.

### Gather Information

👀 Look at the pictures.

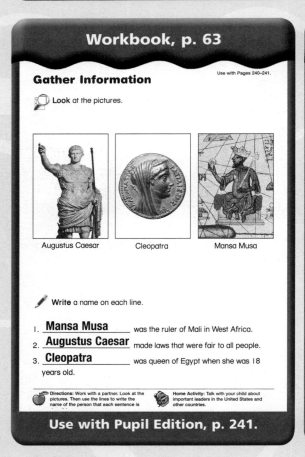

Augustus Caesar    Cleopatra    Mansa Musa

✏️ Write a name on each line.

1. **Mansa Musa** was the ruler of Mali in West Africa.
2. **Augustus Caesar** made laws that were fair to all people.
3. **Cleopatra** was queen of Egypt when she was 18 years old.

**Directions:** Work with a partner. Look at the pictures. Then use the lines to write the name of the person that each sentence is

**Home Activity:** Talk with your child about important leaders in the United States and other countries.

**Use with Pupil Edition, p. 241.**

## Workbook, p. 64

Use with Pages 242–243.

### How Things Have Changed

Match the pictures.

✏️ Draw a radio for the future. **Drawings will vary.**

**Directions:** Top: Match the pictures in column 1 with the pictures in column 2 to show how things have changed. Bottom: Draw a picture to show how a radio might change in the future.

**Home Activity:** Tell your child how a household tool or appliance has changed since you were a child.

**Use with Pupil Edition, p. 243.**

## Workbook, p. 65

Use with Pages 246–249.

### Inventors and Inventions

✏️ Write to tell about each inventor. **Possible answers:**

Thomas Alva Edison **invented the phonograph. He also invented many other things that helped people communicate better.**

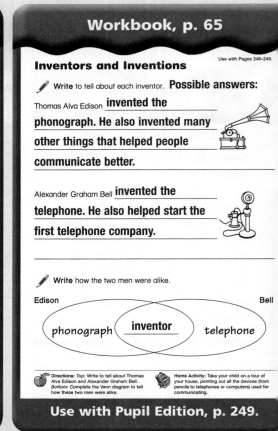

Alexander Graham Bell **invented the telephone. He also helped start the first telephone company.**

✏️ Write how the two men were alike.

Edison          Bell

phonograph ( inventor ) telephone

**Directions:** Top: Write to tell about Thomas Alva Edison and Alexander Graham Bell. Bottom: Complete the Venn diagram to tell how these two men were alike.

**Home Activity:** Take your child on a tour of your house, pointing out all the devices (from pencils to telephones or computers) used for communicating.

**Use with Pupil Edition, p. 249.**

# Workbook Support

## Workbook, p. 66

### How Travel Has Changed
Use with Pages 252–253.

✏️ **Draw** to show 3 ways to travel. **Drawings will vary.**

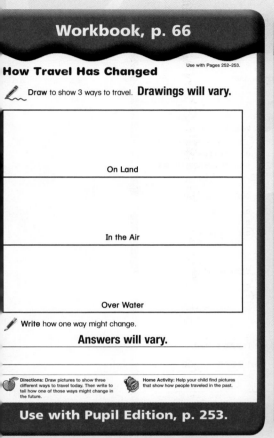

On Land

In the Air

Over Water

✏️ **Write** how one way might change.

**Answers will vary.**

🍎 **Directions:** Draw pictures to show three different ways to travel today. Then write to tell how one of those ways might change in the future.

🎒 **Home Activity:** Help your child find pictures that show how people traveled in the past.

## Use with Pupil Edition, p. 253.

---

## Workbook, p. 67

### Read a Bar Graph
Use with Pages 254–255.

✏️ **Circle** your answer to each question.

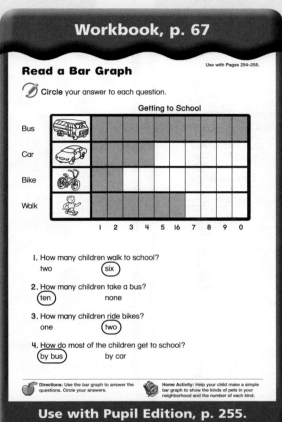

**Getting to School**

| | 1 | 2 | 3 | 4 | 5 | 6 | 7 | 8 | 9 | 0 |

1. How many children walk to school?
   two     (six)

2. How many children take a bus?
   (ten)     none

3. How many children ride bikes?
   one     (two)

4. How do most of the children get to school?
   (by bus)     by car

🍎 **Directions:** Use the bar graph to answer the questions. Circle your answers.

🎒 **Home Activity:** Help your child make a simple bar graph to show the kinds of pets in your neighborhood and the number of each kind.

## Use with Pupil Edition, p. 255.

---

## Workbook, p. 68

### Life Around the World
Use with Pages 258–261.

✏️ **Draw** pictures that show three things about you.

My Picture

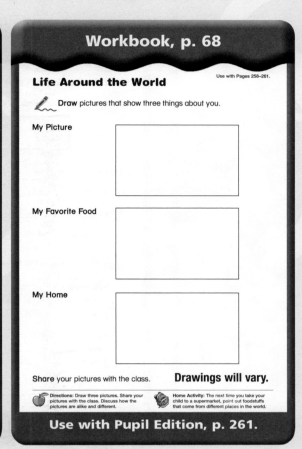

My Favorite Food

My Home

**Share** your pictures with the class. **Drawings will vary.**

🍎 **Directions:** Draw three pictures. Share your pictures with the class. Discuss how the pictures are alike and different.

🎒 **Home Activity:** The next time you take your child to a supermarket, point out foodstuffs that come from different places in the world.

## Use with Pupil Edition, p. 261.

---

## Workbook, p. 69

Use with Unit 6.

✏️ **Circle** a word to complete each sentence.

1. Thomas Alva Edison was a great _____.
   (inventor)     market

2. The phonograph was one of his _____.
   predictions     (inventions)

3. People buy and sell things at a _____.
   world     (market)

4. Telephones are used to _____.
   travel     (communicate)

✏️ **Draw** how the world looks from space. **Drawings will vary.**

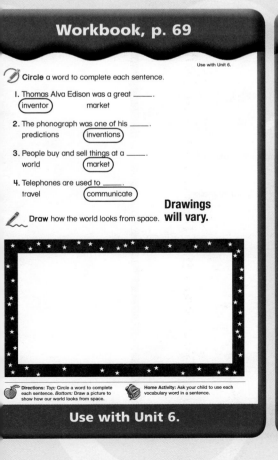

🍎 **Directions:** Top: Circle a word to complete each sentence. Bottom: Draw a picture to show how our world looks from space.

🎒 **Home Activity:** Ask your child to use each vocabulary word in a sentence.

## Use with Unit 6.

---

## Workbook, p. 70

**UNIT 6 Project**   Future World   Discovery SCHOOL

**Drawings will vary.**

✏️ **Draw** a picture of a machine of the future.

✏️ **Write** answers about your machine. **Answers will vary.**

How does the machine help people?

_____

Who will your machine help?

_____

🍎 **Directions:** Top: Draw a machine of the future. Bottom: Answer the questions.

🎒 **Home Activity:** Talk with your child about things people might need in the future.

## Use with Pupil Edition, p. 272.

# Assessment Support

 Use these Assessment Book pages and the ExamView® CD-ROM to assess content and skills in Unit 6. You can also view and print Assessment Book pages from the Teacher Resources CD-ROM.

## Assessment Book, p. 21

### Unit 6: Content Test

✎ **Write** a word from the box to finish each sentence.

| | |
|---|---|
| market | communicate |
| world | invention |

1. Earth is the name of our __**world**__.

2. The printing press was a great __**invention**__.

3. Talking is one way to __**communicate**__.

4. Goods are bought and sold at a __**market**__.

⭐ **Which word completes the sentence?**

1. People who invent things are ____.
   a. worlds     b. markets
   **(c.)** inventors     d. inventions

2. People use telephones to ____.
   a. invention     b. world
   **(c.)** communicate     d. inventor

**Use with Pupil Edition, p. 268.**

## Assessment Book, p. 22

🔍 **Look** at each picture and read the question.

✏ **Circle** the letter of your answer.

1. What do people do here?
   **(a.)** buy things they need
   b. make decorations
   c. borrow books to read

2. What looks very old?
   a. the sink
   b. the TV set
   **(c.)** the stove

3. Who invented this?
   a. Thomas Edison
   **(b.)** Alexander Bell
   c. Mae Jemison

✎ **Write** to complete these sentences. **Possible answers:**

Long ago, people traveled by __**horse and wagon**__.

Today, people travel by __**car**__.

**Use with Pupil Edition, p. 268.**

## Assessment Book, p. 23

### Unit 6: Skills Test

✎ **Write** to predict.

Luis has a pen pal. The pen pal lives in Japan. Luis and his pen pal write to each other often. They tell each other about their families and friends.

One day, Luis got a new pet. He was so excited! He drew a picture of his dog. He put himself in the picture too.

What will Luis do?

__**send the picture to his pen pal**__

Use the bar graph to answer the questions.

**Best Pets**

| | | | | | |
|---|---|---|---|---|---|
| Dogs | | | | | |
| Cats | | | | | |
| Fish | | | | | |
| Birds | | | | | |
| | 1 | 2 | 3 | 4 | 5 |

How many children like dogs? __**4**__

How many children like fish? __**3**__

What pet do the children like best? __**cats**__

**Use with Pupil Edition, pp. 269–270.**

## Assessment Book, p. 24

Nan's family wants to buy a pet. Dad wants a dog. Mom wants a cat. Her brother wants a hamster. Nan wants a goldfish. The family has to decide which pet to buy.

Where can Nan look to gather information about each type of pet?

✏ **Circle** 3 things that would help Nan gather information about pets.

(An encyclopedia)

A dictionary

(The Internet)

A newspaper

(A book about pets)

An atlas

**Use with Pupil Edition, pp. 269–270.**

# Lesson ① Overview

| | | |
|---|---|---|
| **Visiting the Market**<br>pages 238–239 | Children will learn about the role of markets in providing goods and services. |  Time 10–15 minutes<br>**Resources**<br>• Workbook, p. 62<br>• Vocabulary Card  market<br>• Every Student Learns Guide, pp. 106–109 |
| **Gather Information**<br>Pages 240–241 | Children will learn how to gather information to learn about a particular topic. | Time 10–15 minutes<br>**Resource**<br>• Workbook, p. 63 |

# Build Background

## Activity

### Market Day

 **Time** 20 minutes

Describe a market to children. Then have them create a fruit market in the classroom, using fruit, signs, paper bags, and paper money. Invite some children to sell the fruit and others to buy it.

• Have the sellers prepare signs with the prices of their fruits.

• After the buyers have bought fruit, have children exchange roles.

**If time is short,** have children describe a market where goods are sold. Ask them to draw a picture of items for sale.

## Read Aloud

### To Market

**nursery rhyme**

To market, to market

To buy a fat pig,

Home again, home again,

Jiggety jig,

To market, to market

To buy a fat hog,

Home again, home again,

Jiggety jog,

To market, to market

To buy a plum bun,

Home again, home again,

Market is done.

## Lesson 1

# Visiting the Market

### Objective
- Identify the role of markets in the exchange of goods and services.

### Vocabulary
**market** a place where goods are sold (p. 238)

## QUICK Teaching Plan

*If time is short,* discuss the meaning of the word *market.* Explain that goods and services are provided at a market.

- Remind children that goods are things that are grown or made. Tell them that goods are usually bought and sold. Ask children for examples of household goods.

- Remind children that services are jobs in which people help others. Ask them the ways that a waiter in a restaurant provides a service.

## 1 Introduce and Motivate

**Preview** Display the Vocabulary Card **market** and ask children to tell things a family needs. Make a list of the things on the board. Then ask children to tell where these goods can be bought. Tell children that they will be learning about a place where people buy food.

**Warm Up** To activate prior knowledge, ask children to tell if they have ever sold goods (for example, lemonade or cookies). Ask children to identify the goods in the pictures on pp. 238–239.

## 2 Teach and Discuss

### Page 238–239

**1 How do people pay for goods at the market?** With money **Draw Conclusions**

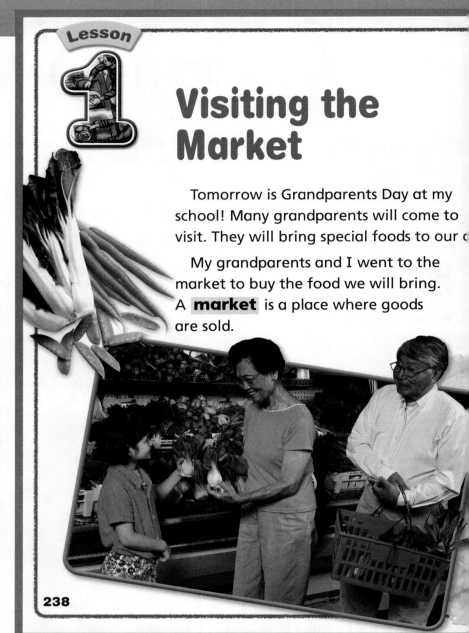

## Lesson 1

# Visiting the Market

Tomorrow is Grandparents Day at my school! Many grandparents will come to visit. They will bring special foods to our c

My grandparents and I went to the market to buy the food we will bring. A **market** is a place where goods are sold.

238

# Practice and Extend

### READING/VOCABULARY
## Predict

- After children have read pp. 238–239, give them a copy of a two-column prediction chart, the first column headed *Today,* the second, *Tomorrow.* Ask children to predict what might happen on Grandparents Day in school.

- In the first column, have children write what Kay's grandparents will do today to prepare for Grandparents Day. (Buy vegetables at the market)

- In the second column, have children fill in their predictions about what the class will do tomorrow for Grandparents Day. (Answers will vary but may include eat the food that the grandparents bring.)

- Ask for volunteers to share their answers orally with the class.

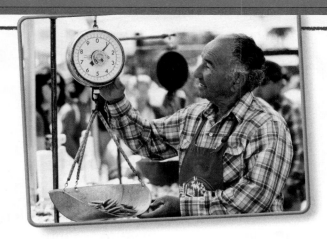

People who work at the market provide services. One worker weighed the vegetables we picked out.

My grandmother said she went to the market every day with her mother and grandmother. They bought food for the family.

**① ② ③**

## What did you learn ?

1. What goods did Kay and her grandparents buy?

2. What service did they use?

3. Kay and her grandparents chose their groceries. They took the groceries to the front of the store. **Predict** what may happen next.

**239**

### SOCIAL STUDIES Background

**Possible Misconceptions**

- Some children may not understand that a grocery store or supermarket is only one kind of market. Crafts, clothing, or electronics can also be sold in a market.

### WEB SITE Technology

You can look up vocabulary words online. Click on *Social Studies Library* and selecting the dictionary at **www.sfsocialstudies.com.**

**Workbook, p. 62**

**Visiting the Market**

Draw stars by 3 goods. **Stars will vary.**

Circle people who provide services.

Color people who use the goods. **Color all people.**

Write a sentence about what happens.

At the market, **people buy and sell goods**

**Also on Teacher Resources CD-ROM.**

---

### SOCIAL STUDIES STRAND
### $ Economics

Explain to children that people depend on one another for goods and services. Usually the goods and services are provided for payment in money. Sometimes, however, people trade goods, such as food, and services rather than pay for them. This exchange is called bartering. Ask children if they have ever traded things.

**② Why do sellers need a market?** Answers will vary but should reflect that sellers need a place to sell their goods. **Apply Information**

**③ What would you do if you wanted to buy your grandparents two flowers but you only had money for one? Support your choice.** Answers will vary but should reflect that children have to make a choice. **Make Decisions**

Tell children that all of the people born at about the same time are part of one generation. Kay belongs to one generation. Kay's mother belongs to another generation. Kay's grandmother belongs to still another generation, and so on. Point out that children may have seen a photograph of a baby, mother, and grandmother. Explain that a photograph like that shows three generations of the same family. Kay shopping with her grandmother and Kay's grandmother shopping with her mother is one example of a family tradition.

## 3 Close and Assess

Ask children to tell what people do at the market. (Buy and sell goods; provide services) Have partners discuss a market they have visited with their family. Ask them to tell what goods were available, what steps were taken in the purchase of an item, and what services were provided.

### ✓ What did you learn ?

1. Kay and her grandparents bought vegetables.

2. Someone at the store weighed the vegetables and wrote the cost on the bag.

3. Possible answer: The grandparents will pay for the groceries.

# Gather Information

## Objective

• Gather information about the lives and accomplishments of selected men and women in the historical period before the Renaissance.

# 1 Introduce and Motivate

**Preview** Ask children to look at the illustrations on pages 240-241. Explain that going to a museum is one way to find out about people who lived long ago. To gather more information about what they had seen, Kay and her grandparents bought postcards. The postcards explained about people from other countries who lived long ago. Tell children that a variety of sources can be used to gather information, such as print resources, technology resources, and community resources.

**Warm Up** To activate prior knowledge, ask volunteers to name things they are interested in and would like to learn more about, such as dinosaurs, collecting shells, baseball, horses, and so on. Write their answers on the board. Ask them to brainstorm places they could find the information they need, which may include books in the library, the Internet, or an interview with an adult.

# Gather Information

Kay's class had to find out about people
**1** long ago. Kay went to the museum with
her grandparents. She learned about other
countries. Kay and her grandparents boug
picture cards that told about some import
leaders who lived long ago.

**Mansa Musa**
West Africa

**2**
**3** Mansa Musa was the ruler of a country in West Africa called Mali.

**Cleopatra**
Egypt

Cleopatra became the queen of Egypt when she was only eighteen years old.

**240**

# Practice and Extend

**ESL** **BUILD BACKGROUND**
**ESL Support**

**Tour of the School Library** Lead children on a tour of the school library or resource center. Have children identify the types of resources found in the library: books, encyclopedias and dictionaries, computers, listening centers, and so on.

**Beginning** Show children some of the items in the library and provide them with the English word for each. Ask them to repeat each word, allow children to handle items where appropriate to reinforce vocabulary.

**Intermediate** Ask children to locate items in the library and have them bring or show each item to you. For example, a dictionary, an encyclopedia, a computer.

**Advanced** Ask children questions that would reflect their vocabulary knowledge. For example, "Where can the meaning of a word be found?" (dictionary) "Where could you look to find out about a favorite animal?" (encyclopedia, book, or Internet).

## Augustus Caesar
### Rome

Augustus Caesar was the leader of many lands. He made laws that were fair to all people.

## Kublai Khan
### China

Kublai Khan was a powerful ruler in China. He believed in treating people fairly.

## Try it!

1. How are these leaders alike and different?

2. Name other ways to gather information about people who lived long ago.

3. **On Your Own** Tell or write an interesting fact about each of these people.

241

### Workbook, p. 63

**Gather Information**

Look at the pictures.

| Augustus Caesar | Cleopatra | Mansa Musa |

Write a name on each line.

1. **Mansa Musa** was the ruler of Mali in West Africa.
2. **Augustus Caesar** made laws that were fair to all people.
3. **Cleopatra** was queen of Egypt when she was 18 years old.

**Also on Teacher Resources CD-ROM.**

## 2 Teach and Discuss

**1 How did Kay gather information about people who lived long ago?** She and her grandparents bought postcards at the museum that told about each leader. Recall and Retell

**2 Who are the leaders Kay learned about? Where were they from?** Mansa Musa from West Africa, Cleopatra from Egypt, Augustus Caesar from Rome, and Kublai Kahn from China. Analyze Information

**3 Why were these leaders important?** They did things to help other people and make their country a better place to live. Draw Conclusions

### Test Talk

**Write Your Answer**

**Which one of these people do you think is the most interesting, and why?** Write your answer. Students answers will vary, but they should use information provided on the postcards to support their choice. Remind them that their answer should be complete as well as correct. Analyze Information

## 3 Close and Assess

Divide the class into small groups. Give each group the name of a person who lived long ago. Ask students to tell how they would gather information about that person.

### Try it!

1. They are alike because they all lived long ago and did important things for their country. They are different because they were from different countries, lived at different times; three were men and one was a woman.

2. Students can gather information about people long ago by using books, encyclopedias, the Internet, and by talking to other people.

3. **On Your Own** Children's postcards will vary.

# Lesson ① Wrap-Up

## MEETING INDIVIDUAL NEEDS
## Leveled Practice

**Market Day**
Ask children to select items, such as necklaces, toy trucks, or videos, to sell at a market. Have them draw pictures of their items and display them in their "booth" in the classroom market.

**Easy** Have children label their pictures. **Reteach**

**On-Level** Have children use their pictures to create a poster for their goods. Tell them to include words describing their goods. **Extend**

**Challenge** Have children write a flyer for the market, listing what goods and services are offered. **Enrich**

## Hands-on Activities

### CURRICULUM CONNECTION
### Reading/Vocabulary

## To Market Again

**Objective** Demonstrate understanding of the lesson vocabulary through reading literature.

**Resource** Vocabulary Card: **market**

**Materials** story about a market

**Learning Style** Auditory/Verbal

**Group**

🕐 **Time** 10–15 minutes

**1.** Read aloud *To Market, To Market* by Anne Miranda.

**2.** Ask children what is real about the story and what is not real.

**3.** Then have them draw one of the vegetables the woman buys for soup.

**4.** Display the Vocabulary Card and have children add the word *market* to their "My Word Book."

To Market, To Market
Anne Miranda

### CURRICULUM CONNECTION
### Music

## Singing at the Corner Grocery Store

**Objective** Sing about the items found in a grocery store.

**Materials** *The Corner Grocery Store & Other Songs* by Raffi (Uni/Rounder, 1992)

**Learning Style** Musical

**Group** 🧍🧍🧍🧍

🕐 **Time** 10–15 minutes

**1.** Play the song "The Corner Grocery Store."

**2.** Play the song again and have children sing along with the song.

**3.** Encourage children to make up verses for other items found at the grocery store.

**4.** Have them add the verses to their "My Word Book."

### CURRICULUM CONNECTION
### Writing

## Rhyme Time

**Objective** Write a poem that rhymes.

**Materials** paper, pencils

**Learning Style** Auditory

**Partners** 🧍🧍

🕐 **Time** 10–15 minutes

**1.** Read the nursery rhyme *To Market* again.

**2.** Ask children to identify the words that rhyme. (*pig/jig, hog/jog, bun/done*)

**3.** Have partners list words that rhyme with one of those rhymes and write them down. (*big, fig, dig, wig; frog, clog, log; fun, begun, none, run, son, sun, ton, one, won*)

**4.** Have partners write a two-line poem using two of their rhyming words.

big
fig
dig
wig

# Lesson ② Overview

**How Things Have Changed**
pages 242–243

Children will explore how technology changes the way people live and work.

⏱ Time 10–15 minutes
Resources
• Workbook, p. 64
• Every Student Learns Guide, pp. 110–113

**Joseph Bruchac**
Pages 244–245

Children will learn about Joseph Bruchac.

⏱ Time 10–15 minutes

# Build Background

## Activity

## My Times

 **Time** 20 minutes

Show children pictures of the way people lived long ago and in the recent past, such as a person reading by candlelight or cooling off with a fan blowing on a block of ice. Have children create a collage from magazine photographs of a modern family in a living room or kitchen. Ask children to discuss how household tools and appliances have changed the way people live.

**If time is short,** show children pictures of the way people lived long ago and in the recent past, and have children tell about how life is different today. Prompt them by asking about how people enjoy music and eating.

## Read Aloud

## Phone Home

### by Emily Kurtz

Off to the bedroom
to tell my sister
how much
I miss her!
But she's gabbing
on her cell phone.

Off to the kitchen
to tell my mom I'll assist her!
But she's gabbing
with—you guessed it—my sister
on her cell phone.

I suppose if I don't want to be alone,
I'll have to get a cell phone
of my own.

## Lesson 2

# How Things Have Changed

## Objectives

- Describe how household tools and appliances have changed.

- Describe how technology has changed recreation.

- Describe how technology has changed the way people work.

**QUICK Teaching Plan**

*If time is short,* discuss how technology has changed at work and home.

- Discuss how the objects in the chart on p. 243 have changed.

# 1 Introduce and Motivate

**Preview** Ask children to read aloud what Kay's grandmother says on p. 242. Show children the bar code on various products. Explain that the scanner "reads" the bars to add up the cost of the items. Then explain that in some places, items are still labeled with the price, which the cashier adds up by punching numbered buttons on a cash register.

**Warm Up** To activate prior knowledge, ask children to read aloud what Kay's grandfather says on p. 242. Ask children how they would use a computer to type their name and print it. Then show children a typewriter. Have them type their name on it. Ask what the differences are between the computer and the typewriter.

# 2 Teach and Discuss

### Page 242

**1 How have computers changed the way people work?** Answers will vary, but may include that they make rewriting and saving stories easier.
**Analyze Information**

## Lesson 2

# How Things Have Changed

We learned many interesting things from the grandparents who visited our class. They told us how work has changed. We learned how some things at home have changed too.

**1** I used a typewriter. Now people use computers!

**2** I used to punch buttons at the store. Now I scan.

# Practice and Extend

### READING SKILL
## Categorize

**Make a Then and Now Chart**

- After children have read pp. 242–243, help them brainstorm a list of things that were commonly used in the past and a list of things that are commonly used now. Remind children that many things that were commonly used in the past are still used today.

- Give children squares of paper. Ask them to draw pictures of the things on the lists.

- Have children make a two-column chart with "Then" and "Now" heading the columns.

- Have children complete the chart by pasting their drawings in the appropriate columns. Remind them to keep related things in the same rows.

My class made a chart to show other ways things have changed. How do you think things might change in the future? **4**

**3**

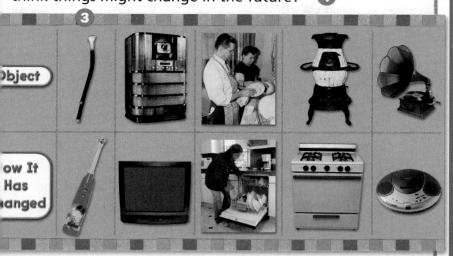

Object

How It Has Changed

## What did you learn ?

1. Tell two ways work has changed.
2. How has something you do for fun changed?
3. **Think and Share** Think of something you use at home. **Predict** how it might change in the future. Draw a picture and write or tell about it.

243

**Workbook, p. 64**

**How Things Have Changed**

Match the pictures.

Draw a radio for the future. **Drawings will vary.**

**Also on Teacher Resources CD-ROM.**

---

**2** **How have store scanners changed the way people work?** Answers will vary, but may include that they make adding the costs of items faster and more accurate. **Analyze Information**

**Page 243**

Discuss how each household tool or appliance in the chart has changed the way families live. Then discuss how the technology in the chart has changed recreation.

**3** **Do all people use the latest things?** Answers will vary but should reflect that not all people use the latest technology. For example, some people might wash dishes by hand. **Analyze Information**

Have children interview their grandparents to find out about recreation when they were children. Then discuss with children how technology has changed recreation from the time when their grandparents were children.

**4** **Do you think the way people have fun has changed?** Answers will vary, but may include that some activities, such as playing computer games, are new, while others, such as playing outdoor sports, are the same. **Hypothesize**

## 3 Close and Assess

Ask children to tell about technology that has changed the way they live. Invite children to make a list with a partner of things that have changed.

## ✓ What did you learn ?

1. Answers will vary but may include that scanning has replaced punching buttons on a cash register, and computers have replaced typewriters.

2. Answers will vary but may include people used to listen to records and now they listen to CDs.

3. **Think and Share** Pictures and descriptions should reflect how something might look in the future.

# CITIZEN HEROES

## Joseph Bruchac

### Objective

• Identify people who exemplify good citizenship and exhibit a love of individualism.

## 1 Introduce and Motivate

**Preview** Tell children that Joseph Bruchac is a Native American who writes down Native American stories. Have them look at the picture on the bottom of p. 245. Explain that Bruchac is signing his name in a book. The signature of a person, called an autograph, is valued by the person purchasing the book. Ask children to read the titles of Bruchac's two books shown on pp. 244–245.

**Warm Up** To activate prior knowledge, ask children to remember what they learned about Native Americans. (Children might remember that they were the first people to live in America and that some hunted for food while others grew food.) Explain to children that many Native Americans, like other peoples around the world, use storytelling as a way to pass along information from parents to children.

## 2 Teach and Discuss

Explain that the word *respect* means to show consideration for someone or something.

### Test Talk

**Locate Key Words in the Text**

**1 What can we learn to respect through many Native American stories?** Each other and the Earth. Have children locate the key words (*respect* and *stories*) in the text that match the key words in the question. **Analyze Information**

---

# CITIZEN HEROES

Joseph Bruchac was born in Saratoga Springs, New York.

## Joseph Bruchac

Joseph lived with his grandparents when he was young. Joseph's grandfather was an Abenaki Indian.

Joseph became interested in the stories told by Native American, or American Indian, elders. Many of the stories told how we should respect each other and the Earth.

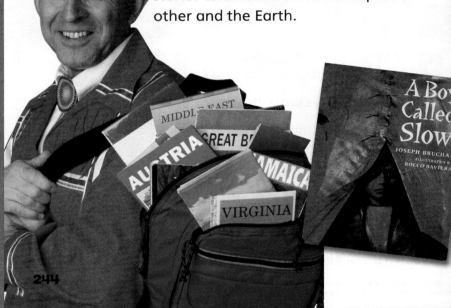

## Practice and Extend

### FYI SOCIAL STUDIES Background

#### About Joseph Bruchac

• Young Joseph would follow his grandfather everywhere. His grandfather showed him how to walk in the woods quietly and to fish.

• Joseph started to write poems when he was in second grade. He liked to read stories about animals.

• Joseph Bruchac showed his love of individualism by writing down the stories told by Native American elders.

• Joseph Bruchac has written more than 50 books for adults and children. His poems, articles, and stories have appeared in more than 500 publications.

• The homelands of the Abenaki (AB uhr NAK ee) tribe were in Maine, New Hampshire, and Vermont.

Today, Joseph Bruchac is a writer. He still listens to stories told by Native American elders. He tells these stories in ❷ many of his books and poems. He also sings songs. Many of the songs tell Native American stories.

Joseph Bruchac respects Native American stories. He thinks it is a good idea to share these stories. He thinks people can learn a lot from them. ❸ ❹

**★ Respect in Action ★**

How does Joseph Bruchac show that he respects Native American stories?

Joseph Bruchac signing one of his books

**245**

### CURRICULUM CONNECTION
### Reading

**The Storyteller's Craft**

Read and discuss any of the following children's books by Joseph Bruchac to children.

- *How Chipmunk Got His Stripes: A Tale of Bragging and Teasing,* by Joseph Bruchac, James Bruchac (illustrator), Jose Aruego (illustrator), and Ariane Dewey (illustrator) (Dial Books for Young Readers, ISBN 0-803-72404-7, 2001) **Easy**

- *Many Nations,* by Joseph Bruchac (Econo-Clad Books, ISBN 0-603-11838-3, 1999), International Reading Teacher's Choice Award **On-Level**

- *Thirteen Moons on Turtle's Back: A Native American Year of Moons,* by Joseph Bruchac and Thomas Locke (illustrator) (Philomel Books, ISBN 0-399-22141-7, 1992) **On-Level**

- *Earth Under Sky Bear's Feet: Native American Poems of the Land, The,* by Joseph Bruchac (Econo-Clad Books, ISBN 0-613-10503-6, 1999) **Challenge**

❷ **Where does Joseph Bruchac get some of his stories from?** He listens to Native American elders.
**Apply Information**

**C** SOCIAL STUDIES STRAND
**Culture**

**Prejudice Reduction** Explain that many Native American stories are about overcoming fear, being helpful, showing respect, and making friends. Tell children that these traditional stories may help them learn to deal with these issues.

❸ **Why does Joseph Bruchac write down the stories he hears?** He wants to share the ways of Native American peoples. He believes other people can learn from them. **Analyze Information**

❹ **What are some ways you can tell a story?** Answers will vary but may include writing a book or poem, singing a song, or speaking to a group. **Apply Information**

## **3 Close and Assess**

Ask children to tell what they learned about Joseph Bruchac. Ask them to discuss with a partner people they respect and how they show their respect.

**★ Respect in Action ★**

Joseph Bruchac listens to stories told by elders and shares them through stories, poems, and songs.

# Lesson ② Wrap-Up

 ## MEETING INDIVIDUAL NEEDS
## Leveled Practice

### Performing Change

Assign groups an object that has changed work, recreation, or tasks in the home. Have groups present performances that show how the object has changed daily life.

**Easy** Assign groups an object such as a washing machine. Help them dramatize how people washed clothes before the washing machine and how people wash clothes in a washing machine. **Reteach**

**On-Level** Assign groups an object such as a car. Help them dramatize how people traveled before the car and how people travel in a car. Have the group explain how the object has changed people's lives. **Extend**

**Challenge** Assign groups an object such as a television. Help them dramatize how people were entertained before television and how people watch television. Have the group explain how the object has changed communication and recreation. **Enrich**

 ## Hands-on Activities

 **CURRICULUM CONNECTION**
### Writing/Vocabulary

## Computers of the Future

**Objective** Demonstrate understanding of the word *change*.

**Materials** drawings of computers, crayons

**Learning Style** Spatial

**Individual**

🕐 **Time** 10–15 minutes

1. Provide children with simple drawings of a computer on large paper. Tell children to make the computer friendlier for the future.

2. Give children suggestions, such as propping a hat on top or decorating areas with stars or stripes.

3. Have children add a sentence about how the computer will change in the future and then show their picture.

 **CURRICULUM CONNECTION**
### Art

## Bar Code

**Objective** Make a bar code.

**Materials** paper, crayons

**Learning Style** Spatial

**Individual** 👤

🕐 **Time** 10–15 minutes

1. Explain to children that a bar code is a band of thick and thin black bars on a white background, printed on items for sale in a store. Tell that these bars are scanned by a computer that lists the price (and other information) about the item. Remind children of the bar codes they saw earlier.

2. Have children draw the back of a cereal box. Tell them to draw a bar code on the lower right side of the box.

3. You may want to display their drawings on the bulletin board.

 **CURRICULUM CONNECTION**
### Reading

## Things Change

**Objective** Tell about changes between the past and present.

**Materials** paper, crayons, book

**Learning Style** Visual/Linguistic

**Group** 👤👤👤👤

🕐 **Time** 10–15 minutes

1. Read with children *When I Was Young in the Mountains* by Cynthia Rylant.

2. Discuss the story with children. Then divide them into groups and have them name the household items (such as the oil lamp, candle, old black stove) and activities (such as pumping water from a well) that have changed since the time of the story. Then have children tell what has replaced the items and activities.

3. Have children draw a picture of one thing from the story that has changed.

# Lesson 3 Overview

## Inventors and Inventions
pages 246–249

Children will learn about inventions that have helped people to communicate better and the inventors who made them.

 **Time 20–30 minutes**

 **Resources**
- Workbook, p. 65
- Vocabulary Cards
  communicate | invention | inventor
- Every Student Learns Guide, pp. 114–117

## Telephones
Pages 250–251

Children will explore the development of the telephone.

**Time 15–20 minutes**

# Build Background

## Activity

### Playing Telephone

 **Time 15 minutes**

Have children play the game *Telephone*. Ask children to sit in a large circle. Start a message around the circle by whispering to the first child Alexander Graham Bell's first words spoken over a telephone: "Mr. Watson, come here. I want you!" Have each child whisper the message to the next child. When the message gets around the circle, have the last child say it out loud. Repeat the original message. Discuss with children the reliability of passing information by word of mouth.

**If time is short,** discuss the telephone as a way for people to communicate with each other.

## Read Aloud

### I've Been Working on the Railroad

**by Bill Basham**

I've been working on the railroad
All the livelong day.
I've been working on the railroad
Just to pass the time away.

Can't you hear the whistle blowing?
Rise up so early in the morn.
Can't you hear the captain shouting?
Dinah, blow your horn.

## Lesson 3

# Inventors and Inventions

## Objectives

- Describe how technology has changed communication.

- Identify historic figures such as Alexander Graham Bell and Thomas Edison who have exhibited a love of inventiveness.

## Vocabulary

**communicate** to give and get information (p. 246)

**invention** something new (p. 246)

**inventor** someone who makes or invents something (p. 247)

### QUICK Teaching Plan

*If time is short,* discuss the meaning of the word *communicate.* Discuss different inventions that people have used to communicate.

- Tell children who Alexander Graham Bell and Thomas Edison were and describe their inventions.

## 1 Introduce and Motivate

**Preview** Display the Vocabulary Card **communicate**. Ask children to name things that people use to give and receive information. Tell children that people not only communicate information but also thoughts and feelings. Then display the Vocabulary Cards **invention** and **inventor**. Explain that an invention is something made for the first time and an inventor is the person who makes the invention.

**Warm Up** To activate prior knowledge, ask children to recall inventions that they have already learned about. Remind children that they learned about Benjamin Franklin, who invented the rocking chair. Explain that they will learn about inventions that help people communicate. Discuss how Americans have customs and celebrations that reflect their love of individualism and inventiveness.

## Lesson 3

# Inventors and Inventions

Telling stories and singing songs are two ways to communicate. You **communicate** when you give and get information.

An **invention** is something new. Many inventions have helped people communicate. The printing press and the telephone are two important inventions people have used to communicate.

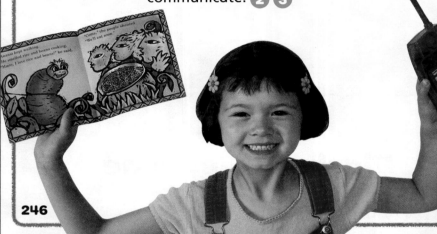

246

# Practice and Extend

### READING/VOCABULARY
### Predict
*Target Skill*

- Tell children that in this lesson they will learn about inventions that help people communicate better.

- Distribute a prediction chart. Ask children to predict what three inventions they might learn about that help people communicate better. Have them write their predictions in the "My Prediction" column.

- After children have read pp. 246–249, tell them to complete the chart by filling in the "What I Actually Learned" column.

### WEB SITE
### Technology

You can look up vocabulary words online. Click on *Social Studies Library* and select the dictionary at **www.sfsocialstudies.com**.

Long ago, there were no machines to copy the pages of a book. Books had to be copied by hand. This took a long time. Then an inventor made a machine called the printing press. An **inventor** is someone who makes or invents something new.

People could use the printing press to make many copies of a page. Books and newspapers could be made more quickly. People in many places around the world were able to get information from the books and newspapers.

Johannes Gutenberg was the inventor of the printing press.

First printing press

## SOCIAL STUDIES
## Background

**Other Inventors and Inventions**

- There were many women inventors. Mary Anderson invented windshield wipers; Beulah Henry, a clock for teaching children time; Margaret Knight, a machine to make square-bottomed paper bags; Grace Hopper, a computer program that could understand the English language and translate it into computer code.

- There were also many African American inventors. Elijah McCoy invented a lubricator for steam engines. Benjamin Banneker constructed the first wooden clock in America. Garrett Morgan invented the yellow caution light.

- Other inventions that have helped us to communicate: telegraph (1837), typewriter (1867), television (circa 1925), and cellular telephone (1979).

# 2 Teach and Discuss

### Page 246

**❶ When two people are together, what do they use besides words to communicate?** Answers will vary but may include talking, making sounds, using facial expressions, and making gestures. **Analyze Information**

**C SOCIAL STUDIES STRAND
Culture**

"Talking" drums is one kind of communication that people have used. People in African villages sent messages by beating drums. This practice is still used today by some people in parts of Africa.

**❷ What inventions are used to communicate besides the printing press and the telephone?** Possible answers: The computer, radio, and television **Make Inferences**

**❸ With whom do you communicate? What do you communicate?** Answers will vary. Children may say that they communicate with their family, friends, and teacher about a variety of things. **Apply Information**

### Page 247

**❹ What way of bookmaking did the printing press replace?** Copying a book by hand **Analyze Information**

**C SOCIAL STUDIES STRAND
Culture**

Tell children that the printing press used metal type that was manually arranged, letter by letter, to form pages of text. This type was inked and pressed onto paper—hence the name *printing press*.

**❺ How did the invention of the printing press increase the spread of information?** Possible answer: More books could easily be made, so more people could read them. **Hypothesize**

Lesson **3**

continued

## Page 248

**6** **What had to be put in place before people miles away from each other could talk by telephone?** Wires between the telephones
**Make inferences**

✓ **Ongoing Assessment**

**If...** children do not understand that wires were needed to connect telephones,

**then...** explain that until recently telephone messages were usually sent over wires by means of electricity.

**7** **How do you think people far away from each other communicated before the telephone was invented?** Answers will vary but may include by letter or telegraph. **Hypothesize**

A man named Alexander Graham Bell invented the telephone. With a telephone, people did not have to be in the same room to talk to each other. They could use the telephone to talk to **6** someone miles away. The telephone **7** helped change the way people communicate.

**Alexander Graham Bell**

1847–1922

Alexander Graham Bell taught at a school for the deaf. He helped start the first telephone company called Bell Telephone Company.

**Thomas Alva Edison**

1847–1931

Thomas Edison made mor than 1,000 inventions. Many of his inventions helped people communicat better. He also invented many other things, such a the light bulb we use toda

248

# Practice and Extend

**ESL** **ACCESS CONTENT**
## ESL Support

**Inventions** Remind children that some inventions help people communicate better. Display pictures with labels of the following: leaf, telephone, flower, radio, dog, printing press, rock. Read the labels aloud as you point to the pictures.

**Beginning** As you reread the labels, one at a time, ask children if and why the object is an invention.

**Intermediate** Have children choose an invention. Then have children tell how the invention helps people communicate.

**Advanced** Have children choose two inventions. Then have children help create a Venn diagram comparing each way of communication.

*For additional ESL Support, use Every Student Learns Guide, pp. 114–117.*

**FYI** **SOCIAL STUDIES**
## Background

**About Alexander Graham Bell**

- Alexander Graham Bell was born in 1847 in Edinburgh, Scotland.

- Influenced by his father, who invented "visible speech" (a way to help the deaf position their vocal organs to make sound), he studied sound.

- He wanted to invent a machine that would transmit sound electronically. In 1876, he was granted a patent for his "electrical speech machine," which we now call a telephone.

- Bell helped found the National Geographic Society, the world's largest nonprofit scientific and educational organization.

Thomas Alva Edison was a famous inventor. One of his inventions was the phonograph. This was the first time people could hear recorded sounds. What do you use to hear recorded sounds?

Today, people around the world communicate in many ways. We even have machines that let people on Earth talk to astronauts in space!

A phonograph from long ago

## What did you learn?

1. Why are Edison and Bell such important **inventors**?

2. How did Alexander Graham Bell change the way people **communicate**?

3. **Think and Share** Recall and retell what you learned about Thomas Alva Edison.

249

**8 How do you think people listened to music before Thomas Edison invented the phonograph?** They listened to live performances. **Apply Information**

### Test Talk

**Use Information from the Text**

**9 How are the activities of Bell and Edison alike and different?** Answers will vary but may include the following. Alike: Both made inventions, the telephone and the phonograph, that send sound to help people communicate. Different: Bell sent sound live. Edison sent recorded sound. Have children look back at the text to make sure they have the right information. **Compare and Contrast**

**10 Why do you think astronauts need to communicate from space?** Possible answer: To get instructions from people on Earth **Analyze Information**

## 3 Close and Assess

Ask children to tell what the word *invention* means. Have them discuss with a partner the inventions that help people communicate.

### ✓ What did you learn?

1. Edison and Bell helped people to communicate better.

2. Alexander Graham Bell made it possible for people who are far away from each other to talk.

3. **Think and Share** Answers will vary but should include that Edison invented the phonograph.

### FYI SOCIAL STUDIES Background

**About Thomas Edison**

- Thomas Edison set up a small chemical laboratory in the cellar of his home when he was only 10 years old.

- Edison invented a transmitter that vastly increased the range of Alexander Graham Bell's telephone.

- Edison received more than 1,000 patents.

- Edison helped form the Edison Electric Light Company. In 1882, the company completed the first permanent, commercial power station.

**Workbook, p. 65**

Inventors and Inventions

Write to tell about each inventor. **Possible answers:**

Thomas Alva Edison **invented the phonograph. He also invented many other things that helped people communicate better.**

Alexander Graham Bell **invented the telephone. He also helped start the first telephone company.**

Write how the two men are alike.

Edison          Bell

phonograph   **inventor**   telephone

**Also on Teacher Resources CD-ROM.**

# Telephones

## Objectives

- Obtain information about a topic using a variety of visual sources, such as pictures.

- Describe how technology has changed communication.

## 1 Introduce and Motivate

**Preview** Ask children to look at the illustrations on pp. 250–251. Ask children to tell whether they have ever seen any telephones that look like those pictured.

**Warm Up** To activate prior knowledge, have children look carefully at the pictures. Have them tell what features are the same on these telephones as on telephones of today. (a speaking part and a listening part)

# Telephones

Alexander Graham Bell invented the telephone in 1876. How do telephones help people? **1**

Earpiece

Alexander Graham Bell makes a telephone call.

Bell's "Box telephone" of 1876–1877 had a combined mouthpiece and earpiece. **2**

Mouthpiece and earpiece combined

In early years, an operator took your number and the number you wanted. Then the operator connected the call.

The first telephone wires were copper with a glass covering. **3**

This wall phone of 1879 was invented by Thomas Edison.

Mouthpiece

250

# Practice and Extend

## CURRICULUM CONNECTION
### Drama

**Telephone Etiquette** Teach children proper telephone manners and telephone safety.

- Bring in two telephones that are not connected. Show children how the phones work.

- Teach children proper phone etiquette. Model a polite way to answer a phone (cordially say "hello"), to ask for a person ("May I speak to LaJeanne, please?"), and to end a conversation. ("It was nice to talk to you.") Have children practice these skills with a partner.

- Suggest to children that they ask older family members how much information they should disclose to a caller.

- Teach children to dial *911* for an emergency. Emphasize that this number is for emergencies only.

By 1885, the mouthpiece and earpiece were combined to form a handset.

Earpiece

"Cradle" telephones like this one were popular by the 1890s. This phone is from 1937.

Hook for earpiece

~piece

Mouthpiece

**4 5** Numbered dial

251

**CURRICULUM CONNECTION**
## Math

### Calculating Telephone Numbers

- Have children write down phone numbers as a result of math problems. For example, say: "The first number is 20 minus 11." Do this for seven numbers.

- Make sure children put the numbers in groups of three, then groups of four, separated by a hyphen.

# 2 Teach and Discuss

Ask children to remember how people communicated over long distances before the invention of the telephone. (by letter or telegraph) Explain to children that it took a while for most homes to get telephone service.

**1 How do you think people's lives changed after they got telephones in their homes?** Answers will vary but might include that they didn't write as many letters and they spent more time on the phone and less time doing other activities. **Hypothesize**

Have children follow along as you read the text. Ask them to point to each picture as you tell about it.

**2 How did people use a "box telephone?"** They spoke and listened through the same piece. **Analyze Pictures**

**3 What were the first telephone wires made of?** Copper **Analyze Information**

**4 How did the invention of the dial on the phone change the way people used the telephone?** It allowed people to make their own connections without an operator. **Cause and Effect**

**5 How are our phones today different from the ones pictured?** They are smaller, lighter, portable, and (most) have buttons not dials. **Compare and Contrast**

# 3 Close and Assess

Ask children to describe how phones have changed from when they were first invented.

# Lesson ③ Wrap-Up

## MEETING INDIVIDUAL NEEDS
### Leveled Practice

**Find Pictures of Communication**

Have children find pictures in magazines or newspapers that show people communicating. Have children pay close attention to any technologies people are using in the pictures. Have children make a collage of their pictures.

**Easy** Have each child tell about one of his or her pictures. Write down the topics on chart paper as children tell about each. Invite volunteers to share a second picture after everyone has had a turn. Display the list in the classroom. **Reteach**

**On-Level** Have children pantomime one of the pictures, for example, talking on the telephone or reading a book. Have the class guess how he or she is communicating. **Extend**

**Challenge** Have children write about some of the pictures they collected. Have them write a sentence for each picture that tells how it stands for communication. **Enrich**

## Hands-on Activities

**CURRICULUM CONNECTION**
### Writing/Vocabulary

# Related Words

**Objective** Demonstrate understanding of the lesson vocabulary.

**Materials** paper, pencils

**Resources** Vocabulary Cards **invention, inventor, communicate**

**Learning Style** Verbal/Linguistic

**Individual** 👤

🕐 **Time** 10–15 minutes

1. Tell children that the word *invent* means to make something new. Explain that adding a syllable to the end of *invent* would change its meaning.

2. Ask children to write two words from the lesson that are related to *invent*.

3. Remind children to add *invention* and *inventor* as well as *communicate* to their "My Word Book."

**CURRICULUM CONNECTION**
### Art

# Business Cards

**Objective** Print multiple copies.

**Materials** rubber stamp, letters and shapes, ink pad, card-size pieces of paper

**Learning Style** Visual/Bodily/Kinesthetic

**Individual** 👤

🕐 **Time** 45 minutes

1. Help children print three "business cards" using a rubber stamp. Explain to them that a rubber stamp works like a printing press.

2. Have children set their name in a rubber stamp. Help children make sure that the letters are right side up and facing in the right direction.

3. Ink the rubber stamp for children. Have them print their name on three "business cards."

4. Invite children to decorate their cards with stars or other shapes.

**CURRICULUM CONNECTION**
### Drama

# All Riiiight!

**Objective** Communicate using nonverbal means.

**Learning Style** Auditory/Visual/Bodily/Kinesthetic

**Partners** 👥

🕐 **Time** 45 minutes

1. Remind children that people can communicate not only without inventions but without words.

2. First, have partners tell words that indicate assent (*yes, okay*) and congratulations or celebration (*all right!, way to go!, yes!*).

3. Then have partners show nonverbal ways of displaying assent (thumbs-up, nodding, OK sign) and congratulations or celebration (handshake, high five, upraised arms).

# Lesson 4 Overview

| | | |
|---|---|---|
| **How Travel Has Changed**<br>pages 252–253 | Children will explore how land transportation in the United States has changed from horse and wagon to the modern automobile. | ⏱ Time 10–15 minutes<br>**Resources**<br>• Workbook, p. 66<br>• Every Student Learns Guide, pp. 118–121 |
| **Read a Bar Graph**<br>pages 254–255 | Children will learn how to interpret a bar graph. | ⏱ Time 10–15 minutes<br>**Resource**<br>• Workbook, p. 67 |
| **Mae Jemison**<br>pages 256–257 | Children will explore the life of Mae Jemison, the first African American woman in space. | ⏱ Time 10–15 minutes |

# Build Background

## Activity

### Modes of Transport

 **Time** 20 minutes

Have children look through magazines to find pictures of things people use to get from one place to another. Have children create a collage with the pictures. Challenge children not to cut out any duplicate types of transportation. Possible types of transportation include: airplane, helicopter, and spaceship; car, truck, bus, motorcycle; train, subway, trolley; ship, submarine, boat; bicycle, skates, skateboard; horse, camel, elephant.

**If time is short,** ask children to brainstorm ways that people get from one place to another.

## Read Aloud

### Over Land

**by Allison Rowe**

Giddy-up, giddy-up,
I travel by horse.
Hold tight to the reins.
Don't fall off, of course.

Swish, swish,
I travel by bike.
Pedal hard and then glide.
It's coasting I like.

Vroom, vroom,
I travel by car.
Looking out the window,
I see near and far.

Don't care how I go,
Old or new,
As long as I
return to you.

## Lesson 4 How Travel Has Changed

### Objective
- Describe how technology has changed transportation.

**QUICK Teaching Plan**

*If time is short,* discuss the different modes of transportation over land.

- Explain that transportation has changed as new things were invented, such as the engine.

- Discuss how many forms of transportation are used to carry goods from place to place.

## 1 Introduce and Motivate

**Preview** Ask children to look at the time line and name the ways people travel that are shown. Ask them to tell which ways they have used to travel.

**Warm Up** To activate prior knowledge, remind children how inventions (printing press, telephone, phonograph) have changed the way people communicate. Tell children that there have also been inventions that changed the way people get from place to place. Explain that the wheel itself was a new invention once. Ask children what means people use to travel with and without wheels.

## 2 Teach and Discuss

**Pages 252–253**

Explain to children that the time line shows a period of time in order from earliest to latest. Discuss each picture. Explain that the horse pulls the wagon. Tell children that another way to say this is: *the horse provides the power for the wagon to move.*

**1** **What provides the power for a bicycle to move?** Pushing on the pedals makes the wheels turn. Make Inferences

**2** **What provides the power for a car to move?** Gas makes the engine run. Make Inferences

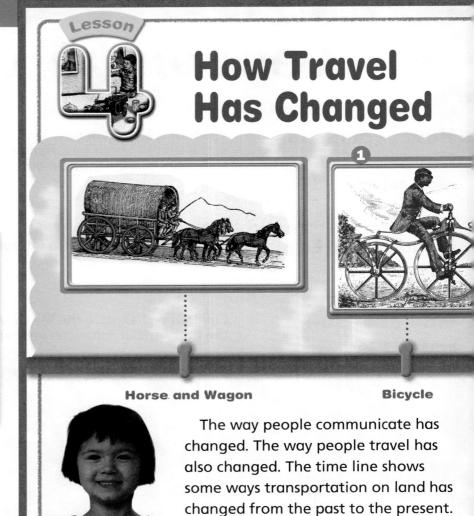

## Lesson 4 How Travel Has Changed

Horse and Wagon          Bicycle

The way people communicate has changed. The way people travel has also changed. The time line shows some ways transportation on land has changed from the past to the present.

252

## Practice and Extend

**READING SKILL**
**Sequence**

**Creating a Time Line** Have children complete a time line for different types of transportation.

- After children have read pp. 252–253, give them a time line with *First, Next,* and *Last* marked off below the line.

- Write the following words on the board: *airplane, spaceship, glider.* Discuss with children these modes of air transportation.

- Ask children to think about which way of air travel came first, next, and last. Then have them draw pictures of the modes of transportation over the appropriate times.

**3** **4**

Old Model T Car                    Car of Today

## What did you learn

1. How has the way we travel on land changed?

2. Name other ways people can travel on land.

3. **Think and Share** **Predict** how people might drive in the future. Draw a picture and tell about it.

253

**FYI** SOCIAL STUDIES **Background**

**Facts About Transportation**

- Besides horses, animals that transport goods are oxen, which pull carts; dogs, which pull sleds; and mules, which carry bags.
- Wheels were solid wood until about 2000 B.C., when spokes were invented to make the wheels lighter and faster.
- The first self-propelled bicycle was invented in 1839 by Kirkpatrick Macmillan in Scotland.

**Workbook, p. 66**

**How Travel Has Changed**

Draw to show 3 ways to travel. **Drawings will vary.**

On Land

In the Air

Over Water

Write how one way might change.
**Answers will vary.**

**Also on Teacher Resources CD-ROM.**

**3** **Which way of travel came first, the bicycle or the Model T car?** Bicycle **Interpret Time Lines**

✓ **Ongoing Assessment**

**If...** children cannot tell which way of travel came before or after another,

**then...** explain that a time line works from left to right. Have children trace the time line from the left (beginning) to the right (end) with their finger.

**4** **How are the ways to travel shown on the time line alike?** Answers will vary but may include that they all move on land. **Compare and Contrast**

**$ SOCIAL STUDIES STRAND**
**Economics**

Explain that many forms of transportation, such as trucks, trains, and ships, are used to carry goods from one place to another. Ask children to tell what kinds of goods a truck might carry. (Possible answers: food, clothing, furniture, appliances, electronics, and other things sold in stores) Discuss advantages and disadvantages of each form of transportation.

## 3 Close and Assess

Ask children to list ways people travel over ice and snow. Have partners draw a picture of two people traveling over ice or snow, one using a motorized means of transportation, the other using a non-motorized means of transportation.

✓ ## What did you learn

1. Answers will vary but may include that many people now use cars that move at fast speeds. As a consequence, travel takes less time.

2. Camel, horse; truck, bus, motorcycle; skateboard, skates, scooter; train; sled

3. **Think and Share** Drawings and oral descriptions should reflect how people might drive in the future. Suggest that children explain what powers their means of transportation.

# Read a Bar Graph

## Objectives
- Obtain information about a topic using a variety of visual sources, such as pictures.
- Create visual and written material, including graphs.

## Vocabulary
**bar graph** a way to compare groups (p. 254)

# 1 Introduce and Motivate

**Preview** Ask children to look at the bar graph on p. 254. Tell them that it compares the quantity of things using bars of different lengths. The more there is of a thing, the longer the bar.

**Warm Up** To activate prior knowledge, ask children to name the places where things travel. (on land, under ground, in the air, in space, on water, under water) Ask children to name where the things on the side of the bar graph travel.

# Read a Bar Graph

A **bar graph** helps you compare groups. Look at this bar graph. The title is at the top of the graph. The pictures on the side of the graph show how Kay's class thinks children will travel to school in the future. ❶ ❷ ❸

**Getting to School in the Future**

254

# Practice and Extend

**CURRICULUM CONNECTION**
**Math**

### Measurement
- Have children "travel" from one starting point to three destinations in the room, such as from the front desk to the board, the window, and the door.
- Help children measure the three distances.
- Write the destinations and the distances on the board.
- Ask children which are the longest and shortest distances.
- Help children create a bar graph comparing the distances they traveled.

Use your finger to follow the bar next to the rocket. Find the number at the bottom of the graph. It shows that seven children think people will travel to school by rocket in the future.

## Try it!

1. What is the title of the **bar graph**?

2. How does Kay's class think most children will travel to school in the future?

3. **On Your Own** Make a bar graph with your class of favorite ways to travel. Predict what most of your class will choose.

255

### Workbook, p. 67

**Read a Bar Graph**

Circle your answer to each question.

Getting to School

| Bus | Car | Bike | Walk |

1 2 3 4 5 6 7 8 9 0

1. How many children walk to school?
   two    (six)

2. How many children take a bus?
   (ten)    none

3. How many children ride bikes?
   one    (two)

4. How do most of the children get to school?
   (by bus)    by car

Directions: Use the bar graph to answer the questions. Circle your answers.    Home Activity: Help your child make a simple bar graph to show the kinds of pets in your neighborhood and the number of each kind.

**Also on Teacher Resources CD-ROM.**

---

## 2 Teach and Discuss

Explain to children that the bar graph shows the number of children in Kay's class who chose a way of travel that they think will be used by children in the future.

### Test Talk

**Use Information from Graphics**

**1 How many children chose the power pack machine?** Four; Tell children to use information from the graph to support their answer. **Interpret Graphs**

**2 Did more children in Kay's class think children in the future will travel by round machine or jet shoes?** Jet shoes **Interpret Graphs**

**3 What way of travel did the fewest number of children choose?** Power pack **Interpret Graphs**

## 3 Close and Assess

Have children vote on their favorite way to travel: bicycle, skateboard, skates, or scooter. Have partners create bar graphs showing the results.

### Try it!

1. "Getting to School in the Future" is the title of the bar graph.

2. Kay's class thinks that most children in the future will travel to school using jet shoes.

3. **On Your Own** Make sure the bar graphs include a title, pictures of ways to travel on the side, and numbers of children along the bottom. Ask children to double check that they have accurately represented the results of the vote.

# Mae Jemison

Read Together · Biography

## Objective

- Identify people who exhibit a love of individualism.

## 1 Introduce and Motivate

**Preview** Write each of the words used to describe Mae Jemison on the board: *doctor, scientist, educator, astronaut.* Help children define each word. (Doctor: a person who treats people who are sick or injured. Scientist: a person who is an expert in studying living things, what things are made of, heat and magnetism, and so on. Educator: a teacher or a specialist in education. Astronaut: a person who travels in space.)

**Warm Up** To activate prior knowledge, point to the picture of the spaceship on p. 256. Explain that this is the space shuttle taking off. Point to the picture of Mae Jemison on the same page. Explain that she is wearing a space suit and holding a helmet. Help children identify some of the patches on the space suit: American flag, wings (the insignia of the United States Air Force), and NASA.

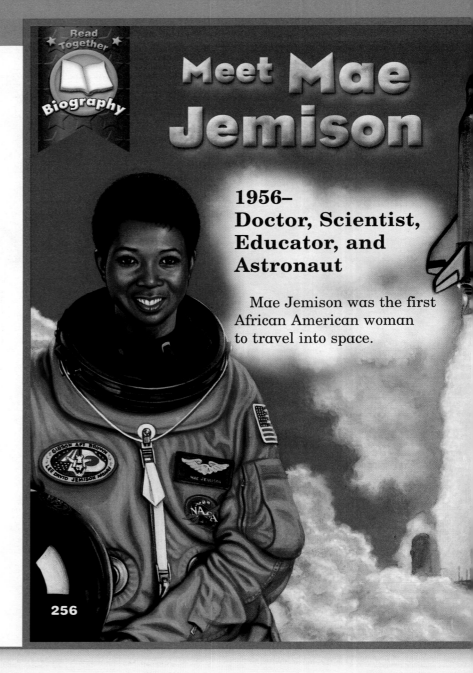

Read Together · Biography

# Meet Mae Jemison

### 1956–
### Doctor, Scientist, Educator, and Astronaut

Mae Jemison was the first African American woman to travel into space.

256

# Practice and Extend

## SOCIAL STUDIES Background

### About Mae Jemison

- Mae Jemison's parents encouraged her to do her best. She was an excellent student. She earned degrees in chemical engineering and medicine.
- After receiving her *Doctor of Medicine* degree, she went to Africa to provide medical care for the Peace Corps crew and U.S. Embassy workers.
- Mae Jemison was one of 15 astronaut candidates selected from 2000 applicants. She flew on one mission into space in 1992. She worked for NASA for more than five years.
- She now works on projects to help developing countries have more technology. Her group is called the Jemison Group, Inc.

## WEB SITE Technology

You may help children find out more about Mae Jemison by clicking on *Meet the People* at **www.sfsocialstudies.com**.

Mae liked science when she was a child. She grew up to become a doctor and scientist. Mae Jemison traveled many places around the world. She helped to care for the people living in each place. ❶

Later, Mae Jemison joined the NASA Space Program. She was the science mission specialist on the space shuttle *Endeavour.* In space, she helped do many experiments. Some of these experiments looked at how being in space affected people and animals. ❷

After she left NASA, Mae Jemison started a group that works on many different projects. The group started a science camp for children. The camp is called ❸ The Earth We Share. At the camp, children from around the world learn about science.

Mae Jemison was born in Decatur, Alabama.

Mae Jemison working in space

### Think and Share

Think about something that interests you. Tell what jobs you might do using your interest.

For more information, go online to *Meet the People* at www.sfsocialstudies.com.

257

## 2 Teach and Discuss

❶ **What did Mae Jemison grow up to become?** Both a doctor and scientist. **Apply Information**

### SOCIAL STUDIES STRAND
### Geography

Explain to children that NASA stands for National Aeronautics and Space Administration. NASA studies and explores science and space. Two of its major facilities are the John F. Kennedy Space Center in Merritt Island, Florida, and the Lyndon B. Johnson Space Center in Houston, Texas. Help children find Merritt Island and Houston on a map.

❷ **What experiments did Mae Jemison perform in space for the NASA Space Program?** Experiments that looked at how being in space affected people and animals **Analyze Information**

Explain to children that an ordinary person may show his or her love of individualism by standing out from others.

❸ **How does Mae Jemison stand out from other people?** Answers will vary but may include: She is a doctor and a scientist. She was an astronaut. She likes to help children from around the world learn about science. **Make Inferences**

## 3 Close and Assess

Ask children to tell about Mae Jemison's accomplishments. Invite them to write a short paragraph telling why people admire her.

**Think and Share**

Children's responses should reflect jobs using their interest.

# Lesson ④ Wrap-Up

## MEETING INDIVIDUAL NEEDS
## Leveled Practice

### I Go With My Family . . .

Read children the book *I Go with My Family to Grandma's* by Riki Levinson, which is widely available in libraries. Show the illustrations of the different ways of traveling used to get to Grandma's house in New York City.

**Easy** Have children name the ways of traveling used in the story. (bicycle, trolley, horse and wagon, train, car, ferry) Have them tell whether people still commonly use these ways of traveling in the United States. **Reteach**

**On-Level** Assign groups one of the illustrations showing ways to travel. Have groups discuss what it would be like to travel in the way shown. Have them tell whether people still commonly use this way of traveling in the United States. **Extend**

**Challenge** Have children select one of the illustrations showing ways to travel. Ask them to imagine that they are the storyteller and to tell about their travels. Have them describe what the ride feels like, what they see, and where they are going. **Enrich**

## Hands-on Activities

### CURRICULUM CONNECTION
### Writing/Vocabulary

## A Mazin'!

**Objective** Demonstrate understanding of the lesson vocabulary.

**Materials** Pencils

**Learning Style** Verbal/Linguistic

**Individual**

🕐 **Time** 10–15 minutes

1. Explain to children that the word *travel* means to go from one place to another.

2. Distribute copies of a maze. Have children take a trip through the maze from home to the park.

3. Explain to children that some of the roads go to the park, but others are dead ends. Tell them that they cannot cross any lines as they travel.

### CURRICULUM CONNECTION
### Science

## Zoom Rockets

**Objective** Create a picture showing travel in the future.

**Materials** paper, crayons

**Learning Style** Visual

**Individual**

🕐 **Time** 10–15 minutes

1. Have children draw a picture of people flying with backpack rockets. Tell children that these rockets enable people to fly among tree tops or over houses, but no higher.

2. Encourage children to create a name for their backpack rocket and share it with the class.

### CURRICULUM CONNECTION
### Music

## Transportation Songs

**Objective** Demonstrate understanding of ways to travel by analyzing songs.

**Materials** Paper, pencils, words to songs if not known

**Learning Style** Auditory/Verbal/Musical

**Group**

🕐 **Time** 10–15 minutes

1. Sing transportation songs with children: "She'll Be Coming Round the Mountain," "I've Been Working on the Railroad," "Row, Row, Row Your Boat," "The Wheels on the Bus."

2. Have children identify and discuss the way of travel in each song.

3. Have children draw one of the ways of traveling that are illustrated in the songs.

# Lesson 5 Overview

**Life Around the World**
pages 258–261

Children will learn about the world and explore how its people are alike and different.

⏱ Time 15–20 minutes

**Resources**
- Workbook, p. 68
- Vocabulary Card world
- Every Student Learns Guide, pp. 122–125

**Laurence Yep**
pages 262–263

Children will learn about Laurence Yep, a Chinese American who writes about the Chinese American way of life.

⏱ Time 10–15 minutes

**It Is Time to Leave**
pages 264–265

Children will learn what people in other countries say when they part.

⏱ Time 10–15 minutes

# Build Background

**Activity**

## Highlight the World

⏱ **Time** 30 minutes

Show children on a globe where the four children from around the world live. Locate their countries and continents. (Carlitos—Argentina—South America; Mónika—Hungary—Europe; Esta—Tanzania—Africa; Daisuke—Japan—Asia) Place stickies with the first letter of the four children's names to their continents. As you point to a letter, say the name and have children repeat it.

**If time is short,** locate the four countries and continents on a globe.

**Read Aloud**

## Couplet

**by Robert Louis Stevenson**

The world is so full
  of a number of things,
I'm sure we should all
  be as happy as kings.

# Lesson 5

## Life Around the World

### Objective
- Compare housing, clothes, and foods from different parts of the world.

### Vocabulary
**world** a name for Earth and everything on it (p. 258)

## QUICK Teaching Plan

**If time is short,** discuss the meaning of the word *world*

- Discuss with children how the clothing, food, and homes of children around the world are alike and different than theirs.

- Have children find the places in the lesson on a globe.

## 1 Introduce and Motivate

**Preview** Display the Vocabulary Card **world** to children. Tell them that a ship can sail around the world. Ask them what countries they would like to sail to and why.

**Warm Up** To activate prior knowledge, ask children to point to ocean and land areas on the picture of the world on p. 258.

## 2 Teach and Discuss

### Page 258

**1 Where do you think the picture of the world was taken from?** It was probably taken from a space satellite or a space shuttle.
**Make Inferences**

---

# Lesson 5

# Life Around the World

The world looks different from way up in space.

From space, Dr. Jemison could look down at the world. The **world** is a nam for Earth and everything on it. Look at th picture. It shows how the world looks from space. **1**

USA

258

## Practice and Extend

### READING SKILL
### Compare and Contrast

- Discuss with children how the children shown on pp. 258–261 are alike and different from them.
- Give children a copy of a Venn diagram.
- Have children pick one of the children they learn about and compare and contrast what the child eats or wears with what they eat or wear.
- Have children fill in the diagram with the information.

From space, everything on the world might look like it is the same. When you are closer, you can see how people around the world are alike and different. Look at the pictures of children around the world. How is the clothing they wear like what you wear? How is it different?

My name is Mónika. I live in Hungary.

My name is Carlitos. I live in Argentina.

My name is Esta. I live in Tanzania.

My name is Daisuke. I live in Japan.

259

**SOCIAL STUDIES STRAND**
## Geography

As you read the captions to children, have them repeat the names and countries. (Daisuke is pronounced dye SOO keh; Tanzania is pronounced TAN zuh NEE uh or tan ZAN ee uh.) Show children where the children of the world live. Locate their countries on a globe. Point out the continents where the countries are located. (Argentina—North America; Hungary—Europe; Tanzania—Africa; Japan—Asia) Invite children to find other countries on the continents.

**2 What country does Mónika live in?** Hungary **Which child lives in Argentina?** Carlitos **Which child lives in Africa?** Esta **Which continent does Daisuke live on?** Asia
**Apply Information/Interpret Maps**

## Test Talk

**Locate Key Words in the Question**
**3 What ways, besides clothing, can people be alike and different?** Answers may vary, but might include: food, homes, customs (e.g., celebrations), work, transportation. Tell children that key words such as *alike* and *different* tell them to look for similarities and contrasts.
**Compare and Contrast**

**FYI** SOCIAL STUDIES
## Background

**About Our World**

- More than two-thirds of Earth's surface is made up of water. The rest is land.
- Earth has four oceans. They are (from largest to smallest) the Pacific, Atlantic, Indian, and Arctic.
- The world's largest country in area is Russia.

**WEB SITE**
## Technology

You can look up vocabulary words online. Click on *Social Studies Library* and select the dictionary at **www.sfsocial studies.com**.

Unit 6 • Lesson 5    **259**

**Pages 260–261**

Discuss the chart with children. As you point to a box, have children point to it. Help children describe ways the children from around the world are alike and different. Encourage children to describe ways that are not in the chart, such as language, climate, and age. Use the DK book *Children Just Like Me* or other books to aid the discussion.

**4** **What is one food that Mónika eats?** Meat and vegetable soup
**Analyze Pictures**

**5** **How is Esta's food different from Daisuke's?** Esta eats beans. Daisuke eats rice cakes wrapped in seaweed. **Analyze Pictures**

**C** **SOCIAL STUDIES STRAND**
**Culture**

Explain to children that music and dance are an important part of each country's culture. A popular folkdance in Hungary is the *czarda.* The Kabuki dance is part of Japanese culture. One type of popular folk music in Argentina is called *creole* music. A famous Argentine dance style is the tango. In Tanzania, Swahili music is very popular. Invite children to discuss other examples of music or dance they might be familiar with. Play tapes or CDs containing music from other countries, ask children to listen for ways in which the types of music are alike and different.

**$** **SOCIAL STUDIES STRAND**
**Economics**

Tell children that people also have different kinds of jobs around the world. These jobs may depend on the needs, wants, and available resources of a place.

**260** Unit 6 • Our Country, Our World

What people eat and where they live can be alike and different too. The chart shows different food and homes from around the world.

| | |
|---|---|
| **Child** |  **Mónika** Hungary |
| **Favorite Food** | 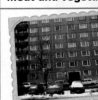 meat and vegetab |
| **Home** | |

260

## Practice and Extend

**ESL** **ACCESS CONTENT**
**ESL Support**

**Telling About Dinner** Discuss with children the steps involved in eating dinner: shopping for food, preparing it, serving it, and cleaning up. Emphasize the interactions between family members in this process. Invite children to describe the process in their native country. If necessary, have them interview a family member to find out more.

**Beginning** Have children draw one of the steps done in their native country. Ask them to describe what they draw.

**Intermediate** Have children work in pairs or groups to mime the process done in their native country.

**Advanced** Have children describe eating dinner in their native country. Then ask them to tell how the experience is alike and different from eating dinner where they live now.

*For additional ESL Support, use Every Student Learns Guide, p. 122–125.*

# he World

**Carlitos**
Argentina

**Esta**
Tanzania

**Daisuke**
Japan

sausage

 **5**

beans

 **6**

rice cakes wrapped
in seaweed

## What did you learn?

1. How are homes around the world alike and different?

2. What does Carlitos eat? How is it different from what Mónika eats?

3. **Think and Share**
   How are these children like you?

**261**

**FYI** **SOCIAL STUDIES**
## Background

### About Tanzania

- Tanzania is located in eastern Africa on the Indian Ocean.

- Elephants, giraffes, lions, zebras, and other wild animals live in Tanzania's vast Serengeti National Park and other areas. Hunting is prohibited or limited in these places.

- Mount Kilimanjaro, Africa's highest mountain (19,340 feet), is in Tanzania.

## Workbook, p. 68

**Life Around the World**

Draw pictures that show three things about you.

My Picture

My Favorite Food

My Home

Share your pictures with the class.  **Drawings will vary.**

**Directions** Draw three pictures. Share your pictures with the class. Discuss how the pictures are alike and different.  **Home Activity:** The next time you take your child to a supermarket, point out foods that come from different places in the world.

**Also on Teacher Resources CD-ROM.**

---

**Problem Solving**

**6 Imagine that one of the children from around the world is coming to visit you. You want to bake cookies for the child but do not know how. What can you do?** Answers will vary, but should include most of the problem-solving steps. Identify the problem: How to bake cookies. With the help of a family member, find recipes and research ingredients available in the kitchen, such as butter, eggs, sugar, and flour. Choose a recipe that uses available ingredients. Solve the problem by asking a family member to help you bake the cookies. **Solve Problems**

## 3 Close and Assess

Ask children to make a drawing of themselves with the children from around the world.

### ✓ What did you learn?

1. Accept all reasonable answers

2. Carlitos eats sausage. Sausage is chopped meat mixed with spices. Sausage is shaped like a tube. Soup is a liquid that is made by boiling meat, fish, or vegetables in water or stock.

3. **Think and Share** Answers will vary, but should reflect what children learned about the clothing, food, and homes of the children around the world.

## Laurence Yep

### Objective
• Identify people who exhibit a love of individualism.

## 1 Introduce and Motivate

**Preview** Tell children that Laurence Yep is a writer who is Chinese American. His father was born in China, but Laurence was born in America. Have children look at the background in the picture on p. 262. Point out the pyramidal tower built over the Cathay House. Then point out the streetcar. Explain that it is a "bus" on rails that provides public transportation along streets. Tell children that the tower and streetcar indicate the location is Chinatown in San Francisco, California.

**Warm Up** To activate prior knowledge, ask children to remember what they learned about Joseph Bruchac. (He writes books for children about Native Americans.)

## 2 Teach and Discuss

**Page 263**

Have children locate China on a globe. Ask them what continent China is on. (Asia) Have students trace with their finger a line from China to San Francisco.

**❶ Why do you think many Chinese people settled in San Francisco, California, when they came to the United States?** It was the first stop in America, across the Pacific Ocean from China. **Draw Conclusions**

**❷ Why do you think where Laurence Yep lived is called Chinatown?** Many Chinese live there. They speak the Chinese language. **Make Inferences**

**262** Unit 6 • Our Country, Our World

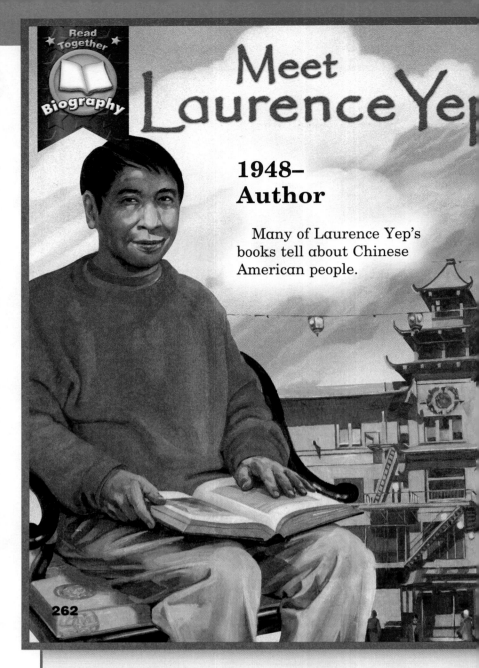

Meet
Laurence Yep

**1948–**
**Author**

Many of Laurence Yep's books tell about Chinese American people.

262

## Practice and Extend

**SOCIAL STUDIES**
**Background**

**About Laurence Yep**

• Laurence Yep's father and mother ran a grocery in San Francisco.

• Laurence Yep sold his first story to a science fiction magazine when he was 18. The magazine paid him one cent for each word.

• *Dragon's Gate* is a historical work of fiction about a 14-year-old Chinese boy who comes to America after the Gold Rush. He works on the railroad.

• *Dragonwings* is the story of a young Chinese immigrant who comes to California in the early 1900's. He works with family members in a laundry.

• The Newbery Medal is awarded annually to the author of the most distinguished American book for children by the Association for Library Service to Children, a division of the American Library Association.

Laurence Yep is Chinese American. He grew up in California. He went to school in a part of San Francisco called Chinatown. Many of the children at his school spoke Chinese. Laurence spoke English. ❶ ❷

Later, Laurence Yep started writing books. He became very interested in the Chinese American way of life. Many of his books are set in Chinese American places such as Chinatown. ❸

Laurence Yep writes books for both children and young adults. His books have won many awards. His books *DragonWings* and *Dragon's Gate* have both won an important award called the Newbery Medal.
❹ ❺

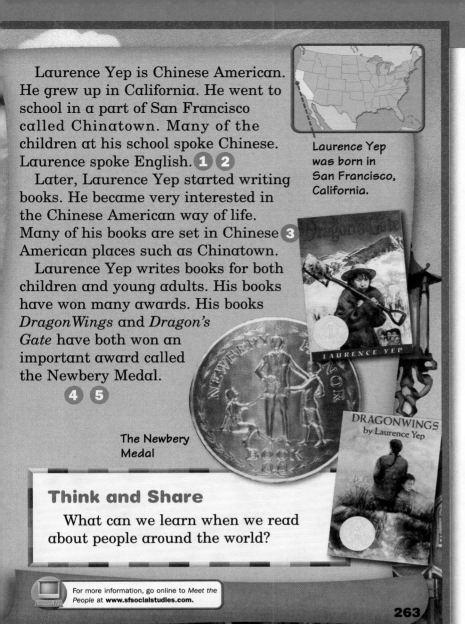

Laurence Yep was born in San Francisco, California.

The Newbery Medal

### Think and Share

What can we learn when we read about people around the world?

For more information, go online to *Meet the People* at **www.sfsocialstudies.com.**

263

---

❸ **What shows Laurence Yep's love of individualism and sets him apart from other writers?** Answers will vary, but may include that he writes about the Chinese American way of life. **Express Ideas**

❹ **How are Joseph Bruchac and Laurence Yep alike and different?** Answers will vary but may include the following. Alike: They were both born in the United States and that they both write about their heritage. Different: Joseph Bruchac often writes down stories that others tell him. Laurence Yep often creates his own stories. Bruchac writes about Native Americans, Yep about Chinese Americans. **Compare and Contrast**

❺ **What important award has two of Laurence Yep's books won?** The Newbery Medal **Recall and Retell**

## 3 Close and Assess

Ask children to tell what they know about Laurence Yep. Ask partners to discuss the way of life of their parents and grandparents.

### Think and Share

Answers will vary but may include that we can learn about the way of life of people around the world.

---

### CURRICULUM CONNECTION
### Literature

**Books by Laurence Yep**

Laurence Yep has written many books for young readers. Read aloud and discuss any of the following picture books.

- *Tiger Woman,* by Laurence Yep and Robert Roth (illustrator) Bridgewater Books, ISBN 0-816-73464-X, 1995) **Easy**

- *Junior Thunder Lord, The,* by Laurence Yep and Robert Van Nutt (illustrator) (Bridgewater Books, ISBN 0-816-73454-2, 1994) **On-Level**

- *Man Who Tricked a Ghost, The,* by Laurence Yep (Econo-Clad Books, ISBN 0-785-78614-7, 1999) **Challenge**

### WEB SITE
### Technology

You may help children find out more about Laurence Yep by clicking on *Meet the People* at **www.sfsocialstudies.com.**

## It Is Time to Leave

### Objective

● Show what people around the world say when they leave.

## 1 Introduce and Motivate

**Preview** Have children look at the photographs of the children and the speech balloons on pp. 264–265. Ask children to guess what the children from around the world are saying. (They might be saying a form of "hello" or "good-bye.")

**Warm Up** To activate prior knowledge, ask children to tell ways to say good-bye in English or other languages. (Examples are *bye, see ya, so long, ciao,* and *aloha.*)

## 2 Teach and Discuss

As you pronounce the sayings for children, have them repeat the sayings. (See pronunciations at the right.)

Put a saying on one side of a flash card and the name of the country where it is spoken on the other side. Have partners learn the saying and the country by using the flash card.

**1 Why do we say something when we leave another person?** Answers will vary, but may include that it is polite and that it makes parting less sad. **Express Ideas**

## It Is Time to Lea

People around the world are alike and different in many ways.

**Good-bye** — United States

NORTH AMERICA

ATLANTIC OCEAN

**Adios** — Bolivia

PACIFIC OCEAN

SOUTH AMERICA

**Adeus** — Brazil

**Au revoi** — France

264

## Practice and Extend

### FYI SOCIAL STUDIES Background

**Pronunciation of Words Meaning "Good-bye"**

● **Adiós** /ah dee OSE/ Bolivia.
● **Adeus** /ah DAY us/ Brazil.
● **Au revoir** /o ruh VWAHR/ France.
● **Sai an jima** /SA uhn JOO muh/ Nigeria.
● **Sayonara** /SY uh NAHR uh/ Japan.
● **Arrivederla** /ah ree vuh DAYR la/ Italy.

### WEB SITE Technology

You may help children find out more about these pages by clicking on *Atlas* at **www.sfsocial studies.com**.

In many countries, people have a saying when they leave another person. ❶ ❷

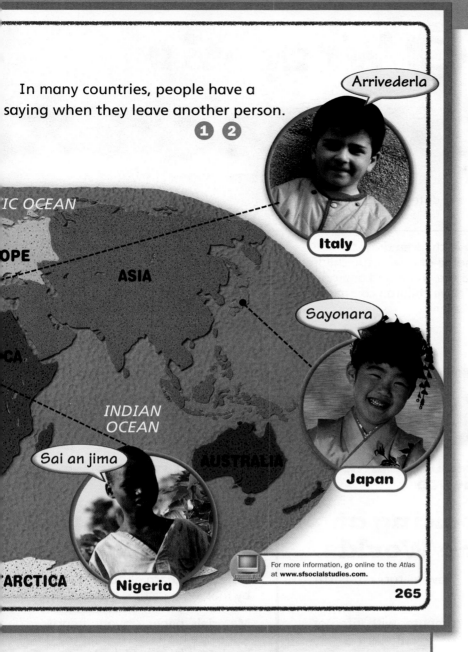

Arrivederla

Italy

Sayonara

Japan

Sai an jima

Nigeria

INDIAN OCEAN

ASIA

AUSTRALIA

ANTARCTICA

For more information, go online to the *Atlas* at **www.sfsocialstudies.com.**

**265**

❷ **How might people say good-bye without using words?** They might • wave, hug, kiss, shake hands, or slap hands. **Apply Information**

# ❸ Close and Assess

Ask children to tell how saying words to people who are leaving shows that people around the world are alike and different. (Alike: They say words when they leave people. Different: They use different words.)

# Lesson ⑤ Wrap-Up

## MEETING INDIVIDUAL NEEDS
## Leveled Practice

### Create Pictures Showing the World
Have children draw pictures showing what it is like to live in different places around the world.

**Easy** Have children draw a picture of the home of one of the children from around the world. **Reteach**

**On-Level** Have children draw two pictures: a home of one of the children from around the world and one of their home. Have children compare the homes. **Extend**

**Challenge** Have children draw two pictures: a home of one of the children from around the world and one of their home. Have children write sentences comparing and contrasting the homes. **Enrich**

## Hands-on Activities

### CURRICULUM CONNECTION
### Writing/Vocabulary

## Asia Puzzle

**Objective** Demonstrate understanding of the lesson vocabulary.

**Materials** puzzle
**Learning Style** Verbal/Linguistic
**Individual** 🧍
⏱ **Time** 15 minutes

1. Display the Vocabulary Card *world*.

2. Tell children that four countries in Asia are China, Vietnam, India, and Japan. Write the names on the board.

3. Distribute the puzzle to children. Tell them to use the names of the countries to complete the puzzle. Explain that some letters have already been filled in.

4. Remind children to add their lesson vocabulary word to their "My Word Book."

### CURRICULUM CONNECTION
### Science

## Looking at the World

**Objective** View pictures of Earth from space.

**Materials** computer with Internet connection
**Learning Style** Visual
**Group** 🧍🧍🧍🧍
⏱ **Time** 15 minutes

1. Help children view current pictures of Earth from space on the Internet.

2. Use the photo gallery at the National Space Science Data Center (**http://nssdc.gsfc.nasa.gov/**) to help children identify continents and approximate locations of cities and countries.

3. Use the Johnson Space Center's Web site (**http://earth.jsc.nasa.gov/**) to help children identify land and water features.

### SOCIAL STUDIES STRAND
### Geography

## Work Around the World

**Objective** Learn about a country by making a picture book.

**Materials** paper, crayons, pencils, reference material, such as the book *Children Just Like Me*
**Learning Style** Verbal/Linguistic
**Group** 🧍🧍🧍🧍
⏱ **Time** 30 minutes

New Zeala

1. Have groups create a two-page picture book about work around the world.

2. Help groups find information about work in a country.

3. Have groups fold a large sheet of paper to make two pages. Have them write the information at the bottom of each page.

4. Have groups illustrate each page and design a cover with the name of the country.

# Ending Unit 6

### End with a Folktale
pages 266–267

Children will listen to and talk about a folktale: "The Farmer's Little Girl" adapted from Aesop.

### Unit 6 Review
pages 268–271

Children will review unit vocabulary words and the unit skills of making a prediction, making a decision, using a bar graph, and making a bar graph. Children will answer questions about what they learned in the unit. Children will learn about several books about our world.

**Resources**
- Workbook, p. 69
- ✓ Assessment Book, pp. 21–24

### Unit 6 Project
page 272

Children will invent a machine of the future. They will also be directed to a Web site where they can learn more about our world.

**Resource**
- Workbook, p. 70

# Wrap-Up

**Activity**

## Welcome to the USA!

Have children make posters to welcome visitors from other countries. Suggest that their posters show activities of what it is like to live in this country—and at least one national symbol, such as the Statue of Liberty.

- Have children cut out pictures from magazines showing people at work, home, or play. Have them draw the national symbol. Then have them make a collage with the pictures and paste them into place on a large sheet of oaktag.

- Help children write a title for their poster. Remind them to spell all the words correctly and to print neatly.

- Display children's posters in the classroom.

**Performance Assessment**
You can use the activity on this page as a performance assessment.

✓ **Assessment Scoring Guide**

| Make Posters About the USA | |
|---|---|
| 6 | Includes one or more pictures that depict life in America, a national symbol, and an appropriate title. Contains no errors in spelling or grammar. |
| 5 | Includes all three required elements but may contain one or two errors in spelling or grammar. |
| 4 | Includes all three required elements but contains errors in spelling and grammar. |
| 3 | Includes two of three required elements. |
| 2 | Includes only one of the required elements. |
| 1 | Pictures chosen do not relate to the topic. |

If you prefer a 4-point rubric, adjust accordingly.

# The Girl and the Milk Pail

## Objective
- Retell stories from selected folktales and legends such as Aesop's fables.

## 1 Introduce and Motivate

**Preview** Explain to children that a folktale is a story handed down by word of mouth by the common people. Further explain that a fable is a kind of folktale that teaches a lesson.

**Warm Up** Explain to children that *moral* means the lesson in the right thing to do taught by the story. Discuss two morals: "Haste makes waste" and "Don't count your chickens before they hatch."

## 2 Teach and Discuss

Read the fable "The Girl and the Milk Pail." Discuss with children what happens in the story. Then have children recall and retell it. Explain that the moral of this story is that you should concentrate on the task at hand.

**1 What was the girl doing while she was walking home with the bucket of milk?**
Thinking about buying new clothes
**Analyze Information**

**2 Predict what will happen after you read that the girl was thinking about other things as she carried the bucket of milk on her head.**
Answers will vary but may include that she's going to drop the bucket. **Predict**

# The Girl and the Milk Pail
**Adapted from Aesop**

1 One day, a little girl went to milk the cow. While she milked, she thought, "I want new clothes." She carried the bucket of milk on her head as she walked home.

2 The little girl began to think. First, she thought about how she would sell the milk at the market. With the money she made, she could buy eggs.

266

# Practice and Extend

**FYI** **SOCIAL STUDIES Background**

**Moral of the Story**

Discuss with children the meaning of the following morals of Aesop's fables.
- Little by little does the trick.
- One good turn deserves another.
- Necessity is the mother of invention.
- Whatever you do, do with all your might.
- Appearances are deceptive.
- An ounce of prevention is worth a pound of cure.
- People are known by the company they keep.

After that, she would feed the chickens that hatched from the eggs. Then she would take the chickens to the market. Finally, she could buy new clothes!

She could not wait. She began to run home. She thought, "How beautiful I will look in my new clothes." She could not hold on to the bucket. It fell off her head! All of the milk spilled out.

*Moral:* Sometimes when you hurry, you only get farther behind.

**267**

 **SOCIAL STUDIES STRAND**
**Economics**

Discuss with children the ways people exchange goods and services at a market. Ask children to identify the steps a family must take to buy clothes, such as working to earn money for goods and making choices about what goods to buy.

**❸ Identify examples of goods in the story.** Answers may include milk, eggs, chickens, and clothes.

**❹ What do you think the girl could have done to prevent spilling the milk?** Answers will vary but may include that she could have paid more attention to carrying the bucket.

## ❸ Close and Assess

- Have children tell the meaning of the story in their own words.

- Have children change the ending of the story.

 **CURRICULUM CONNECTION**
**Literature**

### Aesop's Fables

Children might enjoy reading more of Aesop's fables.

- Go online at **AesopFables.org** to find a collection of Aesop's fables. Read fables with children.
- Discuss with children the moral of the stories. Ask children to retell the stories in their own words.
- Then have children illustrate their favorite fable.

Children might also enjoy reading these books of Aesop's fables: *Aesop for Children, The,* by Mio Winter and Milo Winter (Photographer) (Scholastic Trade, ISBN 0-590-47977-6, 1994) **Easy**; *Aesop's Fables,* by Aesop and Jerry Pinkney (Illustrator) (Seastar Pub Co, ISBN 1-58717-000-0, 2000) **On-Level**; *Aesop's Fables,* by Aesop and Fritz Kredel (Illustrator) (Penguin Putnam Books for Young Readers, ISBN 0-448-06003-5, 1977) **Challenge**

### Resources

- Assessment Book, pp. 21–24
- Workbook, p. 69: Vocabulary Review

# Vocabulary Review

1. inventor
2. market
3. world

 **Answers to Test Prep**

1. c. communicate
2. b. invention

---

**UNIT 6**

## Review

# Vocabulary Review

world
inventor
market

Tell which word completes each sentence.

1. Thomas Edison was a famous _____.

2. A place to buy goods is called a _____.

3. The Earth and everything on it is called the _____.

★  ★  ★  ★  ★  ★  ★  ★

**TEST PREP** Which word completes the sentence?

1. You give and get information when you _____.
   - **a.** market
   - **b.** inventor
   - **c.** communicate
   - **d.** world

2. The telephone was an important _____.
   - **a.** inventor
   - **b.** invention
   - **c.** market
   - **d.** world

**268**

---

# Practice and Extend

## Assessment Options

✓ **Unit 6 Assessment**

- Unit 6 Content Test: Use Assessment Book, pp. 21–22

- Unit 6 Skills Test: Use Assessment Book, pp. 23–24

**TEST PREP Standardized Test Prep**

- Unit 6 tests contain standardized test formats.

✓ **Unit 6 Performance Assessment**

- See p. 272 for information about using the Unit 6 Project as a means of performance assessment.

- A scoring guide for the Unit 6 Project is provided in the teacher's notes on p. 272.

 **Test Talk**

- Test Talk Practice Book

# Skills Review

##  Predict

In your class, vote for your favorite pet. **Predict** which pet will get the most votes.

★ ★ ★ ★ ★ ★ ★ ★

# Gather Information

Suppose you want to gather information about a topic. The library is a good place to start. Books, encyclopedias, newspapers, and the Internet can help you find what you are looking for. Choose one of the people from the list below. Decide if you will use a book, encyclopedia, newspaper, or the Internet to help you learn about that person. Write one sentence about the person you chose.

1. Thomas Jefferson
2. Betsy Ross
3. Martin Luther King, Jr.
4. Neil Armstrong
5. Sally Ride
6. Bill Gates

**269**

---

**WEB SITE Technology**

For more information, you can select the dictionary or encyclopedia from *Social Studies Library* at **www.sfsocialstudies.com**.

---

## Workbook, p. 69

Drawings will vary.

**Also on Teacher Resources CD-ROM.**

---

# Skills Review

## Predict

Children's answers should reflect that predicting means telling what they think will happen next.

- Tell children that what they predict will happen is not necessarily what they wish will happen.
- Remind children that a prediction can never be certain.

Use the following scoring guide.

### ✔ Assessment Scoring Guide

| | Predict the Pet That Gets the Most Votes |
|---|---|
| 6 | Demonstrates clear understanding that voting is an expression of a wish and predicting is telling what will happen, and makes a reasonable prediction. |
| 5 | Understands voting is an expression of a wish and predicting is telling what will happen, and gives a reasonable prediction. |
| 4 | Understands voting and predicting but shows uncertainty when making a prediction. |
| 3 | Understands voting and predicting but makes an unreasonable prediction. |
| 2 | Understands predicting but not voting and makes an unreasonable prediction. |
| 1 | Understands voting but not predicting. |

If you prefer a 4-point rubric, adjust accordingly.

## Gather Information

Children's sentences should reflect something they have learned about the person they chose. Ask children to tell which source they used.

# Skills Review

## Read a Bar Graph

**1.** 10

**2.** Pink

**3.** Blue

## Skills on Your Own

- Children's bar graph should be in the correct format, accurately reflect how the friends travel to school, and have all words spelled correctly.

Use the following scoring guide.

### ✓ Assessment Scoring Guide

| | Use a Bar Graph |
|---|---|
| 6 | Format, results, and spelling are completely correct. Shows attention to detail. |
| 5 | Format, results, and spelling are completely correct. |
| 4 | Format, results, and spelling are mostly correct. |
| 3 | Format and results are completely correct but not spelling. |
| 2 | Format is completely correct but not results and spelling. |
| 1 | Format, results, and spelling are only partially correct. |

If you prefer a 4-point rubric, adjust accordingly.

# Skills Review

## Read a Bar Graph

Kay asked her friends to name their favorite color. Read her bar graph to answer the questions.

**1.** How many friends did Kay ask?

**2.** What color did the most people like?

**3.** What color did three people like?

## Skills On Your Own

Make a bar graph that shows how you and some friends travel to school. Ask your friends how they get to school. Write the ways they get to school on the left. Write numbers on the bottom. Fill in the bar to show how many travel in each way.

**270**

# Practice and Extend

## Revisit the Unit Question

### ✓ Portfolio Assessment

- Have children look back at the list of places made on p. 231.
- Have children list details about a place in the world they would like to visit.
- Ask children to underline countries around the world they learned about in this unit.
- Ask children to draw a picture of the place they would like to visit.
- Ask children to write a sentence about why they want to visit this place.
- Have children add their list, drawings, and sentences to their Social Studies Portfolio.

# What did you learn?

1. What goods and services can you get in a market?

2. Name two inventors who helped change the way people communicate.

3. Name three ways people can be alike and different.

4. **Write and Share** Write about how one thing people use at home has changed.

**Test Talk**

Is your answer complete and correct?

# Read About Our World

Look for books like these in the library.

271

## CURRICULUM CONNECTION
### Literature

**Books About Our Country, Our World**

You may want to read and discuss with children the following books about cultures around the world and the ways technology has changed the ways we live today.

*Travel and Transport Then and Now,* by Alistair Smith, Ruth Russell (designer) and Adrienne Salgado, (illustrator) (Usborne Pub Ltd, ISBN 0-746-03102-5, 2000) **Easy**

*Abuela's Weave,* by Omar S. Castaneda and Enrique O. Sanchez (illustrator) (Lee & Low Books, ISBN 1-880-00020-2, 1995) **On-Level**

*Madlenka,* by Peter Sis (Frances Foster Books, ISBN 0-374-39969-7, 2000) **On-Level**

*Imaginative Inventions: The Who, What, Where, When, and Why, of Roller Skates, Potato Chips, Marbles, and Pie (and More!),* by Charise Mericle Harper (Little, Brown &Co., ISBN 0-316-34725-6, 2001) **Challenge**

---

# What did you learn?

1. You can get goods such as food, clothing, toys, and school supplies, and get services such as aiding you find goods and putting goods in a bag for you.

2. Alexander Graham Bell and Thomas Alva Edison

3. Answers will vary but may include that what people wear, what they eat, and where they live can be alike and different.

4. **Write and Share** Answers will vary but may include household tools, devices, and appliances.

**Test Talk**

**Write Your Answer**
Use *What did you learn?*, Question 4, to model the Test Talk strategy.

**Make sure the answer is correct.**
Children should make sure their written answer has only correct details.

**Make sure the answer is complete.**
Have children include numerous details in their written answer.

*For additional practice, use the Test Talk Practice Book.*

# Read About Our World

You may want to have these books available in the classroom. Read the books aloud for children; then invite them to browse through the books.

*Train Song,* by Harriet Ziefert (Harper Trophy, ISBN 0-531-30204-0, 1990) This book tells the story of a young boy watching a freight train go by. **Easy** *Notable Children's Trade Book in Social Studies*

*Gabriella's Song,* by Candace Fleming (Atheneum, ISBN 0-689-80973-5, 1997) This book is the story of a happy child, Gabriella, who composes a song inspired by Venice. **On-Level** *Parents' Choice Silver Honor*

*Welcoming Babies,* by Margy Burns Knight and Anne Sibley O'Brien (illustrator) (Tilbury House Publishers, ISBN 0-884-48123-9, 1994) This book shows how babies are welcomed into different cultures. **Challenge**

# Unit 6 Project

# Future World

## Objective
- Understand how machines benefit daily life.

## Resource
- Workbook, p. 70

## Materials
shoe boxes, paper, crayons, scissors, glue, string, cardboard tubes, egg cartons, and other common objects

## Follow This Procedure
- Tell children that machines help make work easier. Ask them to think of different kinds of machines people use every day. Write their answers on the board.

- Discuss how each of the machines listed on the board makes work easier.

- Ask children to invent a machine they think people might use in the future.

- Review with children the information that a commercial gives a consumer, such as the product name, what the product does, its price, its benefits and advantages, and where it can be bought.

- Have children create a TV commercial to tell about their inventions.

### ✓ Assessment Scoring Guide

| Future World | |
|---|---|
| 6 | Creates a detailed model of a machine of the future and describes its benefits clearly and thoroughly. |
| 5 | Creates a detailed model and describes its benefits in an acceptable manner. |
| 4 | Creates a detailed model but does not describe its benefits fully. |
| 3 | Creates an acceptable model and somewhat describes its benefits. |
| 2 | Creates a model but cannot describe its benefits. |
| 1 | Creates an incomplete model and cannot describe its benefits. |

If you prefer a 4-point rubric, adjust accordingly.

# UNIT 6 Project

## Future World

**Invent a machine of the future.**

**1 Think** of a machine people might use in the future.

**2 Make** a model of your machine.

**3 Give** a commercial. Tell why people should use your machine.

**4 Ask** your classmates if they would or wouldn't use your machine and why.

### Internet Activity

Go to www.sfsocialstudies.com/activities learn more about inventions.

272

# Practice and Extend

## Hands-on Unit Project

### ✓ Unit 6 Performance Assessment
- The Unit Project can also be used as a performance assessment activity.
- Use the scoring guide to assess each group's work.

## WEB SITE Technology

Children can launch the activity by clicking on *Grade 1, Unit 6* at **www.sfsocialstudies.com/activities.**

### Workbook, p. 70

6 Project Future World

Draw a picture of a machine of the future. **Drawings will vary.**

Write answers about your machine. **Answers will vary.**

How does the machine help people?

Who will your machine help?

**Also on Teacher Resources CD-ROM**

# Reference Guide

## Table of Contents

**R1**

---

# Atlas
### Photograph of the Earth

---

# Atlas
### Photograph of North America

# Atlas

**Map of the World: Continents**

NORTH

ARCTIC OCEAN

WEST

EAST

NORTH
AMERICA

ATLANTIC
OCEAN

PACIFIC
OCEAN

SOUTH
AMERICA

ATLANTIC
OCEAN

EUROPE

ASIA

AFRICA

INDIAN
OCEAN

PACIFIC
OCEAN

AUSTRALIA

ANTARCTICA

SOUTH

# Atlas

**Map of the United States of America**

NORTH

WEST

EAST

SOUTH

RUSSIA

AK

ARCTIC
OCEAN

Greenland
(DENMARK)

CANADA

PACIFIC OCEAN

WA MT ND MN WI MI NY ME
OR ID WY SD IA IL IN OH PA VT NH MA CT RI
NV UT CO NE KS MO KY WV VA NJ DE MD DC
CA AZ NM OK AR TN NC SC
TX LA MS AL GA
FL

ATLANTIC
OCEAN

HI

500 Kilometers

Gulf of Mexico

BAHAMAS

Puerto Rico
(UNITED STATES)

MEXICO

CUBA

DOMINICAN
REPUBLIC

JAMAICA

HAITI

| State or area | Abbreviation |
|---|---|
| Alabama | AL |
| Alaska | AK |
| Arizona | AZ |
| Arkansas | AR |
| California | CA |
| Colorado | CO |
| Connecticut | CT |
| Delaware | DE |
| District of Columbia | DC |
| Florida | FL |
| Georgia | GA |
| Hawaii | HI |
| Idaho | ID |
| Illinois | IL |
| Indiana | IN |
| Iowa | IA |
| Kansas | KS |
| Kentucky | KY |
| Louisiana | LA |
| Maine | ME |
| Maryland | MD |
| Massachusetts | MA |
| Michigan | MI |
| Minnesota | MN |
| Mississippi | MS |
| Missouri | MO |
| Montana | MT |
| Nebraska | NE |
| Nevada | NV |
| New Hampshire | NH |
| New Jersey | NJ |
| New Mexico | NM |
| New York | NY |
| North Carolina | NC |
| North Dakota | ND |
| Ohio | OH |
| Oklahoma | OK |
| Oregon | OR |
| Pennsylvania | PA |
| Rhode Island | RI |
| South Carolina | SC |
| South Dakota | SD |
| Tennessee | TN |
| Texas | TX |
| Utah | UT |
| Vermont | VT |
| Virginia | VA |
| Washington | WA |
| West Virginia | WV |
| Wisconsin | WI |
| Wyoming | WY |

# Atlas

## Map of Our Fifty States

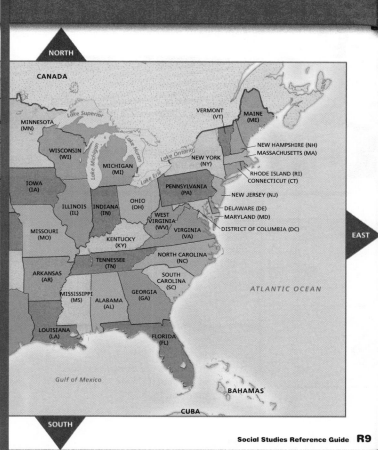

WASHINGTON (WA)
MONTANA (MT)
NORTH DAKOTA (ND)
OREGON (OR)
IDAHO (ID)
SOUTH DAKOTA (SD)
WYOMING (WY)
NEBRASKA (NE)
NEVADA (NV)
UTAH (UT)
COLORADO (CO)
KANSAS (KS)
CALIFORNIA (CA)
ARIZONA (AZ)
NEW MEXICO (NM)
OKLAHOMA (OK)
TEXAS (TX)

PACIFIC OCEAN

RUSSIA
ALASKA (AK)
CANADA
MEXICO
HAWAII (HI)
PACIFIC OCEAN
PACIFIC OCEAN

NORTH
CANADA

MINNESOTA (MN)
Lake Superior
WISCONSIN (WI)
Lake Michigan
MICHIGAN (MI)
Lake Huron
Lake Ontario
Lake Erie
VERMONT (VT)
MAINE (ME)
NEW HAMPSHIRE (NH)
MASSACHUSETTS (MA)
NEW YORK (NY)
RHODE ISLAND (RI)
CONNECTICUT (CT)
PENNSYLVANIA (PA)
NEW JERSEY (NJ)
DELAWARE (DE)
MARYLAND (MD)
DISTRICT OF COLUMBIA (DC)
IOWA (IA)
ILLINOIS (IL)
INDIANA (IN)
OHIO (OH)
WEST VIRGINIA (WV)
VIRGINIA (VA)
MISSOURI (MO)
KENTUCKY (KY)
NORTH CAROLINA (NC)
ARKANSAS (AR)
TENNESSEE (TN)
SOUTH CAROLINA (SC)
MISSISSIPPI (MS)
ALABAMA (AL)
GEORGIA (GA)
LOUISIANA (LA)
FLORIDA (FL)
ATLANTIC OCEAN

WEST
EAST

Gulf of Mexico
BAHAMAS
CUBA
SOUTH

# Geography Terms

**forest**
large area of land where many trees grow

**hill**
rounded land higher than the land around it

**island**
land with water all around it

**lake**
large body of water with land all or nearly all around it

**mountain**
highest land on Earth

**ocean**
a very large body of salt water

**plain**
very large area of flat land

**river**
large stream of water leading to a lake, another river, or ocean

ocean
island
lake
hill

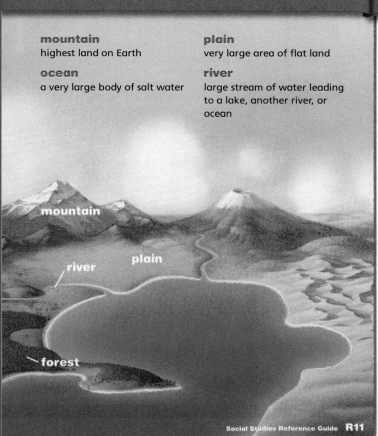

mountain
river
plain
forest

# Picture Glossary

My address is 9 Green Street.

**A**

### address
A way to find a home or another building. My **address** is 9 Green Street. (page 50)

### alike
How things are the same. These houses look **alike.** (page 49)

**B**

### bar graph
A picture that shows how many or how much. This **bar graph** shows how children might get to school in the future. (page 254)

### calendar
A chart that shows the days, weeks, and months of the year. I circled Presidents' Day on the **calendar.** (page 20)

---

### capital
The city where important leaders of a state or country live and work. Washington, D.C., is the **capital** of the United States. (page 220)

### chart
A way to show things using words and pictures. This **chart** shows the jobs we have at home. (page 98)

### citizen
A member of a state and country. I am a **citizen** of the United States of America. (page 218)

### city
A big community where many people live and work. My dad works in the **city.** (page 56)

### colony
A place that is ruled by a country that is far away. Virginia was once a **colony.** (page 202)

### communicate
Give and get information. People can use a telephone to **communicate.** (page 246)

### community
A group of people and the place where they live. I live in a big **community** with many neighborhoods. (page 56)

---

# Picture Glossary

### continent
A very large piece of land. South America is a **continent.** (page 76)

### country
A land where a group of people live. My **country** is the United States of America. (page 16)

### custom
The way people usually do something. It is a **custom** in my family to go to a Chinese New Year parade. (page 62)

**D**

### diagram
A drawing that shows the parts of something. This **diagram** shows the parts of a Native American earth lodge. (page 193)

### different
How things are not the same. Many **different** kinds of homes are in my neighborhood. (page 49)

### directions
North, south, east and west. The **directions** on a map helped us find the park. (page 60)

---

**E**

### Earth
The planet on which we live. My class takes care of the **Earth** by recycling. (page 140)

### endangered
A plant or animal of which very few are living. The mountain gorilla is **endangered.** (page 175)

**F**

### farm
Land people use to raise crops or animals. My family raises corn on our **farm.** (page 57)

### flag
A symbol that stands for a country. The American flag is a **symbol** of our country. (page 16)

### freedom
A person's right to make choices. Many people in the United States show flags to celebrate their **freedom.** (page 198)

## Picture Glossary

**globe**
A round model of the earth. A **globe** shows the earth's land and water. (page 154)

**goods**
Things that are grown or made. A farmer grows **goods** such as fruits and vegetables. (page 108)

**group**
A number of persons or things. I have a **group** of friends at school. (page 9)

**hill**
Land that is higher than the land around it. We climbed to the top of the **hill.** (page 151)

**history**
The story of people and places from the past. I like reading about what people in our country's **history** wore. (page 164)

**holiday**
A special day. Independence Day is a **holiday.** (page 212)

**invention**
Something new. The telephone was an important **invention.** (page 246)

**inventor**
Someone who makes or invents something new. Alexander Graham Bell was a famous **inventor**. (page 247)

**job**
The work people do. My neighbor's **job** is to paint houses. (page 94)

**lake**
A large body of water that has land either totally or almost totally around it. A **lake** is smaller than an ocean. (page 152)

## Picture Glossary

**law**
A rule that people must obey. It is a **law** that cars must stop at stop signs. (page 70)

**leader**
Someone who helps people decide what to do. The **leader** of a community is called a mayor. (page 71)

**map**
A drawing of a real place. This is a **map** of my neighborhood park. (page 54)

**map key**
Tells what the symbols on a map mean. Look at the **map key** to help you read the map. (page 55)

**market**
A place where goods are sold. We buy fruit at the **market**. (page 238)

**money**
Coins or bills that people use to buy goods. **Money** used in different countries can look different. (page 104)

**mountain**
The highest kind of land. The **mountain** has snow on the top. (page 150)

**natural resource**
A useful thing that comes from nature. Water is a **natural resource.** (page 156)

**needs**
Things people must have to live. Food is one of our **needs.** (page 100)

**neighborhood**
A place where people live, work, and play. I like the **neighborhood** where I live. (page 52)

**ocean**
A very large body of salt water. An **ocean** can have many waves. (page 76)

# Picture Glossary

**plain**
A large, mostly flat piece of land. This farm is on a **plain.** (page 151)

**President**
Our country's leader. The **President** of the United States makes many important decisions. (page 215)

**recycle**
A process where things can be made into new things. I put many things in our **recycle** bin at home. (page 172)

**reduce**
To use less of something. I try to **reduce** the amount of paper I use. (page 171)

**reuse**
To use something again. I will **reuse** this shoe box. (page 171)

**river**
A long body of water which usually moves toward a lake or the ocean. We traveled down the **river** in a boat. (page 153)

**route**
A way to get from one place to another. The truck follows a **route** to the store. (page 120)

**rule**
Something that tells us what to do and what not to do. One **rule** we have at school is to only cross the street with the crossing guard. (page 22)

**school**
The place where we learn. I take a bus to **school.** (page 6)

**service**
A job a person does to help others. As a firefighter, my mom provides a **service** to our neighborhood. (page 109)

# Picture Glossary

**state**
A part of a country. Florida is a **state** in our country. (page 75)

**symbol**
A picture that stands for a real thing. The picture shows a **symbol** for a tree. (page 54)

**time line**
A chart that shows the order in which things happen. The **time line** shows it will be windy on Wednesday. (page 146)

**tools**
Things that are used to help people do work. Scissors, a ruler, and a pencil are different kinds of **tools.** (page 108)

**town**
A small community. Our **town** has many small stores. (page 57)

**transportation**
A car, bus, or other way that people and goods move from place to place. A school bus is a kind of **transportation** that takes me to school. (page 124)

**volunteer**
A person who works for free. The **volunteer** helps children cross the street. (page 110)

**vote**
A choice that gets counted. Citizens of the United States **vote** for a new President every four years. (page 218)

**wants**
Things we would like to have. Some of my **wants** are presents and cake. (page 101)

**weather**
How it is outside at a certain place and time. The **weather** is stormy with lightning. (page 142)

**world**
A name for Earth and everything on it. The picture shows how the **world** looks from space. (page 258)

# Index

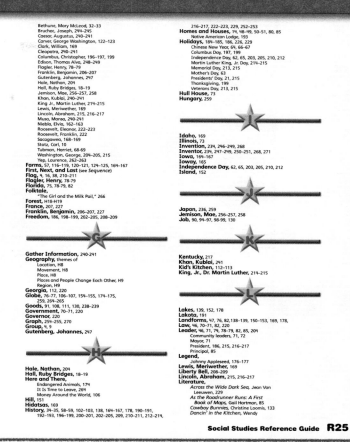

# Credits

**Dorling Kindersley (DK)** is an international publishing company specializing in the creation of high quality reference content for books, CD-ROMs, online materials, and video. The hallmark of DK content is its unique combination of educational value and strong visual style. This combination allows DK to deliver appealing, accessible, and engaging educational content that delights children, parents, and teachers around the world. Scott Foresman is delighted to have been able to use selected extracts of DK content within this Social Studies program. 66-67 from *Celebrations* by Anabel Kindersley and Barnabas Kindersley. Copyright ©1997 by Dorling Kindersley Limited. 126-127 from *Eye Openers: Trucks* edited by Jane Yorke. Copyright ©1991 by Dorling Kindersley Limited. 194-195 from *North American Indian* by David Murdoch. Copyright ©2000 by Dorling Kindersley Limited. 250-251 from *Eyewitness: Invention* by Lionel Bender. Copyright ©2000 by Dorling Kindersley Limited.

**MAPS:** MapQuest.com

**ILLUSTRATIONS:** 4, 46 Tom Barrett 10, 11 Robert Gunn 17, 90, 138 Susan Simon 20, 32 Keith Batchelor 36 Benrei Huang 54 Donna Catanese 60, 62 Robert Krugle 78 Bradley Clark 80 Susan Tolonen 83 David Brion 84, 157 Steven Boswick 114 Laurie Harden 116 Eileen Mueller Neill 122 Stacey Schuett 155, 190 Amy Vangsgard 176 Richard Stergulz 200 Doug Knutson 206 Ann Barrow 208 Tony Nuccio 216 Bill & Debbie Farnsworth 224 Darryl Ligasan 227 Mark Stein 228 Rose Mary Berlin 266 Loretto Lustig 266, 267 Karen Stormer Brooks H17 Jeff Grunewald EM1 Leland Klanderman

**PHOTOGRAPHS:** Every effort has been made to secure permission and provide appropriate credit for photographic material. The publisher deeply regrets any omission and pledges to correct errors called to its attention in subsequent editions. Unless otherwise acknowledged, all photographs are the property of Scott Foresman, a division of Pearson Education. Photo locators are denoted as follows: Top (T), Center (C), Bottom (B), Left (L), Right (R), Background (Bkgd).

**Front Matter:** HH (TC) ©Warren Morgan/Corbis, (TL) ©Comstock Inc., (TR) ©David Roth/Getty Images, (BR) ©Comstock Inc., (BC) ©Jim Cummins/Getty Images, (BL) ©Mitch York/Getty Images H5 ©Bill Losh/Getty Images H6-H7 Colonial Williamsburg Foundation H8 (Bkgd) Frank Siteman/Index Stock Imagery, (R) ©Ken Chernus/Getty Images, (C) ©Kelly/Mooney Photography/Corbis H9 ©Denny Cody/Getty Images H10-H11 Colonial Williamsburg Foundation H12 ©Chad Ehlers/Getty Images H24 Charles Shoffner/Index Stock Imagery Unit 1: 4 (T) Frank Siteman/Index Stock Imagery, (C) David Young-Wolff/PhotoEdit 5 Tom Prettyman/PhotoEdit 8 (BC) ©CMCD/PhotoDisc, (BR) Photodisc, (C) David Young-Wolff/PhotoEdit 9 (Bkgd-L) Mark E. Gibson/Visuals Unlimited 11 (L) SuperStock, (R) ©Peter McGovern/Little League Baseball Museum 12-13 Colonial Williamsburg Foundation 18 (L) ©Corbis-Bettmann, (R) AP/Wide World 19 AP/Wide World 20 © Siede Preis/PhotoDisc 25 (T) Daemmrich Photography, (BR) Bob Daemmrich/Stock Boston, (BL)Getty Images 26, 27 Tony Freeman/PhotoEdit 29 (T) Popperfoto/Archive Photos, (B) Frank Siteman/Index Stock Imagery 30 (B) Jeffry W. Myers/Stock Boston, (T) ©Fox Photos/Hulton Archive/Getty Images 31 (Bkgd) ©PhotoLink/PhotoDisc 33 (T) ©Corbis-Bettmann, (B) ©Corbis 38 (TL) Frank Siteman/Index Stock Imagery, (BL) Tom Prettyman/PhotoEdit 39 (TR) Laura Dwight/PhotoEdit, (BR) Michael Newman/PhotoEdit, (C) Gregg Mancuso/Stock Boston Unit 2: 44 Ellis Vener (C) 46 (T) Michael Newman/PhotoEdit, (TC) SuperStock, (B) Mauritius/Robertstock.com, (BC) ©Hisham F. Ibrahim/PhotoDisc 47 (B) ©A & L Sinibaldi/Getty Images 48 (BL) Daemmrich Photography, (BR) Amy C. Etra/PhotoEdit, (T) ©David Buffington/PhotoDisc 49 (BL) Felicia Martinez/PhotoEdit, (BR) Rhoda Sidney/PhotoEdit 50 (T) Daemmrich Photography 52 (B) ©Michael S. Yamashita/Corbis, (T) Michael Newman/PhotoEdit 56 SuperStock 57 (T) Michele Burgess/Stock Boston, (B) ©1997 Chuck Pefley/Stock Boston 58 The UT Institute of Texan Cultures, No. 74-1401Courtesy of The Houston Public Library 59 Jim Olive Photography 64 ©Kevin Fleming/Corbis 66, 67 Barnabas and Anabel Kindersley/©Dorling Kindersley 68, 69 CAPAY - Coalition for Asian Pacific American Youth 70 (BL) ©David Hiller/PhotoDisc, (BR) ©Hisham F. Ibrahim/PhotoDisc, (BC) Mark C. Burnett/Stock Boston, (TR) Aneal Vohra/Unicorn Stock Photos 73 (CR) Jane Addams Memorial Collection (JAMC negs. A3.132r1r4), Department of Special Collections, The University Library, University of Illinois at Chicago 74 Ellis Vener 79 (B) Richard Cummins/Viesti Collection, Inc., (C) ©Bettmann/Corbis Unit 3: 90 (T) ©Bob Daemmrich/Image Works 91 (TC) Spencer Ainsley/Image Works, (BC) ©R. Hutchings/PhotoEdit, (B) ©David Young-Wolff/Getty Images 102 (TL) Bridgeman Art Library International, Ltd., (BL) ©PhotoDisc, (BR) David Young-Wolff/PhotoEdit 103 (TL) ©Siede Preis/PhotoDisc, (BR) Courtesy Action Products International, Inc. 111 (L) Richard Pasley/Stock Boston, (C), (R) Michael Newman/PhotoEdit 112 Courtesy Pam Woolery 117 (T) Runk/Schoenberger/Grant Heilman Photography, (C) Grant Heilman/Grant Heilman Photography, (B) ©David R. Frazier Photolibrary 118 (T) ©David R. Frazier Photolibrary, (C) Grant Heilman/Grant Heilman Photography, (B) Larry Lefever/Grant Heilman Photography 123 (L) Ingo Spence/Index Stock Imagery, (R) Hulton Archive/Getty Images 124 (TL), (CL) ©Corbis, (BL) ©Photodisc, (BR) Joe Sohm/Image Works 125 (BR) ©Corbis, (B) ©David Young-Wolff/Getty Images, (T) David Young-Wolff/PhotoEdit 126 (C) ©Dorling Kindersley, (B) Stephen Oliver/©Dorling Kindersley, (CL) ©Dave Hopkins 127 (T), (C) Stephen Oliver/©Dorling Kindersley, (TR), (CL), (BR) ©Dave Hopkins Unit 4: 136,137 (Bkgd) Lee Rentz/Bruce Coleman Inc. 138 (T) Kent Wood/Photo Researchers, Inc., (C) ©Wolfgang Koehler, (B) Georg Gerster/Photo Researchers, Inc. 139 (B) Andy Levin/Photo Researchers, Inc., (T) Charlie Ott/Photo Researchers, Inc., (TC) ©Pat O'Hara/Corbis, (BC) ©Robert Glusic/PhotoDisc 141 (C) Bridgeman Art Library International, Ltd., (TR), (BL) Hemera Studio 142 (Bkgd) ©Randy Wells/Getty Images 143 (RBkgd) ©Nick Daly/Getty Images, (LBkgd) ©1989 Joseph Nettis/Stock Boston 148, 149 Smithsonian Institution 150 Lee Rentz/Bruce Coleman Inc. 151 (T) ©Josef Beck/Getty Images, (B) Georg Gerster/Photo Researchers, Inc. 152 (T) ©George Lepp/Corbis, (B) Wolfgang Koehler 153 Myrleen Ferguson Cate/PhotoEdit 156 Michael Godomski/Animals Animals/Earth Scenes 158 ©Emma Lee/PhotoDisc 159 (T) ©Siede Preis/PhotoDisc 160, 161 Courtesy Tree Musketeers 163 (T) Courtesy Elvia E. Niebla, Ph.D., (B) ©Siede Preis/PhotoDisc 164 www.Living History Farms.org 166 (L) Culver Pictures Inc., (C) Living History Farms, (BR) Michael Godomski/Animals Animals/Earth Scenes, (Bkgd) ©Wolf Schussler/PhotoLink/PhotoDisc 169 (B) Obverse ©1999 U.S. Mint. All Rights Reserved. Used with Permission./United States Mint, (T) ©Bettmann/Corbis 174 (T) Tom McHugh/Photo Researchers, Inc., (B) Phillip Colla Photography 175 (T) Lynn M.

Stone/Bruce Coleman Inc., (C) E. Hanumantha Rao/Photo Researchers, Inc., (B) ©Joe McDonald/Corbis Unit 5: 186 (B) ©Museum of the City of New York/Corbis, (BC) ©Joseph Sohm; ChromoSohm Inc./Corbis, (T) ©David & Peter Turnley/Corbis 187 (C) Bob Daemmrich/Daemmrich Photography, (B) Jeff Greenberg/PhotoEdit 189 (L) ©Corbis, (R) Marilyn "Angel" Wynn/Nativestock 191 Chuck Place/Stock Boston 192 ©Corbis-Bettmann 193 American Museum of Natural History/©Dorling Kindersley 194-195 American Museum of Natural History/©Dorling Kindersley 197 The Granger Collection, New York 198 (T) The Granger Collection, New York 199 ©Bettmann/Corbis 202 ©Francis G. Mayer/Corbis 203 The Granger Collection, New York 204 (C) ©Bettmann/Corbis, (B) ©PhotoDisc, (T) © Getty Images 205 Stock Montage Inc. 207 (T) ©Bettmann Archive/Corbis, (B) Courtesy of the Historical and Interpretive Collections of the Franklin Institute 208 (R) ©Gail Mooney/Corbis, (BL) ©Bill Ross/Corbis 209 (BL) ©W. Perry Conway/Corbis, (CR) ©Sandy Felsenthal/Corbis, (T) ©David Muench/Corbis, (BR) Obverse ©U.S. Mint 211 (T) ©Bob Rowan/Progressive Image/Corbis 212 AP/Wide Won 213 (TC) AP/Wide World, (B) Rhoda Sidney/PhotoEdit, (TR) ©Bettmann Archive/Corbis, (TL) ©Bettmann/Corbis, (CR) ©2000 USPS 214 ©Flip Schulke/Corbis 215 (CR) Stock Montage Inc., (T) ©Museum of the City of New York/Corbis 217 (B) ©Morton Beebe/Corbis, (T) ©Corbis-Bettmann 218 David Young-Wolff/PhotoEdit 220 (L) Mark Burnett/Stock Boston, (R) ©Cathlyn Melloan/Getty Images 221 The Granger Collection, New York 222 (R) Courtesy of FDR Library, Hyde Park, NY. (L) AP/Wide World 226 (TL) Library of Congress, (TR) Jeff Greenberg/PhotoEdit, (BL) David Young-Wolff/PhotoEdit, (BR) AP/Wide World Unit 6: 231 (Bkgd) ©Joseph Sohm; ChromoSohm Inc/Corbis 232 (Bkgd) ©Lawrence Manning/Corbis 233 (T) ©Adrain Carroll/Corbis 234 (C) SuperStock, (T) Gary Retherford/Photo Researchers, Inc. 235 (B) ©PhotoDisc, (T) © Getty Images 239 (C) ©David Young-Wolff/Stone 240 (BL) The Granger Collection, (BR) Ancient Art & Architecture Collection Ltd. 241 (TL) SuperStock, (TR) The Granger Collection 243 (TL) National Museum of Dentistry, Baltimore, MD, (TCR) SuperStock, (TCL) ©Schenectady Museum; Hall of Electrical History Foundation/Corbis, (TR) ©C Squared Studios/PhotoDisc, (BCL) ©Chase Swift/Corbis, (TC) ©Bettmann/Corbis, (BCR) ©C Squared Studios/PhotoDisc, (BL) ©David Young-Wolff/Getty Images 245 Courtesy of Fulcrum Publishing 247 (BR) Photo Researchers, Inc., (T) The Granger Collection, New York, (BL) North Wind Picture Archives 248 (R) Library of Congress, (L) SuperStock 249 ©Corbis-Bettmann 250 (TL) Ann Ronan Picture Library, (TC), (R), (BL), (BC) Science Museum/©Dorling Kindersley, (CL) Mary Evans Picture Library 251 Science Museum/©Dorling Kindersley 252 (L) North Wind Picture Archives, (R) The Granger Collection, New York 253 (L) ©Hulton Archive/Getty Images, (R) ©Kim Sayer/Corbis 257 (CR) NASA 258 (BC) ©PhotoDisc 259 Barnabas and Anabel Kindersley/©Dorling Kindersley 260, 261 Anabel and Barnabas Kindersley/©Dorling Kindersley 263 The Newbery Medal was named for eighteenth-century British bookseller John Newbery. It is awarded annually by the Association for Library Service to Children, a division of the American Library Association. Permission has been granted/American Library Association 264 (C), (BR) Barnabas and Anabel Kindersley/©Dorling Kindersley, (BL) ©Will & Deni Mcintyre /Photo Researchers, Inc. 265 (C) Barnabas and Anabel Kindersley/©Dorling Kindersley, (B) ©Jason Lauré, (T) ©Todd Gipstein/Corbis End Matter: R12 Rhoda Sidney/PhotoEdit R13 (B), (BC) SuperStock, (T) Jeff Greenberg/PhotoEdit, (C) Jim Olive Photography R14 (T) ©Kevin Fleming/Corbis, (C) American Museum of Natural History/©Dorling Kindersley, (BR) Amy C. Etra/PhotoEdit, (BL) ©David Buffington/PhotoDisc R15 (C) ©1997 Chuck Pefley/Stock Boston, (B) ©David & Peter Turnley/Corbis, (T) ©Earth Imaging/Stone, (TC) ©Joe McDonald/Corbis R16 (C) David Young-Wolff/PhotoEdit, (BC) ©Josef Beck/Getty Images, (B) Andy Levin/Photo Researchers, Inc. R17 (T) ©Joseph Sohm; ChromoSohm Inc./Corbis, (C) ©Getty Images, (B) Charlie Ott/Photo Researchers, Inc., (BC) ©Bob Daemmrich/Image Works R18 (T) ©Hisham F. Ibrahim/PhotoDisc, (B) Gary Retherford/Photo Researchers, Inc., (TC) Mauritius/Robertstock.com R19 (BC) Michael Newman/PhotoEdit, (TC) ©Wolfgang Koehler, (C) ©Pat O'Hara/Corbis, (B) ©A & L Sinibaldi/Stone R20 (T) Georg Gerster/Photo Researchers, Inc., (TC) ©Museum of the City of New York/Corbis R21 (B) Spencer Ainsley/Image Works, (C) Tom Prettyman/PhotoEdit, (BC) Frank Siteman/Index Stock Imagery, (T) ©Pat O'Hara/Corbis R22 (BC) Michele Burgess/Stock Boston, (B) ©David Young-Wolff/Getty Images R23 (T) Bob Daemmrich/Daemmrich Photography, (BC) Kent Wood/Photo Researchers, Inc., (T) ©R. Hutchings/PhotoEdit, (B) ©PhotoDisc

# Facing Fear: Helping Students Cope with Tragic Events

**American Red Cross**

*Together, we can save a life*

*As much as we would like to protect our children, we cannot shield them from personal or community tragedies. We can, however, help them to be prepared for unforeseen dangerous events and to learn about facing and moving beyond their fears, sadness, and related concerns.*

## Common Responses to Trauma and Disaster

Children experience many common reactions after a trauma. These include reexperiencing the event (for example, flashbacks), avoidance and numbing of feelings, increased arousal, and changes in functioning. These reactions may be manifested in clingy behaviors, mood changes, increased anxieties, increased startle responses (for example, more jumpy with noises), physical complaints, and regressive behavior. Increased aggressive behaviors may also be seen. When the trauma or disaster is human-made, such as a terrorist event, children may react with hurtful talk, behaviors, or play. All of these reactions are normal responses and will, in general, dissipate with time. However, should these persist or increase over time, a referral to a mental health professional might be considered. Similarly, should these reactions result in a danger to self or others, immediate action is warranted.

## Issues of Safety, Security, and Trust

In the aftermath of terrorism or other tragic events, very young children can feel overwhelmed with concerns of safety, security, and trust. They are often unsure where to turn for help. When the safety of their world is threatened, they may feel insecure and fearful. As a result, they may be more anxious and frightened. Children may be more clingy with teachers as well as with parents. This may be due to worry about their own safety as well as the safety of those important to them. Abandonment is a major childhood fear, so children need frequent reassurance they will be cared for and will not be left behind. This message may need to be repeated many times each day. By returning to a regular classroom routine, teachers can help to reinforce a sense of security in young children.

Children's increased fear may also encompass a worry that the trauma will reoccur. Because children this age have not developed a complete sense of time, exposure to replays of the trauma or disaster via television may lead them to believe that the event is happening again and again. This reexposure can result in increasing worry and fear. Limiting this exposure, as well as exposure to adult conversations about the event, may reduce the stress in children.

## Expressing Thoughts and Feelings

Young children may have difficulty putting their thoughts and feelings into words. In order to express these, they may act out ideas through play. Teachers may see play that attempts to recreate the event. Children may repeatedly erect buildings with blocks only to knock them down. Children may pretend to be rescue workers or to be rescued. Children may also become more aggressive or destructive in their play as they act out feelings of anger about what has happened. Teachers may see a direct link to the event (for example, buildings being destroyed) or behaviors seemingly unrelated to the event (such as a game of tag on the playground). Children this age may talk incessantly about the event. To these repetitions, children may gradually add new bits of knowledge that they gain from others. At times, as young children try to make the story "fit" into their concept of the world around them, the repetitions may come to include misinformation or misperceptions of the event. Questions related to the trauma may be equally repetitive. Teachers may answer a child's question only to have the same question repeated within a few minutes. Having the same answer will increase the child's sense of security and help the child process the trauma.

Children this age may have difficulty understanding the results of the event. For example, very young children have magical thinking as well as the belief in the reversibility of loss. Therefore, they may believe that those killed in a disaster will return or that buildings can be easily rebuilt. Children may have many questions and discussions about death and dying. They do not have a mature grasp of the irreversibility of death.

## Identifying Factors to Predict Children at Greatest Risk

Changes in behavior are likely after young children experience a trauma or disaster. One indicator of increased distress may be more whining and irritable behaviors. Young children may have more angry outbursts or temper tantrums, even over seemingly minor events. They may also be more defiant in their behaviors. The opposite may also be seen; some children will become more withdrawn and less engaged in classroom activities.

Children may show a change in functioning. They may have toileting accidents. A return to baby talk is not unusual. Sleep may be disrupted after a trauma, so children may be less rested, which can also produce more irritability. Children may want more help with schoolwork. Not only does this demonstrate increased stress, it also addresses the need for an increased sense of safety and security by having the teacher provide one-on-one attention. At times, children may have problems with attention and concentration on new work presented, which may require multiple presentations of the material. *(continued on the following page)*

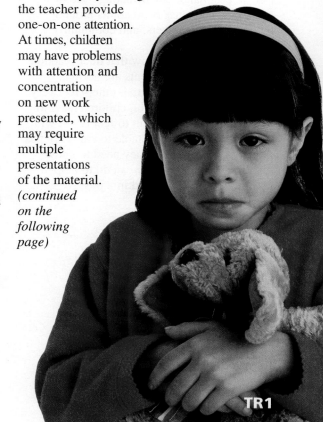

(continued from p. TR1)

## Moving Forward in Spite of Life-Affecting Events

Frightening events, such as the terrorist attacks in the United States on September 11, 2001, the Oklahoma City bombing in 1995, earthquakes, tornadoes, and hurricanes here and in other countries, massive transportation accidents, and war or armed conflict or other military action, impact us all. Events that are caused by human beings can be particularly frightening and raise unique concerns. Terrorist actions and other violent acts are designed to instill fear in individuals and communities, if not countries. Because they happen without warning, there is no time to prepare. This unpredictability leaves us with a heightened sense of vulnerability and anxieties that the event could be repeated again, anywhere. With increased media coverage, even those not directly impacted can be significantly affected by an event. Images make us feel closer to the victims, and we may perceive ourselves as victims of the actions as well. The questions that arise from disasters of human design are difficult, if not impossible, to answer. We want answers to "why" and "how could they" and are often left frustrated by the lack of satisfying responses. This frustration also gives rise to intense feelings of anger. The anger toward the perpetrators may be uncomfortable and difficult to express in productive ways. As adults struggle with reactions and feelings in the aftermath of a terrorist action or tragic event, children are similarly searching for how to best handle their feelings. At all ages, they take cues from adults around them (parents, teachers, and community and national leaders).

Children need to know that their reactions and feelings to such events are normal. They need to recognize that others feel very similarly. Most important, children need to know that they will begin to feel better with time and that it is acceptable to enjoy friends, family, and activities. They need to know that there are things they can do to help themselves move forward in a positive way.

## Activities to Help Children Address Fears

The following activities are designed to help you help your students address their fears and move beyond them.

- **What Happened**—Divide a piece of poster board into five areas. In each area, draw a symbol for one of the senses. As you discuss a trauma/disaster, record what children saw with their eyes, felt inside, heard with their ears, smelled with their nose, and tasted in their mouth.

- **Searching for a Sense of Safety**—Help children list people they can count on and places they can go for safety in an emergency. Remind children that it is important for them to know their own address, phone number, name (first and last), and parents' names (first and last) to give to helpers in order to reunite them with their families.

- **Naming Feelings**—Help children share ideas and feelings with each other by having them draw a picture of a feeling they or other children may have had after a trauma or disaster. Remind them that feelings may vary and that there are no rights and wrongs.

- **Dealing with Feelings**—Distribute strips of paper and ask children to write down or draw some feelings they would like to get rid of. Then tape each strip to the string of a balloon and release the balloon outdoors. Discuss with children how letting go of the balloon might help them let go of bad feelings.

- **Finding Hidden Treasures**—On yellow or gold paper, duplicate coins to serve as "treasure coins." Distribute to children and have them write or draw a good thing, feeling, activity, or person they have in their life. Remind children to use both sides of the coin and to use as many treasure coins as they would like. Invite children to share their treasures. You may also wish to make a treasure chest to store the coins.

## Books for Young Readers

*Smoky Night* Bunting, Eve. Illus. by David Diaz. Harcourt Brace, 1999. Children who witness the Los Angeles riots experience dangerous times.

*A Terrible Thing Happened: A story for children who have witnessed violence or trauma* Holmes, Margaret, and Sasha J. Mudloff. Illus. by Cary Pillo and Thomas Payne. American Psychological Association, 2000. Children explore conscious and subconscious feelings they might have after a traumatic event.

*Thunder Cake* Polacco, Patricia. Paper Star, 1997. A young girl overcomes her fear of thunderstorms as she helps her grandmother make a cake.

*Pip's Magic* Stoll, Ellen. Voyager Picture Book, 1999. A young salamander tries to find the wizard who will help him overcome his fear of the dark.

*My Many Colored Days* Dr. Seuss. Illus. by Lou Fancher and Steve Johnson. Knopf, 1996. Children explore a colorful book about feelings and emotions.

---

 **American Red Cross** **Information on American Red Cross *Facing Fear: Helping Young People Deal with Terrorism and Tragic Events***

The American Red Cross *Facing Fear* curriculum contains lesson plans for teachers and includes hands-on or interactive activities for the classroom that will help students and their families prepare for disastrous situations and equip them with tools to sort out their feelings and fears.

For further information or to obtain copies of the *Facing Fear* curriculum materials, or the curriculum materials that focus on natural disaster preparedness, called *Masters of Disaster*™, contact your local American Red Cross chapter. Visit

http://www.redcross.org to find your nearest Red Cross chapter, and visit www.redcross.org/disaster/masters for specific information on the curriculum. American Red Cross products are available exclusively from local Red Cross chapters in the United States.

*With permission, parts above were adapted from Healing After Trauma Skills, Robin H. Gurwitch and Anne K. Messenbaugh, University of Oklahoma Health Sciences Center.*

# School to Home

## Unit 1

### Newsletter

**Here are the main ideas that we are learning:**

★ A school is a place where people learn.

★ In school, people sometimes work together in a group.

★ A group is made up of people or things.

★ A country is a land where a group of people live.

★ The flag of the United States stands for our country.

★ A rule tells what to do and what not to do.

★ Rules help keep us safe. They also help us treat everyone fairly.

## Fast Facts

- In 1647, Massachusetts passed a law that required the hiring of teachers. Every town that had 50 or more families had to hire a teacher for the children.

- In 2003, there were 6.5 million practicing teachers in the United States, teaching levels from kindergarten through college.

## Family Activities

### Talk Together

Discuss school with your child. Ask him or her to tell about the teacher, the principal, or other school helpers. Help your child compare and contrast his or her school with the schools he or she learns about in class.

### Learn Together

Help your child share things he or she does at school.

✔ Help your child make a list of things he or she does at school each day.

✔ Use a calendar for the current month.

✔ Help your child record any special events at school on the calendar.

✔ Each day have your child tell you the date and draw a picture of something that he or she did at school that day.

### Read Together

 *Owen,* by Kevin Henkes (Greenwillow, ISBN 0-688-11449-0, 1993) Caldecott Honor Book

*Lily's Purple Plastic Purse,* by Kevin Henkes (Greenwillow, ISBN 0-688-12897-1, 1996) ALA Notable Book

*Virgie Goes to School with Us Boys,* by Elizabeth Fitzgerald Howard and E. B. Lewis (illustrator), (Simon & Schuster, ISBN 0-689-80075-2, 2000) ALA Notable Book

 Go online to find more activities at **www.sfsocialstudies.com**

**Thank you for supporting your child's Social Studies education!**

# De la escuela al hogar

## Unidad 1        Boletín

**Estas son las ideas principales que estamos estudiando:**

★ Una escuela es un lugar donde las personas aprenden.

★ En la escuela, la gente a veces trabaja en grupo.

★ Un grupo se compone de personas o cosas.

★ Un país es la tierra donde vive un grupo de personas.

★ La bandera de los Estados Unidos representa a nuestro país.

★ Una regla establece lo que se debe y no se debe hacer.

★ Las reglas nos ayudan a mantenernos fuera de peligro. También nos ayudan a tratar a los demás de una manera justa.

### Datos curiosos

- En 1647, en Massachusetts se aprobó una ley que requería la contratación de maestros. Todos los pueblos con 50 o más familias tenían que contratar un maestro para sus niños. Por lo regular la escuela era un edificio de madera con una sola habitación grande.

- En 2003 había 6.5 millones de maestros trabajando en los Estados Unidos, enseñando desde kindergarten hasta la universidad.

## Actividades en familia

### Para conversar

Hable de la escuela con su niño o niña. Pídale que le hable sobre su maestro o maestra, el director o la directora u otras personas que ayudan en la escuela. Ayúdele a comparar y contrastar su escuela con las escuelas que ha estudiado en clase.

### Para aprender juntos

Use un calendario del mes actual.

✔ Ayude a su niño o niña a anotar los eventos especiales de la escuela en el calendario.

✔ Use un calendario del mes en curso.

✔ Ayude a su niño o niña a apuntar eventos especiales de la escuela en el calendario.

✔ Pida a su niño o niña que todos los días le diga la fecha y que dibuje algo que hizo en la escuela ese día.

### Para leer juntos

*Lila y su bolso de plástico morado,* por Kevin Henkes (Everest, ISBN 84-241-3366-8, 1998)

*Timoteo va a la escuela,* por Rosemary Wells (Altea, ISBN 84-372-1715-2, 1997)

*Pájaros en la cabeza,* por Laura Fernández, (Trillas, ISBN 968-24-1554-31, 1983)

 Para encontrar más actividades, visite **www.estudiosocialessf.com**

**¡Gracias por apoyar la educación de sus hijos en Estudios sociales!**

## Here are the main ideas that we are learning:

★ A neighborhood is a place where people live, work, and play.

★ Many homes in a neighborhood have an address with a number and a street name.

★ A community is a group of people and the place where they live.

★ People in a community can share many different customs.

★ A law is a rule that people must obey.

★ Laws help keep communities safe and clean.

★ A leader helps people decide what to do.

★ A state is a part of a country.

★ A continent is a very large piece of land.

★ An ocean is a very large body of salt water.

### Fast Facts

California has the most people of any state in the United States. Rhode Island has the fewest people. Rhode Island is also the smallest-sized state. The largest-sized state is Alaska.

## Family Activities

### Talk Together

Ask your child to tell about your neighborhood. Talk about the homes and people in your neighborhood. Draw a small circle inside a large circle. Help your child understand that your neighborhood is part of a community just like the small circle is part of the large circle. Talk about the community where you and your child live.

### Learn Together

Help your child explore your neighborhood.

✔ Take a walk through your neighborhood and help your child name the people and places you see.

✔ Ask your child to tell about new buildings or changes you see.

### Read Together

 *My Town,* by Rebecca Treays (EDC, ISBN 0-746-03079-7, 1998) Notable Social Studies Book

*The Little House,* by Virginia Lee Burton (Turtleback, ISBN 0-606-01531-0, 1969) Caldecott Medal

*Urban Roosts: Where Birds Nest in the City,* by Barbara Bash (Little Brown, ISBN 0-316-08312-7, 1992)

 Go online to find more activities at **www.sfsocialstudies.com**

**Thank you for supporting your child's Social Studies education!**

# De la escuela al hogar

## Unidad 2

## Boletín

**Estas son las ideas principales que estamos estudiando:**

★ Un vecindario es un lugar donde la gente vive, trabaja y juega.

★ Muchas de las residencias de un vecindario tienen una dirección con un número y un nombre de calle.

★ Una comunidad es un grupo de personas y el lugar donde viven.

★ Los habitantes de una comunidad pueden compartir muchas costumbres diferentes.

★ Una ley es una regla que las personas deben obedecer.

★ Las leyes ayudan a mantener las comunidades limpias y seguras.

★ Un líder ayuda a la gente a decidir qué hacer.

★ Un estado es una parte de un país.

★ Un continente es una extensión de tierra muy grande.

★ Un océano es una extensión de agua salada muy grande.

### Datos curiosos

California es el estado de los Estados Unidos que más habitantes tiene. Rhode Island es el estado más pequeño y con menos habitantes. Alaska es el estado más grande.

## Actividades en familia

### Para conversar

Pida a su niño o niña que le hable de su vecindario. Hable con su niño o niña de las residencias y personas de su vecindario. Tracen un círculo pequeño dentro de un círculo grande. Ayude a su niño o niña a entender que su vecindario es parte de una comunidad del mismo modo que el círculo pequeño es parte del círculo grande. Hablen sobre la comunidad donde usted y su niño o niña viven.

### Para aprender juntos

Ayude a su niño o niña a explorar su vecindario.

✔ Den un paseo por el vecindario y ayude a su niño o niña a nombrar las personas y lugares que ven.

✔ Pida a su niño o niña que le hable de los nuevos edificios o cambios que vean.

### Para leer juntos

*En la ciudad,* por Erik Forbes y Oki Han (Celebration Press, ISBN 0-673-75859-1, 1996)

*La casita,* por Virginia Lee Burton (Lectorum, ISBN 9-706-29059-8, 1994) Caldecott medal

*La señorita Runfio,* por Barbara Cooney (Puffin Books, ISBN 0-140-56231-1, 1997) Notable Social Studies Book

 Para encontrar más actividades, visite **www.estudiossocialessf.com**

**¡Gracias por apoyar la educación de sus hijos en Estudios sociales!**

# School to Home

**Unit 3**                                              **Newsletter**

## Here are the main ideas that we are learning:

★ A job is the work people do.

★ Needs are things people must have to live. Wants are things people would like to have.

★ Most people work to make money.

★ People can spend or save the money they have.

★ Some workers use tools to grow or make goods.

★ Some workers have service jobs. Some people are volunteers.

★ Transportation moves people and goods from place to place.

## Fast Facts

Five of the fastest growing jobs in the early 2000s are:

• **computer engineers**—people who design or fix computers or computer software

• **computer support specialists**—people who help you when you have a problem with a computer or computer software

• **systems analysts**—people who study the way something is done on a computer and help find ways to make it better

• **database administrators**—people who work with the information on computer software

• **desktop publishing specialists**—people who use computers to make printed materials

## Family Activities

### Talk Together

Ask your child to tell you about the jobs he or she read about at school. Have your child explain why he or she would or would not like to do each job.

### Learn Together

Help your child learn about different jobs.

✔ Write the name of jobs on small pieces of paper.

✔ Put the papers in a bag.

✔ Have your child take a paper from the bag, name the job, and tell something about it.

✔ Take turns drawing papers.

### Read Together

*Sam and the Lucky Money,* by Karen Chinn (Lee and Low, ISBN 1-880-00013-X, 1995)

 *The Night Worker,* by Katie Banks and Georg Hallensleben (illustrator), (Farrar Straus & Giroux, ISBN 0-374-35520-7, 2000) 2001 Charlotte Zolotow Award, ALA Notable Children's Book

*The Boy Who Loved to Draw: Benjamin West,* by Barbara Brenner (Houghton Mifflin, ISBN 0-395-85050-0, 1999) Notable Social Studies Book

 Go online to find more activities at **www.sfsocialstudies.com**

**Thank you for supporting your child's Social Studies education!**

# De la escuela al hogar

## Unidad 3

**Boletín**

## Estas son las ideas principales que estamos estudiando:

★ Un trabajo es la actividad que hacemos para lograr algo.

★ Las necesidades son cosas que la gente debe tener para poder vivir. Los deseos son cosas que a la gente le gustaría tener.

★ La mayoría de la gente trabaja para ganar dinero.

★ Las personas pueden gastar o ahorrar el dinero que tienen.

★ Algunos trabajadores usan herramientas para cultivar, criar o fabricar cosas.

★ Algunos trabajadores tienen empleos de servicio. Algunas personas son trabajadores voluntarios.

★ El transporte permite llevar personas y bienes de un lugar a otro.

### Datos curiosos

Cinco de los empleos de mayor crecimiento a principios del siglo XXI son:

- **ingenieros de computadoras**—personas que diseñan o arreglan computadoras o software para computadoras

- **especialistas de apoyo técnico**—personas que ayudan a resolver problemas con una computadora o software de computadora

- **analistas de sistemas**—personas que estudian la forma en que se hace algo en una computadora y ayudan a encontrar formas de mejorarlo

- **administradores de bases de datos**—personas que trabajan con la información de software de computadora

- **especialistas en autoedición**—personas que usan computadoras para hacer materiales impresos

## Actividades en familia

### Para conversar

Pida a su niño o niña que le hable de los empleos sobre los que ha leído en la escuela. Pídale que le explique por qué le gustaría o no tener esos empleos.

### Para aprender juntos

Ayude a su niño o niña a explorar el mundo del trabajo.

✔ Escriba los nombres de empleos en pequeños pedazos de papel.

✔ Ponga los papelitos en una bolsa.

✔ Pida a su niño o niña que saque un papelito de la bolsa, lea el nombre del empleo y diga algo sobre éste.

✔ Túrnense sacando papelitos.

### Para leer juntos

*En el restaurante,* por Chirstine Loomis (Scholastic, ISBN 0-590-93121-0, 1993)

*Pan dulce,* por Kathleen Contreras y Blanca Dorantes (ilustradora) (Scholastic, ISBN 0-590-29384-2, 1995)

*Tomás y la señora de la biblioteca,* por Pat Mora y Raúl Colón (ilustrador) (Dragonfly, ISBN 0-679-84173-3, 1997) Tomás Rivera Mexican American Children's Book Award

 Para encontrar más actividades, visite **www.estudiosocialessf.com**

**¡Gracias por apoyar la educación de sus hijos en Estudios sociales!**

# School to Home

## Unit 4

### Newsletter

**Here are the main ideas that we are learning:**

★ The weather is how it is outside at a certain place and time.

★ Places on Earth can have different kinds of weather.

★ Earth has different landforms such as mountains, plains, lakes, and rivers.

★ A natural resource is a useful thing that comes from nature.

★ History tells us the story of people and places from the past.

★ Follow the 3 Rs to reduce, reuse, and recycle natural resources.

## Fast Facts

The highest mountain in the United States is Mount McKinley in Alaska. The lowest place is a desert called Death Valley in California. The deepest lake in the United States is Crater Lake in Oregon. It is located in an inactive volcano. There is an island called Wizard Island in the middle of Crater Lake.

Dallol, Ethiopia has the highest average annual temperature in the world: 94 °F. Plateau Station, Antartica has the lowest average annual temperature in the world: -70 °F.

## Family Activities

### Talk Together

Ask your child to tell you things he or she has learned about Earth and its mountains, lakes, rivers, and plains. Then have him or her describe the weather for the day.

### Learn Together

Help your child chart the weather.

✔ Make a weather chart for one week.

✔ Draw seven boxes on a sheet of paper and label the days of the week.

✔ Have your child draw a picture to show the weather for each day.

### Read Together

*I Celebrate Nature,* by Diane Iverson (Dawn Publications, ISBN 1-883-22000-9, 1995) Notable Social Studies Book

*Where Once There Was a Wood,* by Denise Fleming (Henry Holt, ISBN 0-805-06482-6, 2000) Notable Social Studies Book

*Where Does the Garbage Go?* by Paul Showers, Randy and Paul Chewning (illustrators), (HarperCollins, ISBN 0-064-45114-3, 1994)

 Go online to find more activities at **www.sfsocialstudies.com**

**Thank you for supporting your child's Social Studies education!**

# De la escuela al hogar

## Unidad 4

**Boletín**

**Estas son las ideas principales que estamos estudiando:**

★ El tiempo es cómo está el clima en un cierto lugar y momento.

★ Los lugares de la Tierra pueden tener distintas clases de clima.

★ La Tierra tiene accidentes geográficos como montañas, llanuras, lagos y ríos.

★ Un recurso natural es una cosa útil que proviene de la naturaleza.

★ La historia trata de personas y lugares del pasado.

★ Siga las 3 R para reducir, reutilizar y reciclar recursos naturales.

### Datos curiosos

La montaña más alta de los Estados Unidos es el monte McKinley de Alaska. El lugar más bajo es un desierto llamado el Valle de la Muerte en California. El lago más profundo de los Estados Unidos es el lago Crater en Oregón. Está ubicado en un volcán inactivo. Hay una isla llamada Wizard en el medio del lago Crater.

Dallol, Etiopía, tiene la temperatura promedio annual más alta del mundo: 94°F. La Estación Plateau, en la Antártida, tiene la temperatura promedio annual más baja: -70°F.

## Actividades en familia

### Para conversar

Pida a su niño o niña que le cuente cosas que haya aprendido sobre la Tierra y sus montañas, lagos, ríos y llanuras. Después pídale que describa el tiempo que hace ese día.

### Para aprender juntos

Ayude a su niño o niña a llevar en registro del tiempo que hace.

✔ Haga una tabla del clima de una semana.

✔ Dibuje siete cuadros en una hoja de papel y escriba los días de la semana.

✔ Pida a su niño o niña que haga un dibujo del clima de cada día.

### Para leer juntos

*Y hoy... ¿Qué tiempo hará?,* por Paul Rogers y Kazuko (ilustrador), (Scholastic, ISBN 0-590-46834-0, 1993)

*El árbol generoso,* por Shel Silverstein (Litexa, ISBN 980-6053-44-3, 1997)

*Historia verdadera de una princesa,* por Inés Arredondo (CIDCLI, ISBN 968-494-016-5, 1985)

 Para encontrar más actividades, visite **www.estudiosocialessf.com**

**¡Gracias por apoyar la educación de sus hijos en Estudios sociales!**

# School to Home

**Unit 5**          **Newsletter**

## Here are the main ideas that we are learning:

★ Native Americans were the first people to live in North America.

★ Christopher Columbus landed near North America in 1492.

★ The Pilgrims came to North America because they wanted the freedom to practice their own religion.

★ The Pilgrims lived in colonies. Colonies are places that are ruled by a country that is far away.

★ A holiday is a special day when we honor an important person or event.

★ The President is our country's leader.

★ A capital is a city where important leaders of a state or country live and work.

★ A citizen is a member of a state and country.

★ Adult citizens in the United States have a right to vote.

## Fast Facts

In 1800, Washington, D.C. became the nation's capital. The city was named after George Washington.

## Family Activities

### Talk Together

Have your child tell you about the first people to live in North America. Then ask your child about Columbus, the Pilgrims, and the early leaders of our country. Name various holidays and have your child tell why we celebrate each holiday.

### Learn Together

Help your child learn about our country's flag.

✔ Use pieces of paper or strips of cloth to make a flag.

✔ Help your child make the 13 red and white stripes and the blue section with 50 stars.

✔ You may want to make a flag that has only 13 stars for the original 13 colonies.

### Read Together

*I Have Heard of a Land,* by Joyce Carol Thomas and Floyd Cooper (illustrator), (HarperCollins, ISBN 0-06-443617-9, 2000) ALA Notable Book, Coretta Scott King Honor Book, Notable Social Studies Book

*The Boston Coffee Party,* by Doreen Rappaport and Emily Arnold McCully (illustrator), (HarperTrophy, ISBN 0-064-44141-5, 1990)

*The Story of the Statue of Liberty,* by Betsy C. Maestro and Giulio Maestro (illustrator), (HarperCollins, ISBN 0-688-08746-9, 1989)

 Go online to find more activities at **www.sfsocialstudies.com**

**Thank you for supporting your child's Social Studies education!**

# De la escuela al hogar

## Unidad 5

## Boletín

**Estas son las ideas principales que estamos estudiando:**

★ Los indígenas norteamericanos fueron los primeros habitantes de América del Norte.

★ Cristóbal Colón desembarcó cerca de América del Norte en 1492.

★ Los peregrinos llegaron a América del Norte porque querían tener la libertad de practicar su propia religión.

★ Los peregrinos vivían en colonias. Las colonias son lugares gobernados por otro país.

★ Un día festivo es un día especial en el que honramos a una persona o suceso importante.

★ El presidente es el líder de nuestro país.

★ Una capital es una ciudad donde viven y trabajan los líderes importantes de un estado o país.

★ Un ciudadano es miembro de un estado y de un país.

★ Los ciudadanos adultos de los Estados Unidos tienen el derecho a votar.

### Datos curiosos

En 1800, Washington, D.C. se convirtió en la capital de la nación. La ciudad fue nombrada en honor a George Washington.

## Actividades en familia

### Para conversar

Pida a su niño o niña que hable sobre los primeros habitantes de América del Norte. Luego pregúntele sobre Colón, los peregrinos y los primeros líderes de los Estados Unidos. Nombre varios días festivos y pida a su niño o niña que le diga por qué se celebra cada día.

### Para aprender juntos

Ayude a su niño o niña a aprender cosas sobre la bandera de nuestro país.

✔ Use pedazos de papel o tiras de tela para hacer la bandera de los Estados Unidos.

✔ Ayude a su niño o niña a hacer las 13 franjas rojas y blancas y la sección azul con las 50 estrellas.

✔ Quizás prefieran hacer una bandera con sólo 13 estrellas por las 13 colonias originales.

### Para leer juntos

*El niño pastor,* por Kristine L. Franklin y Jill Kastner (ilustradora), (Libros Colibrí, ISBN 0-689-31918-5)

*En 1492,* por Jean Marzolo y Steve Björkman (ilustrador), (Scholastic, ISBN 0590-49442-2, 1995)

*El niño maicero,* por Patricia Van Rhijn y Maribel Suárez (ilustradora), (CIDCLI, ISBN 968-494-042-4, 1991)

 Para encontrar más actividades, visite **www.estudiosocialessf.com**

**¡Gracias por apoyar la educación de sus hijos en Estudios sociales!**

# School to Home

## Unit 6

### Here are the main ideas that we are learning:

★ The world is a name for Earth and everything on it.

★ A market is a place where goods are sold.

★ People who work at a market provide services.

★ You communicate when you give and get information.

★ An invention is something new.

★ An inventor is someone who makes or invents something new.

## Fast Facts

- The fax machine was invented by Alexander Bain of Scotland more than 150 years ago. Long before fax machines were used in homes and most businesses, they were used by police departments and newspapers.

- The sandwich was invented by the Earl of Sandwich in the 1700s. He was so busy he did not want to stop to eat, so he ordered some food to be piled between two slices of bread. The rest is history!

## Family Activities

### Talk Together

Ask your child to tell you who invented the printing press and who invented the telephone. Then ask your child who invented the light bulb we use today. Encourage your child to tell about one of the people in the lesson and the important things he or she did.

### Learn Together

Help your child learn to explore the world.

✔ Look at a newspaper with your child.

✔ Point to pictures or read aloud the headlines about events around the world.

✔ Talk about what is happening and where it is happening.

### Read Together

*Saturday Market,* by Patricia Grossman and Enrique O. Sanchez (illustrator), (Lothrop Lee & Shepard, ISBN 0-688-12176-4, 1994)

*The Great Ball Game: A Muskogee Story,* by Joseph Bruchac and Susan L. Roth (illustrator), (Dial Books for Young Readers, ISBN 0-803-71539-0, 1994)

*The Dragon Prince: A Chinese Beauty and the Beast Tale,* by Laurence Yep and Kam Mak (illustrator), (HarperCollins Juvenile Books, ISBN 0-060-24381-3, 1997)

 Go online to find more activities at **www.sfsocialstudies.com**

**Thank you for supporting your child's Social Studies education!**

# De la escuela al hogar

## Unidad 6

**Boletín**

## Estas son las ideas principales que estamos estudiando:

★ El mundo es otro nombre para la Tierra y todo lo que hay en ella.

★ Un mercado es un lugar donde se vende bienes.

★ La gente que trabaja en un mercado provee servicios.

★ Nos comunicamos cuando damos y recibimos información.

★ Un invento es algo que no existía antes.

★ Un inventor es alguien que hace o inventa algo nuevo.

## Datos curiosos

- La máquina de fax fue inventada por Alexander Bain de Escocia hace más de 150 años. Mucho antes de que las máquinas de fax se usaran en el hogar y en muchos negocios, se usaban en departamentos de la policía y en los periódicos.

- El sándwich fue inventado por el Conde de Sandwich en el siglo XVIII. Estaba tan ocupado que no quería detenerse para comer, así que ordenó que le pusieran algo de comida entre dos rodajas de pan. ¡El resto es historia!

## Actividades en familia

### Para conversar

Pida a su niño o niña que le diga quién invéntó la imprenta y quién invéntó el teléfono. Pregunte a su niño o niña quién inventó la bombilla de luz que usamos hoy. Anime a su niño o niña a que hable sobre una de las personas estudiadas en clase y de las cosas importantes que esta persona hizo.

### Para aprender juntos

Ayude a su niño o niña a explorar el mundo.

✔ Hojee el periódico con su niño o niña.

✔ Señale fotos o lea en voz alta los titulares sobre sucesos mundiales.

✔ Hablen de lo que está pasando y dónde está pasando.

### Para leer juntos

*El gusto del mercado mexicano,* por Nancy María Grande Tabor (Charlesbridge Publishing, ISBN 0-88106-820-9, 1996)

*Aventuras de Maxi, el perro taxista,* por Debra y Sal Barracca (Reading Rainbow, ISBN 0-8037-2009-2, 1996)

*La niña que amaba los caballos salvajes,* por Paul Goble (Alladin, ISBN 0-689-81455-0, 1998) Caldecott Medal

Para encontrar más actividades, visite **www.estudiosocialessf.com**

**¡Gracias por apoyar la educación de sus hijos en Estudios sociales!**

# Calendar Pages

**E**ach month of the year provides new opportunities for children to learn about history, geography, government, good citizenship, economics, culture, and technology through holidays, "firsts," and important birthdays and anniversaries. The 12-month format is ideal for year-round schools and summer schools but also provides a wealth of information for children who attend a standard 9-month school.

The following pages offer an entire year of calendar activities, including:

- A list of facts about the month: birthdays, holidays, and other red-letter days
- Detailed instructions for constructing a bulletin board for each month
- At least one additional activity per month
- A selection of books for children to read about a monthly subject

An extra page is given for you to note state or community celebrations.

**Speech activity, page TR20** ▶

**Pet awards, page TR26** ▼

Softest

Biggest Ears

Don't play with matches

◀ **Fire safety activity, page TR19**

**Hot Dog Day, page TR28** ▲

# Notes

August _____

_____

September _____

_____

October _____

_____

November _____

_____

December _____

_____

January _____

_____

February _____

_____

March _____

_____

April _____

_____

May _____

_____

June _____

_____

July _____

_____

# August

## August

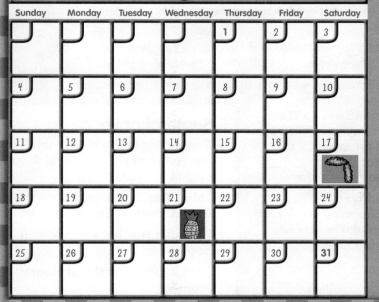

| Sunday | Monday | Tuesday | Wednesday | Thursday | Friday | Saturday |
|---|---|---|---|---|---|---|
| | | | | 1 | 2 | 3 |
| 4 | 5 | 6 | 7 | 8 | 9 | 10 |
| 11 | 12 | 13 | 14 | 15 | 16 | 17 |
| 18 | 19 | 20 | 21 | 22 | 23 | 24 |
| 25 | 26 | 27 | 28 | 29 | 30 | 31 |

## Fill Out the Calendar!

- Provide each child with a blank copy of the monthly calendar.
- Show children where to put the dates for days 1 and 31. Then have them fill in the remaining dates.
- Have children put symbols in date boxes to represent August holidays: a coon-skin cap in the 17 box for David Crockett, and a pineapple in the 21 box for the date Hawaii became our 50th state.
- Ask students to brainstorm symbols for your own classroom or schoolwide events.

### August Facts

- August is the eighth month of the year and has 31 days.
- August is **American Artists' Appreciation Month.**
- **Hawaii** became the 50th state on August 21, 1959.
- **David Crockett** was born on August 17, 1786.

# Activities

## Hawaii

Provide colorful tissue paper squares and large cut-out letters that spell HAWAII. Ask children to place a pencil eraser in the middle of each tissue square, then pull the paper up around the end of the pencil. Place a dot of glue on one of the letters, then press the tissue paper down on the glue. It will form a flower shape. Cover each letter with these tissue paper flowers.

## David Crockett

One thing that David Crockett was famous for was telling tall tales. Explain to children that tall tales are amazing stories. Have a Tall Tale Contest and challenge children to come up with amazing tall tales to share with the class.

## American Artists' Month

For more information on **American Artists' Month,** look for books such as these:

*America My Land, Your Land, Our Land,* by W. Nikola-Lisa (Lee & Low Books, ISBN 1-880000-37-7, 1997)

*Norman Rockwell,* by Mike Venezia (Children's Press, ISBN 0-516-27173-3, 2000)

# September

## September

| Sunday | Monday | Tuesday | Wednesday | Thursday | Friday | Saturday |
|--------|--------|---------|-----------|----------|--------|----------|
|        |        |         |           | 1        | 2      | 3        |
| 4      | 5      | 6       | 7         | 8        | 9      | 10       |
| 11     | 12     | 13      | 14        | 15       | 16     | 17       |
| 18     | 19     | 20      | 21        | 22       | 23     | 24       |
| 25     | 26     | 27      | 28        | 29       | 30     |          |

## Fill Out the Calendar!

- Provide each child with a blank copy of the monthly calendar.
- Show children where to put the dates for days 1, 10, 20, and 30. Then have them fill in the remaining dates.
- Have children put symbols in date boxes to represent September holidays: a hammer and nail in the first Monday box for Labor Day and an apple in the 26 box for Johnny Appleseed's birthday.
- Ask children to brainstorm symbols for your own classroom or schoolwide events.

### September Facts

- September is the ninth month of the year and has 30 days. Autumn begins in September.
- **Labor Day** is celebrated on the first Monday in September.
- **Hispanic Heritage Week** is in September.
- September is **National Honey Month.**
- **Johnny Appleseed** was born on September 26, 1774.

# Activities

## Johnny Appleseed

Fill a burlap sack with Johnny Appleseed items such as apples, apple seeds, a cooking pot, and some stuffed "wild" animals. Have children create a skit about Johnny Appleseed's life.

## Celebrate Autumn

Give each child a long piece of red ribbon. Have children draw colorful fall leaves on yellow, brown, green, orange, and red construction paper. Then have children cut out the leaves and attach them to their ribbons. Hang these "falling leaves" to decorate the room for autumn.

## National Honey Month

For more information on **honey,** look for books such as these:

*From Flower to Honey,* by Robin Nelson (Lerner, ISBN 0-8225-0717-X, 2003)

*Honey,* by Pam Robson (Children's Press, ISBN 0-516-26220-3, 1997)

# October

## October

| Sunday | Monday | Tuesday | Wednesday | Thursday | Friday | Saturday |
|---|---|---|---|---|---|---|
| | | | | 1 | 2 | 3 |
| 4 | 5 | 6 | 7 | 8 | 9 | 10 |
| 11 | 12 | 13 | 14 | 15 | 16 | 17 |
| 18 | 19 | 20 | 21 | 22 | 23 | 24 |
| 25 | 26 | 27 | 28 | 29 | 30 | 31 |

## Fill Out the Calendar!

- Provide each child with a blank copy of the monthly calendar.
- Show children where to put the dates for days 1, 15, and 30. Then have them fill in the remaining dates.
- Have children put symbols in date boxes to represent October holidays: a flame in the second Sunday box for the beginning of Fire Prevention Week, an old sailing ship in the second Monday box for Columbus Day, a globe in the 24 box for United Nations Day, and a torch in the 28 box for the day the Statue of Liberty was dedicated.
- Ask children to brainstorm symbols for your own classroom or schoolwide events.

### October Facts

- October is the tenth month of the year and has 31 days.
- **Columbus Day** is celebrated on the second Monday in October.
- **Fire Prevention Week** is the second week in October.
- **The Statue of Liberty** was dedicated on October 28, 1886.
- October 24 is **United Nations Day.**

# Activities

## United Nations Day

Provide children with books about some of the United Nations member countries. Point out similarities and differences between students and children from these other countries. Have the class make paper plate puppets of children of other nations. Help locate these countries on a world map.

## Fire Prevention Week

Help children name some fire safety rules. Have children make fire safety bookmarks to share with other students in the school. Each bookmark should have one safety tip.

## Statue of Liberty

For more information on the **Statue of Liberty,** look for books such as these:

*Lisa in New York,* by Anne Gutman (Knopf, Distributed by Random House, ISBN 0-375-81119-2, 2002)

*The Statue of Liberty,* by Tristan Boyer Binns (Heinemann Library, 1-58810-121-5, ISBN 2001)

# November

## November

| Sunday | Monday | Tuesday | Wednesday | Thursday | Friday | Saturday |
|--------|--------|---------|-----------|----------|--------|----------|
|  |  |  |  | 1 | 2 | 3 |
| 4 | 5 | 6 | 7 | 8 | 9 | 10 |
| 11 USA | 12 | 13 | 14 | 15 | 16 | 17 |
| 18 | 19 | 20 | 21 | 22 | 23 | 24 |
| 25 | 26 | 27 | 28 | 29 | 30 |  |

## Fill Out the Calendar!

- Provide each child with a blank copy of the monthly calendar.
- Show children where to put the dates for days 2, 4, 6, 8, and continue counting by 2s up to 30. Then have them fill in the remaining dates.
- Have children put symbols in date boxes to represent November holidays: a sandwich in the 3 box for Sandwich Day, USA in the 11 box for Veterans Day, and a turkey in the fourth Thursday box for Thanksgiving.
- Ask children to brainstorm symbols for your own classroom or schoolwide events.

### November Facts
- November is the eleventh month of the year and has 30 days.
- November 11 is **Veterans Day.**
- **Thanksgiving** is the fourth Thursday in November.
- **Sandwich Day** is November 3.

# Activities

## Veterans Day

Veterans Day honors people who fought in our country's wars. Celebrations include flag ceremonies, speeches, and parades. Have children make patriotic hats and flags, then have a parade around the school. Ask a few children to make short speeches about the United States of America.

"We learned about Veteran's Day today . . ."

## Sandwich Day

In honor of Sandwich Day, have children make Super Sandwiches. Give each child a 4" x 18" strip of paper. Have him or her fold it accordion style and draw a sandwich item on each section. Attach a paper "slice of bread" to each end to form a sandwich.

## Thanksgiving

For more information on **Thanksgiving,** look for books such as these:

*I Know an Old Lady Who Swallowed a Pie,* by Alison Jackson (Dutton Children's Books, ISBN 0-525-45645-7, 1997)

*Thanksgiving,* by Mari C. Schuh (Pebble Books, ISBN 0-7368-0981-3, 2002)

# December

## December

| Sunday | Monday | Tuesday | Wednesday | Thursday | Friday | Saturday |
|--------|--------|---------|-----------|----------|--------|----------|
| | | | | 1 | 2 | 3 |
| 4 | 5 | 6 | 7 | 8 | 9 | 10 |
| 11 | 12 | 13 | 14 | 15 | 16 | 17 |
| 18 | 19 | 20 | 21 | 22 | 23 | 24 |
| 25 | 26 | 27 | 28 | 29 | 30 | 31 |

## Fill Out the Calendar!

- **Provide each child with a blank copy of the monthly calendar.**
- **Show children where to put the dates for days 1, 15, and 31. Then have them fill in the remaining dates.**
- **Have children put symbols in date boxes to represent December holidays: a pie in the 1 box for National Pie Day, a present in the 26 box for Boxing Day, and a party hat in the 31 box for New Year's Eve.**
- **Ask children to brainstorm symbols for your own classroom or schoolwide events.**

### December Facts

- December is the twelfth month of the year and has 31 days. Winter begins in December.
- **Hanukah, Christmas,** and **Kwanzaa** are celebrated in December.
- December 1st is **National Pie Day.**
- December 26 is **Boxing Day** in Canada.

# Activities

## Winter

Help children find out what winter weather is like in different states across the country. Have children draw pictures of what they would wear if they visited each of those states in the winter time.

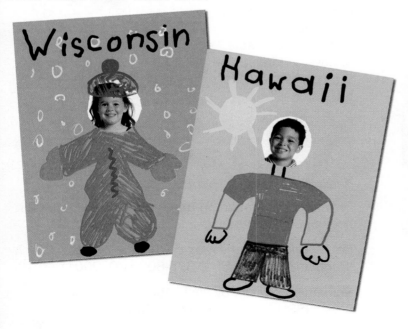

## Boxing Day

Boxing Day in Canada is a day to give gifts to community helpers such as postal workers, trash collectors, and firefighters. Have children make a list of school personnel who have helped keep the school running smoothly through the year. Place hand-made Thank You cards in small decorated boxes and deliver them to your school workers.

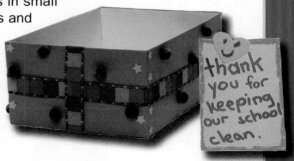

## Kwanzaa

For more information on **Kwanzaa** look for books such as these:

*Kwanzaa,* by David F. Marx (Children's Press, ISBN 0-516-22207-4, 2000)

*Kwanzaa,* by Lola M. Schaefer (Pebble Books, ISBN 0-7368-0663-6, 2001)

# January

## January

| Sunday | Monday | Tuesday | Wednesday | Thursday | Friday | Saturday |
|--------|--------|---------|-----------|----------|--------|----------|
|        |        |         |           |          | 1      | 2        | 3 |

| Sunday | Monday | Tuesday | Wednesday | Thursday | Friday | Saturday |
|--------|--------|---------|-----------|----------|--------|----------|
|        |        |         |           | 1 | 2 | 3 |
| 4 | 5 | 6 | 7 | 8 | 9 | 10 |
| 11 | 12 | 13 | 14 | 15 | 16 | 17 |
| 18 | 19 MLK | 20 | 21 | 22 | 23 | 24 |
| 25 | 26 | 27 | 28 | 29 | 30 | 31 |

## Fill Out the Calendar!

- Provide each child with a blank copy of the monthly calendar.
- Show children where to put the dates for days 1 and 31. Then have them fill in the remaining dates.
- Have children put symbols in date boxes to represent January holidays: a green bean in the 6 box for Bean Day, a kite in the 17 box for Benjamin Franklin's birthday, MLK in the third Monday box for Martin Luther King, Jr. Day, and a puzzle piece in the 29 box for National Puzzle Day.
- Ask students to brainstorm symbols for your own classroom or schoolwide events.

### January Facts

- January is the first month of the year and has 31 days.
- **Martin Luther King, Jr. Day** is celebrated on the third Monday January.
- **Benjamin Franklin** was born on January 17, 1706.
- **National Puzzle Day** is January 29.
- January 6 is **Bean Day.**

# Activities

## Martin Luther King, Jr. Day

One of Dr. Martin Luther King, Jr.'s dreams was that all people could live together in peace. Cut out colorful paper squares and have children create a large mosaic picture by gluing the squares into a bright pattern or picture. Tell children that it takes many colors, shapes, and sizes to make a beautiful design.

## National Puzzle Day

Gather some old jigsaw puzzles and have each child glue some pieces onto a picture frame to create a Puzzle Day creation. Children can add glitter to brighten things up. Put a picture of the class in each frame, or have children place their own pictures in the frames.

## Benjamin Franklin

For more information on **Benjamin Franklin,** look for books such as these:

*Ben Franklin and the Magic Squares,* by Frank Murphy (Random House, ISBN 0-375-80621-0, 2001)

*Benjamin Franklin,* by Philip Abraham (Children's Press, ISBN 0-516-23601-6, 2002)

# February

## February

| Sunday | Monday | Tuesday | Wednesday | Thursday | Friday | Saturday |
|---|---|---|---|---|---|---|
| | | | | 1 | 2 | 3 |
| 4 | 5 | 6 | 7 | 8 | 9 | 10 |
| 11 | 12 AL | 13 | 14 ♥ | 15 | 16 | 17 |
| 18 | 19 ‖ | 20 | 21 | 22 GW | 23 | 24 |
| 25 | 26 | 27 | 28 | | | |

## Fill Out the Calendar!

- **Provide each child with a blank copy of the monthly calendar.**
- **Show children where to put the dates for days 1 and 28. Then have them fill in the remaining dates.**
- **Have children put symbols in date boxes to represent February holidays: a heart in the 14 box for Valentine's Day; a red, white, and blue background in the third Monday box for Presidents' Day; AL in the 12 box for Lincoln's birthday; and GW in the 22 box for Washington's birthday.**
- **Ask children to brainstorm symbols for your own classroom or schoolwide events.**

### February Facts

- February is the second month of the year and has 28 days. It is the shortest month of the year.
- Every four years February has 29 days. This is called a **Leap Year.**
- February is **Black History Month** and **Dental Health Month** is also in February.
- **Valentine's Day** and **Presidents' Day** are in February. Presidents' Day honors all U.S. Presidents. It is celebrated in February because both **George Washington** and **Abraham Lincoln** were born in February.

# Activities

## Valentine's Day

Children can use index cards to make Valentine's Day postcards for their families. Children can decorate the front of the card and practice writing their name and address on the front. Then children can write a Valentine message on the back.

## Presidents' Day—Abraham Lincoln

Make log cabins in honor of President Abraham Lincoln. Start with clean, dry milk cartons. Staple the tops closed. Have children glue brown construction paper to the sides and top. Ask children to draw doors and windows to finish their cabins.

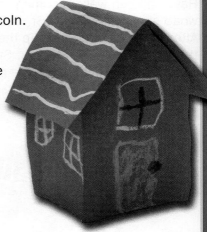

## Black History Month

For more information on **Black History Month,** look for books such as these:

*Martin Luther King, Jr.,* by Pam Walker (Children's Press, ISBN 0-516-23436-6, 2001)

*Rosa Parks,* by Lola M. Schaefer (Pebble Books, ISBN 0-7368-1176-1, 2002)

# March

## March

| Sunday | Monday | Tuesday | Wednesday | Thursday | Friday | Saturday |
|--------|--------|---------|-----------|----------|--------|----------|
|  |  |  |  | 1 | 2 | 3 |
| 4 | 5 | 6 | 7 | 8 | 9 | 10 |
| 11 | 12 | 13 | 14 | 15 | 16 | 17 |
| 18 | 19 | 20 | 21 | 22 | 23 | 24 |
| 25 | 26 | 27 | 28 | 29 | 30 | 31 |

## Fill Out the Calendar!

- Provide each child with a blank copy of the monthly calendar.
- Show children where to put the dates for days 2, 4, 6, 8, and continue counting by 2s up to 30. Then have them fill in the remaining dates.
- Have children put symbols in date boxes to represent March holidays: a "Cat in the Hat" hat in the 2 box for Dr. Seuss's birthday, a shamrock in the 17 box for St. Patrick's Day, and a newspaper in the first Monday in March for the beginning of Newspaper in Education week.
- Ask children to brainstorm symbols for your own classroom or schoolwide events.

### March Facts

- March is the third month of the year and has 31 days. Spring begins in March.
- Theodor **"Dr. Seuss"** Geisel was born on March 2, 1904.
- **St. Patrick's Day** is March 17.
- The first week in March is **Newspaper in Education Week.**

# Activities

## St. Patrick's Day

Have children walk in some paint, then walk across an old white sheet to create a St. Patrick's Day rainbow. Alternately, children can dip their hands in paint and make the rainbow with handprints. Start at the top with a red stripe, then work down to the purple at the bottom. Add a pot of gold at the end of the rainbow!

## Newspaper in Education Week

Gather a variety of newspaper headlines and full-page ads. Ask children to cut out large letters and numbers. Have them use the letters to spell out words and the numbers to do simple math problems.

## Spring

For more information on **spring,** look for books such as these:

*A to Z of Spring,* by Tracy Maurer (Rourke Publishing, ISBN 1-58952-197-8, 2003)

*Spring,* by Cynthia Fitterer Klingel (Child's World, ISBN 1-56766-813-5, 2001)

# April

## April

| Sunday | Monday | Tuesday | Wednesday | Thursday | Friday | Saturday |
|--------|--------|---------|-----------|----------|--------|----------|
|        |        |         |           | 1        | 2      | 3        |
| 4      | 5      | 6       | 7         | 8        | 9      | 10       |
| 11     | 12     | 13      | 14        | 15       | 16     | 17       |
| 18     | 19     | 20      | 21        | 22       | 23     | 24       |
| 25     | 26     | 27      | 28        | 29       | 30     |          |

## Fill Out the Calendar!

- Provide each child with a blank copy of the monthly calendar.
- Show children where to put the dates for days 1 and 30. Then have them fill in the remaining dates.
- Have children put symbols in date boxes to represent April holidays: a globe in the 22 box for Earth Day and a zig-zag in the 29 box for Zipper Day.
- Ask children to brainstorm symbols for your own classroom or schoolwide events.

### April Facts

- April is the fourth month of the year and has 30 days.
- **Earth Day** is April 22.
- April is **Math Education Month** and **National Poetry Month.**
- **Zipper Day** is April 29.

# Activities

## Zipper Day

Thank goodness for zippers! Ask children to name things that have a zipper. Have children cut out pictures of items from catalogs and magazines that have zippers. Make a "Zip It Up!" collage.

## National Poetry Month

Have children write springtime shape poems. Ask children to name spring items such as birds, flowers, and butterflies. Make cardboard patterns of these spring things for children to trace. Each child can choose one item and write his or her poem about that item inside the shape.

## Earth Day

For more information on **Earth Day,** look for books such as these:

*Earth Day,* by Mir Tamim Ansary (Heinemann Library, ISBN 1-58810-220-3, 2002)

*Earth Day,* by David F. Marx (Children's Press, ISBN 0-516-27174-1, 2001)

# May

## May

| Sunday | Monday | Tuesday | Wednesday | Thursday | Friday | Saturday |
|--------|--------|---------|-----------|----------|--------|----------|
|  |  |  |  | 1 | 2 | 3 |
| 4 | 5 | 6 | 7 | 8 | 9 | 10 |
| 11 Mom | 12 | 13 | 14 | 15 | 16 | 17 |
| 18 | 19 | 20 | 21 | 22 | 23 | 24 |
| 25 | 26 USA | 27 | 28 | 29 | 30 | 31 |

## Fill Out the Calendar!

- Provide each child with a blank copy of the monthly calendar.
- Show children where to put the dates for days 1 and 31. Then have them fill in the remaining dates.
- Have children put symbols in date boxes to represent May holidays: a piñata in the 5 box for Cinco de Mayo, the word MOM in the second Sunday box for Mother's Day, and USA in the last Monday box for Memorial Day.
- Ask children to brainstorm symbols for your own classroom or schoolwide events.

### May Facts

- May is the fifth month of the yea and has 31 days.
- **Memorial Day** is the last Monda in May.
- May is **National Book Month,** a **National Transportation Month**
- The Mexican holiday, **Cinco de Mayo,** is celebrated on May 5.
- The second Sunday in May is **Mother's Day.**

## Activities

### National Pet Week

Have children bring in their stuffed animals for National Pet Week. Have a pet show. Ask children to make a special award for each pet.

### National Book Month

How many books can your class read in a month? Keep count by making a book chain. Supply colorful strips of paper in the reading center. Ask children to write the name of each book they read on a paper strip. Make a chain of "books" that stretches across the classroom!

### Cinco de Mayo

For more information on **Cinco de Mayo,** look for books such as these:

*Cinco de Mayo,* by Lola M. Schaefer (Pebble Books, ISBN 0-7368-0661-X, 2001)

*A Look at Mexico,* by Helen Frost (Pebble Books, ISBN 0-7368-0985-6, 2002)

# June

## June

| Sunday | Monday | Tuesday | Wednesday | Thursday | Friday | Saturday |
|--------|--------|---------|-----------|----------|--------|----------|
|        |        |         |           | 1        | 2      | 3        |
| 4      | 5      | 6       | 7         | 8        | 9      | 10       |
| 11     | 12     | 13      | 14  | 15 | 16 | 17 |
| 18 DAD | 19     | 20      | 21        | 22       | 23     | 24       |
| 25     | 26     | 27      | 28        | 29       | 30     |          |

## Fill Out the Calendar!

- Provide each child with a blank copy of the monthly calendar.

- Show children where to put the dates for days 1 and 30. Then have them fill in the remaining dates.

- Have children put symbols in date boxes to represent June holidays: the word DAD in the third Sunday box for Father's Day and a U.S. flag in the 14 box for Flag Day.

- Ask children to brainstorm symbols for your own classroom or schoolwide events.

### June Facts

- June is the sixth month of the year and has 30 days. Summer begins in June.

- **Flag Day** is June 14.

- The third Sunday in June is **Father's Day.**

- June is **National Dairy Month**

- **Zoo and Aquarium Month** is in June.

# Activities

## Flag Day

Make thumbprint flags for Flag Day. Give each child a white piece of paper in the shape of the U.S. flag. Using red and blue ink, have children make thumbprint stripes and a thumbprint blue field on their flag.

## National Dairy Month

Remind children that the milk they drink in school comes from cows. Provide a blackline drawing of a cow for each child, then read the poem, "I Never Saw a Purple Cow." Ask children to decorate their cows using a variety of colors and designs.

## Zoo and Aquarium Month

For more information on **zoos and aquariums,** look for books such as these:

*Curious George Goes to the Aquarium,* edited by Margaret Rey (Houghton Mifflin, ISBN 0-395-36628-3, 1999)

*My Trip to the Zoo,* by Mercer Mayer (McGraw-Hill Children's Pub., ISBN 1-57768-643-8, 2003)

# July

## July

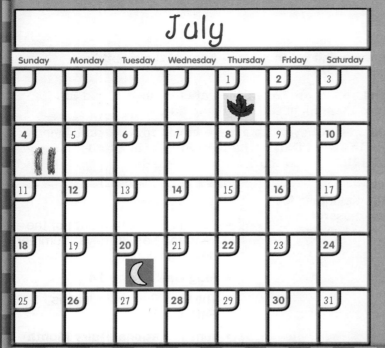

| Sunday | Monday | Tuesday | Wednesday | Thursday | Friday | Saturday |
|--------|--------|---------|-----------|----------|--------|----------|
|  |  |  |  | 1 | 2 | 3 |
| 4 | 5 | 6 | 7 | 8 | 9 | 10 |
| 11 | 12 | 13 | 14 | 15 | 16 | 17 |
| 18 | 19 | 20 | 21 | 22 | 23 | 24 |
| 25 | 26 | 27 | 28 | 29 | 30 | 31 |

## Fill Out the Calendar!

- Provide each child with a blank copy of the monthly calendar.
- Show children where to put the dates for days 2, 4, 6, 8, and continue counting by 2s up to 30. Then have them fill in the remaining dates.
- Have children put symbols in date boxes to represent July holidays: a red maple leaf in the 1 box for Canada Day; a red, white, and blue background in the 4 box for Independence Day; and a moon in the 20 box for the first moon landing in 1969.
- Ask children to brainstorm symbols for your own classroom or schoolwide events.

### July Facts

- July is the seventh month of the year and has 31 days.
- **Independence Day** is July 4.
- The **first Moon landing** was on July 20, 1969.
- July is **National Ice Cream Mon** and **National Hot Dog Month.**
- July 1 is **Canada Day.**

# Activities

## National Hot Dog Month

Welcome to Hot Dog City! Ask children what it would be like if everything was made out of hot dogs! Have children make paper hot dogs, then turn these dogs into houses, offices, cars, and trees by adding windows, wheels, and branches. Ask children to add other hot dog details!

## Canada Day

In honor of Canada Day, display the Canadian flag and ask children what they know about this country. Tell them that the maple leaf is the symbol on the flag of Canada. Cut out maple leaf patterns and have children trace overlapping leaves. Children can fill in each section with a different color to create a vivid design.

## Independence Day

For more information on **Independence Day,** look for books such as these:

*Independence Day,* by David F. Marx (Children's Press, ISBN 0-516-22232-5, 2001)

*Independence Day,* by Robin Nelson (Lerner, ISBN 0-8225-1318-8, 2003)

# Writing Rubrics

# Rubric for Narrative Writing or Dictation

| | **6** | **5** | **4** |
|---|---|---|---|
| **Content Quality and Idea Development** | • focused on topic and purposeful<br>• ideas well developed<br>• relevant, no extraneous material<br>• conveys sense of completeness | • focused on topic<br>• ideas developed<br>• relevant, no extraneous material<br>• conveys sense of completeness | • fairly focused on topic<br>• moderately developed ideas<br>• may include extraneous or loosely related material<br>• conveys some sense of completeness |
| **Voice** | • clear and fitting for topic<br>• expressive and engaging<br>• well-suited for audience and purpose | • clear and fitting for topic<br>• engaging<br>• suited for audience and purpose | • fairly clear and seems to fit topic<br>• fairly engaging style<br>• suited for audience and purpose |
| **Organization** | • logical progression of ideas<br>• sequence very clear | • logical progression of ideas<br>• sequence clear | • organizational pattern apparent<br>• some lapses may occur in organization<br>• sequence fairly clear |
| **Word Choice** | • demonstrates command of language<br>• precise and interesting word choice<br>• wide variety of word choice | • demonstrates command of language<br>• interesting word choice<br>• variety of word choice | • adequate word choice<br>• some variety of word choice |
| **Sentence Fluency** | • uses complete sentences<br>• varied sentence structures and lengths | • uses complete sentences<br>• varied sentence structures | • uses complete sentences<br>• varied sentence structure attempted |
| **Mechanics** | • correct spelling, punctuation, and capitalization<br>• proper grammar and usage | • few errors in spelling, punctuation, and capitalization<br>• proper grammar and usage<br>• errors do not prevent understanding | • mostly correct spelling, punctuation, and capitalization<br>• few errors in grammar and usage<br>• errors do not prevent understanding |
| **If using a four-point rubric** | **4** | **4** | **3** |

| ③ | ② | ① | Cannot be scored |
|---|---|---|---|
| generally focused on topic<br>ideas may be vague<br>some loosely related material<br>conveys some sense of completeness | • somewhat related to topic<br>• insufficient development of ideas<br>• includes extraneous or loosely related material<br>• may lack sense of completeness | • minimally focused on topic<br>• little, if any, development of ideas<br>• lacks sense of completeness | • no focus on topic<br>• no development of ideas<br>• incomplete |
| generally clear and seems to fit topic<br>engaging at times<br>generally suited for audience and purpose | • rarely comes through<br>• basic attempt to engage reader<br>• ill-suited for audience and purpose | • weak<br>• basic attempt to engage reader<br>• not suited for audience or purpose | • no attempt to engage reader<br>• unaware of audience or purpose |
| organizational pattern attempted<br>sequence generally clear | • little evidence of organizational pattern<br>• sequence may be unclear | • no organizational pattern evident<br>• sequence unclear | • no attempt at organization present<br>• no sequence<br>• cannot follow |
| adequate word choice<br>limited, predictable, or occasionally vague word choice<br>some variety of word choice | • word choice limited, inappropriate, or vague<br>• little variety of word choice | • limited or inappropriate word choice may obscure meaning<br>• words/phrases repetitive and show minimal variety | • incorrect word choice<br>• word choice shows no variety |
| uses complete sentences<br>varied sentence structure attempted | • occasional sentence fragment or run-on sentence | • excessive use of sentence fragments or run-on sentences | • no complete sentences |
| generally correct spelling, punctuation, and capitalization<br>some errors in grammar and usage<br>errors do not prevent understanding | • some errors in spelling, punctuation, and capitalization<br>• errors in grammar and usage<br>• errors may prevent understanding | • errors in spelling, punctuation, and capitalization<br>• frequent errors in grammar and usage<br>• errors prevent understanding | • critical errors in spelling, punctuation, and capitalization<br>• critical errors in grammar and usage<br>• errors prevent understanding |
| **3** | **2** | **1** | |

# Rubric for Persuasive Writing or Dictation

| | **6** | **5** | **4** |
|---|---|---|---|
| **Content Quality and Idea Development** | • well-focused on topic<br>• clear position stated<br>• facts and opinions to support position<br>• presents convincing argument<br>• conveys sense of completeness | • focused on topic<br>• clear position stated<br>• ample support<br>• presents convincing argument<br>• conveys sense of completeness | • fairly focused on topic<br>• position apparent<br>• adequate support, though perhaps uneven<br>• may include extraneous or loosely related material<br>• presents reasonable argument<br>• conveys some sense of completeness |
| **Voice** | • clear and fitting for topic<br>• confident and engaging<br>• well-suited for audience and purpose | • clear and fitting for topic<br>• engaging<br>• suited for audience and purpose | • fairly clear and seems to fit topic<br>• fairly engaging<br>• suited for audience and purpose |
| **Organization** | • logical organization with reasons presented in clear order<br>• clearly contains beginning, middle, and end<br>• easy to follow argument | • logical organization with reasons presented in order<br>• contains beginning, middle, and end<br>• easy to follow argument | • organizational pattern apparent<br>• some lapses may occur in organization<br>• vaguely contains beginning, middle, and end<br>• fairly easy to follow argument |
| **Word Choice** | • demonstrates command of language<br>• precise, persuasive, and interesting word choice<br>• wide variety of word choice | • demonstrates command of language<br>• interesting word choice<br>• variety of word choice | • adequate word choice<br>• some variety of word choice |
| **Sentence Fluency** | • uses complete sentences<br>• varied sentence structures and lengths | • uses complete sentences<br>• varied sentence structures | • uses complete sentences<br>• varied sentence structure attempted |
| **Mechanics** | • correct spelling, punctuation, and capitalization<br>• proper grammar and usage | • few errors in spelling, punctuation, and capitalization<br>• proper grammar and usage<br>• errors do not prevent understanding | • mostly correct spelling, punctuation, and capitalization<br>• few errors in grammar and usage<br>• errors do not prevent understanding |
| **If using a four-point rubric** | **4** | **4** | **3** |

| ③ | ② | ① | Cannot be scored |
|---|---|---|---|
| generally focused on topic<br>position may be present<br>some support included, but erratic development<br>includes loosely related material<br>presents mediocre argument<br>conveys some sense of completeness | • somewhat related to topic<br>• position may be unclear<br>• inadequate support<br>• includes extraneous or unrelated material<br>• may lack sense of completeness | • minimally focused on topic<br>• position unclear<br>• little, if any, development of support<br>• lacks sense of completeness | • no focus on topic<br>• no position<br>• no development of support<br>• incomplete |
| generally clear and seems to fit topic<br>engaging at times<br>generally suited for audience and purpose | • rarely comes through<br>• basic attempt to engage reader<br>• ill-suited for audience and purpose | • weak<br>• basic attempt to engage reader<br>• not suited for audience or purpose | • no attempt to engage reader<br>• unaware of audience or purpose |
| organizational pattern attempted<br>frequent lapses in organization<br>attempts to contain beginning, middle, and end<br>generally easy to follow argument | • little evidence of organizational pattern<br>• somewhat difficult to follow argument | • no organizational pattern evident<br>• difficult to follow argument | • no attempt at organization present<br>• cannot follow argument |
| adequate word choice<br>limited, predictable, or occasionally vague word choice<br>some variety of word choice | • word choice limited, inappropriate, or vague<br>• little variety of word choice | • limited or inappropriate word choice may obscure meaning<br>• words/phrases repetitive and show minimal variety | • incorrect word choice<br>• word choice shows no variety |
| uses complete sentences<br>varied sentence structure attempted | • occasional sentence fragment or run-on sentence | • excessive use of sentence fragments or run-on sentences<br>• sentences difficult to understand | • no complete sentences |
| generally correct spelling, punctuation, and capitalization<br>some errors in grammar and usage<br>errors do not prevent understanding | • some errors in spelling, punctuation, and capitalization<br>• errors in grammar and usage<br>• errors may prevent understanding | • errors in spelling, punctuation, and capitalization<br>• frequent errors in grammar and usage<br>• errors prevent understanding | • critical errors in spelling, punctuation, and capitalization<br>• critical errors in grammar and usage<br>• errors prevent understanding |
| **3** | **2** | **1** | |

# Rubric for Expressive/Descriptive Writing or Dictation

| | **6** | **5** | **4** |
|---|---|---|---|
| **Content Quality and Idea Development** | • well-focused on topic<br>• ideas supported with interesting and vivid details<br>• "paints a picture" for reader<br>• conveys sense of completeness | • focused on topic<br>• ideas supported with details<br>• sustains interest of reader<br>• conveys sense of completeness | • fairly focused on topic<br>• ideas supported with adequate detail<br>• may include extraneous or loosely related material<br>• conveys some sense of completeness |
| **Voice** | • clear and fitting for topic<br>• thoughtful, expressive, and engaging<br>• well-suited for audience and purpose | • clear and fitting for topic<br>• expressive and engaging<br>• suited for audience and purpose | • fairly clear and seems to fit topic<br>• fairly engaging with some expression<br>• suited for audience and purpose |
| **Organization** | • logical progression of ideas<br>• easy to follow | • logical progression of ideas<br>• easy to follow | • organizational pattern apparent<br>• some lapses may occur in organization<br>• fairly easy to follow |
| **Word Choice** | • demonstrates command of language<br>• precise, vivid, and interesting word choice<br>• wide variety of word choice | • demonstrates command of language<br>• interesting word choice<br>• variety of word choice | • adequate word choice<br>• some variety of word choice |
| **Sentence Fluency** | • uses complete sentences<br>• varied sentence structures and lengths | • uses complete sentences<br>• varied sentence structures | • uses complete sentences<br>• varied sentence structure attempted |
| **Mechanics** | • correct spelling, punctuation, and capitalization<br>• proper grammar and usage | • few errors in spelling, punctuation, and capitalization<br>• proper grammar and usage<br>• errors do not prevent understanding | • mostly correct spelling, punctuation, and capitalization<br>• few errors in grammar and usage<br>• errors do not prevent understanding |
| **If using a four-point rubric** | **4** | **4** | **3** |

| ③ | ② | ① | Cannot be scored |
|---|---|---|---|
| generally focused on topic<br>ideas may be vague<br>some details included<br>some loosely related material<br>conveys some sense of completeness | • somewhat related to topic<br>• inadequate details<br>• includes extraneous or unrelated material<br>• may lack sense of completeness | • minimally focused on topic<br>• little, if any, development of ideas<br>• lacks sense of completeness | • no focus on topic<br>• no development of ideas<br>• incomplete |
| generally clear and seems to fit topic<br>engaging at times<br>generally suited for audience and purpose | • rarely comes through<br>• basic attempt to engage reader<br>• ill-suited for audience and purpose | • weak<br>• basic attempt to engage reader<br>• not suited for audience or purpose | • no attempt to engage reader<br>• unaware of audience or purpose |
| organizational pattern attempted<br>generally easy to follow | • little evidence of organizational pattern<br>• somewhat difficult to follow | • no organizational pattern evident<br>• difficult to follow | • no attempt at organization present<br>• cannot follow |
| adequate word choice<br>limited, predictable, or occasionally vague word choice<br>some variety of word choice | • word choice limited, inappropriate, or vague<br>• little variety of word choice | • limited or inappropriate word choice may obscure meaning<br>• words/phrases repetitive and show minimal variety | • incorrect word choice<br>• word choice shows no variety |
| uses complete sentences<br>varied sentence structure attempted | • occasional sentence fragment or run-on sentence | • excessive use of sentence fragments or run-on sentences<br>• sentences difficult to understand | • no complete sentences |
| generally correct spelling, punctuation, and capitalization<br>some errors in grammar and usage<br>errors do not prevent understanding | • some errors in spelling, punctuation, and capitalization<br>• errors in grammar and usage<br>• errors may prevent understanding | • errors in spelling, punctuation, and capitalization<br>• frequent errors in grammar and usage<br>• errors prevent understanding | • critical errors in spelling, punctuation, and capitalization<br>• critical errors in grammar and usage<br>• errors prevent understanding |
| **3** | **2** | **1** | |

# Rubric for Expository Writing or Dictation

| | **6** | **5** | **4** |
|---|---|---|---|
| **Content Quality and Idea Development** | • well-focused on topic<br>• ideas supported with interesting details<br>• conveys sense of completeness | • focused on topic<br>• ideas supported with details<br>• conveys sense of completeness | • fairly focused on topic<br>• ideas supported with adequate detail, but development may be uneve▮<br>• may include extraneous or loosely related material<br>• conveys some sense of completeness |
| **Voice** | • clear and fitting for topic<br>• engaging<br>• well-suited for audience and purpose | • clear and fitting for topic<br>• engaging<br>• suited for audience and purpose | • fairly clear and seems to fi▮ topic<br>• fairly engaging<br>• suited for audience and purpose |
| **Organization** | • logical progression of ideas<br>• excellent transitions<br>• easy to follow | • logical progression of ideas<br>• good transitions<br>• easy to follow | • organizational pattern apparent<br>• some lapses may occur in organization<br>• some transitions<br>• fairly easy to follow |
| **Word Choice** | • demonstrates command of language<br>• precise, interesting word choice<br>• wide variety of word choice | • demonstrates command of language<br>• precision in word choice<br>• variety of word choice | • adequate word choice<br>• some variety of word choic▮ |
| **Sentence Fluency** | • strong topic sentence<br>• uses complete sentences<br>• varied sentence structures and lengths | • good topic sentence<br>• uses complete sentences<br>• varied sentence structures | • adequate topic sentence<br>• uses complete sentences<br>• varied sentence structure attempted |
| **Mechanics** | • correct spelling, punctuation, and capitalization<br>• proper grammar and usage | • few errors in spelling, punctuation, and capitalization<br>• proper grammar and usage<br>• errors do not prevent understanding | • mostly correct spelling, punctuation, and capitalization<br>• few errors in grammar and usage<br>• errors do not prevent understanding |
| **If using a four-point rubric** | **4** | **4** | **3** |

| ③ | ② | ① | Cannot be scored |
|---|---|---|---|
| generally focused on topic<br>some loosely related material<br>some details included, but erratic development | • somewhat related to topic<br>• inadequate details<br>• includes extraneous or unrelated material<br>• may lack sense of completeness | • minimally focused on topic<br>• little, if any, development of ideas<br>• lacks sense of completeness | • no focus on topic<br>• no development of ideas<br>• incomplete |
| generally clear and seems to fit topic<br>engaging at times<br>generally suited for audience and purpose | • rarely comes through<br>• basic attempt to engage reader<br>• ill-suited for audience and purpose | • weak<br>• basic attempt to engage reader<br>• not suited for audience or purpose | • no attempt to engage reader<br>• unaware of audience or purpose |
| organizational pattern attempted<br>few transitions<br>generally easy to follow | • little evidence of organizational pattern<br>• no transitions<br>• somewhat difficult to follow | • no organizational pattern evident<br>• difficult to follow | • no attempt at organization present<br>• cannot follow |
| adequate word choice<br>limited, predictable, or occasionally vague word choice<br>some variety of word choice | • word choice limited, inappropriate, or vague<br>• little variety of word choice | • limited or inappropriate word choice may obscure meaning<br>• words/phrases repetitive and show minimal variety | • incorrect word choice<br>• word choice shows no variety |
| adequate topic sentence<br>uses complete sentences<br>varied sentence structure attempted<br>generally simple sentence structures | • weak topic sentence<br>• occasional sentence fragment or run-on sentence<br>• limited to simple sentence structure | • topic sentence not evident<br>• excessive use of sentence fragments or run-on sentences<br>• limited to simple sentence structure<br>• sentences difficult to understand | • no topic sentence<br>• no complete sentences<br>• sentence structure basic/below grade level |
| generally correct spelling, punctuation, and capitalization<br>some errors in grammar and usage<br>errors do not prevent understanding | • some errors in spelling, punctuation, and capitalization<br>• errors in grammar and usage<br>• errors may prevent understanding | • errors in spelling, punctuation, and capitalization<br>• frequent errors in grammar and usage<br>• errors prevent understanding | • critical errors in spelling, punctuation, and capitalization/below grade level<br>• critical errors in grammar and usage/below grade level<br>• errors prevent understanding |
| **3** | **2** | **1** | |

# Notes

# Unit 1 Bibliography

*Froggy Goes to School,* by Jonathan London and Frank Remkiewicz (illustrator), (Puffin, ISBN 0-14-056247-8, 1998) **Easy**

*My First Day of School,* by Patrick K. Hallinan (Hambleton-Hill, ISBN 1-57102-154-X, 2000) **Easy**

*My Teacher Sleeps in School,* by Leatie Weiss and Ellen Weiss (illustrator), (Econo-Clad Books, ISBN 0-808-57413-2, 1999) **Easy**

 *Owen,* by Kevin Henkes (Greenwillow, ISBN 0-688-11449-0, 1993) **Easy** *Caldecott Honor Book, 1994*

*School from A to Z,* by Bobbie Kalman (Crabtree Publishing, ISBN 0-86505-418-5, 1999) **Easy**

*See You Tomorrow, Charles,* by Miriam Cohen and Lillian Hoban (illustrator), (Bantam Books, ISBN 0-440-41151-3, 1997) **Easy**

*Double Trouble in Walla Walla,* by Andrew Clements and Sal Murdocca (illustrator), (Millbrook Press, ISBN 0-7613-0275-1, 1997) **On-Level**

*Lilly's Purple Plastic Purse,* by Kevin Henkes (Greenwillow, ISBN 0-688-12897-1, 1996) **On-Level** *ALA Notable Book*

*No Good in Art,* by Miriam Cohen and Lillian Hoban (illustrator), (Morrow, ISBN 0-688-84234-8, 1980) **On-Level**

*Rex and Lilly Schooltime,* by Laurene Krasny Brown and Marc Brown (illustrator), (Little Brown, ISBN 0-316-10920-7, 1997) **On-Level**

*Teammates,* by Peter Golenbock (Harcourt, ISBN 0-15-200603-6, 1990) **On-Level**

*When Jo Louis Won the Title,* by Belinda Rochelle and Larry Johnson (illustrator), (Houghton Mifflin, ISBN 0-395-81657-2, 1996) **On-Level**

*Yoko,* by Rosemary Wells (Hyperion Press, ISBN 0-7868-0395-9, 1998) **On-Level**

*Marianthe's Story: Painted Words, Spoken Memories,* by Aliki (Greenwillow, ISBN 0-688-15661-4, 1998) **Challenge**

*Mary McLeod Bethune,* by Eloise Greenfield (Harper Trophy, ISBN 0-064-46168-8, 1994) **Challenge**

*More Than Anything Else,* by Marie Bradby and Chris Soentpiet (illustrator), (Orchard Books, ISBN 0-531-09464-2, 1995) **Challenge**

*Nobody's Mother Is in Second Grade,* by Robin Pulver and G. Brian Karas (illustrator), (Dial Books for Young Readers, ISBN 0-8037-1210-3, 1992) **Challenge**

*Story of Ruby Bridges, The,* by Robert Coles (Scholastic, ISBN 0-590-57281-4, 1995) **Challenge**

*Toll-Bridge Troll, The,* by Patricia Rae Wolff and Kimberly Bulcken Root (illustrator), (Voyager Picture Book, ISBN 0-152-02105-1, 2000) **Challenge** *ALA Notable Book, 1996*

*Virgie Goes to School with Us Boys,* by Elizabeth Fitzgerald Howard and E. B. Lewis (illustrator), (Simon & Schuster, ISBN 0-689-80076-2, 2000) **Challenge** *ALA Notable Book*

*Bringing History Home,* by M. Gail Hickey (Allyn & Bacon, ISBN 0-205-28169-9, 1998) **Teacher Reference**

*Hands Around the World,* by Susan Milord (Williamson, ISBN 0-913-58965-9, 1992) **Teacher Reference**

*Through My Eyes,* by Ruby Bridges (Scholastic, ISBN 0-590-18923-9, 1999) **Teacher Reference**

Look for this symbol throughout the Teacher's Edition to find **Award-Winning Selections**.

# Unit 2 Bibliography

**Carpenters,** by Vicky Franchino (Compass Point Books, ISBN 0-756-50006-0, 2000) **Easy**

**Fire Fighters,** by Lucia Raatma (Compass Point Books, ISBN 0-756-50009-5, 2000) **Easy**

**Letter Carriers,** by Alice K. Flanagan (Compass Point Books, ISBN 0-756-50010-9, 2000) **Easy**

**Mayors,** by Alice K. Flanagan (Compass Point Books, ISBN 0-756-50064-8, 2001) **Easy**

 **My Town,** by Rebecca Treays (EDC, ISBN 0-746-03079-7, 1998) **Easy** *Notable Social Studies Book*

 **Officer Buckle and Gloria,** by Peggy Rathmann (Putnam, ISBN 0-399-22616-8, 1995) **Easy** *Caldecott Medal 1996*

**Police Officers,** by Alice K. Flanagan (Compass Point Books, ISBN 0-756-50011-7, 2000) **Easy**

**As the Roadrunner Runs: A First Book of Maps,** by Gail Hartman (Bradbury, ISBN 0-02-743092-8, 1994) **On-Level**

**Aurora Means Dawn,** by Scott Russell Sanders and Jill Kastner (illustrator), (Aladdin, ISBN 0-689-81907-2, 1998) **On-Level**

**City Mouse–Country Mouse and Two More Mouse Tales from Aesop,** by John C. Wallner (illustrator), (Scholastic, ISBN 0-590-41155-1, 1987) **On-Level**

**Home Album, A,** by Peter Roop and Connie Roop (Heinemann, ISBN 1-57572-602-5, 1998) **On-Level**

**How to Make an Apple Pie and See the World,** by Marjorie Priceman (Alfred A. Knopf, ISBN 0-673-61098-5, 1994) **On-Level**

 **Little House, The,** by Virginia Lee Burton (Turtleback, ISBN 0-606-01531-0, 1969) **On-Level** *Caldecott Medal, 1943*

**Me on the Map,** by Joan Sweeney and Annette Cable (illustrator), (Dragonfly, ISBN 0-517-88557-3, 1998) **On-Level**

**My New York,** by Kathy Jakobsen (Little Brown, ISBN 0-316-45653-5, 1993) **On-Level**

**Philharmonic Gets Dressed, The,** by Karla Kuskin (HarperCollins, ISBN 0-06-443124-X, 1986) **On-Level**

**Raising Yoder's Barn,** by Jane Yolen and Bernie Fuchs (illustrator), (Little Brown, ISBN 0-316-96887-0, 1998) **On-Level**

 **Uptown,** by Bryan Collier (Henry Holt, ISBN 0-805-05721-8, 2000) **On-Level** *Coretta Scott King Award*

**Wee Sing Around the World,** by Pamela Conn Beall and Susan Hagen Nipp (Penguin Putnam, ISBN 0-8431-3740-1, 1994) **On-Level**

**Where I Live,** by Christopher Wormell (Dial, ISBN 0-8037-2056-4, 1996) **On-Level**

**Journey, The,** by Sarah Stewart and David Small (illustrator), (Farrar Straus & Giroux, ISBN 0-374-33905-8, 2001) **Challenge**

 **Miss Rumphius,** by Barbara Cooney (Viking, ISBN 0-140-50539-3, 1985) **Challenge** *Notable Social Studies Book*

**New Coat for Anna, A,** by Harriet Ziefert and Anita Lobel (illustrator), (Econo-Clad Books, ISBN 0-833-51245-5, 1999) **Challenge**

 **Smoky Night,** by Eve Bunting and David Diaz (illustrator), (Harcourt Brace, ISBN 0-152-01884-0, 1999) **Challenge** *Caldecott Medal Winner*

**Urban Roosts: Where Birds Nest in the City,** by Barbara Bash (Little Brown, ISBN 0-316-08312-7, 1992) **Challenge**

**Window,** by Jeannie Baker (Greenwillow, ISBN 0-688-08918-6, 1991) **Challenge**

**Discovery Channel School** Video *Two Children, Two Cultures* 25 minutes.

 Look for this symbol throughout the Teacher's Edition to find **Award-Winning Selections**.

# Unit 3 Bibliography

*Career Day,* by Anne F. Rockwell (HarperCollins Children's Book Group, ISBN 0-06-027565-0, 2000) **Easy**

*Cowboy Bunnies,* by Christine Loomis (Putnam, ISBN 0-399-22625-7, 1997) **Easy**

 *My Town,* by Rebecca Treays (EDC, ISBN 0-746-03079-7, 1998) **Easy** *Notable Social Studies Book*

*Sam and the Lucky Money,* by Karen Chinn (Lee and Low, ISBN 1-880-00013-X, 1995) **Easy**

*3 Pigs Garage,* by Peter Lippman (Workman Publishing International Ltd., ISBN 0-7611-1361-4, 1998) **Easy**

*Trucks That Build,* by Lars Klove (Simon & Schuster, ISBN 0-689-81762-2, 1999) **Easy**

*Buzby,* by Julia Hoban and John Himmelman (illustrator), (Harper Audio, ISBN 0-694-70044-4, 1996) **On-Level**

*Dancin' in the Kitchen,* by Wendy Gelsanliter and Frank Christian (Putnam, ISBN 0-399-23035-1, 1998) **On-Level**

*Dream Jar, The,* by Bonnie Pryor (Morrow, ISBN 0-688-13062-3, 1996) **On-Level**

*Jamal's Busy Day,* by Wade Hudson and George Ford (illustrator), (Just Us Books, ISBN 0-940975-21-1, 1991) **On-Level**

*Little Red Hen (Makes a Pizza), The,* by Philemon Sturges (Dutton, ISBN 0-525-45953-7, 1999) **On-Level**

*Night Worker, The,* by Katie Banks and Georg Hallensleben (illustrator), (Farrar Straus & Giroux, ISBN 0-374-35520-7, 2000) **On-Level** *2001 Charlotte Zolotow Award, ALA Notable Children's Book*

*Tight Times,* by Barbara Shook Hazen and Trina Shart Hyman (illustrator), (Viking, ISBN 0-14-050442-7, 1983) **On-Level**

*Window Music,* by Anastasia Sven (Viking, ISBN 0-670-87287-3, 1998) **On-Level**

*Worksong,* by Gary Paulsen (Harcourt Brace, ISBN 0-152-00980-9, 1997) **On-Level**

*Animal Rescue: The Best Job There Is,* by Susan E. Goodman (Simon & Schuster, ISBN 0-689-81794-0, 2000) **Challenge**

*Boy Who Loved to Draw: Benjamin West, The,* by Barbara Brenner (Houghton Mifflin, ISBN 0-395-85050-0, 1999) **Challenge** *Notable Social Studies Trade Book*

*Magic School Bus Gets Programmed, The,* by Joanna Cole (Scholastic Books, ISBN 0-590-18731-7, 1999) **Challenge**

*Mama & Papa Have a Store,* by Amelia Lau Carling (Dial Books for Young Readers, ISBN 0-8037-2044-0, 1998) **Challenge** *Pura Belpré Honor, 2000*

*Weed Is a Flower: The Life of George Washington Carver, A,* by Aliki (Aladdin, ISBN 0-671-66490-5, 1988) **Challenge**

*Steven Caney's Kids' America,* by Steven Caney (Workman, ISBN 0-911-10480-1, 1978) **Teacher Reference**

**Discovery Channel School Video** *Technology at Work* 49 minutes.

Look for this symbol throughout the Teacher's Edition to find **Award-Winning Selections**.

# Unit 4 Bibliography

**Big Blue Whale,** by Nicola Davies and Nick Maland (illustrator), (Candlewick, ISBN 1-56402-895-X, 1997) **Easy**

**The Tiny Seed,** by Eric Carle (Simon and Schuster Children's Publishing, ISBN 0-689-84244-9) **Easy**

**I Took a Walk,** by Henry Cole (Greenwillow, ISBN 0-688-15115-9, 1998) **Easy**

**Morning, Noon, and Night,** by Jean Craighead George and Wendell Minor (illustrator), (HarperCollins, ISBN 0-060-23628-0, 1999) **Easy**

**This Is the Way We Go to School,** by Edith Baer (Scholastic Trade, ISBN 0-590-43162-5, 1992) **Easy**

**Whatever the Weather,** by Karen Wallace (DK, ISBN 0-789-44750-9, 1999) **Easy**

**Backyard,** by Donald M. Silver and Patricia J. Wynne (illustrator), (McGraw-Hill, ISBN 0-070-57930-X, 1997) **On-Level**

**Birdsong,** by Audrey Wood and Robert Florczak (illustrator), (Voyager, ISBN 0-152-02419-0, 2001) **On-Level** **Notable Social Studies Book**

**Bob's Recycling Day,** by Annie Auerbach (Simon Spotlight, ISBN 0-689-84379-8, 2001) **On-Level**

**EcoArt!: Earth-Friendly Art & Craft Experiences for 3- to 9-Year-Olds,** by Laurie Carlson (Williamson Publishing, ISBN 0-913-58968-3, 1992) **On-Level**

**Great Kapok Tree: A Tale of the Amazon**

**Rain Forest, The,** by Lynne Cherry (Voyager Picture Book, ISBN 0-152-02614-2, 2000) **On-Level**

**Legend of the Bluebonnet, The,** by Tomie dePaola (Putnam Publishing Group, ISBN 0-399-20937-9, 1986) **On-Level**

**Picture Book of Sacagawea, A,** by David A. Adler and Dan Brown (illustrator), (Holiday House, ISBN 0-823-41485-X, 2000) **On-Level**

**Prairie Boy's Winter, A,** by William Kurelek (Houghton Mifflin, ISBN 0-395-36609-7, 1984) **On-Level**

**Tell Me a Season,** by Mary McKenna Siddals (Clarion Books, ISBN 0-395-71021-9, 1997) **On-Level**

**Where Once There Was a Wood,** by Denise Fleming (Henry Holt, ISBN 0-805-06482-6, 2000) **On-Level** **Notable Social Studies Book**

**Storm Book, The,** by Charlotte Zolotow (HarperTrophy, ISBN 0-064-43194-0, 1989) **Challenge**

**Sunflower Garden,** by Janice May Udry (Harvey House, ISBN 0-817-84471-6, 1969) **Challenge**

**Turtle Bay,** by Saviour Pirotta and Nilesh Mistry (illustrator), (Farrar Straus & Giroux, ISBN 0-374-37888-6, 1997) **Challenge** **Notable Social Studies Book**

**Where Does the Garbage Go?** by Paul Showers; Randy and Paul Chewning (illustrators), (HarperCollins, ISBN 0-064-45114-3, 1994) **Challenge**

**Mapmaking with Children: Sense of Place Education for the Elementary Years,** by David Sobel (Heinemann, ISBN 0-325-00042-5, 1998) **Teacher Reference**

**Discovery Channel School** Video **Dynamic Earth** 52 minutes. **Invention: Recycling** 27 minutes.

 Look for this symbol throughout the Teacher's Edition to find **Award-Winning Selections**.

# Unit 5 Bibliography

***Cheyenne Again,*** by Eve Bunting and Irving Toddy (illustrator), (Clarion Books, ISBN 0-395-70364-6, 1995) **Easy**

***First Thanksgiving Feast, The,*** by Joan Anderson and George Ancona (photographer), (Clarion Books, ISBN 0-395-51886-5, 1989) **Easy**

***George the Drummer Boy,*** by Nathaniel Benchley and Don Bolognese (illustrator), (HarperCollins Children's Books, ISBN 0-060-20501-6, 1977) **Easy**

***Hooray for the Fourth of July,*** by Wendy Watson (Houghton Mifflin, ISBN 0-618-04036-6, 2000) **Easy**

 ***I Have Heard of a Land,*** by Joyce Carol Thomas and Floyd Cooper (illustrator), (HarperCollins, ISBN 0-06-443617-9, 2000) **Easy** *ALA Notable Book, Coretta Scott King Honor Book, Notable Social Studies Book*

***Ox-Cart Man,*** by Donald Hall and Barbara Cooney (illustrator), (Puffin, ISBN 0-140-50441-9, 1983) **Easy** *Caldecott Medal, 1980*

***T Is for Texas,*** by Anne Bustard (Voyageur, ISBN 0-896-58113-6, 1989) **Easy**

***To Be a Drum,*** by Evelyn Coleman and Aminah Brenda Lynn Robinson (illustrator), (Albert Whitman, ISBN 0-807-58007-4, 2000) **Easy**

***Boston Coffee Party, The,*** by Doreen Rappaport and Emily Arnold McCully (illustrator), (HarperTrophy, ISBN 0-064-44141-5, 1990) **On-Level**

***Cranberry Thanksgiving,*** by Wende Devlin and Harry Devlin (Aladdin, ISBN 0-689-71429-7, 1990) **On-Level**

***Dakota Dugout,*** by Ann Warren Turner and Ronald Himler (illustrator), (Aladdin, ISBN 0-689-71296-0, 1989) **On-Level** *ALA Notable Book*

***How Jackrabbit Got His Very Long Ears,*** by Heather Irbinskas and Kenneth J. Spengler (illustrator), (Rising Moon, ISBN 0-873-58566-6), 1994) **On-Level**

***Midnight Ride of Paul Revere, The,*** by Henry Wadsworth Longfellow and Jeffery Thompson (illustrator), (National Geographic Society, ISBN 0-792-27674-4, 2000) **On-Level**

***Picture Book of Eleanor Roosevelt, A,*** by David A. Adler and Robert Casilla (illustrator), (Holiday House, ISBN 0-823-40856-6, 1991) **On-Level**

***Sam the Minuteman,*** by Nathaniel Benchley and Arnold Lobel (illustrator), (HarperTrophy, ISBN 0-064-44107-5, 1987) **On-Level**

***Star-Spangled Banner, The,*** Francis Scott Key and Peter Spier (illustrator), (Yearling Books, ISBN 0-440-40697-8, 1992) **On-Level**

***Across the Wide Dark Sea: The Mayflower Journey,*** by Jean Van Leeuwen and Thomas B. Allen (illustrator), (Dial Books for Young Readers, ISBN 0-803-71166-2, 1995) **Challenge**

***Flag We Love, The,*** by Pam Muñoz Ryan and Ralph Masiello (illustrator), (Charlesbridge Publishing, ISBN 0-881-06844-6, 2000) **Challenge**

***Peppe the Lamplighter,*** by Elisa Bartone and Ted Lewin (illustrator), (Mulberry Books, ISBN 0-688-15469-7, 1997) **Challenge** *Caldecott Honor Book, 1994*

***Story of the Statue of Liberty, The,*** by Betsy C. Maestro and Giulio Maestro (illustrator), (Mulberry Books, ISBN 0-688-08746-9, 1989) **Challenge**

***Children's Book of America, The,*** by William J. Bennett (Simon & Schuster Trade, ISBN 0-684-84930-5, 1998) **Teacher Reference**

***History Workshop: Reconstructing the Past with Elementary Students,*** by Karen L. Jorgensen (Heinemann, ISBN 0-435-08900-5, 1993) **Teacher Reference**

**Discovery Channel School Video** ***Heroes of American History*** 42 minutes.

 Look for this symbol throughout the Teacher's Edition to find **Award-Winning Selections**.

# Unit 6 Bibliography

**Aesop for Children, The,** by Milo Winter (photographer), (Scholastic Trade, ISBN 0-590-47977-6, 1994) **Easy**

**How Chipmunk Got His Stripes: A Tale of Bragging and Teasing,** by Joseph Bruchac; James Bruchac, Jose Aruego, and Ariane Dewey (illustrators). (Dial Books for Young Readers, ISBN 0-803-72404-7, 2001) **Easy**

**Market Day: A Story Told with Folk Art,** by Lois Ehlert (Harcourt Brace, ISBN 0-152-02158-2, 2000) **Easy**

**On Market Street,** by Arnold Lobel and Anita Lobel (illustrator), (Greenwillow, ISBN 0-688-80309-1, 1981) **Easy**

**Saturday Market,** by Patricia Grossman and Enrique O. Sanchez (illustrator), (Lothrop Lee & Shepard, ISBN 0-688-12176-4, 1994) **Easy**

**Tiger Woman,** by Laurence Yep and Robert Roth (illustrator), (Bridgewater Books, ISBN 0-816-73464-X, 1995) **Easy**

**Train Song,** by Diane Siebert (Harper Trophy, ISBN 0-785-71735-8, 1990) **Easy Notable Children's Trade Book in Social Studies**

**Travel and Transport Then and Now,** by Alistair Smith, Ruth Russell (designer), and Adrienne Salgado (illustrator), (Usborne Publishers Ltd., ISBN 0-746-03102-5, 2000) **Easy**

**Abuela's Weave,** by Omar S. Castaneda and Enrique O. Sanchez (illustrator), (Lee & Low Books, ISBN 1-880-00020-2, 1995) **On-Level**

**Aesop's Fables,** by Aesop and Jerry Pinkney (illusrator), (North-South Books, ISBN 1-58717-000-0, 2000) **On-Level**

**Alexander Graham Bell: A Photo-Illustrated Biography,** by Greg Linder (Bridgestone Books, ISBN 0-736-80202-9, 1999) **On-Level**

**Gabriella's Song,** by Candace Fleming (Atheneum, ISBN 0-689-80973-5, 1997) **On-Level Parents' Choice Silver Honor**

**Great Ball Game: A Muskogee Story, The,** by Joseph Bruchac and Susan L. Roth (illustrator), (Dial Books for Young Readers, ISBN 0-803-71539-0, 1994) **On-Level**

**I Spy a Freight Train: Transportation in Art,** by Lucy Micklethwait (Greenwillow, ISBN 0-688-14700-3, 1996) **On-Level**

**Junior Thunder Lord, The,** by Laurence Yep and Robert Van Nutt (illustrator), (Bridgewater Books, ISBN 0-816-73454-2, 1994) **On-Level**

**Madlenka,** by Peter Sis (Frances Foster Books, ISBN 0-374-39969-7, 2000) **On-Level**

**Many Nations,** by Joseph Bruchac (Econo-Clad Books, ISBN 0-603-11838-3, 1999) **On-Level International Reading Association Teacher's Choice Award**

**Market,** by Ted Lewin (Lothrop Lee & Shepard, ISBN 0-688-12161-6, 1996) **On-Level**

**Picture Book of Thomas Alva Edison, A,** by David A. Adler; John Wallner and Alexandra Wallner (illustrators), (Holiday House, ISBN 0-823-41246-6, 1996) **On-Level**

**Thirteen Moons on Turtle's Back: A Native American Year of Moons,** by Joseph Bruchac and Thomas Locke (illustrator), (Philomel Books, ISBN 0-399-22141-7, 1992) **On-Level**

**To Market, to Market,** by Anne Miranda and Janet Stevens (illustrator), (Harcourt Children's Books, ISBN 0-15-216398-0, 2001) **On-Level**

**When I Was Young in the Mountains,** by Cynthia Rylant (Penguin Putnam Books for Young Readers, ISBN 0-525-42525-X, 1982) **On-Level**

**Aesop's Fables,** by Aesop and Fritz Kredel (illustrator), (Penguin Putnam Books for Young Readers, ISBN 0-448-06003-5, 1977) **Challenge**

**Dragon Prince: A Chinese Beauty and the Beast Tale, The,** by Laurence Yep and Kam Mak (illustrator), (HarperCollins Juvenile Books, ISBN 0-060-24381-3, 1997) **Challenge**

**Earth Under Sky Bear's Feet: Native American Poems of the Land, The,** by Joseph Bruchac (Econo-Clad Books, ISBN 0-613-10503-6, 1999) **Challenge**

**Imaginative Inventions: The Who, What, Where, When, and Why of Roller Skates, Potato Chips, Marbles, and Pie (and More!),** by Charise Mericle Harper (Little, Brown & Co., ISBN 0-316-34725-6, 2001) **Challenge**

**Mae Jemison: The First African American Woman Astronaut,** by Liza N. Burby (Powerkids Press, ISBN 0-823-95027-1, 1998) **Challenge**

**Man Who Tricked a Ghost, The,** by Laurence Yep (Troll Communications, ISBN 0-8167-3031-8, 1999) **Challenge**

**Wake Up, World!: A Day in the Life of Children Around the World,** by Beatrice Hollyer (Henry Holt & Company, ISBN 0-805-06293-9, 1999) **Challenge**

**Welcoming Babies,** by Margy Burns Knight and Anne Sibley O'Brien (illustrator), (Tilbury House Publishers, ISBN 0-884-48123-9, 1994) **Challenge**

**Discovery Channel School Video Inventors and Inventions** 60 minutes.

Look for this symbol throughout the Teacher's Edition to find **Award-Winning Selections.**

# Main Idea and Details

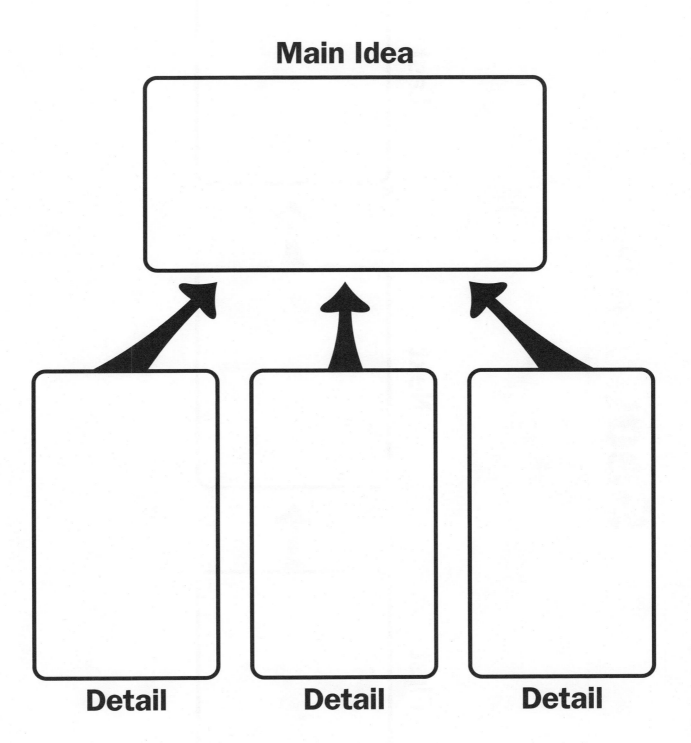

**Main Idea**

**Detail**          **Detail**          **Detail**

**kidspiration** Find a 30-day Kidspiration trial at www.inspiration.com/sf.

Grade 1 • Graphic Organizers **TR45**

# Sequence

**First**

**Next**

**Last**

# Sequence

# Cause and Effect

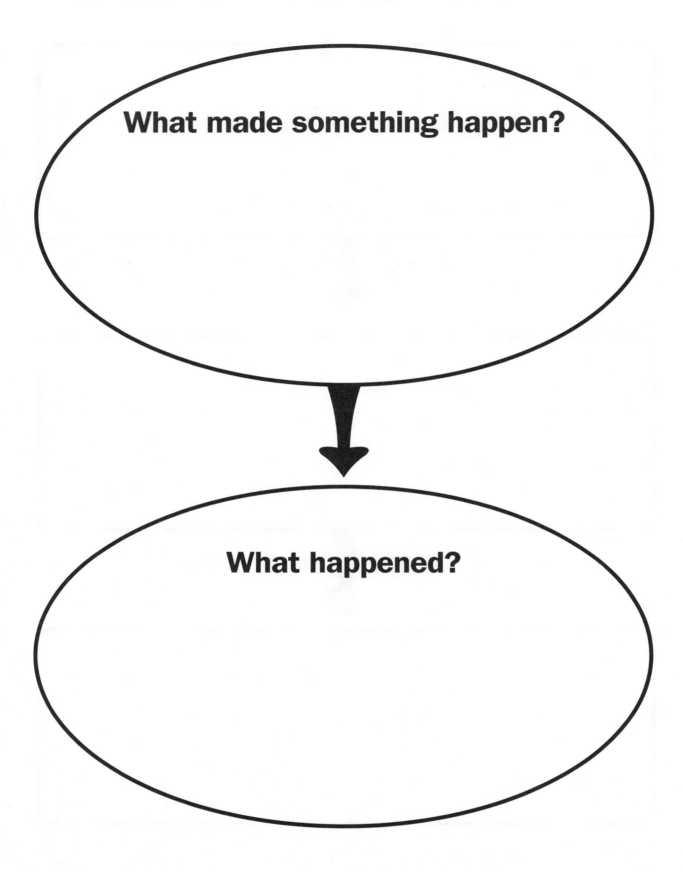

What made something happen?

What happened?

# Cause and Effect

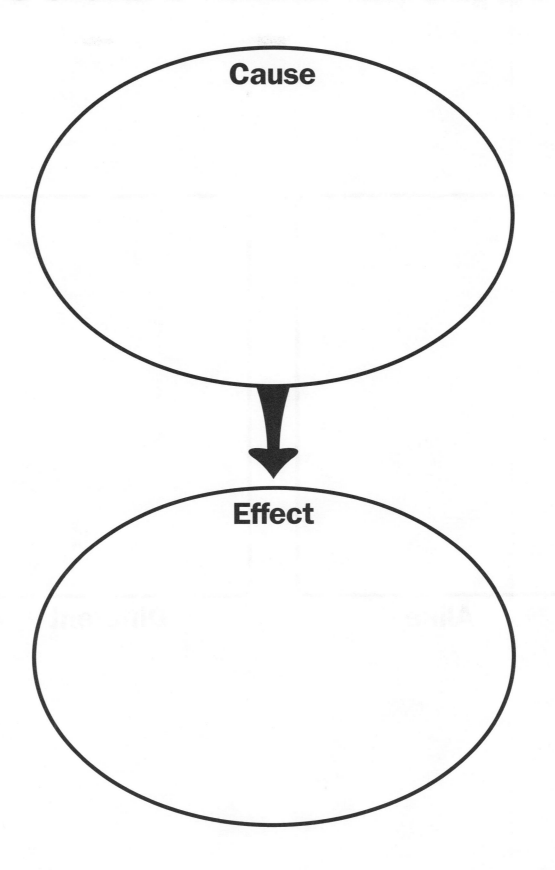

**Cause**

**Effect**

**kidspiration** Find a 30-day Kidspiration trial at www.inspiration.com/sf.

Grade 1 • Graphic Organizers **TR49**

# Compare and Contrast

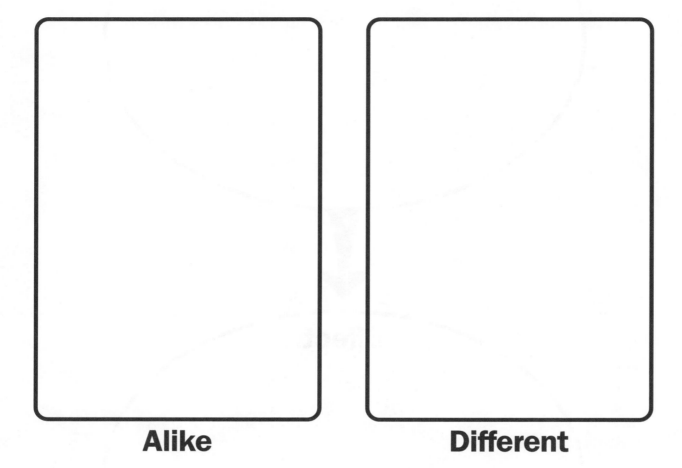

**Alike**

**Different**

**kidspiration** Find a 30-day Kidspiration trial at www.inspiration.com/sf.

# Compare and Contrast

# Predict

# Predict

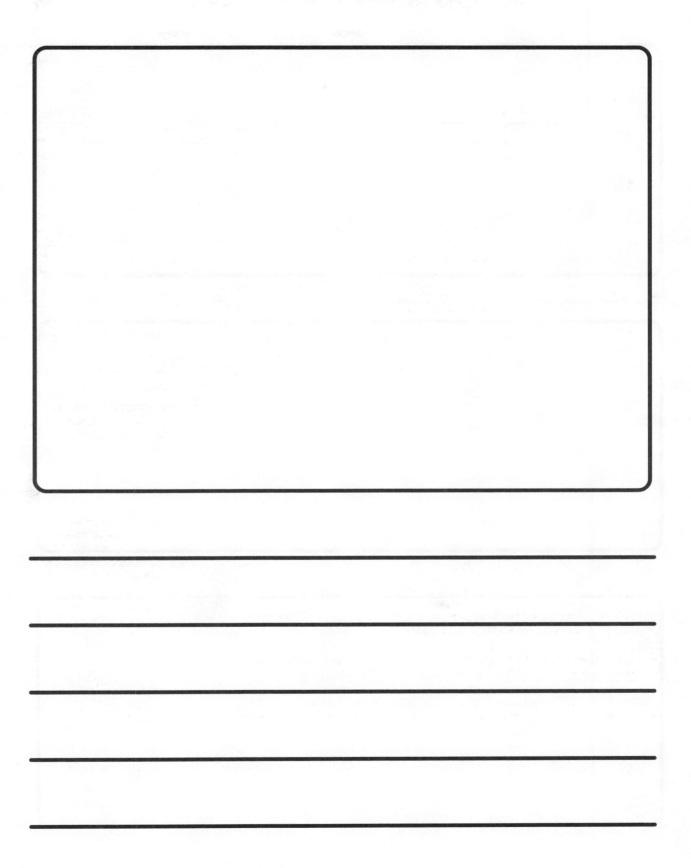

**kidspiration** Find a 30-day Kidspiration trial at www.inspiration.com/sf.

Grade 1 • Graphic Organizers **TR53**

# Recall and Retell

# K-W-L Chart

Topic _____

| What We **K**now | What We **W**ant to Know | What We **L**earned |
|---|---|---|
| | | |

K-W-L Interactive Reading Strategy was developed and is reprinted by permission of Donna Ogle, National-Louis University, Evanston, Illinois.

**kidspiration** Find a 30-day Kidspiration trial at www.inspiration.com/sf.

Grade 1 • Graphic Organizers   **TR55**

# Categorize

| Category 1 | Category 2 | Category 3 | Category 4 |
|---|---|---|---|
|  |  |  |  |
|  |  |  |  |
|  |  |  |  |

**kidspiration** Find a 30-day Kidspiration trial at www.inspiration.com/sf.

# Social Studies Daily Journal

**Today I learned...**

**Some new words I learned are...**

**One thing I found interesting is...**

**I would like to learn more about...**

kidspiration Find a 30-day Kidspiration trial at www.inspiration.com/sf.

Grade 1 • Graphic Organizers **TR57**

# Solve a Problem

**STEP 1:** Name the problem.

**STEP 2:** Find out more about the problem.

**STEP 3:** List ways to solve the problem.    **STEP 4:** Talk about the best way to solve the problem.

Option A

Advantages

Disadvantages

Option B

Advantages

Disadvantages

**STEP 5:** Solve the problem.    **STEP 6:** How well was the problem solved?

© Scott Foresman

# Make a Decision

**STEP 1:** Tell what decision you need to make.

**STEP 2:** Gather Information.

**STEP 3:** List your choices.    **STEP 4:** Tell what might happen with each choice.

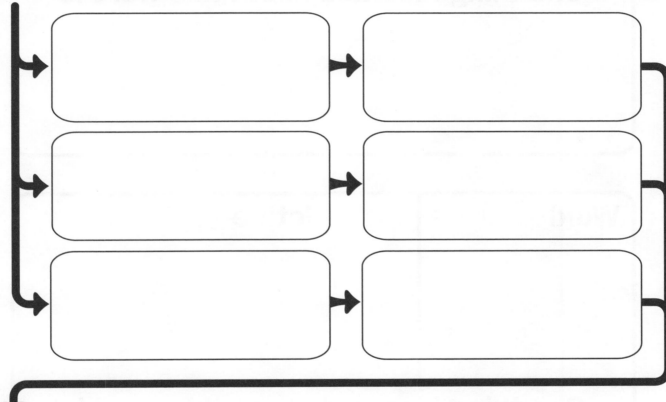

**STEP 5:** Make a decision.

# Vocabulary Organizer

| Word | Picture |
|------|---------|

**One thing I learned about this word is**

| Word | Picture |
|------|---------|

**One thing I learned about this word is**

kidspiration Find a 30-day Kidspiration trial at www.inspiration.com/sf.

# Concept Web

**kidspiration** Find a 30-day Kidspiration trial at www.inspiration.com/sf.

Grade 1 • Graphic Organizers  **TR61**

# Descriptive Writing

**Draw a picture.**

**Describe your picture.**

_____

_____

_____

_____

# Write About Social Studies

**Name the topic.**

[ ]

**List things I know about the topic.**

[ ]

**Write about the topic.**

**Sentence 1**

_____

_____

**Sentence 2**

_____

_____

**Sentence 3**

_____

_____

# Graph Paper

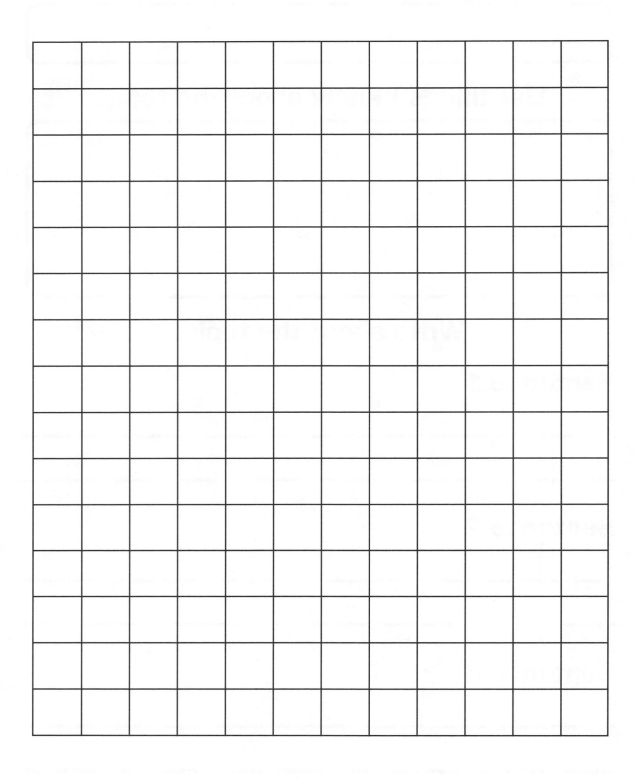

# Time Line

**kidspiration** Find a 30-day Kidspiration trial at www.inspiration.com/sf.

Grade 1 • Graphic Organizers **TR65**

# Grid

Name _____    Date _____

**The World**

0   1,000   2,000 Miles
0 1,000 2,000 Kilometers
Scale accurate only at Equator

Equator

The World

© Scott Foresman

Name _____ Date _____

## North America

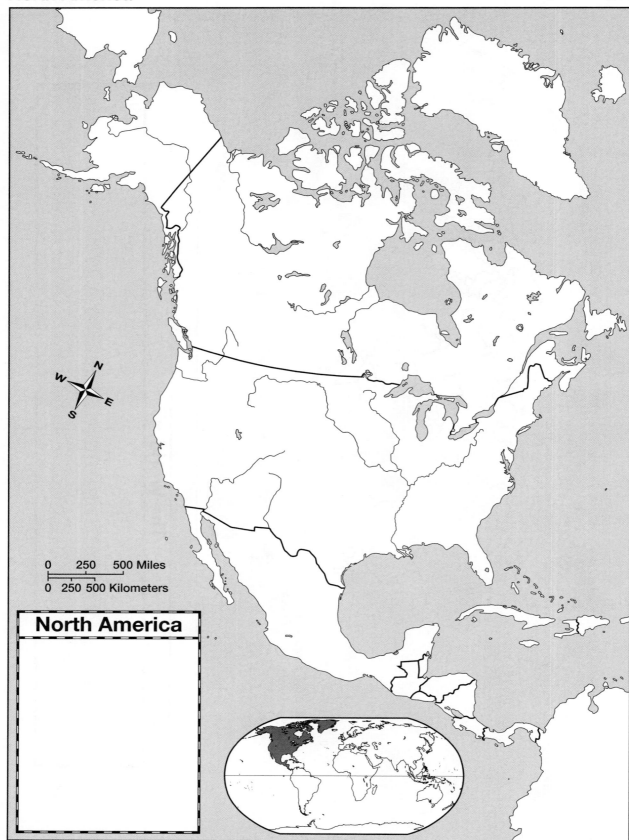

Name _____  Date _____

**The United States**

The United States

200 Miles
0   100   200 Kilometers

100 Miles
0   100   100 Kilometers

200 Miles
0   200 Kilometers

© Scott Foresman

# Calendar

| Sunday | Monday | Tuesday | Wednesday | Thursday | Friday | Saturday |
|--------|--------|---------|-----------|----------|--------|----------|
|        |        |         |           |          |        |          |
|        |        |         |           |          |        |          |
|        |        |         |           |          |        |          |
|        |        |         |           |          |        |          |
|        |        |         |           |          |        |          |

**kidspiration** Find a 30-day Kidspiration trial at www.inspiration.com/sf.

# Index

# Index

# Index

**Washington, George,** 204–205, 215

**Workbook**

  **Workbook Support,** 5, 7, 7a–7b, 9, 13, 17, 21, 25, 27, 31, 36a, 39, 47, 49, 49a–49b, 53, 55, 57, 61, 65, 71, 77, 83, 91, 93, 93a–93b, 97, 99, 100a, 101, 105, 111, 119, 121, 125, 131, 134, 139, 141, 141a–141b, 145, 147, 149, 150a, 153, 155, 159, 164a, 167, 173, 179, 182, 187, 189, 189a–189d 191, 193, 195, 199, 201, 205, 209, 215, 221, 227, 230, 235, 237, 237a–237b, 239 241, 243, 249, 253, 255, 261, 269, 272

**Writing**

  **Curriculum Connection,** H5, 1f, 5, 13a, 21a, 27a, 33, 43f, 45, 55a, 69a, 73a, 87f, 99a, 103, 103a, 115, 115a, 127a, 135f, 136, 149, 149a, 155a, 163a, 169a, 175a, 183f, 195a, 201a, 207a, 211a, 217a, 223, 223a, 231f, 241a, 245a, 251a, 257a, 265a

# Credits

## Maps

MapQuest.com, Inc.

## Illustrations

1D Benrei Huang; 1H, 43H, 135H, 183H,; 231H  Matt Straub; 43D Susan Tolonen; 87D April Mosakowski-Hartman; 87H Wendy Rasmussen; 135D Yvonne Gilbert; 183D Darryl Ligasan; 231D Loretta Lustig

## Photographs

Every effort has been made to secure permission and provide appropriate credit for photographic material.  The publisher deeply regrets any omission and pledges to correct errors called to its attention in subsequent editions.

Unless otherwise acknowledged, all photographs are the property of Scott Foresman, a division of Pearson Education.

Photo locators denoted as follows:  Top (T), Center (C), Bottom (B), Left (L), Right (R), Background (Bkgd)

**Front Matter:** SF7 Spencer Ainsley/Image Works; SF12 ©Angelo Cavalli/Getty Images; **Unit 1:** 13A Getty Images; 28A ©Frances Benjamin Johnston/Corbis; 35A Getty Images; **Unit 2:** 61A ©Ron Slenzak/Corbis; 62A Getty Images; 70A Getty Images; 74A Getty Images; **Unit 3:** 94A Getty Images; 100A Getty Images; 108A Getty Images; 115A Getty Images; 116A Getty Images; 123A Getty Images; **Unit 4:** 135C Getty Images; 142A ©V.C.L./Paul Viant/Getty Images; 150A (BL) ©Joel W. Rogers/Corbis, (BC) ©Dave Jacobs/Getty Images, (BR) Getty Images; 156A ©Joel W. Rogers/Corbis; 164A Getty Images; 170A ©Richard Cummins/Corbis; **Unit 5:** 195A ©Lindsay Hebberd/Corbis; 202A Corbis; 208A Getty Images; **Unit 6:** 231A ©Joseph Sohm; ChromoSohm Inc/Corbis; 265A Getty Images; **End Matter:** TR3, TR5, TR7, TR9, TR11, TR13 Hallogram Publishing; TR17 ©Burstein Collection/Corbis; TR44 Hemera Technologies; TR45 The Granger Collection

## CATEGORIZE ITEMS

**Identify *Groups*** Children will identify examples of a vocabulary word from Lesson 1. Then children will make sentences using the word.

- After children complete Lesson 1, discuss the meaning of the vocabulary word *group*.

- Say: **I am going to describe some things. If something I describe is a *group*, say "group." If something I describe is not a *group*, say "not a group."**

- Draw a two-column chart on chart paper. As you proceed with the activity, write the things you describe in the first column and *group* or *not a group* in the second column.

### Is It a *Group*?

| | |
|---|---|
| a girl playing the piano | (not a *group*) |
| eleven children in a soccer team | (*group*) |

- After you have filled out the chart, invite children to use the vocabulary word *group* to make sentences that mention each item they identified as a *group*. Model for children. Say: **I said there were eleven children in a soccer team. I could also say that there was a *group* of children in a soccer team. Now you try. I said there were three cats sleeping on a sofa. What could you also say?** (There was a *group* of cats sleeping on the sofa.)

### Vocabulary Writing Extension

**Modeled Writing** Ask children to think of other examples of *groups* and dictate sentences about these *groups* that use the word *group*. Write children's sentences on chart paper.

## CREATE EXAMPLES AND NON-EXAMPLES

**Explore Word Meaning** Children will brainstorm examples and non-examples of new vocabulary words to help them understand each word's meaning.

- After children complete Lesson 2, discuss the vocabulary word *country*.

- Copy the graphic organizers shown below, omitting answers in parentheses.

- Say: **Think about what the word *country* means. What are some examples of *countries*? What are some examples that are not *countries*?** (Possible answers are shown in parentheses.)

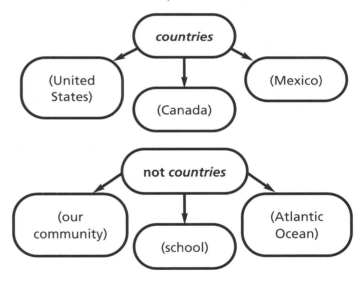

- If necessary, provide children with maps or globes to help them think of examples and non-examples.

- Have children use the vocabulary word *country* in a sentence when they explain their example.

### Vocabulary Writing Extension

**Modeled Writing** Have children dictate sentences using the vocabulary word *country*. Write children's sentences on chart paper.

**Use with:** Lesson 3      pp. 22–25

# MAKE A LIST

**Record *Rules*** Children will practice applying a new vocabulary word in context.

- After introducing the vocabulary word *rule* in the context of Lesson 3, organize children into groups to further explore the word's meaning.

- Assign each group a situation such as eating at the dinner table or visiting a store. Ask groups to brainstorm a list of *rules* for each situation. Say: **Think about eating dinner. What things should you do? What things should you not do? Should you put your feet on the table? Should you use a napkin? What *rules* would you tell someone to follow at the dinner table?**

- As necessary, help each group write down their list of *rules*. See below for an example set of *rules*.

> ***Rules* for Eating Dinner**
> - ***Rule* 1:** Wash your hands.
> - ***Rule* 2:** Do not reach across the table.
> - ***Rule* 3:** Use a napkin.

- Invite each group to present its list of *rules* to the class.

## Vocabulary Writing Extension

**Modeled Writing** Ask children to dictate a list of reasons why people should follow *rules*. Write children's reasons on chart paper.

**Use with:** Lesson 4      pp. 28–31

# SOLVE WORD MEANING

**Use Context Clues** Help students use context clues to figure out the meaning of an unfamiliar word.

- While reading Lesson 1, model the following strategies to help children understand the meaning of the word *future* from the top of page 31.

- Write a list of directions on chart paper.

> **Directions**
> 1. Read
> 2. Think
> 3. Predict

- After reading the text on page 31, explain to children that a reader might be unsure of what the word *future* means. Point to the first direction and say: **First I am going to read the text that comes before the word I do not know. There may be clues in the text that tell me what the word means.** Read the text that precedes *future*.

- Point to the second direction and say: **Now I am going to think about what would make sense. The text says that in the past, the school was small, and now it is bigger. I know that the word *past* means "time that is over." I know that the word *now* means "what is happening at this time."**

- Point to the third direction. Say: **Now help me predict what the word *future* means.** (*Future* probably means "time that is going to happen.")

- Discuss children's answers and model how to confirm the definition with a dictionary.

## Vocabulary Writing Extension

**Modeled Writing** Have children dictate sentences that predict what their school or their community will look like in the future. Sentences should start with the phrase *in the future*. Record children's predictions on chart paper.

**Use with:** Lesson 1                    pp. 50–53

## ANSWER YES/NO QUESTIONS

**Explore Context** Children will answer yes/no questions about a vocabulary word to demonstrate an understanding of its meaning.

- Introduce the vocabulary word *neighborhood* in the context of Lesson 1. Be sure that children understand that a *neighborhood* is a place where people live, work, and play.

- Ask children a series of yes/no questions. Have children answer *yes* or *no*. Then have children use the word *neighborhood* to explain their reasoning.

- Draw a two-column chart on chart paper, omitting answers in parentheses. As you proceed with this activity, write each question in the first column and then *yes* or *no* in the second column.

- Model for children. Ask: **Is a *neighborhood* a place where people only work? No, a *neighborhood* is also a place where people live and play.**

- Ask: **Does a *neighborhood* have stores?** (Yes, people in a *neighborhood* work and shop in stores.)

### What Is a *Neighborhood*?

| | |
|---|---|
| Is a *neighborhood* a place where people only work? | (no) |
| Does a *neighborhood* have stores? | (yes) |
| Is a forest where only bears live a *neighborhood*? | (no) |
| Does a *neighborhood* have streets? | (yes) |

### Vocabulary Writing Extension

**Modeled Writing** Have children dictate sentences that describe their school's *neighborhood*. Write children's descriptions on chart paper.

**Use with:** Lesson 2                    pp. 56–57

## MAKE A K-W-L CHART

**Share Knowledge** Help children share background knowledge and focus their learning by making a K-W-L chart.

- Before you read Lesson 2, guide children in creating a K-W-L chart for the vocabulary word *community*.

| What We <u>K</u>now | What We <u>W</u>ant to Know | What We <u>L</u>earned |
|---|---|---|
| | | |

- Draw a blank K-W-L chart on chart paper. Write the vocabulary word *community* above the chart. Ask: **What do we already <u>K</u>now about *communities*?** (Possible answers may include that they are places where people live and that they are bigger than neighborhoods.) Write children's answers in the "What We <u>K</u>now" column of the chart.

- Next, ask: **What do we <u>W</u>ant to know about *communities*?** (Possible answer: What are some different kinds of *communities*? In what ways do they differ?) Write children's answers in the second column.

- After Lesson 2, ask children to use the vocabulary word *community* as they tell what they learned. Record responses in the third column of the chart.

### Vocabulary Writing Extension

**Modeled Writing** Have children dictate sentences that tell about their *community*. Write children's sentences on chart paper.

# Vocabulary Activities

**Use with:** Lessons 3–4          pp. 62–65, 70–71

## ASSOCIATE WORDS

**Think About Words** Associate words that describe community *customs, laws,* and *leaders*.

- After children complete Lessons 3 and 4, present child-friendly definitions of the word *custom* from Lesson 3 and the vocabulary words *law* and *leader* from Lesson 4. Definitions can be found in the Picture Glossary. Provide children with rich background knowledge about each word to help them make word associations later.

> - A *custom* is a usual way of doing something. Things people do over and over in the same way and at the same times are *customs*.
> - A *law* is a rule that everybody must follow. You have to obey the *law*.
> - A *leader* helps a group of people decide what they should do.

- Next, present children with words and/or phrases and ask them which of the vocabulary words they associate with each word or phrase.

> - Which word goes with *rule*? (*law*)
> - Which word goes with "watch fireworks on July 4th"? (*custom*)
> - Which word goes with "makes choices for other people"? (*leader*)

### Vocabulary Writing Extension

**Modeled Writing** Have children dictate sentences that relate two of these vocabulary words. For example, children could write a sentence about a *leader* making *laws*. Write children's sentences on chart paper.

**Use with:** Lesson 5          pp. 74–77

## START A REFERENCE BULLETIN BOARD

**Post Words for Reference** Post definitions and pictures of vocabulary words on a bulletin board for children to use as a reference.

- After children complete Lesson 5, discuss the vocabulary words *state, continent,* and *ocean*.
- Write the vocabulary word *state* at the top of a large card. Divide the card into three sections as shown below.

| state | | |
|---|---|---|
| **Definition** | **Examples** | **Picture** |
| | | |

- Say: **What is a good definition for the vocabulary word *state*?** (Possible answer: A *state* is part of a country.) Write the definition on the card in the section labeled *Definition*.
- Ask: **What are some examples of *states*?** If necessary, help children use the map on page 75 to find examples. Write the examples on the card in the section labeled *Examples*.
- Ask: **What would be a good picture to draw to remind us what *state* means?** (Possible answer: an outline of our *state*) Draw the picture in the section labeled *Picture*.
- Repeat this activity with the other Lesson 5 vocabulary words. Post the finished card on a bulletin board. Tell students to refer to the bulletin board if they need to remember what a vocabulary word means.

### Vocabulary Writing Extension

**Modeled Writing** Have children dictate a sentence about the meaning of a Lesson 5 vocabulary word. Write children's sentences on chart paper.

**Use with:** Lessons 1, 3      pp. 94–97, 104–105

## TALK ABOUT WORDS

**Build Personal Context** Children will associate a vocabulary word from Lesson 1 and words from Lesson 3 with their own experiences to help them incorporate the words into their speaking vocabularies.

- After children complete these lessons, discuss the vocabulary word *job* from Lesson 1 and the words *spend* and *save* from Lesson 3. Be sure that children understand the meaning of each word.
- Ask children prompts that require them to apply the words to their own lives.

> - **Describe a *job* you would like to have when you grow up.** (Possible answer: A *job* I would like to have is to be a police officer.)
> - **Describe a time when you would like to *spend* money.** (Possible answer: A time when I would like to *spend* money is when I see a book in the bookstore that I want to read.)
> - **Describe a time when you would like to *save* money.** (Possible answer: A time when I would like to *save* money is when I want to buy something that costs a lot of money, like a new bike.)

- Remind children to use the vocabulary words in their answers. Discuss children's responses as a class.

### Vocabulary Writing Extension

**Modeled Writing** Ask children to dictate a class plan they would like to follow for *saving* and *spending* any money they might earn or receive. Write the class plan on chart paper.

**Use with:** Lesson 2      pp. 100–101

## CATEGORIZE WORDS

**Sort *Needs* and *Wants*** Children will categorize objects as things people *need* or things people *want*.

- After children complete Lesson 2, discuss the meaning of the vocabulary words *needs* and *wants*. Make sure that children understand that *things people need* are things people must have to live, and *things people want* are things people would like to have.
- Copy the chart below, omitting answers in parentheses.
- Say: **I am going to name some objects. Think about each object carefully. Is it something people *need* or something people *want*? Tell me why.**
- Name objects such as a shirt, a puppy, water, a new set of crayons, vegetables, and a soccer ball. Make sure that children use the vocabulary words *needs* and *wants* in their responses. Record each object in the appropriate column.

| Things People *Need* | Things People *Want* |
| --- | --- |
| (shirt) | (puppy) |
| (water) | (new set of crayons) |
| (vegetables) | (soccer ball) |

### Vocabulary Writing Extension

**Shared Writing** Ask children to write two sentences. One should tell an example of something they *need* and the other should tell something they *want*. Write children's sentences on chart paper while children copy the sentences on their own paper.

# Unit 3
# Vocabulary Activities

## CREATE INTERVIEW QUESTIONS

**Use New Words Together** Children will use words from Lessons 4 and 5 to write interview questions.

- After children complete Lessons 4 and 5, discuss the vocabulary words *tools, goods, service*, and *volunteer* from Lesson 4; the word *worker* from Lesson 4; and the word *interview* from Lesson 5.

- Be sure children understand that an *interview* is when one person asks another person questions to get information from that person. Review with children the kinds of questions Ben asks the farmer in Lesson 5.

- Ask children to think of a set of questions to ask a *worker* and a set of questions to ask a *volunteer*. Remind students to use the vocabulary words *tools, goods*, and *service* in their questions.

| *worker* questions | *volunteer* questions |
|---|---|
|  |  |

- Say: **We are going to** *interview* **a** *worker*. **What** *interview* **questions might we ask a** *worker*? **One question we could ask is "What** *tools* **do you use when you do your job?" What are others?** (Possible answer: Do you earn money by making *goods*? What kind of *service* do you provide?) Repeat this activity to help children think of questions to ask a *volunteer*.

- List children's questions on chart paper.

### Vocabulary Writing Extension

**Modeled Writing** Have children dictate a list of things *workers* do and a list of things *volunteers* do. Remind children to use the word *worker* and the vocabulary words *tools, goods, services*, and *volunteer*. Write children's lists on chart paper.

## EXAMINE WORD PARTS

**Analyze Words** Explain to children that some word parts give clues to a vocabulary word's meaning.

- After children complete Lesson 6, discuss the meaning of the vocabulary word *transportation*. Be sure children understand that *transportation* means "something, such as a car, a truck, or a bus, that moves people and goods from place to place."

- Write the vocabulary word *transportation* on chart paper. Then copy the graphic organizer shown below. Explain that *trans* means "across" and that *port* means "to move." Tell children that the word *transport* means "to move across." Say: **When people use** *transportation*, **they are moving themselves or goods from one place to another.**

| *trans* "across" | + | *port* "to move" | = | *transport* "to move across" |
|---|---|---|---|---|

- Point out that knowing about these word parts can help children figure out other new words.

- Follow a similar procedure for the word *portable*. Ask children to guess what the word *portable* means. After children have made their guesses, explain that the word *portable* means "able to be moved." People use the word *portable* to describe something that can be moved.

### Vocabulary Writing Extension

**Shared Writing** Have children write sentences using the vocabulary word *transportation* and the word *portable*. Model for them by writing, *A school bus is a kind of* <u>transportation</u>. *We carried a* <u>portable</u> *radio to the beach with us.* Write children's sentences on chart paper while children copy the sentences on their own paper.

**Use with:** Lesson 1        pp. 142–145

## CREATE A TIME LINE

**Chart *Weather*** Children will create a time line to increase their understanding of the Lesson 1 vocabulary word *weather*.

- After children complete Lesson 1, discuss the meaning of the vocabulary word *weather*. Review different words that describe *weather*, such as *hot, cold, rainy, clear, moist, dry, cloudy,* and *sunny*.

- Draw this time line on chart paper (omitting the answers in parentheses) and have children copy it.

**Time Line of *Weather***

| Monday | Tuesday | Wednesday | Thursday | Friday |
|--------|---------|-----------|----------|--------|

(cold)

(dry)

- Try to start the time line on a Monday. Record the *weather* for subsequent days on a daily basis. Ask: **What is the *weather* like today? Is it *hot* or *cold*? Is it *moist* or *dry*?** Remind children to use the vocabulary word *weather* in their answers.

- Write key *weather* words under the appropriate days. Have children record answers on their own time lines. Encourage them to draw pictures of clouds, suns, raindrops, and so on, to help them remember what the *weather* words mean.

- At the end of the week, review children's *weather* time lines. Ask children to use their time lines to describe the *weather* for the past week.

### Vocabulary Writing Extension

**Modeled Writing** Have children dictate a story starter in which they describe the setting, including details about the *weather* conditions. Remind children to use *weather* words in their descriptions. Write children's story starters on chart paper.

**Use with:** Lesson 2        pp. 150–153

## MAKE CHOICES

**Distinguish Among Words** Ask children questions that provide an example and build context for a vocabulary word. Give students a choice of two vocabulary words and have them tell you which is the correct answer.

- After Lesson 2, discuss the vocabulary words *mountain, plain, lake,* and *river*.

- Ask children questions that can be answered correctly using only one of the words. Be sure children think through their choices, decide which word fits the example, and explain their reasoning.

- **If you are walking on the highest kind of land, are you walking on a *mountain* or a *plain*?** (a *mountain*)

- **If you are sailing on a narrow body of water, are you sailing on a *lake* or on a *river*?** (a *river*)

- **If you are able to grow many different kinds of food, are you farming on a *plain* or on a *river*?** (a *plain*)

- **If you are swimming in water that is totally surrounded by land, are you swimming in a *lake* or in a *mountain*?** (a *lake*)

- Be sure children use vocabulary words in their answers. Discuss children's choices with the class.

### Vocabulary Writing Extension

**Shared Writing** Have children write sentences that use Lesson 2 vocabulary words. Sentences should explain what each kind of land and water is. Model for them by writing, *A <u>mountain</u> is a kind of land that is very high.* Write children's sentences on chart paper while children copy the sentences on their own paper.

# Vocabulary Activities

**Use with:** Lessons 3, 5  pp. 156–159, 170–173

## DO EXTENDED READING

**Read About *Natural Resources*** Children will read about different kinds of *natural resources* and write a description of one kind.

- After children complete Lessons 3 and 5, discuss the vocabulary term *natural resource* and the words *reduce, reuse*, and *recycle*.

- Draw a concept web on chart paper and have children brainstorm types of *natural resources*. Ask: **What are some *natural resources* we read about in Lessons 3 and 5?** (Possible answers are shown below.) Remind children to use the vocabulary term *natural resource* in their answers.

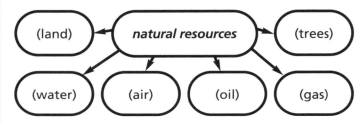

- Ask children to choose a *natural resource* in which they are interested and read more about it. Help them find library books and Internet Web sites related to their topics and do extended reading.

- Help children write one paragraph about their topic. Remind them to use the vocabulary term *natural resource* in their paragraph.

### Vocabulary Writing Extension

**Modeled Writing** Ask children to dictate a list of suggestions for ways that the *natural resources* they researched can be saved. Ask children to try to use the vocabulary term *natural resource* and the words *reduce, reuse*, and *recycle* in their suggestions. Write children's suggestions on chart paper.

**Use with:** Lesson 4  pp. 164–167

## MAKE A PRESENTATION

**Research History** Children will research the Lesson 4 vocabulary word *history*.

- After Lesson 4, discuss with children the vocabulary word *history*. Make sure they understand that the vocabulary word *history* means "the story of people and places from the past."

- Organize children into small cooperative groups. Say: **I am going to help you use a computer to write a class report about the *history* of our community. We will find out three things.**

> ### Things to Research
> 1. Who first lived here?
> 2. How did our community get its name?
> 3. How old is our community?

- Guide children in using the Internet to find out these facts about the *history* of their community. Help children compile the facts into a report. If possible, help children use the computer to add photos of their community to their report.

- Be sure to use the vocabulary word *history* at every opportunity while conducting this research.

- If possible, help children use the computer to make a multimedia presentation, including available pictures and sound effects.

- Have children present their *history* reports to other classrooms in the school.

### Vocabulary Writing Extension

**Shared Writing** Have children dictate a few sentences about the *history* of their community. Write children's sentences on chart paper while children copy the sentences on their own paper.

# Vocabulary Activities

---

**Use with:** Lesson 1                                                    **pp. 190–191**

## THINK ABOUT CONTEXT

**Explore Homonyms** Children will practice figuring out which meaning a multiple-meaning word has in different contexts.

- After children complete Lesson 1, discuss the meaning of the word *squash*. Explain to children that *squash* is a homonym. A homonym is a word that sounds the same and is spelled the same as another word, but has a different meaning.

- Draw the graphic organizer shown below on chart paper.

- Say: **The word *squash* can mean "to press against something until it is soft and flat" or "a kind of food eaten as a vegetable." Which meaning does the word *squash* have in Lesson 1?** ("a kind of food eaten as a vegetable")

- Read sentences such as those shown below and have children use context to figure out which meaning *squash* has in each case.

> - **If you sit on the box, you will *squash* it.** ("press against")
> - **We ate *squash* and beans for dinner.** ("food")

### Vocabulary Writing Extension

**Modeled Writing** Invite children to dictate sentences that use the word *squash* in two different ways and invite their classmates to use context to figure out which meaning *squash* has in each case. Write children's sentences on chart paper.

---

**Use with:** Lessons 2–3                                              **pp. 196–199, 202–205**

## MAKE A WORD MAP

**Map New Words** Help children explore the meaning of vocabulary words by charting them in word maps.

- After children complete Lessons 2 and 3, discuss the meaning of the vocabulary words *freedom* from Lesson 2 and *colony* from Lesson 3.

- Tell children that you are going to chart the vocabulary word *freedom* in a word map. Explain that a word map can help them investigate the meaning of a vocabulary word.

- Copy the graphic organizer shown below.

**What It Is**                                                    **What It Is Not**

*freedom*

- Say: **We read about *freedom* in Lesson 2. Tell me in your own words what *freedom* is.** (Possible answer: being able to do what you want to do) Write children's answers in the *What It Is* box.

- Say: **Now think about what *freedom* is not. Describe in your own words an example of what *freedom* is not.** (Possible answer: having a king tell you what to do) Write children's answers in the *What It Is Not* box.

- Repeat this routine with the vocabulary word *colony* from Lesson 3.

### Vocabulary Writing Extension

**Shared Writing** Have children write descriptions of people in the United States enjoying *freedom*. Remind students to use the vocabulary word *freedom* in their descriptions. Write children's descriptions on chart paper while children copy the descriptions on their own paper.

**Use with:** Lesson 4      pp. 208–209

## LOOK AT WORD PARTS

**Divide Compound Words** Help children investigate word meaning by breaking a compound word into its individual words.

- After children complete Lesson 4, point out that the word *gateway* is a compound word. Write *gateway* on chart paper and ask: **What two words form the word *gateway*?** (*gate* and *way*)

- Copy the graphic organizer shown below, omitting answers in parentheses.

- Say: **Think about the word *gate*. What does it mean?** (Possible answer: "a door in a wall or fence") **Now think about the word *way*. What does it mean? I will give you a hint. What does the word *way* mean when we are talking about traveling from one place to another?** (Possible answer: "the path you take to get somewhere")

- Guide children to understand that the word *gateway* means "a way in and out."

| gate ("a door in a wall or fence") | + | way ("the path you take to get somewhere") | = | *gateway* ("a way in and out") |

- Ask children to look at the picture of the Gateway Arch on page 209. Ask: **Why might an arch be a good symbol for a place that is known as the "*gateway* to the west?"** (Possible answer: An arch is something you can pass through to get to somewhere else.)

### Vocabulary Writing Extension

**Independent Writing** Ask children to draw and label a picture of a *gateway*.

---

**Use with:** Lessons 5–6      pp. 212–215, 218–221

## ANALYZE FEATURES

**Compare People** Help children complete a semantic feature analysis chart.

- Discuss with children the meanings of the vocabulary word *President* from Lesson 5, the vocabulary word *citizen* from Lesson 6, and the word *governor* from Lesson 6.

- After children complete these lessons, draw the semantic feature analysis chart shown below, omitting answers in parentheses.

- As you read each characteristic, have children tell you if it describes a vocabulary word (+) or it does not (–). Complete the chart using appropriate marks.

|  | member of a state and country | leader | works to make state laws | works with leaders around the world |
|---|---|---|---|---|
| *President* | (+) | (+) | (−) | (+) |
| *citizen* | (+) | (−) | (−) | (−) |
| *governor* | (+) | (+) | (+) | (−) |

### Vocabulary Writing Extension

**Shared Writing** Ask children to write descriptions of what a *President*, a *citizen*, and a *governor* does. Remind children to use the vocabulary words *President, citizen*, and *governor* in their descriptions. Write children's descriptions on chart paper while children copy the descriptions on their own paper.

## MAKE A SYNONYM CONCEPT WEB

**Explore Similar Meanings** Children will brainstorm words that are similar in meaning to a vocabulary word.

- After introducing the vocabulary word *market* in Lesson 1, invite children to brainstorm words with similar meanings. Say: **We have just learned that a *market* is a place where goods are sold. Think about places where you buy goods. What are these places called?** Record answers in a concept web such as the sample one shown below.

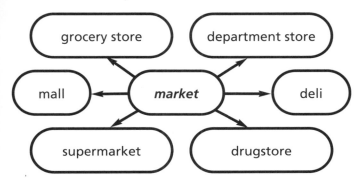

- If you have bilingual children in the class, include words from other languages in the concept web.
- Discuss with children the slight differences in meaning among the words they brainstormed. Provide them with examples of how they could use the different words in sentences. Say: **A *deli* is a *market* where many already-prepared foods are sold. I could go to the *deli* to buy cheese.**

### Vocabulary Writing Extension

**Shared Writing** Ask children to write sentences that use the word *market* and its synonyms. Remind them to use the vocabulary word *market*. Write children's sentences on chart paper while children copy the sentences on their own paper.

## LEARN NEW MEANINGS

**Examine Word Meaning** Children will learn a new meaning for a familiar word.

- After children complete Lesson 2, discuss the word *button*. Ask: **What meaning do you think of when you hear the word *button*?** (Children will most likely say that *button* means "a flat object that fastens or decorates clothing.")
- Explain that the word *button* has another meaning. Point out the sentence on page 242 that reads *I used to punch buttons at the store*. Explain that the grandmother is talking about using a cash register. Show children a picture of a cash register and ask: **Where are the *buttons* on a cash register? What are they used for?** Help children figure out that the *buttons* on a cash register are the keys that a cashier pushes to input prices.
- Explain to children that the word *button* can also mean "a knob pushed to make something work." Draw the graphic organizer shown below on chart paper. Help children think of things other than cash registers that have this kind of *button*, such as elevators and computers.

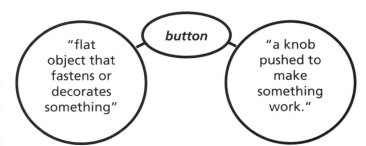

### Vocabulary Writing Extension

**Interactive Writing** Have children write sentences that use the different meanings of the word *button*. Help children by writing on chart paper letters or words they do not know how to write. Have children read their sentences to the class. Invite their classmates to use context to figure out the meaning of *button* in each sentence.

# Unit 6 Vocabulary Activities

## COMPLETE A CLOZE PARAGRAPH

**Use Words in Context** Have children use vocabulary words to fill in the blanks in a paragraph.

- After Lessons 3 and 5, write the Lesson 3 vocabulary words *communicate, invention,* and *inventor,* and the Lesson 5 vocabulary word *world* in random order in a word bank on chart paper. Then write the following:

> Do you like to _____ by telephone?
> Its _____ is Alexander Graham Bell.
> The telephone is an _____ that many people use today. It lets people from all over the _____ talk to each other

- Say: **This paragraph is missing several words. Use context clues to figure out which vocabulary word goes in each blank. Look at the first sentence. I can tell that the word that goes here is a verb. This sentence needs a word that describes something you can use a telephone for. Now look at our word bank.** *Inventor, invention,* **and** *world* **are nouns, and** *communicate* **is a verb. Can you** *communicate* **using a telephone?** (yes) **I will write** *communicate* **in the blank.**
- Work with children to fill in the rest of the Cloze paragraph using vocabulary words.

### Vocabulary Writing Extension

**Interactive Writing** Have children write a few sentences about a device they could invent to help people all over the world *communicate* with each other. Help children by writing on chart paper letters or words they do not know how to write. Remind children to use the vocabulary words *inventor, invention, communicate,* and *world* in their sentences.

## MAKE A VENN DIAGRAM

**Compare Words** Children will make a Venn diagram to compare similarities and differences.

- After Lesson 4, review the meaning of the word *bicycle* and the terms *horse and wagon, old Model T car,* and *car of today.* Write this word and these terms on chart paper. Copy the Venn diagram shown below on chart paper.

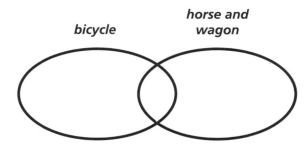

- Say: **Think how a** *bicycle* **and a** *horse and wagon* **are alike and different. How are these two ways to travel alike?** (Possible answers may include that both are forms of transportation and both have wheels.) Record children's answers in the overlapping section.
- Ask: **What is something that is true only for a** *bicycle*? (Possible answers may include that a *bicycle* has two wheels and is powered by someone pedaling.) Record children's answers.
- Ask: **What is something that is true only for a** *horse and wagon*? (Possible answers may include that a *horse and wagon* has four wheels and is powered by a horse.) Record children's answers.
- Repeat this routine and make a Venn diagram comparing *old Model T cars* with *car of today.*

### Vocabulary Writing Extension

**Interactive Writing** Have children write a paragraph describing similarities and differences between two kinds of transportation. Write on chart paper letters or words they may not know how to write.

## Put Reading First

---

**Use with:** Time for School     **pp. 1–42**

## PHONEMIC AWARENESS
### Identify Phonemes

**Work with Phonemes** Guide children in phonemic awareness by having them identify and work with individual phonemes in spoken vocabulary words. For example, have them identify the initial and final phonemes of the vocabulary words *school* and *group* from Lesson 1.

- Lead children in saying the vocabulary word *school*. Then ask: **What is the first sound in the word** *school*? **The first sound in the word** *school* **is /s/. What is the last sound in the word** *school*? **The last sound in the word** *school* **is /l/.** Model the routine several times before children do it.

- Use this routine to identify initial and final phonemes in other vocabulary words.

---

**Use with:** Time for School     **pp. 1–42**

## PHONICS
### Write Beginning Phonemes

**Spell Initial Sounds** As you discuss pictures of the vocabulary words for Unit 1, ask children to make first-letter labels for each word.

- Make picture cards for the vocabulary words.

- Show the picture cards to children. For example, say: **This card shows a** *group* **of children. This card stands for the word** *group*. **What is the first sound in the word** *group*? **The first sound in the word** *group* **is /g/.** Model the routine several times before children do it.

- Provide children with self-stick notepaper. Have children write the letter that stands for the first sound in the vocabulary word *group*. Attach one of the self-stick notes to the picture card for *group*.

- Use this routine throughout Unit 1 to help children identify initial letter-sound associations.

---

**Use with:** Time for School     **pp. 1–42**

## BUILDING FLUENCY
### Choral Reading

**Read in Unison** On chart paper, write "The Wheels on the Bus" as it appears on page 1h of the Teacher's Edition. Sing the song with children several times, tracking the print.

- Organize children into two groups for a choral reading, with each group reading alternate verses.

- Monitor each child's reading for fluency.

---

**Use with:** Time for School     **pp. 1–42**

## TEXT COMPREHENSION
### Make a Story Map

**Put Events in Order** Create a story map to help children understand the main ideas of a lesson.

- Copy the story map shown below, omitting the answers in parentheses. Ask the bolded questions. Continue until the story map is complete.

> **What happened first?** (In the past, the school was small, with few children.)

> **What happened next?** (Next, people moved to the area. The school was too small.)

> **What happened last?** (A bigger school was built. Now all the children can fit in the school. What will happen in the future?)

- Use this routine for other Unit 1 lessons that contain sequential events, such as Lesson 2.

## Put Reading First

---

**Use with:** In My Community          pp. 43–86

# PHONEMIC AWARENESS
## Identify Rimes and Onsets

**Work with Syllables** Help children identify rimes and onsets in spoken one-syllable vocabulary words. For example, examine the word *state* from Lesson 5.

- Say: **Say the word *state* with me. What is the first part of the word *state*?** (The first part of the word *state* is /st/.) **What is the last part of the word *state*?** (The last part of the word *state* is /āt/.) Be sure children repeat the vocabulary word in their answers.

- Model this routine before asking children to identify the onsets and rimes in other Unit 2 words.

---

**Use with:** In My Community          pp. 43–86

# PHONICS
## Long Vowel Sounds

**Words with Silent e** As you begin Lesson 1, write the word *home* on chart paper. Read the word aloud. Call attention to the spelling pattern.

- Begin a list of words in Unit 2 that have the CVCe pattern. Invite volunteers to add to the list.

| | |
|---|---|
| *home* (page 50) | *pine* (page 51) |
| *alike* (page 52) | *like* (page 58) |
| *make* (page 63) | *time* (page 65) |
| *nine* (page 66) | *state* (page 75) |

---

**Use with:** In My Community          pp. 43–86

# BUILDING FLUENCY
## Read Aloud Repeatedly

**Read a Song** On chart paper, copy the song shown below from page 62a of the Teacher's Edition.

> **Flag Song**
>
> Our flag shines bright and true,
> Waving red, white, and blue,
> Looking so grand.
>
> Protecting all who come,
> Welcoming everyone,
> To our homeland.

- Model reading, tracking the print. Say: **Now read the song together with me.**

- Ask children to reread the song orally several times. Monitor each child's reading for fluency.

- Use this routine with other poems and songs.

---

**Use with:** In My Community          pp. 43–86

# TEXT COMPREHENSION
## Generate Questions

**Think of Questions** Point out that good readers often ask themselves questions to help them understand what they are reading.

- Model generating questions about pages 62–63 in Lesson 3. Ask: **What customs do we have on holidays? What customs do we have in our neighborhood?**

- Turn to pages 64–65 in Lesson 3. Say: **Let's ask ourselves questions about this section. What might we ask?** (What does this text tell us about how people celebrate Chinese New Year?)

- Guide children in deciding when and how to apply this routine to other lessons throughout Unit 2.

## Put Reading First

---

**Use with:** Work! Work! Work!  pp. 87–134

## PHONEMIC AWARENESS
### Phoneme Segmentation

**Segment Vocabulary Words** Use phoneme segmentation to help children break vocabulary words into separate sounds. For example, segment the vocabulary word *job* from Lesson 1.

- Lead children in a call-and-response activity to practice segmenting words. Say: **I say *job*, you say /j/ /o/ /b/. Go!**
- Repeat, encouraging children to respond with the segmented word.
- Continue with other short vocabulary words from Unit 3, such as *needs* and *wants* from Lesson 2 and *tools* and *goods* from Lesson 4.

---

**Use with:** Work! Work! Work!  pp. 87–134

## BUILDING FLUENCY
### Partner Reading

**Read an Interview** Use "Interview with a Farmer" on pages 116–119 as a script for partner reading.

- Model reading the script with a fluent reader.
- Organize children into pairs and assign parts. Have children practice their reading several times and then perform it.
- Monitor each child's reading for fluency.
- Use this routine with other sections of text throughout Unit 3 to help build children's fluency.

---

**Use with:** Work! Work! Work!  pp. 87–134

## PHONICS
### Embedded Phonics

**Distinguish Phonemes** Help children understand that some written letters have different sounds in different words.

- Read the first paragraph of Lesson 4 on page 108. Then write the vocabulary words *tools* and *goods* on chart paper. Point to *tools* and *goods* and have children read the words with you several times.
- Ask: **Which letter is found twice in both *tools* and *goods*?** (the letter o) Circle *oo* in *tools* and *goods*.
- Ask: **How do the letters *oo* sound in the word *tools*?** (The letters *oo* in *tools* sound like /ü/.) **How do the letters *oo* sound in the word *goods*?** (The letters *oo* in *goods* sound like /ú/.)
- Use this routine to help children learn other letter-sound relationships, such as the vowel sounds in *love* and *grow* on page 116.

---

**Use with:** Work! Work! Work!  pp. 87–134

## TEXT COMPREHENSION
### Use Mental Imagery

**Create Mental Pictures** Remind children that good readers often create pictures in their mind to help them understand what they read. Model this strategy for children while reading Lesson 6. Copy the chart below. The text is from page 125.

- Say: **I am going to create pictures in my mind while I read the text. This will help me understand what the vocabulary word *transportation* means.**

| What the Text Says | What I Picture |
|---|---|
| *Transportation* moves people and goods from place to place. | • people in a boat<br>• apples in a truck |

- Have children draw sketches of things they could picture in their minds while reading this section of text.
- Help children use this routine as they read Unit 3.

## Put Reading First

**Use with:** Our Earth, Our Resources — pp. 135–182

## PHONEMIC AWARENESS
### Phoneme Substitution

**Substitute Initial Phonemes** Use initial phoneme substitution to give children practice manipulating sounds in words. As an example, use the vocabulary word *lake* from Lesson 2.

- Direct children to say *lake*. Then say: **Change /l/ to /b/. What is the new word?** (*bake*) Continue asking children to substitute the initial sound by changing /b/ to /t/, /t/ to /m/, and /m/ to /k/.
- Use this routine to have children practice substituting initial phonemes in other single-syllable words found throughout Unit 4, such as *hill* on page 151, *cut* on page 157, *land* on page 170, and *can* on page 172.

**Use with:** Our Earth, Our Resources — pp. 135–182

## BUILDING FLUENCY
### Tape-Assisted Reading

**Read a Legend** Help children practice fluent reading by reading along with a tape recording of a selection.

- Tape-record the legend on pages 176–177. Have children turn to pages 176–177 and follow along with the recording, pointing to each word as it is read.
- Have children listen to the tape and read along.
- Have children continue to read along with the tape until they can read the text by themselves. Then tape-record children reading the text. Monitor each child's reading for fluency.

**Use with:** Our Earth, Our Resources — pp. 135–182

## PHONICS
### Identify Onsets and Rimes

**Explore Letter Sounds** Help children identify onsets and rimes in vocabulary words. For example, examine the vocabulary word *plain* from Lesson 2.

- Write the vocabulary word *plain* on chart paper. Point to the word and have children read it with you. Have children write *plain* on their own paper.
- Ask: **What is the first part of the word *plain*? Underline it.** (The first part of the word *plain* is /pl/.) **What is the last part of the word *plain*? Draw a circle around it.** (The last part of the word *plain* is /ān/.)
- Repeat this routine with other one-syllable words throughout Unit 4, such as *snow* (page 145) and *hill* (page 151).

**Use with:** Our Earth, Our Resources — pp. 135–182

## TEXT COMPREHENSION
### Multiple-Strategy Instruction

**Use Reciprocal Teaching** Work together with children to apply comprehension strategies. List the strategies on chart paper.

> - Ask Questions
> - Recall and Retell
> - Explain
> - Predict

- As you read pages 156–157 with children, ask: **What is a question you could ask about *natural resources*?** (What are some kinds of *natural resources*?) **Now, recall and retell things that come from trees.** (Trees can give us wood, food, and paper.) **Explain what you think the word *lumber* means.** (wood that can be used to build homes) After you have read page 157, say: **Predict what may come next.** (The text probably will talk about other *natural resources* and how we use them.)
- Use this routine as children read Unit 4.

## Put Reading First

**Use with:** This Is Our Country          **pp. 183–230**

# PHONEMIC AWARENESS
## Phoneme Identity

**Recognize Sounds** Help children recognize identical sounds in different vocabulary words. For example, examine the words *colony* from Lesson 3 and *citizen* and *capital* from Lesson 6.

- Say: **Listen carefully. Which two words begin with the same sound: *colony*, *citizen*, *capital*?** (*colony* and *capital*) **What sound do *colony* and *capital* begin with?** (/k/)
- Repeat this routine with groups of other words in Unit 5 that have the same initial sounds, such as *native* (page 190) and *north* (page 190), and *people* (page 196) and *Pilgrims* (page 198).

**Use with:** This Is Our Country          **pp. 183–230**

# BUILDING FLUENCY
## Child-Adult Reading

**Read a Story** Use the story "Little Rabbit" on page 188 to practice reading with individual children. The adult reading may be you, a parent, a classroom aide, or a tutor.

- Model reading the story individually with a child. Use your voice to emphasize changes indicated by punctuation, such as pausing for commas and periods and showing excitement for exclamation marks.
- Say: **Now you read the story.** Provide assistance and encouragement as needed. Monitor each child's reading for fluency. Have the child reread the passage until his or her reading is fluent.

**Use with:** This Is Our Country          **pp. 183–230**

# PHONICS
## Analogy-Based Phonics

**Use Similar Parts** Help children use known word parts to identify unknown vocabulary words. For example, examine the vocabulary word *vote* from Lesson 6.

- Copy the graphic organizer shown below.

> note
> _ote

- Point to *note* and say: **Read this word with me.** (*note*) **If I change the *n* to a *v*, what is the new word?** (*vote*) Discuss the meaning of *vote*.
- Repeat this routine with other words throughout Unit 5, such as *corn* on page 191 and *king* on page 196. (*torn, horn, corn; ring, sing, king*)

**Use with:** This Is Our Country          **pp. 183–230**

# TEXT COMPREHENSION
## Monitor Comprehension

**Apply a Strategy** Explain that good readers frequently stop and think about whether they understand what they are reading. Help children practice this strategy.

- Use Lesson 3 to model monitoring comprehension. Say: **As I read, I realized that I'm not sure what a *colony* is. I need to go back and reread the part that explains what a *colony* is.**
- Ask: **What is something in this lesson that you do not understand?** (Answers will vary. Suggest that if children do not understand something they read, they should keep reading to see if there is more information that will help them.)
- Encourage children to ask themselves whether or not they understand as you read the remaining lessons in Unit 5. Stop and use this routine from time to time until children can use it on their own.

# No Child Left Behind

## Put Reading First

**Use with:** Our Country, Our World          pp. 231–272

## PHONEMIC AWARENESS
### Phoneme Addition

**Make New Words** Use phoneme addition to give children practice manipulating sounds in words. For example, use the words *other* and *us* from Lesson 2.

- Write *other*. Then say: **I will add /m/ to the beginning of *other*. What is the new word?** (*mother*) Repeat with the word *us*. Have children add the sound /b/ to make *bus*.

- Use this routine to practice adding sounds to other words throughout Unit 6, such as changing *out* (page 239) to *shout* or *way* (page 243) to *sway*.

**Use with:** Our Country, Our World          pp. 231–272

## PHONICS
### Vowel Sounds

**Read r-Controlled Vowels** Before starting Lesson 1, review r-controlled vowels. Write the word *mat*. Ask: **What sound does the letter *a* have in *mat*?** (/a/) Erase the letter *t* and replace it with *r*. Explain to children that now the letter *a* sounds like /är/.

- Write the Lesson 1 vocabulary word *market* on chart paper. Ask: **What sound does the letter *a* have in the word *market*?** (/är/)

- As you read the lessons in Unit 6, call attention to words with r-controlled vowels. Introduce children to the sound the r-controlled vowel will make before you introduce the word itself.

| | |
|---|---|
| *work* (page 239) | *chart* (page 243) |
| *information* (page 246) | *transportation* (page 252) |

**Use with:** Our Country, Our World          pp. 231–272

## BUILDING FLUENCY
### Model Fluent Reading

**Read a Poem** On chart paper, write the following poem from page 258a of the Teacher's Edition.

> The world is so full
> of a number of things,
> I'm sure we should all
> be as happy as kings.

- Model reading the poem for children, emphasizing the rhyme words *things* and *kings*.

- Ask: **Did you hear how I paused after the comma in the second line? The comma tells me to pause before I keep reading.**

- Have children read the poem with you, pausing when you do and emphasizing the same words. Monitor each child's reading for fluency.

**Use with:** Our Country, Our World          pp. 231–272

## TEXT COMPREHENSION
### Cooperative Learning

**Use Prior Knowledge** Explain that good readers use what they already know about a topic to help them understand text. Divide children into small groups.

- Help each group preview the text before reading Lesson 1. Say: **Look at the pictures. Talk about them with one another. Then read the headings on pages and captions on pictures. Talk with one another about what you already know about visiting a market. Make a list.**

- Invite each group to share its list with the class.

- Encourage children to use this routine when reading text in other lessons throughout Unit 6.